W9-AOY-591

ANNUAL REVIEW OF PSYCHOLOGY

ANNUAL REVIEW OF PSYCHOLOGY

VOLUME 45, 1994

LYMAN W. PORTER, *Editor*
University of California, Irvine

MARK R. ROSENZWEIG, Editor
University of California, Berkeley

ANNUAL REVIEWS INC. 4139 EL CAMINO WAY P.O. BOX 10139 PALO ALTO, CALIFORNIA 94303-0897

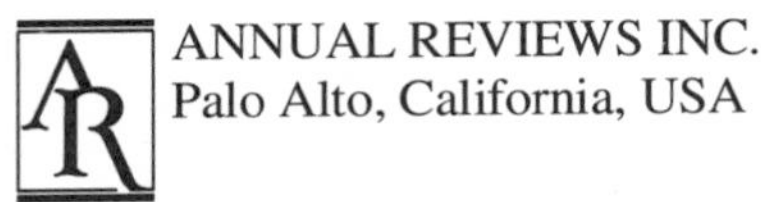

ANNUAL REVIEWS INC.
Palo Alto, California, USA

International Standard Serial Number: 0066-4308
International Standard Book Number: 8243-0245-1
Library of Congress Catalog Card Number: 50-13143

The paper used in this publication meets the minimum requirements of American National Standards for Information Sciences—Permanence of Paper for Printed Library Materials, ANZI Z39.48-1984

Typesetting by Ruth McCue-Saavedra and the Annual Reviews Inc. Editorial Staff

PRINTED AND BOUND IN THE UNITED STATES OF AMERICA

PREFACE

This is the last of 21 volumes (1974–1994) of the *Annual Review of Psychology* (*ARP*) to be co-edited by Mark R. Rosenzweig and Lyman W. Porter. Mark Rosenzweig also co-edited the previous five volumes with Paul Mussen (1969–1973). We welcome our successors, Editor Janet T. Spence and Associate Editors John M. Darley and Donald J. Foss.

We are grateful to the many colleagues and collaborators who have made the years with the *ARP* fulfilling and rewarding. Among these are the knowledgable and congenial psychologists who have volunteered their expertise for five-year terms on the Editorial Committee of the *ARP*. The annual meetings of the Editorial Committee have provided lively informal surveys of the state of the field and of its most exciting developments. The value of the *ARP* rests on the committee's skill and dedication, and on its wise choice of authors. During our co-editorship we are fortunate to have had the skillful collaboration of three talented production editors: Jean Heavener (1968–1986), Ike Burke (1987–1992), and Amy Marks (1993). We have served with four dedicated Editors-in-Chief of Annual Reviews, starting with Professor J. Murray Luck, who started the Annual Reviews organization by founding the *Annual Review of Biochemistry* in 1932. The others have been Robert Schutz (1968–1973), William Kaufmann (1973–1992), and Robert H. Haynes (1993). During many of these years, Chief Executive Officer and Treasurer John S. McNeil earned our admiration by playing a major role in keeping the not-for-profit Annual Reviews organization going despite difficult periods in the publishing industry.

The change of Editors is a time for looking back and taking stock, as well as for looking ahead. The *ARP* has seen several changes and improvements during this period. Special chapters on current topics were first included in Volume 26. The master list of topics has been revised periodically to keep it up-to-date. A chapter on psychology in each of the host countries of the quadrennial International Congress of Psychology has been included since 1976, starting with France. In 1986, we had a chapter on psychology in Israel, the host country of that year's International Congress of Applied Psychology. Since then, each even-numbered year has seen a chapter on psychology in the host country of one or the other international congress, and there have also been occasional chapters on psychology in other countries or regions. Volume 30 included a prefatory chapter by Jean Piaget, and most subsequent volumes have started with a chapter by a distinguished psychologist treating an enduring question with which that person has long been concerned.

Some technical changes have benefitted readers. Citation in chapters was changed in 1980 from numerical to the more informative use of author and year. Since 1979, larger type has made reading easier. Also since 1979, each chapter has started with a table of contents. In 1989, the cumulative indexes began expanding to cover the present ten-year period. Since 1993 readers can search a computer diskette for authors, chapter titles, and key words for all 26 of the Annual Review series.

We look forward to reading future volumes of the *ARP* produced by the new editors—without our having to recruit authors, counsel some of them on their chapter plans, massage some prose into trimmer form, and catch occasional errors of usage or spelling—in other words, to share the benefits of readers of the *ARP*, while relinquishing the often interesting, but always time-consuming duties of editors. At the same time, we will miss the stimulating annual meetings of the Editorial Committee and the interaction with the authors of review chapters.

Mark R. Rosenzweig
Lyman W. Porter

ANNUAL REVIEWS INC. is a nonprofit scientific publisher established to promote the advancement of the sciences. Beginning in 1932 with the Annual Review of Biochemistry, the Company has pursued as its principal function the publication of high quality, reasonably priced Annual Review volumes. The volumes are organized by Editors and Editorial Committees who invite qualified authors to contribute critical articles reviewing significant developments within each major discipline. The Editor-in-Chief invites those interested in serving as future Editorial Committee members to communicate directly with him. Annual Reviews Inc. is administered by a Board of Directors, whose members serve without compensation.

1994 Board of Directors, Annual Reviews Inc.

Management of Annual Reviews Inc.

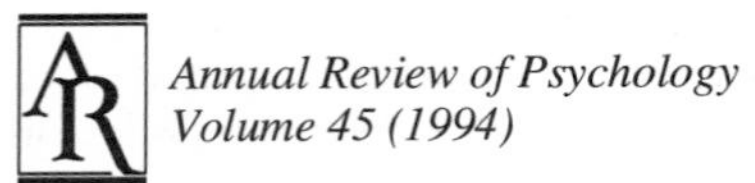

Annual Review of Psychology
Volume 45 (1994)

CONTENTS

INDEXES

ERRATA

We note with regret an error in Volume 44 of the *Annual Review of Psychology.*

page 77: The last sentence should read: "It does seem likely, however, that the ultimate elaboration of the mechanisms underlying behaviorally induced alterations of immune function will have important clinical and therapeutic implications."

SOME RELATED ARTICLES IN OTHER *ANNUAL REVIEWS*

From the *Annual Review of Sociology,* Volume 19 (1993)

Sociological Perspectives on Life Transitions, Linda K. George
Recent Advances in Longitudinal Methodology, Trond Petersen
Perspectives on Organizational Change in the US Medical Care Sector, Mary L. Fennell and Jeffrey A. Alexander
Minority Identity and Self-Esteem, J. R. Porter and R. E. Washington

From the Annual Review of Medicine, Volume 44 (1993)

Neuromodulation Techniques for Medically Refractory Chronic Pain, Barry Landau and Robert M. Levy
Special Aspects of Neuropsychiatric Illness in Women: With a Focus on Depression, Jean A. Hamilton and Uriel Halbreich
Aging—Causes and Defenses, George R. Martin, David B. Danner, and Nikki J. Holbrook
Methods, Successes, and Failures of Smoking Cessation Programs, Edwin B. Fisher, Jr., Edward Lichtenstein, Debra Haire-Joshu, Glen D. Morgan, and Heather R. Rehlberg

From the *Annual Review of Public Health,* Volume 14 (1993)

Regression Analysis for Correlated Data, Kung-Yee Liang and Scott L. Zeger
Risk Perception and Communication, Baruch Fischhoff, Ann Bostrom, and Marilyn Jacobs Quadrel
Poverty and Cultural Diversity: Challenges for Health Promotion Among the Medically Underserved, Jon F. Kerner, Linda Dusenbury, and Jeanne S. Mandelblatt
A Review of Smoking in Pregnancy: Effects on Pregnancy Outcomes and Cessation Efforts, R. Louise Floyd, Barbara K. Rimer, Gary A. Giovino, Patricia D. Mullen, and Susan E. Sullivan
Harm Reduction: A Public Health Response to the AIDS Epidemic Among Injecting Drug Users, Don C. Des Jarlais, Samuel R. Friedman, and Thomas P. Ward
Heterosexual Transmission of HIV: The Role of Other Sexually Transmitted Infections and Behavior in Its Epidemiology Prevention and Control, Sevgi Okten Aral

From the *Annual Review of Neuroscience,* Volume 16 (1993)

Integrative Systems Research on the Brain: Resurgence and New Opportunities, Theodore H. Bullock
Processing of Temporal Information in the Brain, Catherine E. Carr
How Parallel are the Primate Visual Pathways?, W. H. Merigan and J. H. R. Maunsell
The Processing of Single Words Studied with Positron Emission Tomography, S. E. Petersen and J. A. Fiez
Neuroanatomy of Memory, S. Zola-Morgan and L. R. Squire
Computational Models of the Neural Bases of Learning and Memory, Mark A. Gluck and Richard Granger

Annu. Rev. Psychol. 1994. 45:1–23

NEUROPSYCHOLOGICAL ASSESSMENT

Arthur L. Benton

Departments of Neurology and Psychology, University of Iowa, Iowa City, Iowa 52242

KEY WORDS: assessment, brain disease, brain-behavior relationships, clinical evaluation, tests

---

CONTENTS

INTRODUCTION

The primary purpose of neuropsychological assessment is to draw inferences about the structural and functional characteristics of a person's brain by evaluating an individual's behavior in defined stimulus-response situations. Al-

0066-4308/94/0201-0001$05.00

though rating scales, which are a form of naturalistic observation, are also used for this purpose, neuropsychological assessment relies almost entirely on tests, i.e. the elicitation of specific behavioral responses to specific stimuli under controlled conditions.

Nature and Scope

Neuropsychological assessment is more objective and more precise than the conventional behavioral evaluation of the clinical neurologist. Moreover, by means of instrumentation (e.g. the tachistoscope, reaction time apparatus, and diverse test materials) and through manipulation of stimulus properties (e.g. strength and duration), and response requirements (e.g. verbal vs nonverbal), neuropsychological assessment permits the study of behavioral characteristics that are not accessible to clinical observation. Although neuropsychological assessment is sufficiently different from clinical evaluation to be considered a distinctive set of procedures, the two approaches are similar in that both deal with the patient's behavior. In fact, the neuropsychological examination has been characterized as both a refinement and an extension of the neurological examination (Benton 1985).

The scope of neuropsychological assessment has expanded enormously in recent decades to encompass areas beyond clinical neurology and the traditional differentiation between organic and functional conditions in psychiatry. It plays an indispensable role in detecting cerebral dysfunction in various situations in which there is usually no clear anatomic evidence of alterations in the brain. Such situations include evaluating the effects of environmental and industrial toxins (Hartman 1988, Johnson 1990); the behavioral sequelae of carotid endarterectomy (Diener et al 1984) and cardiac surgery (Juolasmaa et al 1981); and the cognitive changes associated with alcoholism (Parsons et al 1987), chronic obstructive pulmonary disease (Adams et al 1980), and eating disorders (Hamsher et al 1981, Jones et al 1991, Szmukler et al 1992); as well as monitoring the outcome of diverse treatments (Mohr & Brouwers 1991). Neurological studies of old age and dementia use neuropsychological test data as the basic criteria against which the behavioral significance of specific brain changes such as cortical atrophy, ventricular enlargement, neurofibrillary tangles, and dendritic loss are evaluated.

A Bit of History

Neuropsychological assessment originated in the ad hoc attempts of physicians in the late nineteenth and early twentieth centuries to evaluate the mental capacities of patients with brain disease (particularly aphasics) more precisely than could be accomplished by the clinical examination of the period. Requiring a patient with expressive aphasia to indicate with his fingers how many letters or syllables were in a word, asking him to nod in assent or denial in response to a series of absurd statements, or having him draw designs from memory are some examples of these early procedural maneuvers. Far ahead of his time, the German neuropsychiatrist Rieger (1888) assembled a battery of 40 tests designed to assess diverse cognitive and perceptual capacities, as well as speech and motor skills. It is doubtful that the battery was used much outside of Rieger's clinic but it did serve as a model for the later test batteries and mental status examinations published by Heilbronner (1905), Rossolimo (1911), Poppelreuter (1917), Franz (1919), Gelb & Goldstein (1920), Lipmann (1922), and Wells (1927). In addition, intelligence test scales such as the Binet (Terman 1916, Terman & Merrill 1937), the Army Alpha (Yerkes 1919) and the Wechsler-Bellevue Scales (Wechsler 1939) were widely used for neuropsychological assessment. By 1943 a variety of specialized tests (Conkey 1938, Shipley 1940, Benton & Howell 1941, Goldstein & Scheerer 1941, Wells & Ruesch 1942, Hunt 1943) were available to clinical examiners and researchers for assessing the cognitive capacities of patients with brain disease. These tests provided the background for those neuropsychological assessment procedures, most notably the Halstead-Reitan test battery (Halstead 1947, Reitan 1955), that were devised after World War II and are in current use.

ASSESSMENT PROCEDURES AND THEIR APPLICATIONS

This section describes a few of the tests used to evaluate different aspects of cognition and some of the findings gained from their application. Detailed reviews of the topic are provided by the comprehensive compendia of Lezak (1983) and Spreen & Strauss (1991).

Standard Test Batteries

The use of standard test batteries such as the Wechsler Adult Intelligence Scales (Wechsler 1981, Lezak 1983, Spreen & Strauss 1991), the Halstead-Reitan Battery (Boll 1981, Lezak 1983) and the Luria-Nebraska Neuropsychological Battery (Golden 1981, Lezak 1983), in which the same set of diagnostic tests is given to all patients, is the most common approach to clinical neuropsychological assessment. These test batteries also figure prominently in clinical studies that involve searching the files for case material relevant to the research question. The use of these tests ensures effective communication and provides a stable basis for comparing the performances of different individuals and diagnostic groups; however, this approach also has serious limitations. Some tests in these batteries are of dubious value and the administration of a fixed set of tests cannot possibly answer all the questions that arise in clinical practice or research. Moreover, habitual use of these tests, which is of great practical convenience, tends to discourage exploration of more effective assessment procedures (cf Benton 1985, 1992; Walsh 1992).

Verbal Capacities and Aphasia Testing

Assessment of language skills is a major component of general clinical and educational psychometrics because test performance is correlated more closely with scholastic and occupational achievement than is any other type of measure. Some of the tests used for language skills assessment have been adapted for neuropsychological purposes as probes to detect cerebral dysfunction in general and, in particular, to assess the functional efficiency of the left "language dominant" cerebral hemisphere. Special tests, also devised for this purpose, include the Token Test (De Renzi & Vignolo 1962, De Renzi & Faglioni 1978), which was designed specifically to evaluate oral verbal understanding in the poorly educated, even illiterate, patient with a limited lexicon. Using stimuli that require knowing only the names of colors and familiar shapes and the meanings of such terms as "touch," "large," and "small," the Token Test determines the precision with which commands of varying complexity (e.g. "touch the yellow circle and [or] the red square") are carried out. Used in virtually every language community in the world, the test has proven to be a useful measure for assessing and monitoring oral speech understanding in both aphasic and ostensibly nonaphasic patients (Boller & Vignolo 1966). Since test performance involves a short-term memory component, it is not surprising that many nonaphasic patients with brain disease perform poorly on the Token Test. Comparisons of patients with unilateral brain damage have shown that defective performance is far more frequent in patients with left hemisphere lesions than in those with right hemisphere lesions. Since failure is not generally accompanied by the more obvious signs of aphasic disorder, it is sometimes conceptualized as an expression of "latent" or "subclinical" aphasia.

Controlled word association tests, which require the subject to produce words beginning with a given letter of the alphabet, also have found wide application in neuropsychological assessment. Originally devised by Thurstone (1938) as a measure of what he called the verbal fluency factor, different versions of the test are now used for a variety of purposes. In aphasic patients, who almost always perform badly, changes in test performance can indicate either recovery or further progression of the disability. Test performance in nonaphasic patients has been found to be particularly sensitive to the presence of left frontal lobe disease although failure is also encountered in some patients with focal lesions in other regions of the brain (Benton 1968, Perret 1974, Cavalli et al 1981).

Controlled oral word association is one of the more discriminating measures for separating normal elderly persons from those with early dementing illness (Eslinger et al 1985). Interestingly, oral word association is relatively invulnerable to the effects of aging (at least until the age of 80 years) while written word association shows an earlier decline (Schaie & Parham 1977, Benton et al 1981). Slower writing and greater concern about spelling on the part of older subjects are quite possibly the determinants of this difference in rate of decline in performance.

"Aphasia" is the label for an aggregate of disabilities the overall effect of which is a breakdown in verbal communication. The diagnostician must analyze the aggregate into its components to identify those primarily responsible for the communication impairment and to relate them to cerebral dysfunction. The procedures developed for these purposes may be divided into three types: 1. Brief screening instruments (administration time = 15–20 min) designed to ascertain whether or not a patient does in fact have an aphasic disorder and which aspects of language appear to be most affected. The Sklar Aphasia Scales (Sklar 1973) and Reitan's Aphasia Screening Test (1984) are examples. 2. Test batteries of intermediate length (administration time = 30–35 min) that probe basic language performances (e.g. naming, repetition, verbal-ideational fluency, understanding of oral and written speech, spelling) and provide a performance profile that is useful for diagnosis and rehabilitation. The Multilingual Aphasia Examination (Benton & Hamsher 1989, Rey & Benton 1991) is an example. 3. Detailed examinations (administration time = 1–2 hr), frequently guided by anatomic and linguistic considerations, assess a large variety of verbal and nonverbal performances to identify specific aphasic syndromes and the deranged neural mechanisms producing distinctive performance profiles. The Boston Diagnostic Aphasia Examination (Goodglass & Kaplan 1983) is a prominent example.

Although aphasia assessment has a long history, adequately standardized test batteries are a comparatively recent development. Their use has not only proven effective in the clinic to monitor change in status and as a guide to rehabilitation strategies, but it has also forced changes in traditional concepts about the nature of aphasic disorders and their lesional localization. For example, the classic taxonomy (Broca's aphasia, Wernicke's aphasia, conduction aphasia, etc) has not been validated by objective analysis, which has shown that less than half of aphasic patients fit into the categories of the system (Albert et al 1981, Reinvang 1985). Conversely, application of the test batteries has disclosed the existence of unsuspected symptom-combinations such as sensory modality-specific and semantic category-specific impairments in naming (Spreen et al 1966, Damasio 1990, Tranel 1991). On the anatomical side, detailed studies have highlighted the significance of the anterior temporal region of the left hemisphere, as well as the traditional posterior temporal localization, for the mediation of naming performances (Tranel 1992a).

Visuoperceptual Capacities

The impetus for the development of perceptual tests, which are primarily measures of visuoperceptual and visuospatial abilities, came from clinical investigation that linked specific impairment in these abilities with disease of the right hemisphere. One effect of this demonstration was to transform the long-held doctrine of exclusive left hemisphere "dominance" for language and cognition into that of "asymmetry of hemispheric function" and this in turn generated the hundreds of studies of "hemispheric specialization" that have appeared in the past 25 or 30 years.

Many tests designed to probe the capacity for visual analysis and synthesis have been developed for clinical evaluation and research purposes. Studies of hemispheric differences in complex visual discrimination have found that failure is extraordinarily frequent in brain-diseased patients; however, no clear indications have been found of a specific hemispheric contribution to performance (Meier & French 1965, Newcombe 1969, Bisiach et al 1979, Benton et al 1983). Patients with right hemisphere lesions generally perform more poorly than those with left hemisphere lesions but the difference is not impressive, probably because these rather difficult tasks make demands on sustained attention and the capacity for searching behavior as well as on specific visuoperceptual ability. Other visuoperceptual tasks such as figure-ground differentiation have yielded comparable results (Russo & Vignolo 1967, Corkin 1979). Most studies have associated the presence of aphasic disorder with failing performance.

Facial recognition has been the subject of intensive study in animal and human subjects. The discovery of an apparently specific loss of the ability to recognize familiar faces (prosopagnosia) and its association with disease of the right hemisphere in some patients aroused great interest among clinicians, and later among experimentalists, because of the implications of the phenomenon for conceptions of cerebral localization and the nature of perceptual processes (Hécaen & Angelergues 1962, Meadows 1974, Rosenfeld & Van Hoesen 1979). Since this curious disability was rarely encountered, a number of researchers developed tests to assess the capacity to discriminate unfamiliar faces on the assumption that a larger number of patients might show it in a milder form that would not give rise to a clinical complaint (Warrington & James 1967, Benton & Van Allen 1968, De Renzi et al 1968). The assumption proved to be incorrect in that prosopagnosia and defective discrimination of unfamiliar faces were found to be largely independent disabilities (Benton & Van Allen 1972, Malone et al 1982).

At the same time, application of these tests demonstrated that impairment in the discrimination of unfamiliar faces possessed clinical and theoretical significance in its own right. Defective performance is shown by a relatively large proportion of nonaphasic patients with lesions in the inferior temporal and occipital region of the right hemisphere and tests of this type are often used in clinical neuropsychological assessment. (Lezak 1983, Spreen & Strauss 1991). Stimulated by these findings, experimentalists have used these tests to analyze components of information processing and identify the neural mechanisms mediating these complex perceptual performances (Damasio et al 1990; Benton & Tranel 1992; Sergent et al 1992b, c; Tranel 1992b).

A variety of tests assessing visuospatial capacities have found that defective performance is associated with posterior lesions of the right hemisphere (Benton et al 1983, Lezak 1983, Spreen & Strauss 1991, Benton & Tranel 1992). It has been demonstrated clearly that this defect is distinct from impaired object and face perception, even though both types of disability are characteristic of patients with right hemisphere disease. Dissociation in performance level is observed frequently: patients with inferior occipitotemporal lesions show defective complex figure and face perception and those with superior occipitoparietal lesions show impaired spatial cognition (Newcombe & Russell 1969, Newcombe et al 1987). The postulation from experimental animal studies of two cortical visual systems, one subserving object recognition and the other subserving the appreciation of spatial relationships, is consistent with these clinical findings (Ungerleider & Mishkin 1982, Mishkin et al 1983).

Visuoconstructional abilities also have been assessed by a variety of tasks including copying line drawings and assembling blocks (Critchley 1953, Benton 1962, Warrington 1969, Benton et al 1983). These tasks differ widely in difficulty level and make varying demands on sustained attention, capacity for deliberation, perceptual acuity, motor skill, and on the appreciation of spatial relationships. As a result, clinical studies using these tasks have not generated consistent findings. Although many studies have reported more frequent and more severe constructional disability in patients with right hemisphere lesions, other studies have not found this difference. Nor is it clear that there are performance differences associated with the anteroposterior dimension within a hemisphere. There are suggestions that impaired performance has different determinants according to the side of lesion; defective constructional activity is more closely related to impaired perception of spatial relations in right hemisphere–damaged patients than in those with left hemisphere lesions (Mack & Levine 1981, Griffiths & Cook 1986). It is apparent that the concept of "visuoconstructional disability" or "constructional apraxia" needs more precise operational definition if it is to be optimally useful (Benton 1989a, Benton & Tranel 1992).

Audition

Audioperceptual tests have played a relatively minor, but significant, role in neuropsychological assessment. Dichotic listening procedures (Sparks et al

1970, Damasio & Damasio 1979, Rubens et al 1985, Hugdahl 1988) and tests of the identification of nonverbal meaningful sounds (Spreen et al 1965, Vignolo 1969, Varney 1980), of phoneme discrimination (Tallal & Newcombe 1978, Varney & Benton 1979, Varney 1984), and of diverse aspects of auditory discrimination (Sanchez-Longo & Forster 1957, Milner 1962, Vignolo 1969) have been used. These studies have brought to light the association of impairment in the discrimination of meaningless sounds with right hemisphere disease and conversely (but with some striking exceptions) the association of impairment in the discrimination of nonverbal meaningful sounds (e.g. a dog barking or a bell ringing) with aphasic disorder. Defective auditory localization has been shown to be associated with right temporal lobe lesions. The dependence of oral-verbal understanding on phoneme discrimination also has been demonstrated.

Somesthesis

Different aspects of somesthetic information processing such as tactile formboard learning (Reitan & Wolfson 1985), tactile maze learning (Corkin 1965), tactile-visual form perception (Benton et al 1983), perception of the direction of linear stimulation on the skin surface (Carmon & Benton 1969, Fontenot & Benton 1971), and tactile object identification (Benton 1972) have been studied in clinical populations. Although patients with unilateral lesions in either hemisphere show defects on the contralateral hand (often associated with basic sensory impairment), only those with right hemisphere lesions are likely to show defects on the ipsilateral hand as well. The one exception to this rule is tactile object identification (stereognosis) where bilateral impairment is more closely associated with left hemisphere disease (Benton 1972). As with audition, the basic distinction appears to be between meaningless configurations that are preferentially processed by mechanisms in the right hemisphere and meaningful configurations that are preferentially processed by left hemisphere mechanisms.

Motor Skills and Praxis

MOTOR SKILLS The "motor system" involves a large number of cortical and subcortical areas that interact to control a variety of movements that differ greatly in their complexity and cognitive requirements. Clinical neurology has traditionally focused on damage to the primary motor system (i.e. motor cortex, pyramidal and extrapyramidal systems) in order to probe for contralateral deficits referable to unilateral damage. This assumption, based on the well-known contralateral organization of the motor system, is valid for some but not all motor tasks. Although simple performances such as finger tapping speed and grip strength have been shown to be impaired in the limb contralateral to unilateral damage, more complex motor skills such as peg board dexterity and static and kinetic steadiness tasks, as measured by the Wisconsin Motor Steadiness battery (cf Reitan & Davison 1974), have been found to be impaired bilaterally with unilateral damage to either the right or the left hemisphere (Haaland & Delaney 1981). Moreover, the left hemisphere in right-handed subjects is dominant for the control of many complex motor tasks such as gesturing, the manipulation of objects, the maintenance of posture, and the imitation of movement sequences (Haaland & Yeo 1989).

PRAXIS The concept of apraxia refers to loss of the ability to execute purposeful acts on verbal command or on imitation in the absence of motor weakness, movement disorders, sensory defects, or akinesia that might produce the disability. Gestural praxis (e.g. waving goodbye, saluting) and manipulative praxis involving the actual or pretended use of objects are the two types most frequently assessed in the clinic. Standard sets of tasks are available for clinical and investigative use (Poeck 1986, Heilman & Gonzalez-Rothi 1985). Impairment in praxis is closely associated with aphasic disorder. However, not all aphasic patients are apraxic and on occasion the disability is found in nonaphasic patients. Unilateral apraxia, indicative of a lesion in the corpus callosum, as well as the more frequent bilateral form may be encountered (Heilman & Gonzalez-Rothi 1985). A related disorder, impairment in the ability to pre-plan complex motor sequences and difficulty in alternating hand postures, is shown by patients with Parkinson's disease (Harrington & Haaland 1991).

Learning, Memory, and Orientation

In no aspect of cognition has the relationship between human and animal neuropsychology been closer than in the domain of learning and memory. Early clinical studies demonstrated the crucial role of diencephalic structures (particularly the mammillary bodies) and the hippocampal formation of the mesial temporal lobes in the mediation of learning and memory performances. This in turn provided the impetus for analogous animal studies, which generated findings that confirmed and amplified the clinical observations. Discussions of the present status of our understanding of the cortical and subcortical "memory systems" of the brain can be found in recent contributions of Squire (1987), Damasio (1989), Damasio & Damasio (1990), and Squire et al (1993).

Research in the neuropsychology of human memory has generated many questions regarding the distinguishing features of diencephalic and temporal lobe amnesia, the role of the basal forebrain, the anatomic correlates of impairment in factual (declarative) memory and perceptuomotor (procedural) memory, the temporal pattern of retrograde amnesia, the diagnostic significance of memory performances in old age and age-associated dementing illness, and the temporal course of anterograde or posttraumatic amnesia. In line with this recognition of the multidimensional nature of the memory disorders produced by brain disease, a large variety of test procedures, assessing virtually every aspect of learning, retention, and orientation, have been developed to help answer these questions (cf Lezak 1983, Spreen & Strauss 1991, Tranel 1992).

The differentiation between factual and perceptuomotor learning and retention has been demonstrated to have a solid foundation. Many Alzheimer patients who are severely impaired in factual memory show relatively preserved capacity for perceptuomotor learning (Eslinger & Damasio 1986, Knopman & Nissen 1987). Conversely, patients with Huntington's disease (with pathologic involvement of the basal ganglia) show clear impairment in perceptuomotor learning with preserved capacity for at least certain aspects of factual learning (Butters 1984). Measures of reproductive learning and retention that make demands on "working memory" (cf Goldman-Rakic & Friedman 1991) have been found to be sensitive indices of incipient dementing illness (Poitrenaud & Barrere 1973, Jones et al 1992). Occasionally, a specific impairment in recent memory, as reflected in loss of temporal orientation, indicates the onset of dementia (Eslinger et al 1985). The question of whether or not the amnesic syndrome produced by hippocampal damage differs significantly from that referable to diencephalic disease has not been answered (cf Squire 1987).

"Executive Functions" and Abstract Reasoning

The concept of "executive functions" arose in the 1960s to refer to a congeries of important human cognitive capacities, including judgment, mental flexibility, creativity, decision making, self-awareness, and planning, that had been mostly ignored in American (but not European) psychological thought. Goldstein's (1939, 1944) concept of the "abstract attitude" encompassed many of these characteristics. Goldstein emphasized the close association of impairment in the abstract attitude to frontal lobe disease and this immediately endowed the concept with neuropsychological significance. Hebb (1945) criticized the concept as being much too broad to be useful. The same criticism can be leveled at the concept of executive functions. Yet despite its resistance to precise definition, "executive functions" refer to a series of important cognitive capacities that neuropsychological assessment generally ignored in favor of more manageable categories such as speech, perception, and memory. However, in the last two decades, a deliberate attempt has been made to use diagnostic procedures that evaluate some of these capacities, particularly flexibility of response (or its negative counterpart, perseveration), planning ability, and self-awareness.

The Wisconsin Card Sorting Test or WCST (Berg 1948, Grant & Berg 1948, Milner 1963, Heaton 1981) was devised to measure abilities to identify abstract categories and to shift cognitive set. The test requires the subject to sort a set of cards according to selected dimensions, which are changed from time to time during the course of examination. The subject must formulate a hypothesis about the correct sorting principle and be capable of changing the hypothesis when feedback from the examiner indicates that it is incorrect. Thus the test provides measures of both conceptual thinking and cognitive flexibility. Milner's (1963, 1964) pioneering studies of patients with frontal and nonfrontal excisions for relief of epilepsy found consistently poor performance in patients with frontal dorsolateral excisions in contrast to the variable and generally better performances of patients with nonfrontal excisions. Perseverative errors were the primary determinant of failure in the frontal patients.

Subsequent studies have only partially supported these initial findings. Drewe (1974) and Heaton (1981) confirmed that frontally injured patients performed on a lower level than those with nonfrontal lesions but they also found considerable variability with many frontal patients performing on a normal level. More recent studies by Grafman et al (1990) and Anderson et al (1991) found no difference in the performance of frontal and nonfrontal patients. Thus, it appears that on balance the WCST is an excellent test for assessing cognitive flexibility and it is useful for detecting the presence of cerebral dysfunction. However, without information provided by other test performances, its localizing significance is questionable.

The Porteus Maze Test (Porteus 1915, 1959, 1965) specifically assesses "planfulness" and the capacity to inhibit immediate response in favor of deliberation. This venerable test is still widely used in clinical practice and research. A modern variant is Elithorn's Perceptual Mazes (1955). On tests of this type, the sensitivity of performances to the presence of brain disease has been well established (Klebanoff et al 1954, Bechtoldt et al 1962). There is also a distinct trend for patients with frontal lobe disease to fail. Their performance is characterized by impulsivity and rule-breaking behavior (Tow 1955, Smith & Kinder 1959, Smith 1960, Walsh 1978). A "frontal lobe" patient occasionally will show unremarkable performance on a battery of tests, except for failure on the Porteus Mazes (Ackerly & Benton 1947, Smith 1960). However, defective performance is not specific for frontal lobe disease. Benton et al (1963) and Archibald et al (1967) found that on the Elithorn Perceptual Mazes, the performances of patients with right hemisphere lesions were generally inferior to those of patients with left hemisphere lesions. It may be that the Elithorn Mazes make greater demands on perceptual analysis than does the Porteus or that the determinants of performance on the two tests are different in frontal and nonfrontal patients, with frontal patients making more impulsive and rule-breaking errors and the nonfrontals being slower and somewhat confused.

RATING SCALES

Rating scales are based on observations of a patient's behavior during the course of an examination, in the hospital, or in everyday life that are made by the examiner, hospital personnel, or relatives, respectively. Most mental status examinations are a mixture of a series of brief tests of cognitive function and observation of diverse characteristics such as grooming, facial expression, mood, and awareness of disability. Ratings of behavioral competence rely on reports that cover such characteristics as a patient's ability to find his way about, eating habits, urinary and fecal continence, and appropriateness of affective behavior. Blessed et al's Dementia Scale (1968), adopted by Hachinski et al (1975), is an example of an observational rating scale that assesses 22 personal characteristics and behavioral capacities that are prime determinants of social competence. With a range of scores from 0 to 34, the scale provides a quantitative estimate of the severity of behavioral incompetence. Overall & Gorham's Brief Psychiatric Rating Scale (1962) is another observational rating scale that is particularly appropriate for the evaluation of psychiatric patients, with its emphasis on such behavioral characteristics as "mannerisms and posturing," "depressive mood," and "blunted affect." However, it also has been used successfully with brain-diseased patients.

These rating scales have proven clinically valuable as a guide to management and disposition and as an index of change of status over time. However, they also have specific neuropsychological significance. For example, Blessed et al (1968) found that scores on their Dementia Scale correlated somewhat more closely ($r = .64$) with counts of senile plaques in the brains of demented patients than scores on their "Information-Memory-Concentration" test battery ($r = .52$). Similarly, high scores on the Brief Psychiatric Rating Scale have been found to be related to the presence of computed tomographic (CT) and EEG abnormalities in head-injured patients (Levin & Grossman 1978).

NEUROPSYCHOLOGICAL INFERENCE: NATURE AND PROBLEMS

Because one distinctive purpose of neuropsychological assessment is to draw inferences about the condition of the brain, neuropsychological tests sometimes have been assumed to be different in nature from clinical, educational, and vocational tests. This is certainly a misconception. All that distinguishes these different tests are the purposes to which they are put. The same test (e.g. the WAIS or the Rorschach) can be used as a measure of intelligence or personality, or for vocational guidance or neuropsychological inference. There are tests such as the Kohs Block Designs and Raven's Progressive Matrices that were originally designed as nonverbal measures of general intelligence but are now mostly used as specific neuropsychological assessment procedures to probe for the presence of focal brain disease.

Another common misconception is that neuropsychological assessment as a procedure is comparable in nature to those carried out in radiological, pathological, and EEG facilities. The fact that neuropsychological test findings emerge from a laboratory and are reported in quantitative terms fosters this impression. However, the neuropsychological examination is a clinical behavioral examination and not a generator of sub-behavioral (physiochemical, physiological, anatomic) information as is the case for the diverse laboratory resources associated with medical practice. In all probability the neuropsychological examination is as reliable and objective as these medical procedures (see Berbaum & Platz 1988, Kundel 1989, Lillington 1989, and Davis et al 1992 for discussions of the serious problems encountered in radiology and pathology). The behavioral data developed from the neuropsychological examination is simply a different kind of data from the structural or functional data furnished by conventional laboratory techniques.

It is a truism that all specific behaviors, including the responses elicited by a neuropsychological test, have multiple determinants. In addition to the factor of cerebral abnormality, which is the neuropsychologist's focus of interest, defective test performances may be produced by inadequate cooperation or effort, medication, deliberate simulation or exaggeration of disability, disorders of mood, hostility or mistrust, and poor task adjustment on the part of culturally deviant subjects. Neuropsychologists generally consider the possible influence of these factors on level and quality of performance before they judge what the performance indicates about the state of the brain.

Considerable attention has been paid to some of these factors (Franzen et al 1990, Jones et al 1992, Hinkin et al 1992, Sweet et al 1992). Varying degrees of depression in mood, which is a frequent accompaniment, or product, of both neurological and nonneurological disease, as well as a common occurence in the normal elderly, is a prominent example. The neuropsychologist's opinion is often sought about the extent to which depression may contribute to observed impairment (or complaints) of poor memory or retardation in thought processes in a patient who may or may not show evidence of brain disease. The task is not an easy one. The use of self-report depression inventories as criterion measures is particularly suspect. As Sweet et al (1992) point out, some severely depressed patients admitted for inpatient treatment have normal scores on a depression inventory. Conversely, some normal elderly persons have high scores on self-report inventories such as the Zung Depression Scale and the Beck Depression Inventory (Zung & Green 1973, Zemore & Eames 1979). These score elevations are perhaps understandable in view of age-associated physical limitations and moderately pessimistic attitudes.

The frequency of depression, whether established on the basis of clinical diagnostic criteria or inventory scores, is high in both brain-diseased and functional psychiatric patients (Caine 1986, Starkstein & Robinson 1991, Sweet et al 1992). The extensive literature on the effects of depression on cognitive function is inconsistent. This outcome is not surprising given the variability in the definition of depression and in the neuropsychological measures used, as well as the failure to control for significant variables such as age, severity of depression, education, and chronicity. Although the majority of studies have found that the presence of depression is associated with some degree of impairment in cognitive function (or in the case of most brain-diseased patients, with incremental impairment), some studies have reported negative results. It is unclear which performances are most vulnerable to depression in mood; investigators have implicated too great a variety to serve as a useful guide. There are also conceptual problems such as whether depression should be regarded as a nonneurological factor potentially affecting performance or as a complicating cerebral dysfunction, perhaps one primarily involving derangement of right hemisphere mechanisms (Kronfol et al 1978, Flor-Henry 1979). A recent review by Sweet et al (1992) summarizes our present understanding of these issues and offers suggestions for the direction of future research.

If defective neuropsychological test performances by depressed patients can be viewed as the result of weak motivation, the deliberate simulation or exaggeration of cognitive disability is its counterpart, i.e. defective performance, produced by strong negative motivation. With the broadening of disability insurance coverage, the striking increase of civil litigation for brain injuries allegedly caused by malpractice or neglect, and the frequent recourse to mental incompetence as a defense in criminal proceedings, the question of deliberate simulation or exaggeration of cognitive impairment has become a major issue in forensic neuropsychology. Testifying as an expert witness for the plaintiff in the courts, the neuropsychologist is often challenged by the defense to prove that the behavioral deficits upon which the inference of brain injury is based are not the products of deliberate simulation or exaggeration of disability. Conversely, serving as an expert for the defense, the neuropsychologist has the responsibility to probe carefully for evidence of simulation or exaggeration in examining (or reviewing the examination of) the plaintiff. The problem goes beyond the forensic arena. A person may be convinced that he is cognitively impaired and his test performances may be influenced to conform to that conviction. To complicate matters, there is the longstanding tendency for clinicians to regard complaints of cognitive impairment on the part of patients without firm evidence or history of serious brain injury (e.g. the "postconcussional syndrome" following apparently trivial head trauma) as the product of simulation, exaggeration, or "functional overlay" (Trimble 1981, Robertson 1988, Benton 1989b).

The problem of simulation and exaggeration is recognized by knowledgeable clinicians to be both complex and subtle and one that requires careful evaluation of the patient's history, character (particularly "sociopathic" tendencies) and symptomatic presentation (Rogers 1988). The neuropsychologist will take all these factors into account, but it is in respect to symptomatic presentation, particularly to the extent that it involves cognitive impairment, that neuropsychological assessment makes a distinctive contribution (Pankratz 1988, Schretler 1988). Two approaches to the detection of gross exaggeration of cognitive incompetence have been developed. The first is the administration of a series of easy tasks on which even nonaphasic severely brain-damaged patients succeed. The ingenious tests of Rey (1941, 1964, Lezak 1983) are examples of these maneuvers. A second approach is to note whether a patient's performance conforms to expectations based on his alleged brain injury; a qualitatively deviant performance which is below expectations is interpreted as evidence of simulation (Benton & Spreen 1961, Spreen & Benton 1963, Heaton et al 1978, Pankratz 1983, Hayward et al 1987, Binder & Willis 1991). Both approaches have proven useful in detecting or confirming simulation.

On the other hand, the possibility of a modest exaggeration of cognitive disability associated with litigation or personal maladjustment may be more difficult to assess. Brain injury itself may produce emotional instability with disturbances in attention and concentration that adversely affect a variety of test performances. Repeated testing with the expectation that there should be improvement in performance and the interpolation of easy tasks are helpful in deciding whether nonneurological motivational factors are determining performance level. In many cases only a probability judgment at a modest level of confidence can be offered.

These examples of depression and simulation have been deliberately chosen to illustrate some of the more difficult problems in the field of neuropsychological assessment. The great majority of cases referred to neuropsychologists are not complicated by significant extraneous issues of this nature. Competent neuropsychological evaluation is usually quite effective in bringing the presence of cerebral dysfunction to light. In this connection it is worth noting that cerebral abnormality is not synonymous with the presence of an identifiable brain lesion. There is no necessary isomorphism between a brain lesion and its clinical manifestations.

The literature of clinical neurology indicates that, although the consequences of identified brain lesions are broadly predictable, clear exceptions to the rule are not uncommon. One example is the study by Katzman et al (1988) of the autopsy findings in 137 nursing home residents who had been classified during life as demented or nondemented on the basis of careful neuropsychological assessment. Of the 29 subjects who had been classified as nondemented, the autopsy findings in 10 (34%) were characteristic of Alzheimer's disease. Conversely, of the 108 subjects who had been classified as demented, 12 (11%) showed no pathological changes. Other examples of this inconsistency are the lack of correspondence between the extent of pontine lesions identified by magnetic resonance imaging (MRI) and the severity of their sequelae (Biller et al, 1986) and the inability of clinicians to distinguish between transient ischemic attacks (TIAs) with or without evidence of infarction as disclosed by CT scan (Koudstaal et al 1991). Finally, it is well known that frontal lobe disease may produce a broad spectrum of clinical pictures, including no behavioral alterations at all, the "frontal lobe syndrome" (itself a variable mixture of deficits), depression, schizophreniform reactions, or dementia.

This variability is understandable. Apart from the fact that these remarkable neurodiagnostic techniques are not absolutely accurate indicators of the presence and extent of brain lesions, the structural abnormalities they disclose cannot reflect the changes in cerebral function associated with diaschisis, restoration of function over time, and alterations in between-hemispheric communication or in the propagation of information through extensive neuronal networks. The direction these functional changes take is determined not by the lesion but by the capacities of the unaffected parts of the brain. Interindividual variation in these capacities is considerable, depending upon both known and unknown factors including age, educational background, gender, and presumably, genetic endowment. In children, there is the added factor of maturational change in the post-injury period. Thus, a case can be made that, given an adequate data base, neuropsychological assessment is probably in a better position to elucidate the functional status of brain functions (as distinguished from the presence and locus of a lesion) in a patient than are other currently used clinical procedures.

Two contemporary developments have decisive implications for the future of neuropsychological assessment. The first development is the advent of new investigative techniques such as the determination of rate of cerebral blood flow (rCBF), positron emission tomography (PET), and single photon emission tomography (SPECT), employed singly or in combination, to probe the regional activity of the brain at rest or during task performances. These techniques have added a new dimension to the exploration of brain-behavior relationships. Studies using these techniques in association with neuropsychological test procedures have yielded results that complement earlier findings with normal subjects and patients with focal brain lesions and also have generated unexpected new information. For example, the association of some verbal performances with left hemisphere activation and others with bilateral activation, of visuospatial performances with right hemisphere activation, and the crucial role of the right inferior occipitotemporal region for facial identification have been demonstrated (Gur et al 1987 a, b; Deutsch et al 1988; Posner et al 1988; Sergent & Signoret 1992a, b, c; Sergent et al 1992 a, b; for reviews, see Haxby et al 1991, Petersen et al 1992).

The second development is the incorporation of advances in cognitive psychology into neuropsychological investigation. The research of Sergent and her coworkers on facial identification (cited above) provides an illustration. The perception of objects can occur at different hierarchical levels. The most basic level is the simple recognition of an object as a member of its class (e.g. a building as a building; a face as a face). At a second superimposed level is the recognition of an object as belonging to a category within its class (e.g. house/office building/barn; face of a man/woman/boy/girl). A third level is the identification of a particular building or face (e.g. one's home/Sears Tower; Ronald Reagan/Aunt Mary). Employing a combined PET/MRI technique and specific cognitive tasks to detect and localize cerebral activation during the performance of these tasks, Sergent's studies have generated results indicating differential activation according to the nature of the task. Judging the orientation of sine wave gratings produced maximal activation of striate and extrastriate cortex in both hemispheres; object recognition produced maximal activation of the posterior region of the left hemisphere, specifically Brodmann areas 19, 20, 21 and 37; face-gender judgments evoked activity in the right extrastriate cortex, and the identification of specific faces produced additional activation in the fusiform and superior temporal gyri in both hemispheres. The interpretation of findings such as these is still quite problematic. As the authors point out, observed activation of an identified cerebral area does not necessarily mean that it is essential for a specific task performance but only that it is participating in the mediation of that performance. A complex task such as the identification of a familiar face involving perception, memory, and verbal identification must engage a number of spatially disparate brain mechanisms.

The leading investigators in this field agree that it is still in its infancy and that many formidable problems of a technical and conceptual nature remain to be mastered. Yet the studies and reviews of Petersen et al (1990, 1992), Frith et al (1991), Wise et al (1991), Zeki et al (1991), and Sergent & Signoret (1992b,c) demonstrate the substantial advances that already have been made. There can be no doubt that a new level in understanding the nature of the brain mechanisms underlying behavior and cognition has been attained. The challenge that this poses for neuropsychological assessment is obvious. It must now adapt its procedures and conceptualizations to accord with this new knowledge.

ACKNOWLEDGMENTS

I am grateful to Charles G. Matthews, Kathleen Haaland and Jack Fletcher for their valuable contributions and to Ann Reedy for her skillful preparation of the manuscript. Dedicated to Harold P. Bechtoldt on the occasion of his eightieth birthday.

Literature Cited

Ackerly SS, Benton AL. 1947. Report of a case of bilateral frontal lobe defect. *Proc. Assoc. Res. Nerv. Ment. Dis.* 27:479–504

Adams KM, Sawyer KD, Krale PA. 1980. Cerebral oxygenation and neuropsychological adaptation. *J. Clin. Neuropsychol.* 3:189–208

Albert ML, Goodglass H, Helm NA, Rubens AB, Alexander MP. 1981. *Clinical Aspects of Aphasia.* New York: Springer-Verlag

Anderson SW, Damasio H, Jones RD, Tranel D. 1991. Wisconsin Card Sorting Test performance as a measure of frontal lobe damage. *J. Clin. Exp. Neuropsychol.* 13:909–22

Archibald YM, Wepman JM, Jones LV. 1967. Performance on nonverbal cognitive tests following unilateral cortical injury to the right and left hemispheres. *J. Nerv. Ment. Dis.* 145:25–36

Bechtoldt HP, Benton AL, Fogel ML. 1962. An application of factor analysis in neuropsychology. *Psychol. Rec.* 12:147–56

Benton AL. 1962. The Visual Retention Test as a constructional praxis task. *Conf. Neurol.* 22:141–55

Benton AL. 1968. Differential behavioral effects in frontal lobe disease. *Neuropsychologia* 6:53–60

Benton AL. 1972. Hemispheric cerebral dominance and somesthesis. In *Psychopathology: Essays in Honor of Joseph Zubin,* ed. Hammer M, Salzinger, K, Sutton S, pp. 227–42. New York: Wiley

Benton AL. 1985. Some problems associated with neuropsycho logical assessment. *Bull. Clin. Neurosci.* 50:11–15

Benton AL. 1989a. Constructional apraxia. In *Handbook of Neuropsychology,* ed. F Boller, J Grafman, 2:387–94. Amsterdam: Elsevier

Benton AL. 1989b. Historical notes on the postconcussion syndrome In *Mild Head Injury,* ed. HS Levin, HM Eisenberg, AL Benton. New York: Oxford Univ. Press

Benton AL. 1992. Clinical neuropsychology: 1960–1990. *J. Clin. Exp. Neuropsychol.* 14:407–17

Benton AL, Elithorn A, Fogel ML, Kerr M. 1963. A perceptual maze test sensitive to brain damage. *J. Neurol. Neurosurg. Psychiatry* 26:540–44

Benton AL, Eslinger PJ, Damasio AR. 1981. Normative observations on neuropsychological test performances in old age. *J. Clin. Neuropsychol.* 3:33–42

Benton AL, Hamsher K. 1989. *Multilingual Aphasia Examination.* Iowa City: AJA Assoc. 2nd ed.

Benton AL, Hamsher K, Varney NR, Spreen O. 1983. *Contributions to Neuropsychological Assessment.* New York: Oxford Univ. Press

Benton AL, Howell IL. 1941. The use of psychological tests in the evaluation of intellectual function following head injury. *Psychosom. Med.* 3:138–51

Benton AL, Spreen O. 1961. Visual memory test: the simulation of mental incompetence. *Arch. Gen. Psychiatry* 4:79–83

Benton AL, Tranel D. 1992. Visuoperceptual, visuospatial and visuoconstructive disorders. In *Clinical Neuropsychology,* ed. KM Heilman, E Valenstein, pp. 165–213. New York: Oxford Univ. Press. 3rd ed.

Benton AL, Van Allen MW. 1968. Impairment in facial recognition in patients with cerebral disease. *Cortex* 4:344–58

Benton AL, Van Allen MW. 1972. Prosopagnosia and facial discrimination. *J. Neurol. Neurosurg. Psychiatry* 15:167–72

Berbaum KS, Platz C. 1988. Perception testing in surgical pathology. *Hum. Pathol.* 19:1127–31

Berg EA. 1948. A simple objective test for measuring flexibility in thinking. *J. Gen. Psychol.* 39:15–22

Biller J, Adams HP, Dunn V, Simmons Z, Jacoby CG. 1986. Dichotomy between clinical findings and MR abnormalities in pontine infarction. *J. Comput. Assist. Tomogr.* 10:379–85

Binder LM, Willis SC. 1991. Assessment of motivation after financially compensable minor head trauma. *Psychol. Assess.* 3:175–81

Bisiach E, Nichelli P, Sala C. 1979. Recognition of random shapes in unilateral brain damaged patients: A reappraisal. *Cortex* 15:491–99

Blessed G, Tomlinson BE, Roth M. 1968. The association between quantitative measures of dementia and of senile change in the cerebral grey matter of elderly subjects. *Br. J. Psychiatry* 114:797–811

Boll TJ. 1981. The Halstead-Reitan neuropsychology battery. See Filskov & Boll 1981, pp. 577–607

Boller F, Vignolo LA. 1966. Latent sensory aphasia in hemisphere-damaged patients: An experimental study with the Token Test. *Brain* 89:815–31

Butters N. 1984. The clinical aspects of memory disorders: contributions from experimental studies in amnesia and dementia. *J. Clin. Exp. Neuropsychol.* 6:17–36

Caine ED. 1986. The neuropsychology of depression: the pseudodementia syndrome. In *Neuropsychological Assessment of Neuropsychiatric Disorders,* ed. I Grant, KM Adams, pp. 221–43. New York: Oxford Univ. Press

Carmon A, Benton AL. 1969. Tactile perception of direction and number in patients with unilateral brain disease. *Neurology* 19:525–32

Cavalli M, DeRenzi E, Faglioni P, Vitale A. 1981. Impairment of right brain-damaged patients on a cognitive linguistic task. *Cortex* 17:545–56

Conkey R. 1938. Psychological changes associated with head injuries. *Arch. Psychol.* 33(232):5–22

Corkin S. 1965. Tactually-guided maze learning in man: effects of unilateral cortical excisions and bilateral hippocampal lesions. *Neuropsychologia* 3:339–51

Corkin S. 1979. Hidden-figures-test performance: lasting effects of unilateral penetrating head injury and transient effects of bilateral cingulotomy. *Neuropsychologia* 17:585–605

Critchley M. 1953. *The Parietal Lobes.* London: Arnold

Damasio AR. 1989. Time-locked multiregional activation: a systems-level proposal for the neural substrates of recall and recognition. *Cognition* 33:25–62

Damasio AR. 1990. Category-related recognition defects as a clue to the neural substrates of knowledge. *Trends Neurosci.* 13:95–98

Damasio AR, Tranel D, Damasio H. 1990. Face agnosia and the neural substrates of memory. *Annu. Rev. Neurosci.* 41:89–108

Damasio H, Damasio AR. 1979. "Paradoxic" ear extinction in dichotic listening: possible anatomic significance. *Neurology* 19:644–59

Damasio H, Damasio AR. 1990. The neural basis of memory, language and behavioral guidance: advances with the lesion method in humans. *Neurosciences* 2:277–86

Davis PC, Gray L, Albert M, Wilkinson W. 1992. The consortium to establish a registry for Alzheimer's disease (CERAD): Part III. Reliability of a standardized MRI evaluation of Alzheimer's disease. *Neurology* 42:1676–80

De Renzi E, Faglioni P. 1978. Normative data and screening power of a shortened version of the Token Test. *Cortex* 14:41–49

De Renzi E, Faglioni P, Spinnler H. 1968. The performance of patients with unilateral brain damage on face recognition tasks. *Cortex* 4:17–34

De Renzi E, Vignolo LA. 1962. The Token Test: A sensitive test to detect disturbances in aphasics. *Brain* 85:665–78

Deutsch G, Bourbon T, Papanicolaou AC, Eisenberg HM. 1988. Visuospatial tasks compared via activation of regional cerebral blood flow. *Neuropsychologia* 26:445–52

Diener HC, Hamster W, Seboldt H. 1984. Neuropsychological functions after carotid endartectomy. *Eur. Arch. Psychiatry Neurol. Sci.* 234:74–77

Drewe EA. 1974. The effect of type and area of brain lesion on Wisconsin Card Sorting Test performance. *Cortex* 10:159–70

Elithorn A. 1955. A preliminary report on a perceptual maze test sensitive to brain damage. *J. Neurol. Neurosurg. Psychiatry* 18:287–92

Eslinger PJ, Damasio AR. 1986. Preserved motor learning in Alzheimer's disease: Implications for anatomy and behavior. *J. Neurosci.* 6:3006–9

Eslinger PJ, Damasio AR, Benton AL, Van Allen MW. 1985. Neuropsychologic detection of abnormal mental decline in older persons. *J. Am. Med. Assoc.* 253:670–74

Filskov SB, Boll TJ, eds. 1981. *Handbook of Clinical Neuropsychology.* New York: Wiley

Flor-Henry P. 1979. On certain aspects of the localization of the cerebral systems regulating and determining emotion. *Biol. Psychiatry* 133:677–98

Fontenot DJ, Benton AL. 1971. Tactile perception of direction in relation to hemispheric locus of lesion. *Neuropsychologia* 9:83–88

Franz SI. 1919. *Handbook of Mental Examination Methods.* New York: Macmillan

Franzen MD, Iverson GL, McCracken LM. 1990. The detection of malingering in neuropsychological assessment. *Neuropsychol. Rev.* 1:247–79

Frith CD, Friston KJ, Liddle PF, Frackowiak RSJ. 1991. A PET study of word finding. *Neuropsychologia* 29:1137–48

Gelb A, Goldstein K. 1920 *Psychologische Analyse Hirnpathologischen Fälle.* Leipzig, Germany: Barth

Golden C. 1981. A standardized version of Luria's neuropsychological tests. See Filskov & Boll 1981, pp. 608–42

Goldman-Rakic PS, Friedman HR. 1991. The circuitry of working memory revealed by anatomy and metabolic imaging. In *Frontal Lobe Function and Dysfunction,* ed. AS Levin, HM Eisenberg, AL Benton, pp. 72–91. New York: Oxford Univ. Press

Goldstein K. 1939. *The Organism.* New York: American Book

Goldstein K. 1944. The mental changes due to frontal lobe damage. *J. Psychol.* 17:187–208

Goldstein K, Scheerer M. 1941. Abstract and concrete behavior: an experimental study with special tests. *Psychol. Monogr.* 43:1–151

Goodglass H, Kaplan E. 1983. *The Assessment of Aphasia and Related Disorders.* Philadelphia: Lea & Febiger

Grafman J, Jonas B, Salazar A. 1990. Wisconsin Card Sorting Test performance based on location and size of neuroanatomical lesion in Vietnam veterans with penetrating head injuries. *Percept. Mot. Skills* 71: 1120–22

Grant DA, Berg EA. 1948. A behavioral analysis of degree of reinforcement and ease of shifting to new responses in a Weigl-type card-sorting problem. *J. Exp. Psychol.* 38:404–11

Griffiths K, Cook M. 1986. Attribute processing in patients with graphical copying disability. *Neuropsychologia* 24:371–83

Gur RC, Gur RE, Obrist WD, Skolnick BE, Reivich M, et al. 1987a. Age and regional cerebral blood flow at rest and during cognitive activity. *Arch. Gen. Psychiatry* 44: 617–21

Gur RC, Gur RE, Silver FL, Obrist WD, Skolnick BE, et al. 1987b. Regional cerebral blood flow in stroke: Hemispheric effects of cognitive activity. *Stroke* 18:776–80

Haaland KY, Delaney HD. 1981. Motor deficits after left or right hemisphere damage due to stroke or tumor. *Neuropsychologia* 19:17–27

Haaland KY, Yeo RA. 1989. Neuropsychological and neuroanatomic aspects of complex motor control. In *Neuropsychological Function and Brain Imaging,* ed. ED Bigler, RA Yeo, E Turkheimer, pp. 219–40. New York: Plenum

Hachinski VC, Iliff LD, Zilhka E, DuBoulay GH, McAllister VL, et al. 1975. Cerebral blood flow in dementia. *Arch. Neurol.* 32:632–37

Halstead WC. 1947. *Brain and Intelligence.* Chicago: Univ. Chicago Press

Hamsher K, Halmi KA, Benton AL. 1981. Prediction of outcome in anorexia nervosa from neuropsychological status. *Psychiatry Res.* 4:79–88

Harrington DL, Haaland KY. 1991. Sequencing in Parkinson's disease. *Brain* 114:99–115

Hartman DE. 1988. *Neuropsychological Toxicology: Identification and Assessment of Human Neurotoxic Syndromes.* New York: Pergamon

Haxby JV, Grady CL, Ungerleider LG, Horwitz B. 1991. Mapping the functional anatomy of the intact human brain with brain work imaging. *Neuropsychologia* 29:539–55

Hayward L, Hall W, Hunt M, Zubrick SR. 1987. Can localized brain impairment be simulated on neuropsychological test profiles? *Aust. NZ. J. Psychol.* 21:87–93

Heaton RK. 1981. *Wisconsin Card Sorting Test Manual.* Odessa, Fla: Psychol. Assess. Res.

Heaton RK, Smith HH, Lehman RAW, Vogt AT. 1978. Prospects for faking believable deficits on neuropsychological testing. *J. Consult. Clin. Psychol.* 46:892–900

Hebb DO. 1945. Man's frontal lobes: A critical review. *Arch. Neurol. Psychiatry* 54:10–24

Hécaen H, Angelergues R. 1962. Agnosia for faces (prosopagnosia). *Arch. Neurol.* 7:92–100

Heilbronner K. 1905. Zur klinisch-psychologischen Untersuchungstechnik. *Mon.schr. Psychiatr. Neurol.* 17:115–32

Heilman KM, Gonzalez-Rothi LJ. 1985. Apraxia. In *Clinical Neuropsychology,* ed. KM Heilman, E Valenstein, pp. 131–50. New York: Oxford Univ. Press. 2nd ed.

Hinkin CH, Van Gorp WG, Satz P, Weisman JD, Thommes J, Buckingham S. 1992. Depressed mood and its relationship to neuropsychological test performances in HIV-1 seropositive individuals. *J. Clin. Exp. Neuropsychol.* 14:285–97

Hugdahl K. 1988. *Handbook of Dichotic Listening: Theory, Methods and Research.* New York: Wiley

Hunt HF. 1943. A practical clinical test for organic brain damage. *J. Appl. Psychol.* 27:375–86

Johnson BL, ed. 1990. *Advances in Neurobehavioral Toxicology.* Chelsea, Mich: Lewis

Jones BP, Duncan CC, Brouwers P, Mirsky AF. 1991. Cognition in eating disorders. *J. Clin. Exp. Neuropsychol.* 13:711–28

Jones RD, Tranel D, Benton A, Paulsen J. 1992. Differentiating dementia from "pseudodementia" early in the clinical course: utility of neuropsychological tests. *Neuropsychology* 6:13–21

Juolasmaa A, Outakoski J, Hirvenoja R, Tienari P, Sotaniemi K, Takkunen J. 1981. Effect of open heart surgery on intellectual performance. *J. Clin. Neuropsychol.* 3:181–97

Katzman R, Terry R, DeTeresa R, Brown T, Davies P, et al. 1988. Clinical pathological, and neurochemical changes in dementia: A subgroup with preserved mental status and numerous neocortical plaques. *Ann. Neurol.* 23:138–44

Klebanoff SG, Singer JL, Wilensky H. 1954. Psychological consequences of brain lesions and ablations. *Psychol. Bull.* 51:1–41

Knopman DS, Nissen MJ. 1987. Implicit learning in patients with probable Alzheimer's disease. *Neurology* 37:784–88

Koudstaal PJ, Van Gijn J, Lodder J, Frenken CWG, Vermeulen M, et al. 1991. Transient ischemic attacks with and without a relevant infarct on computed tomographic scans cannot be distinguished clinically. *Arch. Neurol.* 48:916–20

Kronfol Z, Hamsher K, Digre K, Waziri R. 1978. Depression and hemisphere functions: changes associated with unilateral ECT. *Br. J. Psychiatry* 132:560–67

Kundel HH. 1989. Perception errors in chest radiography. *Semin. Pulm. Med.* 10:203–9

Levin HS, Grossman RG. 1978. Behavioral sequelae of closed head injury: a quantitative study. *Arch. Neurol.* 35:720–27

Lezak MD. 1983. *Neuropsychological Assessment.* New York: Oxford Univ. Press. 2nd ed.

Lillington GA. 1989. Decision analysis in pulmonary medicine. *Semin. Pulm. Med.* 10:191–94

Lipmann O. 1922. *Handbuch Psychologischer Hilfsmittel der Psychiatrischen Diagnostik.* Leipzig, Germany: Barth

Mack JL, Levine RN. 1981. The bases of visuoconstructional disability in patients with unilateral cerebral lesions. *Cortex* 17:515–32

Malone DR, Morris HM, Kay MC, Levin HS. 1982. Prosopagnosia: A double dissociation between the recognition of familiar and unfamiliar faces. *J. Neurol. Neurosurg. Psychiatry* 45:820–22

Meadows JC. 1974. The anatomical basis of prosopagnosia. *J. Neurol. Neurosurg. Psychiatry* 37:489–501

Meier MJ, French LA. 1965. Lateralized deficits in complex visual discrimination and bilateral transfer of reminiscence following unilateral temporal lobectomy. *Neuropsychologia* 3:261–72

Milner B. 1962. Laterality effects in audition. In *Interhemisphere Relations and Cerebral Dominance,* ed. VB Mountcastle, pp. 244–57. Baltimore: Johns Hopkins Press

Milner B. 1963. Effects of different brain lesions on card sorting. *Arch. Neurol.* 9:90–100

Milner B. 1964. Some effects of frontal lobectomy in man. In *The Frontal Granular Cortex and Behavior,* ed. JM Warren, K Akert, pp. 177–95. New York: McGraw-Hill

Mishkin M, Ungerleider L, Macko KA. 1983. Object vision and spatial vision: two cortical pathways. *Trends Neurosci.* 6:414–17

Mohr E, Brouwers P. 1991. *Handbook of Clinical Trials: The Neurobehavioral Approach.* Amsterdam: Swets & Zeitlinger

Newcombe F. 1969. *Missile Wounds of the Brain.* London: Oxford Univ. Press

Newcombe F, Ratcliffe G, Damasio H. 1987. Dissociable visual and spatial impairments following right posterior cerebral lesions. *Neuropsychologia* 25:149–61

Newcombe F, Russell WR. 1969. Dissociated visual perceptual and spatial deficits in focal lesions of the right hemisphere. *J. Neurol. Neurosurg. Psychiatry* 32:73–81

Overall JE, Gorham DR. 1962. The Brief Psychiatric Rating Scale. *Psychol. Rep.* 10:799–812

Pankratz L. 1983. A new techique for the assessment and modification of feigned memory deficit. *Percept. Mot. Skills* 57:367–72

Pankratz L. 1988. Malingering on intellectual and neuropsychologial measures. See Rogers 1988, pp. 169–92

Parsons O, Butters N, Nathan PE, eds. 1987. *Neuropsychology of Alcoholism.* New York: Guilford

Perret E. 1974. The left frontal lobe of man and the suppression of habitual responses in verbal categorical behaviour. *Neuropsychologia* 12:323–30

Petersen SE, Fiez JA, Corbetta M. 1992. Neuroimaging. *Curr. Opin. Neurobiol.* 2:217–22

Petersen SE, Fox PT, Snyder AZ, Raichle ME. 1990. Activation of extrastriate and frontal cortical areas by visual words and word-like stimuli. *Science* 249:1041–44

Poeck K. 1986. The clinical examination for motor apraxia. *Neuropsychologia* 24:129–36

Poitrenaud J, Barrere H. 1973. Valeur de l'examen psychométrique dans le pronostic de l'affaiblissement intellectuel chez le sujet agé. *Rev. Psychol. Appl.* 23:185–96

Poppelreuter W. 1917. *Die Psychische Schädigungen durch Kopfschuss im Kriege 1914–1916.* Leipzig, Germany: Voss

Porteus SD. 1915. Mental tests for the feebleminded: a new series. *J. Psycho-Asthenics* 19:213

Porteus SD. 1959. *The Maze Test and Clinical Psychology.* Palo Alto, Calif: Pacific Books

Porteus SD. 1965. *Porteus Maze Test. Fifty Years Application.* Palo Alto, Calif: Pacific Books

Posner MI, Petersen SE, Fox PT, Raichle ME. 1988. Localization of cognitive operations in the human brain. *Science* 240:1627–31

Reinvang I. 1985. *Aphasia and Brain Organization.* New York: Plenum

Reitan RM. 1955. Investigation of the validity of Halstead's measure of biological intelligence. *Arch. Neurol.* 73:28–35

Reitan RM. 1984. *Aphasia Screening Test.* Tucson, Ariz: Reitan Neuropsychol. Lab.

Reitan RM, Davison L. 1974. *Clinical Neuropsychology: Current Status and Applications,* pp. 378–79. Washington, DC: Winston

Reitan RM, Wolfson D. 1985. *The Halstead-Reitan Neuropsychological Test Battery.* Tucson, Ariz: Neuropsychol. Press

Rey A. 1941. L'examen psychologique dans les cas d'encéphalopathie traumatique. *Arch. Psychol.* 28:286–340

Rey A. 1964. *L'Examen Clinique en Psychologie.* Paris: Presses Univ. France

Rey GJ, Benton AL. 1991. *Exámen de Afasia Multilingüe.* Iowa City: AJA Assoc.

Rieger C. 1888. Beschreibung der Intelligenzstörungen in Folge einer Hirnverletzung. *Verh. Phys. Med. Ges. Würzburg* 22:65–134; 23:95–150

Robertson A. 1988. The post-concussional syndrome then and now. *Aust. NZ. J. Psychiatry* 22:396–403

Rogers R. 1988. *Clinical Assessment of Malingering and Deception.* New York: Guilford

Rosenfeld SA, Van Hoesen GW. 1979. Face recognition in the monkey. *Neuropsychologia* 17:503–9

Rossolimo G. 1911. Die psychologischen. *Klin. Psychiatr. Nerv. Krankh.* 6:295–326

Rubens AB, Froehling BS, Slater G, Anderson D. 1985. Left ear suppression on verbal dichotic tests in patients with multiple sclerosis. *Ann. Neurol.* 18:459–63

Russo M, Vignolo LA. 1967. Visual figure-ground discrimination in patients with unilateral cerebral disease. *Cortex* 3:113–27

Sanchez-Longo LP, Forster FM. 1957. A clinical test for sound localization and its application. *Neurology* 7:655–63

Schaie KW, Parham IA. 1977. Cohort-sequential analysis of adult intellectual development. *Dev. Psychol.* 13:649–53

Schretler DJ. 1988. The use of psychological tests to identify malingered symptoms of mental disorder. *Clin. Psychol. Rev.* 8:451–76

Sergent J, Ohta S, McDonald B. 1992a. Functional neuroanatomy of face and object processing. *Brain* 115:15–36

Sergent J, Signoret J-L. 1992a. Functional and anatomical decomposition of face processing: evidence from prosopagnosia and PET study of normal subjects. *Philos. Trans. R. Soc. London* 335:55–62

Sergent J, Signoret J-L. 1992b. Implicit access to knowledge derived from unrecognized faces in prosopagnosia. *Cereb. Cortex* 2:389–400

Sergent J, Signoret J-L. 1992c. Varieties of functional deficits in prosopagnosia. *Cereb. Cortex* 2:375–88

Sergent J, Zuck E, Levésque M, McDonald B. 1992b. Positron emission tomography study of letter and object processing: empirical findings and methodological considerations. *Cereb. Cortex* 2:68–80

Shipley WC. 1940. A self-administered scale for measuring intellectual impairment and deterioration. *J. Psychol.* 9:371–77

Sklar M. 1973. *Sklar Aphasia Scale.* Los Angeles: Western Psychol. Serv.

Smith A. 1960. Changes in Porteus Maze scores of brain-operated schizophrenics after an eight-year interval. *J. Ment. Sci.* 106:967–78

Smith A, Kinder E. 1959. Changes in psychological test performances of brain-operated subjects offer eight years. *Science* 129:149–50

Sparks R, Goodglass H, Nickel B. 1970. Ipsilateral versus contralateral extinction in dichotic listening resulting from hemispheric lesions. *Cortex* 6:249–60

Spreen O, Benton AL. 1963. The simulation of mental deficiency on a visual memory test. *Am. J. Ment. Defic.* 67:909–13

Spreen O, Benton AL, Fincham R. 1965. Auditory agnosia without aphasia. *Arch. Neurol.* 13:84–92

Spreen O, Benton AL, Van Allen MW. 1966. Dissociation of visual and tactile naming in amnesic aphasia. *Neurology* 16:807–14

Spreen O, Strauss E. 1991. *A Compendium of Neuropsychological Tests.* New York: Oxford Univ. Press

Squire LR. 1987. *Memory and Brain.* New York: Oxford Univ. Press

Squire LR, Knowlton B, Musen G. 1993. The structure and organization of memory. *Annu. Rev. Psychol.* 44:453–95

Starkstein SE, Robinson RG. 1991. The role of the frontal lobes in affective disorder following stroke. In *Frontal Lobe Function and Dysfunction,* ed. HS Levin, HM Eisenberg, AL Benton, pp. 288–303. New York: Oxford Univ. Press

Sweet JJ, Newman P, Bell B. 1992. Significance of depression in clinical neuropsychological assessment. *Clin. Psychol. Rev.* 12:21–45

Szmukler GI, Andrewes D, Kingston K, Chen K, Stargatt R, Robb S. 1992. Psychological impairment in anorexia nervosa: Before and after refeeding. *J. Clin. Exp. Neuropsychol.* 14:347–52

Tallal P, Newcombe F. 1978. Impairment of auditory perception and language comprehension in dysphasia. *Brain Lang.* 5:13–24

Terman LM. 1916. *The Measurement of Intelligence.* Boston: Houghton Mifflin

Terman LM, Merrill MA. 1937. *Measuring Intelligence.* Boston: Houghton Mifflin

Thurstone LL. 1938. *Primary Mental Abilities.* Chicago: Univ. Chicago Press

Tow PM. 1955. *Personality Changes Follow-*

ing Frontal Leucotomy. London: Oxford Univ. Press

Tranel D. 1991. Dissociated verbal and nonverbal retrieval and learning following left anterior temporal damage. *Brain Cogn.* 15:187–200

Tranel D. 1992a. Functional neuroanatomy: neuropsychological correlates of cortical and subcortical damage. In *Textbook of Neuropsychiatry,* ed. SC Yudofsky, RE Hales, pp. 57–88. Washington, DC: Am. Psychiatric Press

Tranel D. 1992b. Neuropsychological assessment. *Psychiatr. Clin. N. Am.* 15:283–99

Trimble MR. 1981. *Post-traumatic Neurosis: From Railway Spine to the Whiplash.* New York: Wiley

Ungerleider L, Mishkin M. 1982. Two cortical visual systems. In *Analysis of Visual Behavior,* ed. DJ Ingle, MA Goodale, pp. 549–86. Cambridge, Mass: MIT Press

Varney NR. 1980. Sound recognition in relation to aural language comprehension in aphasic patients. *J. Neurol. Neurosurg. Psychiatry* 43:71–75

Varney NR. 1984. Phonemic imperception in aphasia. *Brain Lang.* 21:85–94

Varney NR, Benton AL. 1979. Phonemic discrimination and aural comprehension among aphasic patients. *J. Clin. Neuropsychol.* 1:65–73

Vignolo LA. 1969. Auditory agnosia. In *Contributions to Clinical Neuropsychology,* ed. AL Benton, pp. 172–208. Chicago: Aldine

Walsh K. 1992. Some gnomes worth knowing. *Clin. Neuropsychol.* 6:119–33

Walsh KW. 1978. *Neuropsychology: A Clinical Approach.* Edinburgh: Churchill Livingstone

Warrington E. 1969. Constructional apraxia. In *Handbook of Clinical Neurology,* ed. PJ Vinken, GW Bruyn, 4:67–83. Amsterdam: North-Holland

Warrington E, James M. 1967. An experimental investigation of facial recognition in patients with unilateral lesions. *Cortex* 3:317–26

Wechsler D. 1939. *The Measurement of Adult Intelligence.* Baltimore: Williams & Wilkins

Wechsler D. 1981. *WAIS-R Manual.* New York: Psychol. Corp.

Wells FL. 1927. *Mental Tests in Clinical Practice.* New York: World Book

Wells FL, Ruesch J. 1942. *Mental Examiner's Handbook.* New York: Psychol. Corp.

Wise R, Chollet F, Hadar U, Friston KJ, Hoffner E, et al. 1991. Distribution of cortical neural networks in word comprehension and word retrieval. *Brain* 114:1803–17

Yerkes RM. 1919. Report of the Psychology Committee of the National Research Council. *Psychol. Rev.* 26:83–149

Zeki S, Watson JDG, Lueck CJ, Friston KJ, Kennard C, Frackowiak RS. 1991. A direct demonstration of functional specialization in human visual cortex. *J. Neurosci.* 11:641–49

Zemore R, Eames N. 1979. Psychic and somatic symptoms of depression among young adults, institutionalized and non-institutionalized aged. *J. Gerontol.* 34:716–72

Zung W, Green RL. 1973. Detection of affective disorders in the aged. In *Pharmacology and Aging,* ed. C Eisdorfer, WE Fann, pp. 213–24. New York: Plenum

Annu. Rev. Psychol. 1994. 45:25–50

COGNITIVE APPROACHES TO EMOTION AND EMOTIONAL DISORDERS

A. Mathews

MRC Applied Psychology Unit, Cambridge CB2 2EF, England

C. MacLeod

Department of Psychology, University of Western Australia, Perth, Western Australia

KEY WORDS: anxiety, depression, attention, interpretation, memory

---

CONTENTS

0066-4308/94/0201-0025$05.00

INTRODUCTION

The Relationship of Cognition and Emotion

At the beginning of the last decade, diametrically opposed positions were taken up in a public debate about the relationship between cognitive processes and emotion. At one extreme it was claimed that emotion is completely independent of cognition (Zajonc 1980), and at the other, that cognitive appraisals were invariably necessary for the production of emotion (Lazarus 1982, 1984). Since then, the view that cognitive processes are closely related to emotion has been steadily gaining ground, although disagreement continues about the direction and extent of the relationship (Izard 1993). Some of this debate has been associated with confusion about the meaning or definition of cognition: opponents of cognitive models of emotion focused on conscious intentional processes, noting that these seem to have properties quite distinct from feelings and preferences. However, most cognitive psychologists believe that it is useful to distinguish between strategic and automatic processes, with the latter being relatively independent of conscious intent or effort (see Johnson & Hasher 1987). Proponents of cognitive theories assume that some of the critical processes involved in emotion are automatic (e.g. spreading activation, Bower 1992) and non-conscious (e.g. primary appraisal, Lazarus 1993). If it is assumed that automatic and non-conscious processes may be involved in emotion, then many of the objections to cognitive models appear much less compelling. This does not imply that all emotional reactions are equally amenable to cognitive explanations: different emotions probably vary in the level of processing involved. Some simple fears may be represented sub-cortically (LaDoux 1989), while more complex emotions require extensive involvement of higher level processing (Johnson & Multhaup 1992).

Despite their widespread acceptance, cognitive models of emotion have had problems. Some findings, such as mood state–dependent recall, that were initially influential in the development of these models have since proven unreliable (Bower 1987, 1992). Other effects of emotional state that have been interpreted as resulting from automatic activation, such as mood-congruent shifts in subjective judgments (Johnson & Tversky 1983, Bower 1983), can be abolished by reminding subjects about the source of their mood (Schwartz & Clore 1983). Similarly, the negative recall bias found in depression can also be obtained by asking normal subjects to act as if they were depressed (Perrig & Perrig 1988). Even more problematic, instances of significant incongruence between mood state and the emotional valence of recalled events have been reported (Parrott & Sabini 1990, see also Rinck et al 1992). Such findings are difficult to account for solely in terms of invariant automatic processes linking mood with memory. One emerging conclusion is that understanding the relationship between cognition and emotion requires us to consider the interface between automatic and strategic (intentional) processes. Although automatic processes are usually involuntary, effortless, and operating outside of awareness, there are instances in which some but not all of these characteristics apply (Bargh 1989). Thus, it is possible that the cognitive factors involved in emotion could be automatic in one sense but not in another. Also, the factors may interact in such a way that intentional strategies can sometimes modify automatic operations. For this reason, after reviewing evidence for the role of attentional, interpretative, and memorial processes in emotion, we will examine to what extent each may be considered to meet criteria for automatic or strategic processing.

Scope of this Review

Our review of research on cognitive processes in emotion gives priority to studies that may help in understanding individual differences in emotionality, and particularly differences in vulnerability to pathological emotional states. Two general types of study are therefore of special interest: those comparing groups differing on trait measures of negative emotionality and those that contrast individuals with or without emotional disorders such as depression or anxiety states. In most of this research the implicit or explicit hypothesis is that differences in how individuals process emotional information may be a causal factor in the development or maintenance of emotional disorders. This hypothesis is tempting, because the cognitive differences observed often seem to promote or maintain a negative emotional state. Thus, depressed individuals recall relatively more unhappy events than do normal mood controls, and this may in turn maintain depressed mood (Teasdale 1988). The potential for a circular effect will be greater the more that the available memories are depressogenic in nature (e.g. associated with internal, stable, and global attributions). Similarly, the more that nervous individuals attend to threatening cues in their environment, the more they will encode information about potential hazards, again allowing a circular relationship between selective processing and anxious mood (Mathews 1990).

We also focus on research concerned with the processing of emotional information, rather than that documenting general differences in processing capacity (regardless of the type of information). Many researchers have noted that high levels of anxiety or depression are associated with reduced ability to perform complex cognitive tasks (Mueller 1992, Watts & Cooper 1989). Although there is no universal agreement on the reasons for this restriction, several theoretical accounts suggest that capacity-limited cognitive resources such as working memory are depleted by the emotional state (Eysenck &

Calvo 1992, Ellis & Ashbrook 1988) leaving fewer resources available for the experimenter-imposed task. Thus anxious subjects are no poorer on relatively automatic tasks such as making the inferences necessary to comprehend simple anaphoric references in text, but they are slower to verify an inference that was not forced during reading (Darke 1988). A related view is that depression specifically interferes with the capacity for cognitive initiative (Hertel & Hardin 1990, Hertel & Rude 1991). Thus it may be that depressives are in fact capable of performing at normal levels if they are given specific instructions about the appropriate strategy to adopt, but they may fail to do so spontaneously. These general deficits could occur because the resources required have been depleted by the emotional state or because emotions have changed the priorities accorded by subjects in their allocation of the available resources. The latter possibility implies that deficits may arise, at least in part, because anxious or depressed subjects accord higher priority to processing emotional information.

EMOTION AND SELECTIVE ENCODING

A variety of experimental techniques have been developed to test the hypothesis that elevated levels of anxiety or depression are associated with an encoding bias favoring emotionally negative information. Perhaps the simplest approach has used identification tasks. Several studies have demonstrated that individuals reporting elevated levels of depression (e.g. Powell & Hemsley 1984) or anxiety (e.g. Burgess et al 1981, Foa & McNally 1986) display a disproportionate ability to identify or detect emotionally negative stimulus words. Performance on such tasks may be influenced systematically by guessing strategies that operate when encoding operations have only partially resolved the identity of any stimulus word. If anxious and depressed subjects favor emotionally negative words in their guesses, then the observed pattern of results would represent a response bias rather than selective encoding.

Interference Tasks

In order to eliminate the possible impact of any individual difference in guessing strategies, emotional words can be presented as distractor stimuli, which subjects must attempt to ignore while performing some central task. Individual differences in relative tendency to encode alternative classes of distractor stimuli may thus be revealed by differences in the patterns of interference effects observed on this central task. One of the most commonly used interference paradigms involves the modification of the well established Stroop task. As predicted, individuals reporting high levels of anxiety display disproportionately long color-naming latencies for threat-related stimulus words, suggesting that these subjects experience particular difficulty ignoring the emotionally negative content of such stimuli (e.g. Mathews & MacLeod 1985, Watts et al 1986, Hope et al 1990, McNally et al 1990, Foa et al 1991). Similar effects on this color-naming interference task have been reported for individuals reporting high levels of depression (e.g. Gotlib & McCann 1984, Williams & Nulty 1986). However, in reviewing this area of research, MacLeod & Mathews (1991a) have argued that the elevated color-naming interference shown by depressed subjects on emotionally negative words might be mediated by co-occurring elevated levels of anxiety within these depressed populations.

Attentional Probe Tasks

The results from interference tasks are less susceptible to response bias accounts than are the results from identification tasks. Nevertheless, any general tendency to selectively reduce the encoding of all stimulus information, when negative distractor stimuli are present, would also result in this pattern of interference. Likewise, even if all distractor information were encoded to exactly the same degree by all subjects, variations in the emotional impact of the aversive stimuli could produce the observed individual differences in color-naming interference. In attentional probe tasks, subjects are briefly exposed to a stimulus array that includes one emotionally negative word and one emotionally neutral word, each of which is presented in a different location. For example, MacLeod et al (1986) presented negative/neutral word pairs on a computer monitor for 500 ms and required subjects to detect the occurrence of small dot probes that could appear in the location of either stimulus word following termination of the display. Consistent with the hypothesis that elevated anxiety should be associated with the allocation of attention toward emotionally negative stimuli, highly anxious individuals alone demonstrated speeded detection latencies for probes occurring in the spatial location of the negative words, relative to probes occurring in the location of the neutral words. Subsequent research using this visual probe paradigm has confirmed the above pattern of findings, suggesting that anxious individuals do indeed attend selectively to emotionally negative stimulus information (e.g. Broadbent & Broadbent 1988, MacLeod & Mathews 1988, Mogg et al 1992).

Attentional probe tasks have yielded less consistent support for the hypothesis that depression would be associated with a similar bias toward emotionally negative stimuli. In a modified probe task, designed to contrast groups differing in depression, Gotlib et al (1988) concluded that depressed subjects showed no tendency to selectively allocate attention toward negatively valenced stimuli or away from emotionally positive stimuli (see also Hill & Dutton 1989). Nevertheless, Gotlib et al's low depression subjects did appear to allocate attention selectively toward emotionally positive stimuli, suggesting that heightened depression may be associated with the loss of an attentional bias favoring such positive information. A similar argument has been made by Matthews & Antes (1992) on the basis of the eye movements displayed by depressed subjects when scanning emotionally toned sections of photographic stimuli. However, once again, neither of these depression studies was able to show that the loss of the positive attentional bias in the high depressed subjects was more directly associated with these individuals' heightened levels of depression, rather than with their similarly elevated levels of anxiety. In a close replication of Gotlib et al's (1988) study, Mogg et al (1991b) used partial correlations to demonstrate that the individual differences in allocation of selective attention were associated more directly with individual differences in level of anxiety rather than depression. Thus, while there is relatively little evidence to suggest that elevated levels of depression are associated with the facilitated processing of emotionally negative information, there is considerable empirical support for the hypothesis that such an encoding bias is associated with elevated levels of anxiety.

Recent reviews (e.g. Eysenck 1992) have noted that there are certain experimental paradigms that typically fail to detect a processing bias; e.g. when subjects are presented with a single processing option on each trial. In contrast, those studies that have revealed an anxiety-linked encoding advantage for negative information typically have presented clearly defined alternative processing options on every trial, each differing in emotional valence, and have assessed the priorities that subjects attach to each of these options. For example, both depressed (Clark et al 1983) and anxious (MacLeod & Mathews 1991b) subjects fail to show any bias on lexical decision latencies for emotionally negative vs neutral words. However, when stimulus strings appeared simultaneously in pairs on the computer screen, anxious subjects did display a relative speeding of lexical decisions for the emotionally negative stimuli (MacLeod & Mathews 1991b). This effect, which also has been reported by Mogg et al (1991a), suggests that elevated anxiety may be associated with a heightened tendency to prioritize the encoding of emotionally negative stimulus information, rather than with an increase in the actual speed or efficiency with which such information is processed.

EMOTION AND SELECTIVE INTERPRETATION

When subjects are asked to rate the probability of experiencing future positive and negative events, higher probability ratings are given for negative events by anxious or depressed individuals (e.g. Butler & Mathews 1983, 1987). Such judgmental biases are not restricted to the estimation of future risk. Subjective evaluations concerning diverse aspects of one's current life circumstances (e.g. Schwartz & Clore 1983), and ratings of one's own performance from videotapes of role-played interview or social situations (e.g. Cane & Gotlib 1985,

Forgas et al 1984), are also negatively biased. It seems likely that these patterns of judgment reflect the operation in anxious and depressed individuals of an interpretative bias that favors emotionally negative interpretations of ambiguous information.

Early studies relied primarily upon self-report measures. Krantz & Hammen (1979) and Butler & Mathews (1983) presented subjects with descriptions of ambiguous scenarios and required subjects to select their most likely response or interpretation from a list of alternative options. As predicted, both anxious and depressed subjects displayed a disproportionate tendency to select the more negative options from these sets of alternatives. However, it is difficult to discount the possible influence of experimenter demand when such transparent dependent measures are employed to assess interpretation. One approach to reducing demand involves presenting subjects with a spelling task that simply requires the written transcription of words from audio tape. Embedded within these stimulus words are a set of homophones that each have one sound but two meanings differing in emotional valence and alternative spellings (e.g. pain/pane, groan/grown, die/dye). Research employing this homophone spelling task has confirmed that highly anxious individuals provide a disproportionate number of negative word spellings for these ambiguous homophones (e.g. Eysenck et al 1987, Mathews et al 1989b). It remains possible that the homophone spelling task reveals response bias rather than a true interpretative effect. If both words come to mind when a homograph is presented, and anxious subjects choose to produce the more negative response option, then the observed pattern of findings would occur.

In response to this problem, Richards & French (1992) introduced a lexical priming paradigm to assess the semantic activation of each possible meaning when ambiguous words were being processed. On critical trials, subjects were presented briefly with an initial prime homograph that had a single spelling but two meanings differing in emotional valence (e.g. shot, arms, beat, stroke), followed by a lexical decision for the target letter string. When the prime-target stimulus onset asynchrony (SOA) was either 750 ms or 1250 ms, highly anxious subjects alone displayed a greater priming effect for target words related to the negative meaning, rather than to the neutral meaning, of the initial homographs. This suggests that the negative meaning of the ambiguous information was indeed activated to a disproportionate degree. When the prime-target SOA was reduced to 500 ms, however, no such anxiety-linked difference was observed in the relative priming effects shown across each category of target word, suggesting that interpretation of the prime homograph may not have occurred automatically.

Using ambiguous sentences rather than single word stimuli, Eysenck et al (1991) attempted to assess interpretation using a delayed recognition memory paradigm. Subjects were exposed to an audiotaped list of sentences including the critical ambiguous sentences that each permitted one emotionally negative and one neutral interpretation (e.g. "The doctor examined little Emily's growth."). Subjects then saw a recognition set that included disambiguated versions of the original ambiguous sentences constrained either to their negative or to their neutral meanings. Eysenck and colleagues found that highly anxious subjects claimed to recognize disproportionately many threatening disambiguations of the previously presented ambiguous sentences. Furthermore, because elevated anxiety was not associated with any increased tendency to falsely recognize emotionally negative foil sentences within this recognition task, Eysenck et al were able to dismiss the possibility that their results might reflect an anxiety-linked response bias in the recognition memory task. However, as Hitchcock & Mathews (1992) pointed out when they obtained somewhat similar results in a subsequent study that employed the same paradigm, it is impossible to determine whether the effects obtained on this recognition memory paradigm reflect an anxiety-linked interpretative bias in "an on-line process, involving the automatic resolution of ambiguity as it occurs" (p. 229). It may be that the original stimuli are stored in a literal form and their ambiguity is only resolved by later elaboration and reflection during the recognition task itself.

To resolve this problem, MacLeod & Cohen (1993) reported an experiment designed to investigate emotion-linked differences in the on-line interpretation of ambiguous text. Under self-paced conditions, subjects read short passages containing an ambiguous sentence with one emotionally negative and one neutral interpretation, followed by a continuation sentence consistent with only one interpretation. High anxiety individuals demonstrated the pattern of comprehension latencies that would be expected if they had consistently imposed the more negative interpretation on the initial ambiguous sentence. In contrast, the pattern of comprehension latencies shown by the low anxiety subjects suggested that these individuals had consistently imposed the less negative meaning on these ambiguous sentences. Based on these studies, it appears that there is strong support for the hypothesis that elevated anxiety is associated with an increased tendency to selectively impose negative interpretations on ambiguous information. This selective interpretation seems to occur on-line, during the initial processing of the ambiguity. Nevertheless, it remains possible that strategic processes may make some contribution to this anxiety-linked interpretative bias. It is less clear whether elevated depression is associated with any increase in negative interpretations of ambiguity. Although depressed subjects certainly report that they make such negative interpretations, experimenter demand effects or response bias explanations cannot be ruled out until more objective procedures have been used with this group.

EMOTION AND SELECTIVE MEMORY

In some studies of autobiographical memory, subjects have been presented with an emotionally neutral cue word and asked to report the first memory brought to mind. Depressed subjects have shown an elevated tendency to report negative memories (e.g. Clark & Teasdale 1982), and the same phenomenon has been reported for anxious subjects (e.g. Burke & Mathews 1992). Using valenced rather than neutral cues, Williams & Broadbent (1986) have shown that depressed individuals demonstrate disproportionately short recall latencies for negative memories relative to positive memories. More recently, Richards & Whittaker (1990) have reported similar findings for anxious individuals, using this same paradigm. Clearly, this may reflect the increased availability of negative memories in anxious and depressed individuals. However, one of the limitations of autobiographical memory research is that it is difficult to determine whether observed individual differences reflect idiosyncratic retrieval processes or variations in the nature of actual past experience. In order to more clearly implicate individual differences in retrieval processes it is necessary to test memory for stimulus information to which all subjects have equivalent previous exposure.

Researchers adopting this approach have exposed subjects to word lists that contain emotionally valenced items, and then unexpectedly assessed memory for these stimulus materials later in the same experimental session (e.g. Bradley & Mathews 1983, Teasdale & Dent 1987). Depressed subjects frequently have shown a relative memory advantage for emotionally negative stimulus words under these conditions, although the presence of such an effect appears to depend on the nature of the encoding task. For example, when the initial encoding task has required subjects to relate each stimulus word to themselves, depressed subjects reliably display a retrieval advantage for the emotionally negative stimuli (e.g. Denny & Hunt 1992, Watkins et al 1992). However, when instructed to encode the words in some other way, depressed individuals do not show a subsequent recall advantage for the negative items (e.g. Bradley & Mathews 1983).

There is much less evidence that elevated anxiety is associated with facilitated recall or recognition of emotionally negative stimuli that have been encoded during the experimental session. Many of those studies using interference tasks that have successfully demonstrated an anxiety-linked selective processing bias favoring negative stimuli, have failed to detect any equivalent anxiety-linked bias in subsequent ability for subjects to recall or recognize the emotional distractor stimuli (e.g. Watts et al 1986, Mogg et al 1989). Indeed, several studies that have been constructed specifically to examine the patterns of selective memory associated with anxiety have found evidence that recall and recognition of emotionally unpleasant information is selectively impaired in highly anxious individuals (e.g. Watts et al 1986, Watts & Dalgleish 1991). Even when such studies have employed exactly the same self-referent encoding task that has been associated so reliably with facilitated incidental memory for negative stimulus words in depressed subjects, the more anxious subjects have shown impaired recall and recognition of the negative stimuli (e.g. Mogg et al 1987, Foa et al 1989). Some studies that have reported enhanced recall or recognition memory for emotionally negative stimuli used words that had different meanings for the subject groups. Nunn et al (1984) and Rusted & Dighton (1991) claimed to have demonstrated an anxiety-linked recall advantage for emotionally negative stimuli when they found that their phobic subjects were better able to recall words related to their specific fear than were non-phobic control subjects. Group differences on the memory tasks cannot be attributed to anxiety-linked differences in memory for threatening stimuli because the critical target stimuli in such studies were emotionally negative for the phobic subjects alone.

There is a modest degree of evidence that clinically anxious patients suffering from panic disorder may display an enhanced ability to recall emotionally threatening stimulus words (e.g. McNally et al 1989, Cloitre & Liebowitz 1991). If this is the case, however, then it seems likely that such a recall bias may represent a specific clinical feature of this particular disorder, rather than a general characteristic of elevated anxiety. The weight of empirical evidence suggests strongly that facilitated ability to recall emotionally negative information is a characteristic of elevated depression, but not of elevated anxiety.

STATE AND TRAIT VARIABLES IN SELECTIVE PROCESSING

Much of the research reported above has compared clinical subjects, who report naturally occurring elevations of depression or anxiety, with normal controls. Such an approach makes it difficult to determine whether observed group differences in selective information processing are associated with mood states or with group differences in enduring personality traits. There are strong indications that emotional state may make a major contribution to these effects. Three lines of evidence implicate depressed mood state in the mediation of memory biases favoring negative information. First, several studies have demonstrated that the induction of depressed mood can elicit a recall advantage for emotionally negative information within a sample of normal students (e.g. Teasdale & Russell 1983). Second, studies that have examined recovery from episodes of clinical depression have found that negative recall bias is reduced or eliminated (Bradley & Mathews 1988, Dobson & Shaw 1987). Finally, it has been demonstrated that diurnal fluctuations in level of mood in clinical depressives is associated with corresponding changes in the magnitude of these individuals' recall advantage for emotionally negative information (e.g. Clark & Teasdale 1982).

Similar evidence suggests that state anxiety may play an important role in mediating anxiety-linked patterns of selective processing. When Mogg et al (1990) induced state anxiety in normal student subjects by using a stressful anagram task, these individuals demonstrated an increased tendency to orient visual attention toward threat-related words. Conversely, several studies have reported that the attentional bias favoring such negative stimuli, typically shown by clinically anxious subjects, is reduced or eliminated following recovery (e.g. Foa & McNally 1986, Watts et al 1986, Lavy et al 1993, Mogg et al 1992). It seems that this also may be true for the biased pattern of interpretation shown by clinically anxious individuals (Mathews et al 1989b, Eysenck et al 1991). Thus it would appear that dysphoric emotional mood states may be necessary before processing advantages for emotionally negative information are observed. However, there is growing evidence that the degree to which mood elicits such processing advantages may depend on an individuals' stable levels of trait vulnerability to those mood states.

Several researchers have reported that depressed mood states elicit more pronounced cognitive biases in those individuals who report a past history of depressive episodes, suggesting a high level of trait vulnerability to this emotion (e.g. Teasdale & Dent 1987, Miranda & Persons 1988, Miranda et al 1990). Similar findings have been reported concerning the patterns of selective attention associated with elevated anxiety. Using the dot probe detection paradigm to assess distribution of visual attention, MacLeod & Mathews (1988) tested separate groups of high trait and low trait anxious students on two occasions, again when state anxiety was low (early in the semester) and once when state anxiety was high (in the week before an important examination). When state anxiety was low, neither the high trait nor the low trait anxious groups showed any selective attentional response to emotionally negative stimuli words. High trait anxious students responded to elevated state anxiety by displaying increased allocation of visual attention toward emotionally threatening examination-related stimulus words. In contrast, low trait anxious subjects responded to the state anxiety elevation by showing a marginally significant effect in the opposite direction. Based on these findings, MacLeod & Mathews concluded that state anxiety only elicits selective attention to threatening stimuli in high trait anxious individuals (see also Broadbent & Broadbent 1988).

In conclusion, it appears that both state and trait variables may make an important contribution to emotion-linked patterns of selective processing. Furthermore, the evidence suggests strongly that these variables exert their influence in an interactive manner. Individual differences in trait vulnerability to anxiety or depression seem to be associated with the patterns of selective information processing that are elicited by elevated levels of anxious or depressed mood state.

HOW SPECIFIC ARE EMOTIONAL BIASES?

Depending on how one thinks emotional information is represented in memory, emotional states could activate all congruent representations; that is, those consistent in valence and meaning with that emotion. Alternatively, only some kinds of congruent information might be activated, such as that involved in causing the emotion or relating to the individual's current concerns. Finally, emotions could be associated with effects that are relatively specific not only to particular cognitive content but also to certain types of cognitive operations on that information.

The idea that all mood-congruent information in memory is more available when subjects are in the corresponding mood state has received some support from the global effects of mood on judgment of valenced events. In sad or anxious moods, all negative events are seen as more probable, rather than just those related to the events inducing that mood (Johnson & Tversky 1983, Bower 1983). However, when subjects are anticipating or imagining a future threatening event, changes in subjective probability are greater for that event than for other similarly valenced events (Butler & Mathews 1987, Constans & Mathews 1993). When made anxious by the prospect of taking an examination, the increase in subjective probability for examination failure is greater than that for being robbed. Thus, there may be specific as well as global effects of emotion on judgment.

Other more specific effects have been documented in research on mood-congruent recall. Depressed subjects show stronger effects for negative trait adjectives (Clark & Teasdale 1985, Watkins et al 1992) than for other negative words, and the negative bias in recall disappears completely when words are encoded in relation to other people rather than to the subject (Bradley & Mathews 1983). In attentional paradigms, although initial data suggested that anxious subjects attend to all emotionally threatening words (MacLeod et al 1986), more recent replications (Mogg et al 1992) have produced convincing evidence that the size of this effect is not the same for all types of similarly valenced stimuli. All congruent information does not seem equally activated in emotional states.

Content-Specificity Effects

Examination of the evidence for more specific selective processing effects suggests that type of emotional state and relevance of content to the current concerns of the individual may be important. This conclusion is clearly supported by the pattern of results for different clinical groups on tasks such as color-naming. Panic disorder is typically associated with excessive concern about somatic sensations, which are interpreted as signs of disease, collapse, or even imminent death (Clark 1986, Clark et al 1988). These subjects show interference effects when color-naming words that describe physical symptoms or their feared consequences, but not when color-naming other emotional words (Ehlers et al 1988, McNally et al 1992). In contrast, the greatest interference in socially phobic subjects occurs with socially threatening words (Hope et al 1990). Patient groups with specific concerns about other topics similarly show slowing when color-naming words that describe these topics (McNally et al 1990, Foa et al 1991, Cooper & Fairburn 1992). Patients with generalized anxiety disorder (GAD) report worrying excessively and unrealistically about a range of topics and show slowed color-naming with both physically and socially threatening words. However, if the subjects are divided according to their report of which worry troubles them most, the extent of interference is greater with words matching that particular domain (Mogg et al 1989). Similar results are found for the attentional deployment paradigm, in which subjects detect probes in the location of emotional or neutral words. Panic patients are speeded in probe detection only for physically threatening words (Asmundson et al 1992), and the extent of speeding in the same paradigm with generally anxious patients also relates to the match between type of word and major domain of worry for each individual (Mogg et al 1992).

To summarize, attentional effects are greatest when emotional stimuli match the domain of greatest concern to that subject. The same principle appears to hold for interference effects in depression (Williams & Broadbent 1986). We found only one result that seems to challenge this conclusion. Martin et al (1991) reported that their anxious patients showed equivalent color-naming interference (relative to neutral words) for either positive or negative (threatening) words. A possible explanation for this apparently anomalous result is that some of the positive words were the antonyms of words descriptive of typical worries and perhaps were associated semantically with threat (Small & Robins 1988). Mathews & Klug (1993) provide support for this explanation. They divided another set of positive and negative words into those judged to be related (e.g. safe, dying) or unrelated (e.g. mercy, warfare) to the likely concerns of anxious patients. Related words produced more interference than did unrelated words, regardless of valence. This finding further supports the hypothesis that it is the match with current domain of concern, rather than emotional valence or congruence in a general sense, that determines the information that is given processing priority.

Process-Specificity Effects

In an earlier discussion of cognitive processing in emotional disorders, Williams et al (1988) suggested that anxiety and depression are not characterized by uniform biases across all cognitive operations. In this view anxiety states are associated with biases in attention, favoring emotionally threatening stimuli, but less so with similar biases in recall. In contrast, depression is associated with a negative self-related bias in recall, but there are no consistent indications of attentional effects. It is therefore possible that emotional states are associated with biases in specific cognitive operations: early perceptual selection in the case of anxiety and negatively-valenced semantic elaboration leading to better retrieval in depression.

Some findings seem inconsistent with this generalization. Stroop interference is usually thought of as an attentional process (MacLeod 1991), and color-naming negative words does cause interference in depressed subjects (Gotlib & Cane 1987, Williams & Broadbent 1986). Color-naming interference in depressed subjects may be attributable to secondary anxiety (Mogg & Marsden 1990) or to postattentional elaborative processing (Mogg et al 1993), although this issue requires further exploration. More direct tests of attention deployment using the probe method provide less evidence of bias in depression, with several negative or marginal results (MacLeod et al 1986, Gotlib et al 1988, Hill & Dutton 1989). Similarly, not all studies fail to show biased recall in anxiety. McNally et al (1989) found that panic patients recalled words describing fear better than non-fear words, and Mogg et al (1990) also reported similar effects with GAD patients. However, the authors in the last study noted that the parallel pattern of intrusion errors suggested strongly that subjects were using the anxiety-descriptor category to aid recall. Positive results may be more likely when words can easily be categorized as self-descriptive (see Klein & Kihlstrom 1986), thus mimicking the equivalent effect more usually reported in depression. Despite these inconsistent results, the majority of the studies reviewed earlier supported Williams et al's hypothesis.

More definitive findings may emerge if groups are carefully selected to avoid any mixed emotional states and measures are used that can independently assess both early perceptual vs later elaborative processing. The use of paradigms that prevent subjects from reporting on the nature of interfering stimuli or that separate implicit from explicit memory are probably necessary to adequately test the hypothesis that emotional states are associated with specific types of cognitive operation as well as content.

AUTOMATIC AND STRATEGIC PROCESSES

A number of the findings reviewed previously have suggested that mood-congruent recall and mood-related judgment biases can be modified or abolished intentionally. Normal subjects can simulate negative recall biases (Perrig & Perrig 1988), show mood-incongruent recall (Parrott & Sabini 1990), and eliminate any influence of mood on judgments if they are reminded of the reason for their mood state (Schwartz & Clore 1983). Although these demonstrations do not prove that similar biases in emotional disorders are under strategic control, they do raise this possibility.

Effects of Unattended and Masked Stimuli

One method used to determine if attentional or interference effects depend on automatic processes has been to present threatening stimuli during dichotic listening while subjects are attending to other information (e.g. Mathews & MacLeod 1986, Trandell & McNally 1987). Because the interference found on secondary tasks was specific to anxious subjects during exposure to unattended threat words, it could be attributed to preattentive (i.e. nonstrategic) processing. A critique by Holender (1986) raises the interpretive difficulty that rapid voluntary shifts in attention between channels cannot be ruled out. As a result, subsequent efforts to rule out strategic processing have relied on presentation of masked words that subjects cannot report even when asked to do so. In these studies, some words are presented for color-naming in the usual way, while others are presented briefly (e.g. for 20 ms) before being covered by a colored pattern mask, allowing the comparison of interference effects with or without awareness. MacLeod & Hagan (1992) and MacLeod & Rutherford (1992) found evidence that high trait anxious subjects under medical or examination stress showed delayed color-naming of threatening words, even when they were unable to report that any words had been displayed. In anxious patients, masked threatening words have produced interference effects as great as those produced by unmasked threatening words (Mogg et al 1993). Because subjects could not report on which trials the relevant words were actually present, there seems no way that intentional strategies could explain the pattern of interference effects found.

None of the results with masked stimuli showed any evidence of content specificity: in the studies of normals under stress there was no effect of match with current concern, and in the clinical study anxious patients showed equal interference with words that had been rated as relevant to either anxiety or depressive concerns. Furthermore, a group of depressed patients included in the latter study showed no evidence of interference effects with either word set. This suggests that under conditions that reduce the possibility for controlled processing, depressed subjects may not show interference effects, thus supporting the hypothesis that cognitive bias in depression is predominantly postattentive. Preattentive selection in anxiety appears to be relatively global, since even words that were not related to the current source of stress caused interference, provided that they were threatening in meaning. Our previous conclusion about content specificity in anxiety may therefore need to be revised. It seems that the earliest (preattentive) analysis of stimulus meaning may serve only to classify stimuli as related to threat or not. More fine-grained analysis may be required before a match can be made with current concern, leading to more specific interference effects.

Effects of Priming and Mental Load

In general, the above results provide strong support for the idea that the selective bias in anxiety involves at least some automatic processes. If this is the case, then one might expect anxious subjects to show automatic priming (implicit memory) effects following exposure to threatening stimuli. There is some evidence for such priming effects on word stem completion tasks in anxious patients (Mathews et al 1989a, Zeitlin & McNally 1991) and word fragment completion in high trait anxious normal subjects (Richards & French 1991). Yet the convincing lack of evidence for any implicit memory bias in depressed patients (Watkins et al 1992, Denny & Hunt 1992) suggests strongly that automatic priming does not occur in depression, and that the negative bias found in recall of the same words is therefore probably mediated by encoding and/or retrieval strategies. Such an interpretation is of course consistent with the finding that mood-congruent recall bias is observed only for self-encoded words (Bradley & Mathews 1983).

In another approach to the question of automaticity, Bargh & Tota (1988) reasoned that if negative self-judgments in depression were made automatically, then these judgments would not be slowed by requiring subjects to simultaneously maintain a mental load in working memory. Consistent with this expectation, Bargh & Tota found that a mental load delayed depressed subjects when making positive, but not negative decisions about themselves. In a follow-up study, Anderson et al (1992) used the same technique with depressed students required to make judgments about whether negative events might happen to them in the future. Subjects with high depression scores were not slowed by a mental load when making such judgments, but subjects with low or moderate depression were. It therefore seems that such judgments require attentional resources in non-depressed and mildly depressed subjects, but not in severely depressed subjects.

Both automatic and controlled processes seem to be involved in cognitive bias effects. Anxious subjects show the strongest evidence for automatic (non-conscious) processes such as color-naming interference produced by masked words. Mood-congruent recall in depression probably depends on controlled elaborative processes and by implication, the relative absence of such recall effects in anxiety may suggest the intentional avoidance of elaboration. However, other evidence suggests that mood-congruent judgments in depression become increasingly automated as mood worsens or becomes chronic.

CAUSAL STATUS OF SELECTIVE PROCESSING

Emotional disorders are often thought more likely to result when individuals who are high in trait anxiety or depression (neuroticism) come under severe and/or prolonged stress. This conclusion is consistent with research using self-report of psychological distress following life events, showing that individuals with high preexisting levels of neuroticism and negative emotionality were more distressed by life-changes or natural disasters (e.g. Ormel & Wohlfarth 1991, Nolen-Hoeksema & Morrow 1991). Although these studies are consistent with the hypothesis that the manner in which negative information about the stressful event is processed influences the extent of emotional distress, this research is inconclusive because it is correlational in nature.

Teasdale & Dent (1987) compared women who had previously been depressed with those who had never experienced severe depression, to test the hypothesis that a negative bias in recall would be more characteristic of the former group (see also Miranda et al 1990). The women who had been depressed before had higher neuroticism scores, and this measure correlated with poorer recall of positive self-encoded words. The same group also showed better recall of globally negative trait words, but only following induced negative mood. These results were taken as support for the differential activation hypothesis (Teasdale 1988) that depression results when a negative mood activates material in memory having particularly depressogenic properties. In MacLeod & Hagan's (1992) study of women undergoing a stressful diagnostic procedure, color-naming interference scores were correlated with subsequent self-reports of adverse emotional reactions following confirmation of the feared diagnosis. Surprisingly, the best predictor (even better than trait anxiety) was the interference produced by threatening words presented out of awareness. Results from the above studies support the hypothesis that a persisting tendency to selectively process emotionally threatening material represents the cognitive mechanism underlying vulnerability to emotional disorders. In the presence of stressful life events, this trait factor could result in a positive feedback loop between selective encoding and mood state that culminates in emotional disorder.

One difficulty with this hypothesis is that interference with color-naming emotional words can sometimes be paradoxically eliminated by stress manipulations. Mathews & Sebastian (1993) reported that the expected color-naming interference with phobia-related words was abolished when fear was induced by exposing subjects to a real phobic stimulus. Fearful subjects may be able to inhibit interference due to threatening words under these circumstances, although presumably not when they cannot consciously detect the interfering words (see also MacLeod & Rutherford 1992). Vulnerable individuals may use effortful control of this type as a coping strategy, although this strategy is likely to fail under severe stress (Mathews 1993). The causal hypothesis thus requires modification. Stress (or negative mood) may differentially elicit automatic selective encoding of threatening information in vulnerable subjects. Controlled avoidance strategies can counter the consequences of this bias, although since these strategies are resource-limited, they are likely to fail in the face of severe or prolonged stress. Such failure of control may correspond to the onset of emotional disorders.

Selective Processing and Emotional Learning

Little is known about how individual differences in selective processing are acquired or even whether any direct learning is necessary. After finding interference effects from emotional stimuli in children as young as 6–7 years, Martin et al (1992) suggested that selective processing is an integral part of the emotional reaction itself, rather than something that must be learned separately. Still, additional learning may exaggerate or reduce the extent to which emotional information is selectively encoded.

Based on studies of learning by exposure to non-obvious covariations in complex materials, Lewicki et al (1989) has claimed that people learn such covariation rules implicitly: that is, without intention or awareness. Furthermore, it has been suggested that once a covariation rule is acquired, even ambiguous instances will be taken as confirming evidence and thus further strengthen the rule. Hill et al (1991) have argued that self-perpetuating interpretative rules of this type may underlie emotional disorders. Öhman (1993) has reported other evidence that emotional reactions can be acquired and maintained by stimuli that cannot be consciously identified. Skin conductance responses can be conditioned to masked pictures of spiders, snakes, or angry faces, but not to other control pictures, which suggests that the former are biologically prepared to be associated with fear. Intentional processes such as worry may inadvertently enhance such an association after it has been acquired. Thus Jones & Davey (1990) showed that thinking about an aversive event was sufficient to increase the subsequent conditioned response to a cue associated with the event. Cognitive biases also might become self-perpetuating via the illusionary correlation effects reported by Tomarken et al (1989; see also de Jong et al 1992). Snake-phobic subjects markedly overestimated the covariation, which was actually random, between pictures of snakes and mild electric shock. In this way, even without any real contingencies existing, any initial tendency toward selective processing of emotional stimuli could grow stronger over time as a function of exposure to threatening events alone.

IMPLICATIONS FOR THEORIES OF EMOTION

In the study of emotion, as in other areas of psychology, it is usually assumed that understanding normal function precedes understanding of abnormality. Certainly, much of the research described here has been stimulated by cognitive theories about how information is acquired, interpreted, and stored by the normally functioning person. Observations about how systems become dysfunctional can sometimes inform theories of normal function and we believe this may well apply to emotion.

Mood-Memory Network Theory

Bower's (1981, 1987, 1992) seminal network theory has been the stimulation for much of the research we have reviewed. This theory assumes that mood states automatically activate all associated representations in memory. The problems with this theory include: 1. failure to replicate mood state–dependent memory effects, 2. presence of instructional effects on judgmental bias and mood-incongruent recall, 3. failure to find (single) lexical decision effects of mood state, 4. restriction of mood-congruent recall to self-encoded stimuli, 5. specificity of attentional bias to domain of current concern, and 6. facilitation of different types of cognitive operation in different emotions.

Many of these problems may be resolved by further developing or adding to spreading activation theory. Perhaps only information perceived as causally belonging to a mood state will be incorporated within the network, and lexical decisions may not require access to such emotional information (Bower & Mayer 1989). Although additional features may help to deal with some of these problems, it seems increasingly difficult for spreading activation theory to explain all the cognitive consequences of mood states. Part of the difficulty may arise from the fact that the theory only recognizes one type of code, within a single network system, for all types of information; whether for bodily reactions, propositional knowledge, schemas or emotional events. Other theories to account for the range of emotions we experience, and for the distinction between emotions and knowledge, typically assume a hierarchy of codes, from a basic sensori-motor level to higher schematic and conceptual levels (e.g. Leventhal & Scherer 1987). These theories provide a more flexible framework for thinking about the cognitive basis for emotional reactions, even though they make less strongly testable predictions.

Other Cognitive Models of Emotion

According to Oatley & Johnson-Laird's (1987) theory, basic emotions have evolved to serve important biological and social functions, and to determine priorities when conflicts arise in ongoing plans and goals. Fear/anxiety, for example, results when a background goal of ensuring survival and safety is violated, and sadness/depression results from failure of a major plan, or loss of a goal. Emotions impose a relatively stereotyped mode of operations on the cognitive system, consistent with the evolutionary function of that emotion. Thus, fear or anxiety should impose a configuration on the cognitive system that facilitates the operations necessary to avoid danger. If so, then anxiety might reduce the priority given to processing complex memories and increase that given to operations required to maintain perceptual vigilance. In this way, the theory predicts that the mode of processing, as well as the type of information being processed, will vary across emotional disorders, consistent with the pattern of the data reviewed earlier.

Johnson & Multhaup's (1992) theory follows Leventhal's (Leventhal & Scherer 1987) multilevel model more directly. Four hierarchical levels in memory are proposed: two perceptual and two reflective subsystems. The most basic (P1) is concerned with low-level perceptual detection, and feeds information to the next higher subsystem (P2), which encodes at the level of objects and events. The perceptual information from P2 is available to the next module (R1), which is responsible for lower level reflective operations, such as the routine use of schemas to interpret events. At the highest level, R2 controls nonroutine executive operations, receiving information from P2 and R1, and directing their activities. Basic emotional reactions to sensory events, such as fear to sudden looming stimuli, are represented mainly at lower levels. Higher levels are increasingly involved when affect is schema-driven or when it depends on conscious elaboration and recall. The model can account for ability to exercise intentional control over emotional effects on judgment, recall, or attention (R2-level executive control) for automated schema-driven affective decisions in depression (R1) and for preattentive bias without awareness in anxiety states (P1 and P2 alone). The apparent differences between the operations that are biased in anxiety and depression can also be explained as being a function of the processing levels that are primarily involved.

The interacting cognitive subsystems (ICS) approach (Barnard & Teasdale 1991) postulates a set of interconnected modules, each coding for a different type of information. In addition to sensory, perceptual, and body-state subsystems, at the core of the model are propositional and implicational modules, of which the implicational subsystem is most critical for emotion. Propositional codes are concerned with knowledge ("cold" cognition) while implicational codes are concerned with the construction of mental models having personal implications ("hot" cognition). In the same way that propositional schemas integrate information from various sources of knowledge, implicational models are said to integrate at a still higher level, and in particular, to incorporate body-state information. One important difference between ICS and a single mood-memory network is that the former requires that emotional effects operate at the implicational schema level, rather than at the level of propositional or lexical items such as single words (Teasdale & Barnard 1993). Emotional effects are expected only when information is encoded in relationship to its implications for oneself, and not when responses are based on propositional knowledge alone. In this way, ICS can account for some of the phenomena that have created difficulties for models based on a single network. The problem may be that there is too much explanatory power in the absence of precise predictions. In this sense, ICS is a framework for developing hypotheses and not a complete theory.

It is too early to evaluate fully how adequately these multirepresentational models will account for the findings reviewed earlier, but they may help overcome some of the problems encountered with single network models. It is important to note that these models are explicitly consistent with connectionist (or neural network) implementation of each subsystem. However, because each module uses different codes and the information flow between subsystems is restricted, limits are placed on the otherwise undifferentiated flow of information that would occur in a single network. The challenge remains to generate new predictions that will distinguish the various multirepresentational theories that could be proposed.

CONCLUSIONS

Emotional states, both normal and abnormal, are associated with distinctive patterns of processing personally-relevant emotional information. The general finding is that mood-congruent information is given priority, although some striking exceptions to this rule have been noted (e.g. mood-incongruent recall). In emotional disorders, anxiety is strongly associated with attention to threatening stimuli. Depression is reliably associated with the selective recall of negative self-referent information, but not with automatic priming (implicit memory). Automatic components are involved in the tendency for threatening stimuli to cause interference with other tasks in anxious subjects because interference persists in the absence of awareness. There are equally strong indications that strategic components are involved in other tasks such as mood-congruent recall. We have suggested that early automatic (preattentive) analysis of emotional information is relatively global, and perhaps confined to classifying a stimulus as potentially threatening, but that subsequent processing becomes increasingly selective, favoring information that matches current concerns.

The respective influences of current state factors and enduring individual differences are uncertain, but we have proposed that the data is best accounted for by assuming that current emotional state (or the event causing that state) elicits differential tendencies from individuals varying in trait emotionality. Thus anxious mood (or stressful events) leads high, but not low, trait anxious subjects to selectively encode threatening information. Although the causal relationship between processing selectivity and emotional reactions remains unknown, these observations are consistent with the possibility that individual differences in selective encoding represent the cognitive substrate of vulnerability to emotional disorder. We speculate that vulnerable individuals may attempt to use effortful control strategies to restrict the increased intake of threatening information when under stress, and that the eventual failure of such efforts represents the onset of emotional disorder. Finally, we suggest that mood-memory network models, in which a single code represents all emotional and non-emotional information, are not able to account for a number of the findings reported here. Multirepresentational models may offer a way of handling these results, but they need to be examined further before their eventual value can be assessed.

Literature Cited

Anderson SM, Spielman LA, Bargh JA. 1992. Future-event schemas and certainty about the future: automaticity in depressives' future-event predictions. *J. Pers. Soc. Psychol.* 5:711–23

Asmundson GJG, Sandler LS, Wilson KG, Walker JR. 1992. Selective attention toward physical threat in patients with panic disorder. *J. Anxiety Disord.* 6:295–303

Bargh JA. 1989. Conditional automaticity: varieties of automatic influence in social perception and cognition. In *Unintended Thought,* ed. JS Uleman, JA Bargh. New York: Guilford

Bargh JA, Tota ME. 1988. Context-dependent automatic processing in depression: accessibility of negative constructs with regard to self but not others. *J. Pers. Soc. Psychol.* 54:925–39

Barnard PJ, Teasdale JD. 1991. Interacting cognitive subsystems: a systemic approach to cognitive-affective interaction and change. *Cogn. Emot.* 5:1–39

Bower GH. 1981. Mood and memory. *Am. Psychol.* 36:129–48

Bower GH. 1983. Affect and cognition. *Philos. Trans. R. Soc. London Ser. B* 302:387–402

Bower GH. 1987. Commentary on mood and memory. *Behav. Res. Ther.* 25:443–56

Bower GH. 1992. How might emotions affect learning. In *Handbook of Emotion and Memory,* ed. SA Christianson, pp. 3–31. Hillsdale, NJ: Erlbaum

Bower GH, Mayer JD. 1989. In search of mood-dependent retrieval. *J. Soc. Behav. Pers.* 4:121–56

Bradley BP, Mathews AM. 1983. Negative self-schemata in clinical depression. *Br. J. Clin. Psychol.* 22:173–81

Bradley BP, Mathews AM. 1988. Memory bias in recovered clinical depressives. *Cogn. Emot.* 2:235–46

Broadbent DE, Broadbent M. 1988. Anxiety and attentional bias: state and trait. *Cogn. Emot.* 2:165–83

Burgess IS, Jones LN, Robertson SA, Radcliffe WN, Emerson E, et al. 1981. The degree of control exerted by phobic and non-phobic verbal stimuli over the recognition behaviour of phobic and non-phobic subjects. *Behav. Res. Ther.* 19:223–34

Burke M, Mathews AM. 1992. Autobiographical memory and clinical anxiety. *Cogn. Emot.* 6:23–35

Butler G, Mathews AM. 1983. Cognitive processes in anxiety. *Behav. Res. Ther.* 5:51–62

Butler G, Mathews AM. 1987. Anticipatory anxiety and risk perception. *Cogn. Ther. Res.* 91:551–65

Cane DB, Gotlib IH. 1985. Depression and the effects of positive and negative feedback on expectations, evaluations and performance. *Cogn. Ther. Res.* 9:145–60

Clark DM. 1986. A cognitive approach to panic. *Behav. Res. Ther.* 24:461–70

Clark DM, Salkovskis PM, Gelder M, Koehler C, Martin M, et al. 1988. Tests of a cognitive theory of panic. In *Panics and Phobias,* ed. I Hand, H-U Wittchen, pp. 149–58. Berlin/Heidelberg: Springer-Verlag

Clark DM, Teasdale JD. 1982. Diurnal variation in clinical depression and accessibility of memories of positive and negative experiences. *J. Abnorm. Psychol.* 91: 87–95

Clark DM, Teasdale JD. 1985. Constraints on the effects or mood on memory. *J. Pers. Soc. Psychol.* 48:1595–608

Clark DM, Teasdale JD, Broadbent DE, Martin

M. 1983. Effect of mood on lexical decisions. *Bull. Psychon. Soc.* 21:175–78

Cloitre M, Liebowitz MR. 1991. Memory bias in panic disorder: an investigation of the cognitive avoidance hypothesis. *Cogn. Ther. Res.* 15:371–86

Constans JI, Mathews AM. 1993. Mood and the subjective risk of future events. *Cogn. Emot.* In press

Cooper MJ, Fairburn CG. 1992. Selective processing of eating, weight and shape related words in patients with eating disorders and dieters. *Br. J. Clin. Psychol.* 31:363–65

Darke S. 1988. Effects of anxiety on inferential reasoning task performance. *J. Pers. Soc. Psychol.* 55:499–505

de Jong PJ, Merckelbach H, Arntz A, Nijman H. 1992. Covariation detection in treated and untreated spider phobics. *J. Abnorm. Psychol.* 101:724–27

Denny EB, Hunt RR. 1992. Affective valence and memory in depression: dissociation of recall and fragment completion. *J. Abnorm. Psychol.* 101:575–80

Dobson KS, Shaw BF. 1987. Specificity and stability of self-referent encoding in clinical depression. *J. Abnorm. Psychol.* 96:34–40

Ehlers A, Margraf J, Davies S, Roth WT. 1988. Selective processing of threat cues in subjects with panic attacks. *Cogn. Emot.* 2:201–19

Ellis HC, Ashbrook PW. 1988. Resource-allocation model of the effects of depressed mood states on memory. In *Affect, Cognition & Social Behavior,* ed. K Fiedler, J Forgas, pp. 25–43. Gottingen, Germany: Hogrefe

Eysenck MW. 1992. *Anxiety: The Cognitive Perspective.* Hillsdale, NJ: Erlbaum

Eysenck MW, Calvo MG. 1992. Anxiety and performance: the processing efficiency theory. *Cogn. Emot.* 6:409–34

Eysenck MW, MacLeod C, Mathews AM. 1987. Cognitive functioning in anxiety. *Psychol. Res.* 49:189–95

Eysenck MW, Mogg K, May J, Richards A, Mathews AM. 1991. Bias in interpretation of ambiguous sentences related to threat in anxiety. *J. Abnorm. Psychol.* 100:144–50

Foa EB, Feske U, Murdock TB, Kozak MJ, McCarthy PR. 1991. Processing of threat-related information in rape victims. *J. Abnorm. Psychol.* 100:156–62

Foa EB, McNally RJ. 1986. Sensitivity to feared stimuli in obsessive-compulsives: a dichotic listening analysis. *Cogn. Ther. Res.* 10:477–86

Foa EB, McNally R, Murdock TB. 1989. Anxious mood and memory. *Behav. Res. Ther.* 27:141–47

Forgas JD, Bower GH, Krantz SE. 1984. The influence of mood on perception. *J. Exp. Soc. Psychol.* 20:497–513

Gotlib IH, Cane DB. 1987. Construct accessibility and clinical depression: a longitudinal investigation. *J. Abnorm. Psychol.* 96:199–204

Gotlib IH, McCann CD. 1984. Construct accessibility and depression: and examination of cognitive and affective factors. *J. Pers. Soc. Psychol.* 47:427–39

Gotlib IH, McLachlan AL, Katz AN. 1988. Biases in visual attention in depressed and non-depressed individuals. *Cogn. Emot.* 2:185–200

Hertel PT, Hardin TS. 1990. Remembering with and without awareness in a depressed mood: evidence for deficits in initiative. *J. Exp. Psychol: Gen.* 119:45–59

Hertel PT, Rude SS. 1991. Depressive deficits in memory: focusing attention improves subsequent recall. *J. Exp. Psychol.* 120:301–9

Hill AB, Dutton F. 1989. Depression and selective attention to self-esteem threatening words. *Pers. Individ. Differ.* 10:915–17

Hill T, Lewicki P, Neubauer RM. 1991. The development of depressive encoding dispositions: a case of self-perpetuation of biases. *J. Exp. Soc. Psychol.* 27:392–409

Hitchcock P, Mathews AM. 1992. Interpretation of bodily symptoms in hypochondriasis. *Behav. Res. Ther.* 30:223–34

Holender D. 1986. Semantic activation without conscious identification. *Behav. Brain Sci.* 9:1–66

Hope DA, Rapee RM, Heimberg RG, Dombeck MJ. 1990. Representations of the self in social phobia: vulnerability to social threat. *Cogn. Ther. Res.* 14:177–89

Izard CE. 1993. Four systems for emotion activation: cognitive and noncognitive processes. *Psychol. Rev.* 100:68–90

Johnson EJ, Tversky A. 1983. Affect, generalization and the perception of risk. *J. Pers. Soc. Psychol.* 45:20–31

Johnson MK, Hasher L. 1987. Human learning and memory. *Annu. Rev. Psychol.* 38:631–68

Johnson MK, Multhaup KS. 1992. Emotion and MEM. In *Handbook of Emotion and Memory,* ed. SA Christianson. Hillsdale, NJ: Erlbaum

Jones T, Davey CL. 1990. The effects of cued UCS rehearsal on the retention of differential 'fear' conditioning: an experimental analogue of the 'worry' process. *Behav. Res. Ther.* 2:159–64

Klein FB, Kihlstrom JF. 1986. Elaboration organization and the self-reference effect in memory. *J. Exp. Psychol: Gen.* 115:26–38

Krantz S, Hammen C. 1979. Assessment of cognitive bias in depression. *J. Abnorm. Psychol.* 88:611–19

LaDoux JE, Romanski L, Xagoraris A. 1989.

Indelibility of subcortical emotional memories. *J. Cogn. Neurosci.* 1:238–43

Lavy E, van den Hout M, Arntz A. 1993. Attentional bias and spider phobia: conceptual and clinical issues. *Behav. Res. Ther.* 31:17–24

Lazarus RS. 1982. Thoughts on the relations between emotion and cognition. *Am. Psychol.* 37:1019–24

Lazarus RS. 1984. On the primacy of cognition. *Am. Psychol.* 39:124–29

Lazarus RS. 1993. From psychological stress to the emotions: a history of changing outlooks. *Annu. Rev. Psychol.* 44:1–21

Leventhal H, Scherer K. 1987. The relationship of emotion to cognition: a functional approach to a semantic controversy. *Cogn. Emot.* 1:3–28

Lewicki P, Hill T, Sasaki I. 1989. Self-perpetuating development of encoding biases. *J. Exp. Psychol: Gen.* 118:323–37

MacLeod C, Cohen I. 1993. Anxiety and the interpretation of ambiguity: a text comprehension study. *J. Abnorm. Psychol.* 102: 238–47

MacLeod C, Hagan R. 1992. Individual differences in the selective processing of threatening information, and emotional responses to a stressful life event. *Behav. Res. Ther.* 30:151–61

MacLeod C, Mathews AM. 1988. Anxiety and the allocation of attention to threat. *Q. J. Exp. Psychol: Hum. Exp. Psychol.* 38:659–70

MacLeod C, Mathews AM. 1991a. Cognitive-experimental approaches to the emotional disorders. In *Handbook of Behaviour Therapy and Psychological Science: An Integrative Approach,* ed. PR Martin, pp. 115–50. New York: Pergamon

MacLeod C, Mathews AM. 1991b. Biased cognitive operations in anxiety: accessibility of information or assignment of processing priorities. *Behav. Res. Ther.* 29:599–610

MacLeod C, Mathews AM, Tata P. 1986. Attentional bias in emotional disorders. *J. Abnorm. Psychol.* 95:15–20

MacLeod C, Rutherford EM. 1992. Anxiety and the selective processing of emotional information: mediating roles of awareness, trait and state variables, and personal relevance of stimulus materials. *Behav. Res. Ther.* 30:479–91

MacLeod CM. 1991. Half a century of research on the stroop effect: an integrative review. *Psychol. Bull.* 109:163–203

Martin M, Horder P, Jones GV. 1992. Integral bias in naming of phobia-related words. *Cogn. Emot.* 6:479–86

Martin M, Williams R, Clark DM. 1991. Does anxiety lead to selective processing of threat-related information? *Behav. Res. Ther.* 29:147–60

Mathews AM. 1990. Why worry? The cognitive function of anxiety. *Behav. Res. Ther.* 28:455–68

Mathews AM. 1993. Anxiety and the processing of emotional information. In *Progress in Experimental Personality and Psychopathology Research,* ed. L Chapman, J Chapman, D Fowles, pp. 254–80. New York: Springer

Mathews AM, Klug F. 1993. Emotionality and interference with color-naming in anxiety. *Behav. Res. Ther.* 31:57–62

Mathews AM, MacLeod C. 1985. Selective processing of threat cues in anxiety states. *Behav. Res. Ther.* 23:563–69

Mathews AM, MacLeod C. 1986. Discrimination of threat cues without awareness in anxiety states. *J. Abnorm. Psychol.* 95:131–38

Mathews AM, Mogg K, May J, Eysenck M. 1989a. Implicit and explicit memory bias in anxiety. *J. Abnorm. Psychol.* 98:236–40

Mathews AM, Richards A, Eysenck M. 1989b. Interpretation of homophones related to threat in anxiety states. *J. Abnorm. Psychol.* 98:31–34

Mathews AM, Sebastian S. 1993. Suppression of emotional Stroop effects by fear-arousal. *Cogn. Emot.* In press

Matthews GR, Antes JR. 1992. Visual attention and depression: cognitive biases in the eye fixations of the dysphoric and the nondepressed. *Cogn. Ther. Res.* 16:359–71

McNally RJ, Foa EB, Donnell CD. 1989. Memory bias for anxiety information in patients with panic disorder. *Cogn. Emot.* 3:27–44

McNally RJ, Kaspi SP, Riemann BC, Zeitlin SB. 1990. Selective processing of threat cues in posttraumatic stress disorder. *J. Abnorm. Psychol.* 99:398–402

McNally RJ, Riemann BC, Louro CE, Lukach BM, Kim E. 1992. Cognitive processing of emotional information in panic disorder. *Behav. Res. Ther.* 30:143–49

Miranda J, Persons JB. 1988. Dysfunctional attitudes are mood-state dependent. *J. Abnorm. Psychol.* 97:76–79

Miranda J, Persons JB, Byers CN. 1990. Endorsement of dysfunctional beliefs depends on mood state. *J. Abnorm. Psychol.* 99:237–41

Mogg K, Bradley BP, Williams R, Mathews AM. 1993. Subliminal processing of emotional information in anxiety and depression. *J. Abnorm. Psychol.* 102:304–11

Mogg K, Marsden B. 1990. Processing of emotional information in anxious subjects. *Br. J. Clin. Psychol.* 29:227–29

Mogg K, Mathews AM, Bird C, MacGregor-Morris R. 1990. Effects of stress and anxiety on the processing of threat stimuli. *J. Pers. Soc. Psychol.* 59:1230–37

Mogg K, Mathews AM, Eysenck M. 1992. Attentional bias to threat in clinical anxiety states. *Cogn. Emot.* 6:149–59

Mogg K, Mathews AM, Eysenck M, May J. 1991a. Biased cognitive operations in anxiety: artefact, processing priorities or attentional search? *Behav. Res. Ther.* 5:459–67

Mogg K, Mathews AM, May J, Grove M, Eysenck M, Weinman J. 1991b. Assessment of cognitive bias in anxiety and depression using a colour perception task. *Cogn. Emot.* 5:221–38

Mogg K, Mathews AM, Weinman J. 1987. Memory bias in clinical anxiety. *J. Abnorm. Psychol.* 96:94–98

Mogg K, Mathews AM, Weinman J. 1989. Selective processing of threat cues in anxiety states: a replication. *Behav. Res. Ther.* 27:317–23

Mueller JH. 1992. Anxiety and performance. In *Handbook of Human Performance,* ed. AP Smith, DM Jones, pp. 127–60. London: Academic

Nolen-Hoeksema S, Morrow J. 1991. A prospective study of depression and posttraumatic stress symptoms after a natural disaster: the 1989 Loma Prieta earthquake. *J. Pers. Soc. Psychol.* 61:115–21

Nunn JD, Stevenson R, Whalan G. 1984. Selective memory effects in agoraphobic patients. *Br. J. Clin. Psychol.* 23:195–201

Oatley K, Johnson-Laird P. 1987. Towards a cognitive theory of emotions. *Cogn. Emot.* 1:29–50

Öhman A. 1993. Fear and anxiety as emotional phenomena. In *Handbook of Emotions,* ed. M Lewis, JM Haviland. New York: Guilford. In press

Ormel J, Wohlfarth T. 1991. How neuroticism, long-term difficulties, and life situation change influence psychological distress: a longitudinal model. *J. Pers. Soc. Psychol.* 5:744–55

Parrott WG, Sabini J. 1990. Mood and memory under natural conditions: evidence for mood incongruent recall. *J. Pers. Soc. Psychol.* 59:321–36

Perrig WJ, Perrig P. 1988. Mood and memory: mood- congruity effects in the absence of mood. *Mem. Cogn.* 16:102–9

Powell M, Hemsley DR. 1984. Depression: a breakdown of perceptual defence? *Br. J. Psychiatr.* 145:358–62

Richards A, French CC. 1991. Effects of encoding and anxiety on implicit and explicit memory performance. *Pers. Individ. Differ.* 12:131–39

Richards A, French CC. 1992. An anxiety-related bias in semantic activation when processing threat/neutral homographs. *Q. J. Exp. Psychol.* 45:503–25

Richards A, Whittaker TM. 1990. Effects of anxiety and mood manipulation in autobiographical memory. *Br. J. Clin. Psychol.* 29:145–53

Rinck M, Glowalla U, Schneider K. 1992. Mood-congruent and mood-incongruent learning. *Mem. Cogn.* 20:29–39

Rusted J, Dighton K. 1991. Selective processing of threat-related material by spider phobics in a prose recall task. *Cogn. Emot.* 5:123–32

Schwartz N, Clore GL. 1983. Mood, misattribution, and judgements of well-being: informative and directive functions of affective states. *J. Pers. Soc. Psychol.* 3:513–23

Small SA, Robins CJ. 1988. The influence of induced depressed mood on visual recognition thresholds: predictive ambiguity of associative network models of mood and cognition. *Cogn. Ther. Res.* 12:295–304

Teasdale JD. 1988. Cognitive vulnerability to persistent depression. *Cogn. Emot.* 2:247–74

Teasdale JD, Barnard PJ. 1993. *Affect, Cognition and Change.* London: Erlbaum. In press

Teasdale JD, Dent J. 1987. Cognitive vulnerability to depression: an investigation of two hypotheses. *Br. J. Clin. Psychol.* 26:113–26

Teasdale JD, Russell ML. 1983. Differential effects of induced mood on the recall of positive, negative and neutral words. *Br. J. Clin. Psychol.* 22:163–71

Tomarken AJ, Mineka S, Cook M. 1989. Fear-related selective associations and covariation bias. *J. Abnorm. Psychol.* 98:381–94

Trandell DV, McNally RJ. 1987. Perception of threat cues in post-traumatic stress disorder: semantic processing without awareness. *Behav. Res. Ther.* 6:469–76

Watkins P, Mathews AM, Williamson DA, Fuller R. 1992. Mood congruent memory in depression: emotional priming or elaboration? *J. Abnorm. Psychol.* 101:581–86

Watts FN, Cooper Z. 1989. The effects of depression on structural aspects of the recall of prose. *J. Abnorm. Psychol.* 98:150–53

Watts FN, Dalgleish T. 1991. Memory for phobia-related words in spider phobics. *Cogn. Emot.* 5:313–29

Watts FN, McKenna FP, Sharrock R, Trezise L. 1986. Colour naming of phobia related words. *Br. J. Psychol.* 77:97–108

Williams JMG, Broadbent K. 1986. Distraction by emotional stimuli: use of a Stroop task with suicide attempters. *Br. J. Clin. Psychol.* 25:101–10

Williams JMG, Nulty DD. 1986. Construct accessibility, depression and the emotional Stroop task: transient mood or stable structure? *Pers. Individ. Differ.* 7:485–91

Williams JMG, Watts FN, MacLeod C, Mathews AM. 1988. *Cognitive Psychology and Emotional Disorders.* Chichester: Wiley & Sons

Zajonc RB. 1980. Feeling and thinking: Preferences need no inferences. *Am. Psychol.* 35:151–75

Zeitlin SB, McNally RJ. 1991. Implicit and explicit memory bias for threat in post-traumatic stress disorder. *Behav. Res. Ther.* 29:451–57

Annu. Rev. Psychol. 1994. 45:51–78

CONTEMPORARY PSYCHOLOGY IN SPAIN

J.M. Prieto

Faculty of Psychology, Complutense University of Madrid, Spain

R. Fernández-Ballesteros

Faculty of Psychology, Autonomous University of Madrid, Spain

H. Carpintero

Faculty of Philosophy, Complutense University of Madrid, Spain

KEY WORDS: history of psychology, training in psychology, psychological journals, psychological societies, European psychology

---

CONTENTS

0066-4308/94/0201-0051$05.00

INTRODUCTION

The beginnings of modern Spanish psychology are found in the final decade of the nineteenth century (Carpintero 1982). The leading figures until the 1930s were Ramon-y-Cajal, Simarro, and Lafora in Madrid, and Turro and Mira in Barcelona. They maintained regular contacts with leading psychology research groups in France, Germany, Switzerland, and the United Kingdom, and as a result, two International Congresses on Psychotechnics took place in Barcelona in 1921 and 1930.

The Spanish Civil War (1936–1939), which brought to the country a totalitarian regime for more than forty years, impaired normal development of psychology (Carpintero 1984). A massive emigration to Latin America of scholars, scientists, and practitioners followed the war's end in 1939 and the return of psychology as a scientific discipline was slow. Germain led the field's postwar resurgence, and Yela, Pinillos, Siguán, and Secadas were among the first to be active in the field.

Yela introduced factor analysis and multivariate experimental approaches to the study in Spain of intelligence, verbal behavior, personnel selection and psychological testing. Pinillos' initial fields of interest were personality testing and social attitudes; he tried to fill the gap between humanistic and experimental approaches in psychology. His textbook, *Principles of Psychology,* published in 1975, became the most influential of its time. Siguán worked in industrial psychology, focusing on human relations and supervisory training in interpersonal skills and leadership. He also approached migratory movements and bilingualism from a psychological perspective. Secadas was involved in research projects on mental aptitudes and developmental assessment.

In 1980 a five-year curriculum in psychology was established by law. Several universities created Faculties of Psychology and enrollments rose rapidly. Thousands of students came in pursuit of a pre-doctoral degree in psychology (*Licenciatura en Psicologia*). Research teams and lecturing posts grew under this new climate. A new generation of professors favored a fresh approach to research and theory. They reviewed the basis of the core program in psychology and designed new lines of professional action and practice.

PSYCHOLOGY AS A SCIENTIFIC FIELD OF RESEARCH

In the last thirty years Spanish psychologists have contributed to psychology in many basic and applied areas, both from theoretical and empirical perspectives. Only the most well established research programs developed in the last three decades will be considered here. Since it is impossible to cite all the most relevant articles of each important author, an extended bibliography of 1000 references may be requested from the authors of this review.[1]

Basic Processes

Learning has been a central research topic since the early 1960s. While classical conditioning seemed to dominate the experimental scene in the 1960s, operant theory became influential in the 1970s. Pavlovian conditioning (García-Hoz 1985), the role of the local context in the appearance of blocking in serial compound stimuli (Aguado et al 1989), interactions between intra- and extra-maze cues in learning (Chamizo & Mackintosk 1989), drug addiction and conditioning (Campos & Bandres 1986), and preparedness and fear (Huertas 1986) have been studied. There was also significant work on operant conditioning (Bayés 1984) insofar as it concerns programmed learning (Benjumea et al 1988), schedule-induced polydipsia in rats (Pellón & Blackman 1987), extinction as compared to satiation (Cruz 1984), patterning effect in maze learning, and immunization to learned helplessness (Ferrandiz & Pardo 1990). Vicarious learning has also been explored (Luna 1980).

Perceptual and attentional processes have been approached both in isolation and related to other psychological processes. Under the influence of the Gestalt framework, Yela (1952) carried out studies on phenomenal causation. The relevance of stimulus dimensions and structure (Fernández-Trespalacios et al 1988) and the effect of stimulus configuration on discrimination tasks (Luna et al 1985) have been investigated. These authors often have developed complex and specific computational procedures (Jañez 1984) to deal effectively with causality in attentional and perceptual processes (Arnau et al 1992). For instance, the empirical characteristics of visual channels meet the requirements of a kind of wavelet analysis (García-Pérez & Sierra-Vázquez 1992). Sustained attention and vigilance (B. Sierra et al 1983), the processing of non-attended stimuli (Tudela 1985), automatic attention in learning tasks, attentive processing of stimuli (Rechea 1985), and the distribution and shift of attention without eye movements in rapid serial visual presentation tasks (Botella et al 1988) have been explored.

Several groups have studied the various facets of memory: semantic memory (Pitarque et al 1987; Recarte 1985), facilitation with pictures and words (Bajo 1988), episodic memory (Alonso-Quecuty & De Vega 1991), eyewitness accounts (Mira & Diges 1986), conceptual anaphors (Carreiras &

---

[1] In 1994 a special issue of *Applied Psychology: An International Review* will be devoted to "Applied Psychology in Spain." Several sections of this review will be covered in more detail in that journal.

Gernsbacher 1992), concreteness, distinctiveness and recognition (Ruiz-Vargas 1991), words and images as primes in naming tasks (Mayor et al 1988), and long-term retention and meaning of words (Gotor et al 1987).

Delclaux & Seoane (1982) and De Vega (1984) opened up the new area of cognitive psychology. Pinillos (1983) has stressed the renewed interest in the meaning of consciousness for life and its significance for obtaining an adequate view of many psychological issues. Huertas (1992) has studied consciousness in human conditioning and in nonverbal learning. Largely based on previous studies of communication among autistic subjects, Riviere (1991) has developed a coherent theory of the human subject as an "object with a mind" from a perspective both mentalistic and objectivist in accordance with a computational theory of mind.

Abstract thinking and reasoning and logical processes (Del Val 1977); heuristics and categorization, conceptualization, and judgment (González-Marques 1991); multi-level processing in representations, decision making, and problem solving (Martínez-Arias 1991); and syllogistic operations (García-Madruga 1983) have attracted the attention of various groups of researchers.

Psycholinguistic processes have been studied from the perspective of modularity, in which researchers try to analyze the computational structure supporting these processes and to determine the various levels of processing in sentence production (García-Albea et al 1989) and in sentence comprehension (Belinchon et al 1992). Inner active processes in reading, metaphorical expressions as a crossroads for language and thought (Mayor 1985), and the acquisition of linguistic categories have been studied by several researchers interested in applied cognitive approaches (Valle 1991).

The issue of bilingualism has attracted the attention of psychologists (Siguán 1984) because about 60% of the Spanish population live in areas where a second language has an official character and is used in everyday life. Forns & Boada (1993) have been working on referential communication both in monolingual and bilingual children.

Emotion has been studied from both psychophysiological and psychosocial perspectives. Fernández-Dols et al (1991) and Fernández-Dols & Jiménez (1986) have proposed a contextual theory and a taxonomy of emotional situations based on several empirical studies on emotional expression and recognition (Iglesias et al 1989).

Psychobiology

Psychobiological studies in Spain have been developed in close relation to medical school programs in neurosciences. Guillamon & Segovia (1993) and Segovia & Guillamon (1993) have established the existence of a sexually dimorphic system (the vomeronasal system) involved in the control of sexual behavior in mammals.

For two decades Puerto and associates have studied rapid discrimination of rewarding nutrients (1976) and neural mechanisms controlling feeding behavior. Salvador et al (1987) have investigated hormones and competitive human behavior and the pharmacology of aggression.

In the field of human psychophysiology, Vila et al (1992) have carried out a series of studies on the cardiac response in humans to auditory stimulation. These studies have indicated the relationship between stimulus intensity and parametric level of sensory modality with the sympathetic and parasympathetic physiological components as well as several motivational and cognitive correlates. In a similar field, Martínez-Selva et al (1987) are working on individual differences in electrodermal orienting responses. Segura Torres et al (1988) have explored intracranial self-stimulation and its influence on learning and memory.

In the field of neuropsychology, Junqué et al (1990) are working on the role of the fronto-basal system in inhibition, incidental memory, and utilization of knowledge. Nieto et al (1990) are studying functional assymetries of the brain, specifically, the language capabilities of the right hemisphere.

The study of animal behavior in its natural context has become an important topic among psychobiologists. In particular, Sabater-Pi (1974) has conducted studies concerning culture and manufacture of tools in primates. Pelaez (1982) has been working on control mechanisms of primates' social systems.

Social Psychology

Several symposia and conferences on social psychology have been organized, four journals are devoted to this field, and many theoretical contributions have been made (Blanco 1980, Morales 1981, Munné 1986, Torregrosa 1974). During the last decade cross-regional stereotypes and intergroup perceptions have been explored (Sangrador 1981, Ros et al 1987). Research has been conducted on social representation concerning drug addicts and AIDS or HIV sufferers (Echebarria & Paez 1989). Intermember perceptions and dispositions in experimental groups (Huici 1980) and in minority groups (Mugni & Pérez 1991) have been the subject of research. Several facets of the relationship between law and psychology have been explored including visual testimony in the court (e.g. testimony may vary with the presence or absence of blood in a photograph), jury decisions, and delinquency problems (Jimenez-Burillo & Clemente 1986).

The most important research program on environmental psychology concerns basic topics such as visual perception of landscape and cognitive representation of space (Aragonés & Arredondo 1985), the affective quality attributed to places (Corraliza & Aragonés 1988), as well as other applied studies such as residential satisfaction and environmental quality of urban spaces (Amérigo & Aragonés 1990), and educational facilities in schools (Pol & Morales 1986).

Intelligence

Combining psychometric approaches and factor analysis, Yela and a large group of collaborators have been conducting an important research program since the 1950s concerning individual differences in intelligence, verbal aptitudes, and psychomotor abilities. According to Yela, mono- and multi-factorial solutions could be considered compatible. He postulates a general factor solution with specific abilities in accordance with what he has called the heterogenous-continuous dimensionality of human intelligence (Yela 1987).

Several authors have analyzed information-processing components. Each component is classified by function and by level of generality and together are responsible for the persistent appearance of a *g* factor (Martínez-Arias & Yela 1991). Individual differences in representational cognitive strategies for attentional and perceptual tasks and in memory dilemmas and reasoning (Juan-Espinosa & Colom 1989), and in the relation of bilingualism to intelligence (Sánchez-López & Forteza 1987), have been analyzed in detail (cf Sánchez-Cánovas 1986). The relationship between creativity and intelligence (Fernández-Garrido 1980) and between social intelligence and other cognitive abilities have been also approached.

Several groups have been studying both modifiability of intelligence and learning potentials (Calero & Fernández-Ballesteros 1993). Important efforts are being made in the search for psychophysiological correlates of intelligence. Measures investigated include cerebral events preceding motor response in simple and choice reaction time and correlates of event related potentials and dementia (Ortiz & Exposito 1992).

Personality

The field of personality has received great attention in recent years. Eysenck's model of personality has been analyzed and developed, both from correlational and experimental perspectives (Baguena & Belloch 1985). Animal experiments have been carried out to confirm Eysenck's predictions on extraversion and neuroticism in rats (García-Sevilla 1984).

Many other correlational studies have been based on Eysenck's model including examinations of the relationship between extraversion and paranoidism (Carrillo & Pinillos 1983), antisocial behavior, delinquency, and personality (Valverde 1985); verbal fluency and extraversion (Muñiz & Yela 1981); and extraversion and task properties as determinants of incidental recall (Bermúdez et al 1988).

Cattell's theory of personality and motivation has also been the focus of several empirical studies. In the context of questionnaire and objective laboratory test data, second-order factors in Spanish samples closely resemble those of United States samples, however, the primary source-trait structure has been only partially confirmed (Seisdedos 1991).

Based both on Eysenck's and Cattell's theories and on Brengelman's behavioral approach, Pelechano (1973) has been working empirically since 1970 on a theory of personality ("personality and parameters") that explains human performance in terms of interactions including not only personality and motivational dimensions but also situational factors (parameters).

Witkin's theory linking perception and personality gave birth to several research programs dealing with the field dependence-independence (FDI) dimension. A great deal of research has been conducted to establish the construct validity of several FDI measurement devices (Kirchner et al 1989). Other relevant topics have been studied such as the relationship between neuropsychological differentiation and FDI (Manning & Fernández-Ballesteros 1982) and the relationship between FDI and other personality and intelligence variables (Forns & Amador 1990); the results of these studies have supported the view that FDI is much more a cognitive ability than a cognitive style.

In social-learning theory, specifically, in the field of self-control, gratification delay, and aversive stimulation tolerance, Avia & Kanfer (1980) and Blanco & Ruiz (1985) have supported the importance of distraction and self-instruction processes.

Other studies have explored several aspects of personality. For example, Tous (1985) has related individual differences to cognitive and biological variables in information processing.

Psychopathology

In the field of abnormal behavior, several so-called mental problems have been studied. We emphasize three of the most basically psychopathological syndromes: schizophrenia, depression, and anxiety.

In the last ten years many research teams have conducted experimental cognitive research on schizophrenia. This has included experimental research concerning reaction time, perception, memory, and language (Ruiz-Vargas 1987). Vázquez et al (1990) and Obiols et al (1992) have studied the predictive role of attentional deficits and the effects of some drugs in schizophrenic symptoms.

Polaino & Senra (1991) have studied the epidemiology and prevention of depression during childhood and adolescence as well as the measurement of depression. Del Barrio (1990) has explored psychosocial predictors of child depression such as family structure, life events, school achievement, self-esteem, and coping methods.

From an experimental perspective, Ruiz-Caballero & Bermúdez (1992) have developed a research program concerning the relationship between depression and cognitive processes. Vázquez (1987) has been working on judgment of contingency and on the automatic cognitive processes of depressive patients.

Bermúdez (1983) has been working since the 1970s on a research program concerning trait-state anxiety. Miguel-Tobal & Cano-Vindel (1989) have developed a large program to study anxiety and have found the existence of a general trait of anxiety as well as several situational factors accounting for its variance. Finally, Sandín & Chorot (1989) have focused on physiological correlates as well as the basic mechanism associated with increasing and maintaining pathological anxiety.

Health and Clinical Psychology

Health and clinical psychology have shown important developments in Spain during the last decades both in applied and research fields.

Pelechano (1980) and his group have developed community programs that operate both through relatives and at school to treat and prevent psychological problems in children. Cerezo (1991) has developed observational procedures for assessing family interactions and an intervention program for dealing with family problems, child abuse, and other interpersonal problems.

Several research teams have examined the social integration of the handicapped through specific skills training (Martorell et al 1990). Verdugo (1989) has been working on the development, implementation, and evaluation of a standarized program for dealing with physical and mental deficiencies in this special group of subjects. Martin et al (1990) have developed a large research program concerning the evaluation and treatment of mentally retarded subjects.

In the field of clinical psychogerontology, Reig (1992) has explored stress and health status in relation to aging. Pelechano & De Miguel (1992) are involved in the assessment and training of interpersonal skills among old people. Fernández-Ballesteros et al (1992) have developed a large research program concerning the assessment and treatment of psychological problems in the elderly.

Saldaña & Rossell (1988) have used an epidemiological approach to examine dietary behavior and the most important psychosocial predictors and risk factors of obesity, anorexia nervosa, and bulimia. They also have developed a prevention program for these behavioral problems and have been working on remedial treatments of obesity.

Through a series of experimental studies on stuttering, Santacreu (1986) has emphasized the predisposition of electromyogram (EMG) responses to stress in stuttering patients and has developed biofeedback procedures for the treatment of this clinical pathology.

Echeburua et al (1991) are mainly interested in the differential efficacy of several treatments for agoraphobia.

Vallejo & Labrador (1983) are working on the explanation and treatment of pain. Starting with the proposal of a psychobiological model of headache they have found empirical support concerning cognitive variables and defensive response (Labrador & Puente 1988) and they have developed a cognitive-behavioral treatment of headache.

In the field of health psychology and stress, Bayés (1987) and his associates have contributed research on the psychoneuroimmunological bases of health and illness. Flores & Valdés (1986) are involved in research on stress responses, in particular, the investigation of the psychobiological factors of cardiovascular disease as well as the relationships between psychophysiological responses and stress, hypertension, and other health problems. Several groups are also working on the identification of the psychobiological patterns of stress and psychosomatic disorders (Labrador & Crespo 1992).

Several research teams are conducting studies of stressful situations and coping in different populations (Ribera et al 1988) and settings (Rodriguez-Marin 1986). Others are studying methods of coping with physical illness and medical or surgical consequences (Rodriguez-Marin 1992). In the last ten years Ibañez (1988) and associates have developed a research program concerning breast cancer. They have studied several types of psychological and social variables and have established guidelines for when and how to inform the patient and relatives about the illness. Similarly, Rodriguez-Marin et al (1989) have dealt with psychosocial variables related to cancer progression as well as with the patient's ability to cope with chronic pain. Polaino & Lizasoain (1992) have developed an intensive research program concerning hospitalization of children.

Carrobles & Godoy (1987) have developed biofeedback procedures for the treatment of several health problems including myopia, neuromuscular damage, and headaches (Carrobles et al 1981). For example, Guío et al (1989) have initiated an innovative research and behavioral program for the prevention and treatment of myopia by means of behavioral techniques.

Many other health problems have been studied from a psychological point of view (Simon 1993) in areas such as preparation and recovery from surgery, functional gastrointestinal illnesses, neuromuscular control in spastic individuals, and sleep disorders in older adults. Amigo et al (1991) have developed a cognitive-behavioral treatment of essential hypertension. Roales-Nieto (1988) has been working on training in blood glucose discrimination in insulin-dependent diabetes mellitus patients.

Many research teams have been investigating the development, implementation, and evaluation of programs for dealing with important health problems such as drug addiction, AIDS, and bucco-dental diseases. Costa & López (1986) have been working on a community-based model for the development, implementation, and evaluation of health promotion programs.

Psychological Assessment

Both from a theoretical and applied point of view, psychological assessment has developed strongly in recent years. Empirical data have demonstrated that Spanish psychological assessment research shows a profile similiar to that in other countries. The data also show the importance of assessment in every field of psychological practice.

Spanish psychologists have worked to develop a conceptual framework of psychological assessment that is closely related to basic psychology and to the basic process of assessment. Expert system methodology has been introduced to test the conceptual framework (Adarraga & Zaccagnini 1992).

Anguera (1979) and her group have made innovative contributions in the area of observational methodologies—to see and study behavior in natural settings using nonobtrusive measurements, to devise new means for exploring observational units and their implications in field studies, and to emphasize the crucial link between observer and observed in assessment situations. Specific research strategies for field entry and qualitative data collection have been developed, and techniques for recording observational data and methods of time sampling have been introduced in psychological practice.

Self-reports have also been studied from different perspectives. Staats & Fernández-Ballesteros (1987) have explored response distortions owing to feigning of socially desirable responses, the differential predictive value of several reported contents, time and situational influences, multimethod–multitrait analysis, and conceptual appraisal.

In spite of the decline of projective techniques during recent decades, research has been conducted to examine the psychometric properties of such techniques, as well as to test them as perceptual tasks (Marquez & Fernández-Balesteros 1988, Sendin 1987, Vizcarro et al 1987).

Several research teams have tested the value of subjective methods for assessing the self and other subjective constructs. The repertory grid from Kelly (Rivas & Marco 1985), adjective checklists (Avila & Giménez 1991), *Q*-technique from Stephenson (Fierro 1982), and self-biography (Feixas & Villegas 1990) have been thoroughly studied.

Psychophysiological records have been studied in an attempt to establish their correlates with other measurement devices and their diagnostic value as well as to investigate new procedures for analysis (Vila 1992).

Many efforts have been made to adapt into the Spanish context the well-known tests and batteries for neuropsychological assessment, but at the same time new measurement devices have been constructed in order to assess neuropsychological deficits (cf Peña Casanova 1987).

A great deal research on behavioral assessment has been conducted since the 1980s (Fernández-Ballesteros & Carrobles 1981). In recent years critical methodological observations have been made and the integration of psychometric and behavioral approaches to assessment has been defended (Silva 1993).

Tests and other instruments were reviewed several years ago (García-Yague 1975) and the review has been updated by Calonge & Avila in a computer database in 1993.

Computer-based Testing and Traffic Safety

Spain is probably unique in Western countries for establishing, by a governmental directive, the rules and standards for computer-based testing used to assess psychomotor abilities, intelligence, and personality. This is a result of another law concerning traffic safety. Drivers must pass a medical and psychological examination every five or ten years before they can obtain or renew a driver's license. Examinations take place in private centers, which are licensed by the Traffic Department. Drivers are also periodically subjected to psychological testing. Firearm licenses are issued and renewed in the same way.

The Traffic Department Director appoints a committee of experts, currently scholars and one delegate from the department, to approve psychological testing equipment. Manufacturers of testing equipment must obtain approval of (*a*) quality control methods for the equipment, procedures used for the presentation of visual or aural stimuli and for the coding of motor responses, and reliability of the built-in timing system and of cursor movements between fields; (*b*) the theoretical and experimental basis of each psychological test, qualifications and expertise of the team of researchers, and subroutines used for compiling data; (*c*) samples used in the experimental and validation phase of the design as well as reliability and validity indices of each test; and (*d*) sales and post-sales campaigns.

Computer monitors must be high resolution and software must be stored on a ROM basis and be loaded, copied, and unloaded by using a password or alternative protection. Such standards serve as a landmark for psychological research and practice in computer-based testing and in traffic safety programs (Soler & Tortosa 1987; Tortosa et al 1989).

Child and Educational Psychology

Since the early 1920s Claparede and Piaget greatly influenced some Spanish groups working on child and educational problems (Siguán 1982). Del Val

(1975) has provided a detailed picture of children's animism and an interesting analysis of psychological aspects of formal reasoning. Carretero et al (1985) intorduced concrete approaches to the study of cognitive development. Moral development has also received a lot of attention (Beltram 1982, Diaz-Aguado 1982, Pérez-Delgado & García-Ros, 1991). Closely related to these topics are several research projects dealing with the acquisition by young people of social, historical, and scientific concepts that might improve instructional practice (Carretero et al 1991).

Efforts have been made recently to design new curricula and evaluative criteria based on psychological grounds (Coll 1987, Genovard & Gotzens 1990, Rivas & Alcantud 1989). Human information processing has provided the framework for analyzing the cognitive representation of historical time (Carretero et al 1991), active memory processes (De la Mata 1988), selective attention (García 1985), the acquisition of numerical abilities (Bermejo & Lago 1990), and symbolic (Riviere 1990) and social representation (Del Val 1989). Study strategies for school learning have been analyzed by Hernández & García (1991) and a specific program (PIME-3) has been devised to improve the effectiveness of direct instruction.

Palacios (1989) has studied parent/child daily interactions and cognitions. Sex and gender differentiation processes have been studied and summarized both through the analysis of behavioral patterns (Fernández 1988) and through the follow-up of language acquisition (Pérez-Pereira 1991). García-Torres (1990) has analyzed the development of self-concept and self-esteem in cross-sectional as well as longitudinal research programs. Linaza and Maldonado (1987) have studied the influence of games and sports in the psychological development of children.

Cognitive characteristics of deaf and blind children and adolescents have been studied from both applied (Marchesi 1987) and theoretical grounds (Rosa et al 1984). Luciano (1986) have studied the learning and transfer of vocal imitation in children with sever retardation.

Work and Organizational Psychology

Personnel assessment and selection have been the main focus of research in industrial and organizational psychology (Prieto et al 1991). It has been necessary to carry out validity and reliability studies of every psychological instrument used in this domain (Quintanilla 1992). However, confidential reports rather than published papers have been the norm because ownership of data and veto power are still particularly tricky questions. Seisdedos (1993) has analyzed in detail the role of motivational distortion. Motivational distortion is a good predictor of adjustment and intelligent performance in the selection of managers and supervisors. The emphasis on person-job fit has been changed to person-team fit. Everyday work cannot be regarded as an individualistic goal-seeking activity. Effective work performance must be viewed as a positive-sum game. The personnel decision is also a matter of fitting to the team of co-workers performing the job (Prieto 1993). A psychobiological test of morphine-dependency has been devised to assist personnel psychologists in the screening of applicants and the monitoring of job holders (Navarro & Prieto 1992).

Unemployment and contingent (part-time, temporary, or apprenticeship) work have been approached following three basic lines of research: attitudes toward work and employment, psychological effects and consequences, and programs of intervention and action (Peiró 1987). Work transition has been analyzed in two longitudinal studies to clarify the nexus between psychological well-being and vocational guidance, occupational training, job-search activities, and work socialization (Peiró & Moret 1987, Blanch 1989). Forteza & Prieto (1993) have studied and summarized retirement issues and dilemmas.

Research on work motivation has a long history. Forteza (1971) and Munduate & Baron (1989) have partially confirmed the adequacy of bi-factor theories and expectancy theories in the occupational setting. Measurement issues, antecedents, relationship to satisfaction and job performance have been studied regularly (Pereda & García 1986).

The study of stress at work among different occupational groups has been studied in the context of role ambiguity and role conflict. A series of instruments has been developed to clarify the implications on role stress of the structural aspects of the role-set and to establish a causal model of their effects (Peiró et al 1987).

The psychological implications of telemathics (computer-based technologies used in telecommunications) and organizational processess also have been analyzed within the framework of the role-set model (Prieto et al 1990). Laboratory experiments have been conducted to analyze strategic differences in problem solving activities with the support of computers, comparing face-to-face vs video conference dialogues.

Methodology

The study of test theory has been a standard part of the curriculum for graduate students in psychology. A succession of scholars have published several textbooks and monographs on classical test theory (Santisteban 1990, García-Cueto 1993) fundamental statistics in psychology (Amón 1978), and experimental designs (Arnau 1990). Hypothesis testing and statistical inference were core subjects, because the leading figures and pioneers of psychology were trained abroad and carried out successive research projects under the general framework of multivariate methods of analysis. In fact, the analysis of variance and covariance have always been considered special cases of the general linear model in mathematical statistics.

Modern test theory has made rapid advances and has been explained in a textbook by Muñiz (1990). Two innovative contributions in this field must be mentioned. Satorra (1989) has provided a unified approach to the asymptotic theory of alternative test criteria for testing parametric restrictions in the context of covariance structure analysis. García-Pérez & Frary (1991) have developed a polynomial function to the item characteristic curve that utilizes a parameterization of ability different from that used in conventional item response theory. This method accounts directly for factors such as states of knowledge, willingness to guess, mode of test administration, number of options per item, and the response strategy of the examinees.

Decision making models have been reviewed and studied following several research paradigms (Maciá 1990). Strategic decision making seems subject to the same pitfalls as other activities in which individuals or groups are involved.

Teaching has long been an essentially private act. However, succesive reforms in the campus opened up the path to direct and indirect evaluation of teaching activities. In some universities, the present system for identifying teaching adequacies and inadequacies has been devised and validated successfully through cross-sectional and longitudinal analyses (Fernández & Mateo 1992).

The collection and use of information about individual or group performance for the purpose of making sound decisions about existing programs in different settings has changed considerably over time and has become an established field. Program studies and evaluations have been carried out in different areas such as organizational effectiveness and work performance (Quijano 1992), residential programs for the elderly (Fernández-Ballesteros et al 1991), transfer of training, adequacy of social services, and welfare of surgical patients. The incidence of cost-benefit analyses in program administration also has been approached through case studies (Anguera 1992).

Supported by a large group of researchers (Algarabel & Sanmartin 1990), computer applications in psychological research have evolved rapidly during the last decade, mainly in the areas of simulation, artificial intelligence, development of computerized displays and instruments in the laboratory, interfacing for data acquisition, screen control and timing routines, enhancing and degrading visual stimuli, computer interview questionnaires, computer-assisted testing, automated interpretation of profiles, computer reporting of assessment data, computer-aided learning, computer-assisted instruction, and software environments used to produce programs.

History of Psychology

The history of psychology has emerged as a field of study, partly to establish a link between contemporary and past psychology (Rosa et al 1988). For centuries, there was a certain tradition of reflection upon man and his mind and on questions concerning mental ability, giftedness, human passions and disorders, and the assessment of invididuals. Interest in the study of the contribution of medieval authors (such as Petrus-Hispanus, or Averroes) or Rennaissance writers (such as Vives, Huarte, and Pereira) has provided significant knowledge of old views about human mind and behavior. Moreover, interest in the evolution of scientific psychology has encouraged a large body of quantitative research according to sophisticated historiographic methods with the aid of computer analyses. At the same time, the history of psychology has been included as a compulsory course in the curriculum, and as a result, research and teaching posts, a specialized journal, and a society are now devoted to the systematic study of publications, authors, topics, and "invisible colleges and working groups" (Carpintero & Peiró 1981, Quiñones et al 1993). Archival techniques have been proposed as historical research tools for the analysis of psychological literature (Gondra 1985). Caparrós (1980) has identified paradigms as research models in the history of psychology.

PSYCHOLOGY AS A KNOWLEDGE-BASED FIELD OF EXPERTISE

Psychology cannot be reduced to research and academic knowledge. It is also a source of expert knowledge and stable jobs. A university degree in psychology also provides a cultural capital for new graduates to increase their competence and performance in present or future jobs. Psychology in Spain has emerged as a certified knowledge-based discipline, based upon conventional divisions or specialties, and as a labor market, incorporating differents types of practitioners and professional career paths (Prieto 1992).

The youthful nature of Spanish psychologists is seen in the fact that only one out of every five practitioners has more than ten years of professional experience. Women are over-represented—65% are females. The exception is in industrial and organizational psychology where almost two-thirds of practitioners are male. The unemployment rate is below that of the general population and of university graduates.

The occupational classification among psychologists is distributed as follows (Diaz & Quintanilla 1992): 36.7% are in educational psychology; 28.5% are in clinical psychology; 15.5% are in industrial and organizational psychology; 8.8% are in community or social services psychology; 6.0% consider themselves researchers, and 4.5% are devoted to traffic safety psychology issues. Regarding the conditions of employment, 37% might be considered freelance or self-employed practitioners, 33% are civil servants or are employed in different public sector agencies, 21% are employed in private firms, 4% are scholars in state universities, and .5% are more or less permanent

Table 1 Minimum standards for the curriculum in psychology in Spain (1 credit = 10 hours)

Cycle	Course	Credits
First	Basic Psychological Processes	19
	"Research Methods, Designs, and Techniques"	16
	Psychobiology	16
	Developmental Psychology	11
	Social Psychology	9
	Personality	8
	Psychological Assessment	8
	History of Psychology	5
Second	Practicum	9
	"Psychopathology, Intervention Techniques, and Psychological Treatment"	9
	Educational Psychology	9
	Psychology of Groups and Organizations	9
	Psychology of Thought and Language	9

members of national or local governments or parliaments. Finally, 4.5% of practitioners do not indicate the conditions of their employment (e.g. those who receive grants or stipends or who do voluntary work). There were 30,000 registered psychologists as of June 1993.

School psychologists devote themselves to the following activities: counseling parents and teachers; diagnosing, treating, and providing individualized attention to children; and writing reports.

Clinical psychologists work with patients in public or private settings within the following theoretical and methodological orientation (Avila 1989): behaviorism (45.2%), psychoanalysis (34.8%), humanistic psychology (8.2%), systemic approaches (3.2%), and eclecticism (8.6%).

Industrial and organizational psychologists are devoted mainly to personnel assessment, selection, and training, as well as job analysis and performance appraisal. Only a minority devote some time to organizational aspects, marketing, and consumer behavior issues. This group is among the most highly paid of the Spanish practitioners.

Community or social services psychologists work in interdisciplinary workgroups and interact with other experts and professionals to deal with delicate cases of drug addiction, problems with aging, childhood delinquency, rape counseling, housewife syndromes, and domestic aggression. A minor group of forensic psychologists work in prisons or write reports for court trials.

In applied settings psychological action is viewed as a behavioral technology. Practitioners are invited to change situation *A* into *B*, because *B* is more satisfactory for the client or for the citizens. Psychology is accepted insofar as it contributes to the improvement of the quality of life in Spanish society through research and evaluation findings. Significant findings remain confidential or available only to authorized persons. Psychological reports remain unpublished but are indirectly accessible through case study sessions, task forces, joint committees, or informal meetings and talks.

TRAINING IN PSYCHOLOGY

The 1983 Law on the Reformation of Higher Education is the legal foundation for the Spanish higher education system today. Psychology as an academic discipline became structured within the following areas: behavioral sciences methodology, psychobiology, psychology of basic processes, developmental and educational psychology, social psychology, and personality and psychological assessment and treatment.

The University Council established a single degree, *Licenciatura en Psicologia,* and a common core curriculum in psychology, which is formally recognized throughout the country. A minimum of 300 and a maximum of 390 credit hours represents the overall academic load required to obtain this predoctoral degree, which qualifies holders for professional practice. Five years of full-time university study, devoted almost exclusively to psychology courses, are normally required for completion of the *Licenciatura.*

About half of the total curriculum consists of required courses (Table 1). Each university is free to set the number of remaining credits required to insure that students obtain an adequate background in psychology as well as some amount of specialization.

The entrance requirement for this degree is successful completion of secondary education and the completion of a one-year introductory course to the university system. All applicants must take a compulsory general examination for admission to the Faculty of Psychology. Admission quotas for psychology do not exist but a 5% quota is reserved for foreign students. There are no restrictions for students coming from other European Community member countries. Lectures take place from October to June.

Two routes are available for graduate students in psychology: the PhD degree, which takes 2–5 years, emphasizes research in psychology as a behavioral science, and requires completion of a thesis; and the Magister Degree, which takes 1–2 years, emphasizes psychological action and intervention as a behavioral technology, and recommends, but does not require a thesis.

There currently are 920 faculty members who are either tenured professors or lecturers. An ad hoc committee of five members evaluates individual merits and publications of PhD candidates for a tenured position. Applicants write individual reports about the state-of-the-art of the discipline in which they are planning to teach. This report includes a conceptual framework, an overview of research methods and approaches and a review of relevant literature (in at least two languages) in the discipline. Applicants also design the syllabus of a specific course, select instructional strategies, include a specific list of exercises as well as readings, and produce a lesson. The report, syllabus, and lesson are analyzed and discussed by each member of the committee. For a position of senior-professor, the candidate presents an unpublished, completed research project which is also analyzed and discussed by the committee. Each phase of this evaluation process is made during a public session.

Table 2 Journals and magazines of Psychology published in Spain in 1992

Sponsored by Departments or Societies
Anales de Psicología
Anuario de Psicología
Boletin de Psicología
Cognitiva
European Journal of Psychological Assessment
Interaccion Social
Investigaciones Psicologicas
Psicologica
Revista Española de Terapia del Comportamiento
Revista de Historia de la Psicología
Revista de Psicología de la Educacion
Revista de Psicología General y Aplicada
Revista de Psicología Politica
Revista de Psicología Social
Revista de Psicología Social Aplicada
Revista de Psicología de la Salud/Journal of Health Psychology
Revista de Psiquiatría y Psicología Humanista
Sponsored by the *Colegio Oficial de Psicologos*
Anuario de Psicología Juridica
Apuntes de Psicología
Clinica y Salud
Cuadernos de Psicología
Encuentros de Psicología
Enginy
Informacio Psicologica
Intervencion Psicosocial
Papeles del Psicologo
Psicothema
Revista de Psicología del Trabajo y de las Organizaciones Sintesis
Text i Context

JOURNALS AND SOCIETIES

Although a large volume of psychological literature has been published in nonspecialized magazines, the development of psychological journals has paralleled the vicissitudes of Spanish psychology. An average of 400–500 books are published every year under the heading of psychology. About half are translations. The volume of literature provides a general idea of the degree of productivity in the field.

Table 2 classifies existing journals and magazines published regularly by their sponsoring organizations. The *Revista de Psicología General y Aplicada* was launched in 1946 and now covers the whole field of theoretical and applied psychology. It is the official bulletin of the Spanish Society of Psychology. Only two journals accept and publish contributions in both English and Spanish. In 1992 *Evaluación Psicológica/Psychological Assessment* became the *European Journal of Psychological Assessment.* The main bimonthly magazine is *Papeles del Psicologo,* established in 1980 in the *Colegio Oficial de Psicologos,* with a current circulation of 25,000 copies per issue. Each issue of this professionally-oriented magazine includes in-depth dossiers on relevant professional issues, questions, and debates.

The senior scientific and psychological society is the *Sociedad Española de Psicología (SEP),* founded in 1952. Membership is open to university graduates in psychology or related programs. The *SEP* is structured in divisions oriented toward theoretical and experimental issues, and for decades it has promoted annual meetings, periodic congresses, and specialized conventions.

Table 2 (continued)

Sponsored by private organizations
Adicciones
Analisis y Modificacion de Conducta
Clinica y Analisis Grupal
Comunicacion
Energia
Estudios de Psicología
Infancia y Aprendizaje
Psicologemas
Psiquis
Revista de Analisis Transaccional y Psicologia Humanista
Revista de Psicologia
Revista de Psicoterapia
Si...entonces

The *SEP* is the Spanish national member of the International Union of Psychological Science.

During the 1970s and 1980s, new and thematic societies have been created to promote regular exchanges of expertise and scientific knowledge between associates. Among these are the Spanish Society of Psychological Assessment, which in 1990 became the European Association of Psychological Assessment; the Spanish Society of Behavioral Psychology; the Spanish Society of the History of Psychology; the Spanish Society of Rorschach and other Projective Techniques; the Spanish Federation of Sport Psychology; and the Spanish Federation of Associations of Psychotherapy. Each society organizes regular meetings, and in some cases, supports specialized journals and newsletters.

The *Colegio Oficial de Psicologos* was founded on December 31, 1979. The *Colegio* is a professional body whose aims are to protect and promote the interests of Spanish psychologists and practitioners. The existence of the *Colegio Oficial de Psicologos* means that the professional title of psychologist is under legal control and protection. Membership is compulsory for those wishing to accredit themselves as psychologists, and there currently are about 30,000 members. The Spanish Crown and the Spanish Parliament have made the *Colegio* responsible for monitoring and regulating the exercise of Psychology as a profession. The *Colegio* is a self-governing and democratic institution that provides assistance and protection to its members and promotes and defends professional interests, particularly when registered psychologists provide services under a contract of employment. The *Colegio* also regularly sponsors National Congresses, Seminars, and Conventions focusing on theoretical and practical issues and questions of professional interest.

FINAL REMARKS

An effort has been made to review the discipline of psychology in Spain both as a whole and as an expanding field and to discern a common core in what we as psychologists are doing in Spain. Now it is time to take a bird's eye view of the entire picture:

> 1. On the one hand, scientific developments and professional practice in Spain share theoretical frameworks and models with, and address the same topics and follow similar approaches and methods as the worldwide scientific community, showing the predicted convergence in major findings or conclusions and recording some minor discrepancies in specific details. On the other hand, the historical development of psychology seems to be quite culture-specific because the acceptance and recognition of psychology as a scientific, technological, and professional discipline have been encouraged during the political transition toward democracy and societal welfare.

2. Two achievements in 1980 have had important consequences in strengthening psychology as an academic and professional community: the recognition of the Faculty in the university milieu and the recognition of the *Colegio Oficial* in the professional milieu. Both institutional bodies have created a gravitational field and have defined potentials for present and future developments.

3. Legal reforms in the university setting have changed conditions of employment in the campus. The body of tenured professors has increased steadily during the 1980s and it is closely related to an increase in laboratory research, action-research, programs of intervention, and evaluation of programs. As a result, the number of publications and submissions to specialized journals has grown rapidly.

4. Spanish researchers and practitioners have maintained a Janus-faced view toward the existing psychological literature: American and European leading authors, journals, and handbooks were studied and considered quite systematically. Both influences are also found in several Research Institutes in the European Community as well as North and South America. Existing libraries in each faculty have good reference sections in several languages, which benefits both research programs and teaching activities.

5. Until the 1970s there were no regular grants allocated by governmental agencies for experimental research in psychology. The majority of projects were supported by individual initiatives of investigators, departments, and universities. During the 1990s some critical contemporary problems in which psychological knowledge and methods can help have been included among the set of priorities targeted in the National Plan for Scientific and Technological Research Funding. As a result, research and development projects submitted by psychologists on a competitive basis are valued positively and are financed by governmental agencies or local foundations and private firms.

6. Psychology as a field of expertise is gaining many signs of acceptance and esteem. The image of psychologists as a professional group oriented toward the assessment and treatment of mental disorders and behavioral problems has changed. Psychological research and actions are now viewed in the context of normal behavior, effective performance, quality of life and well-being, productivity and competitiveness, career development, artificial intelligence, new technology advances, and environmental issues. This more expanding view increases the probability of stable jobs in public and private organizations. Scholars and leading practitioners, meeting today's challenges, have now started to enjoy the benefits and rewards of societal recognition. These conditions foster further achievements.

Acknowledgments

We acknowledge the collaboration of a large group of colleagues who have discussed with us the content of specific sections of successive drafts. Francisca Martínez organized the reference section and tackled problems as they appeared.

Literature Cited

Adarraga P, Zaccagnini JL. 1992. DAI: a knowledge-based system for diagnosing autism. A case study on the application of artificial intelligence to psychology. *Eur. J. Psychol. Assess.* 8:25–47

Aguado L, Lopez M, Lillo J. 1989. Blocking with serial compound stimuli: the role of local context and second order association. *Q. J. Exp. Psychol. B* 41:3–19

Algarabel S, Sanmartin J. 1990. *Métodos Informaticos Aplicados a la Psicología.* Madrid: Pirámide

Alonso-Quecuty ML, De Vega M. 1991. Metaphor verification in an episodic memory task. In *Learning and Instruction,* ed. M Carretero, M Pope, RJ Simons, JE Pozo, pp. 219–31. Oxford: Pergamon

Amérigo M, Aragonés JI. 1990. Residential satisfaction in council housing. *J. Environ. Psychol.* 10:313–25

Amigo I, Buceta JM, Becoña E, Bueno A. 1991. Cognitive-behavioral treatment of essential hypertension: a controlled study. *Stress Med.* 7(2):99–103

Amón J. 1978. *Estadística para Psicólogos.* Madrid: Pirámide

Anguera MT. 1979. Observational typology: quality and quantity. *Eur.-Am. J. Methodol.* 13(6):449–84

Anguera MT. 1992. Incidence of cost-benefit and cost-effectiveness analysis in Program Administration: a case study. In *Advancing Policy and Program Evaluation: Learning from International Experiences,* ed. J Hudson et al, pp. 181–88. Amsterdam: Elsevier

Aragones JI, Arredondo JM. 1985. Structure of urban cognitive maps. *J. Environ. Psychol.* 5:197–212

Arnau J. 1990. *Diseños Experimentales Multivariados.* Madrid: Alianza

Arnau J, Blanca MJ, Salvador F. 1992. Efecto de la dimensión estimular en el procesamiento global-local. *Rev. Psicol. Gen. Apl.* 45(1):13–21

Avia MD, Kanfer FH. 1980. Coping with aversive stimulation: the effect of training in a self-management context. *Cogn. Ther. Res.* 4(1):73–81

Avila A. 1989. La Psicologia Clinica en España, perspectiva de una decada. *Pap. Psicol.,* pp. 36–37, 84–89

Avila A, Giménez de la Peña A. 1991. Los adjetivos en tareas de evaluación psicológica: propiedades y valor estimular. *Rev. Psicol. Gen. Apl.* 44(4):463–75

Baguena MJ, Belloch A. 1985. *Extraversión, Psicoticismo y Dimensiones Emocionales de la Personalidad.* Valencia, Spain: Promolibro

Bajo MT. 1988. Semantic facilitation with pictures and words. *J. Exp. Psychol.: Learn. Mem. Cogn.* 14:579–89

Bayés R. 1984. Behaviour therapy in Spain. *Eur. Assoc. Behav. Ther. Newsl.* 9:22–32

Bayés R. 1987. Factores de aprendizaje en la respuesta del sistema inmunitario. *Jano* 768:56–66

Belinchon M, Riviere A, Igoa JM. 1992. *Psicologia del Lenguaje. Investigacion y Teoria.* Madrid: Trotta

Beltram J. 1982. El realismo moral: investigacion actual y critica. *Rev. Psicol. Gen. Apl.* 37:229–39

Benjumea S, Caracuel J, Fernández-Serra F, Moreno R, López J, et al. 1988. *Principios y Metodos de la Psicologia del Aprendizaje Aplicados a Ambientes Educativos.* Cadiz, Spain: Univ. Cadiz

Bermejo V, Lago MO. 1990. Developmental processes and stages in the acquisition of cardinality. *Int. J. Behav. Dev.* 13(2):231–50

Bermúdez J. 1983. Análisis funcional de la ansiedad. *Rev. Psicol. Gen. Apl.* 33:617–34

Bermúdez J, Pérez-García AM, Padilla M. 1988. Extraversion and task properties as determinants of incidental recall. *Eur. J. Pers.* 2(1):57–65

Blanch JM. 1989. Valoracion del trabajo y patologia en el paro. In *Juventud, Trabajo y Desempleo, una Perspectiva Psicosociologica,* ed. JR Torregrosa, pp. 365–92. Madrid: Ministerio Trabajo

Blanco A. 1980. La psicología social. Desorientación y aplicación a la realidad española. *Rev. Esp. Invest. Sociol.* 12:159–94

Blanco MS, Ruiz MA. 1985. Consumo atencional y distracción como estrategia de afrontamiento al dolor. *Rev. Psicol. Gen. Apl.* 4:777–92

Botella J, Villar M, Ponsoda V. 1988. Movimientos de la atención en el espacio sin movimientos oculares. *Cognitiva* 1:171–85

Calero MD, Fernández-Ballestero R. 1993. Measuring learning potential. *Int. J. Cogn. Educ. Med. Learn.* 3(1):35–45

Campos JJ, Bandrés J. 1986. Opiáceos y comportamiento. *Jano.* 708:62–71

Caparrós A. 1980. *Los Paradigmas en Psicología.* Barcelona: Horsori

Carpintero H. 1982. The introduction of scientific psychology in Spain (1875–1900). In *The Problematic Science, Psychology in Nineteenth Century Thought,* ed. W Woodward, M Ash, pp. 255–75. New York: Praeger

Carpintero H. 1984. The impact of the Spanish civil war on Spanish scientific psychology. *Rev. Hist. Psicol.* 1/2:91–98

Carpintero H, Peiró JM. 1981. *Psicología Contemporánea: Teoría y Métodos Cuantitativos para el Estudio de su Literatura Cientifica.* Valencia: Alfaplús

Carreiras M, Gernsbacher MA. 1992. Comprehending conceptual anaphors in Spanish. *Lang. Cogn. Process.* 7:281–99

Carretero M, Asensio M, Pozo I. 1991. Cognitive development, historical time representation and causal explanations in adolescence. In *Learning and Instruction. European Research in an International Context,* ed. M Carretero, M Pope, RJ Simons, JI Pozo, 3:28–48. Oxford: Pergamon

Carretero M, Palacios J, Marchesi A. 1985. *Psicología Evolutiva.* Vol. 3 *Adolescencia, Madurez y Senectud.* Madrid: Alianza

Carrillo JM, Pinillos JL. 1983. La correlacion extraversion-paranoidismo en función de la induccion de agresion. *Anal. Modif. Conduct.* 9:169–84

Carrobles JA, Godoy J. 1987. *Biofeedback.* Barcelona: Martínez-Roca

Carrobles JA, Cardona A, Santacreu J. 1981. Shaping and generalization procedures in the EMG-biofeedback treatment of tension headache. *Br. J. Soc. Clin. Psychol.* 20:49–56

Cerezo MA. 1991. *Interacciones Familiares: Un Sistema de Evaluación Observacional.* Madrid: Mepsa

Chamizo VD, Mackintosh NJ. 1989. Latent learning and latent inhibition in maze discriminations. *Q. J. Exp. Psychol. B* 41(1):21–23

Coll C. 1987. *Psicología y Curriculum.* Barcelona: Laia

Corraliza JA, Aragonés JI. 1988. Assessment of emotional environmental dimensions: the affective quality attributed to several places in Madrid. In *Environmental Social Psychology,* ed. D Canter, JC Jesuino, L Soczka, GM Stephenson, pp. 160–71. Dordrecht: Kluwer Academic

Costa M, Lopez E. 1986. *Salud Comunitaria.* Barcelona: Martínez-Roca

Cruz J. 1984. Comparacio de dues techniques d'eliminacio de conducta: extincio i sacietat. *Quad. Psicol.* 8:115–130

De la Mata M. 1988. El desarrollo de las acciones de la memoria. *Infanc. Aprendizaje* 42:3–18

De Vega M. 1984. *Introducción a la Psicología Cognitiva.* Madrid: Alianza

Del Barrio V. 1990. Aspectos socioculturales de la depresión infantil. In *Epidemiología de la Depresión Infantil,* ed. E Domenech, A Polaino. Barcelona: Espax

Delclaux I, Seoane J. 1982. *Psicología Cognitiva y Procesamiento de la Información.* Madrid: Pirámide

Del Val JA. 1975. *El Animismo y el Pensamiento Infantil.* Madrid: Siglo XXI

Del Val JA. 1977. Lógica y psicología del razonamiento. In *Investigaciones sobre Lógica y Psicología,* ed. J Piaget, M Wertheimer, M Henke, RS Woodworth, pp. 17–40. Madrid: Alianza

Del Val JA. 1989. La representacion infantil del mundo social. In *El Mundo Social en la Mente Infantil,* ed. E Turiel, I Enesco, J Linaza, pp. 245–328. Madrid: Alianza

Diaz-Aguado MJ. 1982. Desarrollo del razonamiento moral. *Rev. Psicol. Gen. Apl.* 37:239–46

Diaz R, Quintanilla I. 1992. La identidad profesional del psicologo en el estado español. *Pap. Psicol.* 52:22–74

Echebarria A, Paez D. 1989. Social representation and memory: the case of AIDS. *Eur. J. Soc. Psychol.* 19(6):543–52

Echeburua E, Corral P, García E, Borda M. 1991. La autoexposición y las benzodiacepinas en el tratamiento de la agorafobia sin historia de trastorno de pánico: resultados a largo plazo. *Anál. Modif. Conduct.* 17: 969–91

Feixas G, Villegas M. 1990. Evaluación de textos autobiográficos. *Eval. Psicol./Psychol. Assess.* 6:289–327

Fernández J. 1988. *Nuevas Perspectivas en el Desarrollo del Sexo y el Género.* Madrid: Pirámide

Fernández J, Mateo MA. 1992. Students Evaluation of University Teaching Quality: analysis of questionnaire for a sample of university students in Spain. *Educ. Psychol. Meas.* 52(3):675–86

Fernández-Ballesteros R, Carrobles JAI. 1981. *Evaluacion Conductual.* Madrid: Pirámide

Fernández-Ballesteros R, Izal M, Hernandez J, Montorio I, Llorente G. 1991. Evaluation of residential programs for the elderly in Spain and the US. *Eval. Pract.* 12:159–65

Fernández-Ballesteros R, Izal M, Montorio I, González JL, Diaz P. 1992. *Evaluacion e Intervencion Psicologica en la Vejez.* Barcelona: Martínez-Roca

Fernández-Dols JM, Jiménez A. 1986. The Spanish case: the written expression of emotional routes. In *Experiencing Emotion: A Crosscultural Study,* ed. KR Scherer, HG Wallbott, AB Summerfield, pp. 233–45. Cambridge: Cambridge Univ. Press

Fernández-Dols JM, Wallbott H, Sánchez F. 1991. Emotional category accessibility and decoding of emotion from a facial expression and context. *J. Nonverbal Behav.* 15: 107–23

Fernández-Garrido J. 1980. *Un Modelo para el Estudio de la Creatividad.* Madrid: Univ. Complutense Madrid

Fernández-Trespalacios JL. Shepp BE, Ballesteros S. 1988. *Percepcion del Objeto: Estructura y Procesos.* Madrid: Univ. Natl. Educ. Distancia

Ferrandiz P, Pardo A. 1990. Immunization to

learned helpessness in appetitive non-contingent contexts. *Anim. Learn. Behav.* 18(3):252–56

Fierro A. 1982. *Técnicas de Investigación de la Personalidad.* Salamanca, Spain: Inst. Ciencias Educ.

Flores T de, Valdés M. 1986. Behavior Pattern A: reward, fight or punishment? *Pers. Individ. Differ.* 7(3):319–26

Forns M, Amador JA. 1990. Association of scores on McCarthy scales and field dependence-independence for 7 years old Spanish children. *Percept. Mot. Skill* 70:1291–96

Forns M, Boada H. 1993. Evaluacion de habilidades comunicaturas en situacion referencial: unidades de analis. In *Contribuciones recientes a la Evaluacion Psicologica,* ed. M Forns, MT Anguera. Barcelona: PPU. In press

Forteza JA. 1971. *La Motivacion en el Trabajo: Factores Intrénsecos y Extrínsecos en la Satisfaccion Laboral.* Madrid: Marova

Forteza JA, Prieto JM. 1993. Aging and Work Behavior. In *Handbook of Industrial and Organizational Psychology,* Vol. 4, ed. MD Dunnette, H Triandis. Palo Alto, Calif: Consult. Psychol. In press

García A. 1985. El desarrollo de la atención selectiva y modos de percepción holésticos y analético. *Infanc. Aprendizaje* 48:65–78

García-Albea JE, del Viso S, Igoa JM. 1989. Movement errors and levels of processing in sentence production. *J. Psycholinguist. Res.* 18:145–61

García-Cueto E. 1985. *Introduccion a la Psicometria.* Madrid: Siglo XXI

García-Hoz V. 1985. La representacion del reforzador en el condicionamiento del miedo. *Rev. Psicol. Gen. Apl.* 40:599–630

García-Madruga JA. 1983. Un modelo general sobre el razonamiento silogístico: doble procesamiento y fase de comprobación con verificación. *Rev. Psicol. Gral. Apl.* 38(3):439–66

García-Pérez MA, Frary RB. 1991. Finite state polynomic item characteristic curve. *Br. J. Math. Stat. Psychol.* 44:45–73

García-Pérez MA, Sierra-Vazquez V. 1992. Psychophysical 1-D wavelet analysis and the perception of contrast visual illusions. *Perception* 21:93

García-Sevilla L. 1984. Extraversion and neuroticism in rats. *Pers. Individ. Differ.* 5:511–32

García-Torres B. 1990. Development of self-description in the context of play: a longitudinal study. In *The self-concept: International Perspectives on its development, aspects and applications,* pp. 31–43, ed. L Oppenheimer. New York: Springer-Verlag

García-Yague J. 1975. *Tests Empleados en España.* Madrid: Inst. Nacional Psicol. Aplicada

Genovard C, Gotzens C. 1990. *Psicología de la Instruccion.* Madrid: Santillana

Gondra JM. 1985. La investigación en los archivos psicológicos. In *Estudios de historia de la psicología,* ed. S. Rodríguez, pp. 104–18. Salamanca, Spain: Univ. Salamanca

González-Marqués J. 1991. El razonamiento. See Martínez-Arias & Yela 1991, pp. 303–45

Gotor A, Miralles JL, SanMartin J, Cervera T. 1987. Medidas objetivas y subjectivas de familiaridad y significatividad de las palabras. *Psicologica* 8:137–54

Guío S, Santacreu J, Carrobles JA. 1989. Tratamiento conductual de la miopéa mediante programas de agudeza visual. *Rev. Son. Psicol.* 3:42–59

Guillamon A, Segovia S. 1993. Sexual dimorphism in the Accessory Olfactory System. In *The Development of Sex Differences and Similarities,* ed. M Haug, C Aron, K Olsen, pp. 363–76. Dordrecht: Kluwer Academic

Hernandez P, García L. 1991. *Psicología y Enseñanza del Estudio.* Madrid: Pirámide

Huertas E. 1986. El aprendizaje "preparado" de miedo en humanos. *Estud. Psicol.* 26:107–27

Huertas E. 1992. *El Aprendizaje no Verbal de los Humanos.* Madrid: Pirámide

Huici C. 1980. Initial disposition and intermember perception in experimental groups. *Small Group Behav.* 11(3):297–308

Ibañez E. 1988. La información como estrategia de dominio del estrés en pacientes aquejados de cáncer. *Boll Psicol.* 21:27–50

Iglesias J, Loeches A, Serrano JM, Carretie L. 1989. Muscular basis of infant facial behavior to the stranger approach. *Int. J. Psychophysiol.* 7:237–38

Jañez L. 1984. Visual grouping without low spatial frequencies. *Vision Res.* 24(3):271–74

Jimenez-Burillo F, Clemente M. 1986. *Psicología Social y Sistema Penal.* Madrid: Alianza

Juan-Espinosa M, Colom R. 1989. *Psicología Diferencial y Cognición.* Valencia, Spain: Promolibro

Junqué C, Pujol J, Vendrell P, Bruna O, Jodar M, et al. 1990. Leuko-araiosis on magnetic resonance imaging and speed of mental processing. *Arch. Neurol.* 47:151–56

Kirchner T, Forns M, Amador JA. 1989. Effects of adaptation to the task on solving the group embedded figures test. *Percept. Mot. Skills* 68:1303–6

Labrador FJ, Crespo M. 1992 Evaluacion del estres. In *Introduccion a la Evaluacion Psicologica,* Vol. 2, ed. R Fernández-Ballesteros, pp. 355–70. Madrid: Pirámide

Labrador FJ, Puente ML. 1988. Tratamiento de las cefaleas tensionales: consideraciones actuales y propuestas de intervención. *Anu. Psicol.* 38:67–86

Linaza J, Maldonado A. 1987. *Los Juegos y el Deporte en el Desarrollo Psicologico del Niño.* Barcelona: Anthropos

Luciano MC. 1986. Acquisition, maintenance and generalization of productive intraverbal behavior through transfer of stimulus control procedures. *Appl. Res. Ment. Retard.* 7:1–20

Luna D. 1980. Procesos de retencion en el aprendizaje observacional. *Rev. Psicol. Gen. Apl.* 35:769–84

Luna D, Ruiz M, Fernández-Trespalacios JL. 1985. Análisis de los efectos de las propiedades componentes y configuracionales de los estimulos sobre el proceso perceptual. *Rev. Psicol. Gen. Apl.* 40:855–80

Maciá A. 1990. *Psicología y Teoría de la Decisión.* Madrid: Univ. Natl. Educ. Dist.

Manning L, Fernández-Ballesteros R. 1982. Dependencia-independencia de campo y diferenciacion hemisferica. II. Asimetria izquierda en una tarea de reproduccion de letras. *Rev. Psicol. Gen. Apl.* 37:637–46

Marchesi A. 1987. *El Desarrollo Cognitivo de los Niños Sordos.* Madrid: Alianza

Marquez MO, Fernández-Ballesteros R. 1988. Procesamiento iconico de los estimulos del Rorschach. *Psychol. Assess./Eval. Psicol.* 4:223–37

Martin A, Rubio V, Marquez M, Juan-Espinosa JM. 1990. *Sistema de Evaluacion y Registros del Comportamiento Adaptativo en el Retraso Mental, WV-UAM.* Madrid: Mepsa

Martínez-Arias R. 1991. El proceso de toma de decisiones. See Martínez-Arias & Yela 1991, pp. 411–94

Martínez-Arias R, Yela M. 1991. *Pensamiento e Inteligencia.* Madrid: Alianza

Martínez-Selva JM, Gomez J, Olmos E, Navarro N, Roman F. 1987. Sex and menstrual cycle differences in the habituation and spontaneous recovery of the electrodermal orienting reaction. *Pers. Individ. Differ.* 8:211–17

Martorell C, Peiró JM, Dellacer M, Navarro A, Flores R, Silva F. 1990. Assessing behavioral problems and assets in children and adolescents. *Pers. Individ. Differ.* 11: 1221–26

Mayor J. 1985. Metáfora y conocimiento. In *Actividad Humana y Procesos Cognitivos,* ed. J Mayor, pp. 233–65. Madrid: Alhambra

Mayor J, Sainz J, González Marqués J. 1988. Stroop and priming effects in naming and categorizing tasks using words and pictures. In *Cognitive and Neuropsychological Approaches to Mental Imagery,* ed. M Denis, J Engelkamp, JT Richardson, pp. 69–78. Amsterdam: Nijhoff

Miguel-Tobal JJ, Cano-Vindel A. 1989. Avances en la evaluación de la ansiedad y sus implicaciones en la elección del tratamiento. *Terap. Comport.* 22/23:125–28

Mira JJ, Diges M. 1986. Procesos intervinientes en la evidencia de testigos. In *Psicología Social y Sistema Penal,* ed. F Jimenez-Burillo, M Clemente, pp. 159–84. Madrid: Alianza

Morales JF. 1981. *La Conducta Social como Intercambio.* Bilbao, Spain: Desclée de Brouwer

Mugni G, Pérez JA. 1991. *The Social Influence of Minority Groups.* Cambridge: Cambridge Univ. Press

Munduate L, Baron M. 1989. Análisis de la conducta en el trabajo desde el modelo de expectativa. *Rev. Psicol. Trab. Organ.* 4(11):142–55

Muñiz J. 1990. *Teoría de Respuesta a los Items.* Madrid: Pirámide

Muñiz J, Yela M. 1981. Estudio de las relaciones entre fluidez oral verbal y algunos aspectos de la personalidad. *Rev. Psicol. Gen. Apl.* 36:627–49

Munné F. 1986. *La Construccion de la Psicología Social como Ciencia Teorica.* Barcelona: Alamex

Navarro M, Prieto JM. 1992. A new psycho-biological test to detect morphine-dependent users in the work environment. *Appl. Psychol.* 41(2):175–84

Nieto A, Hernández S, González-Feria L, Barroso J. 1990. Semantic capabilities of the left and right cerebral hemispheres in categorization tasks: effects of verbal pictorial presentation. *Neuropsychologia* 28:1175–86

Obiols JE, Clos M, Corbero E, García-Domingo M, de Trincheréa I, et al. 1992. Sustained attention deficit in young schizophrenic and schizotypic men. *Psychol. Rep.* 71:1131–36

Ortiz T, Exposito J. 1992. EEG topography during letters discrimination in normal and dyslexic children. *Eur. Rev. Appl. Psychol.* 42(3):199–206

Palacios J. 1989. Parent's ideas about the development and education of their children. *Int. J. Behav. Dev.* 13:137–55

Peiró JM. 1987. Desempleo juvenil y socialización para el trabajo. In *Juventud, Trabajo y Desempleo: un Analisis Psicosociologico,* ed. JR Torregrosa, J Berger, JL Alvara. pp. 159–78. Madrid: Ministerio Trabajo

Peiró JM, Melia JL, Zurriaga R. 1987. Structural and relational aspects of role sets and their influence on focal person's role stress. In *The Challenge of Technological Change for Work and Organization: Tools and Strategies for the Nineties,* ed. K De Witte, pp. 337–44. Leuven, Belgium: Univ. Leuven Press

Peiró JM, Moret D. 1987. *La Socializacion Laboral de los Jovenes: la Transicion de la Escuela al Trabajo.* Valencia, Spain: Nau Llibres

Pelaez F. 1982. Greeting movements among adult males in a colony of Baboons. *Papiohamadryas, P. cynocephalus* and their hybrids. *Primates* 23:233–44

Pelechano V. 1973. *Personalidad y Parametros: Tres Escuelas y un Modelo.* Barcelona: Vicens-Vives

Pelechano V. 1980. *Terapia Familiar Comunitaria.* Valencia, Spain: Alfaplús

Pelechano V, De Miguel A. 1992. Entrenamiento en habilidades interpersonales en ancianos. In *Perspectivas en Gerontología y Salud,* ed. A Reig, D Ribera, pp. 77–101. Valencia, Spain: Promolibro

Pellón R, Blackman DE. 1987. Punishment of schedule-induced drinking in rats by signalled and unsignalled delays in food presentation. *J. Exp. Anal. Behav.* 48:417–34

Peña Casanova J. 1987. *La Exploración Neurológica.* Barcelona: MCR

Pereda S, García JM. 1986. Variables personales y causas de satisfacción e insatisfacción en el trabajo en empleados españoles de banca. *Rev. Psicol. Trab. Organ.* 2:101–14

Pérez-Delgado E, Garcí-Ros R. 1991. *La Psicología del Desarrollo Moral.* Madrid: Siglo XXI

Pérez-Pereira M. 1991. The acquisition of gender: what Spanish children tell us. *J. Child Lang.* 18:571–90

Pinillos JL. 1975. *Principios de Psicología.* Madrid: Alianza

Pinillos JL. 1983. *Las Funciones de la Conciencia.* Madrid: Real Acad. Ciencias Morales Politicas

Pitarque A, Soler MJ, Algarabel S. 1987. Facilitación episódica desde el aprendizaje de listas seriales de conceptos no relacionados. *Psicológica* 2:173–85

Pol E, Morales M. 1986. El entorno escolar desde la psicología ambiental. In *Introducción a la Psicología Ambiental,* ed. F Jiménez-Burillo, JI Aragones, pp. 284–302. Madrid: Alianza

Polaino A, Lizasoain O. 1992. Parental stress and satisfaction with children's hospitalization: a prospective study. *Acta Pediátr. Esp.* 50(6):472–79

Polaino A, Senra C. 1991. Measurement of depression: comparison between self-reports and clinical assessments of depressed outpatients. *J. Psychopathol. Behav. Assess.* 13:4

Prieto F, Marti C, Peiró JM, González-Roma V. 1990. Desarrollo tecnológico de los procesos de telecomunicación y su incidencia sobre dimensiones estructurales de la organización. In *Trabajo, Organizaciones y Marketing Social,* ed. JM Peiró, pp. 275–88. Barcelona: PPU

Prieto JM. 1992. A market-based competition in applied psychology. In *General Psychology and Environmental Psychology,* ed. B Wilpert, H Motoaki, J Misumi, pp. 55–69. Hillsdale, NJ: Erlbaum

Prieto JM. 1993. The Team Perspective in Selection and Assessment. In *Advances in Personnel Selection and Assessment,* ed. H Schuler, JL Farr, M Smith, pp. 221–34. Hillsdale, NJ: Erlbaum

Prieto JM, Blasco RD, Quintanilla I. 1991. Recrutement et sélection du personnel en Espagne. *Rev. Eur. Psychol. Appl.* 41(1):47–62

Puerto A, Deutsch JA, Molina F, Roll PL. 1976. Rapid discrimination of rewarding nutrients by the upper gastrointestinal tract. *Science* 192:485–87

Quijano SD. 1992. *Sistemas Efectivos de Evaluacion del Rendimiento: Resultados y Desempeño.* Barcelona: PPU

Quiñones E, Tortosa F, Carpintero H. 1993. *Historia de la Psicología: Textos y Comentarios.* Madrid: Tecnos

Quintanilla I. 1992. *Seleccion y Evaluacion de Personal.* Valencia, Spain: Promolibro

Recarte MA. 1985. Activación en la memoria semántica. *Rev. Psicol. Gen. Apl.* 6:1063–77

Rechea C. 1985. Procesos conscientes, procesos automáticos. In *La Conciencia en la Psicología Actual,* ed. F Valle-Inclán, pp. 87–112. Bilbao, Spain: Univ. País Vasco

Reig A. 1992. Estrés y estado de salud en personas mayores. In *Perspectivas en Gerontología y Salud,* ed. A Reig, D Ribera, pp. 46–59. Valencia, Spain: Promolibro

Ribera D, Reig A, Miquel J. 1988. Psicología de la salud y envejecimiento. Estudio empírico en una residencia de ancianos. *Geriatrika* 4(2):15–24

Rivas F, Alcantud F. 1989. *La Evaluacion Criterial en la Educacion Primaria.* Madrid: Ministerio Educ. Ciencias

Rivas F, Marco R. 1985. *Evaluación Conductual Subjetiva: la Técnica de la Rejilla.* Valencia, Spain: CESPU

Riviere A. 1990. Origen y desarrollo de la función simbólica en el niño. In *Desarrollo Psicologico y Educacion,* Vol. 1, ed. J Palacios, A Marchesi, C Coll, pp. 113–30. Madrid: Alianza

Riviere A. 1991. *Objetos con Mente.* Madrid: Alianza

Roales-Nieto JG. 1988. Blood glucose discrimination in insulin dependent diabetics. Training in feedback and external control. *Behav. Modif.* 12:116–32

Rodriguez-Marin J. 1986. El impacto

psicológico de la hospitalización. *Anál. Modif. Conduct.* 33:421–40.

Rodriguez-Marin J. 1992. Estrategias de afrontamiento y salud mental. In *Influencias Sociales y Psicologicas en la Salud Mental.* ed. JL Alvaro, JR Torregrosa, A Garrido, pp. 103–20. Madrid: Siglo XXI

Rodriguez-Marin J, López S, Pastor MA. 1989. Estrés por hospitalización y estrategias de afrontamiento. *Rev. Psicol. Salud* 1:81–104

Ros M, Cano JJ, Huici C. 1987. Language and intergroup perception in Spain. In *Language and Ethnic Identity,* ed. WB Gudykunst, pp. 87–104. Clevedon, UK: Multilingual Matters

Rosa A, Ochaita E, Moreno E, Fernández E, Carretero M, et al. 1984. Cognitive development in blind children: a challenge to piagetian theory. *Q. Newsl. Lab. Comp. Hum. Cogn.* 6:75–81

Rosa A, Quintana J, Lafuente E. 1988. *Psicología e Historia.* Madrid: Univ. Autónoma Madrid

Ruiz-Caballero JA, Bermúdez J. 1992. Individual differences in depression, induced mood, and perception of emotionally toned words. *Eur. J. Pers.* 6:215–24

Ruiz-Vargas JM. 1987. *Esquizofrenia: un Enfoque Cognitivo.* Madrid: Alianza

Ruiz-Vargas JM. 1991. *Psicología de la Memoria.* Madrid: Alianza

Sabater-Pi J. 1974. An elementary industry of the chimpanzees in the Okorobiko mountains of Rio Muni. *Primates* 14:351–64

Saldaña C, Rossell R. 1988. *Obesidad.* Barcelona: Martínez-Roca

Salvador A, Simón V, Suay F, Llorens L. 1987. Testosterone and cortisol responses to competitive fighting in human males. *Aggress. Behav.* 13:9–13

Sánchez-Cánovas J. 1986. *El Nuevo Paradigma de la Inteligencia Humana.* Valencia, Spain: Tirant Lo Blanch

Sánchez-López MP, Forteza JA. 1987. Bilingüismo e inteligencia. In *Estudios sobre la Inteligencia y Lenguaje,* ed. M Yela, pp. 201–54. Madrid: Pirámide

Sandén B, Chorot P. 1989. The incubation theory of fear/anxiety: experimental investigation in a human laboratory model of Pavlovian conditioning. *Behav. Res. Ther.* 27:9–18

Sangrador JL. 1981. *Estereotipos de las Nacionalidades y Regiones de España.* Madrid: CIS

Santacreu J. 1986. *Tratamiento Conductual de la Tartamudez.* Valencia, Spain: Promolibro

Santisteban C. 1990. *Psicometria: Teoría y Prática den la Construcción de Tests.* Madrid: Norma

Satorra A. 1989. Alternative test criteria in covariance structure analysis: a unified approach. *Psychometrika* 54:131–51

Segovia S, Guillamon A. 1993. Sexual dimorphism in the vomeronasal pathway and sex differences in reproductive behaviors. *Brain Res. Rev.* 18:51–74

Segura Torres P, Capdevila L, Martín Nicolovius M, Morgado I. 1988. Improvement of shuttle-box learning with pre- and post-trial intracranial self-stimulation in rats. *Behav. Brain Res.* 29:111–17

Seisdedos N. 1991. *Monografía Técnica del 16 PF.* Madrid: Tecnicos Especialistas Asociados

Seisdedos N. 1993. Personnel selection, questionnaires and motivational distortion: an intelligent attitude of adaptation. In *Advances in Personnel Selection and Assessment,* ed. H Schuler, JL Farr, M Smith, pp. 91–108. Hillsdale, NJ: Erlbaum

Sendin C. 1987. La estructura factorial del test de Rorschach: un camino para la validez del constructo. *Rorschachiana* 16:152–57

Sierra B, Ruiz-Vargas JM, Zaccagnini JL. 1983. Efectos de la personalidad, ruído, hora del día y tiempos de duración en una tarea de vigilancia visual. In *Sistemas de Producción y Consumo,* ed. I Delclaux, pp. 147–74. Murcia, Spain: Límite

Siguán M. 1982. Piaget en España. *Rev. Psicol. Gen. Apl.* 2:275–84

Siguán M. 1984. *Adquisición Precoz de una Segunda Lengua.* Barcelona: Univ. Barcelona

Silva F. 1993. *Psychometric Foundations and Behavioral Assessment* Newbury Park, CA: Sage

Simon MA. 1993. *Psicología de la Salud: Aplicaciones Clinicas y Estrategias de Intervencion.* Madrid: Pirámide

Soler J, Tortosa F. 1987. *Psicología y Tráfico.* Valencia, Spain: Nau Llibres

Staats A, Fernández-Ballesteros R. 1987. The self-report in personality measurement: a paradigmatic behaviorism approach to psychodiagnostic. *Eval. Psicol./Psychol. Assess.* 3:151–91

Torregrosa JR. 1974. *Teoría en Investigación en la Psicología Social Actual.* Madrid: Inst. Español Opinion Publica

Tortosa F, Montoro L, Carbonell E. 1989. *Psicología y Seguridad vial en España. 60 Años de Historia.* Madrid: Asoc. Española Centros Reconocimiento

Tous JM. 1985. *Psicología de la Personalidad: Diferencias Individuales, Biológicas y Cognitivas en el Procesamiento de Información.* Barcelona: PPU

Tudela P. 1985. Procesos pre-atencionales y procesamiento no consciente. In *Actividad Humana y Procesos Cognitivos,* ed. J Mayor, pp. 41–52. Madrid: Alhambra

Valle F. 1991. *Psicolingüística.* Madrid: Morata

Vallejo MA, Labrador FJ. 1983. Modelo de predisposición psicobiológica para explicar las cefaleas. *Rev. Esp. Ter. Comport.* 1:5–18

Valverde J. 1985. Personalidad delincuente o conducta desadaptada. *Arbor* 494:115–38

Vázquez C. 1987. Judgment of contingency: cognitive biases in depressed and non-depressed subjects. *J. Pers. Soc. Psychol.* 52:419–31

Vázquez C, Fuentenebro F, Sanz J, Gómez I, Calcedo A, et al. 1990. Attentional peformance and positive vs. negative symptoms in schizophrenia. In *European Perspectives of Psychology,* ed. PJ Drenth, JA Sergeant, J Takens, 3:91–106. New York: Wiley

Verdugo MA. 1989. *Programas Conductuales Alternativos: I. Habilidades Sociales.* Madrid: MEPSA

Vila J. 1992. Evaluacion psicofisiologica. In *Introduccion a la Evaluacion Psicologica,* ed. R Fernández-Ballesteros, 2:355–70. Madrid: Pirámide

Vila J, Fernández MC, Godoy J. 1992. The cardiac defense response in humans: effect of stimulus modality and gender differences. *J. Psychophysiol.* 6:140–54

Vizcarro C, Fernández-Ballesteros R, Fernández-Trespalacios JL. 1987. The role of perceptual laws in Rorschach response. *J. Pers. Assess.* 51:115–25

Yela M. 1952. Phenomenal causation at a distance. *Q. J. Exp. Psychol.* 4:139–54

Yela M. 1987. *Estudios sobre Inteligencia y Lenguaje.* Madrid: Pirámide

Annu. Rev. Psychol. 1994. 45:79–129

INTERPERSONAL RELATIONSHIPS

Ellen Berscheid

Department of Psychology, University of Minnesota, Minneapolis, Minnesota 55455

KEY WORDS: relationship, cognition, interaction, trust, love, jealousy, social support, stability

---

CONTENTS

INTRODUCTION

Since Clark & Reis' (1988) review of the relationship domain, the field has experienced phenomenal growth. Relationship scholars now must monitor an increasing number of journals in which relationship theory and research is published as well as the growing number of books and conferences devoted to relationship work. They also must be sensitive to the methodological and analytical techniques the study of interpersonal relationships requires because of the temporal nature of relationships, the dependency of dyadic observations, and the dichotomous nature of important outcome variables (e.g. Bradbury &

Fincham 1991, Godwin 1988, Johnson 1988, Kenny & Kashy 1991, Montgomery & Duck 1991, Morgan & Teachman 1988, Robins 1990).

The profusion of recent writings on relationship phenomena has its source in widening recognition that many of the questions traditionally addressed by the social and behavioral sciences, and by several of the health sciences, directly engage questions about interpersonal relationships. As a result, the multidisciplinary nature of the relationship field has become apparent, and interdisciplinary collaboration and cross-pollinization of theory and technique is increasingly evident. Along with psychology, the disciplines of sociology, of marital and family therapy, and of communication remain vital and sustained contributors to relationship knowledge. Within psychology, developmental psychology, social psychology, and clinical psychology are the largest current contributors to relationship theory and research.

Each discipline tends to address certain types of relationships. Taking an empirically pragmatic and largely atheoretical approach (see Berardo 1990, Lavee & Dollahite 1991, Nye 1988 for reviews), sociologists examine the associations between macro-societal forces and the changing forms and stability of family relationships as well as such outcomes as marital satisfaction. Researchers in marital and family therapy, a field that includes many clinical psychologists, are concerned primarily with identifying the sources of distress within marital relationships and the efficacy of intervention strategies (see O'Leary & Smith 1991), as are many communication researchers who often attempt to identify dysfunctional communication patterns (see Noller & Fitzpatrick 1990). Developmental psychologists address relationships between parents and children and child–peer relationships (Hartup 1989). Collins & Gunnar (1990) recently reviewed some of this work. Lesser interest has been shown in life-span developmental questions pertaining to the relationships of older adults (but see Reis et al 1993, Caspi & Herbener 1990; see Blieszner & Adams 1992 for a review of adult friendship). Social psychologists usually examine young adult relationships, often premarital courtship relationships (see Cate & Lloyd 1992), although they are increasingly likely to range into the marital terrain (e.g. Huston et al 1986).

The matrix of interpersonal relationship knowledge thus is fractured along the lines of relationship type. Type of relationship is substantially confounded with disciplinary approach, with the characteristics of the individuals customarily found within that type of relationship, and with the relationship phenomena of interest. Therefore, it is difficult to conceptually integrate relationship research. It is also difficult to assess progress in the relationship field because such assessment presupposes that relationship scholars have identified and endorse a common goal. In fact, relationship researchers have adopted a variety of goals that are often unique to the type of relationship addressed. Nevertheless, many relationship researchers hope their efforts ultimately will result in a body of knowledge about the causal dynamics of relationships that will transcend relationship type. Whether a superordinate relationship knowledge base can be realized is a fundamental question facing the interpersonal relationship field, and it is likely to remain so for some time.

Generic and Relationship Type Knowledge

Recent consideration of the goal of moving toward a superordinate body of knowledge that crosses the boundaries of relationship type has been evident within sociology. As a result of the decline of the traditional family form and the necessity to broaden the meaning of the term "families" to include an increasingly large number of relationship types, Scanzoni et al (1989) question whether "continuing to think about a concrete subfield called the family is the most fruitful way to proceed" and suggest that "we begin to conceptualize all types of primary relations—for example, child-adult, adult-adult, sex-based and nonsex-based, close and nonclose relationships—in a manner that would facilitate fundamental insights into their commonalities and differences..." (p. 48). Adams (1988), reviewing the past fifty years of family research, wonders whether "family life might be viewed as one type of intimate association" (p. 14) to facilitate more use of general theories of human behavior within family sociology. And Blumstein & Kollock (1988) observe:

> A major organizational hurdle hinders the study of close relationships. The sociological literature possesses numerous atomized research areas focusing on specific kinds of relationships, e.g., friendship, marriage. However, no scientific category system exists for organizing the universe of relationships studies.... While there have been numerous attempts to classify varieties within a given relationship type, especially marriage (e.g. Cuber & Haroff 1965, Fitzpatrick 1984), these approaches show little promise of transcending the boundaries of the particular type of relationship under scrutiny. (p. 472)

Blumstein & Kollock add that the greatest strength of psychology's approach to close relationships is its attempt to conceptualize close relationships generically (e.g. Kelley et al 1983), but they also identify a serious weakness in this approach: "In the psychological literature there is scant recognition that the behavior in a close relationship is shaped by the structural circumstances and cultural definitions of that relationship" (p. 471). One can argue, however, that psychologists' reluctance to cross lines of relationship type within a single study or even within a continuing program of research reflects tacit recognition that societal norms, roles, understandings, and customs are responsible for many of the behavioral regularities within a specific type of relationship. Few mention explicitly the composition of the walls between relationship type that make scaling them so hazardous, however, and fewer directly acknowledge the macro-societal forces that influence behavior within certain relationship types (see Levinger 1990) and that undoubtedly overwhelm opposing psychological forces with some frequency (e.g. Peplau et al 1993). At the same time, however, endorsement of the goal of developing a superordinate knowledge base has become at least nominally accepted, with the construct of relationship closeness often believed to constitute a passport for crossing boundaries of relationship type. The view that a close relationship is one characterized by high interdependence of the partners' behaviors, including their emotions and thoughts (Kelley et al 1983), also has become accepted. More care is now taken with the use of terms that previously were considered synonyms for close, but that since have been theoretically differentiated (e.g. "intimate," see Reis & Shaver 1988).

Many of the processes that underlie relationship phenomena, then, are believed to be causally linked to the closeness of the relationship. For example, Clark & Reis (1988) organized their review of relationship research "around interpersonal processes that affect the course and conduct of interpersonal relationships, rather than, as is common in the literature, relationship types (e.g. friendship, marriage)" (p. 610) and they emphasized processes associated with interdependence. Assessing the closeness of a relationship, or its properties of interdependence, is thus of interest. At least one instrument recently developed to assess interdependence reveals that assuming a relationship is close based on its type (e.g. a family relationship) is an uncertain and unreliable method. Moreover, some relationships nominated by individuals as their closest, irrespective of type, don't seem very close, at least as interdependence is measured by the Relationship Closeness Inventory (Berscheid et al 1989a). An individual's subjective perception of the closeness of a relationship may not well reflect behavioral interdependence because subjective closeness is also a function of feelings of positive sentiment toward the partner (Berscheid et al 1989b). As measured by Aron et al's (1991) Inclusion-of-Other-in-Self Scale, perceived closeness also appears to be associated with stronger interconnections between cognitive representations of the self and the partner, and Aron et al (1992) have suggested that feeling close and behaving close may be relatively independent dimensions of closeness.

Other attempts have been made to surmount the confines of relationship type and to move toward a generic understanding of relationships. From a theoretically based consideration of the structural dynamics of different types of relationships, Blumstein & Kollock (1988) suggest that the relationship property space is defined by five dimensions: kin vs nonkin; sexual-romantic vs nonsexual-romantic; cohabiting vs noncohabiting; hierarchical vs egalitarian; and cross-sex vs same-sex. Alternatively, Scanzoni et al (1989) propose that sexually based primary relations may be a useful classificatory construct because it is positioned midway between the higher-order construct of close and such lower-order constructs as marriage and alternative life styles. Yet another classificatory scheme has been proposed by A. P. Fiske (1992) who argues that one of four fundamental relationship models directs an individual's actions in interaction with others: communal sharing (e.g. where all members of a group are treated equally and share a common identity); authority ranking (e.g. where people attend to each other's status in a hierarchical order); equality matching (e.g. where the behavioral principle of *quid pro quo* predominates); and market pricing (e.g. where people rationally weigh the utility of their behavior in acheiving desired outcomes in interaction with others).

These attempts to identify commonalities underlying certain types of relationships deserve consideration because beyond general endorsement of the desirability of an over-arching relationship knowledge base, and the implicit assumption that knowledge based on relationship type will contribute to that base, little empirical progress toward that goal has been made. For example, it is still rare for a phenomenon to be examined across relationship type (but see Wilmot & Baxter 1983, Ross & Sicoly 1979). Yet, the desirability of a generic relationship knowledge base has been partially responsible for the interdisciplinary character of the relationship field.

The goal of developing a superordinate body of relationship knowledge has no more intrinsic legitimacy than the goal of developing many independent bodies of knowledge, each addressed to a specific type of relationship. Subdirectories of knowledge addressed to a specific type of relationship always will be necessary because some of the conditions influencing behavior within each type of relationship are unique to that type, the properties of the individuals customarily found within certain relationship types often differ, and a number of phenomena occur primarily or even solely within a specific type of relationship. At this stage in the development of the relationship field, however, knowledge that transcends relationship type seems especially valuable for its potential to catapult the relationship field ahead quickly by furthering an understanding of all types of relationships at once.

Overview

The lion's share of this chapter is devoted to relationship cognition, or recent attempts by relationship researchers to understand cognitive processes within relationships and their association with a variety of relationship phenomena. This work promises not only to span relationship type but also to stimulate researchers to acknowledge and confront directly the culturally defined norms, roles, and understandings associated with different types of relationships. Progress along a number of more traditional fronts in relationship theory and research—love, jealousy, social support, and relationship dissolution—is also discussed briefly.

RELATIONSHIP COGNITION

Relationship researchers are beginning to take advantage of the theoretical and empirical fruits of social cognition to further their understanding of interpersonal relationships. At the same time, social cognition theorists and researchers are beginning to recognize that perception and cognition usually take place in the context of ongoing relationships with others. Until recently, social cognition researchers generally confined themselves to the study of cognitive processes as they occur in the laboratory under highly structured and minimal stimulus conditions, the referent of these processes usually being strangers or hypothetical others of no emotional or motivational import to the individual. Fiske (1992) points out that social cognition researchers are rediscovering the fact that social understanding operates in the service of social interaction:

> People make meaning and think about each other in the service of interaction; their interactions depend on their goals, which in turn depend on their immediate roles and the larger culture. People's interpersonal thinking is embedded in a practical context, which implies that it is best understood...by its observable and desired consequences for social behavior. (p. 878)

Many, perhaps most, of an individual's important and enduring goals are either deeply embedded in, or directly implicate, his or her close personal relationships (e.g. Cantor & Malley 1991). As a result, further advances in social cognition may depend on gaining an understanding of cognitive processes as they occur in ongoing association with others with whom the individual is interdependent for the achievement of his or her goals and where the actions that result from those processes have potent consequences for the individual's well-being. Without such knowledge, an understanding of social cognition will be incomplete and it also may be inaccurate (see Fiske & Taylor 1991, p. 557). Thus the rapprochement that has begun between the fields of social cognition and interpersonal relationships has the potential to benefit both endeavors.

Representation of Self and Others

Discovering how people mentally organize and represent information about themselves and about others has been a central task of social cognition research. The mental knowledge structures in which social information is represented usually are called schemas, although there are several other terms for organized representations (e.g. mental models), each with its own theoretical nuances. Schemas have implications for the kinds of social stimuli to which the individual will subsequently attend (e.g. Zadny & Gerard 1974, Berscheid et al 1976), for how newly encountered stimuli will be categorized and then interpreted through the filter of the schema activated by the categorization, and for the retrieval of information from memory (e.g. Brewer & Treyens 1981,

Trafimow & Wyer 1993). Moreover, because schemas often represent expectations about the individual's own behavior, the behavior of another person, and the nature of the interaction likely to take place between the two, schemas often guide the individual's behavior in social interaction, sometimes leading to confirmation of the individual's prior expectations even when those expectations were unwarranted (e.g. Snyder 1984, Miller & Turnbull 1986).

Evidence has supported the long-standing assumption that social information is organized around person categories (e.g. myself, Joe). Most of this evidence, however, has been obtained in laboratory settings in which the structure provided by the minimal stimulus field—often lists of traits associated with person names—encourages, perhaps demands, such an organization. When the stimulus field is richer, as in the natural settings of interest to relationship researchers, person categories may not be dominant (e.g. Cantor et al 1982, Sedikides & Ostrom 1988). Some recent studies suggest that an individual's relationship with another may play an important role in organizing information about that person. For example, a series of studies by A. P. Fiske et al (1991) examines the patterns of substitutions that occur when people confuse one person with another (e.g. calling the person by the wrong name). The investigators find that people tend to confuse those with whom they interact in the same basic relationship mode and conclude that people may often "represent their social world in terms of the kinds of relationships they have with others" (p. 673).

Sedikides et al (1993) provide additional evidence that people may spontaneously organize social information around relationship as well as person categories. Information about individuals known to be in close relationship with one another, as opposed to information presented in proximity about two persons not in relationship, tends to be recalled in ways suggesting that knowledge of the existence of a relationship influences how information about each relationship partner is organized and represented. Attributes of spouses are more frequently confused, for example.

Other evidence is accumulating that relationships with others play an important role in the representation of social knowledge. Sande et al (1988) have found that familiar and liked persons are perceived to possess more traits than unfamiliar, disliked persons, and Prentice (1990) presents evidence that representations of the self and of familiar others show fewer differences on a number of dimensions than do self and unfamiliar other representations. Extending these findings, Andersen & Cole (1990) demonstrate that "significant others" are mentally represented as highly organized person categories that appear to be richer, more distinctive, and also more cognitively accessible than the types of categories more frequently studied (e.g. person stereotypes). Operating as powerful social categories, these representations of significant others should have special influence on how persons who activate these categories are perceived.

Recent evidence also suggests that an individual's relationships with others may influence how information about the self is organized. Markus & Kitayama (1991) argue that current conceptions of the self as an autonomous, independent person whose mental representation is composed of a unique configuration of such internal attributes as traits and abilities is inappropriate for people within many non-Western cultures. An interdependent view of the self seems to prevail in these cultures, whereas Western cultures conceive of the self as an independent entity containing dispositional attributes detached from context. In Japanese culture, for example, the individual's sense of belonging to a social relationship may be so strong that the relationship may be the functional unit of conscious reflection for "it is the 'other' or the 'self-in-relation-to-other' that is focal in individual experience" (p. 225). Thus the self knowledge likely to guide the behavior of those who possess an interdependent view of self may be the self-in-relation to specific others in particular contexts, with social situations serving as the unit of representation rather than a person and his or her cross-situational attributes.

Other theorists of the self also are beginning to examine the relational aspects of self knowledge structures in general and situation-specific self schemas in particular. For example, Baldwin et al (1990) have found that people give lower evaluations of the quality of their task performance when schemas of significant and disapproving others are presumably activated through the subliminal exposure of the scowling face of the department chair to graduate students or, in another condition, the disapproving face of the Pope to Catholics. Baldwin et al speculate that an individual's "sense of identity might always be constructed anew as an emergent product of a matrix of salient interpersonal information, from both ongoing interactions and accessible cognitive structures" (p. 451). Gergen (1991) also argues that conceptions of the self may not be as stable as traditionally assumed because the diversity and multiplicity of an individual's social relationships in modern life may make it difficult for any single conception of self or core identity to develop and be maintained. Self-with-other representations thus may be a useful unit of analysis for research on the self concept, as Ogilvie & Ashmore (1991) demonstrate.

Representations of another person also may be more numerous than traditionally assumed. Srull & Wyer (1989) review evidence suggesting that people often form situation-specific representations of another that are functionally distinct from more general characterizations. Srull & Wyer theorize that the expectations uniquely associated with each other-in-specific-situation schema are likely to guide the individual's behavior in relationship with that person in that situation. Such multiple and situation-specific schemas of others have implications for virtually all questions researchers ask about interaction in relationships, including the feelings and emotions the individual may experience in interaction with that other. Srull & Wyer speculate that "when the behaviors of a person in one situation (or role) tend to differ evaluatively from those performed in another situation (or role), people may not attempt to reconcile the differences and may not even see them as inconsistent" (p. 80) because the two schemas may have been formed and are activated independently. This suggests that partners in long-term relationships may form many partner-in-situation schemas (e.g. partner-as-lover, partner-as-parent), each carrying its own affective tone that becomes salient when that particular schema is activated. Models of social cognition such as Srull & Wyer's are likely to be more useful for research on relationship cognition than previous models that assumed that people form a single cohesive and affectively homogeneous schema of another and that, therefore, could not account for the ambivalence of affect often observed in ongoing relationships (see Berscheid 1982).

Relationship Schemas

The term "relational schema" was introduced by Planalp (1987), who, in Burnett et al's (1987) important collection of papers on relationship knowledge and processes, discussed how people may form schemas that represent their interactions in close relationships. More recently, Baldwin (1992) has provided a valuable review of contributions to the concept of relational schemas, which he defines as "cognitive structures representing regularities in patterns of interpersonal relatedness" (p. 461). Baldwin theorizes that such schemas contain a self schema for how the self is experienced in an interaction situation, a person schema for the partner in the interaction, and a script for the expected interaction pattern that is derived through generalization from repeated similar interaction experiences.

The concept of script is important to relationship researchers because the existence of a relationship is usually defined in terms of the interaction between the partners and it is often the interaction pattern that the researcher wishes to understand, to predict, and in the case of therapeutic intervention, to change. A script may be viewed as an event schema comprised of the expected temporal ordering of events in a situation (e.g. Fiske & Taylor 1991). Like other schemas, scripts guide encoding, memory, and inference. Of particular interest to relationship researchers is what Ginsburg (1988) calls performative scripts, or knowledge structures that guide the individual's sequences of actions, and that "can be expected to facilitate the coordination of action, reduce the effort of interaction, reduce the necessity of attention to small details and allow joint action to be organized in large rather than minute chunks" (p. 30). Scripts and the organized action sequences and interaction expectations they represent are also implicated in affective experiences in the relationship (Berscheid 1983, Fitness & Strongman 1991, Wilson & Klaaren 1992).

The idea of performative scripts as they may effortfully develop in young relationships and become coordinated and routinized over time in many old relationships engages questions of controlled vs automatic processing of information. Bargh (1993) concludes that pure automatic processing has four features: 1. unintentionality, 2. uncontrollability, 3. operation outside of conscious awareness, and 4. efficiency. The cognitive processing of many events in long-term relationships may possess many automatic features because a major factor in the development of automatic processing is repetition and routinization, which allows quick and efficient responses to frequently encountered stimuli.

Scott et al (1991) have outlined some of the implications of the automatic–controlled processing distinction for understanding interaction in close relationships, including communicative behavior. Drawing upon Srull & Wyer's (1989) theory of social cognition, Scott et al have developed a potentially valuable model of information processing in close relationships that recognizes the automatic nature of many routinized communication sequences within relationships. Another provocative application of Srull & Wyer's theory to relationships has been made by Surra & Bohman (1991), who address cognitive processing of information during periods of change in the relationship (i.e. when it is developing or deteriorating) vs periods of stability. Because they address the sequential flow of cognition and action in social interaction, these two heuristically rich models join Bradbury & Fincham's (1989) contextual model of marital interaction in foretelling the nature of much future relationship theorizing. These models also highlight the nature of needed work in social cognition. For example, Srull & Wyer note two limitations of their model of social cognition:

> ...[First,] in the research paradigms in which the model has been evaluated, the information presented has typically described behaviors that were performed at different times and in different situations. The representations formed from temporally or causally related sequences of actions may take on additional complexity. Second, the model focuses on conditions in which subjects receive information about a person for the express purpose of forming an impression of this person. The processing of social information, and the representations that are formed from it, are highly dependent on how one expects to use the information at the time it is encoded.... (p. 58)

Both of these limitations have serious implications for the theory's applicability to relationships because a relationship is defined with reference to the presence of temporally and causally related sequences of partners' actions and also because forming a global impression of the other is an unlikely goal in naturalistic situations, even with strangers. Other models of social cognition are available (e.g. Fiske & Neuberg 1990, Brewer 1988), but they, too, are subject to limitations because they are based on the same kind of evidence.

Still other lacunae in current approaches to social cognition become apparent when one considers their applicability to relationship cognition. For example, short shrift has been given to the problem of attention, which is no problem when the individual is in a laboratory situation where it is his or her task to award undivided attention to the social stimuli at hand and to arrive at the cognitive product requested by the experimenter. But people in relationships are often distracted, tired, and disinterested, and a central question is what relationship events are they likely to attend to, and when. Fiske & Neuberg's (1990) model of social cognition attempts to integrate what is known of attention with subsequent cognitive processes but it is a recent exception to the rule.

Research on automatic processing is yielding new clues to the determinants of attention. If another's behaviors are relevant to the individual's chronically accessible trait constructs (e.g. loyal), the behaviors are more likely to be noticed and remembered, even under attentional overload conditions, as are negative social stimuli such as the other's undesirable behaviors (see Bargh 1993). Chronically accessible constructs are presumed to be unique to an individual and to develop from frequent and consistent experiences within the individual's history of social interaction. Other constructs may be primed by external elements in the stimulus situation, and another's behavior may be more likely to be encoded in terms of these recently primed constructs shortly after the priming event, but more frequently primed constructs become more accessible after a delay of only minutes (Bargh et al 1988, Higgins 1989). Thus, in naturalistic situations, people can be expected to quickly revert to their chronically accessible constructs to interpret another's behavior, especially ambiguous behavior. The chronic accessibility of some person constructs within a relationship schema is undoubtedly one reason why changing an individual's view of the partner in a long-term relationship is difficult. Because the influence of chronically accessible constructs is largely automatic, the individual is likely to interpret the old partner's new behavior in line with old constructs without being aware of doing so—one more reason why interventions seem more useful earlier rather than later in the relationship (see Olson 1990).

Gaps remaining in current models of social cognition, as well as the rapidity with which work in this area is appearing, suggest that such models simply constitute a useful starting point for relationship researchers, and that it would be a mistake for work on relationship cognition to become closely wed to any one existing model. In addition, because the interaction pattern characteristic of two people is the heart of their relationship, it is important that cognitions remain tied to interaction. A good example of how a relationship schema may guide interaction is provided by Bugental and associates' (e.g. Bugental 1993, Bugental et al 1993) investigations of the dynamics of interaction characteristic of families at risk for violence.

Bugental has demonstrated that abusive parents often hold chronically accessible threat-oriented relationship schemas reflecting their belief that negative interactions with children are due to variables controllable by the child but uncontrollable by themselves. When activated in interaction with the child, the schema has been shown to trigger a chain of intra- and interpersonal events that support and perpetuate the schema. Parents who hold a threat-oriented schema are especially alert to threat cues and tend to interpret the child's ambiguous behavior as threatening, thus exaggerating the probability of problems in interaction with the child. Such parents also tend to categorize a specific child on the basis of his or her threat potential (e.g. a naughty child) and to use associated behavioral scripts that reflect their interaction expectations and response patterns, which appear to be played out predictably and automatically. The parent's behavior then tends to elicit the responses the parent expects from the child (i.e. unresponsive behavior resulting in negative outcomes), which then justify the parent's threat-oriented behavior and perpetuate the expectations represented in the schema. Although the evidence supporting this pattern of events comes from a variety of studies using different methodologies, Bugental's computer-simulation experimental paradigm, in which the child's behaviors in response to the adult's is programmed and controlled, is particularly innovative and potentially useful to relationship researchers.

Attributional Processes in Relationships

The role of attribution processes in close relationships, especially distressed marital relationships, has received much attention in recent years. This focus on cognitive and affective behavior in marital interaction represents a departure from the behaviorist approach that emphasized observation and coding of couples' behavior in interaction, often as they discussed their marital problems in the laboratory (see Weiss & Heyman 1990 for a review). Discrepancies between outsiders' interpretations of the interaction and the meanings the interactants' themselves made of it led to the development of cognitively oriented models to guide research on marital communication. For example, Bradbury & Fincham's (1989) contextual model of marital interaction addresses the cognitive and affective processing of communicative events in interaction, recognizing that these are influenced by the cognitive sets the interactants have formed from their previous interactions. Noller and associates (see Noller & Guthrie 1991, Noller & Ruzzene 1991) also emphasize the role of cognition and affect in interaction. Their investigations of accuracy and bias in the decoding of nonverbal messages between spouses, judgments of the partner's affect and intentions during interaction, as well as attributions of the cause of the partner's behavior demonstrate that distressed spouses have difficulty identifying their partner's affect, goals, and intentions during conflictful interactions, and with respect to attributions, tend to put the worst possible interpretation on their partner's motives.

Considerable evidence now documents an association between attributions that cast the partner's behavior in a positive or negative light and relationship satisfaction. There is also some evidence that negative attributions are causally implicated in keeping relationships happy or unhappy. Much of this research has been reviewed recently by Bradbury & Fincham (1990), who played a major role in moving this classic problem in social cognition beyond pencil-and-paper methodology, undertaking the difficult task of tracing the effect of attributional processes on actual interaction in marital and other ongoing relationships (e.g. Fincham & Bradbury 1991, 1992). Fletcher & Fincham (1991b) have incorporated into the Bradbury & Fincham contextual model the distinction between automatic and controlled processing to better account for attributional processes as they occur in interaction. They also provide a valuable discussion of differences in content and process that may characterize attributions made at the controlled and automatic levels.

The automatic–controlled distinction is important in the attribution context because causal reasoning appears to be among the complex cognitive activities that can occur outside of conscious awareness (see Kihlstrom 1987). Read (1987) draws attention to the virtually indisputable fact that many of the inferences about causal connections are made during the initial comprehension phase of perceiving events. "Otherwise, people would simply fail to understand what was going on" (p. 289). Scott et al (1991) speculate that because of schematic automatic processing in close relationships, which directs response without conscious consideration of the antecedent causes of the partner's behavior, "attributions per se may not be as important mediators of interpersonal behavior as one might intuitively expect" and "they may not even be thought about unless the recipient is asked, by an experimenter or another person, to generate them after the fact" (p. 60). The evidence suggests, however, that cognitive processing in any one instance is rarely purely automatic or purely controlled (Bargh 1993) and, moreover, effortful and deliberate puzzling over the cause of the partner's behavior appears to be a common event in the relationship context, even in long-term relationships.

Automaticity in attributional activities raises the question of whether current information about attributional and other cognitive activities presumed to influence interaction is artifactual, to some unknown extent a product of the procedures by which information is obtained about on-line cognition (i.e. cognitive activities that are concurrent with overt interaction behavior). Much research on the role of attributions in interaction is vulnerable to the charge that the procedures by which attributions are examined are irrelevant (in the case of hypothetical situations, "what if your partner...", e.g. Holtzworth-Munroe & Jacobson 1985), intrusive (in the case of thought sampling prompted by a voice over the intercom that periodically asks subjects to tell what they are thinking at that moment, e.g. Berman 1988), or reactive (in the case of video-assisted retrospective thought listing after the fact of interaction, e.g. Ickes et al 1990). Bradbury & Fincham (e.g. 1988) discuss some of the methodological and conceptual problems such procedures raise. These problems reflect those likely to be encountered in other arenas where knowledge of the individual's cognitive activity is desired and where the researcher is dependent on the individual's self-report for that information. The problems attribution researchers have faced in interpreting on-line cognition thus represent a broader conundrum for relationship cognition research. Asking people what they are thinking as they are doing—or, more usually, what they were thinking when they were doing (see Fletcher & Kininmonth 1991)—raises some of the ghosts that used to haunt early introspection research in psychology.

Within the attribution area, the question seems to be shifting somewhat toward identifying the conditions under which people are likely to make spontaneous attributions (e.g. Holtzworth-Munroe & Jacobson 1988). Conscious and effortful examination of cause is likely in the initial stages of a relationship, when important relationship choices are required by changes in the relationship (e.g. Fletcher et al 1987), and when an individual's expectations about another's behavior are violated and that violation may have important consequences for the individual's outcomes (e.g. Weiner 1985). Work by Gilbert (1991) and associates indicates that attention load also influences an individual's causal attribution processes. Gilbert posits a three-stage process: first, another's behavior is immediately characterized in trait terms; second, inferences are made from the trait to a disposition; and, third, possible situational causes for the behavior are considered and may correct the dispositional inference. Dispositional inferences thus are assumed to be made first, quickly and efficiently, but the third stage may be aborted if the individual is cognitively busy and operating under conditions of attention overload.

Efforts to examine when people make spontaneous attributions in naturalistic situations also reveal that attributions of the cause of self-initiated events or behaviors, in the form of excuses or justifications, are a frequent form of attributional activity in relationships. Excusatory self-attributions represent a potentially fruitful area of investigation (see Fincham 1992), one that will be informed by Bradbury & Fincham's (1990) distinction between responsibility and blame attributions, as well as by the traditional and contemporary literature on accounts, or the nature of excuses typically offered by social transgressors and the conditions that influence their likelihood of acceptance (e.g. Scott & Lyman 1968, Schonbach 1990, Gonzales et al 1992).

Autobiographical Memory

Current knowledge structures pertinent to a relationship influence the retrieval from memory of information about that relationship. Relationship researchers have a special interest in autobiographical memory, or memory for personal vs impersonal events, for at least two reasons: first, relationship researchers are usually dependent on self-report for knowledge of the individual's private relationship events as well as past relationship events; and second, an individual's present reconstruction of past relationship events, whether accurate or not, may reflect the meaning of those events to the individual and thus represent the individual's present orientation toward the relationship.

RETROSPECTIVE SELF-REPORT Virtually all relationship researchers recognize that because self-reports are always subjective reconstructions (see Metts et al 1991), they are an uncertain substitute for observation. Thus all endorse the principle that when self-reports are to be taken as isomorphic with what others would have observed, their validity needs to be evaluated against other information. In actual fact, however, self-reports in relationship research are usually considered accurate unless there are compelling reasons to think otherwise. Assumptions of veridicality may be appropriate for certain kinds of factual items such as age at marriage (Field 1981) or for highly objective events (Christensen et al 1983), but other kinds of personal events may not be remembered well, especially if substantial time has elapsed between the event and its recall. Wagenaar (1986), for example, examined his own memories of daily events over a 6-year period and found that his retention function for cued recall dropped from 70 to 35% over a 4-year period.

Identification of the factors influencing personal event memory has become of increasing interest, partly because such knowledge is useful for structuring retrieval conditions to facilitate accurate remembrances (e.g. Schwarz 1990). The principles currently known to govern the nature and quantity of autobiographical memories (e.g. see Cohen 1989, Rubin 1986) might inform interpretations of the reliability and validity of different kinds of self-report more than they have. For example, and in accord with the general shape of the forgetting curve, between one and two thirds of all spontaneously recalled autobiographical memories are of events within the past year. Moreover, it appears that the usual forgetting curve contains two irregularities: (*a*) *childhood amnesia,* where there appears to be an "extra" forgetting of events that occurred during the first 5 years of life, just as Freud supposed (Wetzler & Sweeney 1986); and (*b*) *reminiscense,* where by age 50 and older, there is an increase (beyond what one would expect from the forgetting curve) for events that occurred when the individual was 10 to 30 years old (Rubin et al 1986). In addition, personal events that are likely to be well remembered tend to be unique events, events that have important consequences for the individual, and unexpected events (see Stangor & McMillan 1992 for a review of evidence pertinent to this last).

Emotion-provoking events, which are often consequential to the individual's well-being and are unexpected as well, also tend to be remembered (e.g. Harvey et al 1986), although the individual's temporal distance from the event needs to be taken into consideration. Evidence supporting Taylor's (1991) mobilization–minimization hypothesis suggests that negative events initially may be remembered better than positive ones, but over time there appears to be a preference for positive over negative and neutral events. Wagenaar (1986) found such an effect. Field (1981) found that the number of individuals reporting a happy childhood increased with successive interviews over 40 years. Skowronski et al's (1991) study in a naturalistic setting showed a preference for positive events that happened to the self over a 2-month period, but not for memory of events that happened to a close other. This last study also suggests that the recall advantage of positive self-events will be greatest when the events are neither very usual nor unusual in the individual's life.

The positivity or negativity of the individual's mood at the time of recall also may influence what is recalled (see Forgas 1991), although the effect appears to be more reliable for the recall of mood-congruent material in positive than in negative mood states, with a similar differential reliability of positive and negative mood in producing mood-congruent social judgments (see Clark & Williamson 1989). However, Erber (1991) recently found both positive and negative mood effects, with negative moods increasing the accessibility of mood congruent trait categories. Negative mood has also been found to have a deleterious effect on the ability to solve a complex resource dilemma while positive mood had no effect (Knapp & Clark 1991), a finding with special implications for distressed partners trying to solve difficult relationship problems.

Memory of personal events cannot easily be separated from memory of relationship events because many, if not most, of the former involve the latter. Some relationship researchers, however, have examined how well events within a specific relationship are remembered and have found that agreement between partners, even on highly structured relationship event questionnaires, is not high (see Weiss & Heyman 1990, Christensen et al 1983). Moreover, several biases for memory of relationship events have been demonstrated, including an egocentric bias, or the tendency to ascribe more responsibility for relationship events to oneself than to the partner (Ross & Sicoly 1979). This bias, however, may be partially dependent on the partners' satisfaction with the relationship and whether the event remembered is positively or negatively regarded. In their studies of attributions in satisfied couples, Fincham & Bradbury (1989) found an egocentric bias for negative events, but greater responsibility for positive events was assigned to the partner. Christensen et al (1983) found evidence of an egocentric bias overall in the dating and married couples they studied, but individuals in older relationships attributed more responsibility for negative events to their partners and less to themselves.

Another kind of systematic bias for memory of relationship events has been uncovered. Miell (1987) asked people to depict graphically the strength of one of their four ongoing relationships each week for ten weeks. She found that recall of the strength of a relationship at a time past was based at least as much on the individual's estimation of the current strength of the relationship as it was on the estimation that had actually been made at the time (a recency effect), although individuals had good recall of the pattern of development, if not absolute levels, of strength. McFarland & Ross (1987) found a similar recency effect: The favorability of individuals' recalled impressions of their dating partners tended to be more consistent with their current impressions than actually had been the case. Based on these and other studies, Ross (1989) has theorized that personal recall is an active, constructive, schema-guided process that depends on individuals' implicit theories concerning the stability of their own and another's attributes as well as their current estimations of these attributes. His theory predicts, for example, that people who believe the attribute in question generally stays stable over time will exaggerate the similarity between what is currently true and what was true in the past when, in fact, there has been change along the attribute dimension from past to present.

Some deviations from accuracy thus appear to be systematic. It should be noted, however, that the accuracy of the products of social cognitive processes, or the extent to which they achieve a realistic view of the world, is the subject of current debate. Jussim (1991) argues from his reflection–construction model that the evidence reveals more accuracy than it does the biases and errors that have fascinated researchers in social cognition in recent years. Although in general agreement with an accuracy thesis, Higgins & Bargh's (1987) reminder that people may be motivated to be correct only occasionally seems especially appropriate in the context of ongoing relationships, as illustrated by Gray & Silver's (1990) comparison of former spouses' perceptions of each other and of their divorce. Ex-spouses did not differ in their positive perceptions of themselves and their negative perceptions of their former partner; moreover, both spouses rated themselves more positively than they were rated by their partner with respect to responsibility for the breakup, whether they were a victim or a villain in the breakup, and whether they desired reconciliation. Gray & Silver discuss how ego-enhancing perceptual biases may facilitate adjustment to the divorce situation and may help maintain the partners' change in marital status.

The accuracy of relationship memories may also depend on who is doing the remembering. Ross & Holmberg (1990) found that women are more likely to recall relationship events (e.g. their first date) more vividly and in more detail than are their male partners. Ross & Holmberg speculate that this gender effect may partially stem from the greater importance of relationships to women and the greater tendency of women to reminisce about relationship events. Supporting this view, Acitelli (1992; and see Acitelli & Holmberg 1993) found that when talking about the relationship, women demonstrate more relationship awareness (e.g. awareness of the couple's interaction patterns) than do men. Women also may possess more highly developed relationship schemas because they appear to spend more time in social interaction than do men (e.g. Wong & Csikszentmihalyi 1991), and since good memory has been shown to depend on relating inputs to well-differentiated knowledge structures (e.g. Bower & Gilligan 1979), women's schemas may facilitate the encoding and representation of relationship information.

Finally, memory of relationship events may be a function of the joint memories of both partners. Wegner et al (1985) consider the functional equivalence of individual and transactive memory, with the latter defined as the organized store of knowledge contained in the individual memory systems of both partners and the set of knowledge-relevant transactive communication processes that occur between them. They predict that dysfunctional transactive memory in a relationship forecasts relationship breakdown, and that some of the difficulties accompanying relationship dissolution are the result of the absence of transactive memory.

ACCOUNT NARRATIVES An increasing number of researchers focus on the reconstructive quality of autobiographical memories to learn how people make sense out of past relationship events. The meaning individuals accord to those events is presumed to have a number of implications for their future behavior in that relationship or others, whether or not their memories are congruent with other evidence. *Account narrative* is used here to refer to the stories people construct of relationship events that span a considerable period of time and are presented in relatively unstructured formats in order to distinguish these from the more traditional use of the word "account," which has referred to the individual's publicly offered explanations and justifications of a specific action, often an action performed in the immediate past. It should be noted, however, that "account" is currently used broadly and loosely to refer to both types of activities and to others as well (e.g. see Read 1992). As work in this area progresses, more precise terminology undoubtedly will develop.

Harvey et al (1989), who have been the leaders in the use of account narratives in relationship research, come to the use of account narratives from the framework of classical attribution theories in social psychology. They also have been influenced by Weiss' (1975) study of separated spouses and his impression that the accounts people construct of the dissolution of their relationship are important in helping them adjust to its loss. Harvey et al's (1990) recent theoretical statement focuses on when people are likely to be motivated to construct cohesive account narratives (e.g. after major negative life events such as the loss of a relationship through death or divorce) and the ways in which constructing a coherent account of the troubling events may promote physical and mental health (e.g. through self-esteem enhancement or improved sense of control).

There is evidence of an association between account-making and adaptation to negative life events, but further research is needed to determine if the association is a causal one, and if so, to identify the mediating mechanisms. For example, amount of time elapsed between the event and the measurement of adjustment needs to be considered. According to Harvey et al, accounts take time to construct, and as Ginsburg (1991) observes, time itself often creates psychological distance from the event, which may promote adaptation. For example, Nigro & Neisser (1983) found that recent memories tend to be copy-type memories experienced from the individual's point of view at the time the event took place, but older memories show evidence of reconstruction and of the use of an outside observer's viewpoint, which suggests emotional distancing. Another question concerns the effect of rendering the account publicly. Pennebaker (1989) and associates have shown that the adjustment of survivors of traumatic events is associated with confiding to others about the event. Private construction of an account narrative and sharing the narrative with others, events often associated with each other, may independently contribute to adjustment. Again, it would be useful to have some guidelines for what constitutes an account narrative (e.g. vs an uncohesive collection of thoughts and feelings whose referent is a stressful event).

Like attributions for specific events, account narratives are believed to reflect and maintain current relationship orientations. In their panel study of the experience of couples in first marriages during the first four years, Veroff et al (1993) asked each couple in their first year of marriage to record on tape, together and in their own words, the story of their relationship from the time they first met until the present, and on into the future; they were asked to tell their story again in their third year of marriage. Comparing the affective content of memory changes of couples who had shown a decline in their marital well-being over the two years with those whose well-being had remained stable, Holmes & Veroff (reported in Holmberg & Holmes 1993) found that husbands whose marital well-being had declined over the two years were currently reporting significantly unhappier memories of the same relationship events (e.g. the wedding) than they had reported in their first year when their well-being was higher; similarly, the memories of husbands whose well-being had improved were currently less negative than they had been in the first year. Wives did not show the effect.

Gergen & Gergen (1988) came to account narrative methodology from an interest in the self-narrative, or an individual's account of the association among self-relevant events across time. These theorists carefully draw a distinction between the self-narrative and other related concepts, such as self-schemas, which may be entirely private and even unconsciously held to some degree. Self-narratives are viewed as social constructions that undergo continuous alteration as social interaction progresses, a "linguistic implement constructed by people in relationships to sustain, enhance, or impede various actions" (p. 20). The individual's relationships are thus theorized to play a prominent role in self-narratives, which are believed to be to a large extent "socially derived, socially sustained, and require interdependency of action for their execution..." (p. 53).

The account narrative method has been used to address violence in relationships, a topic of increasing interest to relationship researchers. Felson (reported in Gergen & Gergen 1988) solicited from ex–criminal offenders and mental patients account narratives of incidents of violence in which they had been involved and found that, at least from the perpetrator's viewpoint, the violent action had not been a spontaneous eruption, but rather the predictable outcome of a specific sequence of reciprocal behaviors in social interaction. Using the sequence of behaviors Felson identified, Harris et al (1987) exposed people to stories that began with the first step in the behavioral sequence (i.e. one spouse mildly criticized the other) and then, momentarily interrupting the story at this point, asked them to rate the probability, desirability, and advisability of the other partner making each of a number of possible responses to the spouse's action. The story then continued and individuals learned that the actual reaction of the partner had been to escalate the hostility. The story was halted again while the other partner's probable reactions were rated, with eight escalations made over the length of the story. The rated probability of use of hostile options increased over the eight intervals while the probability of conciliatory options decreased, suggesting to the investigators that "we are tapping a highly conventionalized scenario in the culture" (p. 46).

Using more conventional methods, the general finding that people are unlikely to turn the other cheek when their partner has behaved badly has been replicated by Rusbult et al (1991), who have also developed a theory of accommodation. Accommodation refers to an individual's willingness to react constructively rather than destructively to the partner's negative behavior, and research derived from the theory suggests that accommodation is higher in relationships characterized by higher interdependence, satisfaction, and commitment, for example. Given that destructive behavior generally occurs in all relationships, and frequent findings that distressed couples tend to reciprocate their partner's negative behavior more than satisfied couples do, identifying the factors conducive to accommodation assumes importance. Baumeister et al

(1990) provide additional insight into the dynamics of spiraling negativity. They examined autobiographical accounts of occasions on which the respondent was angered (victim narratives) or had angered another (perpetrator narratives) and found that victims view the provoking act as arbitrary, incomprehensible, and as carrying long-term implications, while perpetrators see it as a meaningful, comprehensible, and isolated incident with no lasting consequences.

Most researchers who use account narratives especially appreciate the power of this method to obtain self-reports that are relatively free of the influence that structured interview questions and questionnaire items impose on respondents' reports. A cynic might say, however, that investigators simply delay their imposition of meaning and structure until the coding stage, a process that many who use this technique spontaneously remark is extremely difficult. Moreover, some researchers regard the account narrative as a qualitative vs a quantitative research technique. Ironically, however, quantitative techniques must be applied if the data are to be useful to people who don't have the time and inclination to wade through sheaves of account narratives. A further irony is that the current use of account narratives appears to derive from two sometimes incompatible perspectives: the information-processing and the ethnographic perspectives. Harvey et al (1989) represent the former, coming to the account narrative method from the information-processing tradition that characterizes virtually all contemporary theory and research in social cognition. Representing the ethnographic tradition, the Gergens (1988) vigorously eschew an information-processing cast being placed on their theory of self-narrative, commenting that "there is something more to life than cognitive processing" (p. 43). They are in good company. Jerome Bruner (1990), one of the founders of the cognitive revolution in psychology, now advocates the use of autobiographical narratives to accomplish what the cognition revolution was intended to achieve before it spun off into activities far afield from psychology's mission to understand human behavior:

> Let me tell you first what I and my friends thought the revolution was about back there in the late 1950s. It was, we thought, an all-out effort to establish meaning as the central concept of psychology—not stimuli and responses, not overtly observable behavior, not biological drives and their transformation, but meaning.... Its aim was to discover and describe formally the meanings that human beings created out of their encounters with the world, and then to propose hypotheses about what meaning-making processes were implicated. It focused upon the symbolic activities that human beings employed in constructing and in making sense not only of the world, but of themselves. Its aim was to prompt psychology to join forces with its sister interpretive disciplines in the humanities and in the social sciences.... [But] very early on...emphasis began shifting from "meaning" to "information," from the construction of

> meaning to the processing of information.... Information is indifferent with respect to meaning. (pp. 2–4)

In the quest to understand interpersonal relationships, these two approaches to human cognition, meaning-making and information-processing, are meeting up with each other once again, so far amicably.

Individual Differences in Relationship Schemas: Security and Trust

Some individual difference variables of current interest to relationship researchers may be usefully viewed, not as static traits, but rather as relatively stable relationship schemas shared by large segments of the population. When viewed as relationship schemas, the ways in which they influence attention to relationship-relevant stimuli are highlighted, as is their influence on encoding and memory of relationship events, on how they guide behavior within the relationship, and on how their modification does or does not correspond to changes in interaction regularities in the relationship.

A great deal of recent research on individual differences in adults' orientation to relationships focuses on the extent to which the individual expects to feel secure within a relationship. Relationship security—and the related constructs of trust in the responsiveness and beneficence of another in time of need, or expectations that another will be a good caregiver—have had a long history in psychology (e.g. Holmes 1991). It is Bowlby's theory of infant attachment (1982), however, that has stimulated much of the recent work on feelings of security in adult relationships.

Bowlby hypothesizes that from event regularities in the first year of life, infants develop inner working models of relationships that mentally represent their expectations about caregivers' responsiveness to satisfying the infant's needs, as well as expectations about the self (e.g. as worthy or unworthy of care). Although presumed to be sensitive to subsequent environmental influences, these early mental representations are hypothesized to be carried forward in some degree to influence the individual's subsequent relationships. Central to Bowlby's theory is the attachment behavioral system, which is assumed to be rooted biologically in natural selection, to be manifested in behavior (e.g. crying) that keeps the child in close proximity to adult caretakers and thus promotes survival, and to have felt security as its goal (e.g. Bretherton 1985). Felt security, which is believed to be experienced subjectively as an emotional bond to the other, is theorized to provide the child with a secure base from which the environment may be explored and a safe haven should threat occur. The quality of the attachment the child has developed for an adult figure, often the mother/caregiver, is frequently assessed via the Strange Situation (Ainsworth et al 1978), which evaluates the child's reactions to episodes of separation and reunion with the caregiver. The pattern of these reactions often permits the child's attachment to the caregiver to be classified as secure, insecure/avoidant, or insecure/anxious-ambivalent.

Inspired by Bowlby's theory, and drawing parallels between processes seemingly associated with adult romantic love and those associated with childhood attachment, Hazan & Shaver (1987) asked adults who were participating in a survey study of their most important romance to indicate which of three descriptive paragraphs best described their feelings. Each paragraph was intended to be an adult analogue of the three Strange Situation classifications, its content designed to determine whether the individual typically feels comfortable being close to, trusting, and depending on others. Whether the individual endorsed the Secure paragraph or one of the two Insecure paragraphs was regarded as a reflection of the individual's attachment style, and that endorsement was found to be associated with the individual's report of experiences in his or her most important romantic relationship and beliefs about romantic love.

Subsequent research has corroborated that endorsement of one of the three paragraphs, or self-classification by one of the many variants of this procedure (e.g. Simpson 1990, Collins & Read 1990), is associated with other self-reports, including retrospective memories of childhood and family events, memories of experiences in past romantic relationships, and reports of experiences in current relationships, as well as with scores on a variety of belief, attitude, and personality (e.g. Shaver & Brennan 1992) scales. Recent research suggests associations with observed behavior within relationships as well (e.g. Mikulincer & Nachshon 1991, for self-disclosure; Simpson et al 1992, for caregiving and careseeking behavior under stress). These items measuring adult attachment style thus appear to possess intrinsic validity (Loevinger 1957).

The theoretical construct of adult attachment style, however, has not yet been sufficiently articulated to dispell a number of ambiguities currently surrounding it. Some of the confusion can be traced to the fact that the word "attached" is commonly used to mean that the individual has positive regard and feelings for another (e.g. Berman 1988) and predates Bowlby's special use of the term and his differentiation of attachment, as it is manifested by attempts to maintain proximity to another, from positive feelings and appraisals associated with the partner. Additional confusion stems from the fact that although the construct of adult attachment has been closely identified with the attachment behavioral system postulated by Bowlby's theory, the two other systems the theory posits, the reproductive behavioral system and the caregiving system, have not yet been well integrated into theorizing about adult attachment style. Shaver et al (1988), however, discuss some of the implications of these three systems for romantic love and Ainsworth (1989) has elaborated on their possible roles in pair bonding beyond infancy, including the sexual pair bonding presumably characteristic of romantic relationships.

Theoretical elaboration addressed to the stability of adult attachment style also would be useful. Some attachment style discourse has seemed to suggest that the classification an adult receives via endorsement of adult attachment style items is the same classification the individual would have received as a child had he or she been assessed in the Strange Situation, although Shaver and colleagues (e.g. Shaver & Brennan 1992) have explicitly stated that such a view is naive. Whether behavior associated with early attachment classification shows continuity is currently the subject of several longitudinal research programs, with some evidence of continuity on some dimensions obtained up to 10 years of age so far (Sroufe et al 1990). There is scant evidence pertaining to the factors that influence the stability of adult attachment style classifications. Kojetin (1993) found that changes 5 months later in attachment style orientations toward romantic relationships in general were systematically associated with actual changes that had occurred in the individual's ongoing romantic relationship. Similarly, Hazan and associates (reported in Shaver & Hazan 1993) found that in a group of adults assessed three times over a period of a year, those whose attachment classification changed (22%) were significantly more likely to have had relationship experiences in this period that disconfirmed their former inner models. These findings suggest that an individual's security orientation may reflect the individual's current relationship experiences as much as a chronic security disposition.

Most theories that address the impact of early relationships on later ones, including Bowlby's, recognize that although an individual's early relationship schemas are important, in healthy individuals such schemas are continuously revised and modified to reflect experience. If individuals typically have different experiences in different types of relationships, it also seems likely that a general schema would become differentiated. It is not yet clear whether adults can be most usefully viewed as having one general security orientation toward all social relationships or whether people show considerable intra-individual variance in security orientations toward different types of relationships. Although the original attachment style items were directed toward romantic relationships, Feeney & Noller's (1990) examination of the correlations between attachment style endorsements and responses on a number of other scales revealed that "the mental model statements dealing with general views of the self and of human relationships discriminated among the three attachment styles much more powerfully than did those items dealing specifically with beliefs about romantic love" (p. 286). Bartholomew's (1990, Bartholomew & Horowitz 1991) examination of individuals' typical experiences across several types of relationships found that people could be classified into four categories defined by a 2 × 2 matrix of positive vs negative self-regard and positive vs negative other-regard. The names of these categories (e.g. secure) were borrowed from attachment research and their content generally corresponds to the results of factor analyses of responses to attachment style items, which often find a primary factor dimension in which secure and avoidant responses are mirror images of each other and a secondary, anxious attachment, factor (see Shaver & Hazan 1993).

Despite this evidence that a single global security orientation may characterize the individual's approach to most relationships, there may be important intra-individual differences among the global security orientation, the expectations of security in certain types of relationships, and expectations of security within actual, ongoing relationships. Kojetin (1993) used the adult attachment style items to assess global security orientation and found the usual distribution of styles (e.g. about 60% secure), but when respondents answered the identical items with respect to their current relationships with their mother, father, best friend, and current romantic partner, most were secure (98% were secure with the friend and about 84% were secure in each of the other relationships). Current work by Ogilvie & Ashmore (1991) suggests that not only do people form relationship schemas custom-tailored to their experiences in a specific relationship, but they may form several situation-specific schemas for that relationship. It seems possible that each may reflect a different security orientation (e.g. Caring-Mom on the weekends; Dismissing-Mom on weekdays).

Holmes (1991) and colleagues have demonstrated that examining the individual's security and trust orientation within a specific relationship helps illuminate the dynamics of interaction in that relationship. Their definition of trust resembles that of the secure adult attachment style: "Attitudes of trust reflect people's abstract positive expectations that they can count on partners to care for them and be responsive to their needs, now and in the future" (Holmes et al 1989, p. 188). An individual's perception of a specific partner's predictability and dependability in response to need is measured by the Trust Scale (Rempel et al 1985), and the theory associated with this scale addresses the development of trust at various stages of the relationship as well as behavioral manifestations of high and low trust within the relationship. The theory predicts, and recent experimental evidence supports, that highly trusting partners may not only assimilate negative information about their partner without impairing their trust, but the presentation of such information may actually result in cognitive activity that bolsters trust and positive appraisals of the partner; similarly, low trust couples appear to discount positive information about their partner in ways that maintain their negative schemas (e.g. Murray & Holmes 1993). Other investigators, working in different contexts, also have found evidence that the imposition of a threat to an existing relationship orientation may sometimes result in cognitive activity that has the effect of preserving the original orientation. For example, the appearance of an attractive, available alternative partner to an individual who is currently committed to a relationship appears to cause devaluation of the attractiveness of the alternative (Johnson & Rusbult 1989, Simpson et al 1990).

Clark and associates' research program also engages the idea of trust in the partner to respond to need (see Clark & Bennett 1992 for a review). They distinguish between a communal orientation to a relationship, where partners expect that benefits will be given in response to needs, and an exchange orientation, where partners expect to receive benefits in response to benefits they have given in the past and to repay currently received benefits in the future. Clark and colleagues have shown that a variety of behaviors exhibited by the partner in interaction are responded to differently depending on which of these two relationship orientations the individual has adopted. Moreover, individuals themselves behave differently in these two types of relationships. Communal partners talk about their own emotions and needs more (Clark & Taraban 1991) and are more likely to track the partner's needs and less likely to tally the partner's inputs (Clark et al 1989) than are exchange partners.

This array of theories and evidence on security and trust strongly suggests that expectations concerning whether care will be received from the relationship partner in response to need may be an important component of most relationship schemas. It may even be the central component—one that is present in every developed relationship schema and one that will exert special influence on all other components of the schema.

There are numerous other individual difference variables in relationship research that might be profitably viewed as chronically accessible relationship schemas. Gender is an example. Gender differences in relationship behavior are pervasive (see C. Hendrick 1988 for a review; Dindia & Allen 1992 for a meta-analysis of self-disclosure studies). No relationship researcher can ignore the possibility of gender differences in any relationship phenomenon, although it has been ignored in some areas (e.g. Beall 1993). Cross & Markus (1993) review some of the theory and evidence relevant to a cognitive approach to identifying how gender influences thought and action in general. Many of the ways that gender influences behavior are undoubtedly associated with differences in how relationships enter into the self-schemas of males and females, as well as content differences in relationship schemas held by men and women. Future research thus might examine: (*a*) the extent to which relationships with others are reflected in the self-schemas of men and women; (*b*) the extent to which schemas for different types of relationships held by men and women are similar or different; and (*c*) where there are gender differences in relationship type schemas, the extent to which these differences reflect different expectations for the behavior of men and women in that type of relationship. Because social constructions of gender are changing rapidly, especially within certain subpopulations, there are likely to be differences between relationship partners in the gender-associated elements of many of their relationship schemas, even when the partners are of the same gender. Moreover, when the relationship schemas of men and women are shared, they often represent different behavioral expectations for men and women within different types of relationships. These differing orientations to social relationships apparently begin very early (e.g. see Maccoby 1990), and it is clear that some are maintained at least through early adulthood (e.g. see Reis & Wheeler 1991). Finally, the extent to which gender differences in relationship behavior reflect power and status schemas, rather than gender schemas per se, should be examined systematically (Berscheid 1993, Geis 1993).

OTHER DEVELOPMENTS

Advances have been made in both theory and research on several traditional issues in interpersonal relationships including love, jealousy, social support, and the identification of the factors associated with relationship dissolution.

Love

The resurgence of interest in love noted by Clark & Reis (1988) continues and theoretical discussions abound (see Sternberg & Barnes 1988). Many taxonomies of types of love have been offered, but few have been developed sufficiently, with a specification of the unique observable manifestations of each type and its causal antecedents and consequences, to guide research. As a result, some investigators have taken an empirically inductive approach to identifying subtypes of love, but with little success. Fehr & Russell (1991) examined the prototypicality of each type of love in the language category "love" and found maternal love to be most prototypical and infatuation the least, but concluded that "the folk definition of love is complex and provides no sharp boundary between love and other, related experiences" (p. 435). As Murstein puts it, "the word love is bandied about more promiscuously than almost any other word in the English language" (1988, p. 13).

Other investigators have taken a psychometric approach to love (Sternberg & Beall 1991), attempting to identify the dimensions that underly the reported experiences of persons in putative love relationships, usually heterosexual courtship (or dating or romantic) relationships. Based on previous social psychological theory and research on love and liking in young adults and on factor analyses of self-reports of dating relationship experiences, Sternberg has developed a triangular theory of love (e.g. 1987, 1988). He hypothesizes that many popularly recognized subtypes of love can be accounted for by different weightings of three components: intimacy, passion, and decision/commitment. Hendrick & Hendrick (1989), however, found little support for this supposition in their factor analysis of college students' responses to the Triangular Theory of Love Scale as well as to other popular love scales, including Davis & Latty-Mann's (1987) Relationship Rating Form, Hatfield & Sprecher's (1986) Passionate Love Scale, Hazan & Shaver's (1987) attachment items, and their own Love Attitudes Scale. The latter assesses love style following Lee's typology (1988), which was developed from a phenomenological examination of experiences in love relationships. These investigators conclude that love means different things to different people in different relationships at different points in time (see Hendrick & Hendrick 1992). Their study illustrates that this is true even when the people sampled are relatively homogeneous and when their responses are confined to a single relationship type.

The limitations of a psychometric approach to phenomena such as love are outlined in Kelley's (1992) discussion of the relationship between common-sense psychology and scientific psychology. In his analysis of how common terms may affect scientific propositions, he observes that in operationalizing a concept, psychologists typically develop a set of questionnaire items working from the common term, trying to exemplify it in a variety of ways. However, "this reasonable procedure sometimes has the unnoticed and unwanted result that the set of indicators comes to include variables measuring the antecedents and/or consequences of the focal variable" (p. 9). For this and other reasons he describes, the psychometric approach to a phenomenon, useful though it may be initially, cannot do the work of theory that specifies the antecedents and consequences of specific behaviors. Kelley also observes that common-sense psychology is most likely to be extensive and valid when it refers to events that exist at the mesolevel (characteristic of most theories of love), and that contradictions between common-sense psychology and scientific psychology are most likely to appear between mesolevel theories and microlevel theories (which involve events that occur rapidly, in seconds and milliseconds, and invisibly, as do some physiological responses). One of the few experiments in the recent love literature may be an illustration. Investigating the misattribution of arousal model of love and the negative-reinforcement alternative, Allen et al (1989) found that extraneous arousal facilitated sexual attraction even when the subjects' attention was directed to the actual arousal source, leading these investigators to hypothesize that sexual arousal is an automatic process that is relatively involuntary and independent of conscious attention. Their microlevel experimental finding might not make good common-sense to lovers, but it does make good microlevel science.

Some psychologists are currently taking an evolutionary approach to the question of love, at least heterosexual love (e.g. Shaver et al 1988, Buss 1988). Buss (1990) has delineated the conceptual differences between evolutionary social psychology and sociobiology, and Scarr (1989) and Brewer & Caporael (1990) discuss some of the questionable applications of the latter to relationship phenomena. Research derived from the evolutionary approach has focused primarily on mate selection preference (e.g. Buss 1988, Kenrick & Trost 1989). Evolutionary models assume all humans have been selected to maximize gene replication and thus reproductive success, but differential biology of reproduction results in gender differences in mate preference. Women, who are assumed to invest more resources in their offspring, are assumed to be sensitive to resource limitations and thus especially desirous of mates who can and will provide resources; men, on the other hand, are assumed to be limited by access to females who are likely to reproduce and thus should be sensitive to characteristics that reflect reproductive capacity (e.g. health).

The mate selection literature is one of the largest in the relationship area (see Surra 1990 for a review), and several studies indicate that men are more likely to report that physical attractiveness, partly a function of youth and health, is important to them while women are more likely to emphasize economic status factors. Buss (1989) finds support for this general hypothesis across many cultures, and Feingold (1992a), in meta-analyses of studies conducted mostly in this culture, finds that the largest gender differences in self-reports of desired attributes in a mate are obtained for cues to resource acquisition (status and ambitiousness), with women more likely than men to value these characteristics. The literature also clearly indicates that women report physical attractiveness as less important to them than men do (Feingold 1990). One can predict this gender pattern in mate preference from perspectives other than the evolutionary one, however, especially from perspectives that consider the universal lower status and power of women (see Howard et al 1987). More studies should examine women's behavior vs their self-reports because the two are often incongruent. Sprecher (1989) asked men and women how attracted they were to an opposite-sex person about whom they read and then asked them to identify the characteristics that influenced their feelings of attraction. The ubiquitous effect, that men put greater emphasis on her physical attractiveness and women on his earning potential, was found even though the results of the experimental manipulation revealed that both men and women were more influenced by physical attractiveness than by any other characteristic. Stevens et al (1990) found that newlyweds' physical attractiveness and educational attainment were significantly correlated, but after statistically controlling for the tendency to marry similar others, the more attractive women were no more likely than the less attractive to be married to men who were highly educated and thus presumably of higher economic status. Feingold (1990) observed that the effect sizes associated with men according more weight to physical attractiveness than women are larger in self-report than in behavioral research paradigms, and he has discussed (1992a) some of the factors that may produce artifactual gender differences in mate preference studies that rely on self-report data.

Possible cultural differences in romantic love also are of current interest. Dion & Dion (1988) review several theories that hypothesize Western individualistic culture to be more conducive to romantic love than collectivist cultures. At least one recent study (Sprecher et al 1992), however, finds remarkable similarities among American, Russian, and Japanese experiences of love in heterosexual relationships, and Hatfield & Rapson (1987) argue that romantic love is virtually universal, occuring at all ages and times across cultures. Anthropologists, who also have become interested in the topic, are currently providing cross-cultural data that support Hatfield & Rapson's view (e.g. Jankowiak & Fischer 1992).

Finally, some are taking a cognitive approach to love. Beach & Tesser (1988) examine several aspects of premarital and marital relationships often associated with love and discuss the implications an individual's higher-order schema of commitment may have for attention to certain aspects of the relationship situation, for the kinds of information about the relationship that will be sought, for the interpretation of ambiguous relationship information, and for the individual's behavior that may result in confirmation of his or her commitment schema. Important gender differences in love schemas are suggested by studies that continue to find that men hold more romantic beliefs than do women (e.g. Sprecher & Metts 1989, Frazier & Esterly 1990).

Jealousy

Interest in jealousy derives from its association with violence and from its frequency as a problem in relationship counseling and therapy. Although jealousy has received concerted attention only within the past decade, theory and research addressed to the problem is now substantial. White & Mullen (1989) provide a useful review of previous thinking and research on jealousy, and Salovey (1991) has collected the views of many contributors to jealousy theory and research.

Current theory and research on jealousy parallels the love literature in a number of respects. First, the almost exclusive focus is on jealousy in romantic premarital and marital relationships. Second, much theoretical discussion is addressed to defining jealousy. It is most often defined with respect to the negative emotions individuals experience in situations presumed to be jealousy-arousing (e.g. Parrott 1991, Buunk & Bringle 1987). Third, self-reports of the kinds of thoughts, feelings, and behaviors that people imagine they would display in putative jealousy-invoking situations, presented in vignettes, are often factor analyzed to identify the dimensions underlying these responses and to construct the several scales now available to assess an individual's propensity for jealousy. Fourth, jealousy is usually viewed as a property of the individual rather than of the relationship. Fifth, examination of the correlates of individual differences in responses to jealousy, often gender differences, characterizes most of the research. Finally, an evolutionary view of jealousy is prominent.

Clanton & Kosins' (1991) study illustrates many of these features. To investigate Bowlby's hypothesis that disrupted attachments with early caretakers often result in anxious attachment, or excessive sensitivity to the possibility of separation or loss of love, Clanton & Kosins examined the associations between the individual's scores on two jealousy scales and those obtained on a number of developmental measures, including an attachment history questionnaire. No significant associations were found between adult jealousy and developmental variables, leading the investigators to conclude that their results challenge the assumptions that adult jealousy is associated with disrupted attachment history and that it is symptomatic of psychopathology.

The evolutionary approach to jealousy, which centers on the uncertainty of paternity problem for males and the resource problem for females, inspired one of the few experiments in the jealousy literature. Buss et al (1992) asked men and women to imagine that their partner had committed emotional infidelity or sexual infidelity and to tell how upset they would be. Not only did more men than women report greater distress over a potential sexual infidelity, but autonomic arousal indicants revealed that men were more physiologically upset during the sexual imagery than the emotional imagery, while women showed the reverse pattern.

Other researchers are broadening their perspective to include situational as well as person determinants of jealousy. Hupka (1991) views jealousy as a social construction that differs across cultures, and after examining archival data from preindustrial societies, found positive correlations between male aggression in jealousy situations and such factors as the importance of marriage, restrictions on premarital and extramarital sexual activities, and emphasis on private ownership of property. Also taking a situational approach and drawing on Tesser's (1988) self-evaluation maintenance model, Salovey & Rodin (1989) distinguish between social-relations jealousy, generated by threat to a previously established unique relationship with another, and social-comparison jealousy or envy, the desire or attempt to possess something belonging to another individual, and they provide experimental evidence to support their theoretical framework. Salovey & Rodin's model is easily applicable to all relationship types, and because jealousy and envy are common relationship problems, it would be desirable if jealousy research expanded beyond the romantic relationship.

White and associates (1991, White & Mullen 1989) offer the most ambitious theory of romantic jealousy. It combines the usual intrapersonal perspective with postulation of an interpersonal jealousy system that includes the relationships between the individual and the partner, between the partner and the rival, between the individual and the rival, and the triadic relationship of all three persons. Moreover, the theory recognizes that each actor in the triangle is embedded within larger friendship and kin systems and that persons in these systems are often deeply implicated in jealousy episodes. Tangential support for this proposition comes from studies by Parks & Eggert (1991), who demonstrate that people in an individual's social communication network influence the initiation, development, and deterioration of romantic relationships. It thus seems likely that network members play an important role in the development and outcome of jealousy episodes as well, perhaps by helping the individual interpret the situation and by facilitating or inhibiting certain coping responses. Finally, White's systems view predicts that jealousy episodes may destabilize the original relationship but stabilize the system in which that relationship is embedded, or under other circumstances, a jealousy episode may stabilize an unstable relationship.

Social Support

Much of the practical import of relationship research derives from the central role relationships play in human happiness and physical and mental health. Interest in articulating that role has grown dramatically in recent years, primarily as a result of findings from large scale epidemiological studies of the determinants and distribution of disease that strongly implicate social relationships in mortality and morbidity. Two features of the data reviewed by Atkins et al (1991) concerning the role of close relationships in the epidemiology of cardiovascular disease highlight why the topic of social support has captured so much interest. First, the weight of these studies not only suggests that low social support is a risk factor for heart disease but that the strength of association for mortality among the socially isolated is at least as strong as it is for other risk factors, including the well-publicized smoking risk factor, even when all other known risk factors are statistically controlled. Second, this association has been obtained even though the measures of social support used have been broad and undifferentiated, often consisting simply of notation of the individual's marital status combined with rough, often subjective, measures of social network size. Although these epidemiological data are correlational, and may reflect illness causing disruption in social support or third variables causing both illness and low social support, Atkins et al conclude that a fine-grained examination of the evidence strongly indicates a causal relationship from social support to mortality. But despite interest in this association for over a decade, the causal mediators remain elusive.

Influenced by the measures used in epidemiological studies, the notion of social support was initially confused conceptually and empirically with size of social network. As Vaux (1988) observes in his comprehensive review of the literature, social support is now viewed as a transactional process between the individual and his or her support network that requires consideration of the features of the network of persons who provide assistance, the specific behaviors that assist, and the individual's perceptions of support received or available.

Perceived support measures have been used much more frequently than observational measures partly because of the influence of the stress-buffering model of social support (Cohen & Wills 1985). This model assumes that actions by others not perceived as supportive are unlikely to reduce psychological distress, and conversely, actions not intended to be supportive but that are perceived as such still might have a buffering effect. That there may be discrepancies between the individual's perception of support and the actual receipt of intended support by others is underscored by two of the few observational studies in the social support literature. Cutrona (1990) asked one of a pair of students to play the role of helper while the other student disclosed a stressful experience that had occurred within the previous 6 months. No type of supportive behavior significantly affected the recipients' perception of support, despite the fact that two observers of the interaction corroborated the helpers' perception that their actions were supportive. Using a similar observational paradigm, Cutrona & Suhr (1993) found that for wives, only the number of support behaviors they had actually received from their husbands was associated with their perceptions of the supportiveness of that interaction; in contrast, husbands' perceptions of their wives' supportiveness were influenced primarily by their mood and degree of marital satisfaction.

More observational and experimental evidence is needed to complement and untangle the mass of correlational studies of social support, especially those examining the factors associated with perceived support. Much research has focused on such individual difference variables as extraversion and neuroticism (e.g. Bolger & Eckenrode 1991), and more recently, social skills. Riggio & Zimmerman (1991) find that socially skilled people perceive that they have more informational and emotional support than the less skilled, but there have been no experimental attempts to demonstrate that successful social skill training for the unskilled expands their social support networks and the support they actually receive. Such evidence is vital to understanding the social support implications of such correlational data. For example, social skill is likely to be associated with other personal characteristics known to be associated with support (e.g. physical attractiveness, see Feingold 1992b).

Expectations of support are also likely to influence perceived support. Pierce et al (1990) suggest that such expectations may be a component of cognitive working models of social support that guide the individual's behavior and the evaluation of others' behavior in situations in which support is needed. These investigators also provide evidence that relationship-based perceptions of support are distinct from global perceptions, but that both contribute to feelings of loneliness (Pierce et al 1991). Fincham & Bradbury (1990b) note that their spousal attribution research suggests that whether the individual sees the other's behavior as voluntary and motivated by selfless concerns will influence whether the behavior is perceived as supportive.

One of the few experimental programs addressed to social support has been initiated by Winstead & Derlega (1991), who have attempted to explicate Hobfoll & London's (1986) finding that among Israeli women whose husbands and kin were serving in the military, those who had more intimates to talk to and who received more social support appeared to experience more, not less, psychological distress. To examine the question experimentally, the investigators led one of a pair of same-sex friends to anticipate guiding a tarantula through a maze. In the interaction period before the stressful event, the other friend was instructed to: (*a*) talk only about personal feelings concerning the task; (*b*) talk only about the task itself; or (*c*) limit conversation to topics unrelated to the task. Winstead & Derlega found that depression and anxiety scores were higher, not lower, in the disclosure-of-feelings condition than in the problem-solving and unrelated-talk conditions. These findings are particularly interesting given the number of support groups composed of persons who are confronting difficulties similar to those faced by the individual and who are encouraged to express their feelings. Further experimentation might be usefully informed by recent work on emotional contagion (Hatfield et al 1992).

In addition to experimental and observational studies that examine actual interaction between supporters and recipients, researchers are taking a closer look at the social networks from which support is obtained. Bolger & Eckenrode (1991) find that different segments of the network may be differentially associated with support. Of special promise for social support as well as other relationship questions is Surra & Milardo's (1991) distinction between interactive networks, consisting of people with whom one engages in face-to-face interaction, and psychological networks, composed of people with whom the individual feels close or believes to be important. There may be little overlap between these two networks. In one study, 75% of the individuals identified by respondents were members of only one network. Moreover, there was no significant correlation between the sizes of the two networks, nor was there an association between size of the psychological network and frequency of daily interaction with persons in the network. This suggests that people with larger psychological networks aren't necessarily more socially active and those with smaller psychological networks aren't necessarily socially isolated. Surra & Milardo are chiefly interested in how the characteristics of the two networks influence relationship development, but the distinction is relevant to many social support questions (see Milardo 1992), particularly to the kinds of support (e.g. tangible, emotional) that are likely to be available to redress different kinds of distress, a factor emphasized by some support models (e.g. Hobfoll 1988, Cutrona 1990).

Another issue receiving attention is whether the kind of event that generates a need for social support may affect the size of the support network (e.g. see Leatham & Duck 1990). Rands (1988) found that 8 months after separation, the networks of divorced persons showed a 40% drop from their pre-divorce network (identified retrospectively by respondents), a decrease not compensated for by new additions. Starker et al (1993), however, found that geographical relocation produced surprisingly little change in network size. Most people had a functioning network in place within 3 months of the move. Although network size was stable, the relationships in it were not; less than 25% of the network members were named at 3-, 6-, and 21-month assessment points. If the stressful event does reduce support because of shrinkage of the network or as a result of other factors, perceived erosion of support will contribute to the negative impact of the event on the individual (Kaniasty & Norris 1993).

Finally, recent models of social support are also more likely to recognize that interactions with others, including close others, often induce stress as well as reduce it (e.g. Hobfoll 1988, Pierce et al 1991). In fact, Coyne & Downey (1991) conclude that "we may need to turn the concept of social support on its head" (p. 413). The perception of low social support may reflect the absence of a supportive relationship, but there is evidence that it also may signify the presence of an ongoing negative relationship that both produces deleterious stressful effects on the individual and impairs coping with that stress. Moreover, because the evidence also suggests that the positive effects of supportive relationships may not be as great as the negative effects of dysfunctional relationships (e.g. Rook 1984), Coyne & Downey observe that the current focus on social transactions presumed to convey support and buffer stress needs to be supplemented with studies of how dysfunctional relationships work their ill effects on the individual. Some of those studies are being stimulated by interest in how stressful events, including stressful relationship events, influence immunocompetence (e.g. Cohen et al 1992, Kiecolt-Glaser et al 1988; and see Weisse 1992), morbidity (see Burman & Margolin 1992 for a review of the association between marital relationship and general health), and mortality (see Stroebe & Stroebe 1987 for partner loss).

Relationship Dissolution

Demographers Martin & Bumpass (1989) estimate that about two thirds of all first marriages in this country will end in divorce. Actuarial prediction of a couple's likelihood of marital success or of stability, a prominent goal for at least four decades, now appears to have been achieved, with some researchers claiming predictive accuracies of more than 80% (e.g. Olson 1990, Buehlman et al 1992). Identification of the factors causally associated with relationship dissatisfaction and dissolution continues to be of great interest. This has led to an increasing number of prospective studies that examine the correlation between personal and relationship factors assessed at an earlier point in time and later relationship stability. Most of these are studies of premarital dating relationships. Although such studies almost always have the virtue of being theory-driven in the selection of factors presumed to be causally implicated in relationship stability, data are usually obtained from only one partner, the subjects frequently are nonrandom college student volunteers, and measurements are typically taken at only two points, with the interval between them short, usually only a few weeks or months. Relatively short intervals are usually adequate to permit identification of factors associated with stability in premarital dating relationships, however. For example, in one study where the current romantic relationship additionally had been identified as the individual's closest, 42% had dissolved 9 months later (Berscheid et al 1989b). Short-term longitudinal studies are more problematical with marital relationships, given the low base-rate of divorce, and as a result, Gottman & Levenson (1992) have proposed a cascade model of marital dissolution to identify precursors of divorce that have higher base-rates than divorce itself.

Prospective studies of premarital relationship dissolution often derive their hypotheses from the social exchange theories. Drigotas & Rusbult (1992) have proposed a dependence model of dissolution, in which dependence on a relationship is assumed to be high when desirable outcomes in the current relationship are perceived to be unavailable elsewhere. Support for their model is provided by the results of two studies in which participants reported on the status of their relationships every week for approximately two months. In another prospective study, Felmlee et al (1990) administered a relationship questionnaire to students early and then again late in the semester. Using information provided by the participants about the duration of the relationship, a hazard analysis revealed that the rate at which relationships dissolved was a function of comparison level for alternatives, amount of time spent together, racial dissimilarity, support from the partner's social network, and duration of relationship.

These two studies and several other prospective studies (e.g. Simpson 1987) highlight the importance of examining the social context of the relationship in addition to factors internal to the relationship, as does Surra & Milardo's (1991) work on the effects of social networks on developing premarital relationships. This perspective is noticeably absent in the marital stability literature, but a recent study by White & Booth (1991) suggests it shouldn't be. These investigators examined the association between marital happiness and marital stability in a national panel of married individuals interviewed in 1980 and 1988. They found that associated with dissolution are both relationship satisfaction and the extent to which there are few alternatives to and many barriers against dissolving the present relationship. White & Booth conclude that "the rise in the divorce rate has occurred not because marriages are less happy, but because, in the presence of falling barriers and rising alternatives, the threshold of marital happiness necessary to prompt divorce is lower than it used to be" (p. 19). It should be noted, however, that marriages also may be unhappier than they once were (Glenn & Weaver 1988).

Marital quality, or satisfaction or adjustment, has remained a ubiquitous variable in the marital literature, deriving much of its interest from its presumed association with marital stability even though as White (1990) observes, the empirical evidence to support this assumption is still surprisingly sparse. Glenn (1990) characterizes the body of quantitative research on marital quality conducted in the 1980s as immense, lacking in unity, only tangentially derived from theory, and marked by disagreement on the best way to assess marital quality (see Sabetelli 1988). It would be useful if a standard measure of relationship quality appropriate to many types of relationships were adopted. S. Hendrick (1988) has offered a generic measure of relationship satisfaction that is applicable to many types of close relationships and is brief, yet still possesses sound psychometric properties, including substantial correlation with at least one longer measure of dyadic adjustment. At present, most measures of relationship quality focus on the marital relationship, and the products of even these often are not comparable (Crane et al 1990).

Glenn also concludes that the bulk of the research on marital quality has "produced only a modest increment in understanding of the causes and consequences of marital success" (p. 818), where success is viewed as satisfaction in an intact marriage. Because most studies of satisfaction correlate measures obtained at a single point in time, stability is not examined. Several important longitudinal studies of marital success have been undertaken in recent years, however. Huston and associates (e.g. Huston et al 1986, Huston & Vangelisti 1991) have followed couples from courtship through the early years of marriage, gathering information from both members of the couple at four intervals (as newlyweds and 14 months, 27 months, and 10 years after the wedding). Attempting to predict later (up to 3 years) changes in satisfaction from earlier socioemotional patterns, these investigators have found that both husbands' and wives' early satisfaction appears to produce spousal behaviors that reinforce their initial levels of satisfaction; when husbands are initially satisfied, their wives maintain relatively high levels of affectional expression, and when wives are dissatisfied early, their husbands come to behave more negatively. Data from this project also document significant declines in love and marital satisfaction over the first year of marriage and indicate that much of the decline in satisfaction in the early stages of marriage that was previously attributed to the advent of parenthood simply is the result of the relationship's advancing age. Glenn (1989) strikes an additional pessimistic note for heterosexual relationships by estimating that marital success decreases monotonically with age of the marriage for the first 10 years, and perhaps for as long as 25 years.

Age of the relationship is an important factor in satisfaction, and thus to the many variables associated with satisfaction. Teachman & Polonko (1990) provide evidence that the reason premarital cohabitation is often associated with marital instability may be that cohabitants usually have spent more time together than have noncohabitants. When the length of time couples have been together is considered, regardless of their marital status, cohabitation prior to marriage (and the variables associated with cohabitation, e.g. lesser commitment to marriage) appears not to be associated with marital stability.

Large-scale national surveys that examine the association between demographic factors and stability help identify those factors that are likely to be associated with marital quality and differential marital interaction patterns. Such factors as race, age at marriage, and socioeconomic status are among the factors that continue to be associated with divorce (see White 1990). There are also several couple factors implicated in dissolution. Performing hazard analyses on data pooled from several National Longitudinal Surveys, Tzeng (1992) finds that for first marriages, the risk of separation or divorce is highest among couples with heterogamous age, heterogamous education, and any husband-wife work arrangement other than the traditional one of "male only in the work force."

In Kurdek's (1993) 5-year prospective study of a relatively large sample of newlywed couple volunteers, personal demographic variables also emerge as potent statistical predictors of dissolution. These variables performed as well or better than psychological (e.g. personality) and relationship (self-report of relationship dependence) variables in the statistical prediction of marital instability. The personality trait of neuroticism, however, was strongly associated with instability, as it was in Kelly & Conley's (1987) examination of the personality antecedents of marital instability in a panel of couples who were followed from their engagements in the 1930s until 1980. Husband's neuroticism, wife's neuroticism, and husband's impulse control (all as assessed in the 1930s) were positively correlated with instability.

Prospective questionnaire studies are complemented by investigations that include observational data of couple interaction to help identify the interaction patterns characteristic of couples whose marriages later deteriorate or improve over time. Previous studies examining differences in interaction patterns between satisfied and distressed couples, usually as they discuss a marital problem in the laboratory, have revealed that distressed couples display more negative affect, greater reciprocity of negative affect, and often greater reciprocity of positive affect as well (e.g. see Weiss & Heyman 1990). Interest in identifying the patterns of affect that may be associated with later dissolution continues (e.g. Gottman & Levenson 1992), and several of the affective patterns characteristic of satisfied and dissatisfied couples appear to be prospectively associated with relationship dissolution. For example, Filsinger & Thoma (1988) collected interaction data from 21 premarital couples "seriously considering marriage" and then followed them via questionnaire assessments over a 5-year period. Later relationship instability was associated with negative reciprocity, positive reciprocity, and the extent to which the woman had interrupted the man in the observed interaction 5 years earlier. Interruption level was not associated with relationship satisfaction at the time of the interaction, which is interpreted by the authors to "support the notion that behavioral patterns of interaction predate later relationship distress" (p. 785). However, as the authors discuss, interruption is likely to be only symptomatic of other unidentified factors that weakened the relationship over time.

In addition to affective patterns, a pattern of interaction in which one partner's attempt to discuss a relationship problem is met by the other partner's avoidance or withdrawal from interaction appears to differentially describe satisfied and distressed couples. Generally believed to be an especially intractable and destructive marital interaction pattern, the demand-withdraw pattern has received a great deal of attention. Roberts & Krokoff (1990) found that in dissatisfied couples, husband's withdrawal in interaction tended to be followed by the wife's display of hostility but no such pattern was evident in satisfied couples. Withdrawal was also one of three interaction characteristics identified by Gottman & Krokoff (1989) as prospectively associated with later marital satisfaction. Defensiveness and stubbornness are the other two. Although this study also appeared to find that the interaction pattern associated with concurrent marital satisfaction was different from the pattern associated with changes in satisfaction some years later, Woody & Costanzo (1990) persuasively argue that this particular finding was more likely an artifact of the statistical analysis performed.

Christensen and associates' (e.g. Christensen & Heavey 1990) research program is an exemplar of how a variety of research methodologies, including experimentation, can complement each other to illuminate the causal dynamics of an interaction pattern. These investigators first established that couples can report accurately the presence of the demand-withdraw pattern in their interactions as their self-reports corresponded to their observed behavior in the laboratory. Moreover, this demand-withdraw pattern was shown to be highly associated with marital dissatisfaction, as well as with the closeness-separateness dilemma in which one partner wants more independence and privacy and the other wants more closeness and intimacy in the relationship. Finally, both self-reports and laboratory observation revealed, as clinicians have suspected, that the woman is usually the demander and the man the withdrawer. Two causal explanations for this gender difference have been investigated experimentally: an individual differences explanation that focuses on stable gender differences (e.g. personality), and a conflict structure explanation where the higher status and power typically enjoyed by men may lead them to avoid discussions of conflict because they have little interest in change. Couples were observed discussing two of their conflicts about child-rearing, one focusing on a change desired by the woman and the other on a change desired by the man. Although there was a main effect for demander gender, with the wives doing more demanding, there also was evidence that a change in the conflict structure caused the partners' demand-withdraw behaviors to change. When the wife wanted the husband to change, the probability that a wife demand–husband withdraw pattern would appear in the interaction was significantly higher than a husband demand–wife withdraw pattern appearing, but when the husband wanted the wife to change, there were no differences in the probability of appearance of these two patterns (i.e. the husband was as likely to be the demander and his wife the withdrawer as the reverse). This interaction between gender and conflict structure in the demand-withdraw pattern has been replicated by Heavey et al (1993), who also found that the presence of the wife demand–husband withdraw pattern in interaction was associated with declines in the wife's satisfaction one year later, while the husband demand–wife withdraw pattern was associated with an increase in wives' later satisfaction.

Researchers are currently attempting to identify the specific gender-associated individual differences responsible for the gender main effect in the demand-withdraw pattern. Gottman & Levenson (1988) speculate that men tend to withdraw emotionally from heated discussion in an attempt to regulate their levels of negative arousal, hypothesizing that men show greater autonomic arousal to stress and recover more slowly than women do. Fitness & Strongman (1991) review the little evidence relevant to this conjecture, as well as gender differences in affective expression that may produce the effect. Gender differences in power also may be responsible because attempting to change the conflict structure in one laboratory discussion may not be wholly successful if there is a pervasive structural power difference in the relationship. Gottman & Levenson's (1986) report that most of the husbands' negative affect in a conflictful discussion consisted of anger and contempt, while most of the wives' negative affective expressions were fear, sadness, and "whining," also suggests such a power differential.

Experiments are rare in the vast literature of attempts to identify the factors associated with marital satisfaction and stability. Thus an experiment conducted by Markman et al (1988) stands out. Premarital couples who were participating in a longitudinal study of relationship development were matched on four variables assumed to be relevant to later instability (e.g. relationship satisfaction), and then couples from each set were randomly selected to serve as a no-treatment control or to be invited to participate in a premarital intervention program where training in communication, problem-solving, and other skills was provided. Assessments taken soon after the intervention indicated that treatment couples had learned the skills the intervention program taught but they exhibited no differences in relationship quality compared to controls at this point. After one and a half years, however, intervention couples were significantly more satisfied with their relationships than were control couples and after 3 years they showed higher levels of relationship satisfaction, sexual satisfaction, and lower levels of problem intensity. The investigators suspect that the effectiveness of their premarital intervention program was at least partially due to the fact that relationship dissatisfaction, and the stable negative interaction patterns associated with it, had not yet become entrenched and resistant to change.

CONCLUDING COMMENTS

Current directions in relationship research may be summarized quickly. First, there has been a gratifying increase in the number of prospective and longitudinal studies, although, as in other areas of research, their causal implications are sometimes exaggerated. Second, the immediate social context of a relationship is deservedly receiving more notice (see Milardo & Wellman 1992), and innovative ways of conceptualizing social networks are appearing along with useful hypotheses about their influence on various relationship phenomena. Third, although actual observation of interaction is still infrequent, it now appears in areas it didn't before, such as social support. Fourth, Clark & Reis' (1988) call for experimentation wasn't heard by many. The individual difference and psychometric approaches dominate, which is partially a reflection of the difficulty of experimentation with ongoing relationships. Experimentation also requires strong causal theory, however. Mesolevel theories that address person-situation interactions are not in great evidence, macrolevel theories tend to be ignored within psychology, and microlevel theories are almost nonexistent. Even Levenson & Gottman's (1983) heavily cited finding that physiological linkage was associated with marital satisfaction has yet to be replicated in their own or another laboratory. Sixth, Clark & Reis's (1988) observation that there is little integration of the two types of research that predominate in the relationship literature—laboratory experiments involving strangers and correlational studies or surveys of people in ongoing relationships—remains true. And, finally, there is growing interest in relationship cognition.

The movement toward an examination of cognitive processes as they occur in the context of actual ongoing social relationships is the most recent illustration of the mutual dependence between basic theory and research in psychology and theory and research in interpersonal relationships (see Kelley 1983). Wider recognition that the relationship arena is the ultimate destination of many, if not most, of the products of basic theory and research in social cognition is destined to enrich both endeavors. There are potential hazards as well as benefits for relationship research, however. For example, it will be tempting to construct questionnaires that purport to assess relationship beliefs and expectations and to avoid the hard work of demonstrating their actual manifestations in interaction or their effect on the relationship in other concrete ways. It will also be tempting to put the causes of social interaction behavior and outcomes in some mysterious cognitive structure and leave it at that.

In addition to keeping strong ties between cognition and relationship interaction and outcomes, it also will be necessary to trace how the relationship-relevant mental representations were formed in the first place. Research on adult attachment style has called attention to the fact that relatively stable relationship orientations—or schemas or inner models—come from somewhere, although just where remains to be discovered. This effort to identify the genesis of adult relationship orientations is somewhat dependent on the efforts of developmental psychologists. Unfortunately, theory and research directly addressed to the development of children's understandings of social relationships—particularly the rules, norms, and expectations associated with different types of relationships—is still surprisingly limited, although there appears to be growing interest in children's understanding of friendship (e.g. La Gaipa 1987; see Flavell et al 1993).

Finally, it is desirable that an interest in relationship cognition leads researchers to give more attention to the individual's relationship-associated plans and goals (e.g. see Reis 1990 for friendship goals), which have so far played a surprisingly limited role in relationship theory and research. This is one more reason why the meaning-making perspective and the account narrative method, which underscore the role relationships play in the setting of goals and the plans devised to achieve them (e.g. see McAdams 1993), deserve to thrive in the relationship domain.

ACKNOWLEDGMENTS

For their valuable comments on an earlier draft, the author would like to express her gratitude to Harold H. Kelley, University of California, Los Angeles; Harry Reis, University of Rochester; Robert Sternberg, Yale University; and Eugene Borgida and Mark Snyder, University of Minnesota.

Literature Cited

Acitelli LK. 1992. Gender differences in relationship awareness and marital satisfaction among young married couples. *Pers. Soc. Psychol. Bull.* 18:102–10

Acitelli LK, Holmberg D. 1993. Reflecting on relationships: the role of thoughts and memories. See Perlman & Jones 1993, pp. 71–100

Adams BN. 1988. Fifty years of family research: what does it mean? *J. Marr. Fam.* 50:5–17

Ainsworth MDS. 1989. Attachments beyond infancy. *Am. Psychol.* 44:709–16

Ainsworth MDS, Blehar MC, Waters E, Wall S. 1978. *Patterns of Attachment: A Psychological Study of the Strange Situation.* Hillsdale, NJ: Erlbaum

Allen JB, Kenrick DT, Linder DE, McCall MA. 1989. Arousal and attraction: a response-facilitation alternative to misattribution and negative-reinforcement models. *J. Pers. Soc. Psychol.* 57:261–70

Andersen SM, Cole SW. 1990. "Do I know you?": The role of significant others in general social perception. *J. Pers. Soc. Psychol.* 59:384–99

Aron A, Aron EN, Smollan D. 1992. Inclusion of other in the self scale and the structure of interpersonal closeness. *J. Pers. Soc. Psychol.* 63:596–612

Aron A, Aron EN, Tudor M, Nelson G. 1991. Close relationships as including other in self. *J. Pers. Soc. Psychol.* 60:241–53

Atkins CJ, Kaplan RM, Toshima MT. 1991. Close relationships in the epidemiology of cardiovascular disease. See Jones & Perlman 1991b, pp. 207–31

Baldwin MW. 1992. Relational schemas and the processing of social information. *Psychol. Bull.* 112:461–84

Baldwin MW, Carrell S, Lopez DF. 1990. Priming relationships schemas: my advisor and the Pope are watching me from the back of my mind. *J. Exp. Soc. Psychol.* 26:435–54

Bargh JA. 1993. The four horsemen of automaticity: awareness, intention, efficiency, and control in social cognition. In *Handbook of Social Cognition,* ed. RS Wyer, TK Srull. Hillsdale, NJ: Erlbaum. 2nd ed. In press

Bargh JA, Lombardi WJ, Higgins ET. 1988. Automaticity of chronically accessible constructs in person x situation effects in person perception: it's just a matter of time. *J. Pers. Soc. Psychol.* 55:599–605

Bartholomew K. 1990. Avoidance of intimacy: an attachment perspective. *J. Soc. Pers. Relat.* 7:147–78

Bartholomew K, Horowitz LM. 1991. Attachment styles among young adults: a test of a four-category model. *J. Pers. Soc. Psychol.* 61:226–44

Baumeister RF, Stillwell A, Wotman SR. 1990. Victim and perpetrator accounts of interpersonal conflict: autobiographical narratives about anger. *J. Pers. Soc. Psychol.* 59:994–1005

Beach SRH, Tesser A. 1988. Love in marriage: a cognitive account. See Sternberg & Barnes 1988, pp. 330–55

Beall AE. 1993. A social-constructionist view of gender. See Sternberg & Beall 1993. In press

Berardo FM. 1990. Trends and directions in family research in the 1980s. *J. Marr. Fam.* 52:809–17

Berman W. 1988. The role of attachment in the post-divorce experience. *J. Pers. Soc. Psychol.* 54:496–503

Berscheid E. 1982. Attraction and emotion in interpersonal relationships. In *Affect and Cognition,* ed. MS Clark, ST Fiske, pp. 37–54. Hillsdale, NJ: Erlbaum

Berscheid E. 1983. Emotion. See Kelley et al 1983, pp. 110–68

Berscheid E. 1993. Foreword. See Sternberg & Beall 1993. In press

Berscheid E, Graziano W, Monson T, Dermer M. 1976. Outcome dependency: attention, attribution, and attraction. *J. Pers. Soc. Psychol.* 34:978–89

Berscheid E, Snyder M, Omoto AM. 1989a. Issues in studying close relationships: conceptualizing and measuring closeness. See Hendrick 1989, pp. 63–91

Berscheid E, Snyder M, Omoto AM. 1989b. The Relationship Closeness Inventory: assessing the closeness of interpersonal relationships. *J. Pers. Soc. Psychol.* 57:792–807

Blieszner R, Adams RE. 1992. *Adult Friendship.* Newbury Park, CA: Sage

Blumstein P, Kollock P. 1988. Personal relationships. *Annu. Rev. Sociol.* 14:467–90

Bolger N, Eckenrode J. 1991. Social relationships, personality and anxiety during a major stressful event. *J. Pers. Soc. Psychol.* 61:440–49

Bower GH, Gilligan SG. 1979. Remembering information related to one's self. *J. Res. Pers.* 13:404–19

Bowlby J. 1982. *Attachment and Loss* Vol. 1: *Attachment.* New York: Basic Books. 2nd ed.

Bradbury TN, Fincham FD. 1988. Assessing spontaneous attributions in marital interaction: methodological and conceptual considerations. *J. Soc. Clin. Psychol.* 7:122–30

Bradbury TN, Fincham FD. 1989. Behavior and satisfaction in marriage: prospective mediating processes. See Hendrick 1989, pp. 119–43

Bradbury TN, Fincham FD. 1990. Attributions in marriage: review and critique. *Psychol. Bull.* 107:3–33

Bradbury TN, Fincham FD. 1991. The analysis of sequence in social interaction. In *Personality, Social Skills, and Psychopathology: An Individual Differences Approach,* ed. DG Gilbert, JJ Connolly, pp. 257–89. New York: Plenum

Bretherton I. 1985. Attachment theory: retrospect and prospect. In *Growing Points of Attachment Theory and Research,* ed. I

Bretherton, E Waters, pp. 3–35. Chicago: Univ. Chicago Press
Brewer MB. 1988. A dual process model of impression formation. In *Advances in Social Cognition* ed. TK Srull, RS Wyer, 1:1–36. Hillsdale, NJ: Erlbaum
Brewer MB, Caporael LR. 1990. Selfish genes vs. selfish people: sociobiology as origin myth. *Motiv. Emot.* 14:237–43
Brewer WF, Treyens JC. 1981. Role of schemata in memory for places. *Cogn. Psychol.* 13:207–30
Bruner J. 1990. *Acts of Meaning*. Cambridge: Harvard Univ. Press
Buehlman KT, Gottman JM, Katz LF. 1992. How a couple views their past predicts their future: predicting divorce from an oral history interview. *J. Fam. Psychol.* 5:295–318
Bugental DB. 1993. Communication in abusive relationships: cognitive constructions of interpersonal power. In *Functional Language—Dysfunctional Communication,* ed. JM Widman, H Giles. Special Issue *Am. Behav. Sci.* In press
Bugental DB, Blue J, Cortez V, Fleck K, Kopeikin H, et al. 1993. Social cognitions as organizers of autonomic and affective responses to social challenge. *J. Pers. Soc. Psychol.* 64:94–103
Burman B, Margolin G. 1992. Analysis of the association between marital relationships and health problems: an interactional perspective. *Psychol. Bull.* 112:39–63
Burnett R, McGhee P, Clarke DD, eds. 1987. *Accounting for Relationships: Explanation, Representation and Knowledge.* New York: Methuen
Buss DM. 1988. Love acts: the evolutionary biology of love. See Sternberg & Barnes 1988, pp. 100–18
Buss DM. 1989. Sex differences in human mate preferences: evolutionary hypotheses tested in 37 cultures. *Behav. Brain Sci.* 12:1–49
Buss DM. 1990. Evolutionary social psychology: prospects and pitfalls. *Motiv. Emot.* 14:265–86
Buss DM, Larsen RJ, Westen D, Semmelroth J. 1992. Sex differences in jealousy: evolution, physiology, and psychology. *Psychol. Sci.* 3:251–55
Buunk B, Bringle RG. 1987. Jealousy in love relationships. In *Intimate Relationships: Development, Dynamics and Detererioration,* ed. D Perlman S. Duck, pp. 123-48. Beverly Hills, CA: Sage
Cantor N, Malley J. 1991. Life tasks, personal needs, and close relationships. See Fletcher & Fincham 1991a, pp. 101–26
Cantor N, Mischel W, Swartz JC. 1982. A prototype analysis of psychological situations. *Cogn. Psychol.* 14:45–77
Caspi A, Herbener ES. 1990. Continuity and change: assortative marriage and the consistency of personality in adulthood. *J. Pers. Soc. Psychol.* 58:250–58
Cate RM, Lloyd SA. 1992. *Courtship.* Newbury Park, CA: Sage
Christensen A, Heavey CL. 1990. Gender and social structure in the demand/withdraw pattern of marital conflict. *J. Pers. Soc. Psychol.* 59:73–81
Christensen A, Sullaway M, King C. 1983. Systematic error in behavioral reports of dyadic interaction: egocentric bias and content effects. *Behav. Assess.* 5:131–42
Clanton G, Kosins DJ. 1991. Developmental correlates of jealousy. See Salovey 1991, pp. 132–77
Clark MS, ed. 1992. *Emotion and Social Behavior. Review of Personality and Social Psychology,* Vol. 14. Newbury Park, CA: Sage
Clark MS, Bennett ME. 1992. Research on relationships: implications for mental health. In *The Social Psychology of Mental Health,* ed. DN Ruble, PR Costanzo, ME Oliveri, pp. 166–93 New York: Guilford
Clark MS, Mills JR, Corcoran DM. 1989. Keeping track of needs and inputs of friends and strangers. *Pers. Soc. Psychol. Bull.* 15:533–42
Clark MS, Reis HT. 1988. Interpersonal processes in close relationships. *Annu. Rev. Psychol.* 39:609–72
Clark MS, Taraban C. 1991. Reactions to and willingness to express emotion in communal and exchange relationships. *J. Exp. Soc. Psychol.* 27:324–36
Clark MS, Williamson GM. 1989. Moods and social judgements. In *Handbook of Social Psychophysiology,* ed. H Wagner, A Manstead, pp. 347–70. New York: Wiley
Cohen G. 1989. *Memory in the Real World.* London: Erlbaum
Cohen S, Kaplan JR, Cunnick JE, Manuck SB, Rabin BS. 1992. Chronic social stress, affiliation, and cellular immune response in non human primates. *Psychol. Sci.* 3:301–4
Cohen S, Wills TA. 1985. Stress, social support, and the buffering hypothesis. *Psychol. Bull.* 98:310–57
Collins NL, Read SJ. 1990. Adult attachment, working models, and relationship quality in dating couples. *J. Pers. Soc. Psychol.* 58:644–63
Collins WA, Gunnar MR. 1990. Social and personality development. *Annu. Rev. Psychol.* 41:387–416
Coyne JC, Downey G. 1991. Social factors and psychopathology: stress, social support and coping process. *Annu. Rev. Psychol.* 42:401–25
Crane DR, Allgood SM, Larson JH, Griffin W. 1990. Assessing marital quality with distressed and nondistressed couples: a comparison and equivalency table for three fre-

quently used measures. *J. Marr. Fam.* 52:87–93

Cross SE, Markus HR. 1993. Gender in thought, belief, and action. See Sternberg & Beall 1993. In press

Cutrona CE. 1990. Stress and social support: in search of optimal matching. *J. Soc. Clin. Psychol.* 9:3–14

Cutrona CE, Suhr JA. 1993. Social support communication in the context of marriage: an analysis of couples' supportive interactions. In *The Communication of Social Support: Messages, Interactions, Relationships, and Community,* ed. B Burleson, T Albrecht, I Sarason. Newbury Park, CA: Sage. In press

Davis KE, Latty-Mann H. 1987. Love styles and relationship quality: a contribution to validation. *J. Soc. Pers. Relat.* 4:409–28

Dindia K, Allen M. 1992. Sex differences in self-disclosure: a meta-analysis. *Psychol. Bull.* 112:106–24

Dion KL, Dion KK. 1988. Romantic love: individual and cultural perspectives. See Sternberg & Barnes 1988, pp. 264–89

Drigotas SM, Rusbult CE. 1992. Should I stay or should I go? a dependence model of breakups. *J. Pers. Soc. Psychol.* 62:62–87

Duck SW, ed. 1988. *Handbook of Personal Relationships: Theory, Research and Interventions.* Chichester: Wiley

Duck SW, Silver RC, eds. 1990. *Personal Relationships and Social Support.* London: Sage

Erber R. 1991. Affective and semantic priming: effects of mood on category accessibility and inference. *J. Exp. Soc. Psychol.* 27:480–98

Feeney JA, Noller P. 1990. Attachment style as a predictor of adult romantic relationships. *J. Pers. Soc. Psychol.* 58:281–91

Fehr B, Russell JA. 1991. The concept of love viewed from a prototype perspective. *J. Pers. Soc. Psychol.* 60:425–38

Feingold A. 1990. Gender differences in effects of physical attractiveness on romantic attraction: a comparison across five research paradigms. *J. Pers. Soc. Psychol.* 59:981–93

Feingold A. 1992a. Gender differences in mate selection preferences: a test of the parental investment model. *Psychol. Bull.* 112:125–39

Feingold A. 1992b. Good-looking people are not what we think. *Psychol. Bull.* 111:304–41

Felmlee D, Sprecher S, Bassin E. 1990. The dissolution of intimate relationships: a hazard model. *Soc. Psychol. Q.* 53:13–30

Field D. 1981. Retrospective reports by healthy intelligent elderly people of personal events of their adult lives. *Int. J. Behav. Dev.* 4:77–97

Filsinger EE, Thoma SJ. 1988. Behavioral antecedents of relationship stability and adjustment: a five-year longitudinal study. *J. Marr. Fam.* 50:785–95

Fincham FD. 1992. The account episode in close relationships. See McLaughlin et al 1992, pp. 167–82

Fincham FD, Bradbury TN. 1989. Perceived responsibility for marital events: egocentric or partner-centric bias? *J. Marr. Fam.* 51:27–35

Fincham FD, Bradbury TN, eds. 1990a. *The Psychology of Marriage: Basic Issues and Applications.* New York: Guilford

Fincham FD, Bradbury TN. 1990b. Social support in marriage: the role of social cognition. *J. Soc. Clin. Psychol.* 7:147–62

Fincham FD, Bradbury TN. 1991. Cognition in marriage: a program of research on attributions. See Jones & Perlman 1991a, pp. 159–204

Fincham FD, Bradbury TN. 1992. Attributions and behavior in marital interaction. *J. Pers. Soc. Psychol.* 63:613–28

Fiske AP. 1992. The four elementary forms of sociality: framework for a unified theory of social relations. *Psychol. Rev.* 99:689–723

Fiske AP, Haslam N, Fiske ST. 1991. Confusing one person with another: what errors reveal about the elementary forms of social relations. *J. Pers. Soc. Psychol.* 60:656–74

Fiske ST. 1992. Thinking is for doing: portraits of social cognition from daguerreotype to laserphoto. *J. Pers. Soc. Psychol.* 63:877–89

Fiske ST, Neuberg SL. 1990. A continuum of impression formation, from category-based to individuating processes: influences of information and motivation on attention and interpretation. In *Advances in Experimental Social Psychology,* ed. MP Zanna, 23:1–74. New York: Academic

Fiske ST, Taylor SE. 1991. *Social Cognition.* New York: McGraw-Hill. 2nd ed.

Fitness J, Strongman K. 1991. Affect in close relationships. See Fletcher & Fincham 1991a, pp. 175–202

Flavell JH, Miller PH, Miller SA. 1993. *Cognitive Development.* Englewood Cliffs, NJ: Prentice Hall. 3rd ed.

Fletcher GJO, Fincham FD, eds. 1991a. *Cognition and Close Relationships.* Hillsdale, NJ: Erlbaum

Fletcher GJO, Fincham FD. 1991b. Attribution processes in close relationships. See Fletcher & Fincham 1991a, pp. 7–36

Fletcher GJO, Fincham FD, Cramer L, Heron N. 1987. The role of attributions in the development of dating relationships. *J. Pers. Soc. Psychol.* 53:481–89

Fletcher GJO, Kininmonth L. 1991. Interaction in close relationships and social cognition. See Fletcher & Fincham 1991a, pp. 235–56

Forgas JP. 1991. Affect and cognition in close

relationships. See Fletcher & Fincham 1991, pp. 151–74

Frazier PA, Esterly E. 1990. Correlates of relationship beliefs: gender, relationship experience, and relationship satisfaction. *J. Soc. Pers. Relat.* 7:331–52

Geis FL. 1993. Self-fulfilling prophecies: a social psychological view of gender. See Sternberg & Beall 1993. In press

Gergen KJ. 1991. *The Saturated Self: Dilemmas of Identity in Contemporary Life.* New York: Basic Books

Gergen KJ, Gergen MM. 1988. Narrative and the self as relationship. In *Advances in Experimental Social Psychology,* ed. L Berkowitz, 21:17–56. New York: Academic

Gilbert DT. 1991. How mental systems believe. *Am. Psychol.* 46:107–19

Ginsburg GP. 1988. Rules, scripts and prototypes in personal relationships. See Duck 1988, pp. 23–39

Ginsburg GP. 1991. Accounting for accounts. *Contemp. Psychol.* 36:1082–83

Glenn ND. 1989. Duration of marriage, family composition, and marital happiness. *Natl. J. Soc.* 3:3–24

Glenn ND. 1990. Quantitative research on marital quality in the 1980s: a critical review. *J. Marr. Fam.* 52:818–31

Glenn ND, Weaver CN. 1988. The changing relationship of marital status to reported happiness. *J. Marr. Fam.* 50:317–24

Godwin DD. 1988. Causal modeling in family research. *J. Marr. Fam.* 50:917–28

Gonzales MH, Manning DJ, Haugen JA. 1992. Explaining our sins: factors influencing offender accounts and anticipated victim responses. *J. Pers. Soc. Psychol.* 62:958–71

Gottman JM, Krokoff LJ. 1989. Marital interaction and satisfaction: a longitudinal view. *J. Consult. Clin. Psychol.* 57:47–52

Gottman JM, Levenson RW. 1986. Assessing the role of emotion in marriage. *Behav. Assess.* 8:31–48

Gottman JM, Levenson RW. 1988. The social psychophysiology of marriage. In *Perspectives on Marital Interaction,* ed. P Noller, MA Fitzpatrick, pp. 182–99. Clevedon, England: Multilingual Matters

Gottman JM, Levenson RW. 1992. Marital processes predictive of later dissolution: behavior, physiology, and health. *J. Pers. Soc. Psychol.* 63:221–33

Gray JD, Silver RC. 1990. Opposite sides of the same coin: former spouses' divergent perspectives in coping with their divorce. *J. Pers. Soc. Psychol.* 59:1180–91

Harris LM, Gergen KJ, Lannamann JW. 1987. Aggression rituals. *Commun. Monogr.* 53:252–65

Hartup WW. 1989. Social relationships and their developmental significance. *Am. Psychol.* 44:120–26

Harvey JH, Agnostinelli G, Weber AL. 1989. Account-making and the formation of expectations about close relationships. See Hendrick 1989, pp. 39–62

Harvey JH, Flanary R, Morgan M. 1986. Vivid memories of vivid loves gone by. *J. Soc. Pers. Relat.* 3:359–73

Harvey JH, Weber AL, Orbuch TL. 1990. *Interpersonal Accounts: A Social Psychological Perspective.* Cambridge: Blackwell

Hatfield E, Cacioppo JT, Rapson RL. 1992. Primitive emotional contagion. See Clark 1992, pp. 151–77

Hatfield E, Rapson RL. 1987. Passionate love: new directions in research. In *Advances in Personal Relationships,* ed. WH Jones, D Perlman, 1:109–39. Greenwich, Conn: JAI

Hatfield E, Sprecher S. 1986. Measuring passionate love in intimate relations. *J. Adolesc.* 9:383–410

Hazan C, Shaver P. 1987. Romantic love conceptualized as an attachment process. *J. Pers. Soc. Psychol.* 52:511–24

Heavey CL, Layne C, Christensen A. 1993. Gender and conflict structure in marital interaction: a replication and extension. *J. Consult. Clin. Psychol.* 61:16–27

Hendrick C. 1988. Roles and gender in relationships. See Duck 1988, pp. 429–48

Hendrick C, ed. 1989. *Close Relationships. Review of Personality and Social Psychology,* Vol. 10. Newbury Park, CA: Sage

Hendrick C, Clark MS, eds. 1990. *Research Methods in Personality and Social Psychology. Review of Personality and Social Psychology,* Vol. 11. Newbury Park, CA: Sage

Hendrick C, Hendrick SS. 1989. Research on love: does it measure up? *J. Pers. Soc. Psychol.* 56:784–94

Hendrick SS. 1988. A generic measure of relationship satisfaction. *J. Marr. Fam.* 39:543–48

Hendrick SS, Hendrick C. 1992. *Romantic Love.* Newbury Park, CA: Sage

Higgins ET. 1989. Knowledge accessibility and activation: subjectivity and suffering from unconscious sources. In *Unintended Thought,* ed. JS Uleman, JA Bargh, pp. 75–123. New York: Guilford

Higgins ET, Bargh JA. 1987. Social cognition and social perception. *Annu. Rev. Psychol.* 38:369–425

Hobfoll SE. 1988. *The Ecology of Stress.* New York: Hemisphere

Hobfoll SE, London P. 1986. The relationship of self concept and social support to emotional distress among women during war. *J. Soc. Clin. Psychol.* 12:87–100

Holmberg D, Holmes JG. 1993. Reconstruction of relationship memories: a mental models approach. In *Autobiographical Memory and the Validity of Retrospective*

Reports, ed. N Schwarz, S Sudman. New York: Springer-Verlag. In press

Holmes JG. 1991. Trust and the appraisal process in close relationships. See Jones & Perlman 1991a, pp. 57–104

Holmes JG, Rempel J, Ashmore K. 1989. Trust in close relationships. See Hendrick 1989, pp. 187–220.

Holtzworth-Munroe A, Jacobson NS. 1985. Causal attributions of married couples: When do they search for causes? What do they conclude when they do? *J. Pers. Soc. Psychol.* 48:1398–412

Holtzworth-Munroe A, Jacobson NS. 1988. Toward a methodology for coding spontaneous causal attributions: preliminary results with married couples. *J. Soc. Clin. Psychol.* 7:101–12

Howard JA, Blumstein P, Swartz P. 1987. Social or evolutionary theories? Some observations on preferences in human mate selection. *J. Pers. Soc. Psychol.* 53:194–200

Hupka RB. 1991. The motive for the arousal of romantic jealousy: its cultural origin. See Salovey 1991, pp. 252–70

Huston TL, McHale S, Crouter A. 1986. When the honeymoon's over: changes in the marriage relationship over the first year. In *The Emerging Field of Personal Relationships,* ed. R Gilmour, S Duck, pp. 109–43. Hillsdale, NJ: Erlbaum

Huston TL, Vangelisti AL. 1991. Socioemotional behavior and satisfaction in marital relationships. *J. Pers. Soc. Psychol.* 61:721–33

Ickes W, Bissonnette V, Garcia S, Stinson LL. 1990. Implementing and using the dyadic interaction paradigm. See Hendrick & Clark 1990, pp. 16–44

Jankowiak WR, Fischer EF. 1992. A cross-cultural perspective on romantic love. *Ethnology* 31:149–55

Johnson DJ, Rusbult CE. 1989. Resisting temptation: devaluation of alternative partners as a means of maintaining commitment in close relationships. *J. Pers. Soc. Psychol.* 57:967–80

Johnson DR. 1988. Panel analysis in family studies. *J. Marr. Fam.* 50:949–55

Jones WH, Perlman D, eds. 1991a. *Advances in Personal Relationships,* Vol. 2. London: Kingsley

Jones WH, Perlman D, eds. 1991b. *Advances in Personal Relationships,* Vol. 3. London: Kingsley

Jussim L. 1991. Social perception and social reality: a reflection—construction model. *Psychol. Rev.* 98:54–73

Kaniasty K, Norris FH. 1993. A test of the social support deterioration model in the context of natural disaster. *J. Pers. Soc. Psychol.* 64:395–408

Kelley HH. 1983. Epilogue: an essential science. See Kelley et al 1983, pp. 486–503

Kelley HH. 1992. Common-sense psychology and scientific psychology. *Annu. Rev. Psychol.* 43:1–23

Kelley HH, Berscheid E, Christensen A, Harvey HH, Huston TL, et al. 1983. *Close Relationships.* San Francisco: Freeman

Kelly EL, Conley JJ. 1987. Personality and compatibility: a prospective analysis of marital stability and marital satisfaction. *J. Pers. Soc. Psychol.* 52:27–40

Kenny DA, Kashy DA. 1991. Analyzing interdependence in dyads. See Montgomery & Duck 1991, pp. 275–85

Kenrick DT, Trost MR. 1989. A reproductive exchange model of heterosexual relationships: putting proximate economics in ultimate perspective. See Hendrick 1989, pp. 92–118

Kiecolt-Glaser JK, Kennedy S, Malkoff S, Fisher L, Speicher CE, Glaser R. 1988. Marital discord and immunity in males. *Psychosom. Med.* 50:213–29

Kihlstrom JF. 1987. The cognitive unconscious. *Science* 237:1445–52

Knapp A, Clark MS. 1991. Some detrimental effects of negative mood on individuals' ability to solve resource dilemnas. *Pers. Soc. Psychol. Bull.* 17:678–88

Kojetin BA. 1993. *Adult attachment styles with romantic partners, friends and parents.* PhD thesis. Univ. Minn., Minneapolis. 56 pp.

Kurdek LA. 1993. Predicting marital dissolution: a 5-year prospective longitudinal study of newlywed couples. *J. Pers. Soc. Psychol.* 64:221–42

La Gaipa JJ. 1987. Friendship expectations. See Burnett et al 1987, pp. 134–57

Lavee Y, Dollahite DC. 1991. The linkage between theory and research in family science. *J. Marr. Fam.* 53:361–73

Leatham G, Duck S. 1990. Conversations with friends and the dynamics of social support. See Duck & Silver 1990, pp. 1–29

Lee JA. 1988. Love-styles. See Sternberg & Barnes 1988, pp. 38–67

Levenson RW, Gottman JM. 1983. Marital interaction: physiological linkage and affective exchange. *J. Pers. Soc. Psychol.* 45:587–97

Levinger G. 1990. *Figure versus ground: micro and macro perspectives on personal relationships.* Presented at Meet. Int. Soc. Study Pers. Relat., Oxford Univ.

Loevinger J. 1957. Objective tests as instruments of psychological theory. *Psychol. Rep.* 3:635–94

Maccoby EE. 1990. Gender and relationships: a developmental account. *Am. Psychol.* 45:513–20

Markman HJ, Floyd FJ, Stanley SM, Storaasli RD. 1988. Prevention of marital distress: a longitudinal investigation. *J. Consult. Clin. Psychol.* 56:210–17

Markus HM, Kitayama S. 1991. Culture and the self: implications for cognition, emotion, and motivation. *Psychol. Rev.* 98:224–53

Martin T, Bumpass L. 1989. Recent trends in marital disruption. *Demography* 26:37–52

McAdams DP. 1993. *Stories We Live By: Personal Myths and the Making of the Self.* New York: Morrow

McFarland C, Ross M. 1987. The relation between current impressions and memories of self and dating partners. *Pers. Soc. Psych. Bull.* 13:228–38

McLaughlin ML, Cody MJ, Read SJ. 1992. *Explaining One's Self to Others: Reason-giving in a Social Context.* Hillsdale, NJ: Erlbaum

Metts S, Sprecher S, Cupach WR. 1991. Retrospective self-reports. See Montgomery & Duck 1991, pp. 162–78

Miell D. 1987. Remembering relationship development: constructing a context for interactions. See Burnett et al 1987, pp. 60–73

Mikulincer M, Nachshon O. 1991. Attachment styles and patterns of self-disclosure. *J. Pers. Soc. Psychol.* 61:321–31

Milardo RM. 1992. Comparative methods for delineating social networks. *J. Soc. Pers. Relat.* 9:447–61

Milardo RM, Wellman B. 1992. The personal is social. *J. Soc. Pers. Relat.* 9:339–42

Miller DT, Turnbull W. 1986. Expectancies and interpersonal processes. *Annu. Rev. Psychol.* 37:233–56

Montgomery BM, Duck S, eds. 1991. *Studying Interpersonal Interaction.* New York: Guilford

Morgan SP, Teachman JD. 1988. Logistic regression: description, examples, and comparisons. *J. Marr. Fam.* 50:929–36

Murray SL, Holmes JG. 1993. Seeing virtues in faults: negativity and the transformation of interpersonal narratives in close relationships. *J. Pers. Soc. Psychol.* In press

Murstein BI. 1988. A taxonomy of love. See Sternberg & Barnes 1988, pp. 13–37

Nigro G, Neisser U. 1983. Point of views in personal memories. *Cogn. Psychol.* 15:467–82

Noller P, Fitzpatrick MA. 1990. Marital communication in the eighties. *J. Marr. Fam.* 52:832–43

Noller P, Guthrie D. 1991. Studying communication in marriage: an integration and critical evaluation. See Jones & Perlman 1991b, pp. 37–74

Noller P, Ruzzene M. 1991. Communication in marriage: the influence of affect and cognition. See Fletcher & Fincham 1991, pp. 203–34

Nye FI. 1988. Fifty years of family research, 1937–1987. *J. Marr. Fam.* 50:305–16

Ogilvie DM, Ashmore R. 1991. Self-with-other representation as a unit of analysis in self-concept research. In *The Relational Self,* ed. RC Curtis, pp. 282–314. New York: Guilford

O'Leary KD, Smith DA. 1991. Marital interactions. *Annu. Rev. Psychol.* 42:191–212

Olson DH. 1990. Marriage in perspective. See Fincham & Bradbury 1990a, pp. 402–19

Parks MR, Eggert LL. 1991. The role of social context in the dynamics of personal relationships. See Jones & Perlman 1991b, pp. 1–34

Parrott WG. 1991. The emotional experiences of envy and jealousy. See Salovey 1991, pp. 3–30

Pennebaker JW. 1989. Confession, inhibition, and disease. In *Advances in Experimental Social Psychology,* ed. L Berkowitz, 22:211–44. New York: Academic

Peplau LA, Hill CT, Rubin Z. 1993. Sex-role attitudes in dating and marriage: a 15-year followup of the Boston Couples Study. *J. Soc. Issues* In press

Perlman D, Jones WH, eds. 1993. *Advances in Personal Relationships,* Vol. 4. London: Kingsley

Pierce GR, Sarason BR, Sarason IG. 1990. Integrating social support perspectives: working models, personal relationships, and situational factors. See Duck & Silver 1990, pp. 173–89

Pierce GR, Sarason IG, Sarason BR. 1991. General and relationship-based perceptions of social support: are two constructs better than one? *J. Pers. Soc. Psychol.* 61:1028–39

Planalp S. 1987. Interplay between relational knowledge and events. See Burnett et al 1987, pp. 175–91

Prentice D. 1990. Familiarity and differences in self- and other-representations. *J. Pers. Soc. Psychol.* 59:369–83

Rands M. 1988. Changes in social networks following marital separation and divorce. In *Families and Social Networks,* ed. RM Milardo, pp. 127–46. Newbury Park, CA: Sage

Read SJ. 1987. Constructing causal scenarios: a knowledge structure approach to causal reasoning. *J. Pers. Soc. Psychol.* 52:288–302

Read SJ. 1992. Constructing accounts: the role of explanatory coherence. See McLaughlin et al 1992, pp. 3–19

Reis HT. 1990. The role of intimacy in interpersonal relations. *J. Soc. Clin. Psychol.* 9:15–30

Reis HT, Lin Y, Bennett ES, Nezler JB. 1993. Change and consistency in social participation during early adulthood. *Dev. Psychol.* 29:633–45

Reis HT, Shaver P. 1988. Intimacy as an interpersonal process. See Duck 1988, pp. 367–89

Reis HT, Wheeler L. 1991. Studying social interaction with the Rochester Interaction Record. In *Advances in Experimental Social Psychology,* ed. M Zanna, pp. 269–318. New York: Academic

Rempel JK, Holmes JG, Zanna MP. 1985. Trust in close relationships. *J. Pers. Soc. Psychol.* 49:95–112

Riggio RE, Zimmerman J. 1991. Social skills and interpersonal relationships: influences on social support and support seeking. See Jones & Perlman 1991a, pp. 133–55

Roberts LJ, Krokoff LJ. 1990. A time-series analysis of withdrawal, hostility, and displeasure in satisfied and dissatisfied marriages. *J. Marr. Fam.* 52:95–105

Robins E. 1990. The study of interdependence in marriage. See Fincham & Bradbury 1990a, pp. 59–86

Rook K. 1984. The negative side of social interaction: impact on psychological well-being. *J. Pers. Soc. Psychol.* 5:1097–108

Ross MA. 1989. The relation of implicit theories to the construction of personal histories. *Psychol. Rev.* 96:341–57

Ross M, Holmberg D. 1990. Recounting the past: gender differences in the recall of events in the history of a close relationship. In *Self-inferences Processes: The Ontario Symposium,* ed. JM Olson, MP Zanna, 6:135–52. Hillsdale, NJ: Erlbaum

Ross M, Sicoly F. 1979. Egocentric biases in availability and attribution. *J. Pers. Soc. Psychol.* 37:322–36

Rubin DC, ed. 1986. *Autobiographical Memory.* Cambridge: Cambridge Univ. Press

Rubin DC, Wetzler SE, Nebes RD. 1986. Autobiographical memory across the lifespan. See Rubin 1986, pp. 202–21

Rusbult CE, Verette J, Whitney GA, Slovik LF, Lipkus I. 1991. Accommodation processes in close relationships: theory and preliminary research evidence. *J. Pers. Soc. Psychol.* 60:53–78

Sabetelli RM. 1988. Measurement issues in marital research: a review and critique of contemporary survey instruments. *J. Marr. Fam.* 50:891–915

Salovey P, ed. 1991. *The Psychology of Jealousy and Envy.* New York: Guilford

Salovey P, Rodin J. 1989. Envy and jealousy in close relationships. See Hendrick 1989, pp. 221–46

Sande GN, Goethals G, Radloff CE. 1988. Perceiving one's own traits and others': the multifaceted self. *J. Pers. Soc. Psychol.* 54:13–20

Scanzoni J, Polonko K, Teachman J, Thompson L. 1989. *The Sexual Bond: Rethinking Families and Close Relationships.* Newbury Park, CA: Sage

Scarr S. 1989. Sociobiology: the psychology of sex, violence, and oppression? *Contemp. Psychol.* 34:440–43

Schonbach P. 1990. *Account Episodes: The Management of Escalation of Conflict.* Cambridge: Cambridge Univ. Press

Schwarz N. 1990. Assessing frequency reports of mundane behaviors: contributions of cognitive psychology to questionnaire construction. See Hendrick & Clark 1990, pp. 98–119

Scott CK, Fuhrman RW, Wyer RS Jr. 1991. Information processing in close relationships. See Fletcher & Fincham 1991, pp. 37–68

Scott MB, Lyman S. 1968. Accounts. *Am. Sociol. Rev.* 33:46–62

Sedikides C, Olsen N, Reis HT. 1993. Relationships as natural categories. *J. Pers. Soc. Psychol.* 64:71–82

Sedikides C, Ostrom TM. 1988. Are person categories used when organizing information about unfamiliar sets of persons? *Soc. Cogn.* 6:252–67

Shaver PR, Brennan KA. 1992. Attachment styles and the "big five" personality traits: their connections with each other and with romantic relationship outcomes. *Pers. Soc. Psychol. Bull.* 18:536–45

Shaver PR, Hazan C. 1993. Adult romantic attachment: theory and evidence. See Perlman & Jones 1993, pp. 29–70

Shaver PR, Hazan C, Bradshaw D. 1988. Love as attachment: the integration of three behavioral systems. See Sternberg & Barnes 1988, pp. 68–99

Simpson JA. 1987. The dissolution of romantic relationships: factors involved in relationship stability and emotional distress. *J. Pers. Soc. Psychol.* 53:683–92

Simpson JA. 1990. Influence of attachment styles on romantic relationships. *J. Pers. Soc. Psychol.* 5:971–80

Simpson JA, Gangestad SW, Lerma M. 1990. Perception of physical attractiveness: mechanisms involved in the maintenance of romantic relationships. *J. Pers. Soc. Psychol.* 59:1192–201

Simpson JA, Rhodes WS, Nelligan JS. 1992. Support seeking and support giving within couples in an anxiety-provoking situation: the role of attachment styles. *J. Pers. Soc. Psychol.* 62:434–46

Skowronski JJ, Betz AL, Thompson CP, Shannon L. 1991. Social memory in everyday life: recall of self-events and other-events. *J. Pers. Soc. Psychol.* 60:831–43

Snyder M. 1984. When belief creates reality. In *Advances in Experimental Social Psychology,* ed. L Berkowitz, 18:247–305. New York: Academic

Sprecher S. 1989. The importance to males and females of physical attractiveness, earning potential and expressiveness in initial attraction. *Sex Roles* 21:591–607

Sprecher S, Aron A, Hatfield E, Cortese A, Potapova E, Levitskaya A. 1992. *Love: American style, Russian style, and Japan-*

ese style. Presented at Meet. Int. Soc. Study Pers. Relat., Orono, Maine

Sprecher S, Metts S. 1989. Development of the "Romantic Beliefs Scale" and examination of the effects of gender and gender-role orientation. *J. Pers. Soc. Relat.* 6:387–411

Sroufe LA, Egeland B, Kreutzer T. 1990. The fate of early experience following developmental change: longitudinal approaches to individual adaptation in childhood. *Child Dev.* 61:1363–73

Srull TK, Wyer RS. 1989. Person memory and judgment. *Psychol. Rev.* 96:58–83

Stangor C, McMillan D. 1992. Memory for expectancy-congruent and expectancy-incongruent information: a review of the social and social developmental literatures. *Psychol. Bull.* 111:42–61

Starker JE, Morgan DL, March S. 1993. Analyzing change in networks of personal relationships. See Perlman & Jones 1993, pp. 229–60

Sternberg RJ. 1987. Liking versus loving: a comparative evaluation of theories. *Psychol. Bull.* 102:331–45

Sternberg RJ. 1988. Triangulating love. See Sternberg & Barnes 1988, pp. 119–38

Sternberg RJ, Barnes ML, eds. 1988. *The Psychology of Love.* New Haven, Conn: Yale Univ. Press

Sternberg RJ, Beall AE. 1991. How can we know what love is? An epistemological analysis. See Fletcher & Fincham 1991a, pp. 257–78

Sternberg RJ, Beall AE. 1993. *Perspectives on the Psychology of Gender.* New Haven, Conn: Yale Univ. Press. In press

Stevens G, Owens D, Schaefer EC. 1990. Education and attractiveness in marriage choices. *Soc. Psychol. Q.* 53:62–70

Stroebe W, Stroebe MS. 1987. *Bereavement and Health: The Psychological and Physical Consequences of Partner Loss.* Cambridge: Cambridge Univ. Press

Surra CA. 1990. Research and theory on mate selection and premarital relationships in the 1980s. *J. Marr. Fam.* 52:844–65

Surra CA, Bohman T. 1991. The development of close relationships: a cognitive perspective. See Fletcher & Fincham 1991a, pp. 281–305

Surra CA, Milardo RM. 1991. The social psychological context of developing relationships: interactive and psychological networks. See Jones & Perlman 1991b, pp.1–36

Taylor SE. 1991. Asymmetrical effects of positive and negative events: the mobilization-minimization hypothesis. *Psychol. Bull.* 110:67–85

Teachman JD, Polonko KA. 1990. Cohabitation and marital stability in the United States. *Soc. Forces* 69:207–20

Tesser A. 1988. Toward a self-evaluation maintenance model of social behavior. In *Advances in Experimental Social Psychology,* ed. L Berkowitz, 21:181–227. New York: Academic

Trafimow D, Wyer RS. 1993. Cognitive representation of mundane social events. *J. Pers. Soc. Psychol.* 64:365–76

Tzeng M. 1992. The effects of socioeconomic heterogamy and changes on marital dissolution for first marriages. *J. Marr. Fam.* 54:609–19

Vaux A. 1988. *Social Support: Theory, Research, and Intervention.* New York: Praeger

Veroff J, Douvan E, Hatchett S. 1993. Marital interaction and marital quality in the first year of marriage. See Perlman & Jones 1993, pp. 103–37

Wagenaar W. 1986. My memory: a study of autobiographical memory over six years. *Cogn. Psychol.* 18:225–52

Wegner DM, Giuliano T, Hertel PT. 1985. Cognitive interdependence in close relationships. In *Compatible and Incompatible Relationships,* ed. W Ickes, pp. 253–76. New York: Springer-Verlag

Weiner B. 1985. "Spontaneous" causal thinking. *Psychol. Bull.* 97:74–84

Weiss RL, Heyman RE. 1990. Observation of marital interaction. See Fincham & Bradbury 1990a, pp. 87–117

Weiss RS. 1975. *Marital Separation.* New York: Basic Books

Weisse CA. 1992. Depression and immunocompetence: a review of the literature. *Psychol. Bull.* 111:475–89

Wetzler SE, Sweeney JA. 1986. Childhood amnesia: an empirical demonstration. See Rubin 1986, pp. 191–201

White LK. 1990. Determinants of divorce: a review of research in the eighties. *J. Marr. Fam.* 52:904–12

White LK, Booth A. 1991. Divorce over the life course. *J. Fam. Issues* 12:5–21

White GL. 1991. Self, relationship, friends, and family: some applications of systems theory to romantic jealousy. See Salovey 1991, pp. 231–51

White GL, Mullen PE. 1989. *Jealousy: Theory, Research and Clinical Strategies.* New York: Guilford

Wilmot W, Baxter L. 1983. Reciprocal framing of relationship definitions and episodic interaction. *West. J. Speech Commun.* 47:205–17

Wilson TD, Klaaren KJ. 1992. "Expectation whirls me around": the role of affective expectations in affective experience. See Clark 1992, pp. 1–31

Winstead BA, Derlega V. 1991. An experimental approach to studying social interaction and coping with stress among friends. See Jones & Perlman 1991a, pp. 107–32

Wong MM, Csikszentmihalyi M. 1991. Affiliation motivation and daily experience: some issues on gender differences. *J. Pers. Soc. Psychol.* 60:154–64

Woody EZ, Costanzo PR. 1990. Does marital agony precede marital ecstasy? A comment on Gottman and Krokoff's "Marital Interaction and Satisfaction: A Longitudinal View". *J. Consult. Clin. Psychol.* 58:499–501

Zadny J, Gerard HB. 1974. Attributed intentions and informational selectivity. *J. Exp. Soc. Psychol.* 10:34–52

Annu. Rev. Psychol. 1994. 45:131–69

CONSUMER PSYCHOLOGY

Alice M. Tybout

Kellogg Graduate School of Management, Northwestern University, Evanston, Illinois 60208

Nancy Artz

School of Business, Economics, and Management, University of Southern Maine, Portland, Maine 04103

KEY WORDS: information processing, judgments, decision making, marketing communications, literature review

---

CONTENTS

INTRODUCTION

Interest in consumer psychology continues to grow. Consumer psychology accounts for a substantial portion of consumer research (Zinkhan et al 1992) and is the focus of a journal launched in 1992, the *Journal of Consumer Psychology*. We strive to provide coverage of topics that have captured signif-

0066-4308/94/0201-0131$05.00

icant research attention and to identify the progress made. This review is organized into three primary sections. We begin with an overview of how consumers process information and how such processing affects judgment and decision making. We emphasize the role of contextual factors and individual differences in moderating these processes. Next, we examine research on how consumers respond to marketer-initiated stimuli such as advertisements, sales promotions, prices, and products, and how consumers' values moderate such responses. Finally, we discuss briefly the contributions to consumer psychology made by alternative approaches to experimental and survey research procedures.

INFORMATION PROCESSING, JUDGMENT, AND DECISION MAKING

Much of the work in consumer psychology examines how consumers process information and form judgments and how memory and judgment affect consumers' decision making. Research on information processing and judgment draws heavily on the theories and research methods of cognitive and social psychology. Thus, elaboration and cognitive resources serve as central constructs and experimental procedures are common in consumer psychology research. Theories borrowed from psychology are tested for robustness and are enriched by examining moderating and mediating conditions made salient by the consumption role and setting.

In contrast, consumer decision making research has roots in economics and sociology, as well as psychology; consequently, research in this area draws upon a broader range of concepts and methods. In particular, costs and normative pressures play a significant role in models of consumer decision processes; and quantitative model building using survey and aggregate-level data complements experimental approaches. Recent contributions to this area emerge from efforts to integrate insights from the different discipline bases.

Information Processing and Judgment

A common assumption in consumer psychology is that the impact of a message on learning and judgment is influenced by the elaboration the message receives in a rich associative memory network. Recent research investigates factors that affect elaboration, and thereby the learning and judgment of a message. Work also examines the role of cognitive resources with the idea that elaboration is a resource-demanding activity. Finally, considerable attention has been given to the ways in which individual differences and contextual factors affect processing and judgment.

ELABORATION It is well documented that the vividness of a stimulus message affects learning and persuasiveness of the message. Recent work qualifies this observation by identifying preconditions for vividness effects. Specifically, the recall advantage of vivid pictorial information can be neutralized by prompting people to elaborate on the stimulus material (Costley & Brucks 1992, Unnava & Brunkrant 1991a). Similarly, the greater attitudinal impact of vivid information in relation to pallid presentations can be eliminated by encouraging stimulus elaboration (McGill & Anand 1989b). These outcomes imply that elaboration of a stimulus message can enhance learning and the favorableness of judgments whether vividness or some other device is used to induce elaboration.

Music is another factor that appears to stimulate elaboration. MacInnis & Park (1991) note that two characteristics of music, the extent to which it arouses emotion-laden memories and its correspondence to other ad cues, influence the extent of message processing. This observation is consistent with Scott's (1990) view that music represents a form of language.

Message elaboration also is influenced by whether consumers relate information to themselves and to their own experiences. Relating a message to positive self-experiences inhibits message learning (Baumgartner et al 1992) and enhances ad evaluation (Baumgartner et al 1992, Bone & Ellen 1992). Self-reference also enhances brand evaluation, provided that the links between the advocated product and the self are made salient (Debevec & Romeo 1992). Apparently, the positive affect in self-associations is transferred to the ad and/or to the brand, but the resource demands attendant to self-associations undermine detailed message learning.

RESOURCE AVAILABILITY Because elaboration of stimulus information is a resource-demanding activity, variations in resource availability affect message processing and evaluation. Consistent with this notion is the repeated finding that when audience involvement is low, peripheral cues such as the message source affect judgment, presumably because processing such cues requires few cognitive resources. By contrast, when involvement is high, more resource-demanding central cues such as the message content determine judgment. Along these lines, Schumann et al (1990) demonstrate that for low involvement consumers, advertising wearout can be forestalled by cosmetic variation in the ad execution (a peripheral cue), and for high involvement consumers by a substantive variation in the ad content. Similarly, Maheswaran & Meyers-Levy (1990) observe that under low involvement, limited processing results in persuasion being determined by the favorableness of the message frame such that positively framed messages are more persuasive than negatively framed ones. However, the more detailed processing that occurs under high involvement appears to focus attention on message consequences, with the result that negatively framed messages are more persuasive (see also Homer & Yoon 1992).

Other studies qualify existing notions of how involvement affects central and peripheral processing. There is evidence that a message source can operate as either a central or a peripheral cue (Homer & Kahle 1990) and that some processing of central and peripheral cues occurs at both high and low levels of involvement (Andrews & Shimp 1990).

The importance of cognitive resources in stimulating elaboration is also documented in work on the congruity between a new product description or experience and an activated schema. Moderate incongruity is found to induce greater information search (Ozanne et al 1992, Stayman et al 1992) and more favorable evaluation than either extreme incongruity or congruity (Meyers-Levy & Tybout 1989, Stayman et al 1992). Apparently, incongruity prompts the activation of resources and subsequent processing leads to successful resolution of moderate incongruity (but not extreme incongruity), a satisfying process that is reflected in enhanced product evaluations.

Finally, several other devices appear to enhance the resources available and thereby the extent of elaboration. When people are not highly involved in an issue, a near miss in achieving a favorable outcome stimulates greater elaboration than a more distant miss, but when issue involvement is high no such effect of temporal proximity is observed (Meyers-Levy & Maheswaran 1992). Repeating a message also enhances the resources available for elaboration (Anand & Sternthal 1990). When the message is complex, repetition induces elaboration of its content, which increases appeal persuasiveness. When the message is simple, repetition, at least up to a point, results in elaboration of counterarguments thereby reducing persuasion. It should be noted, however, that repetition can also induce favorable judgments without stimulating message elaboration by enhancing the perception of familiarity (Hawkins & Hoch 1992).

ELABORATION, RESOURCES, AND JUDGMENTS Studies of inference-making offer insight into how elaboration and cognitive resources operate in the judgment process. When data about a product attribute is missing, consumers often do not infer the attribute's value (Dick et al 1990), even though they may be cognizant of this gap in information (Simmons & Lynch 1991). This is probably because making appropriate inferences about missing attributes requires resources that consumers are often unable or unwilling to devote to the task. However, when personal or situational factors do activate substantial cognitive resources (Gardial & Biehal 1991, Stayman & Kardes 1992, Yi 1990b), inferences about missing attributes are based on accessible and diagnostic information (Dick et al 1990, Ross & Creyer 1992).

Complex inferencing also occurs when information is acquired through conversation (a neglected mode of communication in consumer research), and this is argued to affect both elaboration of message arguments and memory

(Thomas 1992). Obviously, not all inferential processing is detailed and effortful. Erroneous inferences, such as confusing one brand with another, may occur when consumers lack the ability and motivation to do detailed processing and instead employ heuristics (see Foxman et al 1990, 1992).

The role of elaboration and resources in judgment is also illustrated by work on product categorization and on interference effects. An effortful and normatively correct analytical categorization rule appears to be employed only when consumers' memory load is light, relevant attribute information is perceptually salient, and an intentional processing goal is provided. When these conditions are not met, categorization is based on salient but noncriterial attributes (Hutchinson & Alba 1991). Similarly, the presence of competing brand information may inhibit elaboration of focal brand information at encoding, and thereby undermine focal brand recall and evaluation, but this interference may be offset by reducing the resources required at retrieval (Keller 1991b). Likewise, prompting retrieval of a brand may interfere with efforts to recall other brands in the same category (by inhibiting the activation of alternative pathways), though not the recall of an elaborately encoded preferred brand (Miniard et al 1990b, see also Keller 1991a).

More generally, there is evidence that extensive elaboration can have varying effects on memory and judgment. It may provide multiple retrieval pathways, thereby enhancing recall, while at the same time cuing a broad array of concepts that can interfere with access to a particular piece of information (see Meyers-Levy 1989b). Increasing elaboration also may shift the focus of elaboration between the message and one's own thoughts (Anand & Sternthal 1990). Thus, predicting the specific effects of elaboration requires considerable calibration of materials and procedures to the subjects and setting of interest.

CONCEPTUAL DEVELOPMENTS Recent work on elaboration reinforces the view that elaboration mediates the judgments people make, and the extent to which people engage in elaboration depends on the resources available for this task (see also Petty et al 1991 for a longitudinal review). An extension of this concept is the view that there are two types of elaboration: relational, which is sensitive to linkages between objects, and item-specific, which is sensitive to the uniqueness of an object (Kent & Machleit 1990, Meyers-Levy 1991). Initial findings suggest that this distinction may represent an important advance in explaining the judgment process. Similarly, the importance of involvement to elaboration has stimulated work that distinguishes enduring and situational involvement and examines the unique effects of each type of involvement (Andrews et al 1990, Laczniak et al 1989, Richins et al 1992, Venkatraman 1989). Currently, it appears that a simple additive model is adequate to account for the impact of these two types of involvement, though verification of this view awaits further research. Finally, the role of incongruity in elaboration has prompted work to distinguish between two dimensions of incongruity: expectancy and relevance (Heckler & Childers 1992).

On the dependent variable side, several measures have been suggested to enhance detecting the process by which judgments are made. For example, although miscomprehension or noncomprehension of messages is pervasive (see Jacoby & Hoyer 1989), understanding of the comprehension process is limited. Mick (1992) provides insight into this issue by identifing four levels of comprehension and noting that deeper comprehension is associated with greater learning and more favorable judgments. Rothschild & Hyun (1990) find that stimulus recognition can be predicted by certain patterns of electrical response on EEG measures.

INDIVIDUAL DIFFERENCES IN PROCESSING Considerable research has examined how individual differences affect information processing and judgment. For example, men's categorization strategy is more sensitive to hemispheric primes than is women's, perhaps reflecting men's greater hemispheric specialization (Meyers-Levy 1989a). When processing persuasive communications, men exhibit a conceptually-driven orientation, which is manifested in their focus on overall message themes and the schematic knowledge that it triggers (Meyers-Levy & Maheswaran 1991). By contrast, women appear to be data-driven in that they are more reliant on the details of the message (Meyers-Levy & Sternthal 1991).

While these gender differences may be attributable to socialization processes that encourage men to be agentic or goal-oriented and women to be communal and externally focused, some qualification is appropriate. Gender differences only emerge when stimulus and task demands do not overwhelm the relatively subtle differences in men's and women's processing orientations. Gender can also influence consumers' response to the content of product messages: consumers are found to prefer products that are described in terms congruent with their self-perceived schema for masculinity or femininity (Worth et al 1992).

Prior knowledge also affects processing and judgment. Both experts and novices can be motivated to engage in detailed message processing, but the type of information that prompts such processing and the nature of the elaboration varies. Attribute information prompts experts to engage in detailed, evaluative elaboration, whereas benefit information leads novices to detailed, but relatively literal elaboration (Maheswaran & Sternthal 1990). Consistent with this general view, Gardial & Biehal (1991) observe that experts' inferencing about missing information increases when an ad claim is factual and decreases when the claim is evaluative, while novices fail to make inferences irrespective of claim type. Thus, recent research reinforces the view that experts are more conceptually-driven and novices are more data-driven, an observation that suggests an interesting parallel between gender and expertise.

The impact of consumers' age on judgment processes also remains a topic of research interest. John & Sujan (1990a) find that young children are more prone to using perceptually salient attributes rather than more relevant, underlying attributes in categorizing products. But this tendency to ignore underlying attributes can be overcome by a prompt to consider such information when children are 6–7 years old, though not when they are 4–5 years old. This suggests that 6–7 year olds' deficit stems from the failure to invoke the appropriate strategy, whereas 4–5 year olds' deficit reflects a diminished ability to employ such a strategy. Four to five year olds, however, do use the perceptual attribute information in a diagnostic manner (John & Sujan 1990b). In sum, even very young children are more sophisticated than previously thought, and this sophistication increases systematically with age. Because of the difficulties young children have distinguishing between similar categories, such as competing product classes, additions to a choice set from one category affect choices in a competing category to a greater extent for younger children than for older children (John & Lakshmi-Ratan 1992).

Peracchio (1992) explores age differences in learning about events such as how one exchanges an unwanted product. Like John, she finds that relative to older children, younger children exhibit learning deficits that can be overcome when the presentation of the experimental materials and the response formats are tailored to their encoding and retrieval capabilities. Along these lines, Macklin & Machleit (1989) have developed and validated the Preschool Attitude Scale (PSA), which accommodates the processing capabilities of children 3–5 years old, and Peracchio (1990) has outlined how experimental procedures can be tailored to young children's competencies.

Processing differences also exist at the opposite end of the age spectrum. It appears that deficits previously reported for the elderly may be attributable to their increased field dependence and that this processing limitation can be overcome when perceptual cues make the appropriate decision making strategy highly salient (Cole & Gaeth 1990, see also related findings by Ensley & Pride 1991).

CONTEXT EFFECTS Research has examined how context, or the background in which a target stimulus is presented, affects judgments of the target. Evidence suggests that the affect associated with a contextual conditioning stimulus becomes associated with a target unconditioned stimulus when consumers recognize the relationship between the two (Allen & Janiszewski 1989, Shimp et al 1991). Similarly, consumers' attitudes toward an ad are influenced by the affect associated with the editorial environment in which the ad is presented

(Kamins et al 1991, Mathur & Chattopadhyay 1991, Schumann & Thorson 1990, Yi 1990a).

Context also appears to influence the cognitions activated about a contiguously presented target and thus affect target evaluation (Herr 1989, Yi 1990a, 1990c). Herr finds that contextual information affects target evaluation, but only for consumers who are knowledgeable about the product category. For these people, an assimilation effect occurs if the contextual information is composed of moderate exemplars of the category and the target product is ambiguous, whereas a contrast effect is found when extreme exemplars compose the context or when the target is unambiguous.

A third dimension of context is its resource-demanding nature (see Mundorf et al 1991). Context appears to usurp cognitive resources that might otherwise be available for processing a target. Janiszewski (1990a) reports that the comprehension of an attended target is interfered with by the concurrent presentation of an unattended context. However, this deficit can be overcome when stimulus analysis engages one hemisphere and context engages the other (Janiszewski 1990b). Anand & Sternthal (1992) observe that a program context affects the resources available for evaluating a contiguously presented target ad. Meyers-Levy (1989a) demonstrates that contexts can be devised to prompt the activation of resources fostering either holistic or more differentiated categorization judgments.

Future research might address how the affective, cognitive, and resource dimensions of context interrelate to determine target evaluations. Such investigations should take precautions to distinguish between context effects induced by a change in the mental representation of a target and those that merely involve an adjustment in the use of a response scale (Lynch et al 1991).

Models of Processing Outputs

ATTITUDE TOWARD THE AD Research on the antecedents and consequences of consumers' attitude toward the ad (A_{ad}) has focused on the dual-mediation model in which A_{ad} is hypothesized to have both a direct effect on attitude toward the brand (A_b) and an indirect effect via brand cognitions (C_b). While some findings cast doubt on the indirect link (e.g. MacKenzie & Lutz 1989) or raise questions about the direction of the causal relationship between A_{ad} and A_b (e.g. Madden & Ajzen 1991), a meta-analysis of 47 data studies suggests that the dual-mediation model provides a reasonable account of extant data (Brown & Stayman 1992).

Despite the support for the dual-mediation model, there is substantial variation in the strength of A_{ad} effects, in part, as a result of how A_{ad}, C_b, and A_b are defined and measured. An indirect effect of A_{ad} on A_b is observed when a cognitive response measure of C_b is employed, but not when a close-ended measure of C_b is used (Muehling et al 1991). Further, the link between C_b and A_b is stronger, and the direct role of A_{ad} on A_b is diminished when image attributes are incorporated into measures of C_b (Mittal 1990). A_{ad}'s direct effect on A_b is not limited to low involvement situations (e.g. Dröge 1989), but rather is present irrespective of the level of involvement when it is measured as an overall index composed of consumers' responses to both peripheral (non-claim) and central (claim) cues in the ad (Miniard et al 1990a). More generally, A_{ad} effects tend to be strengthened by methods that minimize other sources of variation (e.g. use of homogeneous subject pools, laboratory settings; see Brown & Stayman 1992). Further research should attend to issues of construct validity and to the magnitude of A_{ad} effects under natural viewing conditions.

Situational and individual difference factors that affect motivation to process the ad also contribute to variation in A_{ad} effects. Specifically, when motivation to process a message is low, ad execution elements are the primary determinants of A_{ad}, and thus A_{ad} has a substantial, direct effect on A_b. When motivation to process the message is high, both ad execution and ad claim elements may influence A_{ad}, and as a result, A_{ad} has indirect (i.e. mediated by C_b), as well as direct effects on A_b (but see specific studies for nuances on this general pattern of outcomes, Dröge 1989, Hastak & Olson 1989, Laczniak & Carlson 1989, MacKenzie & Spreng 1992, Miniard et al 1990a, Muehling et al 1991; see Homer 1990 for some contrary evidence).

On the basis of the considerable evidence for A_{ad} effects on A_b, one plausible conclusion is that advertisers should strive to develop well-liked ads. A recent study, however, suggests that the immediate, positive effect of a likable ad on brand attitude may mask a liability at delay. This may result when attention at encoding is limited so that elaboration of a likable ad occurs at the expense of elaboration on the brand claims and brand claim information becomes inaccessible at a later time. As a result, brand attitude after a delay may be less favorable for a highly likable ad than for a neutral one (see Chattopadhyay & Nedugnadi 1992). Further research is needed to explore the conditions under which a favorable A_{ad} will be an asset versus a liability.

The weight of evidence for A_{ad} effects on A_b has generated interest in the antecedents of A_{ad}. MacKenzie & Lutz (1989) examine effects of advertising, advertiser, and ad credibility and find that advertiser credibility mediates the relationship between advertising credibility and ad credibility. Burke & Edell (1989) explore how the feelings evoked by an ad affect both A_{ad} and A_b. They find that upbeat, warm, and negative dimensions of feelings influence A_{ad} and A_b, either directly or indirectly. These effects are robust over ad repetition levels, product categories, and measurement delay periods (see also Homer & Yoon 1992 for related findings, see Batra & Holbrook 1990 for a typology of affective responses to advertising, and see Stayman & Batra 1991 for the storage and retrieval of affective responses in memory). Further research examining feelings both as an antecedent to A_{ad} and to A_b is needed.

INTENTIONS AND BEHAVIOR A second line of research explores the conditions under which attitudes and other variables predict intentions and behavior. One approach has been to explore aspects of attitude strength that increase attitude-behavior consistency. Several studies indicate that providing direct experience or increasing the number of exposures to an ad advocating a product enhances attitude accessibility, and thus, the attitude-behavior correlation (Berger & Mitchell 1989, Fazio et al 1989). Direct experience and repeated ad exposure also have been shown to influence attitude confidence, a second dimension of attitude strength (Berger & Mitchell 1989). Attitude confidence appears to have a greater moderating effect on attitude-behavior consistency than does accessibility when consumers are engaged in deliberative (high involvement/personally relevant) decision making (Berger 1992). Perhaps this occurs because consumers focus on diagnostic information in deliberative situations and confidence is related to diagnosticity. If so, accessibility may have greater influence than confidence when consumers make spontaneous decisions, though further research is needed to examine this idea.

Similarly, Bagozzi and colleagues (Bagozzi & Yi 1989, Bagozzi et al 1989) suggest that attitude-behavior consistency may be contingent on how well-formed intentions are and how much effort is required to enact a behavior. Bagozzi & Warshaw (1990) explore the observation that consumers often perceive behavior to be subject to impediments, and therefore, to require effort or trying. They propose and provide some initial empirical support for a theory of trying.

Bagozzi et al (1992) examine variables that moderate the attitude-behavior relationship. They contrast state-oriented consumers, who are thought to be deliberative and not easily moved to act, with action-oriented consumers, who are characterized by an inherent readiness to act. The intentions of state-oriented consumers are influenced primarily by normative considerations, whereas the intentions of action-oriented consumers are determined by attitudes.

A number of studies have pursued the role of normative pressure or interpersonal influence in determining intentions and behavior. LaTour & Manrai (1989) demonstrate that interpersonal pressure to comply (normative influence) interacts with information about how one's behavior can help others (informational influence) to increase blood donation behavior substantially. Frenzen & Davis (1990) report that social ties between buyers and sellers increase purchase likelihood, though not the amount purchased. Childers & Rao (1992) document cultural variation in the extent to which consumers are influenced by reference groups and observe that the intergenerational family may be an important reference group for private products and necessities, where little peer influence is likely. Fisher & Price (1992) provide a framework for understanding how superordinate group influence and perceived consumption visibility combine to affect normative outcomes (i.e. expected social approval from referents), and thereby influence intentions to adopt a product (see also Stayman & Deshpande's 1989 discussion of perceived ethnicity). Rose et al (1992) report that group conformity pressure is more likely to be resisted if the individual makes attributions to explain the group behavior. Finally, two studies explore methods of measuring individual differences in sensitivity to interpersonal influence. Bearden et al (1989) offer a validated scale (incorporating both informational and normative factors), for measuring consumers' susceptibility to interpersonal influence. Bearden & Rose (1990) examine an alternative individual difference scale, Lennox & Wolfe's attention to social comparison information (ATSCI) scale, and observe that ATSCI moderates the relative importance of normative consequences on behavior intentions and that higher ATSCI scores are associated with greater conformity in a social setting.

There also have been efforts to incorporate feelings/emotions into the prediction of behavior. Batra & Ahtola (1990) suggest separating attitude into a sensory/hedonic component and a utilitarian/functional component. These two components are argued to have roots in different product attributes and to influence overall attitude toward the product and behavior differentially as a function of the type of product and the consumer's purchase goals. By contrast, Allen et al (1992) treat emotion as distinct from attitudes and find that self-reports of emotive experiences associated with past behaviors account for substantive variance in behavior beyond that captured by traditional attitude measures (which are largely utilitarian in Batra & Ahtola's categorization scheme). This line of work may advance understanding of behaviors for which attitudes provide little insight (e.g. habitual behaviors).

Finally, recent work suggests that the prediction of behavior may be facilitated by focusing on the psychological states associated with individual difference variables rather than on observable individual differences. For example, perceptual age increases with chronological age, but is more youthful for married, high income individuals; and younger perceptual age is associated with more active lifestyles and high self-confidence and fashion interest (Wilkes 1992). Similarly, felt ethnicity is a better predictor of consumption choices than simple ethnic classification (Stayman & Deshpande 1989).

CHOICE PROCESSES The current literature on choice processes explains consumers' choices and related behaviors in terms of cost/benefit or effort/accuracy tradeoffs that are adaptive for consumers given their ability and motivation to process information in various settings. (see Alba et al 1991, Bettman et al 1991, Payne et al 1992 for recent longitudinal reviews of the literatures on memory and decision making, consumer decision making, and behavioral decision research, respectively).

The literature on information search provides an illustration of such tradeoffs (see Ozanne et al 1992). Processing costs are increased by search activities such as adding alternatives to the consideration set, examining more attribute information for each alternative, and considering multiple sources of information (Hauser & Wernerfelt 1990). Consumers seem to consider these costs as justified when their subjective knowledge is high and prior experience is limited. These conditions enable them to benefit from further information, as well as reduce the likelihood that a satisfactory alternative has already been identified (Srinivasan & Ratchford 1991, Urbany et al 1989a). Increasing the similarity of alternatives in the consideration set is also thought to influence the perceived benefits of search, though the direction of this effect is difficult to anticipate; further search may be seen either as helpful in discriminating between the alternatives or as unnecessary because the similarity between alternatives reduces choice risk (Urbany et al 1989a). Finally, consumers appear more willing to bear the cost of extensive search when the added information facilitates the strategy that they are trying to use (e.g. creating images of the alternatives as a basis for choice; see McGill & Anand 1989a) or when bargaining is not an option (Brucks & Schurr 1990).

These insights into when consumers will search are important because there is evidence that search affects subsequent choice. For example, the likelihood of purchase and of brand switching is reduced when situational factors such as time pressure and lack of familiarity with a store decrease consumers' ability and motivation to search (Park et al 1989). By contrast, the innovativeness of consumers' choices is enhanced by gathering large quantities of detailed information from impartial sources (Ross & Robertson 1991).

The process by which consumers choose between alternatives also reflects a balancing of costs and benefits. Strategies that minimize effort are employed when they are perceived to produce satisfactory or "good enough" choices or when consumers lack the motivation to engage in more effortful decision making. Thus, consumers may choose a brand in the consideration set on the assumption that familiarity implies popularity and good quality (Hoyer & Brown 1990). Brand accessibility also may influence preference and choice without altering brand evaluations; consumers have been found to choose the most preferred brand from among the set of those that readily come to mind (Nedungadi 1990). More generally, Simonson (1989) suggests that consumers favor brands whose choice can be justified easily and intuitively, a tendency that can explain attraction and compromise biases in choice. Corfman (1991) observes that consumers with low task involvement compare brands in an abstract, holistic manner to minimize their effort.

High task demands encourage strategies that simplify the choice process (Klein & Yadav 1989). Accordingly, framing effects have been observed when the choice task requires consumers to recall brand information from memory, but not when the information is available during decision making (Dhar & Simonson 1992, see also Qualls & Puto 1989 for a discussion of framing effects in the context of industrial buying). Similarly, consumers select a broad variety of products to cope with the demanding task of simultaneously choosing multiple items from a product category for consumption over time (Simonson 1990b, Simonson & Winer 1992). Consumers also appear to increase their effort to simplify, as evidenced by more biased choices, when the similarity among brands increases task demands (Glazer et al 1991).

Particular attention has been devoted to investigating choices involving noncomparable alternatives (i.e. products from different categories), a task that would seem to challenge consumers' decision making capabilities. As the noncomparability of products in a consideration set increases, bases of comparison necessarily become more abstract (Corfman 1991). Of interest is whether more abstract comparison allows consumers to cope with task demands by capitalizing on efficient, conceptually-driven processing (top-down) or by activating the greater cognitive resources needed to engage in effortful, constructive processing (bottom-up). Corfman (1991) suggests that low involvement consumers use abstraction as a simplification strategy, implying a top-down approach. Johnson (1989) argues that comparison of multiple products from different categories is likely to evoke a hierarchical top-down process, but comparison of single products from multiple categories leads to more effortful bottom-up processing. Park & Smith (1989) qualify the latter notion by demonstrating that even choice between single, noncomparable products will be top-down if a well-defined goal is provided or can be inferred from the comparability of products at the level of general needs. Thus, consumers faced with noncomparable alternatives operate as cognitive misers who devote substantial resources to the task only when less effortful approaches cannot be employed. Recent work by Alba et al (1992) extends research on noncomparable choice by noting that simplifying strategies also are evoked when within category alternatives are noncomparable because equivalent attribute information is not available.

Consumers often simplify choice processes, but they remain sensitive to task complexities such as the level of perceived risk. Huber & Klein (1991) observe that the rigidity with which consumers employ attribute cutoffs in a noncompensatory model reflects the quality of available data, while Kahn & Meyer (1991) find that variability in attribute importance weights is affected by whether the attribute is framed as a loss or a gain. McGill & Anand (1989a) find greater evidence of a conservative, noncompensatory approach to choice when evoking prior experience is not an appropriate strategy (i.e. when choosing for someone else).

Research has also explored individual differences in choice. Protocols collected by Gardner & Hill (1989) suggest that individuals in a positive mood employ choice processes that reflect greater concern for needs high in Maslow's hierarchy, are more experientially based, and include more sensory thoughts than do individuals in a negative mood. Steenkamp & Baumgartner (1992) find that consumers seek more variety and take more risk in their choices as their optimum stimulation level increases.

Another issue is how consumers combine input from multiple sources during choice. When husbands and wives make joint decisions, equity is a key concern and leads to choices centered within the negotiation set (Menasco & Curry 1989). When groups make decisions, a shared cognitive structure is thought to emerge from group interactions and this structure appears to function like individuals' cognitive structures in guiding choice (Ward & Reingen 1990).

Finally, a comparison of actual supermarket choices over an extended period of time with those observed in a one-time laboratory simulation revealed that the laboratory data provided reasonable approximations of market shares and consumers' promotion sensitivity (Burke et al 1992). Nevertheless, caution in generalizing from the lab to the field is appropriate because certain laboratory procedures such as concurrent verbalization have been found to affect memory and, therefore, choice (Biehal & Chakravarti 1989).

POST-PURCHASE SATISFACTION Researchers continue to attend to the affect following choice and product experience. Historically, postpurchase satisfaction has been conceptualized as a function of the extent to which product experience confirms/disconfirms product performance expectations (see van Raaij 1991). Hoch & Deighton (1989) suggest that product experience is subjective; therefore, the effects of such experience are determined by consumers' familiarity with the domain, their motivation to learn, and the ambiguity of the information environment. Consistent with this view, Miniard et al (1992a) find that when the consumption experience is ambiguous, preconsumption mood affects satisfaction.

Other research explores affective antecedents of satisfaction in greater detail. Westbrook & Oliver (1991) identify prototypes of emotional response associated with various levels of satisfaction and suggest that two distinct emotional responses, pleasure linked to surprise and pleasure linked to interest, accompany high satisfaction. Individual differences in the desired emotional intensity of product experiences also may moderate the link between emotion and satisfaction (Hanna & Wagle 1989). These emotional responses and preferences warrant attention in future research.

A variety of factors beyond product experience also influence satisfaction. Satisfaction is enhanced by using a product more frequently and in unanticipated ways (Ram & Jung 1991), and by moderate deviation (versus no deviation or extreme deviation) from product category expectations (Stayman et al 1992). Further, satisfaction is greater when the transaction is perceived to be fair, which can be the case even when consumers have an advantage over the merchant (Oliver & Swan 1989a, b).

Interest is growing in dynamic effects of postpurchase satisfaction. Tse et al (1990) conceptualize satisfaction as a multidimensional process that unfolds over time. Mazursky & Geva (1989) demonstrate that although postpurchase satisfaction is an important predictor of subsequent purchase intentions immediately after the product experience, its relative importance declines over time. Bolton & Drew (1991) observe that satisfaction affects judgments of service quality and value. More generally, Simonson (1990a) observes that choices affect consumers' inferences about the importance of attributes in the choice process.

While the satisfaction literature explores affect resulting from a product choice, the literature on regret and responsibility examines the related notion that foregone product experiences influence judgments. Simonson (1992) finds that anticipating how one would feel about a wrong decision leads to more immediate purchase and greater preference for a well-known higher-priced brand over a lesser-known, lower-priced brand. Further, errors in choice caused by selection of lesser-known, lower-priced brands lead to greater responsibility but less regret than errors associated with well-known, higher-priced brands. McGill (1990) observes that product failure is less likely to be attributed to the manufacturer when consumers are perceived as having been able to avoid the failure (see also Hui & Bateson 1991). Counterfactual reasoning provides a framework for understanding these outcomes and for further research on the topic (see Kahneman & Miller 1986).

RESPONSES TO MARKETER-INITIATED STIMULI

The research described in this section focuses on how consumers respond to specific variations in marketing stimuli. Advertising stimuli continue to capture the greatest attention from consumer psychologists, but the effects of sales promotion, pricing, and product variations are also explored. New measures of consumers values that are likely to moderate responses to these marketing stimuli are noted.

Advertising

Recent research adds to the extensive literature on the effects of advertising variations on information processing, attitude, and choice. The research retains its traditional focus on message content and executional cues and increasingly examines media planning issues, such as those pertaining to advertising repetition effects and the impact of programming on contiguously presented ads.

FACTUAL CONTENT OF CLAIMS Researchers interested in the effects of message content continue to focus on the distinction between factual messages based on arguments and lectures and those subjective, evaluative, feeling-based messages often associated with drama (Wells 1989). Factual claims are considered more believable than evaluative claims (Ford et al 1990). They also directly lead to expressions of belief in the appeal as a result of increased cognitive argumentation/response (Deighton et al 1989); they prompt more inferences by experts perhaps because they serve as better memory retrieval cues (Gardial & Biehal 1991); but they may decrease viewing time as a result of diminished arousal and less favorable emotional/attitudinal reaction (Olney et al 1991). Moreover, factual messages are seen as increasingly convincing and persuasive as an individual's need for cognition increases (Venkatraman et al 1990). Factual ads appear to focus attention on claims, making credibility a salient issue, and allowing the viewer to draw a conclusion based on product information, which may be attractive to those with the ability (expertise) and motivation (need-for-cognition) to do so.

In contrast, evaluative ads evoke a more holistic and emotional response in which verisimilitude and the ability of the ad to elicit feelings guide attitude (Deighton et al 1989). These ads might be effective when cognitive resources are limited. An unequivocal interpretation of the processing differences is difficult, however, because the factual/evaluative distinction encompasses a variety of differences (e.g. in credibility, verifiability, involvement, imagery, and directness of audience address).

COMPARATIVE ADVERTISING CLAIMS Using a categorization framework, Snyder (1992) argues that the valence of the anchor used to position the new brand in a category influences the effectiveness of comparative advertising. She finds that brand attribute evaluation is more favorable with direct comparison, which uses a highly favorable exemplar as an anchor, than with indirect comparison, which implies only a moderately favorable prototype as an anchor. Further, both forms of comparative advertising are more favorable than noncomparative advertising, which does not provide any favorable anchor. Others report that the extent of processing influences comparative advertising effects. Dröge's (1989) findings suggest that comparative advertising generates greater message elaboration, which reduces the impact of A_{ad} as a peripheral cue in the formation of A_b. Similarly, Muehling et al (1990) find that comparative advertising generates greater perceived message relevance, self-reported attention, message elaboration, and message recall than noncomparative advertising.

A number of factors moderate the relative effect of comparative and non-comparative advertising (see Rogers & Williams 1989). Comparative ads enhance purchase intentions for low-share brands by attracting attention, but diminish intentions for established brands by increasing awareness of competitive brands and creating confusion about the ad sponsor (Pechmann & Stewart 1990). Gotlieb & Sarel (1991) find that comparative advertising enhances purchase intentions when a higher credibility source activates higher message involvement (i.e. greater message processing), and Pechmann & Ratneshwar (1991) demonstrate that brand familiarity and the typicality of the focal attribute moderate the categorization and inferential processes elicited by direct comparative ads.

OTHER CLAIM VARIATIONS Researchers have examined several claim variations that have failed to exhibit reliable effects in prior research. Fazio et al (1992) demonstrate that delaying brand identification until the end of an ad can be advantageous for unfamiliar brands because it may strengthen the associations between the brand and the product category, thereby facilitating later brand retrieval. Sawyer & Howard (1991) and Stayman & Kardes (1992) demonstrate that ads with omitted conclusions are more persuasive than those with explicitly stated conclusions when the audience is involved and, therefore, motivated to draw the omitted conclusion. Similarly, questions at the end of a commercial are more effective at generating information processing than are concluding statements (Howard & Burnkrant 1990). Other researchers have examined two-sided ads, which although generally viewed as highly credible, rarely have been found to be more persuasive than one-sided ads. Pechmann (1992) demonstrates that two-sided ads can enhance product judgments when the featured attributes are negatively correlated (as opposed to uncorrelated), because favorable correlational inferences as well as increased perceptions of advertiser honesty are available to offset the disclosure of negative information. Kamins et al (1989) find that two-sided ads enhance evaluations and purchase intentions in the context of celebrity endorsements because the higher credibility of the ad complements the celebrity, who is generally likable but not particularly credible.

PICTORIAL IMAGES AND VIVID STIMULI There is evidence that picture-based information is processed similarly to verbal information in that both generate the same types of inferences (Smith 1991) and that product-relevant information in pictures can serve as arguments in high involvement processing (Miniard et al 1991). Why, then, do pictures dominate verbal information in inference formation (Smith 1991) and enhance memory? It appears that pictures, like other forms of vivid stimuli such as concrete language (Kelley et al 1989), self-related ad copy (Bone & Ellen 1992), and in-person rather than printed information

(Herr et al 1991), increase attention and prompt elaboration, making pictorial information more accessible. This greater accessibility may manifest itself in enhanced learning (Unnava & Burnkrant 1991a) and in more favorable product judgments when other highly diagnostic information is not accessible (Costley & Brucks 1992, Herr et al 1991). Similarly, the attractiveness of an ad picture influences choice only when brand attribute information is nondiagnostic (Miniard et al 1992b).

HUMOR Weinberger & Campbell (1990/1991) document that the effect of humor is dependent on product type and the relevance of the humor to the product. Humorless ads prompt greater recall and persuasion for high involvement products associated with thinking decisions. By contrast, relevant humor produces superior recall for high involvement products and superior persuasion for low involvement products when decisions are feeling-based. Further, the effectiveness of humor is enhanced when it is relevant (Scott et al 1990), and humorous ads are more persuasive than nonhumorous ads when consumers have favorable preexisting attitudes, but humor may be counterproductive with negative preexisting attitudes (Chattopadhyay & Basu 1990). These studies suggest that humor increases attention and processing, while prior attitude and the relevance of the humor to the product moderate the direction of processing.

MUSIC The literature has moved beyond the narrow view that music in advertising influences product preferences via classical conditioning. In fact, Kellaris & Cox (1989) demonstrate that the previously reported classical conditioning effects may have been because of demand artifacts. It is now clear that music can play a role in both peripheral and central routes to persuasion (MacInnis & Park 1991). Music can influence consumers via their mood (see Bruner 1990). For example, Alpert & Alpert (1990) report that sad music has a negative effect on listener mood yet enhances purchase intentions compared to happier music. In addition, music uses processing resources, which leaves fewer available to process product-relevant information. This diminishes recall of product information (Gorn et al 1991) and also forestalls advertising wearout from repetition (Anand & Sternthal 1990). Finally, music can influence consumers by conveying semantic content in a way that may be less likely to generate counterarguing than a verbal message (Scott 1990).

SOURCE EFFECTS Source research has shifted away from its traditional focus on source credibility toward advertiser reputation and celebrity endorsement (but see Ratneshwar & Chaiken 1991). Advertiser reputation has effects similar to that of source credibility (Goldberg & Hartwick 1990, MacKenzie & Lutz 1989). Celebrity expertise, but not trustworthiness or attractiveness, positively influences purchase intention (Ohanian 1991). McCracken (1989b) argues that the celebrity endorsement process is more than the effect of source expertise, trustworthiness, and attractiveness on the acquisition of product information. Celebrity effectiveness results from the transfer to the endorsed product of the symbolism associated with the celebrity. Consistent with this concept of meaning transfer, Cohen (1992) finds that advertisements with Asian spokespersons produce more favorable attitudes toward high technology engineering products than do ads with white spokespersons, while the reverse is observed for products associated with status.

ADVERTISING CONTEXT AND AFFECTIVE STATE There is growing evidence that mood that is induced by the advertising context, or that is brought to the viewing situation, affects consumer response to advertising (Schumann & Thorson 1990, but see Murry et al 1992). The affective tone of reactions to a typical ad are biased in the direction of the mood (Batra & Stayman 1990, Mathur & Chattopadhyay 1991, Yi 1990a). However, Kamins et al (1991) observe that the direction of the bias is moderated by the affective tone of the ad: bias is in the direction of the mood with happy ads but in the opposite direction for sad ads. Thus, persuasion appears to be greater when there is congruence between the mood and the affective tone of the ad.

Positive moods can decrease the extent of message processing (Batra & Stayman 1990, Kuykendall & Keating 1990) or increase it (Mathur & Chattopadhyay 1991). Factors that might account for the conflicting results include the specific mood induced, message medium (broadcast or print), type of ad (emotional or rational), source of mood induction (media vehicle or prior induction), and the viewer's desire to maintain the context-induced mood (Schumann & Thorson 1990). Future research may also find that context-induced mood leads the viewer to focus on different elements of the ad (see Gardner & Hill 1989).

Mood is not the only dimension of the viewer's state influenced by program context (Hoffman & Batra 1991). Involving contexts can increase the effectiveness of advertising in terms of recall, attitudes, and intention (Sullivan 1990). Contexts that increase physiological arousal appear to impair the acquisition of information from ads initially (Mundorf et al 1991), but may eventually enhance ad learning and intensify attitudinal and behavioral responses (Singh & Hitchon 1989).

Most research examining the effect of advertising context has focused on the mood or arousal level induced by the context. However, Murry et al (1992) found that a viewer's liking of a program has a greater influence on advertising evaluation than does the induced mood. As discussed earlier, other researchers have examined context effects associated with classical conditioning (Allen & Janiszewski 1989, Shimp et al 1991), encoding interference (Janiszewski

1990a, Keller 1991b), assimilation/contrast (Herr 1989), and priming (Kleine & Kernan 1991).

AD REPETITION The literature on advertising repetition has gone beyond a narrow view of advertising wearout as a diminished attitudinal response following multiple exposures to an ad. Anand & Sternthal (1990) demonstrate that high levels of repetition can enhance, rather than diminish, attitudinal response when messages are extremely easy to process. Other research emphasizes how the effect of repetition is not the same for all elements of attitude. Wearout can occur for the affective evaluation of the ad itself without simultaneously occurring for the viewer's cognitive evaluation of advertising content (Hughes 1992). Moreover, ad repetition can increase attitude accessibility, attitude confidence, and attitude-behavior-consistency even as it fails to enhance the evaluative component of advertising (Berger 1992, Berger & Mitchell 1989; see also Hawkins & Hoch 1992).

The literature has examined partial ad repetition resulting from the use of varied executions (Schumann et al 1990, Unnava & Burnkrant 1991b) and coordinated TV-radio campaigns. Edell & Keller (1989) find that radio executions of previously seen TV ads are processed differently than multiple TV executions. Radio repetition discourages evaluative processing because resources are spent mentally replaying the TV video.

MACRO EFFECTS OF ADVERTISING A few researchers have examined the effect of advertising as an entity on consumers' reactions. Contrary to most prior survey research, which found that TV has a minimal influence on children's preferences, a quasi-experiment by Goldberg (1990) demonstrates that exposure to TV commercials increases children's awareness of products and influences household consumption behavior (e.g. increasing the number of cereals in the home). Richins (1991) suggests that the idealized images of beauty pervasive in advertising encourage consumers to raise their standards for what is ideal attractiveness and lower, at least temporarily, satisfaction with their own appearance. Interestingly, attitudes toward the ad and brand were favorable even though self-satisfaction is lower. This illustrates that consumer psychologists need to examine factors beyond ad and brand attitudes to understand the full impact of advertising on consumers. Future research might examine the effect of self-satisfaction on consumption behavior as well as the effect of idealized advertising images on happiness.

CONCLUSION Progress has been made in understanding consumer response to advertising. However, the tendency to examine each of the various aspects of advertising in isolation raises the need for an integrated approach to the study of how executional elements affect information processing goals and strategies, and thereby influence persuasion. MacInnis et al (1991) provide a conceptual framework that organizes the literature on advertising stimuli by categorizing the various executional elements according to their effects on motivation, opportunity, and ability to process advertising information (see also MacInnis & Jaworski 1989).

Sales Promotion

Researchers interested in nonadvertising forms of promotions have focused primarily on the effects of price promotions (see section on pricing), and on the longstanding view that promotions designed to increase short-term sales may have a negative, longer-term effect on repurchase rates. Fewer studies examine effects specific to the different forms of sales promotion.

NEGATIVE EFFECTS OF SALES PROMOTION The results of research on the negative effect of promotions on repurchase behavior are mixed (Blattberg & Neslin 1989). Some studies provide support for the negative effect predicted by self-perception theory, reference price theory, and other theoretical frameworks (Kalwani et al 1990, Kalwani & Yim 1992; see Kahn & Louie 1990 and Ortmeyer & Huber 1990 for a review of the theory), while others do not (Davis et al 1992). Neslin & Shoemaker (1989) argue that the literature fails to provide convincing evidence of a negative effect because of methodological limitations inherent in the use of aggregate-level repurchase probabilities (i.e. repurchase rates may be lower after promotions because promotions attract households with low repurchase probabilities rather than because promotions reduce individual repurchase probabilities). Others identify moderating variables that specify when negative effects are likely. Promotions appear more likely to reduce repurchase rates for nonusers of the brand (Ortmeyer & Huber 1990), for those loyal to other brands (Chakraborty & Cole 1991, Kahn & Louie 1990), and when only one brand in the product category is promoted (Kahn & Louie 1990).

OTHER SALES PROMOTION ISSUES Gaeth et al (1990) recommend the use of multi-product bundles (a product and a tie-in product sold as one bundle), given that the tie-in product has a much larger effect on the bundle's evaluation than would be expected on the basis of its monetary value. Howard & Barry (1990) find that systematic evaluation of a sweepstake prize is bypassed when sweepstake winners do not expect to win. For those winners, the evaluation of the prize is based more on their positive reaction to winning than on a careful appraisal of the information available about the prize.

In conclusion, sales promotion research focuses on short- and long-term effects of promotional price reductions. Additional knowledge is needed about the factors that moderate and mediate the effect of all forms of sales promotions on short-term sales and long-term brand evaluation and repurchase. This type of knowledge can close the gap between our behavioral theoretic explanations of promotion effects and the scanner-data-based empirical models (Davis et al 1992, Ortmeyer & Huber 1990).

Pricing

Internal reference price (IRP) has emerged as an explanatory concept in the price literature. IRP, often defined as the consumer's expected price, is viewed as a standard of comparison for evaluating a product's price. IRP has many antecedents although their relative role is unclear (Lichtenstein & Bearden 1989). Specifically, a consumer's IRP is related positively with past prices, new prices (Jacobson & Obermiller 1990, Urbany & Dickson 1991), future expected prices (Jacobson & Obermiller 1990), inflation (Kalwani et al 1990), and external reference prices (ERP) supplied in advertising, especially when consumers lack confidence in their IRP and the ERP is believable (Lichtenstein & Bearden 1989, Lichtenstein et al 1991, Biswas & Blair 1991). IRP is negatively related to the frequency and depth of price promotions (Kalwani et al 1990, Kalwani & Yim 1992; see Krishna et al 1991 and Krishna 1991 regarding the accuracy of consumer perceptions of price promotions).

Prices below IRP are generally considered to increase short-term brand evaluation and choice, although the effect of price-IRP deviations on consumer response is not monotonic. A region of relative price insensitivity surrounds the IRP, such that only price changes outside that region have a significant impact on consumer choice (Kalwani & Yim 1992). This may result, in part, from IRP haziness related to consumers' poor knowledge of actual market prices (Urbany & Dickson 1991, Dickson & Sawyer 1990). Asymmetric response to price-IRP deviations may also occur. Consistent with prospect theory, Kalwani et al (1990) report that consumers react more strongly to price losses (i.e. IRP higher than price) than to price gains, but Krishnamurthi et al (1992) find the opposite for brand switchers and no asymmetry in the choice decisions for loyal customers. Resolution of these conflicting results awaits improved measurement of IRP.

The studies above focus on IRP development and the general form of the effect when price deviates from IRP. The challenge for researchers is to identify when non-IRP mechanisms affect consumer response to price and price promotions. A conceptual framework developed by Diamond (1990) suggests that IRP will play a role in the consumer's evaluation of sales promotions for moderately involving, complex decisions but not high or low involvement decisions. In high involvement decisions, the actual price will be treated as one factor in a compensatory decision process while in low involvement decisions, heuristic processing may replace numerical processing of price. The latter situation may explain why the price promotion signal, rather than price cut itself, can influence consumer response (Mayhew & Winer 1992, Dickson

& Sawyer 1990), especially when the consumer is lower in need-for-cognition (Inman et al 1990).

Consumer attributions and perceptions also play a role in responses to price information. Price increases are perceived to be fairer when cost justifications are provided (Urbany et al 1989b), and the favorableness of consumers' response to price promotions increases with the favorableness of their attributions for the promotion offering (Lichtenstein et al 1989). Gupta & Cooper (1992) explain why advertised discounts have minimal influence on purchase intentions for discounts below a threshold level and above a saturation point and why the threshold is lower for a name brand than a store brand in terms of consumers' selective perception, discount believability, and the ability of the name brand to maintain perceptions of quality (see Grewal & Compeau 1992, for a discussion of how ERP may alter quality perceptions as well as alter IRP).

Product

Product oriented research has addressed the role of price as an indicator of product quality, the evaluation of brand extensions, and the effects of country-of-origin.

PRICE-QUALITY RELATIONSHIP The use of price as an indicator of product quality is consistent with the ideas that consumers are heuristic processors and that judgments are based on accessible, diagnostic information. Consumers rely on price as a quality indicator and thus seek higher-priced products when quality is important to product performance but quality information is not available (Tellis & Gaeth 1990). Similarly, low-knowledge consumers are more apt to use price as an indicator of quality than consumers with higher knowledge, who are more likely to have diagnostic information (Gaeth et al 1990). However, extremely knowledgeable consumers also rely more heavily on extrinsic quality cues such as price to assess the quality of products like apparel, perhaps because they know that price is a valid indicator of quality (i.e. diagnostic) in those product categories (Rao & Sieben 1992).

Product durability may moderate the use of price as an indicator of quality. A meta-analysis by Rao & Monroe (1989) finds that price consistently serves as a quality cue for nondurable goods, but not for durable goods. In contrast, Lichtenstein & Burton (1989) argue that price is more often used as a quality cue for durables than nondurables. It appears that some consumers have a propensity to use price as a quality cue for durable goods while other consumers have the same propensity for nondurable goods, but it is not known what characteristics distinguish the two groups of consumers (Lichtenstein & Burton 1989). Finally, Dodds et al (1991) report that the presence of additional quality cues such as brand name diminish the use of price as an indicator of quality for durable goods, while Rao & Monroe (1989) conclude the opposite based on their review of studies involving nondurable products (see Kirmani 1990, Kirmani & Wright 1989 for evidence that perceived advertising cost can also influence perceived quality).

Pechmann & Ratneshwar (1992) examine the formation of consumer assessments of the relationship between price and quality. When the consumer is able to discriminate between brands on the basis of price and quality, assessments are determined by actual price-quality relationship. But when they cannot discriminate, prior beliefs about price-quality relationships determine judgments. Rao & Bergen (1992) argue that some consumers knowingly pay a price premium when they cannot ascertain quality before the purchase as a way to motivate sellers to provide higher quality, and that this tendency increases with an increase in quality consciousness. Rao & Sieben (1992) demonstrate a link between quality perceptions and the prices acceptable to consumers. When the price of the product is not available as a quality cue, low-knowledge consumers appear to greatly discount the product's quality, and as a result have a lower acceptable price range than higher-knowledge consumers, who presumably have more knowledge about product quality and market prices.

BRAND EXTENSIONS AND PRODUCT CATEGORY PERCEPTIONS Categorization theory (see Loken & Ward 1990) has fueled promising research on how brand extensions are characterized and evaluated. Consumers' response to a brand extension is guided by the mental frame that the flagship brand provides and by its similarity to the flagship (Schmitt & Dube 1992). Specifically, when a brand and an extension are seen as similar in terms of product features or abstract concepts (i.e. status), brand extensions are evaluated more favorably (Boush & Loken 1991, Park et al 1991), and the quality of the flagship brand positively influences brand extension attitudes (Aaker & Keller 1990). However, when dissimilarity between the flagship and the extension is made accessible by a contextual prime, the effect of the flagship brand image on the extension is reduced (Schmitt & Dube 1992). Category structure appears to shape the evaluation process as well as the evaluation outcome. Attitudes toward typical brand extensions tend to be computed from attributes of the extension, while extremely typical and atypical extensions are processed in a more global way involving affect transfer (Boush & Loken 1991, see also Aaker & Keller 1990).

Other research examines multiple extensions of a particular brand. Keller & Aaker (1992) find that a successful intervening extension increases the evaluation of the last extension only for an average-quality initial brand, while an unsuccessful intervening extension decreases evaluations of the last extension only for a high-quality initial brand. Boush & Loken (1991) find that high-similarity extensions do better when there have been fewer previous extensions, while moderate-similarity extensions do better when there have been a large number of previous extensions.

Future research is needed to assess further factors that moderate the effect of brand extensions on the flagship brand (see Aaker & Keller 1990, Keller & Aaker 1992), and to explore how category structure affects the likelihood of brand confusion and the evaluation of new and repositioned products (see Foxman et al 1990, 1992; Hutchinson & Alba 1991; Loken & Ward 1990; Meyers-Levy & Tybout 1989; Ozanne et al 1992; Stayman et al 1992; Sujan & Bettman 1989).

COUNTRY-OF-ORIGIN EFFECTS A growing interest in globalism has fueled research addressing country-of-origin effects on product evaluations. Country-of-origin can directly influence product evaluations as one of several product features that combine to influence product evaluation (Hong & Wyer 1989, 1990) or by providing an image that serves as the central concept around which a product impression is formed (Han 1989). Country-of-origin can indirectly affect product evaluations by influencing the consumer's interpretation of product-attribute information. This indirect effect is predominant when consumers are unfamiliar with a country's products (Han 1989) or have previously formed an evaluative concept of the product based on country-of-origin because that concept can guide the processing of attribute information received later (Hong & Wyer 1990). Hong & Wyer (1989) suggest that country-of-origin information stimulates consumer interest, which leads them to think more extensively about product-attribute information and the evaluative implications of that information. More research is needed to understand how country-of-origin impressions are formed and to explore whether country-of-origin is indeed a unique product feature with effects that are distinct from those associated with other product features.

Consumer Values

Consumers' values are likely to moderate responses to marketing stimuli by influencing processing motivation. One value receiving attention recently is materialism. Materialists are those who view possessions as central to their lives and consider acquisition to be a measure of success that is essential to life satisfaction (Corfman et al 1991, Fournier & Richins 1991; see also Rudmin & Kilbourne 1993). Richins & Dawson (1992) provide a measure of individual differences in materialism that can be used to test the effect of material values on response to marketing stimuli such as advertising, and findings by Tse et al (1989) suggest that materialism, as reflected in advertising, varies across cultures. A related but conceptually distinct concept is consumers' attachment to possessions or the extent to which they use possessions to develop and maintain their self-concept (see Ball & Tasaki 1992 for a validated scale).

Other research has extended efforts to measure more general consumer values as a basis for segmentation. This is appropriate because previous psychographic segmentation measures, such as VALS and LOV, have explained little variance in behavior beyond that accounted for by demographics (Novak & MacEvoy 1990). Kamakura & Novak (1992) identify four value segments, based on security, maturity, achievement, and essential enjoyment, that offer better predictions of consumer beliefs, attitudes, and behavior than the LOV basis of segmentation (see also Kamakura & Mazzon 1991). These segments are consistent with Schwartz & Bilksky's (1990) theory of the psychological structure of human value systems.

ALTERNATIVE APPROACHES TO CONSUMER PSYCHOLOGY

Traditional consumer research involves the operationalization of constructs, statistical testing of hypotheses, and measurement of phenomena that can be plausibly explained with psychological constructs. Postmodern research philosophies and methods employ alternative approaches to understanding consumers and consumption (Hirschman & Holbrook 1992, Sherry 1991). Researchers have specifically advocated naturalistic inquiry and ethnographic analysis (Arnould 1989, Belk et al 1989, Belk 1991), literary criticism and explication (Stern 1989a, b), semiotics (McQuarrie & Mick 1992), historical method (Lavin & Archdeacon 1989), existential-phenomenology (Thompson et al 1989), relativism/constructionism (Peter & Olson 1989, Peter 1991), critical relativism (Anderson 1989), and critical theory (Murray & Ozanne 1991).

Active debate continues in the general field of psychology as to whether postmodernism will supplant, transform, expand, or be irrelevant to the contemporary science of psychology (Kvale 1992b, Gergen 1992, Michael 1992, Chaiklin 1992, respectively). A prominent postmodern view is that the study of psychology will shift its focus from the individual self and internal psychological processes toward the social construction of self and human activity embedded in a cultural context (Kvale 1992a).

By contrast, within the narrower field of consumer research, early debates that pitted positivism against postpositivism (see Hirschman 1989) have led to clarification of premises underlying traditional consumer research [including that it cannot be correctly characterized as postivistic (see Hunt 1991)], and to agreement on the value of critical pluralism. Whether this pluralism will involve separate or intersecting research programs across philosophies and methods remains an issue of discussion. Some researchers view postmodern knowledge claims as incommensurable with traditional consumer psychology knowledge claims (Anderson 1989, Ozanne & Hudson 1989, Thompson et al

1989), while others contend that although the knowledge claims may differ, there is no philosophical or practical basis for believing that claims will be incommensurable or rival (Hunt 1991).

Assuming commensurability, it is worthwhile to identify ways that alternative research might enrich traditional consumer psychology. Current evidence suggests that nontraditional research can uncover new constructs, introduce multimethodological perspectives that allow for triangulation of results across research traditions, propose contextual/moderating factors, question the appropriateness of assumptions in conceptual models, and reveal the multidimensional nature of variables studied by suggesting the range of constructs that a single variable may tap and by highlighting the complexity of individuals' consumption experiences.

Arnould's (1989) study of diffusion in Niger demonstrates how ethnography can broaden the theory of preference formation and diffusion of innovation by highlighting limitations to Western assumptions. Specifically, his findings contradict the notions that humans universally long for novelty and will actively evaluate products through logic-deductive comparisons of attribute bundles. This work also enriches the construct of innovation by conceptualizing novel goods as a medium allowing competition between alternative world views in a society (i.e. acceptance of various innovations reinforces premarket, Western market, or Islamic ethnonationalist paradigms coexisting in Niger).

McQuarrie & Mick (1992) demonstrate the value of triangulating across research methods in their study of resonance, a rhetorical element of advertising that allows multiple meanings. Their semiotic analysis calls attention to this neglected advertising executional cue, provides a rich conceptualization of the way multiple meanings are embedded in a text, and explains why and for whom resonance will evoke positive affect (i.e. the effect is greater for individuals who successfully decode the multiple meanings and for individuals with a greater tolerance for ambiguity). McQuarrie & Mick's use of traditional experimental methods demonstrates that resonance enhances attitudes, and their phenomenological interviewing complements the experimental findings by demonstrating that personal experiences of resonance converge with the theorized meaning constructions.

The McQuarrie & Mick study represents one of the many research projects based on semiotic, literary, and anthropological approaches to the study of communication that enrich the information processing perspective of traditional advertising research. Other research finds that the meaning communicated by advertising is idiosyncratic and personalized and not affixed denotatively (Mick & Politi 1989, Domzal & Kernan 1992). Life projects and life themes, constructs new to consumer research, capture individual and sociocultural motivations that may moderate the connotative meaning communicated by ads (Mick & Buhl 1992). Advertising context determines the connotative meaning of an object (i.e. the perceived use of the product) and may even affect the denotative meaning (i.e. the semantic category identifying an object, Kleine & Kernan 1991). The same concept of meaning transfer explains why the transfer of cultural meaning from the celebrity to the product is successful when the meanings of the celebrity and the product match (McCracken 1989b). Finally, literary criticism and explication have been used to assess advertising themes, images, and implied consumer values, and to identify elements that may affect the information people acquire from ads (Stern 1989a, b).

Other postmodern studies provide insights into consumer values and motivations that complement the work on measurment of consumer values. These studies tend to focus on the experiential dimension of consumer behavior and to view human activity as embedded in a cultural-constituted world, and thus produce an enriched conceptualization of the motivations driving consumption (see also Belk et al 1991).

Consumption can be a vehicle for experiencing sacredness when secular goods acquire personal, transcendent meaningfulness. Belk et al (1989) identify how sacralization results from consumer behaviors such as rituals and gift-giving (see Belk 1989, Hirschman & LaBarbera 1989, O'Guinn & Belk 1989). Wallendorf & Arnould (1991) examine the particular meaning of Thanksgiving rituals and identify deliberate actions, like removing product packaging, that individuals use to decommodify mass-marketed branded products and symbolically transform them into personally meaningful products. Others find that gift-giving is more than an overt action that strengthens social ties: gift-giving can precipitate fantasies with negative overtones, cause internal stress, and threaten social ties (McGrath et al 1993; Sherry et al 1992a, b). The notion of time has been explored with emphasis on the temporal embeddedness of consumption (Sherry 1991). Bergadaà (1990) interprets time as part of a perceived temporal orientation with consequences for consumer planning and actions. Consumers oriented toward the future act in a more self-determining way, while those oriented to the present react in a more exogenously-determined fashion.

Consumers also use the symbolic meaning of possessions to construct self-identity, especially during life transitions [see also Ball & Tasaki's attachment scale (1992)]. Material artifacts are crucial to immigrants' self-identity (Mehta & Belk 1991), and possessions had sacred, material, personal, familial, and communal meanings for Mormons during their mid-nineteenth-century migration (Belk 1992). The homeless value possessions for their symbolic representation of the past, present, and future (Hill 1991, Hill & Stamey 1990). McCracken (1989a) describes how material goods can be used to create a sense of "homeyness," which in turn provides a meaningful context for the family's construction of itself.

Finally, research on the motivational aspect of impulsive and compulsive buying complements work on emotion and affect associated with mainstream consumer behaviors. O'Guinn & Faber (1989) find that compulsive consumption may be motivated by the desire to enhance self-perceptions via positive interpersonal interactions with salespersons. This implies that notions such as self-esteem, extroversion, and self-monitoring may play an important role in consumption. Hoch & Loewenstein (1991) suggest that self-control in consumption involves a conflict between the psychological forces of desire and willpower. Hirschman's (1992) phenomenological analysis implies that consumers may engage in compulsive consumption to create and maintain a stable sense of self in response to role transitions or a dysfunctional family. Thompson et al's (1990) existential-phenomenological description of the everyday consumer experiences of married women views impulse buying as "an act of freedom within a restricted situation [that] relieves participants from considering perceived constraints and pondering the purchase decision."

CONCLUSION

Three broad themes underlie much of the recent work in consumer psychology. First, the basic notion of elaboration is being extended by research examining the antecedents, dynamics, and types of elaboration that can occur and by exploring the unique effects of these dimensions of elaboration. These efforts parallel similar work in the more general psychology literature. Second, there is a growing interest in variables that characterize the rich context in which consumer information processing, judgment, and decision making typically occur. This is reflected both in representations and/or manipulations of contextual factors in controlled studies and in the adoption of methods that preserve the richness of context (i.e. postmodern approaches). Finally, the view that consumers are wholly analytical and rational has given way to a more humanistic perspective. This is seen in the attention to heuristic processing and to emotional responses in research employing traditional methods (see Cohen & Areni 1991). It is also reflected in efforts to capture consumption experiences and their meanings via alternative research methods. The last two themes cut across research methods and philosophical orientations, suggesting that traditional and postmodern researchers may have more in common than is reflected in the limited dialogue between them.

This review is an occasion to assess the more general impact of consumer psychology research. Recent articles reflecting on the contributions and progress in the larger field of consumer research have struck a pessimistic note. Wells (1993) argues that two decades of research have yielded limited insight of practical value, mostly because the focus on control (e.g. student subjects, laboratory settings) has produced research with little relevance to the real world and because researchers resist revising their theories to make them more relevant even when data imply that such revision is required. Armstrong (1991) observes that consumer researchers are unable to predict outcomes from a sample of published studies at better than a chance level, implying that their expertise as consumer researchers is questionable.

In contrast, our view is more optimistic. Although further research on many topics is needed, as noted throughout this review, the themes we detect suggest that theories of consumer psychology are increasing in their complexity and their ability to capture decision making and consumption experiences. Main effect predictions are being supplanted by interactions that specify the preconditions for observing outcomes. Indeed, one interpretation of Armstrong's findings is that recognition of real world complexity confounded consumer researchers' ability to predict accurately main effect outcomes. Further, progress is best assessed by looking across individual studies and researchers (see Brinberg et al 1992). From this perspective, there is evidence of theory revision and extension. For example, notions of central and peripheral processing have been modified to accommodate new data and exploration of different aspects of elaboration is beginning. Notions of consumer information processing, judgment, and decision making are proving useful in addressing marketplace issues such as brand extensions and global competition. As these trends continue, consumer psychology will offer an increasingly valuable framework from which to approach the design of solutions to real world problems.

Literature Cited

Aaker DA, Keller KL. 1990. Consumer evaluations of brand extensions. *J. Mark.* 54:27–41

Alba JW, Hutchinson JW, Lynch JG Jr. 1991. Memory and decision making. See Robertson & Kassarjian 1991, pp. 1–49

Alba JW, Marmorstein H, Chattopadhyay A. 1992. Transitions in preference over time: the effects of memory on message persuasiveness. *J. Mark. Res.* 24:406–16

Allen CT, Janiszewski CA. 1989. Assessing the role of contingency awareness in attitudinal conditioning with implications for advertising research. *J. Mark. Res.* 26:30–43

Allen CT, Macheleit KA, Kleine SS. 1992. A comparison of attitudes and emotions as predictors of behavior at diverse levels of behavioral experience. *J. Consum. Res.* 18:493–504

Alpert JI, Alpert MI. 1990. Music influences on mood and purchase intentions. *Psychol. Mark.* 7:109–33

Anand P, Sternthal B. 1990. Ease of message processing as a moderator of repetition effects in advertising. *J. Mark. Res.* 27:345–53

Anand P, Sternthal B. 1992. The effects of program involvement and ease of message counterarguing on advertising persuasiveness. *J. Consum. Psychol.* 1:225–38

Anderson PF. 1989. On relativism and interpretivism—with a prolegomenon to the "why" question. See Hirschman 1989, pp. 10–23

Andrews JC, Durvasula S, Akhter SH. 1990. A framework for conceptualizing and measuring the involvement construct in advertising research. *J. Advert.* 19:27–40

Andrews JC, Shimp TA. 1990. Effects of involvement, argument strength, and source characteristics on central and peripheral processing of advertising. *Psychol. Mark.* 7:195–214

Armstrong JS. 1991. Prediction of consumer behavior by experts and novices. *J. Consum. Res.* 18:251–56

Arnould EJ. 1989. Toward a broadened theory of preference formation and the diffusion of innovations: cases from Zinder Province, Niger Republic. *J. Consum. Res.* 16:239–67

Bagozzi RP, Baumgartner H, Yi Y. 1992. State versus action orientation and the theory of reasoned action: an application to coupon usage. *J. Consum. Res.* 18:505–18

Bagozzi RP, Baumgartner J, Yi Y. 1989. An investigation into the role of intentions as mediators of the attitude-behavior relationship. *J. Econ. Psychol.* 10:35–62

Bagozzi RP, Warshaw PR. 1990. Trying to consume. *J. Consum. Res.* 17:127–40

Bagozzi RP, Yi Y. 1989. The degree of intention formation as a moderator of the attitude-behavior relation. *Soc. Psychol. Q.* 52:266–79

Ball AD, Tasaki LH. 1992. The role and measurement of attachment in consumer behavior. *J. Consum. Psychol.* 1:155–72

Batra R, Ahtola OT. 1990. Measuring the hedonic and utilitarian sources of consumer attitudes. *Mark. Lett.* 2:159–70

Batra R, Holbrook MB. 1990. Developing a typology of affective responses to advertising. *Psychol. Mark.* 7:11–25

Batra R, Stayman DM. 1990. The role of mood in advertising effectiveness. *J. Consum. Res.* 17:203–14

Baumgartner H, Sujan M, Bettman JR. 1992. Autobiographical memories, affect, and consumer information processing. *J. Consum. Psychol.* 1:53–82

Bearden WO, Netemeyer RG, Teel JE. 1989. Measurement of consumer susceptibility to interpersonal influence. *J. Consum. Res.* 15:473–81

Bearden WO, Rose RL. 1990. Attention to social comparison information: an individual difference factor affecting consumer conformity. *J. Consum. Res.* 16:461–71

Belk RW. 1989. Materialism and the modern U. S. Christmas. See Hirschman 1989, pp. 115–35

Belk RW, ed. 1991. *Highways and Buyways: Naturalistic Research from the Consumer Behavior Odyssey.* Provo, UT: Assoc. Consum. Res.

Belk RW. 1992. Moving possessions: an analysis based on personal documents from the 1847–69 Mormon migration. *J. Consum. Res.* 19:339–61

Belk RW, Wallendorf M, Sherry JF Jr. 1989. The sacred and the profane in consumer behavior: theodicy on the Odyssey. *J. Consum. Res.* 16:1–38

Belk RW, Wallendorf M, Sherry JF Jr, Holbrook MB. 1991. Collecting in a consumer culture. See Belk 1991, pp. 178–215

Bergadaà MM. 1990. The role of time in the action of the consumer. *J. Consum. Res.* 17:289–302

Berger IE. 1992. The nature of attitude accessibility and attitude confidence: a triangulated experiment. *J. Consum. Psychol.* 1:103–23

Berger IE, Mitchell AA. 1989. The effect of advertising on attitude accessibility, attitude confidence, and the attitude-behavior relationship. *J. Consum. Res.* 16:269–79

Bettman JR, Johnson EJ, Payne JW. 1991. Consumer decision making. See Robertson & Kassarjian 1991, pp. 50–84

Biehal G, Chakravarti D. 1989. The effects of concurrent verbalization on choice processing. *J. Mark. Res.* 26:84–96

Biswas A, Blair EA. 1991. Contextual effects of reference prices in retail advertisements. *J. Mark.* 55:1–12

Bolton RN, Drew JH. 1991. A multistage model of customers' assessments of service quality and value. *J. Consum. Res.* 17:375–84

Bone PF, Ellen PS. 1992. The generation and consequences of communication-evoked imagery. *J. Consum. Res.* 19:93–104

Boush DM, Loken B. 1991. A process-tracing study of brand extension evaluation. *J. Mark. Res.* 28:16–28

Blattberg RC, Neslin SA. 1989. Sales promotion: the long and the short of it. *Mark. Lett.* 1:81–97

Brinberg D, Lynch JG Jr, Sawyer AG. 1992. Hypothesized and confounded explanations in theory tests: a Bayesian analysis. *J. Consum. Res.* 19:139–54

Brown SP, Stayman DM. 1992. Antecedents and consequences of attitude toward the ad: a meta-analysis. *J. Consum. Res.* 19:34–51

Brucks M, Schurr PH. 1990. The effects of bargainable attributes and attribute range knowledge on consumer choice processes. *J. Consum. Res.* 16:409–19

Bruner GC II. 1990. Music, mood, and marketing. *J. Mark.* 54:94–104

Burke MC, Edell JA. 1989. The impact of feelings on ad-based affect and cognition. *J. Mark. Res.* 26:69–83

Burke RR, Harlam BA, Kahn BE, Lodish LM. 1992. Comparing dynamic consumer choice in real and computer-simulated environments. *J. Consum. Res.* 19:71–82

Cafferata P, Tybout AM. 1989. *Cognitive and Affective Responses to Advertising.* Lexington, Mass: Lexington

Chaiklin S. 1992. From theory to practice and back again: What does postmodern philosophy contribute to psychological science? See Kvale 1992a, pp. 194–208

Chakraborty G, Cole C. 1991. Coupon characteristics and brand choice. *Psychol. Mark.* 8:145–59

Chattopadhyay A, Basu K. 1990. Humor in advertising: the moderating role of prior brand evaluation. *J. Mark. Res.* 27:466–76

Chattopadhyay A, Nedungadi P. 1992. Does

attitude toward the ad endure? The moderating effects of attention and delay. *J. Consum. Res.* 19:26–33

Childers TL, Rao AR. 1992. The influence of familial and peer-based reference groups on consumer decisions. *J. Consum. Res.* 19:198–211

Cohen J. 1992. White consumer response to Asian models in advertising. *J. Consum. Mark.* 9:17–27

Cohen JB, Areni CS. 1991. Affect and consumer behavior. See Robertson & Kassarjian 1991, pp. 188–240

Cole CA, Gaeth GJ. 1990. Cognitive and age-related differences in the ability to use nutritional information in a complex environment. *J. Mark. Res.* 27:175–84

Corfman KP. 1991. Comparability and comparison levels used in choices among consumer products. *J. Mark. Res.* 28:368–74

Corfman KP, Lehmann DR, Narayanan S. 1991. Values, utility, and ownership: modeling the relationships for consumer durables. *J. Retail* 67:184–203

Costley CL, Brucks M. 1992. Selective recall and information use in consumer preferences. *J. Cons. Res.* 18:464–74

Davis S, Inman JJ, McAlister L. 1992. Promotion has a negative effect on brand evaluations—or does it? Additional disconfirming evidence. *J. Mark. Res.* 29: 143–48

Debevec K, Romeo JB. 1992. Self-referent processing in perceptions of verbal and visual commercial information. *J. Consum. Psychol.* 1:83–102

Deighton J, Romer D, McQueen J. 1989. Using drama to persuade. *J. Consum. Res.* 16:335–43

Dhar R, Simonson I. 1992. The effect of the focus of comparison on consumer preferences. *J. Mark. Res.* 29:430–40

Diamond WD. 1990. Schemas determining the incentive value of sales promotions. *Psychol. Mark.* 7:163–75

Dick A, Chakravarti D, Biehal G. 1990. Memory-based inferences during consumer choice. *J. Consum. Res.* 17:82–93

Dickson PR, Sawyer AG. 1990. The price knowledge and search of supermarket shoppers. *J. Mark.* 54:42–53

Dodds WB, Monroe KB, Grewal D. 1991. Effects of price, brand, and store information on buyers' product evaluations. *J. Mark. Res.* 28:307–19

Domzal TJ, Kernan JB. 1992. Reading advertising: the what and how of product meaning. *J. Consum. Mark.* 9:48–64

Dröge C. 1989. Shaping the route to attitude change: central versus peripheral processing through comparative versus noncomparative advertising. *J. Mark. Res.* 26:193–204

Edell JA, Keller KL. 1989. The information processing of coordinated media campaigns. *J. Mark. Res.* 26:149–63

Ensley EE, Pride WM. 1991. Advertisement pacing and the learning of marketing information by the elderly. *Psychol. Mark.* 8:1–20

Fazio RH, Herr PM, Powell MC. 1992. On the development and strength of category-brand associations in memory: the case of mystery ads. *J. Consum. Psychol.* 1:1–13

Fazio RH, Powell MC, Williams CJ. 1989. The role of attitude accessibility in the attitude-to-behavior process. *J. Consum. Res.* 16:280–88

Fisher RJ, Price LL. 1992. An investigation into the social context of early adoption behavior. *J. Consum. Res.* 19:477–86

Ford GT, Smith DB, Swasy JL. 1990. Consumer skepticism of advertising claims: testing hypotheses from economics of information. *J. Consum. Res.* 16:433–41

Fournier S, Richins ML. 1991. Some theoretical and popular notions concerning materialism. *J. Soc. Behav. Pers.* 6:403–14

Foxman ER, Berger PW, Cote JA. 1992. Consumer brand confusion: a conceptual framework. *Psychol. Mark.* 9:123–41

Foxman ER, Muehling DD, Berger PW. 1990. An investigation of factors contributing to consumer brand confusion. *J. Consum. Affairs* 24:171–89

Frenzen JK, Davis HL. 1990. Purchasing behavior in embedded markets. *J. Consum. Res.* 17:1–12

Gaeth GJ, Levin IP, Chakraborty G, Levin AM. 1990. Consumer evaluation of multi-product bundles: an information integration analysis. *Mark. Lett.* 2:47–57

Gardial S, Biehal G. 1991. Evaluative and factual ad claims, knowledge level, and making inferences. *Mark. Lett.* 2:349–58

Gardner MP, Hill RP. 1989. Consumers' mood states and the decision-making process. *Mark. Lett.* 1:229–38

Gergen KJ. 1992. Toward a postmodern psychology. See Kvale 1992a, pp. 17–30

Glazer R, Kahn BE, Moore WL. 1991. The influence of external constraints on brand choice: the lone-alternative effect. *J. Consum. Res.* 18:119–28

Goldberg ME. 1990. A quasi-experiment assessing the effectiveness of TV advertising directed to children. *J. Mark. Res.* 27:445–54

Goldberg ME, Hartwick J. 1990. The effects of advertiser reputation and extremity of advertising claim on advertising effectiveness. *J. Consum. Res.* 17:172–79

Gorn GJ, Goldberg ME, Chattopadhyay A, Litvack D. 1991. Music And information in commercials: their effects with an elderly sample. *J. Advert. Res.* 31:23–32

Gotlieb JB, Sarel D. 1991. Comparative advertising effectiveness: the role of involvement and source credibility. *J. Advert.* 20:38–45

Grewal D, Compeau LD. 1992. Comparative price advertising: informative or deceptive? *J. Public Policy Mark.* 11:52–62

Gupta S, Cooper LG. 1992. The discounting of discounts and promotion thresholds. *J. Consum. Res.* 19:401–11

Han CM. 1989. Country image: halo or summary construct? *J. Mark. Res.* 26:222–29

Hanna N, Wagle JS. 1989. Who is your satisfied customer? *J. Consum. Mark.* 6: 53–61

Hastak M, Olson JC. 1989. Assessing the role of brand-related cognitive responses as mediators of communication effects on cognitive structure. *J. Consum. Res.* 15:444–56

Hauser JR, Wernerfelt B. 1990. An evaluation cost model of consideration sets. *J. Consum. Res.* 16:393–408

Hawkins SA, Hoch SJ. 1992. Low-involvement learning: memory without evaluation. *J. Consum. Res.* 19:212–25

Heckler SE, Childers TL. 1992. The role of expectancy and relevancy in memory for verbal and visual information: What is incongruency? *J. Consum. Res.* 18:475–92

Herr PM. 1989. Priming price: prior knowledge and context effects. *J. Consum. Res.* 16:67–75

Herr PM, Kardes FR, Kim J. 1991. Effects of word-of-mouth and product-attribute information on persuasion: an accessibility-diagnosticity perspective. *J. Consum. Res.* 17:454–62

Hill RP. 1991. Homeless women, special possessions, and the meaning of "home": an ethnographic case study. *J. Consum. Res.* 18:298–310

Hill RP, Stamey M. 1990. The homeless in America: an examination of possessions and consumption behaviors. *J. Consum. Res.* 17:303–21

Hirschman EC. 1989. *Interpretive Consumer Research.* Provo, UT: Assoc. Consum. Res. 209 pp.

Hirschman EC. 1992. The consciousness of addiction: toward a general theory of compulsive consumption. *J. Consum. Res.* 19:155–79

Hirschman EC, Holbrook MB. 1992. *Postmodern Consumer Research: The Study of Consumption as Text. Newbury Park, Calif: Sage. 146 pp.*

Hirschman EC, LaBarbera PA. 1989. The meaning of Christmas. See Hirschman 1989, pp. 136–47

Hoch SJ, Deighton J. 1989. Managing what consumers learn from experience. *J. Mark.* 53:1–20

Hoch SJ, Loewenstein GF. 1991. Time-inconsistent preferences and consumer self-control. *J. Consum. Res.* 17:492–507

Hoffman DL, Batra R. 1991. Viewer response to programs: dimensionality and concurrent behavior. *J. Advert. Res.* 31:46–56

Homer PM. 1990. The mediating role of attitude toward the ad: some additional evidence. *J. Mark. Res.* 27:78–86

Homer PM, Kahle LR. 1990. Source expertise, time of source identification, and involvement in persuasion: an elaborative processing perspective. *J. Advert.* 19:30–39

Homer PM, Yoon S. 1992. Message framing and the interrelationships among ad-based feelings, affect, and cognition. *J. Advert.* 21:19–33

Hong ST, Wyer RS Jr. 1989. Effects of country-of-origin and product-attribute information on product evaluation: an information processing perspective. *J. Consum. Res.* 16:175–87

Hong ST, Wyer RS Jr. 1990. Determinants of product evaluation: effects of the time interval between knowledge of a product's country of origin and information about its specific attributes. *J. Consum. Res.* 17:277–88

Howard DJ, Barry TE. 1990. The evaluative consequences of experiencing unexpected favorable events. *J. Mark. Res.* 27:51–60

Howard DJ, Burnkrant RE. 1990. Question effects on information processing in advertising. *Psychol. Mark.* 7:27–46

Hoyer WD, Brown SP. 1990. Effects of brand awareness on choice for a common, repeat-purchase product. *J. Consum. Res.* 17:141–48

Huber J, Klein NM. 1991. Adapting cutoffs to the choice environment: the effects of attribute correlation and reliability. *J. Consum. Res.* 18:346–57

Hughes GD. 1992. Realtime response measures redefine advertising wearout. *J. Advert. Res.* 32:61–77

Hui MK, Bateson JEG. 1991. Perceived control and the effects of crowding and consumer choice on the service experience. *J. Consum. Res.* 18:174–84

Hunt SD. 1991. Positivism and paradigm dominance in consumer research: toward critical pluralism and rapprochement. *J. Consum. Res.* 18:32–44

Hutchinson JW, Alba JW. 1991. Ignoring irrelevant information: situational determinants of consumer learning. *J. Consum. Res.* 18:325–45

Inman JJ, McAlister L, Hoyer WD. 1990. Promotion signal: proxy for a price cut? *J. Consum. Res.* 17:74–81

Jacobson R, Obermiller C. 1990. The formation of expected future price: a reference price for forward-looking consumers. *J. Consum. Res.* 16:420–32

Jacoby J, Hoyer WD. 1989. The comprehension/miscomprehension of print communication: selected findings. *J. Consum. Res.* 15:434–43

Janiszewski C. 1990a. The influence of nonattended material on the processing of advertising claims. *J. Mark. Res.* 27:263–78

Janiszewski C. 1990b. The influence of print advertisement organization on affect toward a brand name. *J. Consum. Res.* 17:53–65

John DR, Lakshmi-Ratan R. 1992. Age differences in children's choice behavior: the impact of available alternatives. *J. Mark. Res.* 29:216–26

John DR, Sujan M. 1990a. Age differences in product categorization. *J. Consum. Res.* 16:452–60

John DR, Sujan M. 1990b. Children's use of perceptual cues in product categorization. *Psychol. Mark.* 7:277–94

Johnson MD. 1989. The differential processing of product category and noncomparable choice alternatives. *J. Consum. Res.* 16:300–9

Kahn BE, Louie TA. 1990. Effects of retraction of price promotions on brand choice behavior for variety-seeking and last-purchase-loyal consumers. *J. Mark. Res.* 27:279–89

Kahn BE, Meyer RJ. 1991. Consumer multiattribute judgments under attribute-weight uncertainty. *J. Consum. Res.* 17:508–28

Kahneman D, Miller DT. 1986. Norm theory: comparing reality to its alternatives. *Psychol. Rev.* 93:136–53

Kalwani MU, Yim CK. 1992. Consumer price and promotion expectations: an experimental study. *J. Mark. Res.* 29:90–100

Kalwani MU, Yim CK, Rinne HJ, Sugita Y. 1990. A price expectations model of customer brand choice. *J. Mark. Res.* 27:251–62

Kamakura WA, Mazzon JA. 1991. Value segmentation: a model for the measurement of values and value systems. *J. Consum. Res.* 18:208–18

Kamakura WA, Novak TP. 1992. Value-system segmentation: exploring the meaning of LOV. *J. Consum. Res.* 19:119–32

Kamins MA, Brand MJ, Hoeke SA, Moe JC. 1989. Two-sided versus one-sided celebrity endorsements: the impact on advertising effectiveness and credibility. *J. Advert.* 18:4–10

Kamins MA, Marks LJ, Skinner D. 1991. Television commercial evaluation in the context of program induced mood: congruency versus consistency effects. *J. Advert.* 20:1–14

Kellaris JJ, Cox AD. 1989. The effects of background music in advertising: a reassessment. *J. Consum. Res.* 16:113–18

Keller KL. 1991a. Cue compatibility and framing in advertising. *J. Mark. Res.* 28:42–57

Keller KL. 1991b. Memory and evaluation effects in competitive advertising environments. *J. Consum. Res.* 17:463–76

Keller KL, Aaker DA. 1992. The effects of sequential introduction of brand extensions. *J. Mark. Res.* 29:35–50

Kelley CA, Gaidis WC, Reingen PH. 1989. The use of vivid stimuli to enhance comprehension of the content of product warning messages. *J. Consum. Affairs* 23:243–66

Kent RJ, Machleit KA. 1990. The differential effects of within-brand and between-brand processing on the recall and recognition of television commercials. *J. Advert.* 19:4–14

Kirmani A. 1990. The effect of perceived advertising costs on brand perceptions. *J. Consum. Res.* 17:160–71

Kirmani A, Wright P. 1989. Money talks: perceived advertising expense and expected product quality. *J. Consum. Res.* 16:344–53

Klein NM, Yadav MS. 1989. Context effects on effort and accuracy in choice: an enquiry into adaptive decision making. *J. Consum. Res.* 15:411–21

Kleine RE III, Kernan JB. 1991. Contextual influences on the meanings ascribed to ordinary consumption objects. *J. Consum. Res.* 18:311–24

Krishna A. 1991. Effect of dealing patterns on consumer perceptions of deal frequency and willingness to pay. *J. Mark. Res.* 28:441–51

Krishna A, Currim IS, Shoemaker RW. 1991. Consumer perceptions of promotional activity. *J. Mark.* 55:4–16

Krishnamurthi L, Mazumdar T, Raj SP. 1992. Asymmetric response to price in consumer brand choice and purchase quantity decisions. *J. Consum. Res.* 19:387–400

Kuykendall D, Keating JP. 1990. Mood and persuasion: evidence for the differential influence of positive and negative states. *Psychol. Mark.* 7:1–9

Kvale S. 1992a. *Psychology and Postmodernism.* London: Sage. 230 pp.

Kvale S. 1992b. Postmodern psychology: a contradiction in terms? See Kvale 1992a, pp. 31–57

Laczniak RN, Carlson L. 1989. Examining the influence of attitude-toward-the-ad on brand attitudes. *J. Bus. Res.* 19:303–11

Laczniak RN, Muehling DD, Grossbart S. 1989. Manipulating message involvement in advertising research. *J. Advert.* 18:28–38

LaTour SA, Manrai AK. 1989. Interactive impact of informational and normative influence on donations. *J. Mark. Res.* 26:327–35

Lavin M, Archdeacon TJ. 1989. The relevance of historical method for marketing research. See Hirschman 1989, pp. 60–68

Lichtenstein DR, Bearden WO. 1989. Contextual influences on perceptions of merchant-supplied reference prices. *J. Consum. Res.* 16:55–66

Lichtenstein DR, Burton S. 1989. The relationship between perceived and objective price-quality. *J. Mark. Res.* 26:429–43

Lichtenstein DR, Burton S, Karson EJ. 1991. The effect of semantic cues on consumer perceptions of reference price ads. *J. Consum. Res.* 18:380–91

Lichtenstein DR, Burton S, O'Hara BS. 1989. Marketplace attributions and consumer evaluations of discount claims. *Psychol. Mark.* 6:163–80

Loken B, Ward J. 1990. Alternative approaches to understanding the determinants of typicality. *J. Consum. Res.* 17: 111–26

Lynch JG Jr, Chakravarti D, Mitra A. 1991. Contrast effects in consumer judgments: changes in mental representations or in the anchoring of rating scales? *J. Consum. Res.* 18:284–97

MacInnis DJ, Jaworski BJ. 1989. Information processing from advertisements: toward an integrative framework. *J. Mark.* 53:1–23

MacInnis DJ, Moorman C, Jaworski BJ. 1991. Enhancing and measuring consumers' motivation, opportunity, and ability to process brand information from ads. *J. Mark.* 55:32–53

MacInnis DJ, Park CW. 1991. The differential role of characteristics of music on high- and low-involvement consumers' processing of ads. *J. Consum. Res.* 18:161–73

MacKenzie SB, Lutz RJ. 1989. An empirical examination of the structural antecedents of attitude toward the ad in an advertising pretesting context. *J. Mark.* 53:48–65

MacKenzie SB, Spreng RA. 1992. How does motivation moderate the impact of central and peripheral processing on brand attitudes and intentions? *J. Consum. Res.* 18:519–29

Macklin MC, Machleit KA. 1989. Measuring preschool children's attitude. *Mark. Lett.* 1:253–65

Madden TJ, Ajzen I. 1991. Affective cues in persuasion: an assessment of causal mediation. *Mark. Lett.* 2:359–66

Maheswaran D, Meyers-Levy J. 1990. The influence of message framing and issue involvement. *J. Mark. Res.* 27:361–67

Maheswaran D, Sternthal B. 1990. The effects of knowledge, motivation, and type of message on ad processing and product judgments. *J. Consum. Res.* 17:66–73

Mathur M, Chattopadhyay A. 1991. The impact of moods generated by television programs on responses to advertising. *Psychol. Mark.* 8:59–77

Mayhew GE, Winer RS. 1992. An empirical analysis of internal and external reference prices using scanner data. *J. Consum. Res.* 19:62–70

Mazursky D, Geva A. 1989. Temporal decay in satisfaction—purchase intention relationship. *Psychol. Mark.* 6:211–27

McCracken G. 1989a. "Homeyness": a cultural account of one constellation of consumer goods and meanings. See Hirschman 1989, pp. 168–84

McCracken G. 1989b. Who is the celebrity endorser? Cultural foundations of the endorsement process. *J. Consum. Res.* 16:310–21

McGill AL. 1990. Predicting consumers' reactions to product failure: Do responsibility judgments follow from consumers' causal explanations? *Mark. Lett.* 2:59–70

McGill AL, Anand P. 1989a. The effect of imagery on information processing strategy in a multiattribute choice task. *Mark. Lett.* 1:7–16

McGill AL, Anand P. 1989b. The effect of vivid attributes on the evaluation of alternatives: the role of differential attention and cognitive elaboration. *J. Consum. Res.* 16:188–96

McGrath MA, Sherry JF Jr, Levy SJ. 1993. Giving voice to the gift: the use of projective techniques to recover lost meanings. *J. Consum. Psychol.* 2:171–91

McQuarrie EF, Mick DG. 1992. On resonance: a critical pluralistic inquiry into advertising rhetoric. *J. Consum. Res.* 19:180–97

Mehta R, Belk RW. 1991. Artifacts, identity, and transition: favorite possessions of Indians and Indian immigrants to the United States. *J. Consum. Res.* 17:398–411

Menasco MB, Curry DJ. 1989. Utility and choice: an empirical study of wife/husband decision making. *J. Consum. Res.* 16:87–97

Meyers-Levy J. 1989a. Priming effects on product judgments: a hemispheric interpretation. *J. Consum. Res.* 16:76–86

Meyers-Levy J. 1989b. The influence of a brand name's association set size and word frequency on brand memory. *J. Consum. Res.* 16:197–207

Meyers-Levy J. 1991. Elaborating on elaboration: the distinction between relational and item-specific elaboration. *J. Consum. Res.* 18:358–67

Meyers-Levy J, Maheswaran D. 1991. Exploring differences in males' and females' processing strategies. *J. Consum. Res.* 18:63–70

Meyers-Levy J, Maheswaran D. 1992. When timing matters: the influence of temporal distance on consumers' affective and persuasive responses. *J. Consum. Res.* 19: 424–33

Meyers-Levy J, Sternthal B. 1991. Gender differences in the use of message cues and judgments. *J. Mark. Res.* 28:84–96

Meyers-Levy J, Tybout AM. 1989. Schema congruity as a basis for product evaluation. *J. Consum. Res.* 16:39–54

Michael M. 1992. Postmodern subjects: towards a transgressive social psychology. See Kvale 1992a, pp. 74–87

Mick DG. 1992. Levels of subjective comprehension in advertising processing and their relations to ad perceptions, attitudes, and memory. *J. Consum. Res.* 18:411–24

Mick DG, Buhl C. 1992. A meaning-based model of advertising experiences. *J. Consum. Res.* 19:317–38

Mick DG, Politi LG. 1989. Consumers' interpretations of advertising imagery: a visit to the hell of connotation. See Hirschman 1989, pp. 85–96

Miniard PW, Bhatla S, Lord KR, Dickson PR, Unnava HR. 1991. Picture-based persuasion processes and the moderating role of involvement. *J. Consum. Res.* 18:92–107

Miniard PW, Bhatla S, Rose RL. 1990a. On the formation and relationship of ad and brand attitudes: an experimental and causal analysis. *J. Mark. Res.* 27:290–303

Miniard PW, Bhatla S, Sirdeshmukh D. 1992a. Mood as a determinant of postconsumption product evaluations: mood effects and their dependency on the affective intensity of the consumption experience. *J. Consum. Psychol.* 1:173–95

Miniard PW, Sirdeshmukh D, Innis DE. 1992b. Peripheral persuasion and brand choice. *J. Consum. Res.* 19:226–39

Miniard PW, Unnava HR, Bhatla S. 1990b. Investigating the recall inhibition effect: a test of practical considerations. *Mark. Lett.* 2:27–34

Mittal B. 1990. The relative roles of brand beliefs and attitude toward the ad as mediators of brand attitude: a second look. *J. Mark. Res.* 27:209–19

Muehling DD, Laczniak RN, Stoltman JJ. 1991. The moderating effects of ad message involvement: a reassessment. *J. Advert.* 20:29–38

Muehling DD, Stoltman JJ, Grossbart S. 1990. The impact of comparative advertising on levels of message involvement. *J. Advert.* 19:41–50

Mundorf N, Zillmann D, Drew D. 1991. Effects of disturbing televised events on the acquisition of information from subsequently presented commercials. *J. Advert.* 20:46–53

Murray JB, Ozanne JL. 1991. The critical imagination: emancipatory interests in consumer research. *J. Consum. Res.* 18:129–44

Murry JP Jr, Lastovicka JL, Singh SN. 1992. Feeling and liking responses to television programs: an examination of two explanations for media-context effects. *J. Consum. Res.* 18:441–51

Nedungadi P. 1990. Recall and consumer consideration sets: influencing choice without altering brand evaluations. *J. Consum. Res.* 17:263–76

Neslin SA, Shoemaker RW. 1989. An alternative explanation for lower repeat rates after promotion purchases. *J. Mark. Res.* 26:205–13

Novak TP, MacEvoy B. 1990. On comparing alternative segmentation schemes: the List of Values (LOV) and Values and Life Styles (VALS). *J. Consum. Res.* 17:105–9

O'Guinn TC, Belk RW. 1989. Heaven on earth: consumption at Heritage Village, USA. *J. Consum. Res.* 16:227–38

O'Guinn TC, Faber RJ. 1989. Compulsive buying: a phenomenological exploration. *J. Consum. Res.* 16:147–57

Ohanian R. 1991. The impact of celebrity spokespersons' perceived image on consumers' intention to purchase. *J. Advert. Res.* 31:46–54

Oliver RL, Swan JE. 1989a. Consumer perceptions of interpersonal equity and satisfaction in transactions: a field survey approach. *J. Mark.* 53:21–35

Oliver RL, Swan JE. 1989b. Equity and disconfirmation perceptions as influences on merchant and product satisfaction. *J. Consum. Res.* 16:372–83

Olney TJ, Holbrook MB, Batra R. 1991. Consumer responses to advertising: the effects of ad content, emotions, and attitude toward the ad on viewing time. *J. Consum. Res.* 17:440–53

Ortmeyer G, Huber J. 1990. Brand experience as a moderator of the negative impact of promotions. *Mark. Lett.* 2:35–45

Ozanne JL, Brucks M, Grewal D. 1992. A study of information search behavior during the categorization of new products. *J. Consum. Res.* 18:452–63

Ozanne JL, Hudson LA. 1989. Exploring diversity in consumer research. See Hirschman 1989, pp. 1–9

Park CW, Iyer ES, Smith DC. 1989. The effects of situational factors on in-store grocery shopping behavior: the role of store environment and time available for shopping. *J. Consum. Res.* 15:422–33

Park CW, Milberg S, Lawson R. 1991. Evaluation of brand extensions: the role of product feature similarity and brand concept consistency. *J. Consum. Res.* 18:185–93

Park CW, Smith DC. 1989. Product-level choice: a top-down or bottom-up process? *J. Consum. Res.* 16:289–99

Payne JW, Bettman JR, Johnson EJ. 1992. Behavioral decision research: a constructive processing perspective. *Annu. Rev. Psychol.* 43:87–131

Pechmann C. 1992. Predicting when two-sided ads will be more effective than one-sided ads: the role of correlational and correspondent inferences. *J. Mark. Res.* 29:441–53

Pechmann C, Ratneshwar S. 1991. The use of comparative advertising for brand positioning: association versus differentiation. *J. Consum. Res.* 18:145–60

Pechmann C, Ratneshwar S. 1992. Consumer covariation judgments: theory or data driven? *J. Consum. Res.* 19:373–86

Pechmann C, Stewart DW. 1990. The effects of comparative advertising on attention, memory, and purchase intentions. *J. Consum. Res.* 17:180–91

Peracchio LA. 1990. Designing research to reveal the young child's emerging competence. *Psychol. Mark.* 7:257–76

Peracchio LA. 1992. How do young children learn to be consumers? A script-processing approach. *J. Consum. Res.* 18:425–40

Peter JP. 1991. Philosophical tensions in consumer inquiry. See Robertson & Kassarjian 1991, pp. 533–47

Peter JP, Olson JC. 1989. The relativist/constructionist perspective on scientific knowledge and consumer research. See Hirschman 1989, pp. 24–28

Petty RE, Unnava R, Strathman AJ. 1991. Theories of attitude change. See Robertson & Kassarjian 1991, pp. 241–80

Qualls WJ, Puto CP. 1989. Organizational climate and decision framing: an integrated approach to analyzing industrial buying decisions. *J. Mark. Res.* 26:179–92

Ram S, Jung HS. 1991. How product usage influences consumer satisfaction. *Mark. Lett.* 2:403–11

Rao AR, Bergen ME. 1992. Price premium variations as a consequence of buyers' lack of information. *J. Consum. Res.* 19:412–23

Rao AR, Monroe KB. 1989. The effect of price, brand name, and store name on buyers' perceptions of product quality: an integrative review. *J. Mark. Res.* 26:351–57

Rao AR, Sieben WA. 1992. The effect of prior knowledge on price acceptability and the type of information examined. *J. Consum. Res.* 19:256–70

Ratneshwar S, Chaiken S. 1991. Comprehension's role in persuasion: the case of its moderating effect on the persuasive impact of source cues. *J. Consum. Res.* 18: 52–62

Richins ML. 1991. Social comparison and the idealized images of advertising. *J. Consum. Res.* 18:71–83

Richins ML, Bloch PH, McQuarrie EF. 1992. How enduring and situational involvement combine to create involvement responses. *J. Consum. Psychol.* 1:143–54

Richins ML, Dawson S. 1992. A consumer values orientation for materialism and its measurement: scale development and validation. *J. Consum. Res.* 19:303–16

Robertson TS, Kassarjian HH. 1991. *Handbook of Consumer Behavior.* Englewood Cliffs, NJ: Prentice-Hall. 614 pp.

Rogers JC, Williams TG. 1989. Comparative advertising effectiveness: practitioners' perceptions versus academic research findings. *J. Advert. Res.* 29:22–37

Rose RL, Bearden WO, Teel JE. 1992. An attributional analysis of resistance to group pressure regarding illicit drug and alcohol consumption. *J. Consum. Res.* 19:1–13

Ross WT Jr, Creyer EH. 1992. Making inferences about missing information: the effects of existing information. *J. Consum. Res.* 19:14–25

Ross WT Jr, Robertson TS. 1991. Information processing and innovative choice. *Mark. Lett.* 2:87–97

Rothschild ML, Hyun YJ. 1990. Predicting memory for components of TV commercials from EEG. *J. Consum. Res.* 16:472–78

Rudmin FW, Kilbourne WE. 1993. The meaning and morality of voluntary simplicity: history and hypotheses on deliberately denied materialism. *Queen's School of Business Working Paper #93-15.* Queen's University, Kingston, Ontario.

Sawyer AG, Howard DJ. 1991. Effects of omitting conclusions in advertisements to involved and uninvolved audiences. *J. Mark. Res.* 28:467–74

Schmitt BH, Dube L. 1992. Contextualized representations of brand extensions: Are feature lists or frames the basic components of consumer cognition? *Mark. Lett.* 3:115–26

Schumann DW, Petty RE, Clemons DS. 1990. Predicting the effectiveness of different strategies of advertising variation: a test of the repetition-variation hypotheses. *J. Consum. Res.* 17:192–202

Schumann DW, Thorson E. 1990. The influence of viewing context on commercial effectiveness: a selection-processing model. *Curr. Issues Res. Advert.* 12:1–24

Schwartz SH, Bilsky W. 1990. Toward a theory of the universal content and structure of values: extensions and cross-cultural replications. *J. Pers. Soc.* 58:878–91

Scott C, Klein DM, Bryant J. 1990. Consumer response to humor in advertising: a series of field studies using behavioral observation. *J. Consum. Res.* 16:498–501

Scott LM. 1990. Understanding jingles and needledrop: a rhetorical approach to music in advertising. *J. Consum. Res.* 17:223–36

Sherry JF Jr. 1991. Postmodern alternatives: the interpretive turn in consumer research. See Robertson & Kassarjian 1991, pp. 548–91

Sherry JF Jr, McGrath MA, Levy SJ. 1992a.

The dark side of the gift. *J. Bus. Res.* 26:1–19
Sherry JF Jr, McGrath MA, Levy SJ. 1992b. The disposition of the gift and many unhappy returns. *J. Retail.* 68:40–65
Shimp TA, Stuart EW, Engle RW. 1991. A program of classical conditioning experiments testing variations in the conditioned stimulus and context. *J. Consum. Res.* 18:1–12
Simmons CJ, Lynch JG Jr. 1991. Inference effects without inference making? Effects of missing information on discounting and use of presented information. *J. Consum. Res.* 17:477–91
Simonson I. 1989. Choice based on reasons: the case of attraction and compromise effects. *J. Consum. Res.* 16:158–74
Simonson I. 1990a. The effect of buying decisions on consumers' assessment of their tastes. *Mark. Lett.* 2:5–14
Simonson I. 1990b. The effect of purchase quantity and timing on variety-seeking behavior. *J. Mark. Res.* 27:150–62
Simonson I. 1992. The influence of anticipating regret and responsibility on purchase decisions. *J. Consum. Res.* 19:105–18
Simonson I, Winer RS. 1992. The influence of purchase quantity and display format on consumer preference for variety. *J. Consum. Res.* 19:133–38
Singh SN, Hitchon JC. 1989. The intensifying effects of exciting television programs on the reception of subsequent commercials. *Psychol. Mark.* 6:1–31
Smith RA. 1991. The effects of visual and verbal advertising information on consumers' inferences. *J. Advert.* 20:13–23
Snyder R. 1992. Comparative advertising and brand evaluation: toward developing a categorization approach. *J. Consum. Psychol.* 1:15–30
Srinivasan N, Ratchford BT. 1991. An empirical test of a model of external search for automobiles. *J. Consum. Res.* 18:233–42
Stayman DM, Alden DL, Smith KH. 1992. Some effects of schematic processing on consumer expectations and disconfirmation judgments. *J. Consum. Res.* 19:240–55
Stayman DM, Batra R. 1991. Encoding and retrieval of ad affect in memory. *J. Mark. Res.* 28:232–39
Stayman DM, Deshpande R. 1989. Situational ethnicity and consumer behavior. *J. Consum. Res.* 16:361–71
Stayman DM, Kardes FR. 1992. Spontaneous inference processes in advertising: effects of need for cognition and self-monitoring on inference generation and utilization. *J. Consum. Psychol.* 1:125–42
Steenkamp JEM, Baumgartner H. 1992. The role of optimum stimulation level in exploratory consumer behavior. *J. Consum. Res.* 19:434–48
Stern BB. 1989a. Literary criticism and consumer research: overview and illustrative analysis. *J. Consum. Res.* 16:322–34
Stern BB. 1989b. Literary explication: a methodology for consumer research. See Hirschman 1989, pp. 48–59
Sujan M, Bettman JR. 1989. The effects of brand positioning strategies on consumers' brand and category perceptions: some insights from schema research. *J. Mark. Res.* 26:454–67
Sullivan GL. 1990. Music format effects in radio advertising. *Psychol. Mark.* 7:97–108
Tellis GJ, Gaeth GJ. 1990. Best value, price-seeking, and price aversion: the impact of information and learning on consumer choices. *J. Mark.* 54:34–45
Thomas GP. 1992. The influence of processing conversational information on inference, argument elaboration, and memory. *J. Consum. Res.* 19:83–92
Thompson CJ, Locander WB, Pollio HR. 1989. Putting consumer experience back into consumer research: the philosophy and method of existential-phenomenology. *J. Consum. Res.* 16:133–46
Thompson CJ, Locander WB, Pollio HR. 1990. The lived meaning of free choice: an existential-phenomenological description of everyday consumer experiences of contemporary married women. *J. Consum. Res.* 17:346–61
Tse DK, Belk RW, Zhou N. 1989. Becoming a consumer society: a longitudinal and cross-cultural content analysis of print ads from Hong Kong, the People's Republic of China, and Taiwan. *J. Consum. Res.* 15:457–72
Tse DK, Nicosia FM, Wilton PC. 1990. Consumer satisfaction as a process. *Psychol. Mark.* 7:177–93
Unnava HR, Burnkrant RE. 1991a. An imagery-processing view of the role of pictures in print advertisements. *J. Mark. Res.* 28:226–31
Unnava HR, Burnkrant RE. 1991b. Effects of repeating varied ad executions on brand name memory. *J. Mark. Res.* 28:406–16
Urbany JE, Dickson PR. 1991. Consumer normal price estimation: market versus personal standards. *J. Consum. Res.* 18:45–51
Urbany JE, Dickson PR, Wilkie WL. 1989a. Buyer uncertainty and information search. *J. Consum. Res.* 16:208–15
Urbany JE, Madden TJ, Dickson PR. 1989b. All's not fair in pricing: an initial look at the dual entitlement principle. *Mark. Lett.* 1:17- 25
van Raaij FW. 1991. The formation and use of expectations in consumer decision making. See Robertson & Kassarjian 1991, pp. 401–18
Venkatraman MP. 1989. Involvement and risk. *Psychol. Mark.* 6:229–47

Venkatraman MP, Marlino D, Kardes FR, Sklar KB. 1990. The interactive effects of message appeal and individual differences on information processing and persuasion. *Psychol. Mark.* 7:85–96

Wallendorf M, Arnould EJ. 1991. "We gather together": consumption rituals of Thanksgiving Day. *J. Consum. Res.* 18:13–31

Ward JC, Reingen PH. 1990. Sociocognitive analysis of group decision making among consumers. *J. Consum. Res.* 17:245–62

Weinberger MG, Campbell L. 1990/1991. The use and impact of humor in radio advertising. *J. Advert. Res.* 30:44–52

Wells WD. 1989. Lectures and dramas. See Cafferata & Tybout 1989, pp. 13–20

Wells WD. 1993. Discovery-oriented consumer research. *J. Consum. Res.* 19:489–505

Westbrook RA, Oliver RL. 1991. The dimensionality of consumption emotion patterns and consumer satisfaction. *J. Consum. Res.* 18:84–91

Wilkes RE. 1992. A structural modeling approach to the measurement and meaning of cognitive age. *J. Consum. Res.* 19:292–301

Worth LT, Smith J, Mackie DM. 1992. Gender schematicity and preference for gender-typed products. *Psychol. Mark.* 9:17–30

Yi Y. 1990a. Cognitive and affective priming effects of the context for print advertisements. *J. Advert.* 19:40–48

Yi Y. 1990b. The indirect effects of advertisements designed to change product attribute beliefs. *Psychol. Mark.* 7:47–63

Yi Y. 1990c. The effects of contextual priming in print advertisements. *J. Consum. Res.* 17:215–22

Zinkhan GM, Roth MS, Saxton MJ. 1992. Knowledge development and scientific status in consumer-behavior research: a social exchange perspective. *J. Consum. Res.* 19:282–91

Annu. Rev. Psychol. 1994. 45:171–95

TEACHING AND LEARNING: NEW MODELS

James J. Gallagher

Frank Porter Graham Child Development Center, University of North Carolina, Chapel Hill, North Carolina 27514

KEY WORDS: thinking processes, teacher roles, reflective teaching, experts/novices, educational reform

CONTENTS

INTRODUCTION

The last decade has seen a considerable shift in emphasis in the relationship between the teacher and the learner. In the past, teachers were typically seen as dispensers of knowledge and students were seen as absorbers of information.

0066-4308/94/0201-0171$05.00

This view has been increasingly supplanted by a portrait of teachers as reflective planners and students as decision-makers who are concerned with what and how they learn (Solas 1992).

Instead of simply loading learners with reams of specific facts and unconnected information, educators are increasingly viewing learners as bundles of knowledge structures that become increasingly sophisticated and hierarchical as they gain experience. Such a shift requires a reassessment of both the learner and the teacher across numerous domains.

THE LEARNER AND KNOWLEDGE STRUCTURES

Intelligence

The manifest diversity of learners in the American educational system has led to many studies and model instructions of how learning proceeds and what factors influence the learning process. In the past decade, our understanding of the construct of intelligence has evolved steadily. We have come a considerable way from the unproductive idea that intelligence is what an IQ test measures. In place of a maturational unfolding of memory, association, and reasoning abilities, we now have models that involve the sequential interaction of the individual with his/her environment and the successive development of knowledge structures, complex networks of facts, associations, higher order generalizations, etc. Also, there has been an emphasis on the executive control processes by which the student makes decisions, uses strategies, and thinks about his/her own thinking process (Sternberg 1986, Gardner 1986, Borkowski & Kurtz 1987, Siegler 1986).

These new model makers have tried to categorize the full range of human abilities instead of focusing (as did Terman or Wechsler) on intelligence test development in which test items were included if they predicted school success or adult performance. These new models are much more complex, with many more dimensions that are of interest to those studying the learner and how to improve learning abilities.

There is substantial evidence from sibling and twin studies in behavior genetics to support important early individual differences in ability to learn (Plomin 1988). New models of how intelligence interacts with environment do not invalidate earlier models based on genetic influence, but rather they emphasize the crystallization of such native abilities that occurs over time.

These developing knowledge structures are influenced by a variety of social and environmental forces. For example, girls have been shown to be equal (on average) to boys in mathematics ability and performance through the fourth grade. After that time, males appear to gain an increasing level of superiority (Brandon et al 1987). Such superiority, however, is assumed to be caused by a societal bias against girls in the fields of math and science, which results in reduced interest and levels of practice at relevant activities in these fields (Reis & Callahan 1989).

Sternberg's model presents the concept of an *executive function* that allows the individual to access knowledge structures in a variety of ways. These strategies for accessing existing information and seeking new knowledge allow for a more effective use of stored knowledge structures. A good example of an executive function application is the use of Parnes' creative problem-solving process to organize a complex problem into stages so it can be attacked (Parnes et al 1977, Treffinger & Isaksen 1992). Full nurturance of the executive function would require teachers to ensure that their students master a variety of problem-solving and problem-finding strategies. In this way, students could effectively access the existing knowledge structures and focus their search techniques to discover additional relevant knowledge.

The knowledge structures of the student can be dense with innumerable linkages, as it is with our knowledge of our home town, its geography, its weather, its people, its industry, etc. On the other hand, knowledge structures can be highly limited. For example, only a limited amount of information can be gained from one visit to London plus some limited reading about the city. The "Aha!" phenomenon, experienced at some time by all students ("Now I see how calculus can solve everyday problems!!!"), represents a newly-perceived linkage between existing knowledge structures that had previously been strangers to one another. An additional teaching responsibility, therefore, is to create an environment for the student to explore such linkages and to bring together disparate parts of the knowledge structure so that what Whitehead (1929) called inert knowledge—knowledge existing in the memory of the individual but unconnected to other bodies of knowledge—becomes usable in relevant situations.

Investigators are increasingly questioning whether thinking can be viewed as a symbolic process apart from the knowledge context in which it appears. Past emphasis in school has been on individual cognition, insistence on symbolic performances, and the mastery of general competencies (Resnick 1989), but there is now increasing evidence suggesting that such requirements are not in line with what we know about how conceptual systems are mastered.

Similarly, Nesher (1989) has pointed out that proponents of artificial intelligence have largely abandoned a general problem-solving strategy in favor of studying intellectual performance within restricted domains. This seems important when we look at instructional goals such as the mastery of thinking skills, which takes enhanced meaning from the context of the whole experience, in light of the content field in which such thinking skills are exercised. When teachers try to encourage the mastery of thinking skills, the most successful programs appear to be organized around particular bodies of knowledge and interpretation—in other words, particular subject matter—rather than around general abilities (Resnick 1987).

There has also been some interest in how one can measure knowledge structure. The key to understanding knowledge structure has been to discover the relationship between concepts. A variety of methods have been used by investigators to determine the individual's conceptual relationships: word association, ordered recall, card sorting, and numerical rating of degrees of relatedness. Such devices can produce a matrix of proximity values (Goldsmith et al 1991). A variety of representational networks that will allow group comparisons, such as between naive and expert groups, have met with some success (Schvaneveldt et al 1988, Goldsmith & Davenport 1990).

Creativity

One goal of many teachers is to encourage their students to think creatively. But how does a teacher help students generate creative or original thought? Creativity, as a construct and a process, has received considerable attention in recent years (Sternberg 1988, Feldhusen & Treffinger 1990, Hayes 1989).

One of the earliest efforts to bring the construct of creativity into educational circles was done by Guilford (1967), whose model of the structure of intellect stressed divergent thinking as one of the components of creativity. More sophisticated measures of divergent thinking are still being pursued, with some success in terms of validity checks on creative performance (Hong & Milgram 1991, Okuda et al 1991, Runco 1993). There is general recognition, however, that the study of the complex nature of creativity calls for a multi-dimensional approach involving many different cognitive, personality, and motivational factors combined to generate creative products by students.

The earlier work of Getzels & Csikszentmihalyi (1976) has shown problem-finding to be one of the most important aspects of the creative process. This process, however, seems almost entirely overlooked in American education, where the teacher traditionally has formulated the problem and then presented it to the student. Some recent efforts have been made to develop a curriculum around the process of problem-finding (Gallagher et al 1992). Research on this topic has also increased, as Sternberg & Lubart (1993) remind us that problem definition (the formulation of the problem) is one of the essential elements in creativity. They note three insight processes that lead to original thinking: (*a*) *selective encoding,* which involves noticing what is potentially relevant to understanding and solving problems; (*b*) *selective comparison,* which involves relating new information to old information; and (*c*) *selective combination,* which involves putting together information that has only distant connections. The role of a comprehensive knowledge structure in effectively using these processes is clear. The more interconnections you have in your knowledge structure, the more you will be able to do the selective comparisons and selective combinations. In looking at famous musicians, Hayes (1989) found that a strong knowledge base was necessary before significant musical compositions were produced. Only 3 of the 500 notable musical compositions in Hayes' study were completed before the tenth year of the composers' careers. Such information is a powerful antidote to those who would claim that creativity is merely a process that can be taught without reference to a content domain (deBono 1985).

A variety of personality traits can also be linked to creative production: tolerance for ambiguity, risk-taking, willingness to persevere, and a high degree of self-esteem (Hennessey & Amabile 1988). These features can be emphasized and differentially rewarded by teachers trying to maximize creative student performance. Delcourt (1993) points out the importance of allowing students to choose problems of their own interest and encouraging creative productivity to motivate students to do extended work on major projects.

Experts and Novices

The study of experts versus novices is one of the most helpful investigations for conceptualizing the knowledge structures of the learner as he/she proceeds with the tasks involved in learning. Chi et al (1988) have summarized the general findings of a variety of studies comparing experts with novices on subject matter ranging from medical diagnosis to chess:

1. Experts excel mainly in their own domains.
2. Experts perceive large meaningful patterns in their domains.
3. Experts are fast: They are faster than novices at performing the skills of their domains and they quickly solve problems with little error.
4. Experts have superior short-term and long-term memory.
5. Experts see and represent problems in their domains at a deeper level than do novices; novices tend to represent problems at a superficial level.
6. Experts spend a great deal of time analyzing problems qualitatively.
7. Experts have strong self-monitoring skills.

One clear extension of these findings is the assumption that learners develop separate knowledge structures in various domains. The more experienced learners become, the more they are able to use this knowledge base to solve problems. Novices, on the other hand, are reduced to dealing with immediate situations—but without the access to knowledge structures that bring essential meaning to new events or new facts.

The exception to this general rule appears in ill-structured problems (Johnson 1988), where the knowledge structure of the expert may or may not play a role in the solution. Solving ill-structured problems may require the deconstruction of part of the existing knowledge structure to accommodate and adapt to the unusual patterns found in such problems. Therefore, the teacher should concentrate on helping students build effective knowledge structures in a domain and encourage students to link various knowledge structures across domains, instead of simply providing more and more information (assuming that the learner is merely a sponge sopping up new facts).

The issue of transferability of knowledge is raised again by Perkins & Salomon (1989). They accept that transfer is very difficult, particularly when the subject has limited content knowledge, but they maintain that it is possible to encourage knowledge transfer by teaching students general strategies or heuristics to use on a rich, domain-specific knowledge base. They conclude that "the approach that now seems warranted calls for the intimate intermingling of generality and context specificity in instruction" (p. 24).

With the emphasis on thinking processes and encouraging students to think about problems or issues, why doesn't such thinking happen more frequently in classrooms? Onosko (1991) used interviews with teachers and administrators and classroom observations to explore barriers to higher order thinking in the classroom. He found six major barriers: the tradition of instruction as knowledge transmission, the need to cover broad curriculum, low expectations of students, large numbers of students, lack of planning time, and a culture of teacher isolation. Onosko pointed out that the assignment of a 2–3 page theme from a teacher with a student load of 125, allowing 15 minutes for critiquing each theme, would add 31 hours to the workload of the teacher! Obviously, some structural changes are needed before the desired instructional environments for higher order thinking can be instituted.

Gifted Students

There is a special group of students whose performance remains something of a mystery, given the above statements about difficulty of transfer and the domain-specific knowledge structures. Many students referred to as gifted apparently do have a certain type of expertise that they can carry over from domain to domain. In short, they appear to be the general problem solvers that artificial intelligence investigators have been unable to create (Perkins & Salomon 1989). It seems clear that gifted students have superior memories and may have some special learning strategies, like chunking, to acquire knowledge rapidly in many domains. Such students also seem to have the motivation to continue working on a topic for a considerable length of time along with the metacognitive strategies that allow them to move more easily across domains (Posner 1988).

A question raised about gifted students is whether the differences in cognitive development between gifted and average students is quantitative or qualitative. In a review of the topic, Rogers (1986) concluded that quantitative differences in cognition could lead to qualitative differences in performance. Kanevsky (1990) also found that gifted students aged 4–8 were able to use constructive strategies to solve puzzles such as the *Tower of Hanoi.* When compared with students of average ability, the gifted students were not only more accurate, but they refused help from the examiner more often (they preferred an autonomous solution) and they seemed to learn from their mistakes more readily. These strategies resulted in superior cognitive performance. It seems that gifted students have a richer knowledge structure in many different domains and that they also have sets of strategies allowing them to cope with difficult problems. Of course such strategies can also be taught to nongifted students (Schack 1993).

Self-Image

How the student views himself/herself becomes an important aspect of the student's willingness or ability to learn. Schunk (1991) points out that there is evidence that self-efficacy predicts such diverse outcomes as academic achievement, social skills, smoking cessation, pain tolerance, athletic performances, career choices, assertiveness, coping with feared events, recovery from heart attack, and sales performance. In this case, self-efficacy is defined as a person's assessment of his/her own capabilities to organize and execute courses of action required to attain designated types of performances. Students can maintain widely varying senses of self-efficacy, depending on the context. They may have a high sense of self-efficacy in reading and a low one in math; they may have an even lower one in social relationships. In Schunk's view, the important point is that self-efficacy is not only a powerful force affecting many important dimensions in the educational situation, but it can be modified by success or failure, by attributions, and even by the timing of rewards or feedback from a situation.

It is often overlooked that self-efficacy is as valid a concept to apply to teacher behavior as it is to student behavior. Teachers with low self-efficacy in certain topic areas may avoid planning instructional activities that they believe may exceed their own limited capabilities. They may expend little effort to find additional materials, or they may not re-teach the content in ways the student might understand better. Teachers who are not confident of their mastery in certain subject areas may keep to the superhighways of the curriculum and avoid the interesting back roads that help the student fill in his/her conceptual map of the area.

Since self-efficacy seems to be a significant factor in the student approach to school and learning, a fundamental question is what factors influence self-efficacy and what factors, in particular, can the school control? Hoge et al (1990) conducted a multiple regression analysis of the effects of grades, school climate, teacher evaluation of work and social habits, student ratings of teachers, and other factors on the self-esteem of 322 students in two public middle schools over a two-year period. A variety of school variables seem to affect the self-esteem of students. For academic self-esteem, the most important factors were feedback from teachers and the school climate, but for self-esteem in particular disciplines the most important aspect seems to be grades received in the discipline. There appear to be different influences, however, at different years of development, suggesting idiosyncratic local influences such as specific teachers.

Self-Regulation

Since the great increase in interest in students' metacognitive processes, there has been a corresponding interest in self-regulated learning—a version of the executive self-monitoring process. Zimmerman & Martinez-Pons (1990) studied 45 boys and 45 girls enrolled in a school for gifted students, divided equally in grades 5, 8, and 11. They compared these students with a similar number of students from regular schools concerning their use of self-regulated learning strategies as measured by a structured interview schedule and their estimates of their own of verbal and mathematical self-efficacy.

Zimmerman & Martinez-Pons found a strong relationship between measures of self-efficacy in both the verbal and mathematical domains with regard to the use of self-regulated strategies. The gifted students reported much higher levels of self-efficacy and usage of self-regulated strategies at all grade levels than did the students from the regular classes. Gifted students displayed greater organizing and transforming, seeking of peer assistance, and reviewing of their notes. As might be expected, these monitoring skills and attitudes of self-efficacy generally increased with advancing grade levels. The investigators believed that direct instruction in models of self-regulation could help all students become more effective learners.

Cultural Values

Obviously, values about learning itself, which are transmitted through the family and peer society, go far in determining a particular student's posture toward learning. This posture, whether enthusiastic or hostile or depressed, can make an enormous difference in the learning capabilities of that student.

One factor related to learning may be the cultural values and practices in which the individual learner is immersed. A sample of 785 randomly selected children entering Kindergarten in a major urban area were examined, and their families interviewed, regarding the children's beginning math skills (Entwisle & Alexander 1990). At the beginning of the year, there were no differences between black and white students in computation or verbal skills and only a modest difference in math reasoning skills. By the end of the first grade, however, these groups differed significantly by race on all three dimensions. As early as the first grade, the academic performance cleavage related to race and socioeconomic factors had begun. A further finding in this study was the belief of parents that boys would do better than girls in math. This apparently caused sons to view themselves as better in math—even though the objective results showed no differences between the two groups. Such higher self-efficacy may link itself to later superior performance.

Another variable affecting the learner is the cultural/ecological environment in which students find themselves. A recent review of research on schooling and achievement of African-American and Asian-American children revealed a stereotype that predicts educational failure for African-Americans and educational excellence for Asian-Americans (Slaughter-Defoe et al 1990).

Studies of African-American families have emphasized the poor socioeconomic conditions, the absent father, and peer groups hostile to education, whereas studies of Asian-American families have stressed family values and academic expectations. Slaughter-Defoe et al (1990) urge a greater effort to research the role of cultural factors impacting on family members and to encourage studies that focus on the diversity of such populations (e.g. Why do many black students succeed and many Asian students do indifferently?). They also emphasize the teacher's role in understanding cultural differences and modifying teaching styles to take into account such differences.

Ogbu (1992) proposes that the minority learner will do well in those cultures in which they are voluntary immigrants, as opposed to involuntary minorities brought to the majority culture against their will—as with blacks in the United States. Ogbu looks at Korean children as an example. These minority children do poorly academically in Japan, where they are essentially colonial forced labor, but they do well academically in the United States, where they come willingly. Cultural values and orientation obviously play a strong role in motivating or inhibiting the learner in the school setting. In a review of the history of motivational research in education, Weiner (1990) points to the interaction of self-concept and culture and concludes that school motivation cannot be divorced from the social fabric in which it is embedded.

Children with Special Needs

Any attempts to discover general principles of learning or general instructional strategies of teaching must take into account and adapt such principles appropriately to individuals who are most different from the norm. The term "exceptional children" has been used to refer to such students and many diverse approaches and programs have been instituted in the schools to help such students reach their learning potential.

For example, children with mental retardation can be divided into two major groups (Hodapp et al 1990): those at the bottom of the general intelligence distribution, and those who have suffered particular genetic, metabolic, or neurological insults. Particularly in the latter case, the children may reveal special learning problems that require modified instructional strategies and content; children in the former case may need modification in the pacing of the curriculum.

Because students with mental retardation appear to have major difficulty in transferring information from one situation to another and in generalizing information, instruction has been adapted in a variety of ways to try to cope with these problems. The direct instruction of needed skills in the social and vocational areas (with vocational skills learned in the job site) is encouraged. The unit approach is used to show directly important interrelationships to students, rather than relying on the students to make necessary connections themselves (Polloway et al 1991).

Strategies such as cooperative learning (Johnson et al 1990) are effective in teaching social skills to children with disabilities, and in aiding their social acceptance in the classroom by students without disabilities. In addition, small group instruction with specific tasks appears helpful in controlling off-task behavior (Brigham et al 1992).

The development of the Individualized Education Program (IEP)—now mandated by law—has aided in the development of particular educational plans and strategies for individual exceptional students. The IEP requires an education team composed of teachers, the principal, and other relevant specialists to develop, with the parent, a set of goals, educational strategies for meeting those goals, and some criteria by which to judge the program's success (Kirk et al 1993).

Children with learning disabilities comprise a significant number of exceptional children in the public schools (almost 5% of the student body) (U.S. Dept. of Education 1991). "Learning disabilities" originally referred to a small number of children with suspected central nervous system problems that caused unusual developmental patterns, but it now applies to many students who are just having trouble in school and who cannot be otherwise labeled (Lerner 1993).

One of the most prevalent devices to improve the achievement of students with learning disabilities has been referred to as the diagnostic-prescriptive model. Attempts are made, through diagnostic testing and interviews, to identify the particular learning problem of the individual student and then to design a remedial program to counteract or bypass the problem. The IEP has been of considerable help in structuring such programs.

Students with learning disabilities often have major problems in coping with academic situations, a lack of problem-solving skills, and an inability to apply strategies to new problems (Coleman 1992, Schumaker et al 1991).

Accordingly, in addition to social skills instruction, there has been an emphasis on teaching such learning and coping strategies directly.

A number of self-management skills have been incorporated into special education programs for students with learning disabilities: self-monitoring, where students become aware of self-impulses and record them; self-evaluation, where students compare their behavior against some standard; self-reinforcement, where students reward themselves after reaching some desired standard of behavior; and self-instruction, where students talk to themselves with verbal encouragement. Such techniques have proven successful for increasing on-task performance (Hughes et al 1989). Whether these self-management techniques also help achieve long-range goals for exceptional children remains to be determined.

A new category within the general domain of special needs children has been the Attention Deficit Hyperactive Disorder (ADHD), which describes children who are easily distracted, hyperactive, and impulsive. These children often have difficulty learning and their teachers have difficulty instructing them. One strategy that seems effective for such children is a combination of direct learning and instruction in the mastery of academic coping skills, combined with medication (Forness & Kavale 1988, Kauffman 1989).

Children with serious behavior problems are another difficult group of students that teachers must cope with. Over 70% of such students are found to have substantial below-grade achievement (Nelson & Pearson 1991), and this group has the highest dropout rate of any group of students (Wagner et al 1991). The instructional strategies used vary from operant conditioning—using positive reinforcement to strengthen positive social skills and negative reinforcement to reduce undesirable behavior (Mulick et al 1991)—to ecological strategies that create healthy educational and living environments in which students can learn positive social and learning skills (Polloway et al 1989).

Applied Behavioral Analysis (ABA) has been used extensively with children with moderate to severe disabilities. It is distinguished by a focus on rather small units of learning with detailed analysis on specific behaviors, together with an analysis of the child's strengths and weaknesses. The desired student behavior is then identified and the events antecedent and consequent to the behavior are changed in order to modify the student's behavior. The child is rewarded following successful completion of the task or learning, and the results over time are charted to indicate the gains made by the student (Van Houten & Rolider 1991).

With the return of many children with disabilities to the regular education program under the philosophy of full inclusion, the classroom teacher will need a larger set of strategies to help children with special needs and will also need direct assistance from special education personnel.

TEACHERS AND THE TEACHING PROCESS

Since the extraordinary production of the *Handbook of Research on Teaching* (Wittrock 1986), there has been increased recognition of the teacher and the teaching process as an important focus of research. As we have seen in the preceding section on the learner, the complexity of developmental cognition, personality, motivation, and the impact of many diverse social forces on all of these student capabilities present a special challenge to the teacher. The teacher is now expected to create enriched learning environments, to design student interactive activities, and to be aware of the specific content he/she is expected to present—all while being reflective on his/her own role in the interactive and sequential process.

Shulman (1987) has stated that the foundation of the new educational reform movement lies in the development of sophisticated teachers who are knowledgeable about educational content, process, and the understanding of students and institutions. Shulman believes that there are four sources for preparation of a sophisticated teacher: 1. the scholarship and content discipline, which refers to the understanding of the structure of the subject matter being taught; 2. the understanding of educational materials and structures, which includes both the scope and sequence of curriculum, tests, and various materials, and an understanding of how institutions such as schools operate; 3. formal educational scholarship, or the processes of schooling, teaching, and learning; and 4. the wisdom of practice, in which long experience becomes significant for teaching a solid knowledge base. Shulman points out that teaching is conducted without an audience of peers, and thus is devoid of a history of practice! Shulman feels the next major task for education is to catalog the educational process and he proposes a case method approach.

Shulman has presented a model of pedagogical reasoning by which the reflective teacher can think about himself/herself, the content, the processes, the needs of individual students, etc, and can make conscious choices about what to teach and how to teach it on the basis of his/her background of knowledge and experience. Table 1 provides a brief outline of the major dimensions of the model. It is unclear how many of the 2.5 million teachers currently working in elementary and secondary schools can reach this sophisticated level of understanding of content and pedagogy.

The earlier discussion of expert-novice knowledge structures of students can be extended to include teachers. What does it take to reach the mastery level, the expertise that Shulman has proposed? Goodlad (1990) has suggested a similar set of impressive goals for the teacher: to possess a knowledge about the nation's government, to have the intellectual tools to participate broadly in the human conversation, to possess the pedagogical knowledge and skills necessary to arrange optimal conditions for learning, and to understand the curriculum assessment and how to sustain renewal.

Experts and Novices

Any teachers meeting Shulman & Goodlad's standards surely qualify as experts in education. A natural question to pose in expert-novice comparisons is whether expert teachers differ from novice teachers in the same way that experts in chess, physics, medical diagnoses, etc, differ from novices in those same fields. Berliner (1987) compared a sample of nine expert teachers with more than five years' experience to a sample of six first-year teachers of mathematics and science. He also compared these two groups to a group of six postulants who were knowledgeable in math and science, but lacked teaching experience (i.e. professional mathematicians and scientists).

Table 1 A Model of Pedagogical Reasoning and Action

Comprehension
Of purposes, subject matter structures, ideas within and outside the discipline
Transformation
Preparation: critical interpretation and analysis of texts, structuring and segmenting, development of a curricular repertoire, and clarification of purposes
Representation: use of a representational repertoire which includes analogies, metaphors, examples, demonstrations, explanations, and so forth
Selection: choice from among an instructional repertoire which includes modes of teaching, organizing, managing, and arranging
Adaption and Tailoring to Student Characteristics: consideration of conceptions, preconceptions, misconceptions and difficulties, language culture, and motivations, social class, gender, age, ability, aptitude, interests, self-concepts, and attention
Instruction
Management, presentations, interactions, group work, discipline, humor, questioning, and other aspects of active teaching, discover or inquiry instruction, and the observable forms of classroom teaching
Evaluation
Checking for student understanding during interactive teaching
Testing student understanding at the end of lessons or units
Evaluating one's own performance and adjusting for experiences
Reflection
Reviewing, reconstructing, reenacting and critically analyzing one's own and the class' performance, and grounding explanations in evidence
New Comprehensions
Of purposes, subject matter, students, teaching, and self
Consolidation of new understandings, and learnings from experience

Source: Shulman 1987

By comparing their classroom and lesson plans given in a hypothetical scenario of having to fill in for an absent teacher (files on the students were given to each teacher), Berliner found that the groups did differ in their plans and their thinking about the situation. The expert teachers had a clear vision of the students and classes they were to teach, they were able to draw upon past experiences on how to work with both rapid- and slow-learning students, and they were able to bring in many ideas beyond the text and the absent teacher's plans in order to organize new lessons. In short, they had a knowledge structure about the classroom and teaching that allowed them to propose key actions that the novices and postulants could not. Berliner raised the question of whether we could establish a laboratory in teacher education to study exemplary cases of schools, teachers, lesson planning, etc.

The expert vs novice comparison of teachers has been extended to include concepts of time and the different ways teachers perceive time in classroom instruction. Tochon & Munby (1993) compared 23 novice and 23 expert teachers (expert teachers had a minimum of seven years experience, and had been recommended by resource personnel) on a simulated exercise and structured interview protocols. They found that the experts were less concerned about time and improvised when their original plans seemed inappropriate. Novices tended to make frequent short-term modifications to their plans, which seemed neither accurate nor sufficiently flexible.

In the case of teachers, as well as other professionals, the expert appears to have developed a knowledge structure that allows him/her to adjust to the needs of the present situation with the confidence that the long-range goals can still be obtained despite temporary setbacks (such as unexpected demands of time). The novice, without the knowledge structure and past experience to draw upon, seems limited to adjustments within the framework of the immediate situation.

Models of Teacher Roles

There has been a growing trend in research to discover something about teachers' thinking from the perspective of the teachers themselves. A new set of methodologies that includes ethnomethodology, phenomenology, and symbolic interactionism has accompanied this trend (Solas 1992). This interest in the personal perception of the teacher has caused many to revisit Kelly's (1963) Personal Construct theory, which attempted to explain the idiosyncratic manner in which individuals view the world. Methodologies such as autobiographies (Butt et al 1990) and the development of a repertory grid, which is constructed through an individual's response to pairs of concepts similar to the semantic differential, encourage teachers to become reflective about their own role in the teaching-learning process.

One similar approach to the study of teaching is reflective practice, which is the study of the practitioner reflecting upon his/her own performance and on the complex series of events involved in teaching a lesson (Schon 1991). Schon points out that using case studies, in which the practitioner reflects upon his/her own practice, turns research into a reflective practice itself. A new set of questions must be confronted when conducting such research, including:

1. What is appropriate for the practitioner to reflect on?
2. What is an appropriate way of observing and reflecting on practice? In what sort of activity is reflection most effectively applied?
3. When we have taken the reflective turn, what constitutes appropriate rigor?
4. What does the reflective turn imply for the researcher's stance toward his enterprise? Toward his subjects? His research activity? Himself?

There is little doubt that both the phenomenological approach to research and the recognition of the importance of the individual's perception of a situation are beginning to play much more important roles in research on teaching—roles that demand new approaches to methodology, consideration of the validity of observations, and the theories of teaching and learning.

The role that the teacher plays in the classroom and the approach that teachers take to teaching often depends on their view of the students. Many teachers will go about their work without reflecting on it too much, but there is a view that teachers become professional only when they reflect on and choose a stance that guides and sustains them in educating these students (Fenstermacher & Soltis 1992).

Fenstermacher & Soltis have identified three separate roles and approaches to teaching:

1. *The executive approach* views the teacher as an executor—a person charged with bringing about certain learnings using the best skills and techniques possible. Carefully developed curriculum materials and research on the effects of teaching are important to this approach.
2. *The therapist approach* views the teacher as an empathetic person charged with helping individuals to grow personally and reach a high level of self-actualization, understanding, and acceptance. Psychotherapy, humanistic psychology, and existential philosophy undergird this view.
3. *The liberationist approach* views the teacher as a liberator—a freer of the individual's mind and a developer of well-rounded, knowledgeable, rational, and moral human beings. The concept of a liberal education fits in well with this approach. (pp. 4–5)

Teachers' choices on what material to cover, their style of presentation, and their interaction with students all depend on which philosophy the teacher maintains about the students and the role of the teacher. Such choices may be made deliberately as part of a total philosophy, or they may be intuitive and nonreflective in nature.

One specific problem for the teacher arises from the complicated discussions of quantitative vs qualitative research and the ensuing philosophical discussions about objective reality: How can teachers talk about objective reality to their students if there is no such thing? Strictly speaking, do we believe that nothing can be reality without an observer, and that all experience is subjective (Allender 1991)?

Surely the sunset exists whether observed or not, but the meaning of that sunset may be different from one student to another (and from one teacher to another), because no one shares exactly the same knowledge structure with others. Thus, that sunset takes on different meaning depending on the knowledge structure into which this particular experience has been placed. The teacher can discuss the physical properties of the sunset, the psychological meanings of the sunset, even the flow of visual and verbal imagery that such an event can provoke, but the teacher is always aware that no two students have really experienced the same thing. The teacher's task is to understand the idiosyncratic views of the student and to encourage the student's wider understanding of the experience by introducing him/her to multiple associations surrounding the event. Yet, there have been few studies linking the reflectiveness of teachers to student outcomes or particular classroom instruction (Kagan 1992).

The attempt to find a wide array of social and personal variables that influence student learning sometimes ignores two basic points: (*a*) students learn what they study, and (*b*) how much students learn depends on how much time they are engaged in that study (Berliner 1990). The time-on-task factor is so obvious that it is often overlooked in the search for more exotic family and social variables.

Increased attention has been given to the social learning that takes place along with the academic learning in the classroom. This is particularly true of both the therapist and liberationist views of teaching. Sometimes it is difficult to tell whether a proposed educational reorganization or the design of small-group work—such as that called for by cooperative learning—has been organized for social objectives, whether it was designed for academic growth, or both (Sapon-Shevin & Schniedewind 1992). As Weinstein (1991) concluded:

> The classroom is not simply a social context in which students learn academic lessons. It is a social context in which students also learn social lessons—lessons about appropriate behavior in various contexts, about one's self as a learner and one's position in a status hierarchy, about relationships with students from other ethnic and racial groups, about the relative value of competition and cooperation, and about friendship. (pp. 520)

Belief Structures of Teachers

The interest in teachers' perspectives has extended into a special area of belief structures. Such structures appear to be created through a form of enculturation, which includes assimilation through individual observation, participation, and imitation—all of the cultural elements in the teachers' personal world (Pajares 1992).

Peterman (1991) suggests that beliefs form a schema-like semantic network. Such a network might contain contradictory beliefs that reside in different domains as well as some core beliefs that may be difficult to change. The idea that beliefs are difficult to change and are resistant even in the face of facts can explain why inservice and preservice training rarely modify belief systems of teachers.

Pajares (1992) synthesized sixteen generalizations from the available literature, including:

1. Beliefs are formed early and tend to self-perpetuate, persevering even against contradictions caused by reason, time, schooling, or experience.
2. Knowledge and beliefs are inextricably intertwined, but the potent affective, evaluative, and episodic nature of beliefs makes them a filter through which new phenomena are interpreted.
3. Belief sub-structures, such as educational beliefs, must be understood in terms of their connections not only to each other but also to other, perhaps more central, beliefs in the system.
4. Beliefs about teaching are well established by the time a student goes to college.
5. Individuals' beliefs strongly affect their behavior. (p. 324–26)

It is clear that those who wish to modify teacher behavior must take into account the belief systems of the teachers they are trying to change.

Some investigators think that belief systems operate in a different fashion than knowledge structures in the sense that such structures may defy logic and maintain contradictory positions concurrently and that they are resistant to change. Some think (Roehler et al 1988) that beliefs are static, representing eternal truths that remain unchanged in the teacher's mind. Such key educational beliefs as the confidence to affect the performance of students (teacher efficacy, the nature of knowledge, epistemological beliefs), perceptions of self and feelings of self-worth (self-esteem), and confidence to perform specific tasks (self-efficacy) are components of a belief system.

The maintenance of such belief systems could explain the resistance to accepting new concepts that require a shift in attitudes and values. It may also explain why so many different versions of cooperative learning or site-based management may be found in schools across the country. Such presentations must conform to the belief systems of the individual operating in those schools. Despite the difficulties in definition and differing understandings of beliefs and belief structures, there is an increasing effort to conduct research on these systems because they appear to shape and direct the behavior of teachers and students.

Ernest (1989) has developed a model of mathematics instruction that is comprised of several components: knowledge, beliefs, and attitudes. Knowledge includes understanding of the subject area itself, knowledge of other subject matter (such as physics or economics), knowledge of how to teach mathematics, and how to organize and manage the learning environment for the teaching of mathematics. Three separate belief systems about mathematics influence the manner in which the subject area is presented. First, there is a problem-driven view of mathematics (that mathematics is a continually expanding field of human inquiry). Second, there is a view that mathematics is a static, unified body of knowledge that is discovered but not created. Third, there is a view that mathematics is a useful collection of facts, rules, and skills (the instrumentalists' view). Finally, attitudes such as enthusiasm and confidence can have a powerful influence on the pupil's view of the subject area.

Several investigators have devised similar sets of components, such as knowledge of subject matter, pedagogical content knowledge, knowledge of other content, knowledge of curriculum, knowledge of learners, knowledge of educational aims, and general pedagogical knowledge (Wilson et al 1987). Such a model of knowledge, beliefs, and attitudes in mathematics can be translated into a variety of topic areas such as language arts, social studies, etc.

The effects of new and anomalous data on knowledge acquisition and established belief systems has been reviewed by Chinn & Brewer (1993). They have identified seven different responses to scientific information that contradicts the students' and teachers' view of scientific theory. Only one of the seven responses involves accepting the data and changing the theory appropriately, while the other six involve discounting the data in various ways. Chinn & Brewer present a series of instructional strategies for promoting reflective theory change in a responsible fashion. Rather than using new data as a reason to throw away solid theoretical positions, they recommend creating a willingness to accept alternative theories.

Teacher Strategies and Educational Theories

Various theories of instruction have focused on the knowledge to be acquired, the initial state of the learner, and the transition between initial state and desired state of knowledge (Gelman & Greeno 1989). The various instructional strategies used to achieve the transition have attracted serious investigation. Bereiter (1990) has attempted to build an educational learning theory focusing on contextual modules. He raises the questions, "How do people acquire knowledge that is more complex than they already have?" and "How do people learn things that are hard to learn?" These contextual modules represent a subset of knowledges, feelings, and skills surrounding a particular setting. Bereiter proposes a schoolwork module, for example, that involves a child's approach to schoolwork—the set of school routines, childrens' affective feelings about school, and childrens' adaptation to the job of schooling. Bereiter feels that such a module develops early, becomes quite stable, and provides a coherent and predictable response to almost anything that happens in school.

On the other hand, Bereiter proposes an intentional learning module organized around the goals of personal knowledge construction, rather than task performance. A part of the knowledge construction goals is the procedural knowledge for problem-solving, problem-finding, etc. This intentional learning may even acquire a moral dimension, regarding an obligation to pursue truth and depth of understanding. The intentional learning model differs from the schoolwork model in that it does not deal with the school context but rather with the abstract concept of learning itself. It is represented by the potential scientist or the seeker-after-knowledge who has a well-developed, intentional learning module in the cognitive structure. The teacher can also be seen in this model.

Brown & Palinscar (1989) have presented a series of instructional strategies, including cooperative learning, scaffolding, Socratic dialogues (see also Adler 1984), and reciprocal teaching, as devices to improve the process of moving knowledge from teacher to student. In scaffolding, the expert (teacher) models the expected behavior or guides the learner through the early stages of understanding. As the students' understanding increases, the aid is gradually withdrawn (hence the name "scaffolding"). The goal of the aid provided is to have it eventually internalized by the student as he/she becomes able to operate independently without being propped up by the scaffolding.

In reciprocal teaching, small groups of students and teachers take turns leading a discussion on a text issue or discussion topic. The exercises feature four strategic activities: questioning, clarifying, summarizing, and predicting. In each of these activities, as in cooperative learning, the teacher is expected to instruct or model to the students how to carry out each activity successfully. Students are assumed to have little experience with these activities or how they are to be executed.

What the teacher does and how he/she does it clearly has an influence upon students. For example, King (1991) trained students working in pairs that were engaged in solving a set of computer-assisted problems to ask strategic questions of workmates in areas of planning (What do we know about the problem so far?), monitoring (Are we getting closer to the goal?), and evaluating (What should we do differently next time?). These students outperformed a group that was merely directed to ask questions, and a control group that received no instructions. This type of strategic questioning can form the base of a general problem-solving strategy, which can transfer more effectively than domain-specific activities, as noted earlier by Perkins & Salomon (1989).

EDUCATIONAL REFORM

Changes in the school program designed to facilitate student learning or teacher presentations can occur along three major dimensions: (*a*) where the instruction takes place, (*b*) what content is to be taught, and (*c*) what skills are to be mastered. The educational restructuring movement of the early 1990s appeared to want to change the school program in all three of these dimensions (U. S. Dept. of Education 1990).

The middle schools movement (George 1988, Oakes 1985, Vars 1987) appeared to restructure the schools into teams of students and teachers and to add a substantial affective dimension to the educational program. The middle school was designed to replace the junior high school, and in the process, change the role of the teacher from information disseminator to facilitator, group planner, team teacher, and interdisciplinary curricular presenter. Needless to say, many teachers placed in this situation were concerned about their lack of preparation for this new role (Coleman & Gallagher 1992).

Educational strategies such as cooperative learning (Johnson & Johnson 1989, Slavin et al 1990, Kagan 1990) proposed a number of variations on a group-learning process, where a task or set of tasks is given to a small group of students who then work together to produce a final product or answer. They may be evaluated both as a member of a team and individually. Such students can even be taught, explicitly, the social skills required for effective group work. Few students know how to work on a project together. They usually need instruction on sharing responsibility, encouraging others, and helping others who have difficulty learning.

One educational practice that has been under fire in this reform agenda is ability grouping, which has long been used as a device to aid teachers by reducing the range of aptitude and performance found in a single classroom. Reducing this range of performance allowed the teacher to provide some modified curriculum for slower-learning and a different set for faster-learning students. There have been several meta-analyses and literature reviews of the extensive literature on the effects of ability grouping (see Slavin 1988, Oakes 1985, Kulik & Kulik 1991), but the reviewers reached different conclusions. Slavin & Oakes (who present a more traditional literature summary) concluded that ability grouping has little value for all students and should be replaced. Kulik & Kulik contended that ability grouping provides major advantages for gifted students when combined with accelerated programming.

Gallagher (1991) pointed out several substantial flaws in the literature on ability grouping, particularly as applied to gifted students. The tests used to compare the special group with the comparison (control) group in a quasi-experimental model were too conceptually simple; the differential curriculum for the advanced group was rarely considered; the students themselves were rarely asked their opinions on grouping; and the children were rarely evaluated in terms of advanced thinking processes, which is one of the clear goals of programs for gifted students.

Other topics of the reform movement, such as site-based management, are designed to empower teachers to play a meaningful role in educational decision-making at the school level. Few attempts to assess the results of this approach are available. Increased levels of accountability and a substantially changed approach to assessment and measurements are other components of a movement that clearly seeks a major recasting of the American educational enterprise (Baker et al 1990).

Much that has been gleaned about the learner has been based on studies of the individual learner. In school, however, the individual learner is rarely in a tutorial situation, but rather is part of a group. The nature of that group has much to do with the individual learner's success. If one is to teach to the *zone of proximal development,* as presented by Vygotsky (1978), then what does the teacher do when that zone varies wildly over 25 students? Such issues highlight the importance of organizational or structural changes to maximize the effects of teaching in group situations. One effect of individual differences in learners is that students with limited knowledge or learning ability appear to need more structure in order to master concepts; children with extensive knowledge and background can often learn more by guided discovery (Snow & Swanson 1992).

TECHNOLOGY

Since the early days of computer-assisted instruction, it has been clear that even technology as advanced as computers and word processors is not going to replace teachers. Instead, it has become increasingly obvious that such tools can be the teacher's friends and can expand the teacher's own potential. The special education field dealing with children with special needs has been active in technology—perhaps because of the many unusual instructional problems that need to be solved for children with sensory problems, learning disabilities, etc (Kirk et al 1993).

Teachers can use optical disc technology to store and retrieve both video and audio information on interactive videodiscs. Distance learning—a two-way interactive video system—allows for teachers in one place to present knowledge to students or teachers in another place. Hypertext and hypermedia can allow for detailed analysis of a literary passage in terms of semantic, syntactic, or comprehension structures. As usual, there has been a lag in the amount of direct research on the relative utility of such devices both for student learning and for expanding the range of teacher activities (Higgins & Boone 1990).

Another device to stir the thinking process of students has been the video disk. The Cognitive and Technology Group at Vanderbilt (1991) has developed a series of video disks that presents problems to the student through an adventure model and allows them to explore solutions through cooperative group activities. They report that lower achieving students gained confidence through their presenting useful ideas to the group. They could contribute because the stimulus was a video rather than a reading assignment.

Sometimes an educational tool is so powerful that it makes a noticable difference in student performance. Bangert-Drowns (1993) has noted the influence the word processor has had in improving student performance. Most of the studies Bangert-Drowns reviewed on the effects of the word processor show improvement in writing skills, particularly for remedial students, but the effect sizes are quite modest. Bangert-Drowns believes that more integrated instruction and metacognition prompts might increase the learning efficiency and production.

RESEARCH DIRECTIONS

What do these changes in how we perceive the roles of the student and that of the teacher imply for the research agenda of the next few years? Based on this review, the near future appears likely to see some of the following:

1. Increased understanding of student knowledge structures and consequent adjustment of teacher strategies to help students build such structures.
2. The increasing use of the case method as a device for illustrating elements of the instructional process and theory.
3. Construction of new models of the teacher-learner interaction.
4. As team teaching and team planning becomes more common, attempts to analyze the instructional work of groups of teachers.
5. A focus on the teacher-technology interaction for more effective instruction.

We are on a path toward a more qualitative approach to the study of the teaching-learning process—one that has, if anything, even more complex multivariate interactions to try and capture through the new research agenda.

Literature Cited

Adler M. 1984. *The Paideia Program: An Educational Syllabus.* New York: Macmillan

Allender J. 1991. *Imagery in Teaching and Learning.* New York: Praeger

Baker E, Freeman M, Clayton S. 1990. *Cognitive Assessment of Subject Matter: Understanding the Marriage of Psychological Theory and Educational Policy in Achievement Testing.* Los Angeles, Calif: UCLA Cent. Res. Eval.

Bangert-Drowns R. 1993. The word processor as an instructional tool: a meta-analysis of word processing in writing instruction. *Rev. Educ. Res.* 63:69–93

Bereiter C. 1990. Aspects of an educational learning theory. *Rev. Educ. Res.* 60:603–24

Berliner D. 1987. Ways of thinking about students and classrooms by more and less experienced teachers. In *Exploring Teachers' Thinking,* ed. J Calderhead, pp. 60–83. London: Cassell Educ.

Berliner D. 1990. What's all this fuss about instructional time? In *The Nature of Time in Schools,* ed. M Ben-Peretz, R Bromme. New York: Teachers College Press

Borkowski J, Kurtz B. 1987. Metacognition and executive control. In *Cognition in Special Children: Comparative Approaches to Retardation in Learning Disabilities and Giftedness,* ed. J Borkowski, J Day. Norwood, NJ: Ablex

Brandon P, Newton B, Hammond O. 1987. Children's mathematics achievement in Hawaii: sex differences favoring girls. *Am. Educ. Res. J.* 24:437–61

Brigham F, Bakkan J, Scruggs J, Mastropieni M. 1992. Cooperative behavior management: strategies for promoting a positive classroom environment. *Educ. Train. Ment. Retard.* 27:3–12

Brown AL, Palinscar AS. 1989. Guided, cooperative learning and individual knowledge acquisition. See Resnick 1989, pp. 393–452

Butt R, Townsend D, Raymond D. 1990. Bringing reform to life: teachers' stories and professional development. *Cambridge J. Educ.* 20:225–68

Chi M, Glaser R, Farr M, eds. 1988. *The Nature of Expertise.* Hillsdale, NJ: Erlbaum

Chinn C, Brewer W. 1993. The role of anomalous data in knowledge acquisition: a theoretical framework and implications for science instruction. *Rev. Educ. Res.* 63:1–49

Cognitive and Technology Group at Vanderbilt. 1991. Anchored instruction and its relationship to situated cognition. *Educ. Res.* 19(3):2–10

Coleman M. 1992. A comparison of how gifted/LD and average/LD boys cope with school frustration. *J. Educ. Gifted* 15:239–65

Coleman M, Gallagher J. 1992. *Middle School Survey Report: Impact on Gifted Students.* Chapel Hill, NC: Gifted Educ. Policy Stud. Program, Univ. NC

deBono E. 1985. *Masterthinker's Handbook.* New York: Int. Cent. Creat. Think.

Delcourt M. 1993. Creative productivity among secondary school students: combining energy, interest, and imagination. *Gifted Child Q.* 37:23–31

Entwisle DR, Alexander KL. 1990. Beginning school math competence: minority and majority comparisons. *Child Dev.* 61:454–71

Ernest P. 1989. The knowledge, beliefs, and attitudes of the mathematics teacher: a model. *J. Educ. Teach.* 15:13–33

Feldhusen J, Treffinger D. 1990. *Creative Thinking and Problem Solving in Gifted Education.* Dubuque, Iowa: Kendall-Hunt. 3rd ed.

Fenstermacher G, Soltis J. 1992. *Approaches to Teaching.* New York: Teachers College Press. 2nd ed.

Forness S, Kavale K. 1988. Psychopharmacologic treatment: a note on classroom effects. *J. Learn. Disabil.* 32:48–55

Gallagher J. 1991. Educational reform, values, and gifted students. *Gifted Child Q.* 35:12–19

Gallagher SA, Stepien WJ, Rosenthal H. 1992. The effects of problem-based learning on problem solving. *Gifted Child Q.* 36:195–200

Gardner H. 1986. *Frames of Mind: The Theory of Multiple Intelligence.* New York: Basic Books

Gelman R, Greeno JG. 1989. On the nature of competence: principles for understanding in a domain. See Resnick 1989, pp. 125–86

George P. 1988. Tracking and ability grouping: which way for the middle school? *Middle School J.* 20:21–28

Getzels J, Csikszentmihalyi M. 1976. *The Creative Vision: A Longitudinal Study of Problem Finding in Art.* New York: McGraw-Hill

Goldsmith T, Davenport D. 1990. Assessing structural similarity in graphs. In *Pathfinder Associative Networks: Studies in Knowledge Organization,* ed. R Schvaneveldt, pp. 75–87. Norwood, NJ: Ablex

Goldsmith T, Johnson P, Acton W. 1991. Assessing structural knowledge. *J. Educ. Psychol.* 83:88–96

Goodlad J. 1990. Better teachers for our nation's schools. *Phi Delta Kappan* 72:185–94

Guilford J. 1967. *The Nature of Human Intelligence.* New York: Fund Adv. Educ.

Hayes JR. 1989. Cognitive processes in creativity. In *Handbook of Creativity,* ed. JA Glover, RR Ronning, CR Reynolds, pp. 135–46. New York: Plenum

Hennessey BA, Amabile TM. 1988. The role of the environment in creativity. In *The Nature of Creativity,* ed. RJ Sternberg, pp. 11–38. New York: Cambridge Univ. Press

Higgins K, Boone R. 1990. Hypertext computer study guides and the social studies achievement of students with learning disabilities, remedial students and regular education students. *J. Learn. Disabil.* 23(9):529–40

Hodapp R, Burock J, Zigler E. 1990. *Issues in the Developmental Approach to Mental Retardation.* New York: Cambridge Univ. Press

Hoge D, Smit E, Hanson S. 1990. School experiences predicting changes in self-esteem of sixth- and seventh-grade students. *J. Educ. Psychol.* 82:117–27

Hong E, Milgram RM. 1991. Original thinking in preschool children: a validation of ideational fluency measures. *Creat. Res. J.* 5:253–60

Hughes C, Ruhl K, Misra A. 1989. Self-management with behaviorally disordered students in school settings: a promise fulfilled. *Behav. Disord.* 14:250–62

Johnson D, Johnson R. 1989. *Cooperation and Competition: Theory and Research.* Edna, Minn: Interaction

Johnson D, Johnson R, Stanne M, Garibaldi A. 1990. Impact of group processing on achievement in cooperative groups. *J. Soc. Psychol.* 130:507–16

Johnson J. 1988. The challenge of substance abuse. *Teach. Except. Child.* 20:29–31

Kagan D. 1992. Professional growth among preservice and beginning teachers. *Rev. Educ. Res.* 62:129–62

Kagan S. 1990. The structural approach to cooperative learning. *Educ. Leadersh.* 47(4):12–15

Kanevsky L. 1990. Pursuing qualitative differences in the flexible use of a problem solving strategy by young children. *J. Educ. Gifted* 13:115–40

Kauffman J. 1989. The regular education initiative as Reagan-Bush education policy: a trickle-down theory of education of the hard to teach. *J. Spec. Educ.* 23:256–78

Kelly G. 1963. *A Theory of Personality.* New York: Norton

King A. 1991. Effects of training in strategic questioning on children's problem solving performance. *J. Educ. Psychol.* 83:307–17

Kirk S, Gallagher J, Anastasiow N. 1993. *Educating Exceptional Children.* Boston, Mass: Houghton Mifflin. 7th ed.

Kulik J, Kulik C. 1991. Ability grouping and gifted students. In *Handbook of Gifted Education,* ed. N Colangelo, G Davis, pp. 178–96. Boston, MA: Allyn, Bacon

Lerner J. 1993. *Learning Disabilities: Theories, Diagnoses, and Teaching Strategies.* Boston: Houghton Mifflin. 7th ed.

Mulick J, Hammer D, Dura J. 1991. Assessment and management of antisocial and hyperactive behavior. In *Handbook of Mental Retardation,* ed. J Matson, J Mulick, pp. 397–412. New York: Pergamon. 2nd ed.

Nelson C, Pearson C. 1991. *Integrating Services for Children and Youth with Emotional and Behavior Disorders.* Reston, Va: Counc. Except. Child.

Nesher P. 1989. Microworlds in mathematics education: a pedagogical realism. See Resnick 1989, pp. 187–126

Oakes J. 1985. *Keeping Track.* New Haven, Conn: Yale Univ. Press

Ogbu J. 1992. Understanding cultural diversity and learning. *Educ. Res.* 21:5–14

Okuda SM, Runco MA, Berger DE. 1991. Creativity and the finding and solving of real-world problems. *J. Psychoeduc. Assess.* 9:45–53

Onosko J. 1991. Barriers to the promotion of higher order thinking in social studies. *Theory Res. Soc. Educ.* 19(4)341–66

Pajares F. 1992. Teacher's beliefs and educational research: cleaning up a messy concept. *Rev. Educ. Res.* 62:307–32

Parnes S, Noller R, Biondi A. 1977. *Guide to Creative Action.* New York: Scribner's Sons

Perkins DN, Salomon G. 1989. Are cognitive skills context-bound? *Educ. Res.* 18:16–25

Peterman F. 1991. *An experienced teacher's emerging constructivist beliefs about teaching and learning.* Presented at Annu. Meet. Am. Educ. Res. Assoc., Chicago

Plomin R. 1988. Environment and genes: determinants of behavior. *Am. Psychol.* 44:105–11

Polloway E, Patton J, Payne J, Payne R. 1989. *Strategies for Teaching Learners with Special Needs.* Columbus, Ohio: Merrill. 4th ed.

Polloway E, Patton J, Smith J, Roderique T. 1991. Issues in program design for elementary students with mild retardation: emphasis on curriculum development. *Educ. Train. Ment. Retard.* 26:142–50

Posner R. 1988. Introduction: What is it to be an expert? In *The Nature of Expertise,* ed. M Chi, R Glaser, M Farr. Hillsdale, NJ: Erlbaum

Reis S, Callahan C. 1989. Gifted females: they've come a long way—or have they? *J. Educ. Gifted* 12:99–117

Resnick L. 1987. *Education and Learning to Think.* Washington, DC: Natl. Acad. Press

Resnick LB, ed. 1989. *Knowing, Learning, and Instruction: Essays in Honor of Robert Glaser.* Hillsdale, NJ: Erlbaum

Roehler L, Duffy G, Herrmann B, Conley M, Johnson J. 1988. Knowledge structures as evidence of the 'personal': bridging the gap from thought to practice. *J. Curric. Stud.* 20:159–65

Rogers K. 1986. Do the gifted think and learn differently? A review of recent research and its implications for instruction. *J. Educ. Gifted* 10:17–39

Runco M. 1993. Divergent thinking, creativity, and giftedness. *Gifted Child Q.* 37:16–22

Sapon-Shevin M, Schniedewind N. 1992. If cooperative learning's the answer, what are the questions? *J. Educ.* 174:11–35

Schack G. 1993. Effects of a creative problem-solving curriculum on students of varying ability levels. *Gifted Child Q.* 37:32–38

Schon DE, ed. 1991. *The Reflective Turn: Case Studies in and on Educational Practice.* New York: Teachers College Press

Schumaker JB, Deshler DD, McKnight RC. 1991. Teaching routines for content areas at the secondary level. In *Intervention for Achievement and Behavior Problems,* ed. G Stover, MR Shinn, HM Walker, pp. 473–94. Washington, DC: Natl. Assoc. School Psychol.

Schunk D. 1991. Self efficacy and academic motivation. *Educ. Psychol.* 26:207–31

Schvaneveldt R, Dearholt D, Durso F. 1988. Graph theoretical foundations of pathfinder networks. *Comput. Math. Appl.* 15:337–45

Shulman LS. 1987. Knowledge and teaching: foundations of the new reform. *Harvard Educ. Rev.* 57:1–22

Siegler R. 1986. *Children's Thinking.* Englewood Cliffs, NJ: Prentice Hall

Slaughter-Defoe DT, Nakagawa K, Takanishi R, Johnson DJ. 1990. Toward cultural/ecological perspectives on schooling and achievement in African- and Asian-American children. *Child Dev.* 61:363–83

Slavin R. 1988. Synthesis of research on grouping in elementary and secondary schools. *Educ. Leadersh.* 46:67–77

Slavin R, Madden N, Stevens R. 1990. Cooperative learning models for the 3 R's. *Educ. Leadersh.* 47(4):22–28

Snow RE, Swanson J. 1992. Instructional psychology: aptitude, adaptation, and assessment. *Annu. Rev. Psychol.* 43:583–626

Solas J. 1992. Investigating teacher and student thinking about the process of teaching and learning using autobiography and repertory grid. *Rev. Educ. Res.* 62:205–25

Sternberg R. 1986. *Intelligence Applied.* San Diego, Calif: Harcourt, Brace, Jovanovich

Sternberg R. 1988. *The Nature of Creativity: Contemporary Psychological Perspectives.* New York: Cambridge Univ. Press

Sternberg R, Lubart T. 1993. Creative giftedness: a multivariate investment approach. *Gifted Child Q.* 37:7–15

Tochon F, Munby H. 1993. Novice and expert teachers' time epistemology: a wave function from didactics to pedagogy. *Teach. & Teach. Educ.* 9:205–18

Treffinger D, Isaksen S. 1992. *Creative Problem Solving: An Introduction.* Sarasota, Fla: Cent. Creat. Learn.

US Department of Education. 1990. *America 2000.* Washington, DC: US Dept. Educ.

US Department of Education. 1991. *Twelfth Annual Report to Congress on the Implementation of P. L. 94–142: The Education for All Handicapped Children Act.* Washington, DC: US GPO

Van Houten R, Rolider A. 1991. Applied behavior analysis. In *Handbook of Mental Retardation,* ed. J Matson, J Mulick, pp. 586–602. New York: Pergamon. 2nd ed.

Vars GF. 1987. *Interdisciplinary Teaching in the Middle Grades: Why and How.* Columbus, Ohio: Natl. Middle School Assoc.

Vygotsky L. 1978. *Mind in Society: The Development of Higher Psychological Processes.* Cambridge: Harvard Univ. Press

Wagner M, Newman L, D'Amico R, Jay E, Butler-Nalin P, et al. 1991. *Youth With Disabilities: How Are They Doing?* Menlo Park, Calif: SRI Int.

Weiner B. 1990. History of motivational researcher in education. *J. Educ. Psychol.* 82(4):616–22

Weinstein C. 1991. The classroom as a social context for learning. *Annu. Rev. Psychol.* 42:493–525

Whitehead A. 1929. *The Aims of Education.* New York: Macmillan

Wilson S, Shulman L, Richert A. 1987. 150 different ways of knowing: representations of knowledge in teaching. In *Exploring Teacher's Thinking,* ed. J Calderhead, pp. 104–24. London: Cassell

Wittrock M, ed. 1986. *Handbook of Research on Teaching.* New York: Macmillan. 3rd ed.

Zimmerman BJ, Martinez-Pons M. 1990. Student differences in self-regulated learning: relating grade, sex, and giftedness to self-efficacy and strategy use. *J. Educ. Psychol.* 82:51–59

Annu. Rev. Psychol. 1994. 45:197–227

PSYCHOLOGY AND ECONOMICS: Perspectives on Risk, Cooperation, and The Marketplace

Lola L. Lopes

College of Business, University of Iowa, Iowa City, Iowa 52242

KEY WORDS: risk, decision making, social dilemmas, cooperation, experimental economics

---

CONTENTS

0066-4308/94/0201-0197$05.00

INTRODUCTION

If it goes too far to say that psychologists and economists view one another with fear and loathing, there is at least suspicion and distaste. Different histories, methods, and goals widen the disciplinary gulf, but most important are the different perspectives that the two fields offer on the human condition.

Since the cognitive revolution, psychologists have seen people as systems for encoding and processing information. Our variables come from the environment (prereceptor and posteffector), but our theories concern internal processes that intervene as stimuli are encoded, interpreted, and finally transmuted into responses. The experiment is our basic tool and classification of variables as independent, dependent, or control permeates the way we think and talk. People become subjects and we call them that incessantly, not realizing that the label grates on nonpsychologists. Laboratory paradigms also affect the way we see the world, as if certain aspects of reality come into being only when someone captures them in an experimental task.

Economists see people as incentive driven, basing their actions on self-interest and rationality. Rationality, in turn, means that people reason logically about choices, using all available information and allowing for the effects that current choices will have on future choices and future outcomes. Economists also believe that this state of affairs is a good one, and that Adam Smith's (1776) "invisible hand" of economic competition usually fashions the sow's ear of selfishness into the silk purse of social good. Until recently, mathematics has been the basic tool of the economist. Indeed, most economists are at least as much mathematicians as social scientists. And just as psychologists construe the world in ways that fit it to the lab, economists construe the world in ways that make it mathematically tractable.

Most people have seen ambiguous drawings: a vase that is also two faces in profile, a beautiful young woman who is also an old hag. Two features of ambiguous figures concern us presently. First, what people see easily or initially is often the product of their experience and expectations. Second, although people can switch between alternate interpretations, no one can simultaneously hold both percepts.

Psychologists and economists have different perspectives on the world. With effort, any of us could learn to see from the other perspective. But we cannot do both at once, and it is not easy to maintain the alien perspective for long. Still, the effort is worthwhile.

A review is a shot at a moving target, made even more uncertain when the reviewer is moving too. The three areas I survey here trace a personal trajectory of interest from cognitive psychology (individual behavior) to business (groups and market behavior). Decision making under risk and uncertainty sprouted from economic roots in the 1950s and it is in this area that psychology and economics have influenced one another most deeply and most beneficially. The study of social dilemmas has rich traditions in both social psychology and economics; however, interactions here have been more superficial, with theory development more parallel than intertwined. Research on experimental markets is solely the province of economists. I include it, however, to illustrate the types of testable questions that economists see as deriving from economic theory, and to suggest how psychological analysis might shed light on market behavior.

DECISION MAKING UNDER RISK AND UNCERTAINTY

Evolution of the Basic Model

The urge is strong to begin "Once upon a time...," because the history of research in risk taking is an epic spanning two continents, several disciplines, and more than three centuries. One theme persists, however: the idea of mathematical expectation, or the weighted average.

In decision making under risk,[1] people must choose among gambles or lotteries. The terms mislead since both connote risks assumed willingly and for fun. What they denote, however, are acts having probabilistic consequences: outcome O_1 occurs with probability P_1, outcome O_2 occurs with probability P_2, and so on for all possible outcomes. In other words, risks are probability distributions over outcomes, and the expected value (EV) is a probability weighted average of the outcomes (i.e. each possible outcome is multiplied by its probability and then summed over outcomes).

By the mid-seventeenth century, scholars were asking themselves "What is a gamble worth?" Huygens, Pascal, and Fermat arrived at the answer: a gamble is worth its EV. This idea is currently accepted in actuarial settings where EV predicts average outcome in the long run. But the seventeenth century idea of EV was based on the substantially different idea of the "fair price" for a gamble. Indeed, modern notions of long runs and probability developed from the idea of fair (or expected) values rather than the other way around (Gigerenzer et al 1989).

By the early eighteenth century, most scholars believed that EV measures a gamble's value. Doubts were sown, however, by a thought problem now known as the St. Petersburg paradox. A fair coin is tossed repeatedly until it comes up tails, at which point the player is paid a sum equal to $\$2^n$, where n is the toss on which tails appears. For $n = 1$, the prize is \$2; for $n = 2$,

1 The term uncertainty is preferred when probabilities are unknown, but the terms are often used interchangeably.

\$4; for $n = 3$, \$8, and so forth. The nettlesome question was how much should a person pay for a single play of the game? If EV is the criterion, the answer is clear: one should pay all one has because the EV of the game is infinite. Intuition, on the other hand, fairly shouts that the value is not more than a few dollars.

Many solutions were proposed for the paradox but only Bernoulli's (1738) suggestion, which we now call expected utility (EU) theory, became prominent. Bernoulli's insight was that EV implicitly assumes that the subjective worth of money (utility) is equal to its objective worth. He reasoned that this would not be true in general. A windfall of \$1000 would be magnificent for a poor man but paltry for a rich man. In other words, money has diminishing marginal utility. Bernoulli expressed his idea using logarithms. If one computes the expectation of the St. Petersburg game after replacing dollar values with their logs, it becomes apparent that the gamble is not worth much. Taking logs effectively compresses higher values, shifting the average downward, and producing risk aversion (i.e. the preference for a sure thing over an actuarially equivalent gamble).

Although Bernoulli's solution was expressed in mathematics, his conception was psychological, lodged in the differing perspectives of rich and poor. Psychologists in the twentieth century would recognize Bernoulli's utility concept as a precursor to modern-day psychophysics. In economics, Bernoulli's model of risk aversion had little impact but diminishing marginal utility figured prominently in nineteenth century consumer economics. The concept fell from favor in the early twentieth century, however, because of difficulties in measurement. When economists realized that they could make do with ordinal measures, the door was shut on measurable utility (Black 1990).

The door stayed shut until von Neumann & Morgenstern (1947) revived the concept (really a distant cousin of the concept) in the course of developing their theory of games. Von Neumann & Morgenstern took an axiomatic approach to risky choice. They proposed a set of axioms that entail two consequences. If a person's preferences among monetary gambles are consistent with the axioms then (*a*) the preferences can be summarized by a utility function on money, and (*b*) the preferences can be modeled as if the person were choosing in order to maximize EU.

Two phrases are key to understanding how the axiomatic approach differs from Bernoulli's. First, the utility function summarizes preferences; it does not cause them. Preferences are primitive; utility is derivative and defined only for choices involving risk. Second, the EU model is an "as if" model. It describes the output of choosing but not the act. There is no psychology in von Neumann & Morgenstern, though they did defend their system as being psychologically plausible (von Neumann & Morgenstern 1947, pp. 20–31).[2]

The new EU theory met with enthusiasm in economics and the axioms were revised to make them ever more clear and compelling. There were also extensions, most notably the work of Savage (1972), that broadened the application of the theory. Savage's theory, called subjectively expected utility (SEU) theory, replaced objective probabilities with subjective probabilities. Whether one is considering objective or subjective probabilities, the crux of EU maximization is that preferences among gambles should be linear in probabilities. Transformations on probabilities that amount to subtracting constants or dividing by constants should leave relative preferences unchanged.

Although American economists were persuaded, trouble was brewing in France. In 1952, Maurice Allais organized a conference in Paris that many leading EU proponents attended. At the conference, Allais challenged EU devotees with a pair of thought problems, now called the Allais paradoxes, that went to the heart of the linearity postulate: in both forms (constant difference and constant ratio), when people are offered the possibility of something wonderful happening for sure (e.g. receiving $1 million), they will not trade it for an almost certain chance at something even more wonderful (e.g. receiving $5 million). When the certainty or near certainty is linearly reduced to low levels, however, preferences shift and people may trade a smidgen of probability for a major improvement in outcome. This violates linearity. The paradoxes rocked the conference and even Savage displayed the forbidden preferences. Still, most American economists remained steadfast in their devotion to EU.

There are two kinds of people in the world: those who read mysteries from front to back and those who cannot resist peeking at the last page. For the latter, it is a sorrow that in life you can't peek. But I am betting that when the history is written on EU, one of the most interesting parts will involve Allais. Of course, we know what has happened since 1952. The next year, Allais (1953) published his conference paper in *Econometrica* (a respected American journal) in French. Only the abstract appeared in English, with an editorial footnote indicating that Allais was publishing the paper on his own responsibility (i.e. over the objections of reviewers). Between 1952 and 1979 Allais' critique was mostly ignored and when it was not, it was discussed in terms of the analysis that Savage provided to explain his own embarrassing preferences (see Lopes 1988). It was not until 1979 that the English text of Allais' article appeared along with commentaries from EU advocates (Allais & Hagen 1979).

---

2 Pope (1983) argues that the defense was inadequate because their model compresses time to one stage. The experience of risk extends over time and must be modeled using two stages, one before and one after the risk is resolved.

Since 1979 there have been two phases of development in what is now called nonexpected utility theory (for reviews see Fishburn 1989, Weber & Camerer 1987). In Phase I, in economics, Machina clarified the restrictions imposed by linearity (1982) and showed the robustness of more general forms of EU (i.e. non-EU) to relaxation of linearity (1987). In psychology, Kahneman & Tversky (1979) offered prospect theory (PT), a powerful descriptive alternative to EU, which proposed that: (*a*) people represent (edit) gambles psychologically; (*b*) the utility function is *S*-shaped about the status quo; and (*c*) outcomes are weighted by nonlinearly transformed probabilities (decision weights). Two significant features of PT are that it handles the Allais paradoxes and that it predicts risk aversion for gains and risk seeking for losses. PT has deeply influenced behavioral decision making (see Payne et al 1992). PT has been less well accepted in economics because the probability weighting function has some awkward mathematical consequences.

Phase II began with a paper by Quiggen (1982) that suggested an alternate way to model nonlinear probabilities. Yaari (1987) and Allais (1986) later independently invented similar models. The main idea (now called rank dependence) is explained easily by concrete example. Consider a gamble that gives a 5% chance of winning $5, a 25% chance of winning $49, and a 70% chance of winning $125. The expected value of this gamble is .05($5) + .25($49) + .70($125) = $100. If EU theory is applied to the gamble, we replace dollars by utilities. If PT is applied, we also replace probabilities by decision weights, but again, this way of treating decision weights leads to mathematical trouble.

Consider, however, that we might reconstrue the gamble as follows: with probability 1 you get $5, with probability .95 you get another $44, and with probability .70 you get still another $76. Nothing changes. The expected value is still 1($5) + .95($44) + .70($76) = $100. All we have done is to write the equation in decumulative form. This is important, however, because it allows transformations on (decumulative) probabilities that do not lead to trouble (see Lopes 1990 for details).

Early formal work on rank dependence was done in economics but there were parallel developments in psychology. Lopes (1984, 1987) observed that subjects talk about gambles in (de)cumulative form and she proposed that risk averse choices might reflect increased attention to the worst outcomes in gambles. Birnbaum et al (1992) pointed out that rank dependence is related to differential weighting in the averaging model of information integration theory (Anderson 1981, pp. 273–276; Birnbaum 1972; Oden & Anderson 1971). Most recently, Tversky & Kahneman (1992) published a decumulative form of PT.

Allais won the Nobel Prize for Economics in 1988, but the official prize citation did not mention the Allais paradox, even though it was the lever that moved EU. I leave it to historians to figure out why and how Allais' challenge was ignored for so long. I suspect the answer may be found in the sociology of science. Language, of course, played a role, but so did style. At a time when American economics had become formal and spare, Allais was informal and emphatic. Perhaps equally important was that Allais' argument was deeply psychological. As Allais put it in the closing pages of his 1953 paper, "Of course it is quite disappointing to have to exert so much effort to prove the illusory character of a formulation whose oversimplification is evident to anyone with a little psychological intuition" (in Allais & Hagen 1979, p. 105). Although change was slow in coming, many recent developments reflect both psychological and economic influence. In the sections following, I describe several active areas of inquiry.

Preference Reversal and Procedural Variance

In attempting to assess the relative importance of probabilities and payoffs in risk taking, Slovic & Lichtenstein (1968) found that the two dimensions correlated differently with different response measures. The pattern suggested that subjects might set higher selling prices for gambles with small probabilities of large prizes but prefer actuarially comparable gambles with moderate prizes and probabilities in direct choice. The prediction was verified subsequently in both laboratory and casino settings (Lichtenstein & Slovic 1971, 1973).

From a psychological perspective, preference reversal is an interesting but unsurprising effect that underscores the importance of understanding how people represent and process information. For economics, however, the finding contradicted an assumption so basic that it had gone unnamed if not unnoticed. The assumption, now called procedure invariance (Tversky et al 1988), says that preferences are not affected by the task that is used to measure them.

Within a decade of the discovery of preference reversal, psychologists and economists had confirmed its existence and demonstrated its robustness (see Slovic & Lichtenstein 1983) though some effort is still being made to eliminate or moderate the effect. For example, Berg et al (1985, see also Chu & Chu 1990) reduced the severity of preference reversals by forcing subjects who reverse to engage in market transactions that lose money, and Casey (1991) reversed the direction of the effect by using buying prices instead of selling prices and increasing the size of the payoffs.

Focus has shifted recently to the process that produces preference reversals. Three conceptually distinct mechanisms have been proposed, each of which locates the cause at a different stage in the judgment process. Goldstein & Einhorn (1987) target the response function, locating the effect in an adjustment process that subjects use to express their internal judgments as bids. Tversky et al (1990) locate the effect in the relative weighting of prizes and probabilities. They propose that compatibility between the monetary prize and the monetary response scale causes prizes to be overweighted in bids. Mellers et al (1992a, b) locate the effect in the process that integrates prizes and probabilities. They show that the task affects whether the integration process is additive or multiplicative.

Preference reversals and other violations of procedure invariance are of practical importance because they undermine the usefulness of some economically-based methods for measuring human values. For example, utility measures obtained using the axioms of expected utility theory depend critically on normatively irrelevant task details (McCord & De Neufville 1985, Hershey et al 1982). Similarly, techniques for valuing nonmarket goods such as clean air or wildlife (a process called contingent valuation) are called into question by discrepancies between theoretically equivalent measures of what people will pay to increase the good and what payment they require to accept a decrement in the good (Coursey et al 1987). Cummings et al (1986) contains a dialog on contingent valuation encompassing both psychological and economic viewpoints.

Reclaiming Descriptive Ground

The impact of normative theory on descriptive models of risk taking cannot be overestimated. The first psychologists to work in the area were inspired by the mathematical achievements embodied in EU and SEU theory, although they soon discovered that neither theory was adequate for describing human behavior. Nonetheless, until the 1980s, three gaps remained in descriptive theory that owed their existence to the fact that none of the three made sense normatively. These concerned single vs repeated plays of gambles, regret and its role in risk taking, and decision making under ambiguity.

REPEATED GAMBLES The problem of single vs repeated plays of gambles goes back to why von Neumann & Morgenstern invented EU theory in the first place. Their interest was in game theory, not risky choice, but they needed to justify the use of mixed strategies (strategies in which a player chooses among moves probabilistically) for games that are played only once. Their axiomatic justification for maximizing EU (published as an appendix to the second edition of their book) did not rely on long-run arguments and so made moot any difference between long and short runs.

The issue remained moot until Lopes (1981) questioned the normative and descriptive appropriateness of applying mathematical expectations to unique decisions. Although some disagreed (Tversky & Bar-Hillel 1983), considerable evidence has since accumulated showing that people distinguish between single and repeated gambles (Keren 1991, Keren & Wagenaar 1987, Montgomery & Adelbratt 1982, Redelmeier & Tversky 1990, Wedell & Böckenholt 1990).

REGRET At one time there was considerable interest (see Lee 1971) in the role of regret in decision making under risk. There were even attempts to incorporate regret into normative theory (Luce & Raiffa 1957) but such attempts failed because they led to undesirable consequences such as intransitivity and non-independence from irrelevant alternatives. Recently, descriptive interest in regret has been rekindled by theorists who use the idea to explain and justify behavior that violates EU (DE Bell 1982; Loomes & Sugden 1982, 1987).

Psychological research is confirming that regret plays an important role in choice and in our experience of outcomes (e.g. Johnson 1986, Landman 1988). In a study of farm couples considering whether to sell grain or hold it in hopes of better prices, Lindemann (1993) found that regret features prominently (though differently) in the thinking of both husbands and wives. As she remarked, "What student of regret theory understands what it is like to measure regret by the bushel as it pours into a combine grain tank?" (p. 153).

AMBIGUITY In discussing personal probability, Savage (1972) noted that we are sometimes sure and sometimes unsure about our probabilities. He considered the proposition that we may have probabilities about probabilities but rejected the idea as difficult. It also seemed pointless because the best one could do with higher order probabilities would be to compute the expectation of the higher order distribution, eliminating distributional information, and returning, inexorably, to the original point value.

Ellsberg (1961) saw ambiguity as the Achilles heel of SEU. He made his point with a thought experiment demonstrating that people's preferences in choices involving ambiguity are often inconsistent and therefore not representable as numerical probabilities. Although psychologists knew about Ellsberg's paradox and produced some research on the topic (see Lee 1971), ambiguity was at most a footnote to SEU until recently. This is particularly noteworthy since we know that public objections to new technologies are exacerbated by uncertainty in risk assessments (Slovic 1987).

Recent interest in ambiguity was stimulated by Einhorn & Hogarth (1985) who suggested that people adjust probability estimates for ambiguity by mentally simulating potential outcomes of the ambiguous process. Curley et al (1986) addressed other psychological sources of ambiguity aversion and Hogarth & Kunreuther (1985, 1989) showed that ambiguity affects insurance prices. Nevertheless, some psychologists retain a residual uneasiness that ambiguity aversion is irrational unless it is justified strategically (Frisch & Baron 1988).

SOCIAL DILEMMAS AND THE PROVISION OF PUBLIC GOODS

The sage Hillel asked, "If I am not for myself, who is for me? And if I am only for myself, what am I?" Economists and psychologists have been asking the same questions for the last several decades. Although it is simplistic to see this work as research on altruism, it does examine conditions that push people one way or another along a continuum that runs from cooperative or group-oriented behavior on one extreme to self-interested or individually-oriented behavior on the other extreme.

The central issues derive from game theory (von Neumann & Morgenstern 1947), the same theory that launched research on risky choice. Game theory predicts that people will choose rationally (i.e. they will use available information to select moves that maximize self-interest) and that they will assume that their opponent is doing the same. The analytical aim is to find combinations of moves called equilibria from which no player is motivated to move. Sometimes a game has only one equilibrium, other times, more than one. In the latter cases, a further goal of analysis is to find conditions (refinements) under which a single equilibrium exists.

Social dilemmas are games that pit individual incentives against group incentives in such a way that the equilibrium is deficient (i.e. the equilibrium pays off less well for players than does some other combination of moves). The most familiar example is the Prisoner's Dilemma (PD) game in which two players decide separately whether to cooperate or defect. The situation is like that facing two partners in crime who have been caught by the police and are being held separately. If either confesses and implicates his partner, the confessor will go free while the partner will get ten years. If both confess, both will get five years. If neither confesses, they will face a minor charge and get one year each. The dilemma arises because the partners are each better off individually to confess (i.e. freedom vs one year if the other keeps mum and five years vs ten years if the other confesses), yet they are better off jointly if both keep mum.

The game just described is a symmetric two-person game, played once, in which players act independently and in which the outcomes are discrete losses that have a well-specified ordinal relation. For each player, there is a dominating alternative (an act that is preferable no matter what the opponent does), and after both players have acted, each will know what the other has done. But any of these features can be varied.

Most experimental studies of two-person games have used the PD payoff structure, though many other structures exist. Anatol Rapoport & Guyer (1966) provide a taxonomy of 78 nonequivalent 2×2 matrices. Games considered interesting from a game theoretical perspective all involve conflict (e.g. Chicken, Leader, Hero) but some considered trivial (e.g. Trust) become interesting psychologically if players derive utility from beating the opponent (McClintock & Liebrand 1988). Games can also be represented in alternate frames (called decomposed games) that differ superficially in the degree to which they highlight cooperative and competitive motives but that derive from a single 2×2 matrix (Pruitt 1967). One particularly interesting feature of decomposed games is that choices can signal intent to cooperate, increasing the likelihood that partners reciprocate on later trials (Komorita 1987).

An *N*-person case of the PD is the Commons Dilemma (CD). The canonical story (Hardin 1968) involves a village field on which residents can graze their cattle freely. It is advantageous for each villager to add to his herd because the addition of a single cow has little effect on the communal resource but benefits the individual substantially. Yet, if every villager follows the same reasoning, the commons is destroyed and all are worse off than if none increased his herd.

Another well-studied *N*-person dilemma is the problem of public goods provision. In public goods (PG) problems, a communal resource can only come into being as individuals contribute to it. Examples are national defense and public television. The problem that arises is that once the good exists, there is no way to prevent noncontributors from free riding (i.e. benefitting from the good without having contributed to it).

PG problems also have features that can be varied. For example, the good need not increase continuously, but instead might appear abruptly at some critical threshold of participation. PG problems are also affected by whether the actions of particular individuals are identifiable or whether a given actor can imagine his or her actions to be critical in determining whether the good is provided.

Social dilemmas and public good problems tend to have separate literatures,[3] but for both problem types, self-interest predicts that people will either defect (PD and CD forms) or free ride (PG forms). On the other hand, daily experience testifies to the power of group norms in restricting selfish behavior. Laboratory studies support both views. Although psychologists and economists would probably agree on empirical findings, the disciplines diverge in what they feel needs further explaining.

Psychology and the Wellsprings of Cooperation

Before game theory, psychologists concentrated on the expression of conflict in attitudes and overt aggression. Game theory shifted attention to the antecedent role played by opposed interests. Anatol Rapoport (see Rapoport & Chammah 1965) was especially influential in promoting the experimental study of two-person PD games. The resulting program of research explored demographic variables such as gender and age, structural variations of payoff matri-

3 Although PD, CD, and PG games have some similarity, economists tend not to group them together. Roth (1988) mentions that he is discussing PD and PG problems together, though the literatures on these problems seldom refer to one another. He does not mention CD problems. Stroebe & Frey (1982) introduce the CD as a classic example of a PG problem, and Dawes (1980) discusses all three forms.

ces, and effects of repeated play (Lee 1971). Writing two decades later, Pruitt & Kimmel (1977) criticized this work for being excessively behavioral (i.e. atheoretical) and for being bound conceptually and methodologically to the laboratory.

Since the early 1970s social psychologists have turned their attention to the motivational and communicative underpinnings of cooperation. A variety of reviews describe the work from different perspectives. McClintock (1972) proposes three major motives that operate in two-person games (individualism, relativism, and cooperation) and describes paradigms for studying them. Dawes (1980) focuses on the roles that communication plays in increasing cooperation in *N*-person games. Stroebe & Frey (1982) relate CD results to research on bystander intervention and social loafing. Messick & Brewer (1983) add consideration of individual and temporal dilemmas and catalog a variety of solutions.[4]

Several generalizations can be drawn from the psychological studies. Communication has been shown to improve cooperation rates in social dilemmas through two routes. Van de Kragt et al (1983) showed that in PG problems requiring a specified number of contributors [the minimum contributing set (MCS) paradigm], subjects who can communicate typically devise strategies that provide the good efficiently (i.e. at minimal social cost) while reducing the risk of defection. Discussion also increases cooperation rates in non-MCS situations, probably by inducing the development of a group identity. Group members forgo defecting when they expect that others will not defect either (Dawes et al 1977, 1988; Orbell et al 1988).

Group identification and in-group bias may also explain the finding that play between individuals in PD games is more cooperative than play between dyads (McCallum et al 1985). Dyads in the latter experiment appeared to be trying to beat the opposing dyad as much as to maximize their own outcomes. Between-group competitiveness can also lead groups to behave conservatively, in which case the good is secured at the price of social inefficiency (Amnon Rapoport & Bornstein 1989).

MCS games have also been useful for specifying how incentives influence cooperation rates. Amnon Rapoport & Eshed-Levy (1989) have shown that both fear and greed motivate free riding, though greed is the more powerful motive. Suleiman & Rapoport (1992) found that although increasing the threshold level for provision of a good increases the average contribution, some subjects behave consistently with EU maximization (lowering their con-

4 I use the term "solving" to mean finding a way to avoid the deficient outcome. This includes social agreements such as laws and sanctions that literally change the payoffs. Some economists would object to the usage, however, arguing that a solution for a PD or CD game must leave the payoff structure intact, because changing it changes the game.

tribution when they expect high contributions from others) while others seem oriented toward cooperation (increasing their contribution when they expect high contributions from others). This is consistent with studies showing that measures of social orientation (individualistic, competitive, cooperative, or altruistic) predict subjects' choices quite well in PD and CD games (Liebrand & van Run 1985, McClintock & Liebrand 1988).

Social psychologists have also studied how groups manage the harvesting of shares from replenishable (i.e. regenerating) resource pools. These tasks commonly use false feedback in order to make subjects believe that others are overusing or underusing the resource. In underuse conditions, most subjects increase their consumption over time. With overuse, however, subjects who trust others to show self-restraint reduce their own consumption whereas non-trusting subjects do not (Messick et al 1983, see also Brann & Foddy 1987). Such tasks have also been used to investigate when subjects will turn to structural solutions to curb overuse (e.g. electing a leader or privatizing the resource). The results show that people opt for structural solutions to resource depletion primarily when they perceive that their level of self-restraint is high compared to others (Samuelson & Messick 1986).

Economics and the Problem of Goodness

As theologians must explain why a benevolent God allows evil to exist, economists must explain why cooperation flourishes in the face of powerful incentives for selfishness. Several excellent reviews summarize the experimental tacks that economists have taken to meeting this challenge. Roth (1988) describes the historical roots of PD and PG experiments. Ledyard (1994) provides well-detailed descriptions of important PG studies and summarizes what is known about factors that influence cooperation. Camerer (1990) discusses a variety of game theoretical tasks and relates them to behavioral decision theory.

Experimental studies using PD tasks began to appear in economics and psychology at around the same time. Manipulations and results were about the same: cooperative choices were not unanimous but they occurred in far greater numbers than self-interest would predict (Lave 1965). Because equilibrium predictions are essentially predictions about long-run behavior, experiments with repeated trials soon displaced one-shot games. With a fixed and known number of trials, game theory predicts defection in every period,[5] but if subjects believe that the game will continue indefinitely, the equilibrium is cooperation.

---

5 This is not strictly true. Kreps et al 1982 have shown that cooperative strategies can exist even in finite games, but the work is beyond the scope of this review.

In surveying the literature, Roth (1988) concludes that there is too much cooperation in experiments with fixed numbers of trials and too little in experiments where the game can be expected to continue. Still, he considers the equilibrium prediction to be reasonably accurate for the end game. He cites evidence from an experiment by Selten & Stoecker (1986) in which they studied subjects' choices in 25 "supergames" each comprising a ten-period repeated PD. The most common pattern was cooperation in the early periods of each supergame, followed by defection, with the initial defection migrating to earlier and earlier periods across supergames.

Research on public goods provision is motivated by the need to discover whether current political institutions can provide public goods fairly and efficiently. The earliest relevant experiments were done in the 1970s. A good example is an experiment by Bohm (1972) that examined whether pricing mechanisms can be used to determine the demand for television. Free riding is an issue here because, depending on how pricing questions are asked, self-interested individuals may overstate or understate the worth of the good. Bohm found, however, that strategically dissimilar pricing tasks produced about the same response and he concluded that estimating demand for public goods would not be a problem.

By the late 1970s psychologists had begun to work on PG problems, but the research that caught the attention of economists was a provocatively titled study, "Economists free ride, does anyone else?," by sociologists Marwell & Ames (1981). The article reported a dozen PG experiments on high school students. Contribution rates typically ranged between 40% and 55%. For a comparison group of economics graduate students, however, the contribution rate was a mere 20%. The authors did not hesitate to gloat.

Not surprisingly, economists rose to the bait, turning again to the issue of repeated trials. Isaac et al (1985) and Kim & Walker (1984) both found initial contribution rates like those of Marwell & Ames, but rates fell to roughly 10% within a few periods. Systematic manipulation of the relative payoffs for selfish and public acts also showed that subjects gave more when they stood to gain more from the public good (Isaac et al 1984).

Ledyard (1994) discusses 19 variables that affect contribution rates strongly or weakly. Those with strong effects have already been mentioned: communication and improved incentives for the public good increase contributions while repetition decreases them. Weak positive effects include common knowledge about individual endowments, symmetry in endowments, existence of a threshold for provision of the good, participants' beliefs about the contributions of others, group identification, and "rebates" of contributions when the good is not provided. Weak negative effects include economics training, experience with the incentive structure, and requirements for unanimous contributions.

Ledyard's assessment of the directional effects and relative importance of these variables would probably be accepted by psychologists, but differences in interpretation would likely remain. Even Ledyard is pessimistic about the efficacy of voluntary mechanisms for providing public goods. He sees a role for economists in designing incentive schemes that enhance group-oriented behavior. Psychologists looking at the same data might see conditions in which cooperation can easily gain an initial edge. In such environments, incentives for cooperation can become intrinsic or endogenous as both individuals and groups benefit. In response to Hillel's questions, then, psychologists might answer with John Donne: "We are both for ourselves and for others because we are part of mankind."

BEHAVIOR IN MARKET SETTINGS

Because individual behavior in risky choice and social dilemmas is often at variance with economic theory, it would seem natural to psychologists to reject the theory, saying in essence that economics doesn't work. Economists, however, judge matters differently. Although economic theory is derived mathematically from propositions about individuals, the goal is not to predict individual behavior. In an economy, people interact through institutions such as markets. Economic theory predicts how institutions affect behavior. From the economist's perspective, if institutions work as predicted, economics works.

Economists have been testing market predictions experimentally since the 1950s. A memoir of the early years (Smith 1993) shows that psychologists were involved from the outset. A classic book in the field, *Bargaining Behavior* (Fouraker & Siegel 1963), was the collaborative work of a psychologist (Siegel) and an economist (Fouraker).[6] Other psychologists involved were Bush, Coombs, Edwards, Estes, Festinger, Toda, and Simon (who if not a psychologist by training, is at least a fellow traveler).

Debate has flared recently over the implications of psychological research for economics. Some psychologists and even some economists argue that violations of assumptions at the individual level invalidate important parts of economic theory in ways that better incentives, learning, and market forces cannot correct. Representative examples of such arguments are Tversky & Kahneman (1986) on violations of description invariance, Kahneman et al (1986) on fairness and the acceptability of business transactions, Kahneman et al (1990) on differences between willingness-to-pay and willingness-to-ac-

6 Siegel, who died young in 1961, was also one of the founders of behavioral decision making.

cept, and Arrow (1982) and Camerer (1992) on the effects of cognitive biases on markets.

Smith (1991) rejects the view that economic rationality requires the conscious rationality of individuals. He and other experimental economists (e.g. Plott 1986) instead see market rationality as emerging from choices governed interactively by institutions (e.g. the rules of the markets in which exchanges take place). In this view, economic rationality cannot be tested independently of the social and economic institutions that shape and support it.

Although every major economic journal now regularly publishes experimental work, the field is still not mainstream and experimental economists have their work cut out to convince theoretical economists about the feasibility and value of subjecting economic ideas to empirical test. Several lucid reviews have been written to inform nonspecialists about the rationale and methods of experimental economics. These reviews provide an excellent summary of the research and many psychologists will be fascinated by the close-up view of a field, very much like their own, inventing itself against a backdrop of indifference and hostility to the very idea of experimentation.

All the reviews cited here summarize basic findings and comment on the role of experiments in economics, but each also provides specialized commentary of particular note. Plott (1982) gives details of laboratory procedures as well as sample instructions and graphs illustrating prototypical results. Smith (1982) provides a more philosophical perspective on methodology and the function of experiments. Milgrom (1989) provides a primer on the operation and theory of auctions including the familiar English auction, sealed-bid auctions, second-price auctions, and Dutch auctions. Roth (1987) surveys experimental design in laboratory research and its role in answering questions and deepening understanding.

Basic Procedures in Experimental Markets

Experimental markets are real markets in that buyers and sellers make profits by exchanging things of value. However, they are also laboratory markets in that experimenters exercise control over critical variables. Experimenters control individual preferences using a technique called induced valuation in which a commodity that has no intrinsic value (e.g. a token) is assigned value according to a predetermined schedule. Sellers buy tokens from experimenters at preset cost and sell them to buyers. In turn, buyers resell the tokens to the experimenters at preset redemption values. Sellers make a profit by selling at a price that exceeds their cost. Buyers make a profit by paying less than the redemption value.

Experimental markets usually take place over a series of periods or "trading days," each lasting anywhere from five to fifteen minutes. Redemption values may be the same or may change from period to period. Traders ordinarily cannot hold commodities over from one period to the next. In most cases, subjects know only their own redemption values. Experimental markets also have few sellers and few buyers. This is significant because competitive markets theoretically work best with large numbers of buyers and sellers.

One of the most important variables to be manipulated or controlled is the institutional organization of the market, which is the set of rules governing exchanges and communications between buyers and sellers. The simplest laboratory markets include auction markets with public outcry, posted-bid and posted-offer markets, sealed-bid and sealed-offer auctions, and negotiated price (telephone) markets. The most common of these is the double auction in which bids to buy and offers to sell are made orally (or by computer), then displayed on a blackboard (or video monitor) by the experimenter. The best recent bid and offer remain standing until they are accepted, canceled, or surpassed by better bids or offers, which then replace them on the display.

Instructions to subjects are typically as neutral as possible. Worksheets are often provided to help subjects keep track of profits. Average payoffs typically exceed subjects' hourly wage-rates and deception of any sort is rare.

Predictions and Prototypical Findings

DOUBLE AND ONE-SIDED AUCTIONS Double auctions are modeled on organized stock and commodity markets in which there are many buyers and many sellers. Predictions for double auctions are obtained by plotting on the same graph the cost and redemption values for sellers and buyers. These constitute supply and demand curves. The place where they cross (supply = demand) is the competitive equilibrium. This gives both the predicted volume (total number) of transactions and the predicted price. One can also look at efficiency (i.e. the degree to which buyers and sellers jointly extract maximum payoffs from the experimenter).

Data from double auctions have shown repeatedly that this institution is highly robust. Given only a few buyers and a few sellers, prices and volume quickly converge to the competitive equilibrium, and efficiency typically goes to 100%. Even in noncompetitive settings that permit monopoly, oligopoly, or collusion among sellers, the public display of bids and offers seems to provide buyers with the information they need to resist excessively high prices (Plott 1982, pp. 1493, 1501, 1505–1511).

In auctions allowing only bids or only offers (one-sided auctions), prices converge slightly off the equilibrium value and the silent parties (those who can only accept or reject) reap the benefit. No one knows for sure why this occurs but two factors may contribute. First, the silent group may anticipate competition among the nonsilent buyers or sellers and hold out for better prices. Second, the enforced silence prevents the silent parties from divulging information about their own values to nonsilent parties (Plott 1982, pp. 1494–1496).

POSTED-PRICE MARKETS Posted-price markets are similar to ordinary retail markets in which sellers set prices. One critical difference is that sellers in retail markets often wait to set prices until they learn what the competition is charging. In the laboratory, however, sellers typically make pricing decisions privately and simultaneously before the start of each market period.

The most robust finding with posted-price markets is slow convergence from the side of the party posting the price. Posted-offer markets typically stabilize above equilibrium while posted-bid markets stabilize below equilibrium. In either case, these markets seem to work against the nonposting side by encouraging nonposters to passively accept prices rather than trying to change them by postponing acceptance. Posted-offer markets also differ from double auctions in that they foster tacit collusion among experienced sellers even when there is no opportunity for overt conspiracy (Plott 1982, pp. 1498–1500, 1511–517).

NEGOTIATED-PRICE MARKETS In negotiated-price markets, buyers and sellers negotiate with one another privately, often by telephone. Buyers can shop among sellers, but contact within buyer and seller groups is prevented. Research on negotiated-price markets has shown that prices converge toward the equilibrium over time but tend to stay a little on the high side. Efficiency is only 80–90% and there is also excess volume. Plott suggests that these deviations arise because some buyers are poorly informed or do not choose to shop (Plott 1982, pp. 1496–1498).

ENGLISH, DUTCH, AND SEALED-BID AUCTIONS For the noneconomist, the canonical auction is the English auction in which an auctioneer offers a single good to a group of buyers. Prices start low and are bid up until only one bid remains. Prices need not start low, however. In the Dutch auction, prices start high and are lowered incrementally until some buyer accepts the offered price.

English and Dutch auctions are public in the sense that buyers know what prices other buyers have offered or considered. Sealed-bid auctions (e.g. which are commonly used in the sale of oil exploration rights) are private in that bidders submit bids to an auctioneer who either awards the good to the highest bidder or provides summary data on current bids and solicits new bids. Sealed-bid auctions can be either first-price (in which the highest bidder wins the good and pays the price he bid) or second-price (in which the highest bidder wins the good but pays only as much as the second highest bid).

For the economist, the key question about auctions is whether the form affects the outcomes. Are prices higher in one auction than another? Is one institution more efficient at ensuring that the good goes to the person who values it most highly? These questions have both theoretical and empirical answers.

In theory, a buyer at an English auction should increase his bid until the price exceeds his willingness-to-pay (i.e. his private value for the good). If all buyers behave this way, the good will eventually be sold to the buyer who values it most at a price equal to the second highest valuation (i.e. the price the next-to-last buyer was unwilling to exceed). The same analysis applies to second-price sealed-bid auctions if buyers bid their true values. The highest bidder (i.e. the person with the highest true value) wins the good at a price equal to the second-highest valuation (Milgrom 1989).

Dutch and first-price sealed-bid auctions are also theoretically equivalent. In both, optimal bids depend on the number of other bidders (N). In first-price auctions, assuming bidders know their own value (v) for the item being auctioned, they should bid a fraction of v, that fraction approaching unity as N increases. Doing so trades off the potential profitability of winning the item cheaply against the increased probability of losing the item as N increases. The same reasoning applies in Dutch auctions. Bidders should set their bids by the same fractional rule and claim the item if the price reaches that level (Milgrom 1989).

Empirical research verifies that English and second-price auctions do generate appropriate and roughly equivalent outcomes. Dutch and first-price auctions, on the other hand, are not behaviorally equivalent. First-price auctions yield both higher prices and greater efficiency. Bidders in Dutch auctions appear to hold back, waiting until offers are well below predicted levels and sometimes losing to bidders with lower true values. One possible explanation is that buyers in Dutch auctions enjoy the suspense of waiting (Smith 1982).

Market Magic and the Assumptions of Economic Theory

As a psychologist who has, until recently, spent only a little time among economists, I used to wonder why economists dismissed evidence that the behavioral assumptions of their theories were wrong. It is now easier to understand. As noted earlier, economics is in some ways as much mathematics as it is social science. The disciplinary duality means that economic theories serve two roles. In the mathematical part of economics, theories yield mathematical results (theorems) that can be used in the generation of still more mathematical results. Attacks on assumptions threaten not only theory, but also the accumulated body of results that flow from theory. It is no wonder that mathematical economists hesitate to throw out their life's work just because experimental subjects don't behave as they might.

In the social science part of economics, theories are frameworks for organizing and interpreting empirical knowledge and results are merely observations generated in the course of testing theory. Behavioral assumptions may be part of the framework but they have no privileged status and are tested anytime the theory is tested. Many theories predict well despite unrealistic assumptions. In these cases we accord the theory "as if" status and get on with the business of using the theory as a heuristic device for exploring reality.

Experimental markets are prime cases in which theoretical predictions are not undone by unrealistic assumptions. This has not necessarily pleased mainstream economists. Instead, their reactions to experimental findings have often been more like "There must be something wrong with these experiments? How can you get competitive outcomes in the absence of complete information?" (Smith 1993, p. 276). For experimentalists, however, the unexpected robustness of the theory is a challenge, a mystery to be pursued in hopes of someday understanding how, in Smith's words, "people are able to get the 'right' answers without consciously performing our logic and calculations" (1989, p. 163).

A particularly compelling example of the mysterious power of markets originated here at the University of Iowa. Forsythe et al (1992) ran a market in 1988 in which the object was to predict the vote shares of the presidential election candidates. The Iowa Presidential Stock Market (IPSM) was run as a computerized double auction in which traders bought and sold shares in the three major candidates (Bush, Dukakis, and Jackson) plus a fourth candidate labeled "Rest-of-Field." Aspiring traders initially paid $2.50 for portfolios that contained one share of each of the four candidates. After posting a deposit to a cash account, traders could trade with one another or purchase additional portfolios around the clock. The market ran from June 1 until 9 AM on November 9, the day after the election. After election returns were final, shares were paid dividends determined by the candidate's share of the popular vote.

Of the 192 traders enrolled in the market, most were students. Still, running forecasts based on prices showed that the IPSM outperformed six major professional polls in predicting the relative showing of Bush and Dukakis. The same was true in the 1992 presidential election (R Forsythe, personal communication, 1993). How can this be? What knowledge might Iowa students have that professional polling firms lack?

The researchers are the first to admit that they do not have all the answers. Their hypothesis is that markets can generate correct prices (i.e. correct predictions) even with many unknowledgeable traders as long as there are a few unbiased traders (marginal traders) willing to take either side of the trade if they see an opportunity for profit. Although the design of the market did not allow for rigorous testing of the marginal trader hypothesis, post hoc analysis has confirmed that a small group of marginal traders (11% of participants) influenced price. This group's trading behavior exhibited no partisanship biases and they earned a significantly higher return than nonmarginal traders.

METHODOLOGICAL AND PHILOSOPHICAL ISSUES

Small and Special Worlds

The laboratory is a microcosm, a small and special world in which situations are sharpened and simplified. Every task is a model of something, scaled down to the limitations of our abilities and our resources. The scaling is critical. When von Békésy (1960) figured out how the ear encodes pitch, direct observation was impossible so he ran experiments on a fluid-filled tank covered with a rubber membrane. Though clearly not an ear, the tank sufficed to demonstrate that traveling waves encode pitch.

Von Békésy could leap from ear to tank and back again because he knew a lot about the physical system he was studying. For example, he knew that geometry did not matter. A rectangular tank with a membrane on the surface would work the same as a coiled membrane surrounded by fluid. He also knew about the Reynolds number, a dimensionless constant[7] that relates density, viscosity, velocity, and length in viscous flows. The Reynolds number is a benchmark for matching systems: if the Reynolds numbers match, the systems match.

Psychologists and economists could use a Reynolds number, but we don't have one. Scaling problems are particularly critical when we use financial incentives to motivate economic thinking. Given limited resources and the need to run many subjects, we conventionally scale payoffs. Sometimes we pay a single trial drawn at random from the larger set. Other times, we pay a fraction of par. Either way, there may be problems. Selecting a gamble at random is theoretically equivalent to dividing probabilities by a constant and could well affect choice (constant ratio paradox). Paying subjects at a fraction of par is theoretically equivalent to offering gambles with fractional outcomes (asking subjects to gamble for pennies). In both cases, scaling only works (i.e. matches task to prototype) if subjects are not thinking too deeply.[8]

Control may also be more easily achieved in physics than in social science. Individual differences are a particular problem, one to which economists are not fully adjusted. For example, Ledyard (1994) is disconcerted by the failure of the free-rider hypothesis to be fully supported or fully rejected. He sees this imprecision as reflecting the fact that economists have not yet achieved sufficient control to be able to identify what is really happening. Psychologists, on the other hand, expect differences and use psychological testing to increase precision (e.g. McClintock & Liebrand 1988).

---

[7] Dimensionless constants are ratios in which quantities that have units are arranged so that the units cancel out.

[8] Agricultural economists occasionally run experiments in third world countries where a dollar goes a long way. In this case, however, one has to worry about "cultural" scaling.

Good Experiments/Bad Experiments

Psychologists will probably be dismayed to learn that experimental economists consider us sloppy experimenters [put delicately, "methodology in experimental economics is more theoretically driven and fastidious than in experimental psychology" (Camerer 1992, p. 247)]. Among the reasons for this is that experimental economics, being the new kid on a hostile block, is more self-conscious about its science. Readers who have been around awhile will recall a similar self-consciousness in neobehaviorism.

There are also differences between behavioral decision making (BDM) and "more theoretically driven and fastidious" fields such as perception and memory. BDM has two quite separate research traditions. One focuses on parametric variations of theoretically driven designs. The other focuses on "word problems" that function more as demonstrations than experiments and that may be reported without even a "Methods" section. Unfortunately for the image of BDM, economists are less aware of parametric research than of demonstration research.

More important, however, is that psychologists and economists worry about different things. Psychologists and economists are both distrustful of each other's subject pools, but for different reasons. Economists worry that psychology subjects expect to be deceived, undoing experimental control (Ledyard 1993). Moreover, psychology subjects seem likely to be poorly motivated because meaningful incentives are lacking (Smith 1991). Psychologists worry that economics subjects are different from noneconomists by virtue of training or "preoccupation with the 'rational' allocation of money and goods" (Marwell & Ames 1981, p. 309).

Psychologists and economists also worry differently about experiments. Economists worry that subjects will not "tell the truth" unless incentives make truth-telling compatible with maximizing utility. Psychologists expect subjects to tell the truth, but worry about experimental demand and select subjects who are naive with respect to the theory under test. Economists worry about demand, too, in the form of cues from the experimenter. Consequently, they write instructions that are as neutral as possible, avoiding words like "maximizing" or "competition" that might set up expectations about desired behavior (e.g. Ledyard 1994; Plott 1982, p. 1490). In contrast, psychologists may instruct subjects to maximize individual outcomes even in social dilemmas (e.g. Kelley & Grzelak 1972, Samuelson & Messick 1986).

This is no time to pick sides. It does appear that economics students behave less cooperatively than noneconomists (Frank et al 1993). If this prevents experimental economists from drawing the kinds of conclusions they want from their experiments, they should be concerned. They should also wonder how experiences in other experiments might affect subjects' behavior. Likewise, psychologists should be concerned if subjects expect deception, and should also consider the ways in which subjects' answers to hypothetical questions might differ from real behavior. This is especially important when real incentives cannot be used (e.g. large stakes or out-of-pocket losses). And everybody should be aware that changes of a single word in instructions can affect outcomes.

There are no universal proscriptions. Using deception as a case in point, it is easy to say "don't deceive subjects." But for all its problems, deception has one clear benefit: a powerful deception experiment is the equivalent of virtual social reality. Done well, it creates laboratory situations that would rarely occur spontaneously or in controlled form. In the same way, it is inappropriate to rule out the use of economics students in experiments. Economics models the economic system, and many of the people who run businesses and set policy have had training in economics. In the small and special world of the experimental economics laboratory, it is not clear what species of student makes the best experimental subject. What is clear is that every experimenter in every discipline has to care deeply that predictions are not just right, but that they are right for the right reasons.

Getting Theory Right

Friedman (1953) argued that the goodness of a theory rests on its predictive accuracy and not on the realism of its axioms. Polanyi (1962) is more to my taste in believing that truth lies in the achievement of contact with reality. Getting theories right is hard to do because wrong theories impose errors on us by conflating phenomena and explanations. It seems to me that one such error in the overlap of psychology and economics has its source in Bernoulli's proposal that risk attitude is a byproduct of how we value money. The idea appears in modern EU theory in the notion that risk aversion is identical with curvature in the utility function. Similarly in PT, risk aversion and risk seeking reflect concave and convex segments in the utility function.

The earliest draft of Yaari's (1987) rank dependent model bore the radical title "Risk aversion without diminishing marginal utility." A later revision amended this by adding "and the dual theory of choice under risk." The published version dropped the radical phrase altogether. Others who have argued that curvature in the utility function is unrelated to risk aversion (Lopes 1984, Wakker 1991) have had no better success. Still, there is plenty to suggest that modeling risk attitude by curvature leads to problems. It isolates risky choice from risk perception, an embarrassing gap that few have tried to fill (but see Lopes 1984, Weber et al 1992). Measured risk attitudes have also been highly variable (Berg et al 1992, McCord & De Neufville 1985, Hershey et al 1982). Even when allowance is made for different risk attitudes on gains and losses, failures of reflection and framing predictions are routine (e.g.

Cohen et al 1987, Fagley & Miller 1987, Fischhoff 1983, Hershey & Schoemaker 1980, Miller & Fagley 1991, Schneider 1992, Schneider & Lopes 1986).

One way to achieve contact with psychological reality is to ask people questions about their behavior. Most economists are leery of asking such questions, and there are good reasons to be cautious, but subjects' insights can sometimes be valuable (see Smith 1993, p. 262). Retrospective protocols based on open-ended questions are often of little use, but protocols that are collected on-line or with cued recall (Russo & Dosher 1983) can provide valuable clues to the reasons for people's actions.

Must the Heart Have Reasons That Reason Cannot Know?

Anatol Rapoport & Chammah (1965) point out that game theorists playing repeated PDs lose (defect) every time when they might as easily win. "Confronted with this paradox, game theoreticians have no answer. Ordinary mortals, however,...hardly ever play DD [mutual defection] one hundred percent of the time.... Evidently the run-of-the-mill players are not strategically sophisticated enough to have figured out that strategy DD is the only rationally defensible strategy, and this intellectual shortcoming saves them from losing" (p. 29).

Rapoport & Chammah were writing in jest (one hopes), but there is scant humor in the proposition that reason offers no solutions for life's conflicts. Economists as much as psychologists look for solutions and for explanations of why cooperation is as prevalent as it is. Frank (1988) proposed the theory that cooperation arises not from reason, but from passion or emotion that leaks out, as it were, through nonverbal cues that signal unambiguously one's intent to cooperate. In this way, cooperators may recognize fellow cooperators and distinguish them from competitors whose words may disguise bad intentions.

I have no prejudice against passion, however leaky, but it seems that the brief against reason has been accepted too readily. Reason in game theory comprises an uneven collection of procedures including (*a*) logical procedures borrowed from mathematics such as backwards induction, (*b*) procedures for simplifying problems such as "first eliminate dominated alternatives," and (*c*) heuristic procedures based on implicit social theories such as "never trust your opponent." Neither of the latter two has the logical force of backward induction, and either could be replaced by an equally reasonable (i.e. rational) procedure.

Anatol Rapoport (1973) reinterprets game theory by suggesting an alternative to simplifying by dominance. Because game theory requires "mutual perception of rationality" (i.e. "I'm rational; you're rational"), players must refrain from making asymmetrical assumptions (i.e. any assumption that players might choose differently). This limits feasible outcomes. Simplifying by feasibility reveals that the only feasible outcomes are DD and CC [mutual cooperation], and of these CC is clearly best.

The social heuristic might also be replaced by something less paranoid. Not everyone is untrustworthy. To behave as if they were assures that the benefits of cooperation will be lost. It is well understood that tit-for-tat[9] is a good strategy for the PD (Axelrod 1984), but no one gets to tit-for-tat without a leap of faith. However, if one thinks of cooperation on early trials as an investment, the leap seems well justified.

Aggregation and Emergent Properties

Economics has been much criticized for being excessively mathematical and practically irrelevant (e.g. Bauer 1988, D Bell 1981, Simon 1986). Smith adds the criticism that economists have failed to understand the locus of market rationality. "That individual rationality is a consciously cognitive phenomenon is fundamental in the rhetoric of microeconomic and game theory… It has been hard for either the theorist or the psychologist to imagine optimal market outcomes being achieved by other than conscious cognition" (Smith 1991, pp. 879–80). "*Theorists* have to assume complete information in order to [do their calculations]. But it does not follow that agents either require such information, or would know how to make the calculations if they had the information" (Smith 1989, p. 161).

Experimental economists look to institutions as the source of intelligence in markets. Buyers and sellers can be cognitively simple, knowing only their own costs and values, yet still achieve outcomes at or near theoretical optima. Much needs explaining, however. For example, Smith (1982) reports that although convergence is rapid and complete in double auctions with incomplete information, giving buyers and sellers information about others' costs and values slows convergence. Why? No one knows.

Experimental market research has spurred changes in economic thinking along three lines: model robustness, constraint in structure, and emergence of complexity from simplicity. The same lines of thought have also been prominent in psychology. In BDM, linear models have been a staple for description (Anderson 1981), for prediction (Dawes & Corrigan 1974), and for prescription (von Winterfeldt & Edwards 1986). We have had to learn that robust models are double-edged swords, however: goodness of fit can be a poor indicator of a model's correctness (Anderson & Shanteau 1977, see also Harrison 1989). Rigorous model tests demand pointed questions.

Very early in the development of BDM, Simon (1956) and Toda (1962) proposed that intelligence can emerge from the interactions of simple organ-

9 Cooperate on Trial 1 and thereafter mimic the opponent's most recent move.

isms with structured environments. In perception, Gibson (1957) challenged the view that massive inference is needed to resolve ambiguous sensory stimulation into unambiguous percepts. The Gibsonian point is that the stimulus is a rich source of information that can be apprehended directly. These views are consistent with the experimental economists' admonition that we should understand the constraints and information in institutions before looking to conscious cognition for explanations.

Finally, recent research on connectionist models has challenged the assumption that intelligence requires conscious execution of explicit rules. Simple computational units interacting in parallel exhibit powerful properties (Rumelhart & McClelland 1986). Human beings have evolved as social organisms. Would it be so surprising if some of our intelligence were lodged in social processes operating without conscious intent? Research on experimental markets may offer a forum in which psychologists (and perhaps sociologists, see Coleman 1986) can explore this possibility.

Changing the World

An important way in which physics and social science differ is that social science changes the world that it models. Physics has changed the world, but even if the theories of physics someday allow us to self-destruct, the laws of physics will apply to the wreckage. With social science, theories change the way people think about themselves, and that changes what people are.

All of us who teach contribute to the change. Whether we intend to or not, we tell students how to think and live. Economics considers itself a normative science, the very term, an oxymoron of ought and is. A text on game theory begins "Strategic thinking is the art of outdoing an adversary, knowing that the adversary is trying to do the same to you" (Dixit & Nalebuff 1991, p. ix). Labels like rational and irrational reinforce the message. Psychology also has normative overtones, conveyed in messages about mental health. It is the cooperative and undemanding child who is well-adjusted. Even when we see the need for teaching someone to be less cooperative, we train for assertiveness, not competitiveness.

Psychology and economics meet in the business college. As a nation we must learn to compete in a global market on terms that we do not like. Shall we destroy our competitors or improve our products? Pay-for-performance or empower workers? The lessons we teach are broader than we know.

Psychologists and economists are not so different as people, but our disciplinary perspectives often lead to different conclusions. As Daniel Bell has remarked, "the social sciences are necessarily partial 'prisms,' selecting out different facets of behavior in order to understand the causes of change and their meanings. And what sets their boundaries is not the 'essential' properties of a subject matter, but the different questions they ask..." (1981, p. 77). To study another discipline in the light of one's own is to look through another prism. The unfamiliar vantage improves one's grasp of the whole.

ACKNOWLEDGMENTS

I thank my colleagues Gregg Oden, Andy Daughety, and Bob Forsythe for the comments and conversations that have enriched this manuscript. Requests for reprints may be mailed to the address on the title page or sent via e-mail to lola-lopes@uiowa.edu.

Literature Cited

Allais M. 1953. Le comportement de l'homme rationnel devant le risque: critique des postulats et axiomes de l'Ecole Americaine. *Econometrica* 21:503–46

Allais M. 1986. The general theory of random choices in relation to the invariant cardinal utility function and the specific probability function. *Working Paper C4475.* Paris: Centre Anal. Econ., École Mines

Allais M, Hagen O, eds. 1979. *Expected Utility Hypotheses and the Allais Paradox.* Boston: Reidel

Anderson NH. 1981. *Foundations of Information Integration Theory.* New York: Academic

Anderson NH, Shanteau J. 1977. Weak inference with linear models. *Psychol. Bull.* 84:1155–70

Arrow KJ. 1982. Risk perception in psychology and economics. *Econ. Inq.* 20:1–9

Axelrod R. 1984. *The Evolution of Cooperation.* New York: Basic Books

Bauer P. 1988. The disregard of reality. *Cato's Letter #3.* Washington, DC: Cato Inst.

Bell D. 1981. Models and reality in economic discourse. In *The Crisis in Economic Theory,* ed. D Bell, I Kristol, pp. 46–80. New York: Basic Books

Bell DE. 1982. Regret in decision making under uncertainty. *Oper. Res.* 30:961–81

Berg JE, Dickhaut JW, O'Brien JR. 1985. Preference reversal and arbitrage. *Res. Exp. Econ.* 3:31–72

Berg JE, Dickhaut JW, McCabe K. 1992. Risk preference instability across institutions: a dilemma. *Working Paper.* Iowa City: Dept. Account., Univ. Iowa

Bernoulli D. 1738. *Exposition of a New Theory on the Measurement of Risk.* Transl. L Sommer, 1967. Farnborough Hants, England: Gregg

Birnbaum MH. 1972. Morality judgments: tests of an averaging model. *J. Exp. Psychol.* 93:35–42

Birnbaum MH, Coffey G, Mellers BA, Weiss R. 1992. Utility measurement: configural-weight theory and the judge's point of view. *J. Exp. Psychol.: Hum. Percept. Perform.* 18:331–46

Black RDC. 1990. Utility. In *The New Palgrave: Utility and Probability,* ed. J Eatwell, M Milgate, P Newman, pp. 295–302. New York: Norton

Bohm P. 1972. Estimating demand for public goods: an experiment. *Eur. Econ. Rev.* 3:111–30

Brann P, Foddy M. 1987. Trust and the consumption of a deteriorating common resource. *J. Confl. Resolut.* 31:615–30

Camerer CF. 1990. Behavioral game theory. In *Insights in Decision Making: A Tribute to Hillel J. Einhorn,* ed. RM Hogarth, pp. 311–36. Chicago: Univ. Chicago Press

Camerer CF. 1992. The rationality of prices and volume in experimental markets. *Organ. Behav. Hum. Decis. Process.* 51:237–72

Casey JT. 1991. Reversal of the preference reversal phenomenon. *Organ. Behav. Hum. Decis. Process.* 48:224–51

Chu Y-P, Chu R-L. 1990. The subsidence of preference reversals in simplified and marketlike settings: a note. *Am. Econ. Rev.* 80:902–11

Cohen M, Jaffray, J-Y, Said T. 1987. Experimental comparison of individual behavior under risk and under uncertainty for gains and for losses. *Organ. Behav. Hum. Decis. Process.* 39:1–22

Coleman JS. 1986. Psychological structure and social structure in economic models. *J. Bus.* 59:S365–69

Coursey DL, Hovis JL, Schulze WD. 1987. The disparity between willingness to accept and willingness to pay measures of value. *Q. J. Econ.* CII:679–90

Cummings RG, Brookshire DS, Schulze WD. 1986. *Valuing Environmental Goods: An Assessment of the Contingent Valuation Method.* Totowa, NJ: Rowman & Allanheld

Curley SP, Yates JF, Abrams RA. 1986. Psychological sources of ambiguity avoidance. *Organ. Behav. Hum. Decis. Process.* 38:230–56

Dawes RM. 1980. Social dilemmas. *Annu. Rev. Psychol.* 31:169–93

Dawes RM, Corrigan B. 1974. Linear models in decision making. *Psychol. Bull.* 81:95–106

Dawes RM, McTavish J, Shaklee H. 1977. Behavior, communication, and assumptions about other people's behavior in a commons dilemma situation. *J. Pers. Soc. Psychol.* 35:1–11

Dawes RM, van de Kragt AJC, Orbell JM. 1988. Not me or thee but we: the importance of group identity in eliciting cooperation in dilemma situations: experimental manipulations. *Acta Psychol.* 68:83–98

Dixit AK, Nalebuff BJ. 1991. *Thinking Strategically: The Competitive Edge in Business, Politics, and Everyday Life.* New York: Norton

Einhorn HJ, Hogarth RM. 1985. Ambiguity and uncertainty in probabilistic inference. *Psychol. Rev.* 92:433–61

Ellsberg D. 1961. Risk, ambiguity, and the Savage axioms. *Q. J. Econ.* 75:643–69

Fagley NS, Miller PM. 1987. The effects of decision framing on choice of risky vs certain options. *Organ. Behav. Hum. Decis. Process.* 39:264–77

Fischhoff B. 1983. Predicting frames. *J. Exp. Psychol.: Learn. Mem. Cognit.* 9:103–16

Fishburn PC. 1989. Foundations of decision analysis: along the way. *Manage. Sci.* 35:387–405

Forsythe R, Nelson F, Neumann GR, Wright J. 1992. Anatomy of an experimental stock market. *Am. Econ. Rev.* 82:1142–61

Fouraker LE, Siegel S. 1963. *Bargaining Behavior.* New York: McGraw-Hill

Frank RH. 1988. *Passions Within Reason: The Strategic Role of the Emotions.* New York: Norton

Frank RH, Gilovich T, Regan DT. 1993. Does studying economics inhibit cooperation? *Working Paper.* Ithaca, NY: Johnson School Manage., Cornell Univ.

Friedman M. 1953. *Essays in Positive Economics.* Chicago: Univ. Chicago Press

Frisch D, Baron J. 1988. Ambiguity and rationality. *J. Behav. Decis. Making.* 1:149–57

Gibson JJ. 1957. Optical motions and transformations as stimuli for visual perception. *Psychol. Rev.* 64:288–95

Gigerenzer G, Swijtink Z, Porter T, Daston L, Beatty J, Krüger L. 1989. *The Empire of Chance: How Probability Changed Science and Everyday Life.* Cambridge: Cambridge Univ. Press

Goldstein WM, Einhorn HJ. 1987. Expression theory and the preference reversal phenomena. *Psychol. Rev.* 94:236–54

Hardin G. 1968. The tragedy of the commons. *Science* 162:1243–48

Harrison GW. 1989. Theory and misbehavior of first-price auctions. *Am. Econ. Rev.* 79:749–62

Hershey JC, Kunreuther, HC, Schoemaker, PJH. 1982. Sources of bias in assessment procedures for utility functions. *Manage. Sci.* 28:936–54

Hershey JC, Schoemaker PJH. 1980. Prospect theory's reflection hypothesis: a critical examination. *Organ. Behav. Hum. Perform.* 25:395–418

Hogarth RM, Kunreuther H. 1985. Ambiguity and insurance decisions. *Am. Econ. Rev.* 75:386–90

Hogarth RM, Kunreuther H. 1989. Risk, ambiguity, and insurance. *J. Risk Uncertain.* 2:5–35

Isaac RM, McCue KF, Plott CR. 1985. Public goods provision in an experimental environment. *J. Public Econ.* 26:51–74

Isaac RM, Walker JM, Thomas SH. 1984. Divergent evidence on free riding: an experimental examination of possible explanations. *Public Choice* 43:113–49

Johnson JT. 1986. The knowledge of what might have been: affective and attributional consequences of near outcomes. *Pers. Soc. Psychol. Bull.* 12:51–62

Kahneman D, Knetsch JL, Thaler RH. 1986. Fairness and the assumptions of economics. *J. Bus.* 59:S285–300

Kahneman D, Knetsch JL, Thaler RH. 1990. Experimental tests of the endowment effect and the Coase theorem. *J. Polit. Econ.* 98:1325–48

Kahneman D, Tversky A. 1979. Prospect theory: an analysis of decision under risk. *Econometrica* 47:263–91

Kelley HH, Grzelak J. 1972. Conflict between individual and common interest in an N-person relationship. *J. Pers. Soc. Psychol.* 21:190–97

Keren G. 1991. Additional tests of utility theory under unique and repeated conditions. *J. Behav. Decis. Making.* 4:297–304

Keren G, Wagenaar WA. 1987. Violation of utility theory in unique and repeated gambles. *J. Exp. Psychol.: Learn. Mem. Cognit.* 13:387–91

Kim O, Walker M. 1984. The free rider problem: experimental evidence. *Public Choice* 43:3–24

Komorita SS. 1987. Cooperative choice in decomposed social dilemmas. *Pers. Soc. Psychol. Bull.* 31:53–63

Kreps DM, Milgrom P, Roberts J, Wilson R. 1982. Rational cooperation in the finitely repeated prisoners' dilemma. *J. Econ. Theory* 27:245–52

Landman J. 1988. Regret and elation following

action and inaction: affective responses to positive versus negative outcomes. *Pers. Soc. Psychol. Bull.* 13:524–36

Lave LB. 1965. Factors affecting co-operation in the prisoner's dilemma. *Behav. Sci.* 10:26–38

Ledyard JO. 1994. Is there a problem with public good provision? In *Handbook of Experimental Economics,* ed. K Kagel, AE Roth. Princeton, NJ: Princeton Univ. Press. In press

Lee W. 1971. *Decision Theory and Human Behavior.* New York: Wiley

Lichtenstein S, Slovic P. 1971. Reversals of preference between bids and choices in gambling decisions. *J. Exp. Psychol.* 89:46–55

Lichtenstein S, Slovic P. 1973. Response-induced reversals of preference in gambling: an extended replication in Las Vegas. *J. Exp. Psychol.* 101:16–20

Liebrand WBG, van Run GJ. 1985. The effects of social motives on behavior in social dilemmas in two cultures. *J. Exp. Soc. Psychol.* 21:86–102

Lindemann BL. 1993. *The effects of social context on grain producers' decisions to sell or hold grain.* PhD thesis. Univ. Iowa

Loomes G, Sugden R. 1982. Regret theory: an alternative theory of rational choice under uncertainty. *Econ. J.* 92:805–24

Loomes G, Sugden R. 1987. Some implications of a more general form of regret theory. *J. Econ. Theory* 41:270–87

Lopes LL. 1981. Decision making in the short run. *J. Exp. Psychol.: Hum. Learn. Mem.* 7:377–85

Lopes LL. 1984. Risk and distributional inequality. *J. Exp. Psychol.: Hum. Percept. Perform.* 10:465–85

Lopes LL. 1987. Between hope and fear: the psychology of risk. *Adv. Exp. Soc. Psychol.* 20:255–95

Lopes LL. 1988. Economics as psychology: a cognitive assay of the French and American Schools of risk theory. In *Risk, Decision, and Rationality,* ed. BR Munier, pp. 405–16. Boston: Reidel

Lopes LL. 1990. Re-modeling risk aversion: a comparison of Bernoullian and rank dependent value approaches. In *Acting Under Uncertainty: Multidisciplinary Conceptions,* ed. GM von Furstenberg, pp. 267–99. Boston: Kluwer

Luce RD, Raiffa H. 1957. *Games and Decisions: Introduction and Critical Survey.* New York: Wiley

Machina MJ. 1982. "Expected utility" analysis without the independence axiom. *Econometrica* 50:277–323

Machina MJ. 1987. Choice under uncertainty: problems solved and unsolved. *Econ. Perspect.* 1:121–54

Marwell G, Ames RE. 1981. Economists free ride, does anyone else? Experiments on the provision of public goods, IV. *J. Public Econ.* 15:295–310

McCallum DM, Harring K, Gilmore R, Drenan S, Chase JP, et al. 1985. Competition and cooperation between groups and between individuals. *J. Exp. Soc. Psychol.* 21:301–20

McClintock CG. 1972. Game behavior and social motivation in interpersonal settings. In *Experimental Social Psychology,* ed. CG McClintock, 271–97. New York: Holt, Rinehart & Winston

McClintock CG, Liebrand WBG. 1988. Role of interdependence structure, individual value orientation, and another's strategy in social decision making: a transformational analysis. *J. Pers. Soc. Psychol.* 55:396–409

McCord MR, De Neufville R. 1985. Assessment response surface: investigating utility dependence on probability. *Theory Decis.* 18:263–85

Mellers BA, Chang S, Birnbaum MH, Ordóñez LD. 1992a. Preferences, prices, and ratings in risky decision making. *J. Exp. Psychol.: Hum. Percept. Perform.* 18:347–61

Mellers BA, Ordóñez LD, Birnbaum MH. 1992b. A change-of-process theory for contextual effects and preference reversals in risky decision making. *Organ. Behav. Hum. Decis. Process.* 52:331–69

Messick DM, Brewer MB. 1983. Solving social dilemmas: a review. *Rev. Pers. Soc. Psychol.* 4:11–44

Messick DM, Wilke H, Brewer MB, Kramer RM, Zemke PE, Lui L. 1983. Individual adaptations and structural change as solutions to social dilemmas. *J. Pers. Soc. Psychol.* 44:294–309

Milgrom P. 1989. Auctions and bidding: a primer. *J. Econ. Perspect.* 3:3–22

Miller PM, Fagley NS. 1991. The effects of framing, problem variations, and providing rationale on choice. *Pers. Soc. Psychol. Bull.* 17:517–22

Montgomery H, Adelbratt T. 1982. Gambling decisions and information about expected value. *Organ. Behav. Hum. Perform.* 29:39–57

Oden GC, Anderson NH. 1971. Differential weighting in integration theory. *J. Exp. Psychol.* 89:152–61

Orbell JM, van de Kragt AJC, Dawes RM. 1988. Explaining discussion-induced cooperation. *J. Pers. Soc. Psychol.* 54:811–19

Payne JW, Bettman JR, Johnson EJ. 1992. Behavioral decision research: a constructive processing perspective. *Annu. Rev. Psychol.* 43:87–131

Plott CR. 1982. Industrial organization theory and experimental economics. *J. Econ. Lit.* 20:1485–527

Plott CR. 1986. Rational choice in experimental markets. *J. Bus.* 59:S301–27

Polanyi M. 1962. *Personal Knowledge: Towards a Post-Critical Philosophy.* Chicago: Univ. Chicago Press

Pope, R. 1983. The pre-outcome period and the utility of gambling. In *Foundations of Utility and Risk Theory with Applications,* ed. BP Stigum, F Wenstøp, pp. 137–77. Boston: Reidel

Pruitt DG. 1967. Reward structure and cooperation: the decomposed prisoner's dilemma game. *J. Pers. Soc. Psychol.* 7:21–27

Pruitt DG, Kimmel MJ. 1977. Twenty years of experimental gaming: critique, synthesis, and suggestions for the future. *Annu. Rev. Psychol.* 28:363–92

Quiggen J. 1982. A theory of anticipated utility. *J. Econ. Behav. Organ.* 3:323–43

Rapoport Amnon, Bornstein G. 1989. Solving public good problems in competition between equal and unequal size groups. *J. Confl. Resolut.* 33:460–79

Rapoport Amnon, Eshed-Levy D. 1989. Provision of step-level public goods: effects of greed and fear of being gypped. *Organ. Behav. Hum. Decis. Process.* 44:325–44

Rapoport Anatol. 1973. *Two-Person Game Theory: The Essential Ideas.* Ann Arbor: Univ. Mich. Press

Rapoport Anatol, Chammah AM. 1965. *Prisoner's Dilemma: A Study in Conflict and Cooperation.* Ann Arbor: Univ. Mich. Press

Rapoport Anatol, Guyer M. 1966. A taxonomy of 2 × 2 games. *Gen. Syst.* 11:203–14

Redelmeier DA, Tversky A. 1990. Discrepancy between medical decisions for individual patients and for groups. *N. Engl. J. Med.* 322:1162–64

Roth AE. 1987. Laboratory experimentation in economics. In *Advances in Economic Theory, Fifth World Congress,* ed. TF Bewley, pp. 269–99. Cambridge: Cambridge Univ. Press

Roth AE. 1988. Laboratory experimentation in economics: a methodological overview. *Econ. J.* 98:974–1031

Rumelhart DE, McClelland JL. 1986. PDP models and general issues in cognitive science. In *Parallel Distributed Processing: Explorations in the Microstructure of Cognition,* Vol. 1: *Foundations,* ed. DE Rumelhart, JL McClelland, pp. 110–46. Cambridge, MA: MIT Press

Russo JE, Dosher BA. 1983. Strategies for multiattribute binary choice. *J. Exp. Psychol.: Learn. Mem. Cognit.* 4:676–96

Samuelson CD, Messick DM. 1986. Inequities in access to and use of shared resources in social dilemmas. *J. Pers. Soc. Psychol.* 51:960–67

Savage LJ. 1972. *The Foundations of Statistics.* New York: Dover. 2nd ed.

Schneider SL. 1992. Framing and conflict: aspiration level contingency, the status quo, and current theories of risky choice. *J. Exp. Psychol.: Learn. Mem. Cognit.* 18:1040–57

Schneider SL, Lopes LL. 1986. Reflection in preferences under risk: who and when may suggest why. *J. Exp. Psychol.: Hum. Percept. Perform.* 12:535–48

Selten R, Stoecker R. 1986. End behavior in sequences of finite prisoner's dilemma supergames: a learning theory approach. *J. Econ. Behav. Organ.* 7:47–70

Simon HA. 1956. Rational choice and the structure of the environment. *Psychol. Rev.* 63:129–38

Simon HA. 1986. Rationality in psychology and economics. *J. Bus.* 59:S209–24

Slovic P. 1987. Perception of risk. *Science* 236:280–85

Slovic P, Lichtenstein S. 1968. Relative importance of probabilities and payoffs in risk taking. *J. Exp. Psychol. Monogr.* 78(3,Pt.2):1–18

Slovic P, Lichtenstein S. 1983. Preference reversals: a broader perspective. *Am. Econ. Rev.* 73:596–605

Smith A. 1776. *An Inquiry into the Nature and Causes of the Wealth of Nations.* Reprinted 1976. Chicago: Univ. Chicago Press

Smith VL. 1982. Microeconomic systems as an experimental science. *Am. Econ. Rev.* 72:923–55

Smith VL. 1989. Theory, experiment, and economics. *J. Econ. Perspect.* 3:151–69

Smith VL. 1991. Rational choice: the contrast between economics and psychology. *J. Polit. Econ.* 99:877–97

Smith VL. 1993. Game theory and experimental economics: beginnings and early influences. *Hist. Polit. Econ.* In press

Stroebe W, Frey BS. 1982. Self-interest and collective action: the economics and psychology of public goods. *Br. J. Soc. Psychol.* 21:121–37

Suleiman R, Rapoport Amnon. 1992. Provision of step-level public goods with continuous contribution. *J. Behav. Decis. Mak.* 5:133–53

Toda M. 1962. The design of a fungus-eater: a model of human behavior in an unsophisticated environment. *Behav. Sci.* 7:164–83

Tversky A, Bar-Hillel M. 1983. Risk: the long and the short. *J. Exp. Psychol.: Learn. Mem. Cognit.* 9:713–17

Tversky A, Kahneman D. 1986. Rational choice and the framing of decisions. *J. Bus.* 59:S251–78

Tversky A, Kahneman D. 1992. Advances in prospect theory: cumulative representation of uncertainty. *J. Risk Uncertain.* 5:297–323

Tversky A, Sattath S, Slovic P. 1988. Contingent weighting in judgment and choice. *Psychol. Rev.* 95:371–84

Tversky A, Slovic P, Kahneman D. 1990. The

causes of preference reversal. *Am. Econ. Rev.* 80:204–17

van de Kragt AJC, Orbell JM, Dawes RM. 1983. The minimal contributing set as a solution to public goods problems. *Am. Polit. Sci. Rev.* 77:112–22

von Békésy G. 1960. In *Experiments in Hearing,* ed. EG Wever. New York: McGraw-Hill

von Neumann J, Morgenstern O. 1947. *Theory of Games and Economic Behavior.* Princeton, NJ: Princeton Univ. Press. 2nd ed.

von Winterfeldt D, Edwards W. 1986. *Decision Analysis and Behavioral Research.* Cambridge: Cambridge Univ. Press

Wakker P. 1991. Separating marginal utility and probabilistic risk aversion. *Working Paper.* Nijmegen, Netherlands: Univ. Nijmegen

Weber EU, Anderson CJ, Birnbaum MH. 1992. A theory of perceived risk and attractiveness. *Organ. Behav. Hum. Decis. Process.* 52:492–523

Weber M, Camerer C. 1987. Recent developments in modelling preferences under risk. *OR Spektrum* 9:129–51

Wedell DH, Böckenholt U. 1990. Moderation of preference reversals in the long run. *J. Exp. Psychol.: Hum. Percept. Perform.* 16:429–38

Yaari ME. 1987. The dual theory of choice under risk. *Econometrica* 55:95–115

Annu. Rev. Psychol. 1994. 45:229–59

HEALTH PSYCHOLOGY: Why Do Some People Get Sick and Some Stay Well?

Nancy Adler

Departments of Psychiatry and Pediatrics, University of California, San Francisco, California 94143-0844

Karen Matthews

Department of Psychiatry, University of Pittsburgh, Pittsburgh, Pennsylvania 15213-2593

KEY WORDS: stress, social support, personality, health behaviors, disease etiology, cardiovascular reactivity to stress, psychoneuroimmunology

CONTENTS

INTRODUCTION

The biomedical community has increasingly recognized the importance of psychological factors in the natural history of disease, prevention of disability and illness, and promotion of recovery. In *Health and Behavior Research* (USDHHS 1991), a report on behavioral research by the National Institutes of Health (NIH), the NIH director indicates, "Our research is teaching us that many common diseases can be prevented, and others can be postponed or well-controlled, simply by making positive life style changes. For these reasons, intensifying such research and encouraging all Americans to make health-enhancing behaviors a part of their daily lives has taken on more and more importance in our efforts to conquer disease" (p. 1). Likewise, *Healthy People 2000* (USDHHS 1991), a report of health promotion and disease prevention objectives for the United States population, notes that "achievement of the agenda depends heavily on changes in human behavior" (p. 8).

Similarly, the psychology community has increasingly embraced questions of essential importance to physical health. Concepts that originated in relation to health problems have become topics of interest themselves. Theories that were developed to account for mental health (e.g. attributional style and depression, or coping with stress and related interventions) are being used to understand and promote good physical health.

As a result, health psychology no longer has clearly demarcated boundaries. Examining the contents of four American Psychological Association (APA) journals that span general psychology and large subdisciplines (*American Psychologist, Psychological Bulletin, Journal of Personality and Social Psychology,* and *Journal of Consulting and Clinical Psychology*), we found that over one third of the articles in 1990–1992 either examined physical health issues or involved concepts from health psychology such as stress or Type A. Specialized journals have also prospered. Division 38 of the APA established *Health Psychology* in 1982, with its almost 1700 members receiving the journal. In 1993, over 8200 APA members received the journal, which is jointly published by Division 38 and the APA. Articles relevant to health psychology also appear in journals in several other fields, including many medical journals.

Although the domain of health psychology is broad and the enormity of its knowledge base is daunting, many of the new developments and concepts in the past five years pertain to three essential questions: First, who becomes sick and why? Second, among the sick, who recovers and why? Third, how can illness be prevented or recovery be promoted? Given the explosion of re-

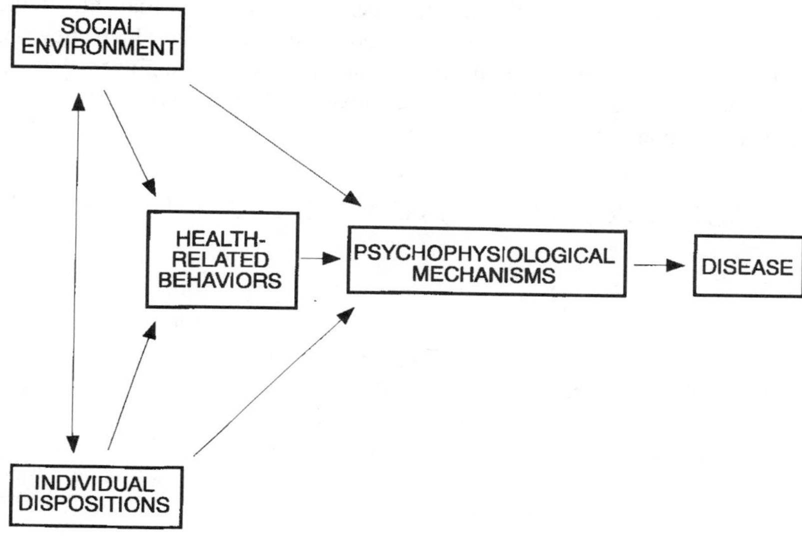

Figure 1 The organization of this review.

search, which precludes a complete review, we had a difficult choice about which question to address. We chose to review the first question—the psychological characteristics of individuals prone to disease and underlying mechanisms accounting for the associations between psychological variables and disease—because it is the basis for the other questions and suggests possibilities for prevention. We applied strict criteria, limiting ourselves whenever possible to longitudinal studies with adequate sample sizes to test predictions about the contribution of psychological variables to the onset of disease. We have excluded for the most part (*a*) cross-sectional studies because of difficulties interpreting cause and effect and (*b*) studies of patients because of biases owing to diagnosis and treatment. More importantly, the latter studies pertain more to the psychological factors in recovery and treatment than to those in the early etiology of disease. We have included some studies of mortality because it is a hard outcome, although we realize that associations between psychosocial factors and mortality could reflect recovery processes as well as etiologic factors.

In this review, we examine two broad domains of variables affecting the onset of disease: factors residing in the social environment and factors residing in the individual (see Figure 1). The double-headed arrow between the two domains signifies the importance of the person-environment interaction. For example, dispositions may predispose individuals to be susceptible to specific environmental elicitors of clinical episodes or dispositions may affect the likelihood that individuals will be exposed to situations to which they are vulnerable. Variables in the environmental and individual domains may affect disease onset through physiological mechanisms and/or through health behaviors that in turn affect these mechanisms.

SOCIAL ENVIRONMENT AS CONTRIBUTOR TO DISEASE

Stress

Individuals who experience stress may be more susceptible to disease. The evidence is strongest for cardiovascular disease, infectious disease, and pregnancy complications. Prospective evidence for the role of stress in the etiology of cancer and endocrine diseases, such as diabetes, thyroid disorder, and Cushings disease, is not substantial (Cox & Gonder-Frederick 1992, Beardsley & Goldstein 1993). Additionally, evidence is stronger for studies using subjective evaluations of stress than for those using other measures. The latter is consistent with the more recent emphasis on contextual, subjective components of stress, including appraisal processes (Lazarus & Folkman 1984).

CARDIOVASCULAR DISEASE Rosengren et al (1991) followed 2000 men with no prior history of myocardial infarction (MI) for 12 years. Those men who reported substantial stress in the previous 1 to 5 years at the initial interview were more likely to experience coronary artery disease over the next 12 years compared to those who indicated no stress or only sporadic instances. Men reporting more stress also reported more adverse health behaviors such as smoking, alcohol abuse, and lack of physical exercise, but disease risk associated with heightened stress was only slightly reduced when these behaviors were controlled for. Severe stress also predicted subsequent risk of stroke (Harmsen et al 1990).

In contrast, several studies failed to find a link between life events and subsequent mortality. In the Multiple Risk Factors Intervention Trial (MRFIT), over 12,000 men who showed no signs of coronary heart disease (CHD) but who were at high risk were followed for 6 years. Although life events predicted angina, neither death due to CHD nor fatal or non-fatal MI was affected by the experience of life events in general or of life events that were clearly undesirable (Hollis et al 1990). The most severe life event, death of a loved one, was unrelated to subsequent mortality in two studies. Levav et al (1988) found that mortality rates over ten years were not significantly higher among parents in Israel who had lost a son either in war or in an accident than in the general population. In a United States population, women whose partners died during the five years in which they participated in a health study showed no higher mortality than age-matched controls (Avis et al 1991).

Research on the health effects of stress has frequently focused on stresses in the work environment, much of it stimulated by Karasek's (1979) model of job strain. The model posits that jobs involving a combination of high demand (e.g. time pressure) and low control (e.g. little latitude over decisions and choice of skills to use) engender mental and physical health problems. Initial studies used individuals' own ratings of their jobs, but such ratings may be influenced by the individual's dispositions, which may themselves influence health outcomes. Karasek et al (1988) developed a system for categorizing occupations, and cross-sectional analyses of two large surveys found that men in high stress occupations had an increased prevalence of MI.

Several studies have established a prospective link between job strain and CHD. Siegrist et al (1990) examined both workers' self-reports of their work environment and scores based on job descriptions for a sample of male, blue-collar workers in Germany. Both types of variables predicted risk of CHD over the next six and a half years. Independent of the association with medical risk factors (e.g. blood lipids and systolic blood pressure), CHD risk increased with high levels of one external indicator of job strain (discrepancy between occupational grades of individuals and their educational levels) and three self-rated measures (low perceived job security, high perceived work pressure, and a vigilant coping strategy). Effects of job strain on risk of CHD were minimal at low medical risk factor levels. However, among individuals at higher medical risk, men in low reward/high effort jobs showed a substantial risk of disease; men in jobs with only one or the other characteristic showed a moderate CHD rate, and those with neither indicator of job strain had little risk. In a subsequent analysis of this data set, Siegrist et al (1992) broadened the set of cardiovascular diseases to include stroke. Biomedical and psychosocial risk factors accounted for almost 85% of the risk of cardiovascular disease. At each level of biomedical risk, the probability of a cardiovascular event increased as job strain indicators increased.

Job strain predicted health problems in two other studies. Among employees of a metal fabrication plant in Finland, job strain, indexed by lack of variety and control and high physical strain, was associated with CHD over a ten-year period. The association remained significant when age, sex and risk factors (e.g. smoking, blood pressure) were controlled (Haan 1988). In a community sample in Sweden, men who had recently retired from high strain jobs (high demand and low scheduling latitude) had a significantly higher relative risk of mortality in the subsequent six years (Falk et al 1992).

Disconfirming evidence of the role of job strain in CHD emerged in a study of Hawaiian men of Japanese ancestry (Reed et al 1989). Over 4000 men, who were in the same occupation at follow-up that they had earlier reported as their usual occupation, were assigned job strain scores based on occupation ratings. Risk of developing CHD over 18 years was not associated with either the demand or the control dimension of their occupation. Men in high job strain occupations, surprisingly, had the lowest incidence rates of disease, although the rates were not significantly lower.

Research on job strain as a contributor to cardiovascular disease is promising, but several important questions remain. First, it is not clear whether classification of occupations sufficiently captures individual experiences. An advantage of classification ratings is that they can be applied to data sets lacking information on individual perceptions. Also, these ratings are uncontaminated by traits of individuals that may affect perceptions of their jobs, and that may also be linked to disease risk. Further work is needed to clarify relationships among job stress as determined by occupational ratings, organizations' descriptions of specific jobs, and workers self-ratings, and the relationship of these to health outcomes. A second question concerns the generalizability of findings. Most of the studies have used male subjects, and many have been done in Scandinavia and other parts of Europe. It is not clear if the measures capture pathogenic aspects of work settings for women and for different national and ethnic groups.

INFECTIOUS DISEASES Stress has also been linked to increased susceptibility to infectious diseases. In one study, medical students reported more instances of infectious disease during exam periods than in comparison months preceding these periods (Glaser et al 1987). Immune indicators such as a reduction in interferons and increased lymphocyte antibodies to the Epstein-Barr virus, suggesting reduced control of the virus at the cellular immune level, also changed in the exam periods. In a sample of married couples keeping daily diaries, undesirable events increased and positive events decreased three to four days before the onset of symptoms of infectious disease (Stone et al 1987). Positive and negative events reported in the two days immediately preceding symptom onset did not differ from average levels, suggesting that reported events were not responsive to early stages of infection, but rather, that the increase in stress contributed to infection risk.

Viral challenge studies, which follow volunteers who are experimentally exposed to viruses, rule out differential exposure to viruses as a potential alternative explanation for the link between stress and infection. These studies also provide clinical verification of infection. Stone et al (1992) exposed subjects to a rhinovirus and observed them for five days. Subjects who developed a clinical cold following the viral challenge had reported a greater number of both positive and negative life events in the prior year. Neither perceived stress nor mood at time of induction related to risk of subsequent cold, which is surprising given the prior study's findings that life events at the time of exposure might lower resistance to infection (Stone et al 1987).

Using a similar protocol to Stone et al's (1987), in which healthy volunteers were assessed and then exposed to one of five respiratory viruses, Cohen et al (1991) found a linear relationship between a stress index encompassing negative life events, negative affect, and perceived stress and the probability of developing a clinical cold following viral challenge. The association held across all five viruses and after controlling for health practices (e.g. smoking, diet, sleep). Subsequent analyses (Cohen et al 1993) showed that life events related differently to biological mediators than did perceived stress or affect. Perceived stress and negative affect predicted infection following viral exposure (determined from culture or increases in antibodies), whereas life events predicted who, among those infected, developed a clinical cold. These findings suggest that aspects of stress may play a different role at different stages of disease onset, and indicate the need for better specification of the stress process and its impact on the body.

PREGNANCY The effect of stress on pathological processes can also be seen in research on pregnancy outcomes such as preterm delivery, birth weight, and Apgar scores. The latter are standardized ratings of newborn functioning encompassing heart rate, respiratory effort, reflex response, muscle tone, and color. Pagel et al (1990) found that women who, in their third trimester, reported more life events in the year before pregnancy, had babies with lower birth weights and lower Apgar scores than those born to women experiencing fewer events. No association with life events during pregnancy was found. Williamson et al (1989) found that although life events during the year before pregnancy were unrelated to obstetrical outcome, an increase in life events from the second to third trimester predicted adverse outcomes (e.g. neonatal death, low 5-minute Apgar, low birth weight). Norbeck & Anderson (1989) and McCormick et al (1990) found no association of life events with obstetrical outcome.

Other studies, incorporating subjective reports, show more consistent results. Lobel et al (1992) found that a latent stress factor, incorporating anxiety, perceived stress, and the impact of life events, predicted both timing of delivery and infant birth weight in a low socioeconomic status sample. Medical risk factors contributed independently to birth outcomes and did not reduce the association of stress and outcome. The experience of adverse working conditions also appears to contribute to complications. Vartiainen (1990) studied women in Finland before conception and followed them throughout their pregnancies. Women who reported having a psychologically stressful job had a higher risk of delivering infants with low Apgar scores; measures of life events were not related to outcome. Among women participating in the National Longitudinal Survey of Labor Market Experience, a significant association of job strain and risk of delivering a low birth weight, preterm infant became nonsignificant in the sample as a whole after controls were entered for education, degree of physical exertion in the job, and health-related behaviors. However, the association remained significant for the subset of women who reported that they didn't want to remain in the work force. These women may have been particularly affected by adverse job characteristics (Homer et al 1990).

Social Connections

The degree to which an individual is connected to others may also influence health. One's degree of social connection has been reflected in measures of social isolation, number of individuals in the social network, and social integration [i.e. involvement in clubs, churches, and other organizations (House et al 1988)], and in measures of perceived support from others, including the type and degree of support (Cohen 1988).

MORBIDITY AND MORTALITY Many studies of social connections are from Scandinavia and use mortality as the outcome. In a sample of elderly Swedish men, Hanson et al (1989) found that social network and social support indicators related independently to mortality. Men who participated less in formal and informal groups, those who reported less emotional support, and those who were unmarried were at greater risk of dying over a five-year period. In a community sample of middle-aged healthy Swedish men, those who were lower on social integration were significantly more likely to suffer a heart attack during a six-year follow-up; those low on social support were also at increased risk but the difference was of borderline statistical significance (Orth-Gomer et al 1993). Social connections may interact with stress to affect health. Falk et al (1992) found mortality especially high among retired Swedish men who were low in social support and high on job strain.

Reynolds & Kaplan's (1990) study of a United States sample provides mixed evidence for the role of social connections in cancer onset. They examined the incidence of newly diagnosed cancer and mortality over a 17-year period in a sample of 6848 adults in Alameda County, California, as related to several aspects of social connection. For men, none of the measures predicted either cancer onset or mortality. For women, social isolation, specifically having fewer contacts with friends and relatives, predicted onset for total cancers across all sites. Lack of church membership and feeling socially isolated predicted increased rates of hormone-related cancers. Relative risk of mortality for all-site cancer was greater for women who scored high on social isolation, had fewer contacts with friends and relatives, and who felt isolated. Relative risk of mortality from hormone-related cancers was higher in women with fewer contacts and who felt isolated.

Vogt et al (1992) found stronger links between social connections and mortality than with onset for a variety of diseases in over 2600 members of a health maintenance organization. Individuals who had social networks of greater scope and size and who had more contacts within them showed lower mortality over 15 years even after adjusting for sociodemographic variables and health status at baseline. Network measures were unrelated, however, to subsequent incidence of cancer, stroke, or hypertension. Network scope (but not size or frequency of contact) significantly predicted relative risk of CHD. Using the same data set, Hibbard & Pope (1993) examined social support at work and in the marital role. Aspects of marriage were unrelated to morbidity or mortality for men, but women who were married and those who reported greater equality with their marriage partner in decision-making were less likely to die over the 15-year span. Women who reported greater social support at work were less likely to die and also had lower rates of stroke over the 15 years. Work stress, but not support, predicted CHD.

Social support during pregnancy appears to contribute to better obstetrical outcomes. Collins et al (1993) found that three aspects of social support measured during pregnancy predicted birth outcomes. Women who received more support and those who received higher quality support delivered babies with higher Apgar scores, and those with more support also had shorter labors; women who reported larger social networks delivered babies who were of higher birth weight. However, the beneficial effects of social support may differ by ethnicity. Norbeck & Anderson (1989) found that support from partners and from mothers contributed substantially to a reduction in complications and increased gestational age at birth in black women. However, among Hispanic women, outcome was unrelated to social support and among whites, social support from mothers was associated with more complications.

EXPERIMENTAL EVIDENCE Experimental studies that manipulate degree of support and show health advantages provide strong evidence for the role of social support. A recent analog study of social support (Kamarck et al 1990) suggests that social resources may reduce cardiovascular reactivity to stress, a possible risk for CHD (see below). In this study, women brought a friend with them to a laboratory experiment. The women either had the friend in the experimental room with them while they performed several challenging tasks and had their blood pressure and heart rate measured, or they had the friend wait in another room. The former group showed smaller cardiovascular responses to challenge than did the latter.

Kennell et al (1991) replicated in a United States sample earlier findings from Guatemala showing fewer birth complications for women randomly assigned a *doula,* a woman who uses talk and touch to aid a woman in labor (Sosa et al 1980, Klaus et al 1986). Kennell et al found that women assigned a *doula* had better outcomes, including shorter labors, fewer caesarean sections, and fewer infants requiring extended hospitalization compared to women receiving standard care or to those assigned a passive observer who only monitored them through labor.

An intervention providing social support during pregnancy to high-risk, poor women in Latin America failed to show positive effects, however (Villar et al 1992). Pregnant women in the first trimester randomly assigned to receive additional visits from a nurse or social worker showed the same rates of complications as those assigned to standard care. The authors argue that the intervention was as intensive as could be expected in a public health effort in a developing country (Villar 1993), but it is not clear how well the support intervention functioned and whether a more intensive or meaningful effort would have shown results. For example, Reite & Boccia (1993) questioned the effectiveness of the social support because it was not provided by someone who had a personal relationship to the woman.

Further clarification is needed about the nature and functioning of social connections and social support. Additionally, it is not clear how support that is experimentally provided mirrors naturally occurring support; resolution of this question will both further our understanding of the function of social support and facilitate the development of more effective interventions.

DISPOSITIONS AS CONTRIBUTORS TO DISEASE

Type A and Hostility

Continuing the trend reported in the last *Annual Review of Psychology* chapter on this topic (Rodin & Salovey 1989), recent prospective studies do not indicate that Type A individuals (i.e. those who are competitive, achievement oriented, easily annoyed, and time urgent) are more likely to be at risk for CHD mortality and MI than their Type B counterparts (Eaker et al 1989, Eaker et al 1992, Matthews 1988, Orth-Gomer & Unden 1990). Moreover, in the MRFIT sample, Type As who reported high levels of life events generally, or loss events specifically, were not at higher risk for CHD mortality or MI than other groups (Hollis et al 1990). Newly recognized is that Type A may be a risk factor for poor health-related quality of life, including chest pain (Eaker et al 1989), general health problems (Shoham-Yakubovich et al 1988), and injuries, especially among Type As that colleagues rated low in amicability (Lee et al 1989).

Type A is a multidimensional concept, and efforts to disentangle coronary-prone and noncoronary-prone components have, with few exceptions, pointed to the importance of hostility, anger, and anger expression in the etiology of CHD. Clinical ratings of potential for hostility based on interview responses were significant predictors of CHD morbidity and mortality in the MRFIT and Western Collaborative Group Study (WCGS) data (Dembroski et al 1989, Hecker et al 1988, Houston et al 1992). The Cook-Medley scores of hostile or cynical attitudes predicted CHD or total mortality in three of six prospective studies that Smith (1992) reviewed.

The aforementioned exceptions include a cluster analysis of WCGS participants who differ in patterns of Type A characteristics: hostile men and controlling, dominant men with little hostility were more prone to CHD (Houston et al 1992). In a sample of blue collar men, those who scored highly on combined dimensions of need for approval, competitiveness, impatience and irritability, and inability to stop working had a higher risk of coronary disease, while being hard driving and perfectionistic did not relate to CHD (Siegrist et al 1990).

Problems of measurement have contributed to the difficulty of estimating the true effect of hostility (or Type A). Measures of hostility and anger are heterogeneous and some overlap with dispositions that may be noncoronary-prone. For example, clinical ratings of potential for hostility have little or no association with Cook-Medley scores (Matthews et al 1992). Three of six factors from a rational analysis of the Cook-Medley scale predicted CHD: cynical attitudes, hostile affect, and aggressive behavior (Barefoot et al 1989). Reanalysis of the Western Electric Study suggested that cynical attitudes, a component of hostile attitudes as measured by the Cook-Medley scores, predicted all cause and CHD mortality, independent of neuroticism. Neuroticism, independent of cynicism, was unrelated to outcomes, except for alcohol-related deaths (Almada et al 1991). Health psychology would benefit from further development of valid measures of the major domains of hostility for use in large scale, prospective studies.

Depression, Distress, and Exhaustion

The concepts of depressive symptoms, distress, and vital exhaustion are all conceptualized as negative mood states, which are somewhat reliable across time, although affected by environmental stress. Below, we review these concepts in relation to risk for cancer and for cardiovascular disease or total mortality.

CANCER RISK Interest in the association of depression and cancer stems from a proposed connection between emotional distress and compromised immune function (see below) and an early prospective study in which Minnesota Multiphasic Personality Inventory (MMPI) depression scores predicted a two-fold increase in death from cancer (Shekelle et al 1981). Hahn & Petitti (1988) examined the incidence of breast cancer in almost 9000 women over 15–20 years. MMPI scale scores for depression and repression/sensitization were similar in women with and without incident breast cancer; the lying score was higher in breast cancer patients. The National Health and Nutrition Examination Survey I cohort was administered the Center for Epidemiologic Studies Depression scale and the depression subscale from the General Well-being Schedule and were followed for 10 years. Neither measure was associated with cancer morbidity or mortality (Zonderman et al 1989). In the Alameda County Study of almost 7000 cancer-free persons, those who scored one standard deviation or above on an 18-item scale of depressive symptoms had similar rates of cancer morbidity and mortality to those with lower scores. However, depressed individuals were at higher risk for early mortality from all causes and from non-cancer related illnesses, which presumably are largely constituted by cardiovascular diseases (Kaplan & Reynolds 1988). It may be biologically naive to expect depression to play a major role in determining all cancers because pathogenic factors differ for different types of cancers.

CARDIOVASCULAR DISEASE RISK Evidence for the role of depression and psychological distress in the etiology of cardiovascular diseases, including hypertension, elevated blood pressure, MI, and cardiac death, is more substantial than it is for cancers.

Anxiety scores predicted change in women's blood pressure across three years controlling for age, parental history of hypertension, diet, obesity, and other predictors of blood pressure status (Markovitz et al 1991). Among middle-aged men in the Framingham Heart Study, anxiety scores predicted 20-year incidence of hypertension, independent of age, obesity, glucose intolerance, smoking, hematocrit, and alcohol intake (Markovitz et al 1993). Among women in that study, those who reported high levels of tension, low educational attainment, and no vacations were at heightened risk for MI or cardiac death (Eaker et al 1992).

In the Evans County study, high scores on the Health Opinion Survey, a measure of psychosomatic symptoms, predicted greater mortality over 12 years controlling for gender, race, and age, as well as preexisting disease and blood pressure (Somervell et al 1989). In a prospective longitudinal study of the elderly, a significant association of high levels of depressive symptoms and low frequency attendance at religious services with incidence of stroke over six years became nonsignificant when statistical controls for age, sex, housing, hypertension, diabetes, physical function, and smoking were entered (Colantonio et al 1992).

Appel and colleagues' concept of vital exhaustion is defined as a mental state characterized by unusual fatigue, a feeling of being dejected or defeated, and increased irritability. Excess fatigue and general malaise may be immediately precursory to a clinical event (i.e. within a few days or weeks). Recent data suggest that vital exhaustion might also be a long-term predictor.

In the Rotterdam Civil Servants Study of men, feelings of vital exhaustion predicted four-year incidence of angina and non-fatal MI, but not cardiac death. The effect for each individual year was not significant by the fourth year, however (Appels & Mulder 1989). In this sample and in the Kaunas-Rotterdam Intervention study, men who reported being burned out or exhausted at the end of the day were at higher risk for subsequent MI (Appels & Schoeten 1991, Appels & Otten 1992).

Interpretation of findings regarding vital exhaustion or distress more generally has been a matter of some debate. Some believe that exhaustion may simply reflect a poorly functioning heart muscle. Others suggest that feelings of mild depression, anxiety, and fatigue, when superimposed on an already compromised heart, may lower the threshold for triggering clinical events. Future studies on mechanisms using new ambulatory technologies (see below) will help disentangle these hypotheses.

Neuroticism and Negative Affectivity

In the last five years controversy emerged about the extent that neuroticism or negative affectivity contaminates relationships between correlated dispositions (e.g. hostile attitudes) and health outcomes. Self-reported health outcomes or diseases diagnosed largely by symptom reports are especially vulnerable to possible confounding. Neuroticism is defined as a broad dimension of individual differences characterized as the tendency to experience negative emotions, including anger, anxiety, and depression. Costa & McCrae (1987) reviewed data suggesting that although neuroticism scores are moderately correlated with chest pain and angina, they are unrelated to MI or cardiac death. Similarly, Watson & Pennebaker (1989) have demonstrated that the disposition of negative affectivity (i.e. persistent differences in the general negative affect level) leads to self-ratings of poor health, but is unrelated to biological markers such as elevated blood pressure or serum lipids in relatively healthy samples.

Our review focuses on studies of health outcomes that are less susceptible to reporting biases (e.g. occurrence of MI, stroke, or cardiac death). However, concern about how dispositions may relate to perceptions of health versus pathophysiological processes or objective clinical events is an important one. Experimentally-induced negative mood increases reports of physical symptoms (Salovey & Birnbaum 1989). Neurotic persons clearly report more stressful events and uncomfortable physical symptoms (Affleck et al 1992, Aldwin et al 1989) and magnify the effects of a given stressful event (Bolger 1990). On the other hand, data reviewed above demonstrate that specific negative emotions relate to specific health outcomes. Furthermore, perceived health predicts mortality, independent of biological risk factors (Kaplan & Comacho 1983), suggesting that self-report provides useful information not captured by biological markers. Finally, self-reported ill health and health-related quality of life are important outcomes themselves because of their influence on utilization of services and the burden they impose on individuals and families (Weiner 1991). Such measures are used to evaluate the effectiveness of many clinical treatments (Kaplan 1988). Whether neuroticism should be viewed only as a nuisance variable, as a disposition that exacerbates the effects of environmental stress, or as a risk factor itself remains unresolved. In the meantime, it is premature to write off associations between psychosocial factors and self-reported health status because of possible contamination from neuroticism or negative affectivity.

Optimism, Explanatory Style, and Self-Esteem

Recent models of disease are emphasizing positive factors, especially those having to do with positive cognitions. Several overlapping concepts—optimistic expectations, optimistic explanatory style, self-efficacy, and high self-esteem—are important determinants of mental health (Scheier & Carver 1992, Taylor & Brown 1988); these may also contribute to physical health outcomes.

Measures of dispositional optimism (i.e. general positive expectations) predicted reports of few physical symptoms in relatively healthy populations (Smith et al 1989), active coping responses during stress (Aspinwall & Taylor 1992), as well as faster physical recovery and high quality of life after bypass surgery (Scheier et al 1989). A non-optimistic explanatory style—making internal, stable, and global attributions for negative events—predicted subsequent physician-diagnosed poor health in mid-life, controlling for initial health status, in a sample of male Harvard undergraduates (Peterson et al 1988). This style was also associated with lowered immunocompetence in elderly individuals (Kamen-Siegel et al 1991).

In contrast, Friedman et al (1993) found that bright children rated highly by parents and teachers on two items, good sense of humor and optimism/cheerfulness, died younger in adulthood. In addition, being conscientious was related to longevity, whereas high self-esteem was unrelated (as a main effect). High self-esteem, however, may interact with stress to affect physical symptoms of illness. On days following a stressful day, individuals with low self-esteem and poor social networks reported more health problems, such as flu, sore throat, and backaches (DeLongis et al 1988). After experiencing a positive life event, students with low self-esteem reported lower physical well being and used the student health center more often than those with high self-esteem (Brown & McGill 1989).

The concepts of optimism, explanatory style, and self-esteem appear to have promise as predictors of physical health, especially in individuals experiencing stressful events or distress. Self-efficacy, a more situation-specific variable, may affect health more through its impact on health-related behaviors (Bandura 1989).

HEALTH-RELATED BEHAVIORS

Health-related behaviors constitute a pathway by which environmental and dispositional variables affect physiological mechanisms and disease risk. In this section, we review evidence for linkage between these variables and health-related behaviors. We also discuss alternative ways of analyzing the role of behavior in disease risk and new issues in health behavior research.

Links with Stress and Support

Individuals under stress may find it more difficult to engage in health-promoting behaviors because of the emotional and behavioral demands of such behaviors. In addition, some individuals may offset stress-induced emotional distress by engaging in behaviors that have health-damaging consequences. Perkins & Grobe (1992) demonstrated that smokers subjected to a stressful task had an increased desire to smoke compared to those experiencing a non-stressful task. In a prospective study of individuals quitting smoking (Cohen & Lichenstein 1990), individuals who had decreasing levels of perceived stress over six months were more likely to remain abstinent over that period.

Social support's impact on health-related behaviors can occur in several ways. Insofar as individuals use health-damaging behaviors to cope with stress, and social support reduces the adverse effects of stress, individuals with more support in the context of stressful experiences may be less likely to engage in health-damaging behaviors. For example, Jennison (1992) reanalyzed several national surveys to examine the influence of recent loss on alcohol use among older adults. More losses (eg. death of spouse) were associated with greater excess use of alcohol. Social support buffered the effects of loss—the relationship of loss to drinking was reduced for those with more support.

Social connections can also provide specific support for engaging in health-promoting behaviors. Individuals who report receiving more support for given health-related behaviors (e.g. exercising, avoiding alcohol or tobacco while pregnant) are more likely to engage in those behaviors (Aaronson 1989, Treiber et al 1991). Zimmerman & Conner (1989) obtained reports of anticipated support among participants in a 7-week worksite program aimed at changing 4 cardiovascular risk behaviors. Anticipated support did not predict change. However, those who reported at follow-up having received more support from others for changing their behavior showed greater behavior change. The best prospective data come from a study of relapse following treatment for alcohol use, smoking, or opiate use. Individuals successfully completing treatment were followed once a week until relapse (for up to 12 weeks). At the first follow-up, indicators of general and of abstinence-specific social support were obtained. Both types related to subsequent risk of relapse. Individuals who had a partner and those who reported greater social participation were less likely to relapse. There was no effect of general functional support but individuals who had more support specifically for abstinence were less likely to relapse (Havassy et al 1991).

Links with Dispositions

Dispositions, too, can affect health-related behaviors. For example, recent data suggest that hostile individuals experience more adverse changes in coronary risk factors over time, thereby contributing to their higher risk (Scherwitz et al 1992). Prospective studies beginning with adolescents and college students and following them for three to twenty years have shown that hostility and Type A behavior predict later smoking and alcohol use, as well as higher lipid levels and body mass index (Siegler et al 1992, Raikkonen & Keltikangas-Jarvenen 1991, Keltikangas-Jarvenen & Raikkonen 1989). Similarly, Anda et al (1990) found in cross-sectional analyses that individuals who were depressed were more likely to smoke. In a 9-year follow-up of these smokers, individuals who were initially depressed were 40% less likely to quit than were smokers who were not depressed.

Analytic Issues

Researchers frequently treat health-related behaviors and risk indicators (e.g. cholesterol level, which may reflect eating habits) as confounders rather than as mediators of relationships between dispositions or environmental variables and health. For example, studies of hostility and CHD test the association controlling for other CHD risk factors such as blood pressure, cigarette smoking, and physical activity. This approach may underestimate the true risk associated with hostility on CHD because, as noted above, hostility influences these risk factors. The same argument would hold for the impact of other variables such as stress and depression.

It may be most useful to use combinations of variables to predict health outcomes, which may not be predicted by a single variable. For example, Linkins & Comstock (1990) found that the combination of depression and smoking strongly predicted cancer incidence in a cohort of over 2000 individuals who were cancer-free at least 2–4 years into a follow-up period of 12 years. A similar interaction was observed by Grossarth-Maticek et al (1988), who found that individuals who felt distant from loved ones and who smoked were at higher risk for cancer. Rather than simply controlling for health-related behaviors and observing if the residual relationship of psychosocial variables with health remains significant, it will be more revealing to test for main effects and interactions of both types of variables.

Other Influences on Health-Related Behaviors

Studies linking stress, social support, and dispositions to health-related behaviors constitute a narrow cut through the vast literature on behavior and health. In the past five years, there has been increasing awareness of the critical role that behavior plays in risk of disease, generating a great deal of research on determinants and consequences of health-related behaviors.

Major shifts have occurred in some health-risk behaviors. Key examples are reductions in smoking prevalence (Lichtenstein & Glasgow 1992), which are credited along with other behavioral changes for a substantial drop in heart disease (USDHHS 1989), and reduction in unsafe sexual behaviors in high-risk gay male populations (Ekstrand & Coates 1990, Catania et al 1990). The processes by which these changes occurred are not fully known, but each involved shifts in social and community norms governing behavior. As a result, more attention is being paid to public health and social approaches to behavior change (Chesney 1993, Lichtenstein & Glasgow 1992). At the same time, research on individual determinants of health-related behaviors has flourished. The Health Belief Model (Rosenstock et al 1988), Theory of Reasoned Action and Theory of Planned Behavior (Ajzen & Fishbein 1980, Ajzen 1985), Self-Efficacy Theory (Bandura 1986), Protection Motivation Theory (Rogers 1983), Self-Regulation Theory (Leventhal et al 1984), and Transtheoretical Stages of Change Model (Prochaska & DiClemente 1984, Prochaska et al 1992) all have been used to elucidate the cognitive and affective factors associated with specific health-related behaviors including cigarette smoking, exercise, diet, breast self-examination, care-seeking, and sun exposure. Increasingly, researchers are combining and elaborating on the models to improve prediction of behavior (e.g. Seydel et al 1990, Boyd & Wandersman 1991, Aspinwall et al 1991, Weinstein 1993). There have been innovations in both individual and community approaches to behavior change. Research evaluating these interventions addresses our third question, regarding ways to prevent disease and promote recovery, but are unfortunately beyond the scope of this review.

Diverse studies on risk behavior point to the importance of placing the health implications of risk behaviors in the context of other costs and benefits of engaging in that behavior. Some models of health-related behavior include only elements that relate to the health risks and benefits of the target behavior. This may be appropriate for simple behaviors, such as obtaining a vaccination, but are not helpful for understanding ongoing lifestyle behaviors, such as eating habits, exercise, and sexual practices. When studies have assessed broader aspects of behavior, better prediction has been achieved. So, for example, studies of condom use have revealed that use is more affected by considerations of the physical and interpersonal aspects of use, including the impact on the pleasure and spontaneity of sex, than by health concerns (Kegeles et al 1989, Hays et al 1990).

Findings that health concerns are generally not the predominant influence on health-risking behaviors has been used as evidence for the irrationality of human behavior. Adolescents have been characterized as being particularly irrational in their behavior patterns. However, empirical tests have shown that adolescents are no less rational than adults. Applications of rational models to adolescent decision-making show that adolescents are consistent in their reasoning and behavior after the salient set of beliefs is assessed (Adler et al 1990). Quadrel et al (1993) demonstrated that adolescents are no more biased in their estimates of vulnerability to adverse health outcomes than are their parents. These and the above findings suggest that interventions aimed at modifying perceived consequences of health-damaging behaviors will be more effective for adults and adolescents if they consider a full range of salient consequences.

New Health Risks

In recent years, the adverse consequences of some behaviors have received greater attention. With the spread of AIDS, there has been increasing concern about unsafe sexual practices. We know a lot about the behavioral epidemiology of the disease and many of the models of health-related behavior have been used to understand sexual risk behaviors. Currently, the only prevention for AIDS requires behavioral change. There has been increasing attention paid to new high-risk populations, including adolescents and women (Ickovics & Rodin 1992), and efforts at prevention span individual to community-level interventions (Coates 1990).

A second area of increasing interest is unintentional injury. Injuries are closely tied to behavior and are the primary cause of death for individuals under age 44 in the United States. Although relatively little empirical work has been done, some studies have examined contributors to injuries in children (Boyce & Sobolewski 1989, Horwitz et al 1988). This will be an increasingly important arena for research and intervention (Spielberger & Frank 1992).

Newly recognized as a potential risk are some health promotion efforts that may have unintended health-damaging consequences. A prominent example is dieting for weight reduction. It has generally been assumed that dieting is beneficial because short-term weight loss is accompanied by improvement in cardiovascular risk factors. However, weight loss is usually not maintained, thereby leading to repeated cycles of loss and regain of weight. Further, many dieters are unsuccessful even in the short run and feel a sense of loss of control and lowered sense of self-worth (Brownell 1991). Of special concern are epidemiological findings suggest that body-weight variability leads to heightened risk for CHD and all cause mortality (Lee & Paffenbarger 1992, Lissner et al 1991). The robustness of these associations and their underlying mechanisms must await further research, but the possibility that unsuccessful dieting is hazardous clearly deserves careful consideration.

Another example of unintended negative consequences of health promotion activities comes from interventions to reduce blood cholesterol levels. Although low or lowered cholesterol levels are associated with reduced risk for CHD mortality and morbidity (Muldoon et al 1990, Rossouw et al 1990), they are also associated with increased risk of death from non-illness related causes, including accident, suicide, and homicide. Low or lowered cholesterol levels are associated with increased aggression and risk-taking behavior, which are thought to be related to altered central serotonergic function (Muldoon & Manuck, 1992), and may explain in part the association between non-illness related death and lowered cholesterol.

PHYSIOLOGICAL MECHANISMS

There has been an explosion of research on physiological mechanisms that may connect psychological variables to disease processes. Below, we review progress in the most active areas, cardiovascular reactivity to stress, and psychoneuroimmunology.

Cardiovascular Reactivity to Stress

Large and frequent increases in cardiovascular responses to stress have been proposed as a key mechanism relating Type A, hostility, and low social support with risk for hypertension and CHD. Considerable progress has been made in the conceptualization and measurement of cardiovascular responses to stress as an individual difference variable. Longitudinal studies ranging from two weeks to four years have demonstrated that the magnitude of blood pressure and heart rate responses to cognitive tasks are reliable over time (Manuck et al 1989b), even among children (Matthews et al 1990). Reliability is further increased if responses to laboratory tasks are statistically averaged (Kamarck et al 1992, Llabre et al 1988).

Recent improvements in noninvasive measures of cardiovascular function using impedance cardiography now allow reliable measurement of hemodynamic factors underlying observed stress-induced changes in blood pressure and heart rate [i.e. total peripheral resistance and cardiac output (Saab et al 1992)]. Based on these measures, individuals appear to fall into several types: (*a*) cardiac output responders, (*b*) total peripheral resistance responders, and (*c*) undifferentiated (Allen et al 1991, Kasprowicz et al 1990). It is not yet known if these types are reliable across time or if they are differentially useful for predicting disease.

The external validity of laboratory task–induced measures of cardiovascular responses has been of considerable interest. Many studies have examined the association between laboratory measures of responses during cognitive challenges and ambulatory measures of blood pressure. Although some studies report associations, especially if the ambulatory measures were taken during the workday (Fredrikson et al 1991), many have not (Pickering & Gerin 1990), leading some to question the validity of laboratory measures of stress responses. Part of the lack of correspondence between ambulatory and laboratory measures is the result of greater variability in posture, time of day, and activity level during ambulatory rather than laboratory measurement (Gellman et al 1990). Perhaps just as important is the greater variability of stress during ambulatory measures, which are typically averaged without regard to the occurrence of stress; laboratory measures are, by definition, averaged only during periods of stress. A recent analysis showed that individuals who exhibit large elevations in blood pressure during laboratory tasks also exhibit elevated ambulatory blood pressure levels, but only for those measures taken during times when participants simultaneously reported being under stress (Matthews et al 1992).

Additionally, most laboratory tasks are asocial [e.g. performing serial subtraction or reaction time tests (Smith et al 1989)]. Life stress is often interpersonal, and cardiovascular responses to laboratory stress and to ambulatory measures will not correlate if individuals differ in how they respond to asocial and social stress. Indeed, Ewart & Kolodner (1993) found that adolescents exhibiting large cardiovascular responses to a stressful interview had elevated ambulatory blood pressure throughout the schoolday; responses to asocial tasks were less predictive of ambulatory levels. An important direction for future research is to classify individuals not only by their responses to asocial stressors, but also to social stressors (Lassner et al 1993).

Increased attention has also been paid to influences of ethnicity, gender, and age on cardiovascular responses to stress. Accumulating data suggest that African-Americans, males, and older individuals exhibit larger blood pressure and total peripheral resistance responses to stress, whereas Caucasian-Americans, females, and younger individuals exhibit larger heart rate and cardiac output responses (e.g. Anderson 1989, Girdler et al 1990, Tischenkel et al 1989). These data are of particular interest because African-Americans, males, and older individuals are at greater risk for cardiovascular diseases.

Despite the above advances, longitudinal data linking cardiovascular responses to psychological stress and risk for cardiovascular disease remain sparse. Menkes et al (1989) followed a group of male medical students for 18–20 years for incidence of hypertension. Students who had exhibited an increase of 20 mm Hg or more in systolic blood pressure while immersing their hands in cold water were more likely to become hypertensive during the follow-up period. This relationship was independent of baseline blood pressure, parental history of hypertension, age, and smoking status. Similar analyses for incidence of MI, sudden death, stroke, and other cardiovascular diseases showed no effect (Coresh et al 1992). In another study, third grade school children performed a video game while their blood pressure and heart rate were monitored. Those children who exhibited the largest stress-induced increases in blood pressure had the greatest increase in resting blood pressure 4 years later, independent of age, body mass index, and resting pressure and heart rate at study entry (Murphy et al 1992). Another study of children aged 7–18 at study entry and their parents showed that cardiovascular responses to serial subtraction, mirror image tracing, and isometric exercise predicted increases in resting pressure 7 years later, adjusted for age, body mass index, resting pressure at study entry, and length of follow-up, in men, women, and boys (Matthews et al 1993). Light et al (1992) reported that among a small subgroup of an initial sample of undergraduate men who were able to be followed, systolic blood pressure and heart rate responses to a reaction time task were related to subsequent blood pressure status 10–15 years later. Clearly, longitudinal studies of reactivity and disease are a pressing need in this area.

Advances in our understanding of psychosocial factors and coronary disease also have emerged from animal model research. Cynomolgus monkeys, when fed a North American diet, develop atherosclerosis that resembles that of humans. Social stress induced by periodic reorganization of housing accelerates atherosclerosis and endothelial dysfunction (paradoxical vasoconstriction) in the coronary arteries of male monkeys (Kaplan et al 1991, Williams et al 1991). Cross-sectional data show that dominant males under social stress and subordinate females (not ovariectomized), regardless of social stress, have the greatest atherosclerosis (Kaplan et al 1991). Perhaps most relevant to our review, male and female monkeys who exhibit the largest heart rate changes in response to threat of capture have the greatest atherosclerosis upon autopsy (Manuck et al 1989a).

Psychological stress may not only lead to exaggerated cardiovascular responses in susceptible individuals, but also to enhanced platelet aggregation, coronary vasoconstriction, plaque rupture, myocardial ischemia, and arrhythmias, all part of the pathogenic process leading to MI or sudden death (see Kamarck & Jennings 1991, Markovitz & Matthews 1991 for reviews). A particularly important series of studies has demonstrated that stress leads to transient myocardial ischemia that is often symptomless or silent in coronary patients (e.g. Rozanski et al 1988) and that those patients who exhibit the largest blood pressure response to mental stress are more likely to experience myocardial ischemia (Krantz et al 1991). The extent that dispositional and environmental factors influence pathophysiological processes other than exaggerated cardiovascular reactivity is largely unknown and is an important area for research.

Immune Competence

Lowered immune competence has been proposed as a key mechanism linking psychological variables with susceptibility to infectious diseases as well as with progression of cancer, AIDS, and other diseases. Ader & Cohen (1993) reviewed animal research on conditioning of the immune system. In this section, we briefly examine human research on psychological influences on the immune system.

Recent meta-analytic (Herbert & Cohen 1993b) and enumerative (Kiecolt-Glaser et al 1992) reviews clearly show that psychological stress lowers immune competence. More specifically, stress can lead to decreased proliferative response of lymphocytes to mitogens such as phytohemagglutin (PHA) and concanavalin A (Con A), as well as to natural killer (NK) cell activity; to fewer circulating B cells, T cells, helper T cells, suppressor/cytotoxic T cells, and large granular lymphocytes; and to increased herpesvirus antibody titers (thought to reflect poor immune competence).

Personal resources or attributes may also modulate the immune system. Increased in vitro immune competence has been found among persons reporting supportive networks (Baron et al 1990) and feelings of belonging (Kennedy et al 1990), and among nonhuman primates with high rates of affiliation during stress (Cohen et al 1992). A prospective study found that caregivers who reported less social support and greater distress at an initial interview showed significantly greater decrements in immune function over the next 13 months (Kiecolt-Glaser et al 1991). A meta-analytic review documented that depression is associated with large decreases in proliferative response of lymphocytes to PHA, Con A, and pokeweed mitogen (PWM), and natural killer cell cytotoxic activity and decreased numbers of NK cells, T cells, B cells, helper T cells, and suppressor/cytotoxic T cells (Herbert & Cohen 1993a). These associations appear stronger among older and hospitalized populations. Finally, recent data suggest that those who exhibit heightened sympathetic responses to stress, indexed by elevations in blood pressure, heart rate, and catecholamines, are most likely to show immuno-suppression during stress (Manuck et al 1991, Zakowski et al 1992).

Given these associations, psychological interventions to alter immune function have been tried. Both a cognitive-behavioral stress management program and exercise program attenuated immunologic changes following notification of HIV-1 seropositivity (Antoni et al 1991, LaPerriere et al 1990). Writing about traumatic personal experiences led to better lymphocyte response to PHA, compared to a control of writing about topics with no emotional element (Pennebaker et al 1988).

Although associations between psychological parameters and functional and enumerative measures of immune measures are now documented, the precise health consequences of changes in immune responses are not known, particularly in determining infection and emergence of initial clinical symptoms. Decreased NK cell activity is a predictor of disease recurrence in patients with early-stage breast cancer (Levy et al 1991); delayed hypersensitivity to skin testing is associated with mortality, unadjusted for age in the elderly (Wayne et al 1990); and poor PHA response is associated with mortality in one sample of the elderly (Murasko et al 1988), but not in another (Wayne et al 1990). At this point, a high priority should be longitudinal studies on psychologically-induced alterations in immune parameters in relation to health outcomes.

SUMMARY AND CONCLUDING COMMENTS

The past five years have witnessed substantial progress in addressing the question, who becomes sick and why? Links of antecedent environmental and individual variables with future disease have become clearer. Firm evidence has emerged that social support, dispositional hostility, and work strain are linked to health outcomes, whereas accumulating evidence suggests that Type A is not linked with CHD, nor depression with all-site cancers. In addition, appraisal of stress appears to play a more important role in health outcomes than does simple exposure to life events.

Progress has occurred despite methodological challenges in studying the etiology of disease. A relatively small number of initially healthy individuals fall ill over even five to ten years (except for upper respiratory disease and flu). Suitable indicators of subclinical disease are often not available for research purposes. For example, coronary angiograms and thallium scans used to measure atherosclerosis require costly or invasive procedures, making their use hard to justify in people with no apparent disease. The influence of psychosocial factors may be more easily detected in studies of recurrence or of course of disease because of greater incidence rates and because frank disease is more easily measured than subclinical disease. Studies have, for example, documented higher rates of recurrence of herpes and breast cancer (Forsén 1991, Levy et al 1991, Kemeny et al 1989, cf Dean & Surtes 1989), of abnormal cardiac responses in heart patients (Follick et al 1988, Zotti et al 1991, Rozanski et al 1988), and of poor glucose control in diabetics (Gonder-Frederick et al 1990) under increased stress.

Health-related psychological concepts are increasingly being refined. In an effort to understand better the health-damaging aspects of psychological factors, distinctions have been made between subjective stress and life events, functions of social support and social network or integration, hostile attitudes and neuroticism, and dispositional optimism and attributional style. We are lagging, however, in developing measurement tools that adequately capture the progress made in refining our concepts. We often infer relationships based on secondary analyses of existing items, rather than using a priori scales with demonstrated external and discriminative validity. Furthermore, work establishing the external validity of self-report measures of stress, neuroticism, social support, hostility, etc is less than desirable, leaving questions about the conceptual underpinnings of our measures. Validated tools are essential for establishing precise linkages between behavior and disease and for adequate characterization of individual risk in studies of prevention and intervention.

In contrast, there has been substantial research on assessment of mechanisms. We now have reliable and internally valid assessments of stress-induced cardiovascular reactivity. Although there are many demonstrations that psychological factors impact on cardiovascular and immune function, it is not yet clear, however, that psychologically-induced alterations in cardiac and immune function are predictive of disease status. This is an important agenda for future research.

Future research on mechanisms as well as on measurement of psychological states will benefit from recent technological advances. Of special relevance are ambulatory monitoring techniques for measurement of physiological states (e.g. myocardial ischemia, blood pressure, glucose sampling) and psychological states (e.g. mood) that record data for immediate relay via telemetry to data storage and for later readout. These techniques will permit health psychologists to address different questions; to assess, in a more refined manner, variability in physiological and psychological states for testing of theory; and to avoid biases owing to retrospective recall and poor sampling techniques.

Research on mechanisms has focused mostly on cardiovascular reactivity and psychoneuroimmunology. New directions in research on mechanisms are emerging, including the effects of stress on body fat distribution (Rebuffé-Scrive et al 1992), which is a newly identified risk factor for cardiovascular disease; development of a suitable animal model for noninsulin-dependent diabetes mellitus that has permitted analysis of genetic and environmental determinants of hyperglycemia (Surwit 1992); and the role of the sympathetic nervous system in accounting for the covariation of insulin sensitivity, blood pressure, and body fat distribution (Donahue et al 1990). The interactions among systems influenced by environmental stress will be an important arena for further investigation.

Finally, health psychology is now seeing the development of more sophisticated models that consider genetic predispositions, environmental challenge, and individual differences in behavior in understanding disease risk. We anticipate that the enormous progress made in studying the relationships between psychological variables and health outcomes in the last few years will be dwarfed by the progress in the next five years as research will benefit from the advances in technology, research on assessment of psychosocial variables and mechanisms, and awareness of the interaction between mechanisms and environmental variables, dispositions, and health-related behaviors.

ACKNOWLEDGMENTS

We gratefully acknowledge the support of the John D. and Catherine T. MacArthur Foundation Research Network on Health-Promoting and Disease-Preventing Behaviors; of NIH grants HL25767 and HL38712 for Dr. Matthews, and HD23880 for Dr. Adler; and of NIMH grant MH19391 for Dr. Adler. We also appreciate the input of Drs. Frances Cohen and Christine Dunkel-Schetter to sections of the review, and the editorial assistance of Ms. Lynae Darbes.

Literature Cited

Aaronson LG. 1989. Perceived and received support: effects on health behavior during pregnancy. *Nurs. Res.* 38:4–9

Ader NA, Cohen N. 1993. Psychoneuroimmunology: conditioning and stress. *Annu. Rev. Psychol.* 44:53–85

Adler NE, Kegeles SM, Irwin CE, Wibbelsman C. 1990. Adolescent contraceptive behavior: an assessment of decision processes. *J. Pediatr.* 116:463–71

Affleck G, Tennen H, Urrows S, Higgins P. 1992. Neuroticism and the pain-mood relation in rheumatoid arthritis: insights from a prospective daily study. *J. Consult. Clin. Psychol.* 60:119–26

Ajzen I. 1985. From intentions to actions: a theory of planned behavior. In *Action Control: From Cognition to Behavior,* ed. J Kuhl, J Beckman, pp. 11–39. New York: Springer-Verlag

Ajzen I, Fishbein M. 1980. *Understanding Attitudes and Predicting Social Behavior.* Englewood Cliffs, NJ: Prentice Hall

Aldwin CM, Levenson MR, Spiro A III, Bosse R. 1989. Does emotionality predict stress? Findings from the Normative Aging Study. *J. Pers. Soc. Psychol.* 56:618–24

Allen MT, Boquet AJ, Shelley KS. 1991. Cluster analysis of cardiovascular responsivity to three laboratory stressors. *Psychosom. Med.* 53:272–88

Almada SJ, Zonderman AB, Shekelle RB, Dyer AR, Daviglus ML, et al. 1991. Neuroticism and cynicism and risk of death in middle-aged men: the Western Electric Study. *Psychosom. Med.* 53:165–75

Anda RF, Williamson DF, Escobedo LG, Mast EE, Giovino GA, Remington PL. 1990. Depression and the dynamics of smoking. *J. Am. Med. Assoc.* 264:1541–45

Anderson NB. 1989. Racial differences in stress-induced cardiovascular reactivity and hypertension: current status and substantive issues. *Psychol. Bull.* 105:89–105

Antoni MH, Baggett L, Ironson G, LaPerriere A, August S, et al. 1991. Cognitive-behavioral stress management intervention buffers distress responses and immunologic changes following notification of HIV-1 seropositivity. *J. Consult. Clin. Psychol.* 59:906–15

Appels A, Mulder P. 1989. Fatigue and heart disease. The association between 'vital exhaustion' and past, present and future coronary heart disease. *J. Psychosom. Res.* 33:727–38

Appels A, Otten F. 1992. Exhaustion as precursor of cardiac death. *Br. J. Clin. Psychol.* 31:351–56

Appels A, Schouten E. 1991. Burnout as a risk factor for coronary heart disease. *Behav. Med.* 17:53–59

Aspinwall LG, Kemeny ME, Taylor SE, Schneider SG, Dudley JP. 1991. Psychosocial predictors of gay men's AIDS risk-reduction behavior. *Health Psychol.* 10:432–44

Aspinwall LG, Taylor SE. 1992. Modeling cognitive adaptation: a longitudinal investigation of the impact of individual differences and coping on college adjustment and performance. *J. Pers. Soc. Psychol.* 63:989–1003

Avis NE, Brambilla J, Vass K, McKinlay JB. 1991. The effect of widowhood on health: a prospective analysis from the Massachusetts Women's Health Study. *Soc. Sci. Med.* 9:1063–2070

Bandura A. 1986. *Social Foundations of Thought and Action: A Social Cognitive Thoery.* Englewood Cliffs, NJ: Prentice Hall

Bandura A. 1989. Human agency in social cognitive theory. *Am. Psychol.* 44:1175–84

Barefoot JC, Dodge KA, Peterson BL, Dahlstrom WG, Williams RB Jr. 1989. The Cook-Medley Hostility Scale: item content and ability to predict survival. *Psychosom. Med.* 51:46–57

Baron RS, Cutrona CE, Hicklin D, Russell DW, Lubaroff DM. 1990. Social support and immune function among spouses of cancer patients. *J. Pers. Soc. Psychol.* 59:344–52

Beardsley G, Goldstein MG. 1993. Psychological factors affecting physical condition. Endocrine disease literature review. *Psychosomatics* 34(1):12–19

Bolger N. 1990. Coping as a personality process: a prospective study. *J. Pers. Soc. Psychol.* 59:525–37

Boyce WT, Sobolewski S. 1989. Recurrent injuries in schoolchildren. *Am. J. Dis. Child.* 143:338–42

Boyd B, Wandersman A. 1991. Predicting undergraduate condom use with the Fishbein and Ajzen and the Triandis Attitude-Behavior Models: implications for public health interventions. *J. Appl. Soc. Psychol.* 21:1810–30

Brown JD, McGill KL. 1989. The cost of good fortune: when positive life events produce negative health consequences. *J. Pers. Soc. Psychol.* 57:1103–10

Brownell KD. 1991. Personal responsibility and control over our bodies: when expectation exceeds reality. *Health Psychol.* 10:303–10

Catania JA, Kegeles S, Coates TJ. 1990. Towards an understanding of risk behavior: an AIDS risk reduction model. *Health Educ. Q.* 17:53–72

Chesney MA. 1993. Health psychology in the 21st century: acquired immunodeficiency syndrome as a harbinger of things to come. *Health Psychol.* 12:259–68

Coates TJ. 1990. Strategies for modifying sexual behavior for primary and secondary prevention of HIV disease. *J. Consult. Clin. Psychol.* 56:57–69

Cohen S. 1988. Psychosocial models of the role of social support in the etiology of physical disease. *Health Psychol.* 7:269–97

Cohen S, Kaplan JR, Cunnick JE, Manuck SB, Rabin BS. 1992. Chronic social stress, affiliation, and cellular immune response in nonhuman primates. *Psychol. Sci.* 3:301–4

Cohen S, Lichtenstein E. 1990. Perceived stress, quitting smoking, and smoking relapse. *Health Psychol.* 9:466–78

Cohen S, Tyrrell DAJ, Smith AP. 1991. Psychological stress and susceptibility to the common cold. *N. Engl. J. Med.* 325:606–12

Cohen S, Tyrrell DAJ, Smith AP. 1993. Negative life events, perceived stress, negative affect, and susceptibility to the common cold. *J. Pers. Soc. Psychol.* 64:131–40

Colantonio A, Kasl V, Ostfeld AM. 1992. Depressive symptoms and other psychosocial factors as predictors of stroke in the elderly. *Am. J. Epidemiol.* 136:884–94

Collins NL, Dunkel-Schetter C, Lobel M, Scrimshaw SC. 1993. Social support in pregnancy: psychosocial correlates of birth outcomes and postpartum depression. *J. Pers. Soc. Psychol.* In press

Coresh J, Klag MJ, Mead LA, Liang KY, Whelton PK. 1992. Vascular reactivity in young adults and cardiovascular disease. A prospective study. *Circulation* 19:218–23

Costa PT Jr, McCrae RR. 1987. Neuroticism, somatic complaints, and disease: Is the bark worse than the bite? *J. Pers.* 55:299–316

Cox DJ, Gonder-Frederick L. 1992. Major developments in behavioral diabetes research. *J. Consult. Clin. Psychol.* 60:628–38

Dean C, Surtes PG. 1989. Do psychological factors predict survival in breast cancer? *J. Psychosom. Res.* 233:561–69

DeLongis A, Folkman S, Lazarus RS. 1988. The impact of daily stress on health and mood: psychological and social resources as mediators. *J. Pers. Soc. Psychol.* 54:486–95

Dembroski TM, MacDougall JM, Costa PT Jr, Grandits GA. 1989. Components of hostility as predictors of sudden death and myocardial infarction in the Multiple Risk Factor Intervention Trial. *Psychosom. Med.* 51:514–22

Donahue RP, Skyler JS, Schneiderman N, Prineas RJ. 1990. Hyperinsulimea and elevated blood pressure: cause, confounder, or coincidence? *Am. J. Epidemiol.* 132:827–36

Eaker ED, Abbott RD, Kannel WB. 1989. Frequency of uncomplicated angina pectoris in Type A compared with Type B persons (the Framingham Study). *Am. J. Cardiol.* 63:1042–45

Eaker ED, Pinsky J, Castelli WP. 1992. Myocardial infarction and coronary death among women: psychosocial predictors from a 20-year follow-up of women in the Framingham Study. *Am. J. Epidemiol.* 135:854–64

Ekstrand ML, Coates TJ. 1990. Maintenance of safer sexual behaviors and predictors of risky sex: the San Francisco Men's Health Study. *Am. J. Public Health* 80:973–77

Ewart CK, Kolodner KB. 1993. Predicting ambulatory blood pressure during school: effectiveness of social and nonsocial reactivity tasks in black and white adolescents. *Psychophysiology* 30:30–38

Falk A, Hanson BS, Isacsson S, Ostergren P. 1992. Job strain and mortality in elderly men: social network, support, and influence as buffers. *Am. J. Public Health* 82:1136–39

Follick MJ, Gorkin L, Capone RJ, Smith TW, Ahern DK, et al. 1988. Psychological distress as a predictor of ventricular arrhythmias in a post-myocardial infarction population. *Am. Heart J.* 116:32–36

Forsén A. 1991. Psychosocial stress as a risk for breast cancer. *Psychother. Psychosom.* 55:176–85

Fredrikson M, Robson A, Ljungdell T. 1991. Ambulatory and laboratory blood pressure in individuals with negative and positive family history of hypertension. *Health Psychol.* 10:371–77

Friedman HS, Tucker JS, Tomlinson-Keasey C, Schwartz JE, Wingard DL, Criqui MH. 1993. Does childhood personality predict longevity? *J. Pers. Soc. Psychol.* 65:176–85

Gellman M, Spitzer S, Ironson G, Llabre M, Saab P, et al. 1990. Posture, place, and mood effects on ambulatory blood pressure. *Psychophysiology* 27:544–51

Girdler SS, Turner JR, Sherwood A, Light KC. 1990. Gender differences in blood pressure control during a variety of behavioral stressors. *Psychosom. Med.* 52:571–91

Glaser R, Rice J, Sheridan J, Fertel R, Stout J, et al. 1987. Stress-related immune supression: health implications. *Brain Behav. Immun.* 1:7–20

Gonder-Frederick LA, Carter WR, Cox DJ, Clarke WL. 1990. Environmental stress and blood glucose change in insulin-dependent diabetes mellitus. *Health Psychol.* 9:503–15

Grossarth-Maticek R, Eysenck HJ, Vetter H. 1988. Personality type, smoking habit and their interaction as predictors of cancer and coronary heart disease. *Pers. Indiv. Diff.* 9:479–95

Haan MN. 1988. Job strain and ischaemic heart disease: an epidemiologic study of metal workers. *Ann. Clin. Res.* 20:143–45

Hahn RC, Petitti DB. 1988. Minnesota Multiphasic Personality Inventory-rated depression and the incidence of breast cancer. *Cancer* 61:845–48

Hanson BS, Isacsson SO, Janzon L, Lindell SE. 1989. Social network and social support influence mortality in elderly men. *Am. J. Epidemiol.* 130:100–11

Harmsen P, Rosengren A, Tsipogianni A, Wilhelmsen L. 1990. Risk factors for stroke in middle-aged men in Goteborg, Sweden. *Stroke* 21:23–29

Havassy BE, Hall SM, Wasserman DA. 1991. Social support and relapse: commonalities among alcoholics, opiate users, and cigarette smokers. *Addict. Behav.* 16:235–46

Hays RB, Kegeles SM, Coates TJ. 1990. High HIV risk-taking among young gay men. *AIDS* 4:901–7

Hecker MHL, Chesney MA, Black GW, Frautschi N. 1988. Coronary-prone behaviors in the Western Collaborative Group Study. *Psychosom. Med.* 50:153–64

Herbert TB, Cohen S. 1993a. Depression and immunity: a meta-analytic review. *Psychol. Bull.* 113:472–86

Herbert TB, Cohen S. 1993b. Stress and immunity in humans: a meta-analytic review. *Psychosom. Med.* 55:364–79

Hibbard J, Pope C. 1993. The quality of social roles as predictors of morbidity and mortality. *Soc. Sci. Med.* 36:217–25

Hollis JF, Connett JE, Stevens VJ, Greenlick MR. 1990. Stressful life events, Type A behavior, and the prediction of cardiovascular and total mortality over six years. *J. Behav. Med.* 13:263–81

Homer J, James SA, Siegel E. 1990. Work-related psychosocial stress and risk of preterm low birthweight delivery. *Am. J. Public Health* 80:173–77

Horwitz SM, Morgenstern H, DiPietro L, Morrison CL. 1988. Determinants of pediatric injuries. *Am. J. Dis. Child.* 142:605–11

House JS, Landis KR, Umberson D. 1988. Social relationships and health. *Science* 241:540–45

Houston BK, Chesney MA, Black GW, Cates DS, Hecker MHL. 1992. Behavioral clusters and coronary heart disease risk. *Psychosom. Med.* 54:447–61

Ickovics JR, Rodin J. 1992. Women and AIDS in the United States: epidemiology, natural history, and mediating mechanisms. *Health Psychol.* 11:1–16

Jennison KM. 1992. The impact of stressful life events and social support on drinking among older adults: a general population survey. *Int. J. Aging Hum. Dev.* 35:99–123

Kamarck TW, Jennings JR. 1991. Biobehavioral factors in sudden cardiac death. *Psychol. Bull.* 109:42–75

Kamarck TW, Jennings JR, Debski TT, Glickman-Weiss E, Johnson PS, et al. 1992. Reliable measures of behaviorally-evoked cardiovascular reactivity from a PC-based test battery: results from student and community samples. *Psychophysiology* 29:17–28

Kamarck TW, Manuck SB, Jennings JR. 1990. Social support reduces cardiovascular reactivity to psychological challenge: a laboratory model. *Psychosom. Med.* 52:42–58

Kamen-Siegel L, Rodin J, Seligman MEP, Dwyer J. 1991. Explanatory style and cell-mediated immunity in elderly men and women. *Health Psychol.* 10:229–35

Kaplan GA, Comacho T. 1983. Perceived health and mortality: a 9-year follow-up of the Human Population Laboratory Cohort. *Am. J. Epidemiol.* 117:292–304

Kaplan GA, Reynolds P. 1988. Depression and cancer mortality and morbidity: prospective evidence from the Alameda County study. *J. Behav. Med.* 11:1–13

Kaplan JR, Adams MR, Clarkson TB, Manuck SB, Shively CA. 1991. Social behavior and gender in biomedical investigations using monkeys: studies in atherogenesis. *Lab. Anim. Sci.* 41:1–9

Kaplan RM. 1988. Health-related quality of life in cardiovascular disease. *J. Consult. Clin. Psychol.* 56:382–92

Karasek RA. 1979. Job demands, job decision latitude and mental strain: implications for job redesign. *Admin. Sci. Q.* 24:285–308

Karasek RA, Theorell T, Schwartz JE, Schnall PL, Pieper CF, Michela JL. 1988. Job characteristics in relation to the prevalence of myocardial infarction in the US Health Examination Survey (HES) and the Health and Nutrition Examination Survey (HANES). *Am. J. Public Health* 78:910–18

Kasprowicz AL, Manuck SB, Malkoff SB, Krantz DS. 1990. Individual differences in behaviorally evoked cardiovascular response: temporal stability and hemodynamic patterning. *Psychophysiology* 26:605–19

Kegeles SM, Adler NE, Irwin CE. 1989. Adolescents and condoms: associations of beliefs with intentions to use. *Am. J. Dis. Child.* 143:911–15

Keltikangas-Jarvinen L, Raikkonen K. 1989. Developmental trends in Type A behavior as predictors for the development of somatic coronary heart disease risk factors. *Psychother. Psychosom.* 52:210–15

Kemeny ME, Cohen F, Zegans LS, Conant MA. 1989. Psychological and immunological predictors of genital herpes recurrence. *Psychosom. Med.* 51:195–208

Kennedy S, Kiecolt-Glaser JK, Glaser R. 1990. Social support, stress, and the immune system. In *Social Support: An Interactional View,* ed. BR Sarason, IG Sarason, GR Pierce, pp. 253–66. New York: Wiley

Kennell J, Klaus M, McGrath S, Robertson S, Hinkley C. 1991. Continuous emotional support during labor in a US hospital. *J. Am. Med. Assoc.* 265:2197–2201

Kiecolt-Glaser JK, Cacioppo JT, Malarkey WB, Glaser R. 1992. Acute psychological stressors and short-term immune changes: What, why, for whom, and to what extent? *Psychosom. Med.* 54:680–85

Kiecolt-Glaser JK, Dura JR, Speicher CE, Trask OJ, Glaser R. 1991. Spousal caregivers of dementia victims: longitudinal changes in immunity and health. *Psychosom. Med.* 53:345–62

Klaus MH, Kennell JH, Robertson SS, Sosa R. 1986. Effects of social support during parturition on maternal and infant morbidity. *Br. Med. J.* 293:585–87

Krantz DS, Helmers KF, Bairey CN, Nebel LE, Hedges SM, Rozanski A. 1991. Cardiovascular reactivity and mental stress-induced myocardial ischemia in patients with coronary artery disease. *Psychosom. Med.* 53:1–12

LaPerriere AR, Antoni MH, Schneiderman N, Ironson G, Klimas N, et al. 1990. Exercise intervention attenuates emotional distress and natural killer cell decrements following notification of positive serologic status for HIV-1. *Biofeedback Self-Regul.* 15:229–42

Lassner JB, Matthews KA, Stoney CM. 1993. Are cardiovascular reactors to asocial stress also reactors to social stress. *J. Pers. Soc. Psychol.* In press

Lazarus RS, Folkman S. 1984. *Stress, Appraisal, and Coping.* New York: Springer

Lee DJ, Niemcryk SJ, Jenkins CD, Rose RM. 1989. Type A, amicability and injury: a prospective study of air traffic controllers. *J. Psychosom. Res.* 33:177–86

Lee IM, Paffenbarger RS. 1992. Change in body weight and longevity. *J. Am. Med. Assoc.* 268:2045–49

Levav I, Friedlander Y, Kark JD, Peritz E. 1988. An epidemiologic study of mortality among bereaved parents. *N. Engl. J. Med.* 319:457–61

Leventhal H, Nerenz DR, Steele DF. 1984. Illness representations and coping with health threats. In *A Handbook of Psychology and Health,* ed. A Baum, J Singer, pp. 219–52. Hillsdale, NJ: Erlbaum

Levy SM, Herberman RB, Lippman M, D'Angelo T, Lee J. 1991. Immunological and psychosocial predictors of disease recurrence in patients with early-stage breast cancer. *Behav. Med.* 17:67–75

Lichtenstein E, Glasgow RE. 1992. Smoking cessation: What have we learned over the past decade? *J. Consult. Clin. Psychol.* 60:518–27

Light KC, Dolan CA, Davis MR, Sherwood A. 1992. Cardiovascular responses to an active coping challenge as predictors of blood pressure patterns 10 to 15 years later. *Psychosom. Med.* 54:217–30

Linkins RW, Comstock GW. 1990. Depressed mood and development of cancer. *Am. J. Epidemiol.* 132:962–72

Lissner L, Odell PM, D'Agostino RB, Stokes J, Kreger BE, et al. 1991. Variability of body weight and health outcomes in the Framingham population. *N. Engl. J. Med.* 324:1839–44

Llabre MM, Ironson GH, Spitzer SB, Gellman MD, Weidler DJ, Schneiderman N. 1988.

How many blood pressure measurements are enough?: an application of generalizability theory to the study of blood pressure reliability. *Psychophysiology* 25:97–106
Lobel M, Dunkel-Schetter C, Scrimshaw S. 1992. Prenatal maternal stress and prematurity: prospective study of socioeconomically disadvantaged women. *Health Psychol.* 11(1):32–40
Manuck SB, Cohen S, Rabin BS, Muldoon MF, Bachen EA. 1991. Prediction of individual differences in cellular immune response. *Psychol. Sci.* 2:111–15
Manuck SB, Kaplan JR, Adams MR, Clarkson TB. 1989a. Behaviorally elicited heart rate reactivity and atherosclerosis in female cynomolgus monkeys (*Macaca fascicularis*). *Psychosom. Med.* 51:306–18
Manuck SB, Kasprowicz AL, Monroe SM, Larkin KT, Kaplan JR. 1989b. Psychophysiologic reactivity as a dimension of individual differences. In *Handbook of Research Methods in Cardiovascular Behavioral Medicine,* ed. N Schneiderman, SM Weiss, PG Kaufman, pp. 365–82. New York: Plenum
Markovitz JH, Matthews KA. 1991. Platelets in coronary heart disease: potential pathophysiologic mechanisms. *Psychosom. Med.* 53:643–68
Markovitz JH, Matthews KA, Kannel WB, Cobb JL, D'Agostino RB. 1993. Psychological predictors of hypertension in the Framingham Study: Is there tension in hypertension? *J. Am. Med. Assoc.* In press
Markovitz JH, Matthews KA, Wing RR, Kuller LH, Meilahn EN. 1991. Psychological, biological, and health behavior predictors of blood pressure change in middle-aged women. *J. Hypertens.* 9:399–406
Matthews KA. 1988. Coronary heart disease and Type A behaviors: update on and alternative to the Booth-Kewley and Friedman quantitative review. *Psychol. Bull.* 104:373–80
Matthews KA, Woodall KL, Allen MT. 1993. Cardiovascular reactivity to stress predicts future blood pressure status. *Hypertension.* In press
Matthews KA, Woodall KL, Engebretson TO, McCann BS, Stoney CM, et al. 1992. Influence of age, sex, and family on Type A and hostile attitudes and behaviors. *Health Psychol.* 11:317–23
Matthews KA, Woodall KL, Stoney CM. 1990. Changes in and stability of cardiovascular responses to behavioral stress. *Child Dev.* 61:1134–44
McCormick MC, Brooks-Gunn J, Shorter T, Holmes JH, Wallace CY, et al. 1990. Factors associated with smoking in low-income pregnant women: relationship to birth weight, stressful life events, social support, health behaviors and mental distress. *J. Clin. Epidemiol.* 43:441–48
Menkes MS, Matthews KA, Krantz DS, Lundberg U, Mead LA, et al. 1989. Cardiovascular reactivity to the cold pressor test as a predictor of hypertension. *Hypertension* 14:524–30
Muldoon MF, Manuck SB. 1992. Health through cholesterol reduction: Are there unforseen risks? *Ann. Behav. Med.* 14:101–8
Muldoon MF, Manuck SB, Matthews KA. 1990. Effects of cholesterol lowering on mortality: a quantitative review of primary prevention trials. *Br. Med. J.* 301:309–14
Murasko DM, Weiner P, Kaye D. 1988. Association of lack of mitogen-induced lymphocyte proliferation with increased mortality in the elderly. *Aging: Immunol. Infect. Dis.* 1:1–6
Murphy JK, Alpert BS, Walker SS. 1992. Ethnicity, pressor reactivity, and children's blood pressure. Five years of observations. *Hypertension* 20:327–32
Norbeck JS, Anderson NJ. 1989. Psychosocial predictors of pregnancy outcomes in low-income black, hispanic, and white women. *Nurs. Res.* 38:204–9
Orth-Gomer K, Rosengren A, Wilhelmsen L. 1993. Lack of social support and incidence of coronary heart disease in middle-aged Swedish men. *Psychosom. Med.* 55:37–43
Orth-Gomer K, Unden AL. 1990. Type A behavior, social support, and coronary risk: interaction and significance for mortality in cardiac patients. *Psychosom. Med.* 52:59–72
Pagel MD, Smilkstein G, Regen H, Montano D. 1990. Psychosocial influences on newborn outcomes: a controlled prospective study. *Soc. Sci. Med.* 30:597–604
Pennebaker JW, Kiecolt-Glaser JK, Glaser R. 1988. Disclosure of traumas and immune function: health implications for psychotherapy. *J. Consult. Clin. Psychol.* 56:239–45
Perkins KA, Grobe JE. 1992. Increased desire to smoke during acute stress. *Br. J. Addict.* 87:1037–40
Peterson C, Seligman MEP, Vaillant GE. 1988. Pessimistic explanatory style is a risk factor for physical illness: a thirty-five-year longitudinal study. *J. Pers. Soc. Psychol.* 55:23–27
Pickering TG, Gerin W. 1990. Cardiovascular reactivity in the laboratory and the role of behavioral factors in hypertension: a critical review. *Ann. Behav. Med.* 12:3–16
Prochaska JO, DiClemente CC. 1984. *The Transtheoretical Approach: Crossing Traditional Boundaries of Therapy.* Homewood: Dow Jones Irwin
Prochaska JO, DiClemente CC, Norcross JC.

1992. In search of how people change. *Am. Psychol.* 47:1102–14

Quadrel MJ, Fischhoff B, Davis W. 1993. Adolescent (in)vulnerability. *Am. Psychol.* 48:102–16

Raikkonen K, Keltikangas-Jarvinen L. 1991. Hostility and its association with behaviorally induced and somatic coronary risk indicators in Finnish adolescents and young adults. *Soc. Sci. Med.* 33:1171–78

Rebuffé-Scrive M, Walsh UA, McEwen B, Rodin J. 1992. Effect of chronic stress and exogenous glucorticoids on regional fat distribution and metabolism. *Physiol. Behav.* 52:583–90

Reed DM, LaCroix AZ, Karasek RA, Miller D, MacLean CA. 1989. Occupational strain and the incidence of coronary heart disease. *Am. J. Epidemiol.* 129:495–502

Reite M, Boccia M. 1993. Letter to the editor. *N. Engl. J. Med.* 328:887

Reynolds P, Kaplan GA. 1990. Social connections and risk for cancer: prospective evidence from the Alameda County Study. *Behav. Med.* 9:101–10

Rodin J, Salovey P. 1989. Health psychology. *Annu. Rev. Psychol.* 40:533–79

Rogers RW. 1983. Cognitive and physiological processes in attitude change: a revised theory of protection motivation. In *Social Psychophysiology*, ed. J Cacioppo, R Petty, pp. 153–76. New York: Guilford

Rosengren A, Tibblin G, Wilhelmsen L. 1991. Self-perceived psychological stress and incidence of coronary artery disease in middle-aged men. *Am. J. Cardiol.* 68:1171–75

Rosenstock IM, Strecher VJ, Becker MH. 1988. Social learning theory and the health belief model. *Health Educ. Q.* 15:175–83

Rossouw JE, Lewis B, Rifkind BM. 1990. The value of lowering cholesterol after myocardial infarction. *N. Engl. J. Med.* 323:1112–19

Rozanski A, Bairey CN, Krantz DS, Friedman J, Resser KJ, et al. 1988. Mental stress and the induction of silent myocardial ischemia in patients with coronary artery disease. *N. Engl. J. Med.* 318:1005–12

Saab PG, Llabre MM, Hurwitz BE, Frame CA, Reineke LJ, et al. 1992. Myocardial and peripheral vascular responses to behavioral challenges and their stability in black and white Americans. *Psychophysiology* 29:384–97

Salovey P, Birnbaum D. 1989. Influence of mood on health-relevant cognitions. *J. Pers. Soc. Psychol.* 57:539–51

Scheier MF, Carver CS. 1992. Effects of optimism on psychological and physical well-being: theoretical overview and empirical update. *Cogn. Ther. Res.* 16:201–28

Scheier MF, Matthews KA, Owens JF, Magovern GJ, Lefebvre RC, et al. 1989. Dispositional optimism and recovery from coronary artery bypass surgery: the beneficial effects on physical and psychological well-being. *J. Pers. Soc. Psychol.* 57:1024–40

Scherwitz LW, Perkins LL, Chesney MA, Hughes GH, Sidney S, Manolio TA. 1992. Hostility and health behaviors in young adults: the CARDIA study. *Am. J. Epidemiol.* 136:136–45

Seydel E, Taal E, Wiegman O. 1990. Risk-appraisal, outcome and self-efficacy expectancies: cognitive factors in preventive behaviour related to cancer. *Psychol. Health* 4:99–109

Shekelle RB, Raynor WJ, Ostfeld AM, Garron DC, Bieliauskas LA, et al. 1981. Psychological depression and 17-year risk of death from cancer. *Psychosom. Med.* 43:117–25

Shoham-Yakubovich I, Ragland DR, Brand RJ, Syme SL. 1988. Type A behavior pattern and health status after 22 years of follow-up in the Western Collaborative Group Study. *Am. J. Epidemiol.* 128:579–88

Siegler IC, Peterson BL, Barefoot JC, Williams RB Jr. 1992. Hostility during late adolescence predicts coronary risk factors at mid-life. *Am. J. Epidemiol.* 136:146–54

Siegrist J, Peter R, Junge A, Cremer P, Seidel D. 1990. Low status control, high effort at work and ischemic heart disease: prospective evidence from blue-collar men. *Soc. Sci. Med.* 31:1127–34

Siegrist J, Peter R, Motz W, Strauer BE. 1992. The role of hypertension, left ventricular hypertrophy and psychosocial risks in cardiovascular disease: prospective evidence from blue-collar men. *Eur. Heart J.* 13(Suppl. D):89–95

Smith TW. 1992. Hostility and health: current status of a psychosomatic hypothesis. *Health Psychol.* 11:139–50

Smith TW, Pope MK, Rhodewalt F, Poulton JL. 1989. Optimism, neuroticism, coping, and symptom reports: an alternative interpretation of the life orientation test. *J. Pers. Soc. Psychol.* 56:640–48

Somervell PD, Kaplan BH, Heiss G, Tyroler HA, Kleinbaum DG, Obrist PA. 1989. Psychologic distress as a predictor of mortality. *Am. J. Epidemiol.* 130:1013–23

Sosa R, Kennell J, Klaus M, Robertson S, Urrutia J. 1980. The effects of a supportive companion on perinatal problems, length of labor, and mother-infant interaction. *N. Engl. J. Med.* 303:597–600

Spielberger CD, Frank RG. 1992. Injury control: a promising field for psychologists. *Am. Psychol.* 47:1029–30

Stone AA, Bovbjerg DH, Neale JM, Napoli A, Valdimarsdottir H, et al. 1992. Development of the common cold symptoms following experimental rhinovirus infection is related to prior stressful life events. *Behav. Med.* 18:115–20

Stone AA, Reed BR, Neale JM. 1987. Changes

in daily event frequency precede episodes of physical symptoms. *J. Hum. Stress* 13:70–74

Surwit RS. 1992. Glycemic responsivity to adrenergic stimulation and genetic predisposition to type II diabetes. In *Perspectives in behavioral medicine: Stress and disease processes,* ed. N Schneiderman, P McCabe, A Baum, pp. 235–48. Hillsdale, NJ: Erlbaum

Taylor SE, Brown JD. 1988. Illusion and well-being: a social psychological perspective on mental health. *Psychol. Bull.* 103:193–210

Tischenkel NJ, Saab PG, Schneiderman N, Nelesen RA, Pasin RD, et al. 1989. Cardiovascular and neurohumoral responses to behavioral challenge as a function of race and sex. *Health Psychol.* 8:503–24

Treiber FA, Baranowski T, Braden DS, Strong WB, Levy M, Knox W. 1991. Social support for exercise: relationship to physical activity in young adults. *Prev. Med.* 20:737–50

US Department of Health and Human Services. 1991. *Health and Behavior Research. NIH Report to Congress.* Washington, DC: USDHHS

US Department of Health and Human Services, Public Health Service. 1989. Advance report of final mortality statistics. *Monthly Vital Stat. Rep.* 40:8

US Department of Health and Human Services, Public Health Service. 1991. *Healthy People 2000: National Health Promotion and Disease Prevention Objectives (Full Report).* Washington, DC: US Govt. Print. Off.

Vartiainen H. 1990. Effects of psychosocial factors, especially work-related stress, on fertility and pregnancy. *Acta. Obstet. Gynecol. Scand.* 69:677–78

Villar J. 1993. Responses to letters to the editor. *N. Engl. J. Med.* 328:888

Villar J, Farnot U, Barros F, Victora C, Langer A, Belizan J. 1992. A randomized trial of psychosocial support during high-risk pregnancies. *N. Engl. J. Med.* 327:1266–71

Vogt T, Mullooly J, Ernst D, Pope C, Hollis J. 1992. Social networks as predictors of ischemic heart disease, cancer, stroke and hypertension: incidence, survival and mortality. *J. Clin. Epidemiol.* 45:659–66

Watson D, Pennebaker JW. 1989. Health complaints, stress, and distress: exploring the central role of negative affectivity. *Psychol. Rev.* 96:234–54

Wayne SJ, Rhyne RL, Garry PJ, Goodwin JS. 1990. Cell-mediated immunity as a predictor of morbidity and mortality in subjects over 60. *J. Gerontol.* 45:M45–M48

Weiner H. 1991. Stressful experience and cardiorespiratory disorders. *Circulation* 83(Suppl. II):2–8

Weinstein ND. 1993. Testing four competing theories of health-protective behavior. *Health Psychol.* 12:324–33

Williams JK, Vita HA, Manuck SB, Selwyn AP, Kaplan JR. 1991. Psychosocial factors impair vascular responses of coronary arteries. *Circulation* 84:2146–53

Williamson HA, LeFevre M, Hector M. 1989. Association between life stress and serious perinatal complications. *J. Fam. Pract.* 5:489–96

Zakowski SB, McAllister CG, Deal M, Baum A. 1992. Stress, reactivity, and immune function in healthy men. *Health Psychol.* 11:223–32

Zimmerman RS, Conner C. 1989. Health promotion in context: the effects of significant others on health behavior change. *Health Educ. Q.* 16:57–74

Zonderman AB, Costa PT, McCrae RR. 1989. Depression as a risk for cancer morbidity and mortality in a nationally representative sample. *J. Am. Med. Assoc.* 262:1191–1215

Zotti AM, Bettinardi O, Soffiantino F, Tavazzi L, Steptoe A. 1991. Psychophysiological stress testing in post-infarction patients: psychological correlates of cardiovascular arousal and abnormal cardiac responses. *Circulation* 83(Suppl.II):25–35

Annu. Rev. Psychol. 1994. 45:261–96

PERSONNEL SELECTION AND PLACEMENT

Frank J. Landy[1] *and Laura J. Shankster*

The Center for Applied Behavioral Sciences, The Pennsylvania State University, University Park, Pennsylvania 16802

Stacey S. Kohler

St. Paul Fire and Marine Insurance Company, St. Paul, Minnesota 55102-1396

KEY WORDS: personnel, selection, performance, psychometrics, assessment

---

CONTENTS

[1] Please contact Frank Landy for a more complete bibliography, including articles that could not be cited here because of chapter length restrictions.

0066-4308/94/0201-0261$05.00

INTRODUCTION

As others have pointed out (e.g. Guion & Gibson 1988), personnel selection is one element of a larger family of decisions. Any single personnel decision is based on an inference drawn from some body of information. In this review, we are less interested in the technology by which these decisions are made than in the logic and theory supporting the decision process. This logic and theory is represented in the basic and applied research literature. For the most part, we consider literature that appeared in 1991 and 1992, although we also include some material from 1993 and some published before 1991 if it is relevant and has not been cited in earlier reviews.

HISTORICAL TREATMENTS

As one might expect following psychology's centennial year, historical treatments of a wide variety of topics have appeared, including personnel selection. Landy (1992a) has provided a biography of Hugo Munsterberg that lays out the philosophical and theoretical roots of the early testing movement. In a subsequent publication (Landy 1993), he covers the testing movement during World War I and interactions among the leaders in industrial testing at that time. Katzell & Austin (1992) present a review of the growth of industrial psychology. Austin & Villanova (1992) published an article on criterion issues that is part history, part theory, and part methodology. Harrell (1992) offers a personal account of the development of the Army General Classification Test and ancillary placement procedures during World War II. Dunnette (1992) traces the evolution of the concept of construct validity. Primoff et al (1992) trace the development of the job element method of job analysis from its World War I days. Finally, *The Industrial and Organizational Psychologist* has presented a number of articles detailing the growth and development of industrial psychology in individual academic training programs (Austin 1992,

Guion 1992, Jeanneret 1991, Katzell 1991, 1992, Landy 1991, 1992, Lawshe & Weiss 1991, Pitariu 1992, Russell 1992, Thompson 1991).

SELECTION AND THE LAW

Since the passage of the Civil Rights Act of 1964, personnel selection has been inextricably bound to laws and court cases. The laws tend to be political instruments and have the effect of sharpening and broadening sociopolitical debates. The best example of such a debate was the controversy surrounding attempts to pass the 1990 and 1991 Civil Rights Acts. In spite of their alleged centrality, theory and practice tend to play a minor role in these debates. In court cases involving tests and testing, on the other hand, research and practice are the foundation for discussion. Finally, issues surrounding practice result because testing occurs in a litigious environment. We treat each of these areas—laws, court cases or litigation, and practice—in reverse order.

Practice

Partly because of the passage of laws such as the Civil Rights Act of 1991 and the Americans with Disabilities Act (1990) (ADA) and partly because of heightened sensitivity, considerable attention has been paid to pre-employment inquiries. Ash (1991) presents a review of relevant regulations governing pre-employment inquiries on a state-by-state basis as well as a consideration of the relative vulnerability to challenge of various common practices. Although the laws are most often framed to protect the applicant, pre-employment inquiries may also serve to protect the public, consumer, or coworker from negligence. Ryan & Lasek (1991) consider defamation and negligence in a review that concentrates on the role of references in pre-employment evaluation of candidates. Sharf (1993) presents a detailed analysis of bio-data instruments from the legal perspective (i.e. the Civil Rights Act of 1991, ADA). Jones and colleagues (Jones et al 1990, Jones 1991a, Arnold & Jones 1992) propose that perceived invasiveness of integrity tests is associated with the personal nature of the questions. For those involved in public sector assessment, an International Personnel Management Association Assessment Council monograph highlights well the advances and issues that involve policy, practice, and relevant legislation (Sproule 1990).

Laws

There have been several significant developments in the law in the past few years. Most notable is the passage of the Americans with Disabilities Act and the Civil Rights Act of 1991. In addition, it is likely that the Age Discrimination in Employment Act will be modified as a result of recent research on aging and work performance (Landy et al 1992).

The ADA has aroused substantial interest in the human resource community. There is a lot of confusion about which disabilities are covered, how an essential task is defined, and what constitutes a medical test. In many instances, a test for psychopathology would be considered a medical test, as would a test of cardiac capacity if cardiovascular strength were not directly related to job performance. ADA stipulates that if a test is considered medical, it may not be administered prior to an offer of employement. As with the Civil Rights Act, working definitions will come from a combination of administrative guidelines and clarification as well as relevant case law. Nevertheless, at a much deeper level, research and theory are likely to be stimulated by the law. For example, Biersdorff & Radke (1991) address provisions of Canadian law similar to those of the ADA that relate to intelligence. They question whether intelligence is essential for many jobs. According to ADA requirements, if an attribute is not required for performing an essential task, then an applicant may request an accommodation or modification of either the testing process or the job if he or she claims a covered disability that is associated with that nonessential attribute. In practice, this might mean that unless it is demonstrated that intelligence is required for accomplishing an essential task, no test that measures intelligence (or any facet of intelligence) could be administered before offering employment to any applicant claiming an impairment that is associated with intellectual functioning.

The Civil Rights Act of 1991 was hotly debated because of the fear that it would inevitably lead to quotas in hiring as a way to avoid litigation. A 1990 version of the bill was vetoed by President Bush and the veto was upheld in Congress. The bill was intended to redress Supreme Court decisions (e.g. Watson, Wards Cove, Hopkins) that appeared to increase the burden on plaintiffs in discrimination cases. Although the new Civil Rights Act diminishes the importance of these earlier decisions, many of the issues raised by these cases remain relevant to personnel practitioners and researchers. Barrett (1990) identifies several of these issues. Two articles (Schmidt 1993, Silva & Jacobs 1993) question the concept of affirmative action in the larger arena of utility and international competitiveness and conclude that the issue is one of values, not technology.

With one exception, it is still too soon to tell if the Civil Rights Act of 1991 will substantially change theory, research, or practice in personnel selection. The new act outlaws race norming of test scores, which means that the development and use of dual hiring or promotion lists will no longer be permitted. Because this was a popular method for remedying past discrimination, it will place a greater burden on both the courts and employers to identify new ways of reducing adverse impact.

The Age Discrimination in Employment Act (ADEA), originally passed in 1967, was amended in 1986 to outlaw forced retirement based on age with the exception of tenured college faculty and public safety employees. Congress mandated that the Department of Labor and the Equal Employment Opportunity Commission (EEOC) complete studies to determine the propriety of those exemptions. Studies completed by the National Research Council (Hammond & Morgan 1991) and Landy et al (1992) both conclude that age is a poor predictor of performance and that the exemptions should be eliminated. The Landy et al study includes a review of age and abilities (both cognitive and physical) and should be useful to industrial gerontology researchers. Congress must decide whether to continue the exemptions or make them permanent by January 1, 1994. If they do nothing, the exemptions will be eliminated.

Litigation

Two reviews of court cases have appeared in the past several years. Beck-Dudley & McEvoy (1991) review 46 cases in which performance evaluation was an issue in hiring or promotion. They conclude that, in many instances, the courts have ignored what personnel psychologists would consider to be critical technical issues and that the courts have provided little direction to employers or employees on what might constitute fair evaluation. From the perspective of personnel research, this is somewhat disappointing but should not diminish our confidence in what we already know. Feild et al (1990) review court cases specifically related to alleged hiring or promotion discrimination in police and fire departments. This review was conducted during a period when the Wards Cove decision represented prevailing case law. Even though the Civil Rights Act of 1991 places a substantial burden of proof back on the shoulders of the defendant/employer, the issues raised by Wards Cove with respect to adverse impact and job relatedness will remain central to the debate about fair testing practices.

Recent decisions in the Ninth Circuit Court have addressed the use of score bands for hiring. Cascio et al (1991) had described a method using standard error to establish confidence intervals about test scores. This technique was challenged and upheld by the Circuit Court of Appeals [979 F.2d 721 (9th Circuit 1992)]. Because the Civil Rights Act of 1991 specifically prohibits race-based scoring, this technique may be attractive to those employers interested in reducing adverse impact through modified appointment procedures.

Although this review does not cover sexual harassment, we note that Terpstra & Baker (1992) provide a review of nine harassment court cases. Finally, in a much publicized state case that addressed the invasiveness of a clinical screening device, the Society for Industrial and Organizational Psychology (SIOP) assisted the American Psychological Association (APA) in developing an Amicus brief that illuminated the scientific issues associated with such practices (paper in preparation).

JOB ANALYSIS

First, it should be noted that Ernest McCormick, who died in 1990, did unique and invaluable work on the theory and practice of job and task analysis and on the development of the PAQ, a widely used standardized instrument for job analysis. Naylor (1991) provides a detailed description of McCormick's accomplishments. Recent literature on job analysis falls into two distinct categories: job analytic methodology and purposes or uses for job analysis information.

Methodology

The use of incumbents and supervisors as Subject Matter Experts (SMEs) in job analysis is common. There has been considerable interest in the characteristics of these SMEs. The research question is whether these attributes affect the judgments SMEs make about jobs. Veres et al (1991) found race to have an impact. In contrast, Landy & Vasey (1991) observed no effect for race but did find experience effects on task ratings. Vance et al (1992) also observed an experience effect on ability ratings. Mathieu et al (1993) found differences between incumbents and supervisors with respect to the task clusters derived from task ratings. Forbinger et al (1992, paper in preparation) considered experience from a different perspective. They detected differences between novice and experienced job analysts as the analysts applied the PAQ (McCormick et al 1989). In addition, regardless of expert status, Forbinger et al found that the meaningfulness and significance of the task statements to the analysts is a salient characteristic. The only inference that seems reasonable at this point is that SME characteristics cannot be ruled out of the job analysis equation.

Fleishman (1991) has continued his work on the development of a comprehensive taxonomy of human abilities implicated in job and task performance. He has published the *Manual for the Ability Requirements Scales* (*MARS*), which describes his well-known abilities taxonomy and provides scales for the use of that taxonomy in job analysis. A text (Fleishman & Reilly 1991) accompanies the manual. Fleishman & Mumford (1991) address the construct validity of the taxonomy. Fleishman's work remains the most comprehensive and applicable in the area of ability analysis.

Purposes

Several researchers have used job analysis procedures to create broad-based structural statements about jobs. Hogan (1991a) has considered physical tasks and proposes a three parameter structure for physical abilities—strength, endurance, and movement quality. Schippmann et al (1991) present an elaborate job analysis of management work by examining prior analyses. They propose

21 task dimensions and 22 skill dimensions. Inwald (1992) has published the *Hilson Job Analysis Questionnaire*, which purports to identify the important personality characteristics required for success in particular jobs. Although the underlying database is still being established, this initiative should be useful. As we discuss later, personality variables have assumed new importance in personnel research and most current job analytic procedures concentrate heavily on skills and abilities and only peripherally on the "other" characteristics that might be critical for success.

Two studies address the use of job analytic procedures for jobs that do not currently exist. Arvey et al (1992c) demonstrate how the task/ability correlation matrix derived from current jobs can be used to forecast the ability demands of future jobs. Manning & Broach (1992) illustrate the use of expert teams to anticipate the changed ability demands on air traffic controllers when an automated procedure is introduced to the control system.

Robinson (1992) has collaborated with PAQ Services in adapting the PAQ database to the problem of worker rehabilitation. He has developed the Worker Rehabilitation Questionnaire, a counselor/therapist assessment of an individual's current capacities, which is used to identify jobs that a client might be able to perform. It seems clear that this technology will be valuable for ADA compliance in a similar manner by identifying ways in which a job might be modified to accommodate a covered disability.

Perhaps the most novel use of job analysis information is in Borman et al's (1992) work. Rather than treating within-job interrater disagreement as measurement error, they consider it a manifestation of time allocation strategies on the part of the respondents (stock brokers) and use an individual's "time spent" ratings to successfully predict sales performance. This suggests similar strategies for importance ratings, frequency ratings, when learned ratings, etc. Simply thinking of these ratings as attributes of individual raters transforms the ratings from dependent to independent variables and opens multiple avenues for investigation.

PREDICTORS

Cognitive

The emergence of industrial/organizational (I/O) psychology is inextricably bound with mental testing. Jastrow & Munsterberg displayed mental tests in 1893 (Landy 1992a). In the early part of the twentieth century, Cattell, Scott, Bingham, Viteles, and other prominent applied and industrial psychologists used tests of cognitive abilities to lay the foundation for the current practice of personnel research (Landy 1993). It is with some embarrassment, then, that we must recognize that little progress is apparent in the conception and understanding of cognitive abilities by I/O psychologists after more than 100 years of mental testing. At best, we are reproducing the debates that Cattell and Binet, or Spearman and Thorndike had about the unitary nature of intelligence.

Ackerman and colleagues have been arguing for the relevance of individual abilities for some time. Ackerman's work represents the modern version of a multiple factor theory of intelligence. The last three *Annual Review* chapters on personnel selection have essentially overlooked work on cognitive abilities. Schmidt et al (1992) make passing reference to cognitive research without offering much description. Schmitt & Robertson (1990) don't mention legitimate cognitive studies at all, nor do Guion & Gibson (1988). This is a symptom of a larger problem. I/O psychology is mired in a quasi-scientific argument about how much variance in performance can be attributed to general intelligence (commonly referred to as psychometric *g*). As a result, I/O psychologists are doing little work in the development and validation of measures of cognitive ability. We are in a state of arrested professional and scientific development that dates to the increased emphasis on cognitive tests following World War II (Katzell & Austin 1992). There seems to be ample value in tests of general mental ability and tests of specific abilities (Carroll 1992, Humphreys 1992, Jensen 1992). There is also growing concern that the seeming robustness of measures of psychometric *g* derives from the homogeneity of criterion tasks considered (Sternberg 1993, Sternberg et al 1993).

Having cursed the darkness, let us now light a candle. Ackerman & Kanfer (Ackerman 1987, 1990, 1992, Ackerman & Kanfer 1993, Kanfer & Ackerman 1989) have published field and experimental data demonstrating the relevance of a multi-ability framework for information processing tasks. Their approach is compatible with, though somewhat less ambitious than, Sternberg's (1985) componential theory of intelligence. Lohman (1993) has applied the more orthodox cognitive science paradigm to the skilled performance problem and has come to the same conclusion with respect to the value of a multi-ability view of the world.

The *g* proponents (e.g. Ree & Caretta 1992) argue that the best way to classify large numbers of applicants/candidates in terms of probable success (in training and on-the-job) is with a measure of general intelligence. It is essentially a utility argument. In spite of the pre-emptive tone of much of the pro-*g* literature, much more needs to be known about these issues before the debate is abandoned. Other research also suggests a continued interest in ability measurement beyond an exclusive psychometric *g* approach. Kanfer & Ackerman (1989) and Murphy (1993) have both suggested an interaction between ability and motivation. Matthews et al (1992) have demonstrated interactions between personality variables and ability levels on a mail-coding task. There is good reason to believe that the relevant question is not whether psychometric g or a measure of a specific ability is a better predictor of job success, but rather what are the limiting conditions (e.g. criteria, work conditions, job titles) to the use of either approach. One such limiting condition is the purpose of testing. Zeidner & Johnson (1991a,b, 1993) have argued that simple predictive efficiency is only one facet of utility and that for purposes of differential placement it is best to consider various ability composites in making personnel assignments. Computer simulations (Scholarios 1992) and reanalyses of existing Armed Services Vocational Aptitude Battery (ASVAB) data sets (Alley & Teachout 1992) were used as support for the composite argument. The reanalyses provided evidence that using a differential placement model would result in performance gains of one third of a standard deviation above current assignment procedures.

Sternberg and colleagues (e.g. Sternberg & Wagner 1992, 1993) have attempted to broaden the debate about general intelligence. Based on his triarchic theory of intelligence, Sternberg (1985) suggests that practical intelligence and tacit knowledge play a role in job success. Schmidt & Hunter (1993) argue that tacit knowledge is nothing more than job knowledge and that the construct is old wine in a new bottle. Both agree that regardless of the name of the construct, job knowledge predicts performance variance unaccounted for by traditional measures of intellectual ability, whether those measures are of the big G or little s variety. The reader should be aware of a theme that will recur throughout this chapter: We are unlikely to get the full picture of job performance if we restrict ourselves to a consideration of traditional measures of ability. Sternberg's work is seldom cited by I/O psychologists, but it should be incorporated into our theory and research if our goal is to improve the understanding of job performance. It is also less important to label the construct as ability or knowledge than it is to recognize that we need to know more about the measurement and application of knowledge. Regardless of its pedigree, the construct implies cognitive activity. The construct of tacit knowledge is particularly relevant to job domains that are not well-structured, mechanistic, or routine, such as management positions. Sternberg has developed measures of practical intelligence and tacit knowledge (Wagner & Sternberg 1987) that warrant inclusion in future studies of managerial performance.

The strong feeling we get from reviewing "progress" in the development of cognitive ability predictors is that the single-factor advocates would like to close off further investigation and declare a technical knockout. This would be a mistake. The availability of models such as those presented by Ackerman (1986), Lohman (1993), and Sternberg (1985), as well as ability taxonomies and data collection protocols such as those presented by Fleishman (1991, Fleishman & Reilly 1991) should encourage additional research in this area.

Physical Abilities

Research on predictors of performance on physically demanding tasks has appeared infrequently in the I/O literature in the past decade. The last several years, however, have yielded a number of high quality articles. Arvey and colleagues have presented a series of articles using public safety positions (police officers and fire fighters) as illustrations of test development and validation (Arvey 1992, Arvey et al 1992a,b). Not surprisingly, they found that strength and endurance were implicated in successful public safety performance and that females generally scored lower on both test performance and job performance with respect to physical attributes. Hogan (1991b) has presented an excellent overview of the theory and practice of measurement of physical abilities in the *Handbook of Industrial and Organizational Psychology* (Dunnette & Hough 1991). She also has reanalyzed a number of data sets to identify underlying dimensions of performance in physically demanding tasks and jobs (Hogan 1991a). Based on those analyses, she has proposed a three parameter model including strength, endurance, and movement quality (defined by flexibility, balance, and coordination requirements). These results agree quite well with the exercise physiology literature (McCardle et al 1991) and with Fleishman's taxonomy of physical abilities (Fleishman & Reilly 1991). Blakley et al (1992) demonstrate the value of isometric strength tests for predicting performance in a wide variety of physically demanding professions. Finally, Sothmann et al (1990) use a combination of laboratory and field tests to estimate the minimal oxygen consumption demands of firefighting tasks. In addition, Landy et al (1992) have completed a review of the physical demands of public safety positions as well as a consideration of the effect of aging on the decline of physical abilities.

Personal Attributes

Increasing attention is being paid to variables other than cognitive and physical abilities in predicting job success. In part, this is the result of continued demonstrations that the addition of personality test scores, bio-data information, and integrity test scores to the more traditional paper and pencil cognitive test scores can improve observed validities. Another attractive aspect of many of these strategies is that they have little or no adverse impact against female or minority job applicants.

PERSONALITY Goldberg has observed a trend in the use of personality tests for selection: "Once upon a time, we had no personalities. Fortunately, times change..." (1993, p. 1). In 1965, Guion & Gottier stopped applied personality testing in its tracks by reviewing the relevant research literature and concluding that there was little predictive value in personality test scores. Coupled with similar comments in Guion's landmark testing book (1965) and the pressures that social critics were putting on the testers (Gross 1962), personality testing appeared to be losing favor. This all changed with the introduction of the new and more sophisticated meta-analytic techniques. Schmitt et al (1984) completed a comprehensive review and meta-analysis of different classes of predictors and criteria and demonstrated that nontrivial predictions about performance could be made from personality test scores. Structure was added by the discovery (or at least articulation) of the "Big Five" personality factors—neuroticism, extroversion, openness to experience, agreeableness, and conscientiousness (Digman 1990). As Goldberg implies, it is now acceptable to examine the role of personality factors in personnel selection.

Considerable attention has been paid to the "Big Five" factors. Barrick & Mount (1991) conducted a meta-analysis of 117 criterion-related validity studies in which personality variables were predictors. The variables were coded in terms of the Big Five structure. Barrick & Mount concluded that the conscientiousness dimension significantly predicted all job performance criteria for all occupational groups represented in the data analyzed. Further, they found significant predictive value for the other four factors for particular combinations of job title and criterion. Tett et al (1991) also conducted a meta-analysis that affirmed the value of the Big Five structure but identified agreeableness as the facet with the greatest predictive potential. Tett et al accounted for the discrepancy by citing parameters (e.g. exploratory vs confirmatory research design) that were used in their analysis but not in the Barrick & Mount analysis. Ones, Mount, Barrick, and Hunter (paper in preparation) have presented a critique of the Tett et al methodology, analysis, and conceptual structure. Nevertheless, all agree that there is value to pursuing the Big Five structure in predicting job performance. Day & Bedeian (1993) have suggested that the critical issue is the extent to which a personality profile for an individual is consistent with the profiles of others in a particular organization. Thus, the argument is not whether the individual is more or less agreeable than some large normative population collapsed across many organizations and settings, but whether that individual is more or less agreeable than the people who work in the same organization and work group as the respondent. Day & Bedeian have cited this personality dissimilarity mechanism to account for the discrepancies between the Barrick & Mount (1991) and Tett et al (1991) conclusions.

There does seem to be some value in agreeing on a taxonomy for purposes of research (if not application). A lot of progress was made in the study of job satisfaction when the research community decided to adopt the Job Description Index (JDI) as the gold standard (Smith et al 1969). The problem is deciding what it means to accept the Big Five structure. Day & Bedeian have operationalized the structure through the Adjective Check List (Gough & Heilbrun 1965). Cortina et al (1992) define the Big Five through subscales of the Minnesota Multiphasic Personality Inventory and the Inwald Personality Inventory (Inwald et al 1983). Kline & Lapham (1991, 1992) use the 68 items of the Professional Personality Questionnaire (Kline & Lapham 1990) to identify Big Five components. Barrick & Mount (1993) use 137 conceptually- and empirically-derived items assembled into an instrument called the Personality Characteristic Inventory (PCI). Hough (1992) presents an informative conceptual analysis of the similarities and dissimilarities among alternative conceptions of the Big Five and suggests that perhaps as many as nine factors might be necessary if the goal of the research is prediction rather than description. Wiggins & Pincus (1992) present a coherent discussion of the status of the Big Five theory in the personality community.

At some point, it will be necessary to agree on which instruments are and which are not reasonable operationalizations of the Big Five (or Nine) constructs. The good news is that this will inevitably occur. The bad news is that for the next several years, the journals will be clogged with narrow methodological examinations and comparisons of alternative measuring devices. It is too early to draw any solid inferences about which personality facets or how many will predict particular job behaviors, but it is evident that there is promise in the research enterprise.

BIO-DATA Schmidt et al (1992) concluded their review of bio-data predictors with a call for greater attention to the constructs and theory supporting the empirical validities. In the last two years, their call has been answered. Hough & Paullin (1993) reviewed methods of scale development and defined three distinct developmental techniques: 1. external (traditional empirical keying), 2. inductive (factor, principal components, or cluster analysis of item responses), and 3. deductive (theory or logic based). The deductive method is often thought to be too transparent, thus encouraging socially desirable responses. Hough & Paullin demonstrated that there were minor differences between subtle and obvious items in fakability and they argued that social desirability should be controlled with instructions and lie scales, not through the use of subtle items.

There are two levels at which theory enters into the development of bio-data. The keying of items (as discussed by Hough & Paullin) is one level. But at a deeper level, the question is "Why use bio-data at all?" Mumford et al (1992) provide such a framework (called the ecology model) and illustrate its application. Mael (1991) intends to address a quite different question but ends up providing useful parametric structure to the bio-data discussion. Mael's manifest question is "What qualifies as a bio-data item?". In the process of concluding that to be classified as bio-data, an item must have an historical content, Mael identifies ten specific parameters on which bio-data items might be considered (e.g. verifiable vs nonverifiable, job relevant vs not job relevant). This will be a useful taxonomic aid in future research and discussion.

INTEGRITY TESTS Like personality tests, it seems as if integrity tests are becoming more acceptable in both personnel research and practice. The APA report on integrity testing (Goldberg et al 1991) was favorable. More recently, a meta-analysis by Ones et al (1993) was quite supportive of this type of testing. Ones et al examined 665 validity coefficients from over 180 studies utilizing 25 different measures of integrity to predict a wide range of criterion variables. They estimated the mean predictive validity coefficient for predicting supervisory ratings to be .41. Their analyses demonstrate that a broad criterion of organizationally disruptive behaviors (e.g. absenteeism, tardiness, violence, substance abuse) is better predicted than a narrow criterion of theft. While moderators have some impact on estimated mean validities, the general conclusion drawn is that the validity of integrity tests is generalizable across situations. Further, this holds for both overt and personality-based integrity tests. This clear endorsement of integrity testing will spur increased research and application. In addition to the individual relationship of integrity test scores to performance, Ones et al (1993) demonstrate that there is substantial incremental validity when combined with cognitive ability tests and that there is no adverse impact against minority job applicants. Not only is the utility enhanced by combining integrity test scores and cognitive ability test scores, but the number of minority applicants likely to be hired using the two measures in combination is increased. The authors conclude that most integrity tests are probably measuring the Big Five personality factor of "conscientiousness" (Barrick & Mount 1991).

In a companion meta-analysis, the same authors (Ones, Viswesvaran, & Schmidt, paper in preparation) partition the data set used for the full meta-analysis to consider the predictability of absenteeism from integrity test scores. In this analysis, 28 studies were reviewed. When considering only absenteeism, the distinction between personality-based and overt integrity tests assumes greater importance. Personality-based tests do considerably better (mean validity = .33) than overt tests (mean validity = .09). The authors explain this difference by noting that most overt tests were developed to predict a single criterion—theft. In contrast, most personality-based tests are directed toward the broader construct of counterproductive behaviors. Thus, it makes sense that when an instance of counterproductive behavior is examined (i.e. absenteeism), personality-based tests would exhibit higher validity coefficients. Other noteworthy publications on this topic include a special issue of *Forensic Reports* (Volume 4(2), 1991) and a recently edited book on pre-employment honesty testing (Jones 1991b).

PREDICTORS: PROCESS

In the last section, we considered predictors from the point of view of what they measured. We now consider how these attributes are measured.

Computer Testing

Computers are useful for control of both stimulus and response variables. On the stimulus side, it is relatively simple to create motion, depth, speed, and other characteristics not easily produced in paper and pencil tests. One can also control the rate of information flow, observing changes in subject strategy as additional information is presented. On the response side, it is possible to measure response latencies, to build examinations around response patterns (as with computerized adaptive testing), and to avoid extra procedural steps such as scoring of response sheets.

Several reviews have nicely summarized the state-of-the-art in computerized testing (Burke 1993, Bartram 1993, Drasgow et al 1993, Sands 1992). As one might expect, perceptual motor tasks are well suited to computer presentation. Park & Lee (1992) describe a combination of cognitive and perceptual motor tests that appear valuable in the selection of pilots. Arthur & Williamson (paper in preparation) present a PC-based test of visual attention that is useful in predicting driving accidents. Bennett (1993) illustrates how the computer can be used to present a wide variety of stimulus material such as computer programming problems, algebra problems, and ill-structured verbal problems. Schmitt, Gilliland, Landis, & Devine (paper in preparation) use the computer to present problems of the electronic workplace often faced by secretaries. The ASVAB has undergone its share of computerized research both in terms of automated presentation (Moreno et al 1991, Sands & Moreno 1991) and adaptive testing formats (Sands 1990). Myers & Schemmer (paper in preparation) demonstrate how the medium can be used to hire nuclear power plant operators.

One of the most useful contributions is Mead & Drasgow's meta-analysis (1993) of the comparability between computerized and paper and pencil cognitive ability tests. Their analysis shows that a critical parameter is speededness of the tests. Power tests produce much the same result regardless of how they are administered but speed tests don't. This is important information given the likely increased pressure on testers to administer tests in non-traditional manners as a result of the Americans with Disabilities Act.

The Interview

As has been the case for the past 30 years, a lot of the recent research on the interview is of limited usefulness. Undergraduate and graduate students are asked to imagine what it must be like to make hiring decisions. They are further asked to imagine that they have interviewed a real person (unlike the paper resume or videotape or fellow student asked to act as an applicant). The sheer resilience of the paradigm is startling. What is most disappointing, however, is that even from the worst of studies, something might have been learned had the researchers stopped to ask themselves what parameters warranted generalization. It might not have been possible to generalize to the hiring environment but it might have been legitimate to make inferences about first impressions or resume review by nonexpert reviewers or some similar parameter. If this type of research is to continue, editors must demand to know what parameters were legitimately sampled and what the target population will be. At the very least, such action will be likely to liberate pages of the applied journals.

There has been some useful research on the interview in the last several years. The two most impressive of these efforts are meta-analyses of the employment interview. McDaniel, Whetzel, Schmidt, and Maurer (paper in preparation) completed a review of over 100 studies with a total *N* exceeding 17,000. They examined several parameters including the extent to which the interview was structured, the criterion measure, the rationale for gathering criterion measures, and the content of the interview. The findings were encouraging and instructive. The major conclusion drawn was that the interview supports valid inferences across a wide range of situations and criteria. What is more impressive, however, is the elaboration of circumstances that endow the interview with its greatest predictive power. The "ideal" interview for predicting job success would be situational and structured. If the criteria were gathered for research purposes and were defined by job performance as opposed to training performance, the validities (corrected for range restriction) would fall in the range of .40–.50. The authors point out factors that might result in either over- or underestimates of the population values but these factors seem to balance each other. The authors also point out that the lack of detail in results of interview studies led them to feel less confident about the meta-analytic results than they would have been had the predictors been cognitive test scores. They call for a taxonomy of interview structure and content. Huffcutt & Woehr (1992) have provided a five parameter model that is a move in the right direction. The parameters include interview questions, response evaluation, methods of combination, interviewers, and the interview environment. The point is not so much that an analysis of these parameters should be done but that when reporting the results of an interview study, at least these parameters should be described so that a more complete and compelling meta-analysis can be conducted in the future. McDaniel et al (paper in preparation) suggest additional parameters. Huffcutt & Woehr (1992) completed a second meta-analysis. They include 112 validity coefficients and, like McDaniel, Whetzel, Schmidt, and Maurer (paper in preparation), conclude that the validity coefficients are quite impressive when the interview is structured. They report a mean value of .57 (corrected for criterion unreliability, range restriction, and sampling error). This value compares favorably with the values of other commonly used predictors.

Searcy et al (1993) completed a third meta-analysis, in which they were considerably more restrictive in their inclusion rules and reviewed a total of 23 studies. The overall estimate of the population value was .49, a value similar to those found in the other two meta-analyses described above. Searcy et al suggest additional moderator variables for future meta-analyses. The results of these three meta-analyses are in close agreement and suggest that the selection interview may be a good deal more valuable than had been previously suggested (e.g. Hunter & Hunter 1984).

Another factor that emerged from these meta-analyses was the enthusiasm for the situational interview. This enthusiasm seems to be justified by additional recent research. Lin et al (1992) found that the situational interview seemed to be less vulnerable to bias from factors such as race of applicant and/or interviewer. Motowidlo et al (1992) have combined the situational interview with the more traditional structured interview and developed a new strategy called structured behavioral interviewing. Although the reported validities are a good deal lower (averaging about .22) than the population estimates of the meta-analyses described above, the values were not corrected for range restriction or unreliability so they are almost certainly underestimates of the respective population values. More work will need to be done on this format before any reasonable conclusion can be drawn but it looks promising. Finally, Graves & Karren (1992) conducted a policy-capturing study on corporate interviewers evaluating hypothetical candidates. They were able to separate the interviewers into effective and ineffective categories based on managerial evaluations and discovered some interesting differences between the two groups. In general, the effective interviewers were more disciplined and paid closer attention to the job requirements that defined the position in question. In addition, the more effective interviewers concentrated on assessing interpersonal skills and oral communication skills. The most intriguing finding, however, may have been the individual differences among effective interviews. The researchers were able to identify 134 distinct strategies that were used for combining information when the purpose was to evaluate candidates' qualifications. Six different patterns were apparent for making hiring recommendations. It would have been interesting to see if one (or a few) of these patterns were more associated with candidate success than others but the applicants were hypothetical so such an analysis was impossible.

Although this may seem like a basic question to be asking after 50 years of programmatic research on the selection interview, it is still worth asking "exactly what is being measured in the interview?" Are we measuring general intelligence, motivation, personality, individual skills and abilities, knowledge, experience? Does the interview tap process or substance? We are reaching a level of sophistication in modeling such that this question, raised often in the 1950s and 1960s as speculation, can be answered with some confidence. If the validity of the interview, the validity of measures of general intelligence, and measures of Big Five personality constructs all generalize across criteria and across situations, it is reasonable to ask if these predictors share some "core" variance or if they all make unique contributions. In addition, we need to consider the measures of knowledge and/or experience that seem to be undisputed contributors to performance. How do all of these components go together in predicting and understanding work behavior? As we point out in our discussion of criteria, researchers are beginning to address these fundamental questions.

Assessment Centers

Assessment centers remain an enigma. They seem to "work" but why? Howard (1992) identifies and refutes six of seven arguments against the continued use of assessment centers, particularly for executive selection. The argument that she has the most trouble countering is that assessment centers have failed to demonstrate construct validity with remarkable regularity. To be specific, the problem has been that there is usually an "exercise" factor that overwhelms (or at least overshadows) the dimensional effect. Assessor ratings seem to be specific to the exercises and do not generalize from exercise to exercise. This is at odds with the underlying notion of assessment centers (i.e. that they help to illuminate stable traits, skills, and abilities of candidates). In each of the last three *Annual Review* chapters on personnel selection, the caution has been made that until, and unless, construct evidence is forthcoming, assessment centers will remain the practitioner's delight and the theoretician/psychometrist's nightmare. Unfortunately, things have not changed much in the past two years even though researchers have been active in looking for ways to improve on the convergent validity of assessment centers. Joyce et al (1992) contrasted traditional dimensional ratings with ratings of managerial function in the hope that the latter would help to diminish the "exercise" factor. They failed. Construct validity was poor for both approaches. Fleenor (1992) examined construct validity for developmental (rather than selection) assessment centers and failed to find any evidence for construct validity of the ratings. Harris et al (1993) investigated two different methods of assigning assessment ratings. The within-exercise scoring scheme required assessors to provide ratings for each candidate on all dimensions at the conclusion of each exercise. In contrast, the within-dimension scoring method required assessors to withhold ratings until the candidate had completed all exercises and then to assign the dimensional ratings for the aggregated exercises, dimension by dimension. This was a strategy that Wherry (Landy & Farr 1983) had toyed with 50 years ago as a way of reducing halo in performance rating scales. In the present study, construct validity evidence was weak for both strategies. The within-dimension strategy didn't work for Wherry either!

Schneider & Schmitt (1992) made the best of a bad situation and tried to determine what it is about exercises that overwhelms the dimensional ratings. They suggested two possibilities—exercise form and exercise content—and studied two levels of form (leaderless group exercise and role play) and content (competitive vs cooperative). They discovered that the active ingredient in the exercise main effect was form. It accounted for 16% of the method variance and content accounted for no variance. Based on their results, Schneider & Schmitt suggest that in order to understand what happens in the assessment process, considerably more attention must be paid to various aspects of assessment centers including parameters such as types of problems, abilities required, number and kind of other participants, etc. We need a taxonomy or a roadmap to plan a serious course of research, because we are no closer to understanding the dynamics of the assessment process than we were ten years ago.

Applicant Reactions

The history of personnel selection has been somewhat pre-Copernican. Concerns have been expressed about the validity, utility, and defensibility of tests. The center of the universe has been the needs and goals of the user. In the last several years, an alternative reality has emerged—the needs and goals of the test-taker. Granted, much of this work is based on the premise that organizations suffer when individuals react negatively to selection or other personnel procedures, but it is a start. At least we are offered a glimpse into another corner of the solar system.

Schuler et al (1993) provide the most extensive treatment of the topic to date in a book that covers virtually all aspects of the interaction between applicant and selection process. In addition, they also consider the reactions of incumbents to various aspects of personnel administration as well as a template for future research. Rynes & Connerley (1992) surveyed 390 applicants about their reactions to various selection devices and concluded that the most positively regarded instruments and procedures were those high on face validity. As one might expect, personality inventories, integrity tests, and drug testing were seen less positively. Reactions seemed to be based on the applicant's confidence in the capacity of the employer to understand and correctly interpret the information they were receiving about the applicant. Rynes (1993) presents a review and theoretical rationale for the study of applicant reactions. As the work of Rynes suggests, job relatedness perceptions are likely to be related to general affective reactions of applicants. Arvey & Sackett (1993) provide a template for considering the possible parameters of selection system fairness from the perspective of various stakeholders, including the applicant.

There have been several studies of applicant reactions to particular devices and approaches. Reactions of applicants to interviews (Liden, Parsons, and Martin, paper in preparation; Powell 1991) and assessment centers (Robertson et al 1991) seem to be affected by both process and substance. Fletcher (1991) found that there was a complex reaction to assessment centers. For example, in the period immediately following participation in the center, there seemed to be a surge of job involvement and motivation, followed later by a sharp drop off in enthusiasm. In addition, the reactions were different for those who had done well versus those who had done poorly. Kluger & Rothstein (1993) report that bio-data instruments were viewed more positively by applicants than cognitive ability tests. The subjects in this study were college students and although the design was a creative one that did induce some realism to the experiment, considerably more field work is required, particularly because this finding is at odds with the results of Smither & Pearlman (1991) reported above. Konovsky & Cropanzano (1991) consider employees' reactions to drug testing and report that a critical variable is the perception of procedural justice by the employee. Practically, this means that things like advanced notice and rights to appeal will influence the reactions of employees to drug tests. Surprisingly, outcome justice (what happens as a result of the test) has much less impact on employee reactions. Jones (1991a,b) presents evidence that employees react more favorably to integrity test items that appear more job related than the more generic clinical assessment devices. But we are considering reactions, not behaviors. We have no idea of the extent to which good or bad recruits abandoned further discussions with the organization as a result of certain devices or practices.

Interest in applicant reactions to selection procedures is likely to continue growing, particularly in light of the substantial treatment provided by the Schuler, Farr & Smith book. It is much too early to speculate about "the" reactions of applicants to particular procedures or devices, but such reactions do occur, are stable, and influence other aspects of applicant behavior, including test performance. There is ample justification for continued research in this area.

Selection of Group Members

In the movie *Moonstruck,* Olivia Dukakis tells Danny Aiello, "What you don't know about women is a lot." The same might be said about the selection of group members. Although there is increasing recognition of the importance of group effectiveness, little empirical work has been done on actual practices. That's the bad news. The good news is that there is greater recognition of the need for such work and a research and practice agenda has begun. Jackson and colleagues (Bantel & Jackson 1989, Jackson 1991, Jackson et al 1991, Jackson et al 1993) have presented logic and data regarding work group composition and the concept of heterogeneity of group members. The underlying hypothesis is that heterogeneity of group members leads to lower cohesion, loyalty, performance, and satisfaction. Since heterogeneity is defined, at least in part, by demographic characteristics, this hypothesis is particularly salient given the inevitability of diversification in the workforce (Jackson 1991, Jackson et al 1993). But as has often been recognized, demographic variables are "boxcars" that simply carry other important differences in personality or values (Day & Bedeian 1993). Prieto (1993) proposes that team selection and composition should be guided by the principle of technostructure and that effective team performance is based on five attributes of group members: ability to gain group acceptance, ability to increase group solidarity, awareness of group consciousness, willingness to share group identification, and ability to manage the impressions of others. Prieto suggests that selection procedures be developed around these attributes using an assessment center format. Finally, Morgan & Lassiter (1992) have reviewed basic literature from social psychology to suggest ways that team selection and training might be done. It is this tone that pervades most of the group selection literature. Group selection is an area that begs for research, and although it will tax the creative talent of a technology and history steeped in the glorification of individual differences, the effort will be suitably rewarded. It seems clear that the most substantial obstacle to improved performance and satisfaction of a workforce is an understanding of small group phenomena as they are manifested in concrete ways in the workplace.

CRITERION ISSUES

The Performance Construct

The most comprehensive and far reaching contributions to the criterion literature in the past several years were made by J. P. Campbell and colleagues. Campbell et al (1993) suggest a theory of performance that depends on three parameters—declarative knowledge, procedural knowledge and skill, and motivation. They further suggest that there may be eight specific performance components or factors that derive from the three building blocks. Examples of these components are job specific task proficiency (e.g. directing air traffic), maintaining personal discipline (e.g. minimal absenteeism), and management/supervision (e.g. helping to overcome crises). In a later paper, Campbell (1993) elaborates on eight functional models of performance that vary from the "classic" (performance is represented by a general factor that covers distinct highly intercorrelated facets) to the "critical deficiency" model (performance is defined by avoiding catastrophic failure). This work derives from the Project A research, a subject covered in earlier Annual Reviews. It provides a much needed construct perspective for performance research. On a somewhat less ambitious scale, Lance et al (1992b) provide data suggesting that the criterion construct space includes multiple performance factors as well as multiple methods for measuring those factors. They further suggest that these method factors not be considered as bias but as performance perspectives. For example, rather than considering a work sample factor as methodological, one might interpret work samples as providing opportunities for maximum rather than typical performance. This might be a fruitful avenue for assessment center researchers to pursue since they seem to be plagued with an "exercise" factor problem.

A final substantive expansion of the issue of the criterion is Borman & Motowidlo's (1993) proposal to add the notion of contextual performance to our consideration of job performance. Contextual performance includes the "extras" that most employers look for in the outstanding employee. These extras are not directly involved in task performance but are similar to constructs such as "citizenship" (Organ 1988) and "prosocial organizational behavior" (Brief & Motowidlo 1986). Examples of contextual performance dimensions include extra effort, volunteering for tasks, helping and cooperating with others, and following rules. Data suggest that as much as 30% of a manager's job may be defined in terms of contextual performance dimensions. In a second study, Motowidlo & Van Scotter (paper in preparation) present additional evidence, in the form of task performance and contextual performance ratings of Air Force mechanics. The results indicate that experience contributes incrementally to an understanding of task performance ratings but ability and personality contribute to contextual performance ratings. The relationship between ability and contextual performance contradicts the earlier Borman & Motowidlo (1993) finding but this may be the result of a substantial restriction of range on the ability dimension. Further, it appears that contextual performance is more likely than task performance to influence personnel decisions (measured as intentions) such as favorable assignments, early promotion, etc. The topic of contextual performance is sure to attract attention in the next several years.

Although the debate surrounding the concept of dynamic criteria was quite active in earlier years (e.g. Ackerman 1989, Austin et al 1989, Barrett et al 1985, Hulin et al 1990), the argument is presently in remission with an occasional flare-up. Barrett et al (1992) have reanalyzed the Hulin et al (1990) data that led to the conclusion that validities decline over time. Barrett et al dismiss most of the studies that formed the Hulin et al database as being largely irrelevant to the typical industrial context. Unfortunately, this does not address dynamic criteria as much as it does the art of meta-analysis. Cascio (1991) raises an interesting point with respect to dynamic criteria. He speculates that many utility studies may have overestimated gains from the use of particular predictors if validities and standard deviations of performance diminish over time. These are two key parameters in utility estimates and they are generally assumed to be constant over the selected tenure value. Statistically, his point is axiomatic. If these values do diminish, then utility gains must be reduced proportionally over time. But at this stage, these declines remain speculative. In fact, the lifespan development and gerontological literatures suggest that there may actually be increases in performance standard deviations over time, and earlier lifespan work (e.g. Lerner 1985, 1986) and industrial research (Deadrick & Madigan 1990) have found evidence of increases in validity coefficients over time. Thus, Cascio may be right that utility estimates may be systematically biased by assumptions regarding the constancies of the validity and variability parameters, but we must be less confident about the direction of that bias for the time being.

Hofmann and colleagues (Jacobs et al 1990, Hofmann et al 1993, Hofmann et al 1992) have introduced a new direction to the debate. In a series of field studies involving public safety officers, baseball players, and insurance sales representatives, they have found some evidence for emerging patterns of change. They argue that the seeming stability of performance measures over time is the result of aggregating over embedded performance change patterns. For example, they found that after five years, three different patterns of performance appear in baseball players. One group continues to get better, one group stays about the same, and another group gets worse. This plays havoc with the utility estimates but it does suggest a potential solution to the dynamic criterion debate—both sides are right. Some people change and others stay the same. The trick is in predicting who will change and in what direction. This avenue of speculation is still too new to offer an endorsement of the implied model but it does warrant additional research effort.

Ratings

Because supervisory ratings continue to be the most commonly used measure of performance in industrial research, it is not surprising that research on performance ratings remains popular. We must admit, however, to a form of selection bias before presenting salient studies. We have not included studies based on university students asked to consider performance scenarios because, as was true of the interview studies with student subjects, the target population for the results is unclear. It is somewhat puzzling that journal editors are not similarly curious about these target populations.

Ratee and rater gender remain salient independent variables in studies of the rating process, and some consensus seems to be emerging. For the past ten years, the field has been moving inexorably toward the final conclusion that well-developed rating procedures accompanied by training of the raters will produce ratings that are minimally biased by demographic characteristics of raters or ratees. Recent studies have refined the designs that examine such dynamics and confirmed earlier conclusions. Sackett & DuBois (1991) re-examined an earlier assertion by Kraiger & Ford (1985) that there was a small but significant same-race-rater advantage in performance ratings. Sackett & DuBois looked at the Kraiger & Ford design and discovered that most of the effect found was owing to the use of peer ratings and laboratory studies. In field studies using supervisory ratings that were done after 1970, no effect appears. In addition, Sackett & DuBois presented data from two large scale studies—one military and one civilian—that also contradict the Kraiger & Ford proposition. An added strength of Sackett & DuBois' analysis is that they were able to analyze data using a within-subjects design. This means that black ratees were each evaluated by the same black and white raters, as was the case for white ratees. This leaves little opportunity to debate the "true" differences between whites and blacks as a confounding variable in explaining rater behavior. Waldman & Avolio (1991) controlled for ability and length of experience in an examination of black-white rating differences and also concluded that differences were trivial after these controls were in place. In an elaborate test of three different designs for examining race effects in supervisory ratings, Oppler et al (1992) concluded that the effects are minimal but that peer ratings may be more susceptible to race effects than supervisory ratings. Hoffman et al (1991) also contrasted peer ratings with supervisory ratings and found little value in peer evaluations. It would seem that we can stop thinking about peer ratings as performance measures and begin thinking of them as variables to be understood—as phenomena rather than devices. Lefkowitz & Battista (paper in preparation) conducted a field study of race and gender differences in ratings and found little effect, although they did find a substantial effect for the extent to which the supervisor liked the subordinate. Not much light was shed on the dynamics of this effect, however. No one seems to have found direct gender or race effects, at least in large scale field studies. The one exception is a study by Sackett et al (1991). They found that the proportion of women in a work group made a difference in ratings assigned. The fewer the number of women in a group, the lower the ratings. No such effect was found for men or for groups analyzed in terms of racial composition. The effect seems to be specific to women. Unfortunately, no data are presented regarding the gender of the raters so we are left with a phenomenon but not much else. Interestingly, Ferris et al (1991) found a similar group composition dynamic in examining the effect of age on performance evaluations. Older supervisors provided higher ratings to work groups with younger members and younger supervisors provided higher ratings to work groups with older members. Again, little can be inferred from this phenomenon because of a confounded design (non-crossed raters) and limited sample (all female hospital employees). Nevertheless, the results of both the Sackett et al and Ferris et al studies are intriguing enough to suggest further study. With the increasing diversity of the workforce by virtue of legislation (ADEA, ADA, and the Civil Rights Acts of 1964 and 1991) and demographic shifts, it is likely that group composition will become a more potent independent variable in examining bias.

There seems to be an emerging consensus (or at least a popular plea) to abandon halo measures as indicators of the psychometric integrity of performance ratings. Murphy et al (1993) suggest that there are many alternative definitions of halo with no one seemingly superior, that it is virtually impossible to separate true halo from illusory halo in field studies, and that available halo measures seem unrelated to rating accuracy and validity. Murphy et al also suggest that halo is a real phenomenon and deserves study, but that it should not be used to evaluate the adequacy of a rating device or process until we know more about what halo is and how it should be measured. To end this section on a theoretical high note, Borman et al (1991) present an expanded model of the substantive (as opposed to process) variables that might be implicated in performance ratings. The model is based on an analysis of Project A data.

It appears that large-scale data sets may be both a curse and blessing. Three of the studies mentioned above (Sackett et al 1991, Sackett & DuBois 1991, Waldman & Avolio 1991) used the same database—the U.S. Employment Service GATB data. Oppler et al (1992) used the Project A database (as did Sackett & DuBois 1991 and Borman et al 1991). These large databases provide an opportunity to test salient structural models; nevertheless, we must be careful that we do not create a science of first term soldiers or GS-12 federal employees that replaces the science of college sophomores. We are clearly learning a lot from these large data sets, but the possibility of sample-specific variance, regardless of sample size, grows with each new study that uses those data. On an optimistic note, however, it is only a matter of time before someone will do a meta-analysis of the area and use GATB–non-GATB or Project A–non-Project A as a parameter. It might be useful to license these two data sets and make them available to all who want them so we might be able to vary experimenters as well. A good description of the breadth and depth of the Project A activities can be found in Campbell & Zook (1991).

VALIDITY

Designs

Construct validity appears to be gaining popularity. During the last several decades, an article would appear every five years reminding researchers and practitioners that construct validity was the beacon to steer toward. The message has been received. In 1990, the Personnel Testing Council of Southern

California devoted its yearly symposium to the topic of construct validity and the papers were published as a group in *Human Performance* (Volume 5, Issues 1 & 2). Among the articles appearing in those issues, Barrett's (1992) provides a broad historical perspective to the issue and gives several excellent examples of construct validity designs in personnel selection; Jeanneret's (1992) integrates job analysis, synthetic validity and construct validation; and Rothstein's (1992) illustrates the relationship between meta-analysis and construct validity. Here we add a cautionary note: It is tempting to substitute the comforting quasi-inductive bells and whistles of meta-analysis for careful theory building based on deductive principles, but that would be a serious mistake for several reasons. First, we have yet to scratch the surface of the pool of potential moderators that might be examined in meta-analytic validity designs. Like neuro-transmitters, more are discovered every day. The challenge is in identifying and incorporating these moderators in the meta-analysis. For example, Russell, Settoon, McGrath, Blanton, Kidwell, et al (paper in preparation) reanalyzed Schmitt et al's (1984) well-known meta-analysis and found that the highest observed validity coefficients were reported by researchers and practitioners who had been employed by private industry for many years. Academic researchers reported lower values. More generally, Lance et al (1992a) demonstrated that much unexplained variance in *r*s can be attributed to unmeasured moderators. Second, meta-analytic and hypothetic-deductive systems must converge for us to have any feeling of confidence about what we think we know. Finally, in many areas of interest, we have yet to accumulate a sufficiently strong database to permit meta-analysis. In any event, we simply point out that the apparently precise estimates derived from meta-analytic strategies should not be confused with "truth." For example, Roth, Campion, and Jones (paper in preparation) demonstrate the effect of the missing data treatment strategy (e.g. listwise vs pairwise deletion) on observed validities. In an important sense, the GIGO (garbage in–garbage out) rule that applies to general multivariate analysis is important to keep in mind with meta-analysis. It is best to think of a meta-analysis as a roadmap to where we want to be. Vance, Brooks & Urban (paper in preparation) present a comprehensive and articulate treatment of the interplay between data and theory in applying construct validation strategies. Arvey (1992) has provided additional examples of how construct validity might be operationalized in personnel selection.

Criterion-related research has virtually disappeared from the scientific journals for a number of reasons (Landy 1992b). This presents a challenge for future meta-analysts and might account for the increasing interest in large-scale databases (e.g. GATB, Project A). Landy (1992b) has edited a special section of two issues of the *Journal of Business Psychology* (Volume 7, Issues 2 & 4), which present a wide range of criterion-related validity studies covering a variety of jobs, predictors, and criteria. It is anticipated that this special section will appear in the journal yearly, permitting public access to traditional empirical validation studies.

META-ANALYSIS AND VALIDITY GENERALIZATION

In a review of the role of meta-analysis and its contribution to the accumulation of scientific knowledge in psychology, Schmidt (1992) presents a rather startling glimpse into the future of the research enterprise. He asserts that "traditional procedures for data analysis and interpretation in individual studies and in research literatures have hampered the development of cumulative knowledge in psychology" (p. 1180) and identifies meta-analysis as a new and more valuable way of viewing the meaning of data. It is clear that Schmidt does not really mean *a* way of viewing the meaning of data, but rather *the* way. As a result, he sees a two-tiered structure for scientific research in psychology. There will be the traditional researchers and the meta-analysts, and the "*meta-analysts will make the scientific discoveries*" (p. 1180, emphasis not added!). This is an extreme point of view and glorifies a technique (meta-analysis) beyond its current limits. As indicated above, we feel that the jury is still out on relevant moderators. Further, we see meta-analysis, if suitably grounded in constructs, as *a* method for theory development and not *the* method. Meta-analysis and traditional empirical research should be complementary and not competitors. In some situations, meta-analysis can illuminate where traditional single study research cannot, but meta-analysis depends heavily on the topics researchers choose to study, the designs employed to study those phenomena, the operations chosen to define variables, etc. In such an environment, it is hard to see how either approach (i.e. traditional or meta-analytic) can be seen as "superior" or pre-eminent.

Validity generalization is a special case of meta-analysis and of particular interest in the area of personnel selection. In spite of the cautionary nature of our remarks above, we agree that validity generalization is an important tool in the bag of the scientist/practitioner. A lot of the discussion and research associated with validity generalization continues to address the viability of the situational specificity hypothesis. Lance et al (1992) reanalyzed 45 previously published meta-analyses using a likelihood-based analytic model proposed by Thomas (1989, 1990) and found some support for the existence of additional moderators, suggesting that we should be more cautious about the generalizability inferences made in earlier studies. James et al (1992) criticize some common validity generalization assumptions, in particular, that variance owing to statistical artifacts (e.g. range restriction on the predictor or unreliability in the criterion) is independent of variance owing to situational moderators. For example, James et al propose that range restriction on the predictor could be affected by recruiting policies or that range restriction on the criterion could be affected by equipment. James et al suggest that the situational specificity hypothesis may be in remission rather than dead. Finally, Ashworth et al (1992) question the role of unrepresented studies in validity generalization analyses. They demonstrate that the Rosenthal file-drawer equation may be ill-suited to validity generalization studies (as opposed to the more general meta-analysis arena). They conclude that in many instances, the hypothesis of a population correlation coefficient of .00 could not be rejected if a different method were used for estimating the effects of unrepresented studies. More specifically, Ashworth et al show that the appearance of only one or two studies with observed validity coefficients of .00 would be enough to reject generalizability. In contrast, the Rosenthal technique suggests that several hundred studies of nonsignificance would have to be uncovered to reject generalizability.

Schmidt et al (1993) demonstrate ways to reduce the variability of observed validities owing to statistical artifacts to a greater extent than ever before, and they argue that the variance left for the situational specificity hypothesis (or more functionally, situational moderators) is getting vanishingly small. Their argument is that the more variability that can be put in the statistical artifact pile, the more trivial unmeasured moderators become. Switzer et al (1992) have suggested using bootstrap standard error estimates as a way of moving away from conventions (e.g. the 75% rule) and toward the more precise statement of confidence intervals. Osburn & Callender (1992) demonstrate that weighting means and variances by sample size is critical only when there are outliers with large *N*s. With the exception of that special condition, there is little difference between weighted and unweighted solutions. Mendoza & Reinhardt (1991) compare the accuracy of six validity generalization procedures. The parameter of greatest importance in choosing an analytic strategy seems to be the selection ratio. When selection ratios were homogeneous across studies, the Taylor Series Approximation 1 seemed to produce the most accurate results. As a final note, it might be helpful to consider an assumption implicit in much of the validity generalization discussion—that jobs and roles within organizations are crystallized rather than dynamic. Ilgen (1993) suggests that this may no longer be true (if it ever was), which means that even if we accept the viability of validity generalization as a post-dictive device, its potential for predictive accuracy may be limited by the dynamic nature of work.

CUT SCORES AND APPOINTMENT PROCEDURES

The Angoff procedure for setting minimum pass scores has received some attention in the last two years. Norcini et al (1991) suggest that optimal results can be achieved when 5 or more judges consider 25 or more common items.

They further suggest that more than 5 judges or more than 25 items do not appreciably reduce error. Plake & Kane (1991) agree that 25 common items are sufficient but found that using more than 5 judges did reduce error. Maurer & Alexander (1992) suggest that the Angoff method can be improved with a combination of procedural and psychometric enhancements. Suggestions for procedural enhancements include picking better judges and giving them frame-of-reference training; suggestions for psychometric enhancement include identification of idiosyncratic ratings and rater calibration.

Cascio et al (1991) suggested a method of applicant appointment from eligible lists that would result in the joint optimization of social (i.e. minority hiring) and economic (utility gain) objectives. The procedure is known as the sliding band and is based on a standard error logic and the mechanics of a fixed band appointment strategy. In fixed band appointment, candidates are placed into predictor score bands and appointments are made from the highest band until that band is exhausted. Then appointments are made from the next band, etc. The sliding band variation allows the appointing authority to move the appointment band down one point if all of the applicants receiving the highest score in that band are appointed; hence, the concept of the "slide." Schmidt (1991) took exception to the procedure on logical, methodological, and statistical grounds, asserting that the data Cascio et al used to show that there were no eventual ability differences in the appointed applicants were anomalous. Sackett & Roth (1991) did a Monte Carlo study to demonstrate empirically that the Cascio et al results (i.e. no ability differences in appointees but substantially enhanced opportunities for minority applicants) would not hold under certain conditions. Zedeck et al (1991) responded by reminding their critics that the issue was not simply utility but the optimization of social and economic goals. At its foundation, the argument remains one of values, not psychometrics. We suspect that the passage of the 1991 Civil Rights Act and its prohibition against race-based scoring will direct considerable attention to both fixed and sliding band appointment procedures, at least in public sector settings. Recent Federal District & Appeals decisions (Officers for Justice et al, U.S.A. and San Francisco Police Officers Assoc. v. Civil Service Commission of the City and County of San Francisco et al) have supported the legality of the sliding band procedure.

CHALLENGES AND OPPORTUNITIES

After reviewing several year's worth of research, we can share some representative observations. We call these observations challenges and opportunities for a reason. We feel that some trends are problematic and should be modified or abandoned. These are the challenges. There are other issues that are exciting and appear fruitful. These are the opportunities.

The continued use of student samples for personnel research is one challenge. Inferences must be severely restricted. The inferential leap from these samples to field applications is seldom warranted. Designs must be made more convincing, inferences must be reconciled with target populations, and more field work must be done. A second challenge is understanding the limits of meta-analytic approaches to theory building and testing. The meta-analytic approach cannot and should not be deified. It is a powerful and illuminating procedure but will always be an aid to and never a substitute for logic. Regardless of the claims of meta-analysis proponents, traditional researchers and theoreticians should stay the course and collaborate rather than compete or accept second-tier status. Finally, we might be better off accepting certain conventions rather than creating finer and finer pockets of disagreement.

The opportunities are so plentiful that it is hard to limit the discussion. An obvious need is for a concentrated examination of group composition and group performance. With respect to individual performance measurement, there is ample justification for a re-examination of the stability of performance over time as well as a continuation of the examination of different qualitative categories of performance (e.g. task vs contextual). On the predictor side of the equation, it is time to stop the fist fights about general intelligence vs specific abilities and get down to the task of understanding cognitive activity in work settings. Fleishman's taxonomy is a good point of departure but it should not be accepted as *the* structure of cognitive activity. There is too little known about this area to accept a convention at this time. Research on the Big Five personality factors will increase geometrically whether we endorse it or not. We would only enter a plea for a bare minimum of methodology and a concentration on substance and theory in this research line. Perhaps journal editors might open a three-year window for addressing questions related to how many factors there are and how they are to be measured and at the end of three years, form a committee to adopt a series of conventions related to the constructs and their measurement. Realistically, we should prepare for a good deal of smoke and heat in this area before we see the light.

Applicant reactions to various personnel devices and procedures are clearly worthy of increased attention. We encourage more attention to applicant behaviors rather than simply affective responses. We need to know a lot more about how SMEs respond to job analysis questionnaires. It is not enough to know that experience makes a difference and race does not. We need to know more about the cognitive operations involved. Finally, there will be enormous payoffs from continued work on the structural models that are meant to represent the interaction of the collection of antecedent conditions (e.g. ability, experience, personality) and consequent conditions (e.g. task performance, contextual performance, individual development). Perhaps the single most obvious opportunity for learning more about the nature of work behavior is the impetus provided by the Americans with Disabilities Act. Currently, personnel researchers have the attention of the business community, public policy advocates, regulatory agencies, and funding agencies by virtue of the ADA. We should embrace the opportunity to do something good for society (i.e. integrate the disabled into the workplace on a rational basis), as well as the opportunity to enhance both the science and practice of industrial and organizational psychology and form alliances with other disciplines (e.g. occupational medicine, exercise physiology, bio-mechanics, industrial engineering). The greatest advances in the science and practice of I/O psychology have occurred when there was a societal need that we could meet. We should recognize this as one of those times.

ACKNOWLEDGMENTS

We would like to acknowledge the contributions of David Day, Jim Farr, Rick Jacobs, and John Mathieu in reviewing early versions of this chapter. In addition, the clerical and technical assistance of Joy Struble, Kirk Basehore, Michelle Albright, and Adam Carroll were invaluable.

Literature Cited

Ackerman PL. 1986. Individual differences in information processing: an investigation of intellectual abilities and task performance during practice. *Intelligence* 10:101–39

Ackerman PL. 1987. Individual differences in skill learning: an integration of psychometric and information processing perspectives. *Psychol. Bull.* 102:3–27

Ackerman PL. 1989. Within-task intercorrelations of skilled performance: implications for predicting individual differences? A comment on Henry & Hulin, 1987. *J. Appl. Psychol.* 74:360–64

Ackerman PL. 1990. A correlational analysis of skill specificity: learning, abilities, and individual differences. *J. Exp. Psychol.: Learn. Mem. Cogn.* 16:883–901

Ackerman PL. 1992. Predicting individual differences in complex skill acquisition: dynamics of ability determinants. *J. Appl. Psychol.* 77(5):598–614

Ackerman PL, Kanfer R. 1993. Integrating laboratory and field study for improving selection: development of a battery for predicting air traffic controller success. *J. Appl. Psychol.* 78(3):413–32

Alley WE, Teachout MS. 1992. *Differential assignment potential in the ASVAB.* Presented at Annu. Meet. Am. Psychol. Assoc., 100th, Washington, DC

Americans with Disabilities Act. 1990. *P. L. 101–336, 104 Statute 327,* 26 July

Arnold DW, Jones JW. 1992. *Assessing invasivness of psychological tests: lawyers' perceptions of job-relevant and personality-oriented items.* Presented at Winter Conf. LA Bar Assoc., Labor and Employ. Law Sect., San Diego

Arvey RD. 1992. Constructs and construct validation: definitions and issues. *Hum. Perform.* 5(1/2):59–69

Arvey RD, Landon TE, Nutting SM, Maxwell SE. 1992a. Development of physical ability tests for police officers: A construct validation approach. *J. Appl. Psychol.* 77(6):996–1009

Arvey RD, Nutting SM, Landon TE. 1992b. Validation strategies for physical ability testing in police and fire settings. *Public Pers. Manage.* 21(3):301–12

Arvey RD, Sackett PR. 1993. Fairness in selection: current developments and perspectives. See Schmitt et al 1993, pp. 240–74

Arvey RD, Salas E, Gialluca KA. 1992c. Using task inventories to forecast skills and abilities. *Hum. Perform.* 5(3):171–90

Ash P. 1991. Law and regulation of preemployment inquiries. *J. Bus. Psychol.* 5(3):291–308

Ashworth SD, Osburn HG, Callender JC, Boyle KA. 1992. The effects of unrepresented studies on the robustness of validity generalization studies. *Pers. Psychol.* 45(2):341–61

Austin JT. 1992. History of industrial/organizational psychology at Ohio State. *Ind.-Organ. Psychol.* 29(4):51–59

Austin JT, Humphreys LG, Hulin CL. 1989. A critical re-analysis of Barrett et al. *Psychol. Bull.* 42:583–96

Austin JT, Villanova P. 1992. The criterion problem: 1917–1992. *J. Appl. Psychol.* 77(6):836–74.

Bantel KA, Jackson SE. 1989. Top management and innovations in banking: Does the composition of the top team make a difference? *Strateg. Manage. J.* 10:107–24

Barrett GV. 1990. Personnel selection after Watson, Hopkins, Atonio, and Martin (Wham). *Forensic Rep.* 3:179–203

Barrett GV. 1992. Clarifying construct validity: definitions, processes, and models. *Hum. Perform.* 5(1&2):13–58

Barrett GV, Alexander RA, Doverspike D. 1992. The implications for personnel selection of apparent declines in predictive validity over time: a critique of Hulin, Henry & Noon. *Pers. Psychol.* 45(3):601

Barrett GV, Caldwell MS, Alexander RA. 1985. The concept of dynamic criteria: a critical re-analysis. *Psychol. Bull.* 38:41–56

Barrick MR, Mount MK. 1991. The big five personality dimensions and job performance: a meta analysis. *Pers. Psychol.* 44(1):1–26

Barrick MR, Mount MK. 1993. Autonomy as a moderator of the relationships between the big five personality dimensions and job performance. *J. Appl. Psychol.* 78(1):111–18

Bartram D. 1993. Emerging trends in computer-assisted assessment. See Schuler et al 1993, pp. 267–88

Beck-Dudley C, McEvoy GM. 1991. Performance appraisals and discrimination suits: Do courts pay attention to validity? *Empl. Responsib. Rights J.* 4(2):149–63

Bennett RE. 1993. Environments for presenting and automatically scoring complex constructed-response items. See Rumsey et al 1993. In press

Biersdorff KK, Radke SA. 1991. Human rights legislation: Will intelligence become a bona fide occupational requirement? *Can. J. Rehabil.* 4(4):203–11

Blakley BR, Quinones MA, Jago IA. 1992. *The validity of isometric strength tests: results of five studies.* Presented at Annu. Meet. Soc. Ind. Organ. Psychol., 7th, Montreal

Borman WC, Dorsey D, Ackerman L. 1992. Time spent responses as time allocation strategies: relations with sales performance in a stockbroker sample. *Pers. Psychol.* 45(4):763–78

Borman WC, Motowidlo SJ. 1993. Expanding the criterion domain to include elements of contextual performance. See Schmitt et al 1993, pp. 71–98

Borman WC, White LA, Pulakos ED, Oppler SH. 1991. Models of supervisory job performance ratings. *J. Appl. Psychol.* 76(6):863–72

Brief AP, Motowidlo SJ. 1986. Prosocial organizational behaviors. *Acad. Manage. Rev.* 11:710–25

Burke MJ. 1993. Computerized psychological testing: impacts on measuring predictor constructs and future job behavior. See Schmitt et al 1993, pp. 203–39

Campbell JP. 1993. Alternative models of job performance and their implications for selection and classification. See Rumsey et al 1993. In press

Campbell JP, McCloy RA, Oppler SH, Sager CE. 1993. A theory of performance. See Schmitt et al 1993, pp. 35–70

Campbell JP, Zook LM, ed. 1991. *Research Report 1597.* U.S. Army Res. Inst. Behav. Soc. Sci., Alexandria, Va.

Carroll J. 1992. Cognitive abilities: the state of the art. *Psychol. Sci.* 3(5):266–70

Cascio WF. 1991. *The impact of dynamic criteria on the assessment of the outcomes of selection and training programs.* Presented at Annu. Meet. Soc. Ind. Organ. Psychol., 6th, St. Louis

Cascio WF, Outtz J, Zedeck S, Goldstein IL. 1991. Statistical implications of six methods of test score use in personnel selection. *Hum. Perform.* 4(4):233–64

Civil Rights Act of 1991. *P. L. 102–166, 105 Statute 1071,* 21 Nov.

Cortina JM, Doherty ML, Schmitt N, Kaufman G, Smith RG. 1992. The "big five" personality factors in the IPI and MMPI: predictors of police performance. *Pers. Psychol.* 45(1):119–40

Day DV, Bedeian AG. 1993. *Effects of personality dissimilarity and psychological climate on role stress, job satisfaction, and job performance: an interactionist perspective.* Presented at Annu. Meet. Soc. Ind. Organ. Psychol., 8th, San Francisco

Deadrick DL, Madigan RM. 1990. Dynamic criteria revisited: a longitudinal study of performance stability and predictive validity. *Pers. Psychol.* 43(4):717–44

Digman JM. 1990. Personality structure: emergence of the five-factor model. *Annu. Rev. Psychol.* 41:417–40

Drasgow F, Olson JB, Keenan PA, Moberg P, Mead AD 1993. Computerized assessment. In *Research in Personnel and Human Resource Management,* ed. GR Ferris, KM Rowland, 11:163–206. Greenwich, Conn: JAI

Dunnette MD. 1992. It was nice to be there: Construct validity then and now. *Hum. Perform.* 5(1&2):157–69

Dunnette MD, Hough LM, eds. 1991. *Hand-*

book of Industrial and Organizational Psychology, Vol. 2. Palo Alto, Calif: Consult. Psychol. Press. 2nd ed.

Feild HS, Buckner KE, Holley WH Jr. 1990. Personnel selection in police and fire departments: a study of employment discrimination case characteristics and outcomes. *Labor Law J.* 41(9):623–32

Ferris GR, Judge TA, Chachere JG, Liden RC. 1991. The age context of performance-evaluation decisions. *Psychol. Aging* 6(4):616–22

Fleenor JW. 1992. *Constructs and development assessment centers: Further troubling empirical findings.* Presented at Annu. Meet. Soc. Ind. Organ. Psychol., 7th, Montreal

Fleishman EA. 1991. *Manual for the Ability Requirement Scales (MARS, revised).* Palo Alto, Calif: Consult. Psychol. Press

Fleishman EA, Mumford MD. 1991. Evaluating classifications of job behavior: a construct validation of the ability requirement scales. *Pers. Psychol.* 44(3):523–75

Fleishman EA, Reilly ME. 1991. *Human Abilities: Their Definition, Measurement, and Job Task Requirements.* Palo Alto, Calif: Consult. Psychol. Press

Fletcher C. 1991. Candidates' reactions to assessment centres and their outcomes: a longitudinal study. *J. Occup. Psychol.* 64(2):117–27

Forbinger LR, Binning JF, Alexander RA. 1992. *Heuristic judgement processes and PAQ ratings: assessing item-induced availability biases.* Presented at Annu. Meet. Soc. Ind. Organ. Psychol., 7th, Montreal

Goldberg LR. 1993. Basic research on personality structure: implications of the emerging consensus for applications to selection and classification. See Rumsey et al 1993. In press

Goldberg LR, Grenier JR, Guion RM, Sechrest LB, Wing H. 1991. *Questionnaires Used in the Prediction of Trustworthiness in Preemployment Selection Decisions.* Washington, DC: Am. Psychol. Assoc.

Gough HG, Heibrun AB. 1965. *The Adjective Checklist.* Palo Alto, Calif: Consult. Psychol. Press

Graves LM, Karren RJ. 1992. Interviewer decision processes and effectiveness: an experimental policy-capturing investigation. *Pers. Psychol.* 45(2):313–39

Gross ML. 1962. *The Brain Watchers.* New York: Random House

Guion RM. 1965. *Personnel Testing.* New York: McGraw Hill

Guion RM. 1992. Can we learn from history? *Ind. Organ. Psychol.* 30(1):25

Guion RM, Gibson WM. 1988. Personnel selection and placement. *Annu. Rev. Psychol.* 39:349–74

Guion RM, Gottier RF. 1965. Validity of personality measures in personnel selection. *Pers. Psychol.* 18:135–64

Hammond P, Morgan HP, eds. 1991. *Ending mandatory retirement for tenured faculty: the consequences for higher education.* Comm. Rep. from the Natl. Res. Council. Washington, DC: Natl. Acad. Press

Harrell TW. 1992. Some history of the army general classification test. *J. Appl. Psychol.* 77(6):875–78

Harris M, Becker A, Smith D. 1993. Does the assessment center scoring method affect the cross-situational consistency of ratings? *J. Appl. Psychol.* 78(4):675–78

Hoffman CC, Nathan BR, Holden LM. 1991. A comparison of validation criteria: objective versus subjective performance measures and self- versus supervisor-ratings. *Pers. Psychol.* 44(3):601–19

Hofmann DA, Jacobs R, Baratta JE. 1993. Dynamic criteria and the measurement of change. *J. Appl. Psychol.* 78(2):194–204

Hofmann DA, Jacobs R, Gerras SJ. 1992. Mapping individual performance over time. *J. Appl. Psychol.* 77(2):185–95

Hogan J. 1991a. Structure of physical performance in occupational tasks. *J. Appl. Psychol.* 76(4):495–507

Hogan J. 1991b. Physical abilities. See Dunnette & Hough 1991, pp. 753–832

Hough L. 1992. The "big five" personality variables—construct confusion: description versus prediction. *Hum. Perform.* 5(1/2):139–55

Hough LM, Paullin C. 1993. Construct-oriented scale construction: the rational approach. In *The Biodata Handbook: Theory, Research and Application,* ed. GS Stokes, MD Mumford, WA Owens, pp. Palo Alto, Calif: Consult. Psychol. Press. In press

Howard A. 1992. *Selecting executives for the 21st century: Can assessment centers meet the challenge?* Presented at Exec. Select. Conf., Cent. for Creative Leadership, Greensboro, NC

Huffcutt AI, Woehr DJ. 1992. *A conceptual analysis of interview structure and the effects of structure on the interview process.* Presented at Annu. Meet. Soc. Ind. Organ. Psychol., 7th, Montreal

Hulin CL, Henry RA, Noon SZ. 1990. Adding a dimension: time as a factor in the generalizability of predictive relationships. *Psychol. Bull.* 107:328–40

Humphreys L. 1992. Commentary: What both critics and users of ability tests need to know. *Psychol. Sci.* 3(5):271–74

Hunter JE, Hunter RF. 1984. Validity and utility of alternative predictors of job performance. *Psychol. Bull.* 96:72–98

Ilgen DR. 1993. Jobs and roles: accepting and coping with the changing structure of organizations. See Rumsey et al 1993. In press

Inwald R. 1992. *Hilson Job Analysis Questionnaire.* Kew Gardens, NY: Hilson Research

Inwald R, Knatz H, Shusman E. 1983. *Inwald Personality Inventory Manual.* New York: Hilson Research

Jackson SE. 1991. Team composition in organizational settings: Issues in managing an increasingly diverse work force. In *Group Processing and Productivity,* ed. S Worchel, W Wood, JA Simpson, pp. 138–73. Newbury Park, Calif: Sage

Jackson SE, Brett JF, Sessa VI, Cooper DM, Julin JA, et al. 1991. Some differences make a difference: Individual dissimilarity and group heterogeneity as correlates of recruitment, promotions, and turnover. *J. Appl. Psychol.* 76(5):675–89

Jackson SE, Stone VK, Alvarez EB. 1993. Socialization amidst diversity: The impact of demographics on work team oldtimers and newcomers. In *Research in Organizational Behavior,* ed. LL Cummings, BM Staw, 15:45–109. Greenwich, Conn: JAI

Jacobs R, Hofmann DA, Kriska SD. 1990. Performance and seniority. *Hum. Perform.* 3(2):107–21

James LR, Demaree RG, Mulaik SA, Ladd RT. 1992. Validity generalization in the context of situational models. *J. Appl. Psychol.* 77(1):3–14

Jeanneret PR. 1991. Growth trends in I/O psychology. *Ind.-Organ. Psychol.* 29(2):47

Jeanneret PR. 1992. Applications of job component/synthetic validity to construct validity. *Hum. Perform.* 5(1/2):81–96

Jensen A. 1992. Commentary: Vehicles of *g*. *Psychol. Sci.* 3(5):275–77

Jones JW. 1991a. Assessing privacy invasiveness of psychological test items: job relevant versus clinical measures of integrity. *J. Bus. Psychol.* 5(4):531–35

Jones JW, ed. 1991b. *Preemployment Honesty Testing: Current Research and Future Directions.* New York: Quorum

Jones JW, Ash P, Soto C. 1990. Employment privacy rights and pre-employment honesty tests. *Empl. Relat. Law J.* 15(4):561–75

Joyce LW, Thayer PW, Pond SB. 1992. *Managerial functions: an alternative to traditional assessment center dimensions?* Presented at Annu. Meet. Soc. Ind. Organ. Psychol., 7th, Montreal

Kanfer R, Ackerman PL. 1989. Motivation and cognitive abilities: an integrative/aptitude-treatment interaction approach to skill acquisition. *J. Appl. Psychol.* 74(4):539–45

Katzell RA. 1991. History of early I/O doctoral programs. *Ind. Organ. Psychol.* 28(4):51

Katzell RA. 1992. History of I/O psychology at NYU. *Ind. Organ. Psychol.* 29(3):61–64

Katzell RA, Austin JT. 1992. From then to now: the development of industrial-organizational psychology in the United States. *J. Appl. Psychol.* 77(6):803–35

Kline P, Lapham SL. 1990. *The PPQ.* London: Psychometric Systems

Kline P, Lapham SL. 1991. The validity of the PPQ: a study of its factor structure and its relationship to the EPQ. *Pers. Individ. Diff.* 12(6):631–35

Kline P, Lapham SL. 1992. The PPQ: a study of its ability to discriminate occupational groups and the validity of its scales. *Pers. Individ. Diff.* 13(2):225–28

Kluger AN, Rothstein HR. 1993. The influence of selection test type on applicant reactions to employment testing. *J. Bus. Psychol.* 8(1):3–26

Konovsky MA, Cropanzano R. 1991. Perceived fairness of employee drug testing as a predictor of employee attitudes and job performance. *J. Appl. Psychol.* 76(5):698–707

Kraiger K, Ford JK. 1985. A meta-analysis of ratee race effects in performance ratings. *J. Appl. Psychol.* 70:56–65

Lance CE, Stennett RB, Mayfield DL. 1992. *A reexamination of selected meta-analysis results: Has the generalizability of research findings been overstated?* Presented at Annu. Meet. Soc. Ind. Organ. Psychol., 7th, Montreal

Lance CE, Stennett RB, Searcy CA. 1992a. *On evaluating the situational specificity hypothesis in meta-analysis.* Presented at Annu. Meet. Southern Manage. Assoc., New Orleans

Lance CE, Teachout MS, Donnelly TM. 1992b. Specification of the criterion construct space: an application of hierarchical confirmatory factor analysis. *J. Appl. Psychol.* 77(4):437–52

Landy FJ. 1991. The I/O family tree. *Ind. Organ. Psychol.* 29(2):31–34

Landy FJ. 1992a. Hugo Munsterberg: victim or visionary? *J. Appl. Psychol.* 77(6):787–802

Landy FJ, ed. 1992b. Test validity yearbook, Vol. 1 & 2. *J. Bus. Psychol.* 7(2/4):111–257, 269–482

Landy FJ. 1993. Early influences on the development of industrial/organizational psychology. In *Exploring Applied Psychology: Origins and Critical Analyses,* ed. TK Fagan, GR VandenBos, pp.79–118. Washington, DC: Am. Psychol. Assoc.

Landy FJ, Bland RE, Buskirk ER, Daly RE, DeBusk RF, et al. 1992. *Alternatives to chronological age in determining standards of suitability for public safety jobs.* Tech. Rep., Cent. Appl. Behav. Sci., Penn State Univ.

Landy FJ, Farr JL. 1983. *The Measurement of Work Performance.* New York: Academic

Landy FJ, Vasey J. 1991. Job analysis: the composition of SME samples. *Pers. Psychol.* 44(1):27–50

Lawshe CH, Weiss HM. 1991. History of industrial/organizational psychology at

Purdue University. *Ind. Organ. Psychol.* 28(4):52

Lerner RM. 1985. Individual and context in developmental psychology: conceptual and theoretical issues. In *Individual Development and Social Change: Explanatory Analysis,* ed. JR Nesselroade, A von Eye, pp. 155–87. San Diego: Academic

Lerner RM. 1986. *Concepts and Theories of Human Development.* San Diego: Academic. 2nd ed.

Lin T-R, Dobbins GH, Farh J-L. 1992. A field study of race and age similarity effects on interview ratings in conventional and situational interviews. *J. Appl. Psychol.* 77(3):363–71

Lohman DF. 1993. Implications of cognitive psychology for ability testing: three critical assumptions. See Rumsey et al 1993. In press

Mael FA. 1991. A conceptual rationale for the domain and attributes of biodata items. *Pers. Psychol.* 44(4):763–92

Manning CA, Broach D. 1992. *DOT/FAA/AM-92/26.* Washington, DC: Off. Aviation Med.

Mathieu JE, Farr JL, Shankster LJ, Landy FJ, Kohler SS. 1993. *An examination of the convergence between incumbents' and managers' job analysis ratings.* Presented at Annu. Meet. Am. Psychol. Assoc., 101st, Atlanta

Matthews G, Jones DM, Chamberlain AG. 1992. Predictors of individual differences in mail-coding skills and their variation with ability levels. *J. Appl. Psychol.* 77(4):406–18

Maurer TJ, Alexander RA. 1992. Methods of improving employment test critical scores derived by judging test content: a review and critique. *Pers. Psychol.* 45: 727–61

McCardle WD, Katch FI, Katch VL. 1991. *Exercise Physiology: Energy, Nutrition, and Human Performance.* Malvern, PA: Lea & Febiger

McCormick EJ, Jeanneret PR, Mecham RC. 1989. *Position Analysis Questionnaire.* Palo Alto, Calif: Consult. Psychol. Press. 2nd ed.

Mead AD, Drasgow F. 1993. Equivalence of computerized and paper-and-pencil cognitive ability tests: a meta-analysis. *Psychol. Bull.* 114: In press

Mendoza JL, Reinhardt RN. 1991. Validity generalization procedures using sample-based estimates: a comparison of six procedures. *Psychol. Bull.* 110(3):596–610

Moreno KE, Sands WA, Vicino FL, Segall DO. 1991. *Research on implementation of computer-based testing.* Presented at Annu. Conf. Military Testing Assoc., 33rd, San Antonio

Morgan B, Lassiter D. 1992. Team composition and staffing. In *Teams: Their Training and Performance,* ed. RW Swezey, E Salas, pp. 75–100. Norwood, NJ: Ablex

Motowidlo SJ, Carter GW, Dunnette MD, Tippins N, Werner S, et al. 1992. Studies of the structured behavioral interview. *J. Appl. Psychol.* 77(5):571–87

Mumford MD, Uhlman CE, Kilcullen RN. 1992. The structure of life history: implications for the construct validity of background data scales. *Hum. Perform.* 5(1/2):109–37

Murphy KR. 1993. Toward a broader conception of jobs and job performance: impact of changes in the military environment on the structure, assessment, and prediction of job performance. See Rumsey et al 1993. In press

Murphy KR, Jako RA, Anhalt RL. 1993. The nature and consequences of halo error: a critical analysis. *J. Appl. Psychol.* 78(4):218–25

Naylor JC. 1991. Ernest J. McCormick (1911–1990): Obituary. *Am. Psychol.* 46(4):438

Norcini J, Shea J, Grosso L. 1991. The effect of numbers of experts and common items on cutting score equivalents based on expert judgment. *Appl. Psychol. Meas.* 15(3):241–46

Ones D, Viswesvaran C, Schmidt F. 1993. Meta-analysis of integrity test validities: findings and implications for personnel selection and theories of job performance. *J. Appl. Psychol.* 78(4):679–703

Oppler SH, Campbell JP, Pulakos ED, Borman WC. 1992. Three approaches to the investigation of subgroup bias in performance measurement: review, results, and conclusions. *J. Appl. Psychol.* 77(2):201–17

Organ DW. 1988. *Organizational Citizenship Behavior: The Good Soldier Syndrome.* Lexington, Mass: Lexington

Osburn HG, Callender J. 1992. A note on the sampling variance of the mean uncorrected correlation in meta-analysis and validity generalization. *J. Appl. Psychol.* 77(2):115–22

Park KS, Lee SW. 1992. A computer-aided aptitude test for predicting flight performance of trainees. *Hum. Factors* 34(2):189–204

Pitariu HD. 1992. I/O psychology in Romania: past, present, intentions. *Ind. Organ. Psychol.* 29(4):29–32

Plake BS, Kane MT. 1991. Comparison of methods for combining the minimum passing levels for individual items into a passing score for a test. *J. Educ. Meas.* 28(3):249–56

Powell GN. 1991. Applicant reactions to the initial employment interview: exploring theoretical and methodological issues. *Pers. Psychol.* 44(1):67–83

Prieto JM. 1993. The team perspective in selection and assessment. See Schuler et al 1993, pp. 221–34

Primoff ES, Eyde LD, Kelly KL. 1992. *Building the criterion into assessment procedures: the job element method.* Presented at Annu. Meet. Am. Psychol. Assoc., 100th, Washington

Ree M, Carretta T. 1992. *The Correlation of Cognitive and Psychomotor Tests. AL-TP-1992–0037.* Armstrong Laboratory, Brooks Air Force Base, Texas

Robertson IT, Iles PA, Gratton L, Sharpley D. 1991. The impact of personnel selection and assessment methods on candidates. *Hum. Rela.* 44(9):963–82

Robinson DD. 1992. *Worker Rehabilitation Questionnaire (WRQ) User's and Technical Manual.* Palo Alto, Calif: Consult. Psychol. Press

Rothstein H. 1992. Meta-analysis and construct validity. *Hum. Perform.* 5(1/2):71–80

Rumsey MG, Walker CG, Harris JH, eds. 1993. *Personnel Measurement: Directions for Research.* Hillsdale, NJ: Erlbaum. In press

Russell CJ. 1992. A conversation with C. H. Lawshe. *Ind. Organ. Psychol.* 29(3):65–68

Ryan AM, Lasek M. 1991. Negligent hiring and defamation: areas of liability related to pre-employment inquiries. *Pers. Psychol.* 44(2):293–319

Rynes SL. 1993. Who's selecting whom? Effects of selection practices on applicant attitudes and behavior. See Schmitt et al 1993, pp. 240–74

Rynes SL, Connerley ML. 1992. Applicant reactions to alternative selection procedures. *J. Bus. Psychol.* 7(3):261–78

Sackett PR, DuBois CL. 1991. Rater-ratee race effects on performance evaluation: challenging meta-analytic conclusions. *J. Appl. Psychol.* 76(6):873–77

Sackett PR, DuBois CL, Noe AW. 1991. Tokenism in performance evaluation: the effects of work group representation on male-female and white-black differences in performance ratings. *J. Appl. Psychol.* 76(2):263–67

Sackett PR, Roth L. 1991. A Monte Carlo examination of banding and rank order methods of test score use in personnel selection. *Hum. Perform.* 4(4):279–95

Sands WA. 1990. *Joint-service computerized aptitude testing.* Presented at Annu. Conf. Military Testing Assoc., 32nd, Orange Beach

Sands WA, ed. 1992. *Technical Report: Computer-based Testing for Personnel Selection and Classification in the Technical Cooperation Program (TTCP) Countries: Australia, Canada, New Zealand, United Kingdom, and United States.* San Diego: Navy Pers. Res. Dev. Ctr.

Sands WA, Moreno KE. 1991. *Computer-based aptitude testing for military personnel selection and classification.* Presented at Annu. Conf. Military Testing Assoc., 33rd, San Antonio

Schippmann JS, Prien EP, Hughes GL. 1991. The content of management work: formation of task and job skill composite classifications. *J. Bus. Psychol.* 5(3):325–54

Schmidt FL. 1991. Why all banding procedures in personnel selection are logically flawed. *Hum. Perform.* 4(4):265–77

Schmidt FL. 1992. What do data really mean? Research findings, meta-analysis, and cumulative knowledge in psychology. *Am. Psychol.* 47(10):1173–81

Schmidt FL. 1993. Personnel psychology at the cutting edge. See Schmitt et al 1993, pp. 497–515

Schmidt FL, Hunter JE. 1993. Tacit knowledge, practical intelligence, general mental ability, and job knowledge. *Curr. Dir. Psychol. Sci.* 2(1):8–9

Schmidt FL, Law K, Hunter J, Rothstein H, Pearlman K, et al. 1993. Refinements in validity generalization methods: implications for the situational specificity hypothesis. *J. Appl. Psychol.*78(1):3–13

Schmidt FL, Ones DS, Hunter JE. 1992. Personnel selection. *Annu. Rev. Psychol.* 43:627–70

Schmitt N, Borman WC, Assoc., ed. 1993. *Personnel Selection in Organizations.* San Francisco: Jossey-Bass

Schmitt N, Gooding RZ, Noe RA, Kirsch MP. 1984. Meta-analyses of validity studies published between 1964 and 1982 and the investigation of study characteristics. *Pers. Psychol.* 37:407–22

Schmitt N, Robertson I. 1990. Personnel selection. *Annu. Rev. Psychol.* 41:289–320

Schneider JR, Schmitt N. 1992. An exercise design approach to understanding assessment center dimension and exercise constructs. *J. Appl. Psychol.* 77(1): 32–41

Scholarios D. 1992. *A comparison of predictor selection methods for maximizing potential classification efficiency.* Presented at Annu. Meet. Am. Psychol. Assoc., 100th, Washington, DC

Schuler H, Farr JL, Smith M, eds. 1993. *Personnel Selection and Assessment: Industrial and Organizational Perspectives.* Hillsdale, NJ: Erlbaum. In press

Searcy C, Woods PN, Gatewood R, Lance C. 1993. *The validity of structured interviews: a meta-analytical search for moderators.* Presented at Annu. Meet. Soc. Ind. Organ. Psychol., 8th, San Francisco

Sharf JC. 1993. Legal and EEO issues impacting on personal history inquiries. In *Biodata Handbook: Theory, Research, and Application,* ed. GS Stokes, MD Mumford,

WA Owens. Palo Alto, Calif: Consult. Psychol. Press. In press

Silva JM, Jacobs RR. 1993. Assessing the impact on performance of increased selection of minority applicants. *J. Appl. Psychol.* 78(4):591–601

Smith PC, Kendall LM, Hulin CL. 1969. *The Measurement of Satisfaction in Work and Retirement.* Chicago, IL: Rand McNally. 186 pp.

Smither JW, Pearlman K. 1991. *Perceptions of the job-relatedness of selection procedures among college recruits and recruiting/employment managers.* Presented at Annu. Meet. Soc. Ind. Organ. Psychol., 6th, St. Louis

Sothmann M, Saupe K, Jasenof D, Blaney J, Fuhrman S, et al. 1990. Advancing age and the cardiorespiratory stress of fire suppression: determining a minimum standard for aerobic fitness. *Hum. Perform.* 3:217–36

Sproule CF, ed. 1990. Recent innovations in public sector assessment. *Pers. Assess. Monogr.* 2(2):1–160

Sternberg RJ. 1985. *Beyond IQ: A Triarchic Theory of Human Intelligence.* New York: Cambridge Univ. Press

Sternberg RJ. 1993. The PRSVL model of person-context interaction in the study of human potential. See Rumsey et al 1993. In press

Sternberg RJ, Wagner RK. 1992. Tacit knowledge: an unspoken key to managerial success. *Tacit Knowledge* 1(1):5–13

Sternberg RJ, Wagner RK. 1993. Practical intelligence and tacit knowledge. *Curr. Dir. Psychol. Sci.* 2(1):1–4

Sternberg RJ, Wagner RK, Okagaki L. 1993. Practical intelligence: the nature and role of tacit knowledge in work and at school. In *Advances in Lifespan Development,* ed. H Reese, J Puckett. Hillsdale, NJ: Erlbaum. In press

Switzer FS III, Paese PW, Drasgow F. 1992. Bootstrap estimates of standard errors in validity generalization. *J. Appl. Psychol.* 77(2):123–29

Terpstra D, Baker D. 1992. Outcomes of federal court decisions on sexual harassment. *Acad. Manage. J.* 35(1):181–90

Tett RP, Jackson DN, Rothstein M. 1991. Personality measures as predictors of job performance: a meta-analytic review. *Pers. Psychol.* 44(4):703–42

Thomas H. 1989. A mixture model for distributions of correlation coefficients. *Psychometrika* 54:523–30

Thomas H. 1990. A likelihood-based model for validity generalization. *J. Appl. Psychol.* 75:13–20

Thompson AS. 1991. The evolution of doctoral training in I/O psychology at Teacher's College, Columbia U. *Ind. Organ. Psychol.* 29(2):47–54

US Court of Appeals, 9th Circuit. 1992. Officers for Justice et al, USA, Plaintiffs, and San Francisco Police Officers Assoc., Intervenor-Appellant, v. Civil Service Commission of the City and County of San Francisco, et al, City and County of San Francisco, et al, Defendants-Appellees. No. 91–16519. Argued and Submitted July 13, 1992. Decided Nov. 5, 1992. [979F. 2d 721 (9th Cir. 1992)]

Vance RJ, Caligiuri PM, Farr JL, Shankster LJ, Tesluk PE. 1992. *Relationship for job experience to job ability ratings.* Presented at Annu. Meet. Acad. Manage., Las Vegas

Veres JG, Green SB, Boyles WR. 1991. Racial differences on job analysis questionnaires: an empirical study. *Public Pers. Manage.* 20(2):135–44

Wagner RK, Sternberg RJ. 1987. Tacit knowledge in managerial success. *J. Bus. Psychol.* 1(4):301–12

Waldman DA, Avolio BJ. 1991. Race effects in performance evaluations: controlling for ability, education, and experience. *J. Appl. Psychol.* 76(6):897–901

Wiggins JS, Pincus AL. 1992. Personality: structure and assessment. *Annu. Rev. Psychol.* 43:473–504

Zedeck S, Outtz J, Cascio WF, Goldstein IL. 1991. Why do "testing experts" have such limited vision? *Hum. Perform.* 4(4):297–308

Zeidner J, Johnson CD. 1991a. *The Economic Benefits of Predicting Job Performance,* Vol. 1: *Selection Utility.* New York: Praeger

Zeidner J, Johnson CD. 1991b. *The Economic Benefits of Predicting Job Performance,* Vol. 3: *Estimating the Gains of Alternative Policies.* New York: Praeger.

Zeidner J, Johnson CD. 1993. Is personnel classification a concept whose time has passed? See Rumsey et al 1993. In press

Annu. Rev. Psychol. 1994. 45:297–332

THE SELF IN SOCIAL CONTEXTS

Mahzarin R. Banaji

Department of Psychology, Yale University, New Haven, Connecticut 06520-7447

Deborah A. Prentice

Department of Psychology, Princeton University, Green Hall, Princeton, New Jersey 08544-1010

KEY WORDS: self-enhancement, social comparison, self-presentation, self-esteem, identity, distinctiveness, gender, culture, motivation

CONTENTS

INTRODUCTION

If the number of papers published on a topic is an accurate indicator of the interest it evokes and the attention it commands, then the self continues to hold center-stage position in psychology. Over 5000 articles about the self have been published since the last *Annual Review of Psychology* chapter on the topic appeared seven years ago (Markus & Wurf 1987). The title of that chapter, "The Dynamic Self-Concept," presaged much of the work to come, for a major focus of research attention in the intervening years has been on how the self is involved in the regulation of social behavior. However, the emphasis has been less on demonstrating the dynamic nature of the self per se than on investigating how that dynamic nature is expressed within specified social contexts. In particular, researchers have examined how individuals pursue goals of self-enhancement, self-knowledge, and self-improvement through processes of social reasoning, social comparison, social interaction, self-presentation, and collective identification. Although individual investigations have focused on determining the precise nature or relative importance of self motives or goals, the overarching concern across investigations has been with delineating strategies used to pursue these goals.

In this review, we examine the strategies of the self in social contexts. We concentrate specifically on studies of how the self directs social cognition and social behavior. We restrict our review to articles published in major journals from 1988 to 1992, with book chapters and additional articles included more sparingly. Thus, the chapter by no means represents an exhaustive review of the literature on the self. Not reviewed here, for example, is the rich history of research on the self that has shaped current interest in this topic (see Markus & Cross 1990). Also absent are studies on the relationship of self and memory (Klein & Loftus 1993, Greenwald & Banaji 1989, Prentice 1990, Skowronski et al 1991), self and mood (Salovey 1992, Sedikides 1992), self-knowledge and its development (Harter 1989, Lewis 1990, Neisser 1988), comparative analyses of self-awareness (Gallup 1991), the relation of self to mental health outcomes (Bandura 1988, Deaux 1992a, Emmons & King 1988, Taylor & Brown 1988), and goal-directed behavior that does not specifically implicate the self (see Buss & Cantor 1989, Pervin 1989). These literatures touch on the concerns of this chapter, but space limitations prevent us from including them.

MOTIVES OF THE SELF

Most recent research on the self has traced its activity to two general sets of motives that we term self-knowledge and self-enhancement (see Kunda 1990; Schlenker & Weigold 1989, 1992; Strube 1990; Swann 1990). Self-knowledge refers to the desire for accurate and certain evidence of one's traits and abilities, and in particular, for evidence that confirms one's self-assessments. The need for self-knowledge is presumably rooted in a more basic need, although whether that need is for consistency (Backman 1988), for uncertainty reduction (Trope 1986), for the ability to predict and control the environment (Swann 1990), or for some combination of these rewards remains unclear (see

Schlenker & Weigold 1992). Self-enhancement refers to the desire for positive feedback about the self and includes both self-protective impulses unleashed by threatening or negative experiences and the ongoing drive to have a positive sense of self. It is presumably rooted in the more basic tendency to seek pleasure and to avoid pain. Although there has been some debate in recent years about the precise nature of specific motives and the needs underlying them, most researchers would agree on some version of these two general sources of goal-directed behavior.

A frequent addition to the short-list of self motives is the need for self-improvement. Self-improvement refers to the desire to bring oneself closer to what one should or would ideally like to be (see Higgins 1987, 1989; Markus & Ruvolo 1989; Taylor & Lobel 1989; Wood 1989). Like self-knowledge and self-enhancement, self-improvement can be either defensive (avoiding feared selves) or offensive (striving for ideal selves). It is presumably rooted in more basic needs for control (Markus & Ruvolo 1989) and/or achievement (Taylor & Lobel 1989, Wood 1989). Although empirical evidence of behaviors directly attributable to a self-improvement motive is, at present, somewhat limited, much research on goal-directed behavior has been predicated on the assumption that such a motive exists (see Cantor & Zirkel 1990 for a review, and Pervin 1989 for many examples). In this review, we include only those studies in which behavior is linked explicitly to a desire to improve oneself.

This discussion of self motives obscures what is perhaps the most remarkable feature of recent research on the self: an implicit agreement among social and personality psychologists on the validity of a motivational perspective. After years of debating whether or not motivation affects social cognition and behavior (see Greenwald 1975, Miller & Ross 1975, Tetlock & Levi 1982), self theorists appear to have settled the issue with a considerable degree of consensus. The legitimation of a motivational approach seems to have come less from a satisfactory resolution of perennial concerns than from a realization that such a resolution was unlikely to be achieved (Tetlock & Levi 1982). Agreement on the ground rules has had both positive and negative consequences. On the positive side, the past half-decade has been a period of remarkable productivity in the study of the self, as researchers have explored the potential of this motivational approach for predicting and explaining social behavior. On the negative side, this period has witnessed a proliferation of self theories and constructs with only modest attention paid to the relations among them.

STRATEGIES OF THE SELF

The pursuit of self-knowledge, self-enhancement, and self-improvement can account for a wide variety of social behaviors. Indeed, these motives appear to influence how people reason about the social world, with whom and on what dimensions they compare themselves, their choice of interaction partners, the way they present themselves both publicly and privately, and their relations to the groups of which they are members. Most recent investigations of the link between the self and social behavior have focused on the strategies that individuals use to satisfy these motives in particular social contexts. The specification of context is important here, because recent research has shied away from all-encompassing strategies like Freud's (1925) defense mechanisms or Festinger's (1957) dissonance reduction. Instead, it has focused on more circumscribed strategies that take into account both the motives driving the self and the opportunities and limitations inherent in the social context. Most of these strategies specify behavior in the domains of social reasoning, social comparison and interaction, self-presentation, and collective identification.

Social Reasoning Strategies

Research on social reasoning strategies has focused on three effects of self-serving motives: 1. how they influence the content and use of cognitive structures, 2. how they bias memory search and evaluation processes, and 3. how they influence attributional processes. Exactly how these strategies serve the self (i.e. what specific motives are invoked) has received little attention. Instead, the emphasis has been on demonstrating motivationally guided departures from rational thought.

SELF-ENHANCING COGNITIVE STRUCTURES When given sufficient leeway, people define positive traits, abilities, and outcomes in a way that makes them self-descriptive. Dunning and colleagues found that people rate self-descriptive traits as highly central to the prototypes of positive qualities, such as intelligence and creativity, and as not at all central to the prototypes of negative qualities, such as submissiveness and aloofness (Dunning et al 1991). They also found that people with low standing on a particular trait or ability define success more leniently than do those with high standing (Dunning & Cohen 1992). These self-enhancing biases are facilitated by the ambiguity of most traits and abilities, which thereby allows for self-serving definitions that can be justified to self and others (Dunning et al 1989, see also Kunda 1987). Moreover, these studies suggest that the effects of motivation end there: Traits and theories that are defined self-enhancingly are used rationally (Dunning & Cohen 1992).

However, additional studies support the role of self-serving motives in the use of traits and categories as well. For example, several investigations have shown that failure in an ability-related domain leads one to evaluate that ability as less central (Hill et al 1989) and as less important (Frey & Stahlberg 1987). In addition, Niedenthal and colleagues have recently provided evidence for the self-serving use of a prototype-matching strategy (Niedenthal & Mordkoff

1991, Setterlund & Niedenthal 1993). Subjects asked to rank-order four kinds of psychotherapists preferred to see the therapist whose prototypical patient was most dissimilar to them on emotions and most similar to them on traits. Interestingly, these results were stronger for comparisons of the prototype with the ideal self than with the actual self (Niedenthal & Mordkoff 1991). Finally, additional studies indicate that a prototype-matching strategy is used more by people high in self-esteem than by those low in self-esteem (Setterlund & Niedenthal 1993), implicating this cognitive strategy in the maintenance of positive self-regard.

BIASED SEARCH AND EVALUATION PROCESSES Self motives are also pursued through biased strategies for accessing, constructing, and evaluating self-knowledge (Kunda 1990). In numerous studies, Kunda and colleagues (Kunda & Sanitioso 1989, Sanitioso et al 1990) have shown that subjects led to believe that a particular trait is associated with success rated themselves higher on that trait and accessed trait-relevant memories more readily than subjects who believed that the opposite trait predicted success. These self-enhancing tendencies were tempered, however, by self-knowledge: Subjects in these studies were constrained in their self-assessments by their prior standing on the trait dimension. Kunda (1990) has proposed that the motivation to self-enhance simply leads people to pose to themselves the hypothesis that they possess the desired trait, which is then confirmed through normal cognitive processes (Kunda et al 1993).

MOTIVATED ATTRIBUTIONAL PROCESSES Self-serving attributions, and in particular, the tendency to make internal attributions for positive outcomes and external attributions for negative outcomes, are perhaps the most well-researched of all motivated reasoning strategies. They were the primary focus of earlier debates about the validity of a motivational approach (Bradley 1978, Miller & Ross 1975, Tetlock & Levi 1982), and were a major impetus for much of the research we have discussed in this section. Recent studies of self-serving attributions have analyzed closely the motives underlying this strategy and have provided some evidence for its self-protective function. Tennen & Herzberger (1987) found that self-esteem predicts attributional style and argued that attributional style differences that are typically associated with depression, in fact, reflect attempts at self-esteem maintenance. Consistent with the contention that attributional style is driven by self-esteem maintenance, Brown & Rogers (1991) demonstrated that arousal plays a mediating role in the use of external attributions to explain failure. However, a field experiment in which subjects were assigned randomly to receive successful or unsuccessful outcomes provided no evidence of self-serving attributions (Taylor & Riess 1989).

Two additional studies have examined other ways in which self motives influence the attribution process. First, Braun & Wicklund (1988) demonstrated a positive correlation between attributions to ability and effort when a task was relevant to an important identity. They argued that the pursuit of self-knowledge leads people to bring identity-relevant factors into line with each other, and thereby reverses the usual negative relation between ability and effort associated with discounting. Second, Krosnick & Sedikides (1990) found evidence for self-enhancement in people's use of consensus information to predict their own behavior, but only among high self-monitors.

SUMMARY Recent research on motivated reasoning has provided more precise accounts of reasoning than of motivation. Theorists have sought to refine their accounts by isolating the effects of motivation in a single stage of the information-processing sequence. In this way, they have departed from earlier accounts that proposed more pervasive motivational effects (e.g. Pyszczynski & Greenberg 1987).

Social Comparison and Interaction Strategies

Interpersonal contexts provide expanded opportunities for the pursuit of self-knowledge, self-enhancement, and self-improvement. In particular, they allow people to choose comparison targets and interaction partners in ways that maximize benefits to the self. Of the many strategies through which self motives can be satisfied in these social contexts (e.g. Swann et al 1992b, Wood 1989, Wood & Taylor 1991), recent empirical studies have focused primarily on the pursuit of self-knowledge in social interactions and of self-enhancement in social comparisons.

SELF-VERIFICATION IN SOCIAL INTERACTIONS One manifestation of a desire for self-knowledge is that people tend to choose interaction partners who see them as they see themselves. Swann and colleagues (Swann et al 1987, 1989, 1990, 1992a,b) have conducted a series of studies of the self-verification process. According to Swann (1987), people use two general strategies to self-verify: They create environments that confirm their self-views, primarily by choosing appropriate interaction partners, and they interpret and remember their interactions as confirming their self-views. The literature contains considerable support for the second of these strategies (see Swann 1987 for a review); recent empirical studies have focused more closely on the first. The critical tests in these studies have concerned people with negative self-views, for whom self-verification and self-enhancement accounts make differential predictions. Both laboratory (e.g. Swann et al 1989) and field studies (e.g. Swann et al 1992a) have demonstrated that people choose and are highly committed to interaction partners who confirm their self-views, even if those self-views are negative.

Swann and colleagues argue that the inclination to choose interaction partners who confirm one's self-views is rooted in a desire to maintain perceptions of predictability and control. Two different types of findings have provided support for this proposal. First, several studies suggest that people seek verification only of self-views of which they are highly certain and confident (Pelham 1991b, Swann et al 1988). It makes sense that one's desire to know social reality would be most threatened by evidence that disconfirms those things of which one is certain. Second, more direct evidence of the motives underlying self-verification was provided by Swann et al (1992b). They analyzed the spontaneous verbalizations of subjects who were choosing interaction partners, and found that those who chose self-verifying partners did so mostly because the confirmation of their self-views put them at ease. Although the desire for positive social feedback also played a role for people with positive self-views, these positivity strivings were independent of self-verification.

SELF-ENHANCING SOCIAL COMPARISONS Whereas recent studies have portrayed social interactions as vehicles for self-verification, they have portrayed social comparisons primarily as opportunities for self-enhancement. In contrast to Festinger's (1954) original emphasis on the use of social comparison to evaluate one's abilities (in which he invoked both self-knowledge and self-improvement motives), recent investigations have examined the self-enhancing properties of downward comparisons (see Wood 1989 for a review). Many of these investigations were inspired by downward comparison theory (see Wills 1981, 1991), which holds that individuals under threat will improve their subjective well-being by comparing themselves with someone less fortunate. Empirical studies have validated this claim, operationalizing threat as negative feedback (Gibbons & McCoy 1991), low self-esteem (Smith & Insko 1987), depression (Pelham 1991a), and illness (Buunk et al 1990). Several of these studies also provided evidence for the information-seeking aims that Festinger posited (and that considerable earlier research has supported; see Wood 1989, Wood & Taylor 1991 for reviews), but their main emphasis was on the use of downward comparison as a self-enhancement strategy.

Although empirical evidence has generally supported the downward comparison framework, it has revealed the need for elaboration on two points, one pertaining to self-esteem and the other to the social context. Several recent studies indicate that level of self-esteem does not influence the extent of downward comparison (as Wills 1981 proposed), but instead the kind of downward comparison strategies people use. Gibbons & McCoy (1991, see Gibbons & Gerrard 1991) found that high self-esteem subjects were more likely to use an active form of downward comparison when threatened (e.g. to derogate the unfortunate comparison target), whereas low self-esteem subjects were more likely to use a passive form (e.g. to experience mood improvement after the comparison opportunity). Similarly, Brown et al (1988) found that high and low self-esteem subjects differed not in how much they enhanced, but in how directly they enhanced. High self-esteem subjects showed more ingroup favoritism when they were actively involved in a group than when they were not, whereas low self-esteem subjects showed more outgroup derogation when they were not actively involved in a group than when they were active (see also Crocker et al 1987). Brown et al (1988) argued, on the basis of these findings, that everybody seeks positive identities but that people low in self-esteem are constrained in their self-enhancement by concerns over whether their positive identities can be defended.

A similar set of arguments applies to the social context. In a recent investigation, Brown & Gallagher (1992) found that the social context moderates the extent to which people use downward social comparison to self-enhance after failure. Subjects who failed privately tended to exaggerate their relative superiority over others, whereas those who failed publicly showed no signs of self-enhancement. Brown & Gallagher again traced this difference to concern over whether their self-presentations could be defended. It is difficult to maintain (with a straight face) that one is superior after having just shown oneself to be a failure. (See Wood 1989 for a more extended discussion of the role of the social context in social comparison.)

EVIDENCE FOR A SELF-IMPROVEMENT MOTIVE In his original formulation of social comparison theory, Festinger (1954) proposed that comparisons would be characterized by a unidirectional drive upward, whereby people would seek comparisons with slightly superior others in order to obtain information on how to improve. Earlier investigations of social comparison in nonthreatening circumstances have provided considerable evidence for the unidirectional drive upward (see Wood 1989). But recent studies have demonstrated that social comparison can serve this function even in groups under threat. For example, Buunk et al (1990) found that cancer patients were able to benefit from both upward and downward comparisons, with upward comparison targets serving mainly as models of self-improvement (particularly for those patients with high self-esteem). Similarly, Taylor & Lobel (1989) argued that people under threat may evaluate themselves in comparison to less fortunate targets, but they prefer to seek information and affiliation from more fortunate others. Thus, downward comparisons are clearly not the only way to deal with threat. Upward comparison strategies may also serve as effective coping strategies.

UNDERLYING MECHANISMS One obvious question raised by the findings reviewed in this section is how to reconcile the evidence for downward comparison, on the one hand, and self-verification, on the other. That is, what factors promote the differential pursuit of self-enhancement and self-knowledge in these social contexts? A partial answer is provided by research on the mechanisms underlying these strategies. Several studies have provided converging evidence that self-enhancement is rooted primarily in the affective system whereas self-verification is rooted primarily in the cognitive system. Some of this evidence comes from Tesser's (1988) research on the self-evaluation maintenance model. According to this model, reactions to another's performance on a task depend on three variables: the quality of the performance, one's closeness to the performer, and the relevance of the task to the self. For high relevance tasks, one compares oneself to the performer and feels better if the performer does poorly than does well (a form of downward comparison). For low relevance tasks, one reflects in the other's performance and feels better if the performer does well than does poorly. Closeness to the performer increases the pain of comparison and the pleasure of reflection. In several studies, Tesser and colleagues (Tesser et al 1988, 1989, see Tesser 1991 for a review) have shown that this strategy of self-evaluation maintenance is driven by arousal. For example, Tesser et al (1988) found that being outperformed by a close other worsened performance of a complex task but improved performance of a simple task, suggesting that the experience was arousing. In a very different investigation, Tesser et al (1989) found that effects predicted by the self-evaluation maintenance model were found under normal conditions but were eliminated when arousal could be misattributed. These and other studies suggest that self-evaluation maintenance, which includes a downward comparison component, is rooted in the affective system (see also Paulus & Levitt 1987).

Further evidence that different mechanisms underlie self-enhancement and self-verification was provided by Swann and his colleagues (Swann et al 1987). Swann et al (1987) presented subjects who had positive or negative self-views with either favorable or unfavorable social feedback. They found that cognitive responses to the feedback were influenced by its consistency with their self-views, whereas affective responses were influenced by its positivity. Swann et al (1990) provided additional support for the cognitive basis of self-verification. In several studies, they found that people preferred consistent feedback under normal conditions, but preferred enhancing feedback when deprived of cognitive resources. Swann et al argued that self-enhancement is driven by a simple preference for favorable social feedback, whereas self-verification involves a more complex process of comparing feedback with representations of the self in memory.

SUMMARY Recent studies of social comparison and social interaction have addressed two separate questions. Social comparison studies have focused on the strategies that people use under threat, and have thereby invoked the affective system and desires for self-enhancement. Social interaction studies, on the other hand, have typically examined choice of interaction partners in the absence of explicit evaluative threat, and thus have invoked desires for self-knowledge. The points of convergence in these two research traditions, particularly regarding the motives and mechanisms underlying the strategies, suggest that they are most usefully conceived as complementary approaches. A view of the self as driven by both self-enhancement and self-knowledge concerns can accommodate all of the existing data.

Self-Presentation Strategies

The task of presenting oneself before others offers yet another forum for the pursuit of self motives. The strategic possibilities in this context seem almost limitless, and indeed, recent studies serve as a testimony to this broad range of possibilities. Less research attention has been given to disentangling the motives underlying these strategies. Most theoretical frameworks have implicitly or explicitly included the three self motives that we have described, typically combining them under the more general goal of constructing desired identities that are both believable (a self-knowledge concern) and beneficial (a self-enhancement/self-improvement concern; see Leary & Kowalski 1990, Schlenker & Weigold 1989, 1992). In addition, some of these models have posited interpersonal motives for self-presentation, including the desire to maximize social and material outcomes (Leary & Kowalski 1990) and to influence the behavior of others (Baumeister 1982).

CONTENTS OF SELF-PRESENTATIONS The contents of self-presentations are influenced by numerous factors including properties of the presenter (e.g. his or her current self-concept, desired and undesired identities) and properties of the social context (e.g. role constraints, the beliefs and values of the audience; see Leary & Kowalski 1990). Several recent studies have outlined strategies that presenters use to self-enhance in contexts that mitigate against positive self-images. For example, Fleming & Rudman (1993) examined self-presentational strategies that people use to insulate themselves from the consequences of negative self-discrepant behaviors. They found that subjects who read counterattitudinal essays about affirmative action in front of an African-American audience member performed various distancing behaviors (e.g. self-embracing posture, lip and mouth movements, disclaimers, excuses) in order to dissociate themselves from their statements. This strategy was apparently quite effective, as it eliminated the need for dissonance-reducing attitude change and served as a discounting cue for naive observers. In another line of research, Cialdini and colleagues (Cialdini & DeNicholas 1989, Finch & Cialdini 1989) investigated self-presentational strategies involving associations with others. They found that subjects who believed they were in a unit relation with another person (a male who was described as sharing their birthday) presented him and their connection with him so as to benefit both parties, even when he was disreputable or a failure. These studies illustrate that people are skilled self-enhancers, even within quite constraining contexts.

Of course, people vary in what they consider to be a desirable identity to present. For example, Jones et al (1990) assigned subjects to play the role of a morally reprehensible person and found that high self-monitors felt better if they succeeded than if they failed, whereas low self-monitors felt better if they failed than if they succeeded. Schlenker & Weigold (1990) found that privately self-conscious subjects presented themselves as autonomous, whereas publicly self-conscious subjects presented themselves as social animals. Chaiken and colleagues (Mori et al 1987, Pliner & Chaiken 1990) found that female subjects moderated their eating behavior in order to present themselves as feminine, consuming less while getting acquainted with a desirable male than with other types of companions. Thus, people differ considerably in how they want to be seen, but they share in common an active pursuit of those desired self-images (see also Doherty et al 1990).

ROLE OF SELF-ESTEEM Self-esteem has also proven to be an important predictor of how people self-present, and in particular, of the extent to which they present themselves in a self-enhancing fashion. Two competing views of the relation between self-esteem and self-presentation have been proposed. First, Baumeister et al (1989) have suggested that people with high self-esteem tend to present themselves in a self-enhancing fashion, characterized by an inclination to accept risks, to focus on their outstandingly good qualities, to engage in strategic ploys, and to call attention to themselves. People with low self-esteem, on the other hand, tend to present themselves in a self-protective fashion, characterized by an inclination to avoid risks, to focus on avoiding their outstandingly bad qualities, to eschew strategic ploys, and to refrain from calling attention to themselves. In support of this framework, Baumeister et al (1993) found that when exposed to evaluative threat, subjects with high self-esteem took greater risks (and as a result, tended to lose more) than subjects with low self-esteem. Similarly, Schlenker et al (1990) found that social pressures (i.e. pressure to make a good impression and to make it publicly) led high self-esteem subjects to be more self-assertive and low self-esteem subjects to be more self-protective in their attributions, especially after they had received failure feedback (see also Brown & Gallagher 1992).

Baumgardner et al (1990) have proposed a very different view of the relation between self-esteem and self-presentation. They began with the premise that self-enhancement is a strategy used to improve affect and that this strategy necessarily takes different forms depending on the favorableness of one's self-regard. People with high self-esteem, because they are certain of their positive self-conceptions, tend to engage in private self-enhancement involving thought and attentional processes. People with low self-esteem, by contrast, need social support for their positive self-conceptions and thus tend to engage in public self-enhancement involving self-presentation. Several empirical studies have provided evidence consistent with this framework (see Baumgardner 1990, Baumgardner et al 1989).

Although these two views make opposite predictions about who will engage in public self-enhancement, they have several points of convergence. In particular, both suggest that a critical factor affecting how people present themselves is the certainty with which they hold their self-conceptions. However, the two accounts differ in what they regard to be the goal of self-presentation. For Baumeister and colleagues, self-presentation is a strategy for securing positive evaluations of the self by others. People with high self-esteem seek to maximize the positivity of these evaluations by adopting a self-assertive style. People with low self-esteem seek to minimize the negativity of these evaluations by adopting a self-protective style. For Baumgardner and colleagues, self-presentation is a strategy for improving self-affect. People with high self-esteem do not need to assert to others that they are good in order to have positive self-regard. People with low self-esteem feel more certain of themselves in public than in private, and thus engage in more public forms of self-enhancement.

These views also differ in the circumstances under which each applies. Most of the studies supporting Baumeister's view involve behavior under threatening conditions (e.g. when the audience expects failure or when subjects have received failure feedback), whereas those supporting Baumgardner's view do not involve an explicit threat. This difference may also account for the differential predictions of the two frameworks (see Baumgardner et al 1990).

SELF-HANDICAPPING Another strategy of self-enhancing presentation that is used under threatening circumstances is self-handicapping. In self-handicapping, people arrange in advance for impediments to a successful performance, thereby ensuring that failure will not threaten their self-esteem (Jones & Berglas 1978). Although self-handicapping is only one of many self-presentational strategies that people can use to ward off threat, it has proven to be an enormously popular topic of research for the past 15 years (Higgins et al 1990).

Like other self-presentational strategies, self-handicapping is influenced by both properties of the presenter and properties of the social context. Shepperd & Arkin (1989a) provide a recent example of research on contextual factors. Subjects were to take either a high- or low-validity aptitude test with an impediment to their performance (i.e. a handicap) either already present or absent in the environment. The question was whether they would choose a handicap themselves. Results indicated that subjects chose a handicap only in anticipation of an important task and only if no preexisting handicap was available in the environment. In a review of the situational influences on self-handicapping, Self (1990) concluded that self-handicapping is most likely when an important aspect of the self is threatened with public disconfirmation, when handicaps are both available and legitimate, and when the performance does not involve tangible rewards.

More attention has been paid lately to how properties of the presenter influence self-handicapping. Rhodewalt et al (1991; see Rhodewalt 1990) have developed a self-report inventory that measures generalized preferences for self-handicapping behavior. This measure has been found to predict both the likelihood that a person will self-handicap and the specific strategies that he or she will employ (see also Hirt et al 1991). Likewise, public self-consciousness has been found to predict the likelihood of self-handicapping (Shepperd & Arkin 1989b). And numerous studies have demonstrated gender differences in the likelihood (Shepperd & Arkin 1989b) and strategies (Hirt et al 1991) of self-handicapping, although these gender differences are still not well understood (see Rhodewalt 1990 for a review).

Not surprisingly, self-esteem is also associated with differences in self-handicapping. Although scores on the self-handicapping scale are inversely related to self-esteem (Rhodewalt 1990), indicating that people low in self-esteem are more likely to self-handicap, recent evidence suggests that people high in self-esteem are also likely to self-handicap if presented with an opportunity to appear outstanding. For example, Rhodewalt et al (1991) found that high self-esteem subjects used self-handicapping both to discount failure and to augment success, whereas low self-esteem subjects used it only to discount failure (and then, only if they scored high on the self-handicapping scale). Similarly, in several investigations, Tice (1991) found that high self-esteem subjects were more likely to handicap if success was meaningful whereas low self-esteem subjects were more likely to handicap if failure was meaningful (see also Tice & Baumeister 1990). These and additional findings support the view that self-presentation serves an enhancing function for people of high self-esteem and a protective function for people of low self-esteem (Baumeister et al 1989).

Finally, several studies have addressed the effectiveness of different types of self-handicapping, both as a discounting cue for the audience and as a self-esteem buffer for the presenter. From the audience perspective (typically, a subject reading a scenario), involuntary handicaps, like depressive symptoms (Schouten & Handelsman 1987) or unintentional low effort (Baumgardner & Levy 1988), appear to serve as more powerful discounting cues for poor performance than do voluntary handicaps (Baumgardner & Levy 1988). Moreover, even when voluntary handicaps reduce negative attributions about ability, they can lead to more negative attributions about other personal characteristics (Luginbuhl & Palmer 1991). However, from the presenter's perspective, self-handicapping can be an effective strategy to ward off the negative feelings that come with failure. Rhodewalt et al (1991) found that self-handicapping reduced the dampening influence of failure on both self-esteem and mood, whereas it had no effect on the positivity associated with success. Thus, for the presenter, self-handicapping may be a valuable strategy indeed.

SUMMARY Research on self-presentation has continued to reveal just how skillful people are at constructing strategies to negotiate difficult social circumstances. The view of the self underlying this research is quite consistent with the enhancement- and knowledge-seeking creature we have been describing. However, self-presentation research has also accorded the social context (including the audience and properties of the situation) a powerful role in determining an individual's goals and behaviors. Indeed, this work provides an excellent illustration of how the self both shapes and is shaped by the social context. We will see more evidence for this theme in the literature on collective identification.

Collective Identification Strategies

The relation of the individual to the collective has traditionally been a central issue in social psychology. In this section, we examine recent advances in the study of how the self influences and is influenced by identification with social groups. This literature reflects the growing conviction among many researchers that self structure and process must be considered with reference to entities larger than the individual (Brewer 1991; Crocker & Major 1989; Deaux 1992a,b, 1993; McCann 1990; Markus & Cross 1990; Morgan & Schwalbe 1990; Serpe & Stryker 1987; Stryker 1991). Empirical support for this contention is accumulating, but the theoretical statements remain more impressive at the present time. These statements can be classified, according to their primary focus, into two categories: self-enhancement and self-esteem maintenance theories and distinctiveness theories.

SELF-ENHANCEMENT THEORIES Most recent research on self-collective relations has been guided by social identity theory and its successors. The original formulation of social identity theory (Tajfel 1972, Tajfel & Turner 1986) stated that individuals strive to maintain or enhance their self-esteem by their membership in social groups that permit either positive or negative identification. More recently, self-categorization theory has incorporated this assumption into a more explicit account of the self (Turner 1985, Turner et al 1987, Turner & Oakes 1989). Self-categorization theory defines the self-concept as comprised of two components: personal identity and social identity. Personal identity refers to the self-categorization or cognitive grouping of the self based on intrapersonal similarities and differences from other individuals. Social identity refers to the social categorization of the self based on interpersonal similarities or differences derived from group membership (e.g. Californian, Zoroastrian, female). Of particular interest are the conditions under which people are more likely to categorize themselves primarily in terms of their personal or social identity and the consequences of such categorization.

Considerable research has addressed the second of these questions, and much of it has examined the effects of shifting focus from personal to social identity on subsequent behavior. These studies have shown that this shift in focus (known as depersonalization) leads individuals to behave as group members, producing increased evidence for such group behaviors as stereotyping, cooperation and competition, norm formation, conformity, and polarization (Abrams et al 1990, Brewer & Schneider 1990, Hogg 1992, Oakes & Turner 1990, Turner 1991, Turner et al 1987).

More recently, attention has turned to the questions of how and why variability in self-categorization emerges. Here, Turner and colleagues (see Turner et al 1994) subscribe to Bruner's (1957) emphasis on the accessibility of particular categories as a function of past experience, present circumstances, and immediate motives and goals. The relative prominence of personal versus social identity derives from the degree of fit between category specifications and the stimulus to be represented. For example, Hogg & Turner (1987) found that males and females used gender in judgments of self more when they made intergroup rather than intragroup comparisons (see also Oakes et al 1991).

The notion of fit has also been used to generate predictions about the role of social context in self-judgment (Turner et al 1994). For example, several studies have shown that self-categorization becomes more inclusive as comparative context expands to include those seen as different from self (increasing perceived differences between *us* and *them* compared to differences between *me* and *you*) (Haslam & Turner 1992, Gaertner et al 1989, Wilder & Thompson 1988). Additional evidence suggests that these results reflect the influence of social context on the way social categories are defined. Specifically, McGarty et al (1992) found that changes in ingroup/outgroup boundaries altered judgments of common social categories (e.g. categories such as psychologist and American). Such experiments have been interpreted to implicate a view of self as neither fixed nor chaotic, but as a dynamic process that works in lawful relation to the social context (Turner et al 1994).

Social identity and self-categorization theories have inspired numerous related accounts of collective identification. For example, Cheek (1989) has proposed a view of personal and social identities in which they are not defined by the immediate social context but instead are stable, enduring properties of individuals. In Cheek's formulation, personal identity refers to one's self-knowledge and self-evaluation, whereas social identity includes the characteristics of self that emerge in interaction with others (e.g. attraction, popularity). Support for a dispositional view of these identities has come from correlational research relating individual differences in personal and social identity to numerous traits and behaviors, including altruism, social appropriateness, achievement, and uniqueness (for discussion of individual differences in identity effects see also Abrams 1992, Hinkle & Brown 1990).

Another perspective on collective identification has emerged from a closer consideration of the relation between self-esteem and group membership (Crocker & Major 1989). An examination of the empirical literature on this point reveals an apparent contradiction: Studies have consistently failed to demonstrate the association between membership in a stigmatized group and low global self-esteem that would be predicted by social identity and other theories. Crocker & Major (1989) proposed instead that members of stigmatized groups can adopt several strategies to deflect negative feedback including 1. attributing it to the group rather than self (Crocker et al 1991), 2. comparing themselves with disadvantaged (ingroup) rather than advantaged (outgroup) others, and 3. selectively devaluing those dimensions on which their group is known to perform poorly. In a related inquiry, Bat-Chava (1994) found that among deaf subjects, the relation between group identification and self-esteem was low overall, but was moderated by the degree of deaf awareness present in the subject's family. If awareness was low (hearing parents and siblings, no use of sign language), the correlation between self-esteem and group identification remained low; if awareness was high, a substantial correlation between these two variables was observed. Such analyses add to a growing body of literature suggesting that the relationship between self-esteem and group identity is not nearly as straightforward as earlier theories would suggest.

In a separate line of work, Crocker & Luhtanen (1990; Luhtanen & Crocker 1991, 1992) have developed and tested a measure of collective self-esteem. They construe collective self-esteem to be an individual difference variable (empirically distinct from personal self-esteem) that measures the extent to which individuals generally evaluate their social groups positively. Crocker & Luhtanen (1990) provided recent evidence in support of this notion of collective self-esteem. Subjects in a minimal group experiment received either success or failure feedback about the performance of their group and then rated above-average and below-average scorers. Results showed that subjects high in collective self-esteem varied their ratings to enhance ingroup performance, whereas subjects low in collective self-esteem did not (nor was this pattern obtained when using the personal self-esteem measure). Similarly, Brown et al (1988) found that high self-esteem subjects (measured by the Texas Social Behavior Inventory, a measure that places emphasis on the social aspects of self-esteem) were more likely than low self-esteem subjects to display ingroup favoritism when they were directly involved in group processes. However, this study also showed that low self-esteem subjects were more likely than high self-esteem subjects to display ingroup favoritism when they were not directly involved in group processes.

In a final, related line of research, Deaux (1991, 1992a,b) has examined how individual experiences combine with social situations to influence identity. Deaux (1993) defines identity as the social categories in which an individual claims membership, and focuses on how people adopt identities by categorizing themselves as members of various groups. This perspective differs from traditional social identity and self-categorization theories primarily in the emphasis it places on the personal meaning that individuals attach to their social categories. As a result, Deaux (1993) views personal and social identity to be very closely linked. On the one hand, personal identity is partly defined by group memberships and on the other, identification with social categories is colored by personal meanings. She and her colleagues have explored this notion of identity by asking subjects to name the identities they claim and then to provide the characteristics associated with each identity.

Additional arguments for a more flexible view of personal and social identity have been offered by Abrams (1992, Abrams & Hogg 1988). His disagreement with traditional social identity theory concerns its emphasis on the self-esteem maintenance function of collective identification. Abrams contends that identification with a group can, in fact, serve a myriad of functions, ranging from material wealth, power, and control, to self-knowledge, cognitive consistency, and self-efficacy. Moreover, Abrams (1994) has recently argued for the integration of social identity and self-awareness approaches in order to achieve a better understanding of collective behavior.

DISTINCTIVENESS THEORIES A second set of theories has emphasized the role of distinctiveness in determining the collectives that define the self. In an account inspired by social identity theory, Brewer (1991, 1993) has proposed that collective identification is driven by the tension between needs for validation and similarity to others and needs for uniqueness and individuation. According to her optimal distinctiveness theory, social identity is a compromise between assimilation toward others (i.e. those in the ingroup) and differentiation away from others (i.e. those in the outgroup). Among the theory's main assumptions is that individuals will identify most strongly with groups that best resolve this conflict between assimilation and differentiation.

In support of optimal distinctiveness theory, Brewer (1991) reviewed research showing that individuals often act in accordance with their social identity rather than their personal identity, even when the context is not explicitly depersonalizing. For example, numerous studies have shown that people perceive greater discrimination against their groups than against themselves, and that it is the perception of group discrimination that motivates collective action

(Taylor et al 1987, 1990). In a more direct test of the optimal distinctiveness notion, Brewer & Schneider (1990) examined collective identification using a social dilemma task. They found that if a collective identity was not available or if the available collective was large or amorphous, subjects acted in their own self-interest. However, if the available collective was intermediate in size, subjects acted in the collective interest.

Distinctiveness is derived, in part, from group size, leading to the prediction that group identification will be stronger among members of minority than majority groups. This prediction has received support from studies showing that biases in favor of the ingroup increase as the ratio of ingroup to outgroup size decreases (Mullen et al 1992). However, group status complicates this simple prediction, as minority size is often correlated with disadvantages in status, placing distinctiveness and positive social identity in opposition. Recently, Brewer et al (1993) examined the effects of group status, majority status, and depersonalization on ingroup bias. They found that group status and majority status interacted for control subjects, with members of high status majority groups and of low status minority groups providing the most positive evaluations of the ingroup. However, for depersonalized subjects, they found that members of minority groups provided more positive ingroup evaluations than did members of majority groups, irrespective of status.

McGuire & McGuire (1988) have adopted a unique approach to the study of distinctiveness. Pointing out that research on the self has overemphasized reactive measures and evaluative judgments, they have examined the self by asking subjects simply to "Tell us about yourself" or "Tell us about school." Numerous findings have supported their major prediction that distinctive aspects of self would be mentioned more frequently in these spontaneous self-concepts than would nondistinctive aspects. For example, boys and girls mentioned their gender more often as the number of opposite gender members in their family increased. Likewise, children who belonged to ethnic minority groups were more likely to mention their ethnicity than were white children, but were less likely to mention their ethnicity as its representation in their classroom increased. These findings demonstrate the importance of both enduring and immediate social contexts in shaping the self-concept.

SUMMARY Research on collective identification strategies has shown how these strategies reflect both the motives of the self and the influence of the social context. Some investigators have emphasized the agency of individuals, who are guided in their relations with collectives by needs for self-enhancement and self-definition (Brewer 1991, Crocker & Major 1989, Deaux 1993, Turner et al 1994). Others have emphasized the influence of group membership in the spontaneous self-concept (McGuire & McGuire 1988). Taken together, these investigations have provided considerable support for the contention that collectives are not external to individuals, but instead are authentic and significant aspects of the self.

MODERATING VARIABLES

Our discussion has focused on the common psychological and behavioral strategies through which people pursue goals of self-knowledge, self-enhancement, and self-improvement. However, numerous variables moderate the use of these strategies by particular individuals. In some cases, these variables influence the form that a particular strategy takes (e.g. the dimensions of downward comparison, the methods of self-handicapping, the relations between public and private collective self-esteem). In other cases, these variables influence whether a particular strategy is adopted at all (e.g. whether people choose situations using a prototype-matching strategy, whether they self-enhance after failure). We now review explicitly such moderating effects, documenting the influence of social categories, individual difference variables, and culture on the self. We focus especially on how these variables moderate strategies of the self, but also review their effects on related aspects of self-evaluation and self-definition.

Social Categories

Social psychologists trained in psychology have traditionally devoted little attention to how membership in particular social categories shapes the self. However, this topic has been of long-standing interest to sociologists, who see social categories, and more generally social roles and identities, as providing definition and meaning to self (see Markus & Cross 1990 for a review). Recent theoretical perspectives include Stryker's (1991) identity theory, which considers how societal norms that are attached to social category, positional, and role designations are translated into individual identities. Also, Wiley & Alexander (1987) have offered an analysis of the conditions under which social categories and roles should influence the self (e.g. they argue that if one component of a role is gratifying, other aspects of the role will be adopted as well). Here, we review empirical studies that have demonstrated an influence of social category membership on the self, focusing in particular on gender and ethnicity.

GENDER Gender is the most fundamental of human categories, so it is hardly surprising that gender should influence the strategies of the self. We have already reviewed evidence showing gender differences in downward comparison (Gibbons & McCoy 1991), self-presentation (Mori et al 1987), and self-handicapping strategies (Hirt et al 1991). In addition, Josephs et al (1992) found gender differences in the bases for self-esteem, with men deriving self-esteem from achievements that are personally distinguishing and women deriving self-esteem from attachments to important others. But in a related finding, Pratt et al (1990) demonstrated that gender differences in connectedness (females greater than males) disappear in late adulthood, when connectedness becomes important for men as well.

Although research on gender has moved away from simply documenting main effects, some gender differences in self-evaluation and self-definition have been noted. Recent research has shown that women more than men underestimate performance on self-evaluations (Beyer 1990), place less value on physical attractiveness in others (Feingold 1990), score higher on some measures of emotional intensity (Fujita et al 1991, LaFrance & Banaji 1992), report greater happiness and life satisfaction (Wood et al 1989), self-disclose to a greater degree under conditions of close friendships (Dindia & Allen 1992), and disclose information of differing quality to same-sex and opposite-sex partners (Snell 1989).

Additional gender differences have been documented in aspects of the self related to depression. Levit (1991) found that adolescent males make greater use of externalizing ego-defenses (e.g. projection and outward aggression), whereas female adolescents make greater use of internalizing ego-defenses (e.g. turning against the self). Similarly, Block et al (1991), in a study of the antecedent conditions of depressive tendencies, found that girls show less aggression, less self-aggrandizing, and greater overcontrolling than do boys. Further studies have shown that women exhibit a greater tendency to self-focus (Ingram et al 1988), and to amplify their moods by ruminating about their depressed states (Nolen-Hoeksema 1987) than do men. Finally, Rohde et al (1990) found that being female predicted a future diagnosis of depression, but did not predict an increase in depressive symptoms.

Finally, the relation between gender and gender identity has emerged as an important topic of research. Investigations have suggested that gender identity, rather than gender per se, is often the better predictor of behavior. For example, Jose & McCarthy (1988) found that subjects with high masculinity scores on the Bem Sex Role Inventory (Bem 1974) were perceived to talk more and to contribute more good ideas in the course of social interaction, whereas females and subjects with high femininity scores were judged to be more concerned about group members' feelings. Other studies have shown that gender identity influences behaviors as diverse as me–not me judgments on trait adjectives (Payne et al 1987) and choice of ego defense style (Levit 1991). These and similar findings have led to the development of a new procedure to measure the contribution of gender in terms of diagnosticity (Lippa 1991).

SATISFACTION WITH THE PHYSICAL SELF Among the various dimensions of self, none is as visible as one's physical self or body. Social psychologists have traditionally paid little attention to this facet of self, but its importance is beginning to be recognized (Cash & Pruzinsky 1990). In particular, Cash (1990) has recently documented the ways that bodily attributes affect self-perceptions. Additionally, Fallon (1990) has reviewed the influence of culture on the formation and maintenance of body image, the differential influence of cultural standards on individuals within social categories of sex, culture, and class, and the suffering caused by unnatural cultural ideals of body image.

Empirical evidence for the impact of the physical self on self-evaluation and self-definition, especially among women, has been provided by Chaiken, Pliner, and their colleagues. Pliner et al (1990) conducted a survey of more than 600 women and men, ranging in age from 10 to 79 years, in which they measured concern with body weight, eating, physical appearance, and global and appearance-specific self-esteem. Women reported more concern than men about body weight, eating, and physical appearance, and showed lower appearance self-esteem than men at all ages. In a related experiment, Chaiken & Pliner (1987) found that a food diary attributed to a male or female target who ate either small or large meals led to different inferences about the target on a variety of dimensions: Male targets were rated similarly regardless of the size of their meal, whereas females were rated as more feminine, more likely to possess feminine personality traits, more concerned about appearance, and more physically attractive if they ate small portions than if they ate large portions.

Additional studies have shown how these gender-specific norms for appearance and eating behavior shape self-presentation strategies. Mori et al (1987) found that females ate reliably less when in the presence of a desirable rather than an undesirable opposite-sex partner, whereas males did not show this sensitivity to partner's attractiveness. Even more impressively, females who had been led to believe that they had masculine rather than feminine interests ate less in the presence of a partner whom they believed was aware of this information. More recently, Pliner & Chaiken (1990) have suggested that although both men and women are concerned about social desirability in eating behavior, women show an additional concern with appearing feminine.

Finally, a separate line of research has provided converging evidence for the relation between physical appearance and self-evaluation, especially among women. Following from Higgins' (1987) self-discrepancy theory, Strauman et al (1991) found that actual-ideal discrepancies among female undergraduates were correlated with dissatisfaction with body mass and appearance-related beliefs about self. In addition, an actual-ideal discrepancy was associated with bulimic-related disorders and an actual-ought discrepancy with anorexic-related disorders in populations of both women and men.

ETHNICITY Social scientists have theorized that ethnicity is central to the self-concept, but surprisingly little empirical research on this topic has appeared in the major personality and social psychology journals (see Phinney 1990 for a review). There are, however, a few very recent findings to suggest that ethnicity influences collective identification strategies and their relation to psychological well-being. First, in an investigation of identity change among Hispanic students at Ivy League universities, Ethier & Deaux (1990) found no relation between perceptions of identity threat (as measured by self-report) and ethnic identity among students entering college, but a large negative correlation was found on later measures. This research also showed that the stronger the perceived threat to one's identity, the more likely that identity was to be viewed negatively (see also Cameron & Lalonde 1994).

In addition, Crocker et al (1991) have provided evidence that ethnicity moderates both relations among components of collective self-esteem and the relation of collective self-esteem to psychological well-being. Among European-, Asian-, and African-American college students, these investigators found systematic differences in the relation between the public self and the private self. European-American students showed a moderate positive correlation between public and private collective self-esteem, suggesting that they view their own social groups largely as they believe others evaluate them. African-American students, on the other hand, showed no correlation between public and private collective self-esteem, suggesting a separation of personal feelings about their groups from beliefs about how others evaluate them. In contrast to both these groups, Asian-American students showed a high positive correlation between public and private collective self-esteem, suggesting that they place a strong emphasis on the connection between themselves and their groups (see Markus & Kitayama 1991). In addition, this study showed that for members of minority groups (African-Americans and Asian-Americans), but not the majority group (European-Americans), collective self-esteem predicted psychological well-being beyond the effects of personal self-esteem. (For a discussion of the effects of race identity on self-esteem see Jones 1992.)

SUMMARY Taken together, these demonstrations of the moderating effects of social categories provide important evidence for the influence of society on the self (Stryker 1991). Social categories differ both in their desirability (as culturally defined) and in what their members consider to be desirable behavior. Thus, the strategies used by members of these categories to pursue self-knowledge and especially self-enhancement are likely to differ as well. The studies in this section, particularly those of Pliner & Chaiken (1990), Ethier & Deaux (1990), and Crocker et al (1994), serve as excellent illustrations of this point.

Individual Differences

Numerous individual differences in personality have also been found to moderate the strategies of the self. By far the most popular moderator among researchers has been self-esteem, although a number of others have received attention as well. In this section, we review recent research on individual differences in self-strategies, focusing especially on studies that have linked individual difference variables directly to concerns with self-knowledge and self-enhancement.

SELF-ESTEEM Common conceptions of self-esteem tend to equate it with the balance of positive and negative conceptions one has about oneself. The more positive self-conceptions and the fewer negative self-conceptions one holds, the higher one's self-esteem. In support of this view, Greenwald et al (1988) demonstrated reliable correlations between self-esteem and the number of items generated in categories such as liked activities, positive qualities, and names of friends.

However, most recent investigations of self-esteem have emphasized not its evaluative component but rather its association with the certainty or clarity of self-conceptions (Pelham & Swann 1989). For example, Baumgardner (1990) demonstrated that individuals with low self-esteem were less certain than those with high self-esteem about possessing a variety of trait attributes. Likewise, Campbell (1990) found that individuals with low self-esteem rated themselves less extremely, less confidently, less quickly, and with less temporal stability than did individuals with high self-esteem. In addition, this study showed that the self-concepts of low self-esteem people, compared with high self-esteem people, were less internally consistent, less congruent with perceptions of current behavior, and less congruent with memory for past behavior (see also Campbell & Fehr 1990).

Most of the moderating effects of self-esteem on motivated strategies have been traced to this association between self-esteem and self-certainty. In particular, differences between individuals with high and low self-esteem in prototype-matching (Setterlund & Niedenthal 1993), downward comparison (Gibbons & McCoy 1991), ingroup favoritism (Brown et al 1988), self-presentation (Baumeister et al 1989, 1993; Baumgardner 1990, Baumgardner et al 1989, Schlenker et al 1990), and self-handicapping (Baumeister et al 1989, Rhodewalt et al 1991, Tice 1991, Tice & Baumeister 1990) have all been attributed to underlying differences in the certainty of their self-conceptions. In addition, Brown and colleagues have recently shown that the self-evaluations of low self-esteem people were more vulnerable to their recent experiences (Brown & Smart 1991) and to their mood (Brown & Mankowski 1993) than were those of high self-esteem people.

Finally, additional studies have suggested that self-certainty is an important predictor of the relation between self-esteem and emotional experience. Kernis et al (1991) found that an inverse correlation between level of self-esteem and depression emerged only for individuals with stable self-esteem (as measured by repeated completion of a self-esteem measure; see Showers 1992a for a related finding). And in a separate investigation, Kernis et al (1989) found that unstable self-esteem was associated with greater tendencies to experience anger and hostility, especially among high self-esteem individuals.

OTHER INDIVIDUAL DIFFERENCES Self-esteem is not the only variable that moderates the strategies of the self. We have already reviewed studies demonstrating the influence of self-monitoring on social reasoning (Krosnick & Sedikides 1990) and of both self-monitoring (Jones et al 1990) and self-consciousness (Schlenker & Weigold 1990) on self-presentation. In these cases, the moderating variables appear to affect the kind of private or public image that the self seeks.

In other cases, moderating variables influence the type of strategy that is adopted. Researchers have identified a number of specific strategies that characterize some individuals but not others. For example, Cantor et al (1987) have distinguished between two types of people who differ in their approaches to challenging situations: Optimists assume the best until proven otherwise and protect self-esteem only in the event of failure; defensive pessimists emphasize the negative possibilities inherent in a situation up front in order to prepare for the possibility of failure and to motivate maximum effort. Each of these self-protective strategies can work very well, but only for individuals disposed to use them. Recent studies have demonstrated that a mismatch between the person and the strategy has negative consequences for both affect and performance (Norem & Illingworth 1993, Showers 1992b). Similar investigations have delineated a self-critical interaction strategy (Powers & Zuroff 1988) and a narcissistic personality style (Raskin et al 1991), each of which serves a self-protective function for particular individuals.

Culture

An additional moderator of self-evaluation and self-definition is culture. In recent years, two influential analyses of culture and the self, one by Markus & Kitayama (1991) and the other by Triandis (1989), have traced differences in self-related thoughts and feelings to differing cultural emphases on independence and individualism, on the one hand, and interdependence and collectivism, on the other. To date, this research has sought primarily to document group differences in the self as a function of geographic location or, even more generally, of simple East-West distinctions. However, the consequences of these cultural differences for motivation and behavior are a source of considerable current interest. Thus, without examining the controversial questions that typically accompany cross-cultural research, we summarize here the two major theoretical perspectives on culture and the self and recent findings that support them.

In his analysis of culture and the self, Triandis (1989) relied on the common distinction between the private self (the assessment of self by the self), the public self (the assessment of self by a generalized other), and the collective self (the assessment of self by a particular reference group). Triandis argued that the probability that an individual will sample each of these three aspects of the self varies across cultures. In individualistic cultures (e.g. the United States) the private self tends to be more complex and more salient than the collective self, and thus is more likely to be sampled. In collectivistic cultures [e.g. Japan, the People's Republic of China (PRC)], the collective self tends to be more complex and more salient than the private self, and thus is more likely to be sampled. Recent empirical studies have provided support for this framework. Trafimow et al (1991) found that private and collective self-cognitions were represented independently in memory, and that subjects from an individualistic culture (the United States) retrieved more cognitions about the private self and fewer about the collective self than did subjects from a collectivistic culture (e.g. the PRC).

Additional investigations have focused on documenting the consequences of these cultural differences in self-sampling. Triandis et al (1990) used subjects from five cultures known to differ a priori in their levels of collectivism (America, Greece, Hawaii, Hong Kong, and the PRC) and five methods to probe aspects of self. They found that the view of self obtained from members of collectivistic cultures showed more group-linked elements, greater perception of homogeneity of ingroup than outgroup, more intimate and subordinate behavior toward the ingroup, and greater emphasis on values that promote the welfare of the ingroup than did the self obtained from members of individualistic cultures. However, further evidence has suggested that these cultural differences in closeness to the ingroup are not observed for all types of ingroups (Triandis et al 1988).

Markus & Kitayama (1991, 1994) provided a related view of culture and the self. In contrast to Triandis' (1989) comprehensive theory of cross-cultural differences, Markus & Kitayama focused their analysis on just one aspect of how people see themselves, namely, their degree of separation from versus connection with others. They distinguished between two types of self-construals: an independent construal, in which the self is a separate and autonomous entity, guided by internal thoughts, feelings, and actions; and an interdependent construal, in which the self is fundamentally connected with others and guided, at least in part, by perceptions of others' thoughts, feelings, and actions. Markus & Kitayama (1991, 1994) argued that Western cultures promote the development of an independent self-construal, whereas many non-Western cultures promote the development of an interdependent self-construal (see also Singelis 1994 for a self-report scale that measures interdependent and independent self-construals).

Markus & Kitayama (1991) maintained that these divergent self-construals have specific consequences for cognition, motivation, and behavior. Recent empirical investigations have begun to document these consequences, focusing especially on cognition. For example, Markus & Kitayama (1991) reported the results of a study in which students raised in the United States showed asymmetries in self-other similarity judgments in favor of self (i.e. self was judged as less similar to other than other to self), whereas students raised in India showed the opposite asymmetry. Similarly, Cousins (1989) found that Japanese and American students differed in their patterns of self-descriptions depending on the interpersonal context. In response to the generic prompt, "Who am I?," Japanese students provided examples of behaviors in specific roles (i.e. one who swims often), whereas American students described themselves with psychological attributes (e.g. easy going). However, in response to a contextualized prompt (e.g. "Who am I with family?," "Who am I with friends?"), Japanese students described themselves with psychological attributes, whereas American students referred to preferences and wishes. These findings illustrate some of the cognitive consequences of independent and interdependent self-construals; their motivational and behavioral consequences remain largely unexplored.

SUMMARY Recent research has provided two useful frameworks within which to examine the moderating effects of culture on the self. The ways in which culture influences both the motives of the self and the psychological and behavioral strategies used to pursue these motives are intriguing topics for future research (see Markus & Kitayama 1991).

INFLUENCE OF STRATEGIES ON THE SELF

Thus far, the self has been seen primarily as a causal agent in the regulation of behavior in a variety of social contexts. But the relation between the self and social behavior is not unidirectional—the strategies that an individual adopts, in turn, affect his or her self-concept. We now examine the influence of motivated strategies on the self, focusing first on the processes that maintain existing assessments of self, and then on the conditions that promote self-concept change.

Self-Maintenance Processes

Most recent research on the self attests to its powerful conservatism (see Greenwald 1980). The literature is replete with examples of how behavior serves to verify, protect, and maintain existing conceptions and evaluations of self (although see Paulus & Reid 1991). Indeed, most of the motivated strategies we have examined thus far appear to function primarily to preserve the self's status quo.

In addition, several more general theories have outlined strategies that serve to maintain the integrity of the self in the face of threat. For example, one formulation of cognitive dissonance theory has posited that dissonance occurs when people behave in ways that violate important elements of their self-concepts, whether those self-concepts are positive or negative (Thibodeau & Aronson 1992). The cognitive inconsistency produced by these violations motivates individuals to reduce dissonance in a way that maintains the self. Thus, strategies for reducing dissonance vary depending on one's self-concept, although given how well most people think of themselves, these strategies typically involve an effort to maintain a sense of the self as both competent and morally good (Thibodeau & Aronson 1992).

A similar view of self-maintenance is provided by self-affirmation theory (Steele 1988). In this view, a threat to the self activates processes that are designed to affirm the general integrity of the self, rather than to resolve any particular threat. Self-affirmation theory differs from dissonance theory in the self-defensive goal it posits (global self-integrity, rather than cognitive consistency) and in the flexibility of strategies that can be used to accomplish that goal. The most impressive empirical evidence in support of this theory has come from studies showing that when subjects experiencing dissonance are allowed to affirm important but unrelated aspects of their self-concepts, they no longer show dissonance-reducing attitude change (see Steele 1988 for a review).

A final, related view of self-maintenance processes is provided by terror management theory (Rosenblatt et al 1989, Solomon et al 1991), according to which a wide variety of social behaviors are directed by the motivation to maintain self-esteem and faith in a cultural worldview. This motivation stems, in turn, from the capacity of these psychological structures to afford protection from the anxiety associated with awareness of personal vulnerabilities and ultimate mortality. Empirical support for this theory has come from two different types of studies, one linking mortality salience to strategies for affirming cultural worldviews (Greenberg et al 1990, 1992a), and the other showing that enhancing self-esteem alleviates anxiety (Greenberg et al 1992b).

These various accounts of self-maintenance processes converge on a view of the self as strongly committed to preserving the status quo, but they also raise the question of whether these different self-protective strategies reflect one or many underlying processes. Recent studies support the common-process account. Tesser & Cornell (1991) found that giving subjects the opportunity to self-affirm eliminated self-enhancing comparison and reflection strategies and, in a separate study, that the use of these latter strategies blocked dissonance-reducing attitude change. These findings complement Steele's (1988) demonstrations of the dissonance-reducing effects of self-affirmation. And in a related investigation, Pyszczynski et al (1993) found that encouraging subjects in a dissonance experiment to express their feelings about writing a counterattitudinal essay reduced subsequent attitude change. These findings all portray a self motivated by maintenance, not maximization: The use of one self-protective strategy appears to eliminate the need for others.

Self-Concept Change

In light of the impressive evidence for maintenance of the self, it is somewhat surprising that self-concepts ever change at all. Indeed, the literature contains many demonstrations of temporary changes in the self-concept, but relatively few examples of enduring self-concept change.

CHANGES IN THE IMMEDIATE SELF-CONCEPT How one thinks about oneself at any particular time is strongly influenced by the immediate social context. Changes in context can produce changes in the working self-concept. We have already reviewed research showing how self-definition, and especially the tendency to identify oneself with social groups, varies depending on the structure of both immediate and enduring contexts (see McGuire & McGuire 1988, Turner et al 1994).

Other research has examined changes in the self-concept as a result of self-presentation. These studies have involved inducing subjects to behave in a particular way and then examining the conditions under which that behavior is internalized. Several independent investigations have shown that behavior is more likely to lead to self-concept change when it is performed publicly rather than privately (Tice 1992), when the target of the presentation has high power rather than low power (Kowalski & Leary 1990), and when the presenter has relatively low self-esteem (Baumgardner et al 1989, Kowalski & Leary 1990) or weak prior self-beliefs (Schlenker & Trudeau 1990). Although these studies certainly attest to the vulnerability of the working self-concept to immediate behavior, it is not clear whether such change is enduring.

ENDURING SELF-CONCEPT CHANGE More substantial changes in the self-concept have been documented during periods of life transition. Several studies have highlighted the active process through which individuals construct new identities during times of change. For example, Deutsch et al (1988) examined changes in the self during the transition to first-time motherhood. In a cross-sectional comparison of women in the planning, pregnant, and post-partum stages of the transition, they found that those in the planning and pregnant stages actively sought information about motherhood and used that information to construct new identities for themselves as mothers. Women in the post-partum stage based their self-definition to a significant extent on direct experiences with their newborn. As another example, Ethier & Deaux (1990, 1992) found that the more threat Hispanic students perceived to their ethnic identity upon entering an Ivy League university, the less strongly they identified with Hispanics over time (see also Zirkel 1992, Zirkel & Cantor 1990 for related studies of goal-pursuit during life transitions).

These demonstrations of self-concept change reflect many of the same processes of identity construction and self-esteem maintenance that usually serve to stabilize the self. Indeed, existing data suggest that self-concept change occurs primarily, and perhaps only, in response to major changes in role or situational demands. This conclusion again coincides with a view of the self as consistent in its motives and conservative in its strategies, yet ultimately responsive to environmental contingencies.

FINAL COMMENT

In recent years, investigators have taken the study of self into numerous social contexts, and have documented how it regulates social behavior. Specific lines of research have examined (*a*) the ways in which normal reasoning processes enhance the self, (*b*) the social comparison strategies used to ward off threat, (*c*) the search for interaction partners that confirm self-views, (*d*) the artful strategies of self-presentation, and (*e*) the causes and consequences of group identification. In more recent efforts, researchers have begun to identify factors that moderate the form and use of these strategies, including social category memberships, individual difference variables, and cultural origins. With these new investigations, they have begun to expand the notion of context to include the societal and cultural norms that shape the self and social behavior. Finally, recent demonstrations of self-concept change during periods of life transition suggest a powerful influence of changing contexts on the outcome of self-regulatory processes. Investigating the workings of the self within these expanded contexts should provide an interesting agenda for future studies.

ACKNOWLEDGMENTS

The order of authors is alphabetical. We thank R. Bhaskar, Nancy Cantor, John Darley, Curtis Hardin, Ned Jones, Dale Miller, and Peter Salovey for their generous comments and many discussions, and Lisa Driscoll for assistance in preparing the manuscript.

Literature Cited

Abrams D. 1992. Processes of social identification. In *Social Psychology of Identity and the Self Concept,* ed. G Breakwell, pp. 57–99. New York: Surrey Univ. Press

Abrams D. 1994. Social self-regulation. *Pers. Soc. Psychol. Bull.* In press

Abrams D, Hogg MA. 1988. Comments on the motivational status of self-esteem in social identity and intergroup discrimination. *Eur. J. Soc. Psychol.* 18:317–34

Abrams D, Wetherell M, Cochrane S, Hogg MA, Turner JC. 1990. Knowing what to think by knowing who you are: self-categorization and the nature of norm formation, conformity and group polarization. *Br. J. Soc. Psychol.* 29:97–119

Backman C. 1988. The self: a dialectical approach. *Adv. Exp. Soc. Psychol.* 21:229–60

Bandura A. 1988. Perceived self-efficacy: exercise of cerebral through self-belief. *Annu. Ser. Eur. Res. Behav. Ther.* 2:27–59

Bat-Chava Y. 1994. Group identification and self-esteem of deaf adults. *Pers. Soc. Psychol. Bull.* In press

Baumeister RF. 1982. A self-presentational view of social phenomena. *Psychol. Bull.* 91(1):3–26

Baumeister RF, Heatherton TF, Tice DM, Hutton DG. 1993. When ego threats lead to self-regulation failure: negative consequences of high self-esteem. *J. Pers. Soc. Psychol.* 64(1):141–56

Baumeister RF, Tice DM, Hutton DG. 1989. Self-presentational motivations and personality differences in self-esteem. *J. Pers.* 57:547–79

Baumgardner AH. 1990. To know oneself is to like oneself: self-certainty and self-affect. *J. Pers. Soc. Psychol.* 58(6):1062–72

Baumgardner AH, Kaufman CM, Cranford JA. 1990. To be noticed favorably: links between private self and public self. *Pers. Soc. Psychol. Bull.* 16(4):705–16

Baumgardner AH, Kaufman CM, Levy PE. 1989. Regulating affect interpersonally: when low esteem leads to greater enhancement. *J. Pers. Soc. Psychol.* 56(6):907–21

Baumgardner AH, Levy PE. 1988. Role of self-esteem in perceptions of ability and effort: illogic or insight? *Pers. Soc. Psychol. Bull.* 14(3):429–38

Bem S. 1974. The measurement of psychological androgyny. *J. Consult. Clin. Psychol.* 42:155–62

Beyer S. 1990. Gender differences in the accuracy of self-evaluations of performance. *J. Pers. Soc. Psychol.* 59(5):960–70

Block JH, Gjerde PF, Block JH. 1991. Personality antecedents of depressive tendencies in 18-year-olds: a prospective study. *J. Pers. Soc. Psychol.* 60:726–38

Bradley GW. 1978. Self-serving biases in the attribution process: A reexamination of the fact or fiction question. *J. Pers. Soc. Psychol.* 36:56–71

Braun OL, Wicklund RA. 1988. The identity-effort connection. *J. Exp. Soc. Psychol.* 24(1):37–65

Brewer MB. 1991. The social self: on being the same and different at the same time. *Pers. Soc. Psychol. Bull.* 17(5):475–82

Brewer MB. 1993. The role of distinctiveness in social identity and group behavior. In *Group Motivation,* ed. M Hogg, D Abrams. England: Harvester-Wheatsheaf. In press

Brewer MB, Manzi JM, Shaw JS. 1993. In-group identification as function of depersonalization, distinctiveness, and status. *Psychol. Sci.* 4:88–92

Brewer MB, Schneider SK. 1990. Social identity and social dilemmas: A double-edged sword. In *Social Identity Theory: Constructive and Critical Advances,* ed. D Abrams, MA Hogg, pp. 169–84. New York: Harvester-Wheatsheaf

Brown JD, Collins RL, Schmidt GW. 1988. Self-esteem and direct versus indirect forms of self-enhancement. *J. Pers. Soc. Psychol.* 55:445–53

Brown JD, Gallagher FM. 1992. Coming to terms with failure: private self-enhancement and public self-effacement. *J. Exp. Soc. Psychol.* 28:3–22

Brown JD, Mankowski TA. 1993. Self-esteem, mood, and self-evaluation: changes in mood and the way you see you. *J. Pers. Soc. Psychol.* 64(3):421–30

Brown JD, Rogers RJ. 1991. Self-serving attributions: the role of physiological arousal. *Pers. Soc. Psychol. Bull.* 17(5):501–6

Brown JD, Smart SA. 1991. The self and social conduct: linking self-representations to prosocial behavior. *J. Pers. Soc. Psychol.* 60(3):368–75

Bruner JS. 1957. On perceptual readiness. *Psychol. Rev.* 64:123–51

Buss DM, Cantor N, ed. 1989. *Personality Psychology: Recent Trends and Emerging Directions.* New York: Springer-Verlag

Buunk BP, Collins RL, Taylor SE, VanYperen NW, Dakof GA. 1990. The affective consequences of social comparison: either direction has its ups and downs. *J. Pers. Soc. Psychol.* 59(6):1238–49

Cameron JE, Lalonde RN. 1994. Self, ethnicity, and social group memberships in two generations of Italian Canadians. *Pers. Soc. Psychol. Bull.* In press

Campbell JD. 1990. Self-esteem and clarity of the self-concept. *J. Pers. Soc. Psychol.* 59(3):538–49

Campbell JD, Fehr B. 1990. Self-esteem and perceptions of conveyed impressions: Is negative affectivity associated with greater realism? *J. Pers. Soc. Psychol.* 58(1):122–33

Cantor N, Norem JK, Niedenthal PM, Langston CA, Brower AM. 1987. Life tasks, self-concept ideals, and cognitive strategies in a life transition. *J. Pers. Soc. Psychol.* 53:1178–91

Cantor N, Zirkel S. 1990. Personality, cognition, and purposive behavior. See Pervin 1990, pp. 135–64

Cash TF. 1990. The psychology of physical appearance: aesthetics, attributes, and images. See Cash & Pruzinsky 1990, pp. 51–79. New York: Guilford

Cash TF, Pruzinsky T. 1990. *Body Images: Development, Deviance, and Change.* New York: Guilford

Chaiken S, Pliner P. 1987. Women, but not men, are what they eat: the effect of meal size and gender on perceived femininity and masculinity. *Pers. Soc. Psychol. Bull.* 13(2):166–76

Cheek JM. 1989. Identity orientation and self-interpretation. See Buss & Cantor, pp. 275–85

Cialdini RB, DeNicholas ME. 1989. Self-presentation by association. *J. Pers. Soc. Psychol.* 57(4):626–31

Cousins SD. 1989. Culture and self-perception in Japan and the United States. *J. Pers. Soc. Psychol.* 56(1):124–31

Crocker J, Luhtanen R. 1990. Collective self-esteem and ingroup bias. *J. Pers. Soc. Psychol.* 58(1):60–67

Crocker J, Luhtanen R, Blaine B, Broadnax S. 1994. Collective self-esteem and psychological well-being among white, black, and Asian college students. *Pers. Soc. Psychol. Bull.* In press

Crocker J, Major B. 1989. Social stigma and self-esteem: the self-protective properties of stigma. *Psychol. Rev.* 94(4):608–30

Crocker J, Thompson LL, McGraw KM, Ingerman C. 1987. Downward comparison, prejudice, and evaluation of others: effects of self-esteem and threat. *J. Pers. Soc. Psychol.* 52(5):907–16

Crocker J, Voelkl K, Testa M, Major B. 1991. Social stigma: the affective consequences of attributional ambiguity. *J. Pers. Soc. Psychol.* 60(2):218–28

Deaux K. 1991. Social identities: thoughts on structure and change. In *The Relational Self: Theoretical Convergences in Psychoanalysis and Social Psychology,* ed. RC Curtis, pp. 77–93. New York: Guilford

Deaux K. 1992a. Focusing on the self: challenges to self-definition and their consequences for mental health. In *The Social Psychology of Mental Health: Basic Mechanisms and Applications,* ed. DN Ruble, PR Costanzo, ME Oliver, pp. 301–27. New York: Guilford

Deaux K. 1992b. Personalizing identity and socializing self. In *The Social Psychology of the Identity and the Self-concept,* ed. G Breakwell, pp. 9–33. London: Academic

Deaux K. 1993. Reconstructing social identity. *Pers. Soc. Psychol. Bull.* 19(1):4–12

Deutsch FM, Ruble DN, Fleming A, Brooks-Gunn J, Stangor C. 1988. Information-seeking and maternal self-definition during the transition to motherhood. *J. Pers. Soc. Psychol.* 55(3):420–31

Dindia K, Allen M. 1992. Sex differences in self-disclosure: a meta-analysis. *Psychol. Bull.* 112(1):106–24

Doherty K, Weigold MF, Schlenker BR. 1990. Self-serving interpretations of motives. *Pers. Soc. Psychol. Bull.* 16(3):485–95

Dunning D, Cohen GL. 1992. Egocentric definitions of traits and abilities in social judgment. *J. Pers. Soc. Psychol.* 63(3):341–55

Dunning D, Meyerowitz JA, Holzberg AD. 1989. Ambiguity and self-evaluation: The role of idiosyncratic trait definitions in self-serving assessments of ability. *J. Pers. Soc. Psychol.* 57(6):1082–90

Dunning D, Perie M, Story AL. 1991. Self-serving prototypes of social categories. *J. Pers. Soc. Psychol.* 61(6):957–68

Emmons RA, King LA. 1988. Conflict among personal strivings: immediate and long-term implications for psychological and physical well-being. *J. Pers. Soc. Psychol.* 54(6):1040–48

Ethier KA, Deaux K. 1990. Hispanics in ivy: assessing identity and perceived threat. *Sex Roles* 22:427–40

Fallon A. 1990. Culture in the mirror: sociocultural determinants of body image. See Cash & Pruzinsky 1990, pp. 80–109

Feingold A. 1990. Gender differences in effects of physical attractiveness on romantic attraction: a comparison across five research paradigms. *J. Pers. Soc. Psychol.* 59(5):981–93

Festinger L. 1954. A theory of social comparison processes. *Hum. Relat.* 7:117–40

Festinger L. 1957. *A Theory of Cognitive Dissonance.* Evanston, IL: Row Peterson

Finch JF, Cialdini RB. 1989. Another indirect tactic of (self-) image management: boosting. *Pers. Soc. Psychol. Bull.* 15(2):222–32

Fleming JH, Rudman LA. 1993. Between a rock and a hard place: self-concept regulating and communicative properties of distancing behaviors. *J. Pers. Soc. Psychol.* 64(1):44–59

Freud S. 1925. *Collected Papers.* London: Hogarth

Frey D, Stahlberg D. 1987. Selection of information after receiving more or less reliable self-threatening information. *Pers. Soc. Psychol. Bull.* 12(4):434–41

Fujita F, Diener E, Sandvik E. 1991. Gender differences in negative affect and well-being: the case for emotional intensity. *J. Pers. Soc. Psychol.* 61(3):427–34

Gaertner SL, Mann J, Murrell A, Dovidio JF. 1989. Reducing intergroup bias: the benefits of recategorization. *J. Pers. Soc. Psychol.* 57:239–49

Gallup GG. 1991. Toward a comparative psychology of self-awareness: species limitations and cognitive consequences. In *The Self: An Interdisciplinary Approach,* ed. GR Goethals, J Strauss, pp. 121–35. New York: Springer-Verlag

Gibbons FX, Gerrard M. 1991. Downward comparison and coping with threat. See Suls & Wills 1991, pp. 317–45

Gibbons FX, McCoy SB. 1991. Self-esteem, similarity, and reactions to active versus passive downward comparison. *J. Pers. Soc. Psychol.* 60(3):414–24

Greenberg J, Pyszczynski T, Solomon S, Rosenblatt A, Veeder M, et al. 1990. Evidence for terror management theory II: the effects of mortality salience on reactions to those who threaten or bolster the cultural worldview. *J. Pers. Soc. Psychol.* 58(2):308–18

Greenberg J, Simon L, Pyszczynski T, Solomon S, Chatel D. 1992a. Terror management and tolerance: Does mortality salience always intensify negative reactions to others who threaten one's worldview? *J. Pers. Soc. Psychol.* 63(2): 212–20

Greenberg J, Solomon S, Pyszczynski T, Rosenblatt A, Burling J, et al. 1992b. Why do people need self-esteem? Converging evidence that self-esteem serves an anxiety-buffering function. *J. Pers. Soc. Psychol.* 63(6):913–22

Greenwald AG. 1975. On the inconclusiveness of "crucial" cognitive test of dissonance versus self-perception theory. *J. Exp. Soc. Psychol.* 11:490–99

Greenwald AG. 1980. The totalitarian ego: fabrication and revision of personal history. *Am. Psychol.* 35(7):603–18

Greenwald AG, Banaji MR. 1989. The self as a memory system: powerful, but ordinary. *J. Pers. Soc. Psychol.* 57:41–54

Greenwald AG, Bellezza F, Banaji MR. 1988. Is self-esteem a central ingredient of the self-concept? *Pers. Soc. Psychol. Bull.* 14(1):34–45

Harter S. 1989. Causes, correlate and the functional role of global self-worth: a life-span perspective. In *Perceptions of Competence and Incompetence Across the Life-span,* ed. J Kolligian, R Sternberg pp. 67–97. New Haven, Conn: Yale Univ. Press

Haslam SA, Turner JC. 1992. Context-dependent variation in social stereotyping 2: the relationship between frame of reference, self-categorization and accentuation. *Eur. J. Soc. Psychol.* 22:251–77

Higgins ET. 1987. Self-discrepancy: a theory relating self and affect. *Psychol. Rev.* 94:319–40

Higgins ET. 1989. Self-discrepancy theory: What patterns of self-beliefs cause people to suffer? *Adv. Exp. Soc. Psychol.* 22:93–136

Higgins RL, Snyder CR, Berglas S, eds. 1990. *Self-Handicapping: The Paradox That Isn't.* New York: Plenum

Hill T, Smith ND, Lewicki P. 1989. The development of self-image bias: a real-world demonstration. *Pers. Soc. Psychol. Bull.* 15(2):205–11

Hinkle S, Brown RJ. 1990. Intergroup comparisons and social identity: some links and lacunae. In *Social Identity Theory: Constructive and Critical Advances,* ed. D Abrams, MA Hogg, pp. 48–70. London/ New York: Harvester-Wheatsheaf/ Springer-Verlag

Hirt ER, Deppe RK, Gordon LJ. 1991. Self-reported versus behavioral self-handicapping: empirical evidence for a theoretical distinction. *J. Pers. Soc. Psychol.* 61:981–91

Hogg MA. 1992. *The Social Psychology of Group Cohesiveness: From Attraction to Social Identity.* New York: Harvester-Wheatsheaf

Hogg MA, Turner JC. 1987. Intergroup behaviour, self-stereotyping and the salience of social categories. *Br. J. Soc. Psychol.* 26:325–40

Ingram RE, Cruet D, Johnson BR, Wisnicki KS. 1988. Self-focused attention, gender, gender role, and vulnerability to negative affect. *J. Pers. Soc. Psychol.* 55(6):967–78

Jones EE, Berglas S. 1978. Control of attributions about the self through self-handicapping strategies: the appeal of alcohol and the role of underachievement. *Pers. Soc. Psychol. Bull.* 4:200–6

Jones EE, Brenner KJ, Knight JG. 1990. When failure elevates self-esteem. *Pers. Soc. Psychol. Bull.* 16:200–9

Jones JM. 1992. Understanding the mental health consequences of race: contributions of basic social psychological processes. In *The Social Psychology of Mental Health: Basic Mechanisms and Applications,* ed. DN Ruble, PR Costanzo, ME Oliver, pp. 301–27. New York: Guilford

Jose PE, McCarthy WJ. 1988. Perceived agentic and communal behavior in mis-sex group interactions. *Pers. Soc. Psychol. Bull.* 14(1):57–67

Josephs RA, Markus HR, Tafarodi RW. 1992. Gender and self-esteem. *J. Pers. Soc. Psychol.* 63(3):391–402

Kernis MH, Grannemann BD, Barclay LC. 1989. Stability and level of self-esteem as predictors of anger arousal and hostility. *J. Pers. Soc. Psychol.* 56:1013–23

Kernis MH, Grannemann BD, Mathis LC. 1991. Stability of self-esteem as a moderator of the relation between level of self-esteem and depression. *J. Pers. Soc. Psychol.* 61(1):80–84

Klein SB, Loftus J. 1993. The mental representation of trait and autobiographical knowledge about the self. In *Advances in Social Cognition,* Vol. 5, ed. TK Srull, RS Wyer. Hillsdale, NJ: Erlbaum. In press

Kowalski RM, Leary MR. 1990. Strategic self-presentation and the avoidance of aversive events: antecedents and consequences of self-enhancement and self-depreciation. *J. Exp. Soc. Psychol.* 26(4):322–36

Krosnick JA, Sedikides C. 1990. Self-monitoring and self-protective biases in use of consensus information to predict one's own behavior. *J. Pers. Soc. Psychol.* 58(4):718–28

Kunda Z. 1987. Motivated inference: self-serving generation and evaluation of causal theories. *J. Pers. Soc. Psychol.* 53(4):636–47

Kunda Z. 1990. The case for motivated reasoning. *Psychol. Bull.* 108(3):480–98

Kunda Z, Fong GT, Sanitioso R, Reber E. 1993. Directional questions direct self-conceptions. *J. Exp. Soc. Psychol.* 29(1):63–86

Kunda Z, Sanitioso R. 1989. Motivated changes in the self-concept. *J. Exp. Soc. Psychol.* 25(3):272–85

LaFrance M, Banaji M. 1992. Toward a reconsideration of the gender-emotion relationship. *Rev. Pers. Soc. Psychol.* 14:178–201

Leary MR, Kowalski RM. 1990. Impression management: a literature review and two-component model. *Psychol. Bull.* 107(1):34–47

Levit DB. 1991. Gender differences in ego defenses in adolescence: sex roles as one way to understand the differences. *J. Pers. Soc. Psychol.* 61(6):992–99

Lewis M. 1990. Self-knowledge and social development in early life. See Pervin 1990, pp. 277–300

Lippa R. 1991. Some psychometric characteristics of gender diagnosticity measures: reliability, validity, consistency across domains, and relationship to the big five. *J. Pers. Soc. Psychol.* 61(6):1000–11

Luginbuhl J, Palmer R. 1991. Impression management aspects of self-handicapping: positive and negative effects. *Pers. Soc. Psychol. Bull.* 17(6):655–62

Luhtanen R, Crocker J. 1991. Self-esteem and intergroup comparisons: toward a theory of collective self-esteem. See Suls & Wills 1991, pp. 211–34

Luhtanen R, Crocker J. 1992. A collective self-esteem scale: self-evaluation of one's social identity. *Pers. Soc. Psychol. Bull.* 18:302–18

Markus H, Cross S. 1990. The interpersonal self. See Pervin 1990, pp. 576–608

Markus H, Kitayama S. 1991. Culture and the self: implications for cognition, emotion, and motivation. *Psychol. Rev.* 98(2):224–53

Markus H, Kitayama S. 1994. A collective fear of the collective: implications for selves and theories of selves. *Pers. Soc. Psychol. Bull.* In press

Markus H, Ruvolo A. 1989. Possible selves: Personalized representations of goals. See Pervin 1989, pp. 211–41

Markus H, Wurf E. 1987. The dynamic self-concept: a social psychological perspective. *Annu. Rev. Psychol.* 38:299–337

McCann CD. 1990. The self and interpersonal relations. In *Self-Inference Processes: The Ontario Symposium,* ed. JM Olson, MP Zanna, 6:191–215. Hillsdale, NJ: Erlbaum

McGarty C, Turner JC, Hogg MA, David B, Wetherell MS. 1992. Group polarization as conformity to the prototypical group member. *Br. J. Soc. Psychol.* 31:1–20

McGuire WJ, McGuire CV. 1988. Content and process in the experience of self. *Adv. Exp. Soc. Psychol.* 21:97–144

Miller DT, Ross M. 1975. Self-serving biases in the attribution of causality: fact or fiction. *Psychol. Bull.* 82:213–25

Morgan DL, Schwalbe ML. 1990. Mind and self in society: linking social structure and social cognition. *Soc. Psychol. Q.* 53(2):148–64

Mori D, Pliner P, Chaiken S. 1987. "Eating lightly" and the self-presentation of femininity. *J. Pers. Soc. Psychol.* 53(4):693–702

Mullen B, Brown R, Smith C. 1992. Ingroup bias as a function of salience, relevance and status: an integration. *Eur. J. Soc. Psychol.* 22:103–22

Neisser U. 1988. Five kinds of self-knowledge. *Philos. Psychol.* 1(1):35–59

Niedenthal PM, Mordkoff JT. 1991. Prototype distancing: a strategy for choosing among threatening situations. *Pers. Soc. Psychol. Bull.* 17:483–93

Nolen-Hoeksema S. 1987. Sex differences in unipolar depression: evidence and theory. *Psychol. Bull.* 101:259–82

Norem JK, Illingworth KSS. 1993. Strategy-dependent effects of reflecting on self and tasks: some implications of optimism and defensive pessimism. *J. Pers. Soc. Psychol.* In press

Oakes PJ, Turner JC. 1990. Is limited information processing capacity the cause of social stereotyping? In *The European Review of Social Psychology,* Vol. 1, ed. W Stroebe, M Hewstone, pp. 111–35. Chichester, England: Wiley

Oakes PJ, Turner JC, Haslam SA. 1991. Perceiving people as group members: the role

of fit in the salience of social categorizations. *Br. J. Soc. Psychol.* 30:125–44
Paulus DL, Levitt K. 1987. Desirable responding triggered by affect: automatic egotism? *J. Pers. Soc. Psychol.* 52(2):245–59
Paulus DL, Reid DB. 1991. Enhancement and denial in socially desirable responding. *J. Pers. Soc. Psychol.* 60(2):307–17
Payne TJ, Connor JM, Colletti G. 1987. Gender-based schematic processing: an empirical investigation and reevaluation. *J. Pers. Soc. Psychol.* 52(5):937–45
Pelham BW. 1991a. On the benefits of misery: self-serving biases in the depressive self-concept. *J. Pers. Soc. Psychol.* 61:670–81
Pelham BW. 1991b. On confidence and consequence: the certainty and importance of self-knowledge. *J. Pers. Soc. Psychol.* 60(4):518–30
Pelham BW, Swann WB. 1989. From self-conceptions to self-worth: on the sources and structure of global self-esteem. *J. Pers. Soc. Psychol.* 57(4):672–80
Pervin LA, ed. 1989. *Goal Concepts in Personality and Social Psychology.* New York: Hillsdale, NJ: Erlbaum
Pervin LA, ed. 1990. *Handbook of Personality: Theory and Research.* New York: Guilford. 738 pp.
Phinney JS. 1990. Ethnic identity in adolescents and adults: review of research. *Psychol. Bull.* 108:499–514
Pliner P, Chaiken S. 1990. Eating, social motives, and self-presentation in women and men. *J. Exp. Soc. Psychol.* 26:240–54
Pliner P, Chaiken S, Flett G. 1990. Gender differences in concern with body weight and physical appearance over the life span. *Pers. Soc. Psychol. Bull.* 16(2):263–73
Powers TA, Zuroff DC. 1988. Interpersonal consequences of overt self-criticism: a comparison with neutral and self-enhancing presentations of self. *J. Pers. Soc. Psychol.* 54(6):1054–62
Pratt MW, Pancer M, Hunsberger B, Manchester J. 1990. Reasoning about the self and relationships in maturity: an integrative complexity analysis of individual differences. *J. Pers. Soc. Psychol.* 59(3):575–81
Prentice DA. 1990. Familiarity and differences in self- and other-representations. *J. Pers. Soc. Psychol.* 59:369–83
Pyszczynski T, Greenberg J. 1987. Toward an integration of cognitive and motivational perspectives on social inference: a biased hypothesis-testing model. *Adv. Exp. Soc. Psychol.* 20:297–340
Pyszczynski T, Greenberg J, Solomon S, Sideris J, Stubing MJ. 1993. Emotional expression and the reduction of motivated cognitive bias: evidence from cognitive dissonance and distancing from victims' paradigms. *J. Pers. Soc. Psychol.* 64:177–86
Raskin R, Novacek J, Hogan R. 1991. Narcissistic self-esteem management. *J. Pers. Soc. Psychol.* 60:911–18
Rhodewalt F. 1990. Self-handicappers: individual differences in the preference for anticipatory, self-protective acts. See Higgins et al 1990, pp. 69–106
Rhodewalt F, Morf C, Hazlett S, Fairfield M. 1991. Self-handicapping: the role of discounting and augmentation in the preservation of self-esteem. *J. Pers. Soc. Psychol.* 61(1):122–31
Rohde P, Lewinsohn PM, Tilson M, Seeley JR. 1990. Dimensionality of coping and its relation to depression. *J. Pers. Soc. Psychol.* 58(3):499–511
Rosenblatt A, Greenberg J, Solomon S, Pyszczynski T, Lyon D. 1989. Evidence for terror management theory: I. The effects of mortality salience on reactions to those who violate or uphold cultural values. *J. Pers. Soc. Psychol.* 57(4):681–90
Salovey P. 1992. Mood-induced self-focused attention. *J. Pers. Soc. Psychol.* 62:699–707
Sanitioso R, Kunda Z, Fong GT. 1990. Motivated recruitment of autobiographical memories. *J. Pers. Soc. Psychol.* 59(2):229–41
Schlenker BR, Trudeau JV. 1990. Impact of self-presentations on private self-beliefs: effects of prior self-beliefs and misattribution. *J. Pers. Soc. Psychol.* 58(1):22–32
Schlenker BR, Weigold MF. 1989. Goals and the self-identification process. See Pervin 1989, pp. 243–90
Schlenker BR, Weigold MF. 1990. Self-consciousness and self-presentation: being autonomous versus appearing autonomous. *J. Pers. Soc. Psychol.* 59:820–28
Schlenker BR, Weigold MF. 1992. Interpersonal processes involving impression regulation and management. *Annu. Rev. Psychol.* 43:133–68
Schlenker BR, Weigold MF, Hallam JR. 1990. Self-serving attributions in social context: effects of self-esteem and social pressure. *J. Pers. Soc. Psychol.* 58(5):855–63
Schouten PGW, Handelsman MM. 1987. Social basis of self-handicapping: The case of depression. *Pers. Soc. Psychol. Bull.* 13(1):103–10
Sedikides C. 1992. Changes in the valence of the self as a function of mood. In *Emotion and Social Behavior: Review of Personality and Social Psychology,* Vol. 14, ed. MS Clark. Newbury Park, CA: Sage
Self EA. 1990. Situational influences on self-handicapping. See Higgins et al 1990, pp. 36–68
Serpe RT, Stryker S. 1987. The construction of self and the reconstruction of social relationships. *Adv. Group Process.* 4:41–66
Setterlund MB, Niedenthal PM. 1993. "Who

am I? Why am I here?": Self-esteem, self-clarity, and prototype-matching. *J. Pers. Soc. Psychol.* In press

Shepperd JA, Arkin RM. 1989a. Self-handicapping: the moderating roles of public self-consciousness and task importance. *Pers. Soc. Psychol. Bull.* 15:252–65

Shepperd JA, Arkin RM. 1989b. Determinants of self-handicapping: task importance and the effects of preexisting handicaps on self-generated handicaps. *Pers. Soc. Psychol. Bull.* 15:101–12

Showers C. 1992a. Compartmentalization of positive and negative self-knowledge: keeping bad apples out of the bunch. *J. Pers. Soc. Psychol.* 62(6):1036–49

Showers C. 1992b. The motivational and emotional consequences of considering positive or negative possibilities for an upcoming event. *J. Pers. Soc. Psychol.* 63(3):474–84

Singelis TM. 1994. The measurement of independent and interdependent self-construals. *Pers. Soc. Psychol. Bull.* In press

Skowronski JJ, Betz AL, Thompson CP, Shannon L. 1991. Social memory in everyday life: recall of self-events and other-events. *J. Pers. Soc. Psychol.* 60(6):831–43

Smith RH, Insko CA. 1987. Social comparison choice during ability evaluation: the effects of comparison publicity, performance feedback, and self-esteem. *Pers. Soc. Psychol. Bull.* 13(1):111–22

Snell WE. 1989. Willingness to self-disclose to female and male friends as a function of social anxiety and gender. *Pers. Soc. Psychol. Bull.* 15(1):113–25

Solomon S, Greenberg J, Pyszczynski T. 1991. A terror management theory of social behavior: the psychological functions of self-esteem and cultural worldviews. *Adv. Exp. Soc. Psychol.* 24:93–159

Steele CM. 1988. The psychology of self-affirmation: sustaining the integrity of the self. *Adv. Exp. Soc. Psychol.* 21:261–302

Strauman TJ, Vookles J, Berenstein V, Chaiken S, Higgins ET. 1991. Self-discrepancies and vulnerability to body dissatisfaction and disordered eating. *J. Pers. Soc. Psychol.* 61(6):946–56

Strube MJ. 1990. In search of self: balancing the good and the true. *Pers. Soc. Psychol. Bull.* 16(4):699–704

Stryker S. 1991. Exploring the relevance of social cognition for the relationship of self and society: linking the cognitive perspective and identity theory. In *The Self-Society Dynamic: Cognition, Emotion, and Action,* ed. JA Howard, PL Callero, pp. 19–41. Cambridge: Cambridge Univ. Press

Suls J, Wills TA, eds. 1991. *Social Comparison.* Hillsdale, NJ: Erlbaum

Swann WB. 1987. Identity negotiation: where two roads meet. *J. Pers. Soc. Psychol.* 53:1038–51

Swann WB. 1990. To be adored or to be known: the interplay of self-enhancement and self-verification. In *Handbook of Motivation and Cognition,* ed. RM Sorrentino, ET Higgins, 2:408–50. New York: Guilford

Swann WB, Griffin JJ, Predmore SX, Gaines B. 1987. The cognitive-affective crossfire: when self-consistency confronts self-enhancement. *J. Pers. Soc. Psychol.* 52(5):881–89

Swann WB, Hixon JG, DeLaRonde C. 1992a. Embracing the bitter "truth": negative self-concepts and marital commitment. *Psychol. Sci.* 3(2):118–21

Swann WB, Hixon JG, Stein-Seroussi A, Gilbert DT. 1990. The fleeting gleam of praise: cognitive processes underlying behavioral reactions to self-relevant feedback. *J. Pers. Soc. Psychol.* 59:17–26

Swann WB, Pelham BW, Chidester TR. 1988. Change through paradox: using self-verification to alter beliefs. *J. Pers. Soc. Psychol.* 54(2):268–73

Swann WB, Pelham BW, Krull DS. 1989. Agreeable fancy or diagreeable truth? Reconciling self-enhancement and self-verification. *J. Pers. Soc. Psychol.* 57(5):782–91

Swann WB, Stein-Seroussi A, Giesler RB. 1992b. Why people self-verify. *J. Pers. Soc. Psychol.* 62(3):392–401

Tajfel H. 1972. La categorisation sociale. In *Introduction a la psychologie sociale,* Vol. 1, ed. S Moscovici, pp. 272–302. Paris: Larousse

Tajfel H, Turner JC. 1986. The social identity theory of intergroup behaviour. In *Psychology of Intergroup Relations,* ed. S Worchel, WG Austin, 2:7–24. Chicago: Nelson-Hall

Taylor DM, Moghaddam FM, Gamble I, Zellerer F. 1987. Disadvantaged group responses to perceived inequality: from passive acceptance to collective action. *J. Soc. Psychol.* 127:259–72

Taylor DM, Wright SC, Moghaddam FM, Lalonde RN. 1990. The personal/group discrimination discrepancy: perceiving my group, but not myself, to be a target for discrimination. *Pers. Soc. Psychol. Bull.* 16(2):254–62

Taylor J, Riess M. 1989. "Self-serving" attributions to valenced causal factors: a field experiment. *Pers. Soc. Psychol. Bull.* 15(3):337–48

Taylor SE, Brown JD. 1988. Illusion and well-being: a social psychological perspective on mental health. *Psychol. Bull.* 103(2):193–210

Taylor SE, Lobel M. 1989. Social comparison activity under threat: downward evaluation and upward contacts. *Psychol. Rev.* 96(4):569–75

Tennen H, Herzberger S. 1987. Depression,

self-esteem, and the absence of self-protective attributional biases. *J. Pers. Soc. Psychol.* 52(1):72–80

Tesser A. 1988. Toward a self-evaluation maintenance model of social behavior. *Adv. Exp. Soc. Psychol.* 21:181–227

Tesser A. 1991. Emotion in social comparison and reflection processes. See Suls & Wills 1991, pp. 115–45

Tesser A, Cornell DP. 1991. On the confluence of self processes. *J. Exp. Soc. Psychol.* 27(6):501–26

Tesser A, Millar M, Moore J. 1988. Some affective consequences of social comparison and reflection processes: the pain and pleasure of being close. *J. Pers. Soc. Psychol. 54(1):49–61*

Tesser A, Pilkington CJ, McIntosh W. 1989. Self-evaluation maintenance and the mediational role of emotion: the perception of friends and strangers. *J. Pers. Soc. Psychol.* 57(3):442–56

Tetlock PE, Levi A. 1982. On the inconclusiveness of the cognition-motivation debate. *J. Exp. Soc. Psychol.* 18(1):68–88

Thibodeau R, Aronson E. 1992. Taking a closer look: reasserting the role of the self-concept in dissonance theory. *Pers. Soc. Psychol. Bull.* 18(5):591–602

Tice DM. 1991. Esteem protection or enhancement? Self-handicapping motives and attributions differ by trait self-esteem. *J. Pers. Soc. Psychol.* 60(5):711–25

Tice DM. 1992. Self-concept change and self-presentation: the looking glass self is also a magnifying glass. *J. Pers. Soc. Psychol.* 63(3):435–51

Tice DM, Baumeister RF. 1990. Self-esteem, self-handicapping, and self-presentation: The strategy of inadequate practice. *J. Pers.* 58:443–64

Trafimow D, Triandis HC, Goto SG. 1991. Some tests of the distinction between the private self and the collective self. *J. Pers. Soc. Psychol.* 60(5):649–55

Triandis HC. 1989. The self and social behavior in differing cultural contexts. *Psychol. Rev.* 96(3):506–20

Triandis HC, Bontempo R, Villareal MJ, Asai M, Lucca N. 1988. Individualism and collectivism: cross-cultural perspectives on self-ingroup relationships. *J. Pers. Soc. Psychol.* 54(2):323–38

Triandis HC, McCusker C, Hui C. 1990. Multimethod probes in individualism and collectivism. *J. Pers. Soc. Psychol.* 59(6):1006–20

Trope Y. 1986. Self-enhancement and self-assessment in achievement behavior. In *Handbook of Motivation and Cognition: Foundations of Social Behavior,* ed. RM Sorrentino, ET Higgins, 1:350–78. New York: Guilford

Turner JC. 1985. Social categorization and self-concept: A social cognitive theory of group behaviour. *Adv. Group Process.* 2:77–122

Turner JC. 1991. *Social Influence.* Pacific Grove, CA: Brooks/Cole

Turner JC, Hogg MA, Oakes PJ, Reicher SD, Wetherell MS. 1987. *Rediscovering the Social Group: A Self-Categorization Theory.* New York: Basil Blackwell

Turner JC, Oakes PJ. 1989. Self-categorization theory and social influence. In *The Psychology of Group Influence,* ed. PB Paulus, 2:233–75. Hillsdale, NJ: Erlbaum

Turner JC, Oakes PJ, Haslam SA, McGarty C. 1994. Self and collective: cognition and social context. *Pers. Soc. Psychol. Bull.* In press

Wilder DA, Thompson JE. 1988. Assimilation and contrast effects in the judgments of groups. *J. Pers. Soc. Psychol.* 54:62–73

Wiley MG, Alexander CN. 1987. From situated activity to self-attribution: the impact of social structural schematic. In *Self and Identity: Psychosocial Perspectives,* ed. K Yardley, T Honess, pp. 105–18. New York: Wiley

Wills TA. 1981. Downward comparison principles in social psychology. *Psychol. Bull.* 90:245–71

Wills TA. 1991. Similarity and self-esteem in downward comparison. See Suls & Wills 1991, pp. 51–78

Wood JV. 1989. Theory and research concerning social comparisons of personal attributes. *Psychol. Bull.* 106(2):231–48

Wood JV, Taylor KL. 1991. Serving self-relevant goals through social comparison. See Suls & Wills 1991, pp. 23–49

Wood W, Rhodes N, Whelan M. 1989. Sex differences in positive well-being: a consideration of emotional style and marital status. *Psychol. Bull.* 106:249–64

Zirkel S. 1992. Developing independence in a life transition. *J. Pers. Soc. Psychol.* 62(3):506–21

Zirkel S, Cantor N. 1990. Personal construal of life tasks: those who struggle for independence. *J. Pers. Soc. Psychol.* 56(1):172–85

Annu. Rev. Psychol. 1994. 45:333–56

IMAGES OF THE MIND: STUDIES WITH MODERN IMAGING TECHNIQUES

Marcus E. Raichle

Departments of Radiology and Neurology, Washington University School of Medicine, St Louis, Missouri 63110

KEY WORDS: brain blood flow, neuroimaging, language, learning, automatic behavior, non-automatic behavior

CONTENTS

INTRODUCTION

In this Decade of the Brain it seems especially appropriate to recall the advice of Sir Charles Sherrington, the great British neurophysiologist:

> ...physiology and psychology, instead of prosecuting their studies, as some now recommend, more strictly apart one from another than at present, will find it serviceable for each to give to the results achieved by the other even closer heed than has been customary hitherto.

At no previous time in our scientific history have we been in a better position to achieve the crucial working relationship between the behavioral and brain sciences that Sherrington envisioned. There was no truly effective way to test specific psychological hypotheses about human behavior in terms of the underlying normal human brain circuitry until Hounsfield's introduction of x-ray computed tomography (CT) in 1973 (Cormack 1963, 1973; Hounsfield 1973). CT not only provided a new way of looking at the human brain in vivo, which had immense clinical significance, but it also stimulated the development of positron emission tomography (PET; Ter-Pogossian et al 1975, Phelps et al 1975) and magnetic resonance imaging (MRI; Lautebur 1973, Hinshaw et al 1977), which made possible the imaging of function as well as anatomy. Complementing the development of these imaging techniques, and crucial to their success in imaging the function of the human brain, was the development of strategies for the measurement of brain blood flow and metabolism, which began in the late 1940s with the pioneering work of Kety, Sokoloff, Lassen, Ingvar, and their many colleagues (see Raichle 1987 for review). As a result of these developments we have moved into the Decade of the Brain with modern imaging devices that safely permit us to localize and monitor accurately the activity of areas in the normal human brain during specific mental tasks. With these techniques, our understanding of the neurobiological basis of human behavior should advance at an unprecedented rate.

Success in this exciting endeavor is dependent on a close working relationship between cognitive scientists who understand how to characterize and study the elements of human behavior and neuroscientists who understand how to study brain function at a system level. This partnership relies on a mutual understanding of brain imaging techniques and how they can be most successfully applied to the study of the human brain. We can expect a new breed of scientist, whom we might call cognitive neuroscientists, to emerge from this partnership, equipped with the interdisciplinary skills necessary to be successful in this challenging area.

This review examines progress in the study of human behavior using functional brain imaging techniques—specifically, those techniques designed to measure changes in brain blood flow or metabolism that accompany changes in neuronal activity. This review focuses on the use of positron emission tomography (PET) simply because it is the most mature technology currently available for functional brain imaging. Lessons learned with PET will certainly apply to other techniques. Functional magnetic resonance imaging (fMRI) is likely to become an increasingly important participant in this research and will be discussed at the end of this review along with the contribution to be made by the several approaches to recording human brain electrical activity.

This review has three goals: 1. to acquaint the reader with current techniques in functional brain imaging including strategies in the design of psychological paradigms used in the imaging study; 2. to acquaint the reader with progress that has been made in relating psychological theory to actual brain circuits; and 3. to introduce the reader to some of the unique and challenging aspects of developing appropriate behavioral tasks that respect the constraints imposed by the imaging techniques and the neurobiology.

I focus on studies of verbal response selection, largely from our own laboratory, for several reasons: 1. the work reflects a substantial input from both cognitive scientists and neuroscientists; 2. results are promising in relating cognitive theories to brain function; 3. important lessons have been learned about how best to conduct this type of research and what conclusions to draw from the results; 4. sufficient imaging research has been done by others to permit an interesting comparison of results; and 5. research in this area demonstrates the role of imaging research in focusing a spectrum of neurobiological data on questions of human brain function.

FUNCTIONAL IMAGING TECHNIQUES

Positron Emission Tomography

Emission tomography produces an image of the distribution of a previously administered radionuclide in any desired section of the body. Positron emission tomography (PET) uses the unique properties of the annihilation radiation that is generated when positrons are absorbed in matter (Raichle 1987) to provide an image that is a highly faithful representation of the spatial distribution of the radionuclide at a selected plane through the tissue. Such an image is effectively equivalent to a quantitative tissue autoradiogram obtained with laboratory animals, but PET has the added advantage that it is noninvasive; hence, studies are possible in living animals and in humans. PET has been used in humans to measure brain blood flow, blood volume, metabolism of glucose and oxygen, acid-base balance, receptor pharmacology, and transmitter metabolism. This review focuses on the measurement of brain blood flow with PET.

Blood Flow and Brain Function

The window through which we examine the functional organization of the normal human brain is based on our ability to measure neuronally-induced changes in local blood flow within the brain tissue. Interest in the relationship between brain blood flow and local functional activity crystallized when Roy & Sherrington (1890) suggested that there was an automatic mechanism that provided for a local variation in blood supply in accordance with local variations in the functional activity of the brain. Subsequent experiments in laboratory animals and humans led to confirmation of these pioneering observations and to the establishment of one of our most sensitive and accurate ways to study the functional anatomy of the normal human brain in vivo (see Raichle 1987 for a review of this literature).

Imaging Strategy

There are several important elements in the strategy for using PET for functional mapping of neuronal activity in the human brain. The deliberate selection of blood flow measured with the PET adaptation of the Kety autoradiographic technique (Herscovitch et al 1983, 1987; Raichle et al 1983), or estimated from the radioactive counts accumulating in brain tissue during 40 sec following the intravenous bolus administration of $H_2{}^{15}O$ (Fox et al 1985, Fox & Mintun 1989), is the most accurate and flexible signal of changes in local neural activity that can be detected with PET (Fox et al 1988). Linearly scaled images of blood flow or radioactive counts in a control state are subtracted from images obtained during functional activation in each subject (i.e. paired image subtraction). The control state and the stimulated state are carefully chosen to isolate, as much as possible, a limited number of mental operations (e.g. Petersen et al 1988). By subtracting blood flow measurements made in the control state from each task state it is possible to identify those areas of the brain concerned with the mental operations unique to the task state. This adds a strategy first introduced to psychology in 1868 by Dutch physiologist Donders, who used reaction time to dissect out the components of mental operations (Donders 1969). In brain imaging work we dissect out the components of mental operation in relation to specific regions of the brain involved in particular mental operations.

Subtraction images form the basis of a data set that is composed of averaged responses across many individual subjects or across many runs in the same individual. Image averaging dramatically enhances the signal-to-noise properties of such data. This enables us to detect even low level responses associated with mental activity (Mintun et al 1989, Fox et al 1988). The statistical analysis of these averaged subtraction images presents many interesting challenges. A number of novel approaches (Fox et al 1988, Worsley et al 1992, Friston et al 1991b) have been developed. In cases where regions of interest within a particular data set can be identified in advance, actual hypothesis testing using more conventional statistical approaches to the data (e.g. ANOVA or paired t-test) can be used (see Squire et al 1992, Raichle et al 1993).

STUDIES OF VERBAL RESPONSE SELECTION

Experimental Observations

Functional imaging work with PET on verbal response selection began with a study of single word processing (Petersen et al 1988, 1989). This initial study introduced a hierarchical design composed of four levels of information processing. Such a design has become fairly standard in this type of imaging work (e.g. Wise et al 1991, Friston et al 1991a, Frith et al 1991, Zatorre et al 1992, Howard et al 1992). In the first level, normal subjects were scanned while fixing their gaze on a fixation point in the middle of a television monitor. In the second level, they continued to maintain their gaze on the fixation point but either passively viewed common English nouns below the fixation point on the monitor, or in a separate scan, passively listened to the same nouns through earphones. In the third level, subjects were asked to repeat the word they either heard or viewed (separate scans were performed for auditory and visual presentation). Finally, in the fourth level, the subjects were asked to say aloud a verb appropriate for the noun that they either saw or heard (again visual and auditory presentation of words occurred in separate scans). Subtracting the

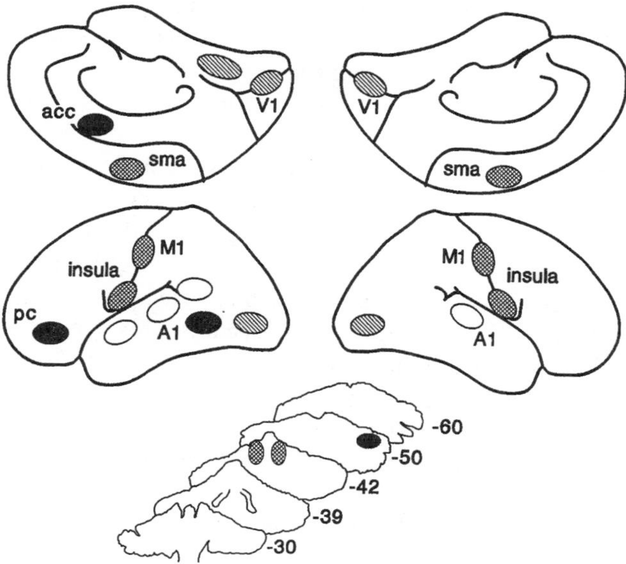

Figure 1. Areas of the normal human brain involved in single word processing as determined by PET measurements of blood flow change (adapted from Petersen et al 1988, 1989). The study looked at three levels of change: passive presentation of nouns (compared to no presentation; visual = diagonal hatching, auditory = clear), repetition aloud of nouns (compared to passive presentation; cross-hatched), and generation aloud of a verb appropriate to the presented nouns (compared to repetition; dark stipple).

first level from the second isolated those areas concerned with either the auditory or visual perception of words. Subtracting the second level from the third isolated those areas of the brain concerned with word output. Subtracting the third level from the fourth isolated those areas concerned with such internal mental operations as selection for action, lexical access, response inhibition (i.e. the tendency to speak the presented word), and semantic analysis. The results of this initial study (Petersen et al 1988, 1989) are summarized in Figure 1.

After publication of this early exploratory work, three additional pieces of information came to light. First, further analysis of Petersen et al's original data suggested an apparent reciprocal relationship between the left prefrontal cortex (active when speaking an appropriate verb for a seen or heard noun but reduced when speaking a seen or heard noun) and the Sylvian-insular cortex bilaterally (active when speaking the seen or heard noun but inactive when speaking an appropriate verb for a seen or heard noun). Second, in a pilot study, after as little as 15 min of practice in generating verbs from the same list of seen nouns, the areas of the brain activated were no different than those activated when speaking the seen noun. Third, performance studies prompted by these observations demonstrated that there was a significant reduction in response times and the occurrence of stereotyped responses across practice blocks in subjects performing the verb generation task.

The above work led to the design and performance of a study (Raichle et al 1993) to test the hypothesis that two distinct anatomical pathways could be used for verb generation. The hypothesis was in keeping with long-standing human lesion and performance data suggesting the existence of two pathways for response selection (e.g. Jackson 1874, Lichtheim 1885, James 1890, Miller et al 1960, Norman & Shallice 1980, Reason & Mycielska 1982) but also provided a direct indication of the actual brain areas involved in the two pathways. We initially hypothesized that a pathway for non-automatic processing involved the anterior cingulate, left prefrontal, and left posterior temporal cortices and the right cerebellar hemisphere; and a pathway for automatic processing involved areas of Sylvian-insular cortex bilaterally. Furthermore, we hypothesized that the use of these two pathways would reflect the degree to which a given response was automatic.

As a test of our hypothesis, we conducted a PET functional imaging study in which normal adult subjects performed the verb generation task on first exposure to a list of 40 visually presented common English nouns (naive condition), immediately after 9 practice blocks on the same list (practiced condition), and then on a new list of words (novel condition). During each block the subjects were urged to say the first word that came to mind and to do so as rapidly as possibly. The words were presented at the rate of one every 1.5

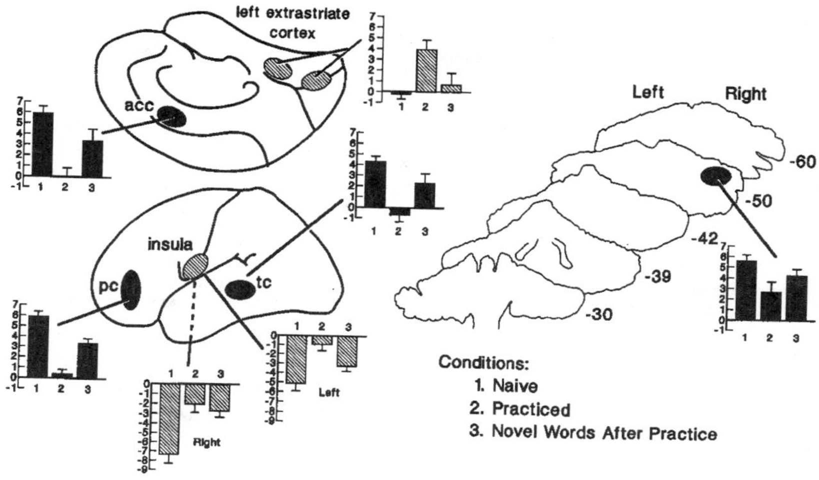

Figure 2. Areas of the normal human brain involved in the generation of verbs for visually presented nouns minus speaking aloud the visually presented nouns as determined by PET measurements of blood flow change (adapted from Raichle et al 1993). See text for experimental details. The vertical bars represent the change in blood flow from the control condition (speaking aloud the presented nouns). The error bars represent one SEM.

sec and remained on the television monitor for 150 msec. Control scans for this study consisted of having the subjects repeat the same words.

The results of this study demonstrated that 7 regions of the brain (Figure 2) showed a significant effect of practice. The results were consistent with the hypothesis (Figure 3) that two pathways exist for the execution of this task. One involves the anterior cingulate, left frontal and left temporal cortices, and the right cerebellum, and the other involves Sylvian-insular cortex bilaterally and the left medial extrastriate cortex. The distinguishing feature of the two pathways was clearly the degree to which the task was learned or automatic.

Previous Imaging Studies of Learning

Several functional imaging studies of learning-related changes in the normal human brain have been reported (Mazziotta et al 1985, Seitz et al 1990, Haier et al 1992, Mazziotta et al 1991, Grafton et al 1992, Friston et al 1992). Each has examined some type of motor skill learning ranging from sequences of finger-to-thumb opposition (Seitz et al 1990, Friston et al 1992) to tasks such as holding a stylus on a revolving target (Mazziotta et al 1991, Grafton et al

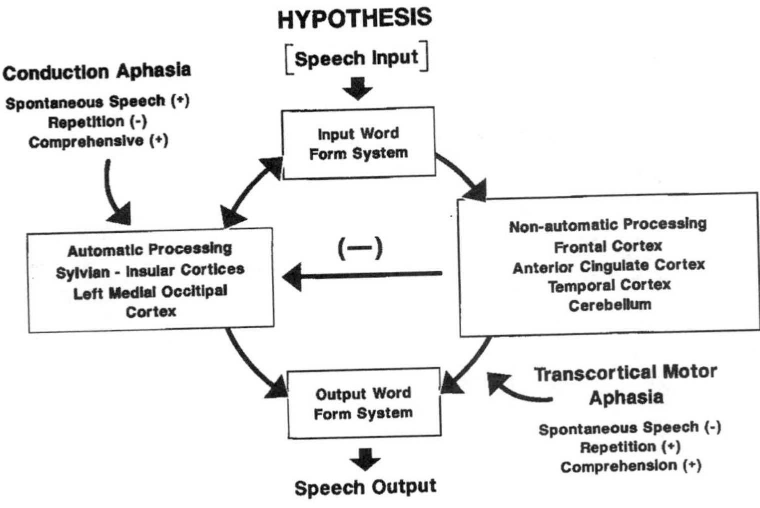

Figure 3. A hypothesis about the two routes available for verbal response selection in the normal human brain and their constituent anatomy. Also shown are those forms of aphasia that have been specifically implicated as affecting one of the two routes.

1992), manipulating complex figures on a computer screen (Haier et al 1992), and signature writing (Mazziotta et al 1985). Four of the studies (Seitz et al 1990, Mazziotta et al 1991, Grafton et al 1992, Friston et al 1992) used measurements of brain blood flow (usual measurement time ≈ 1 min) while the other studies (Mazziotta et al 1985, Haier et al 1992) used measurements of brain glucose metabolism (usual measurement time approximately 45 min). The implications of these different measurement times for behavioral studies of this type are discussed below.

Three of the studies (Mazziotta et al 1991, Grafton et al 1992, Friston et al 1992) controlled the amount of motor activity per scanning session whereas two (Haier et al 1992, Seitz et al 1990) allowed the amount of motor activity to vary with practice. In Mazziotta et al (1985), the effect of learning was assessed by comparing measurements of brain glucose use during a sequence of finger movements (assumed to be novel) with the act of repetitive signature writing, both observed over the approximately 45 min required for the measurement of brain glucose use with PET (Sokoloff et al 1977, Reivich et al 1985). No comment was made about any differences in motor performance on the two tasks or any changes occurring over the period of the measurement.

In the three studies that controlled motor activity during the scanning sessions, one noted no change in primary motor cortex (Friston et al 1992), one noted a decrease (Mazziotta et al 1991), and the other noted an increase (Grafton et al 1992). In the two studies that did not control the amount of motor activity, and consequently observed an increase in the number of motor acts performed during the scanning session, one reported an increase in activity in primary motor cortex (Seitz et al 1990) and one reported a decrease (Haier et al 1992). Two of the groups that controlled motor activity commented about changes in the supplementary motor area (SMA) but reported opposite results: Grafton et al (1992) reported an increase and Friston et al (1992) tentatively reported a decrease. In the one study that neither controlled motor activity nor commented about any aspects of performance (Mazziotta et al 1985), no differences were observed in primary motor cortices or SMA between the novel (finger sequences) and the overlearned task (signature writing). The varied results reported in these six imaging studies of motor learning in normal humans do not permit any conclusions about consistent changes in neuronal activity or organization in primary motor or SMA to be expected from practice and learning of various motor tasks or to anticipate the results of the verb generation task (Raichle et al 1993).

Prompted by these findings, we examined our own data for changes in left and right primary motor cortices and SMA, but found none. We concluded that our subjects did not learn to say the words per se, but rather they learned to select an already learned word on the basis of new stimulus-response associations. One of the studies (Mazziotta et al 1985) commented about changes in the basal ganglia in the overlearned task (signature writing) but none of the other studies including two from the same laboratory (Mazziotta et al 1991, Grafton et al 1992) noted similar changes.

Two of the groups (Seitz et al 1990, Friston et al 1992) studied the cerebellum. Friston et al (1992), who controlled motor activity, noted a decrease and Seitz et al (1990), who allowed motor activity to increase, noted no change. However, the latter authors reasoned that because motor activity had increased with practice, the amount of cerebellar activity per unit of motor activity had actually decreased. Thus both groups postulated a decrease in cerebellar activity as a motor task was learned, suggesting that the cerebellum participates in the learning process. The actual areas of the cerebellum involved in these changes were not specified.

We did not observe any changes in the paramedian regions of the cerebellum (Raichle et al 1993), areas concerned with the actual motoric aspects of speech production (Petersen et al 1989). Again, this is consistent with the hypothesis that it is not the ability to say the word per se that is being learned, but rather, the selection of a specific word on the basis of new stimulus response associations.

Contributions of Constituent Anatomy: Non-Automatic Circuit

Verbal response selection, whether occurring in an automatic or non-automatic manner, represents a distributed brain process with several, widely-separated areas of the brain acting in support of the task. To help unravel the unique operations contributed by each brain area within these circuits, following is a review of known features of the areas revealed in the functional imaging studies of verbal response selection.

The left lateral frontal cortex is a major participant in the naive and novel conditions of the verb generating task. Several previous functional imaging studies have reported activity in inferior frontal cortex under circumstances in which the subjects' responses cannot be based on strong associations with presented stimuli (see Petersen et al 1988, 1989; Wise et al 1991; Frith et al 1991; Friston et al 1991a; Corbetta et al 1991). This is consistent with Goldman-Rakic's (1987) interpretation that the frontal lobe of the cerebral cortex is concerned with internalized knowledge necessary to guide behavior in the absence of informative external cues (i.e. short-term, representation memory). Others have made similar interpretations (e.g. Passingham 1985, Fuster 1989, Duncan 1992). Imaging data would be consistent with that interpretation because when activation is not observed in frontal regions (e.g. during the practiced verb generation condition), the responses produced by the subjects are highly associated with the presented stimuli.

Analysis of patients and nonhuman primates with lesions of the frontal lobes supports this analysis (for reviews see Goldman-Rakic 1987, Fuster 1989, Levin et al 1991). For instance, frontal patients are impaired at performing the Wisconsin card sorting task in which subjects are required to form a sorting principle that is dependent on analysis of the color, number, or shape of items presented on each card. The sorting criterion is covertly changed periodically throughout the test, and subjects must attempt to discern the new principle through trial and error. Frontal patients tend to repeatedly apply a previously correct sorting principle despite feedback that the principle is no longer correct (Milner 1963, Robinson & Furton 1980). Similarly, monkeys performing a visual discrimination task have difficulty overcoming their pre-established preferences for a particular response (Brush et al 1961, Meyer et al 1964). Both patients and monkeys with prefrontal lesions are able to perform well in routine, largely stimulus-driven situations. Luria & Tsvetkova (1964) reported one of the clearest demonstrations of this preserved ability. The patient studied by Luria & Tsvetkova successfully performed constructions in which the actions could be determined by the perceived patterns, but he failed when the perceived pattern had to be decoded into elements forming the basis of the reconstruction. This failure could be overcome, however, by providing a set of simple steps for decoding the pattern.

The anterior cingulate cortex is a prominent constituent of the pathway supporting the naive and novel performance of the verb generating task. Previous functional imaging studies with PET (Petersen et al 1988, 1989; Pardo et al 1990; Frith et al 1991; Corbetta et al 1991; Talbot et al 1991; Jones et al 1991) have also seen activation in this area of the cortex under a variety of experimental conditions. Posner and colleagues (Posner et al 1988, Posner & Petersen 1990) have suggested previously that this area of the cortex is an important component of an anterior attention system in the human brain concerned with selection among competing, complex contingencies. Recent single-unit recording work in monkeys supports that view, showing greater activation for many anterior cingulate neurons when the animals are performing relatively complex sensory-motor tasks compared to more simple conditions (Shima et al 1991). Anatomical tract-tracing studies provide evidence that the anterior cingulate cortex has strong, reciprocal connections to the prefrontal cortex (Goldman-Rakic 1987). This is consistent with the close functional relationship shown in Raichle et al (1993). Patients with large midline lesions including the SMA and anterior cingulate often develop akinetic mutism, a syndrome in which spontaneous speech is extremely rare (Nielsen & Jacobs 1951, Barris & Schuman 1953, Masdeu et al 1978). Extensive studies of patient groups with more focal, psychosurgical anterior cingulate lesions have failed to detect any impairments across a range of motor and cognitive tasks (Ballantine et al 1975, Corkin et al 1979, Corkin 1980), although a recent single-case study suggests some subtle, transient impairments can be detected (Janer & Pardo 1991). A recent comprehensive review summarizes well the current literature on the cingulate cortex (Vogt et al 1992)

Previous work from our laboratory (Petersen et al 1988, 1989) revealed a response in left posterior temporal cortex, at the temporoparietal junction, to the passive presentation of auditory words. Comparing the coordinates of this previously described region to the response observed in the naive and novel conditions of our most recent experiment (Raichle et al 1993) reveals that their centers of mass (Mintun et al 1989) are separated by approximately 16 mm (computed as the vector distance between 2 sets of coordinates). Thus, the posterior temporal activity observed during the naive and novel generation of verbs to visually presented nouns (Raichle et al 1993) lies ventral to the previously described response to passive auditory words by a distance sufficient to suggest that the two areas of activation may be different. Further evidence in support of this hypothesis comes from the observation that the area stimulated by passive auditory words (and also present during repetition and generation of verbs) in our previous work was not active during verb generation to visually presented nouns; whereas the response observed in the more recent experiment was active during verb generation to visually presented nouns but not during passive listening to auditory nouns.

These data (i.e. spatial separation and reciprocally differing responsivity) suggest that at least two areas exist in posterior temporal cortex that are active in the processing of words. There is a more dorsal area that responds to the passive presentation of words (Petersen et al 1988, 1989; Wise et al 1991) and pseudowords (Wise et al 1991). This area is also active when subjects repeat words they hear (Petersen et al 1988, 1989) and when they generate verbs to auditorily presented nouns (Petersen et al 1988, 1989; Wise et al 1991). There also appears to be a more ventral area that is active when subjects generate verbs to visually presented nouns but not during tasks involving the auditory presentation of words (Raichle et al 1993). The more ventral location of this latter area and its apparent involvement with visually and not auditorily presented words suggests that it may be part of the postulated ventral visual processing stream in middle and inferior temporal cortices (Ungerleider & Mishkin 1982).

These findings support the hypothesis that several areas in left posterior temporal cortex are involved in the processing of words. A more dorsal area appears to be concerned with the processing of auditory words (Petersen et al 1988, 1989; Wise et al 1991), whereas a more ventral area appears to be concerned with the processing requirements of visually presented words (Raichle et al 1993). The appearance of activity in left posterior temporal cortex is consistent with its well-established role in language processes (Wernicke 1874). However, the current findings challenge the concept that a single area located in this region has the analysis of words as its major function, regardless of the mode of presentation. Rather, this region of the human brain almost certainly contains a more complex array of processing areas dealing with as yet undefined aspects of word processing. The data from these functional imaging studies in normal human subjects begins to unveil that complexity.

Other, more anterior areas in temporal cortex also have been observed in response to the auditory presentation of words under a variety of task conditions (Petersen et al 1988, 1989; Wise et al 1991; Frith et al 1991; Friston et al 1991a; Zatorre et al 1992). These functional areas are usually bilateral and their response properties suggest that they represent, at least in part, primary auditory cortices. The behavior of these areas (e.g. see Frith et al 1991, Friston et al 1991a) does not seem to be related to the present results.

Contributions of Constituent Anatomy: Automatic Circuit

In contrast to the paramedian regions of the cerebellum, dramatic changes in the right cerebellar hemisphere did accompany the practice-induced changes in reaction time and stereotypy. This complements our previous work (Fiez et al 1992), which concluded that the right cerebellar hemisphere is of critical importance in practice-related learning and the detection of errors in a variety of tasks involving complex nonmotor processing such as generating verbs for the visually presented nouns used in the present study. Our results complement a substantial literature on the role of the cerebellum in learning (Thach 1987, Thompson 1987, Lisberger 1988) and support the hypothesis that some functions performed by the cerebellum may be generalized beyond a purely motor domain (Petersen et al 1989, Fiez et al 1992, Berntson & Torello 1982, Bracke-Tolkmitt et al 1989, Decety et al 1990, Leiner et al 1991, Schmahmann 1991, Akshoomoff et al 1992, Ito 1993).

The Sylvian-insular cortices bilaterally appear to play an important role in the non-automatic pathway for verbal response selection. When subjects attempted the verb generation task for the first time, Sylvian-insular activity was significantly reduced as compared to the control state of simply reading aloud a visually presented noun. In other words, reading aloud a visually presented noun used neurons in these areas but the naive performance of the verb generation task did not. Practice of the verb generation task restored the activity in Sylvian-insular cortices bilaterally to the level of activity found during reading aloud of a visually presented noun.

A recent study of changes in neuronal activity in awake, behaving nonhuman primate premotor cortex while learning conditional visuo-motor associations (Mitz et al 1991) complements our findings in Sylvian-insular cortices. Mitz and colleagues noted that approximately 75% of sampled neurons in premotor cortex significantly increased their activity as the monkeys learned the conditional visuo-motor associations. The increases in neuronal activity closely followed (but did not anticipate) the improvement in the monkeys' performance. In both Mitz et al (1991) and Raichle et al (1993), the subjects learned conditional associations (i.e. one stimulus instructs one response, another stimulus instructs another response). We hypothesize that both studies sampled the activities of populations of neurons with analogous functions. In our study these changes were observed as changes in blood flow rather than actual changes in neuronal firing rate but given the close coupling between neuronal activity and blood flow (Raichle 1987), we think it reasonable to assume that changes in neuronal activity stimulated the observed changes.

In Mitz et al (1991) approximately 25% of the cells sampled decreased their activity with learning. According to the authors, "aside from the sign of the activity change, the properties of cells with activity decreases closely resembled those with increases." We wonder whether the cells that decreased their activity when monkeys learned visuo-motor conditional associations are not analogous to those that caused the blood flow increases we observed in frontal cortex in the naive and novel verb generation conditions and which disappeared when subjects performance changed with practice.

The behavior of the cells studied by Mitz et al parallels the responses we have observed in humans and the tasks studied fall within the same general class, but the gross topography is somewhat different. However, developmental differences, and especially the addition of the capacity for language, may somewhat alter these spatial relationships. Furthermore, we don't know of anyone who provides data on Sylvian-insular cortex under similar experimental conditions.

A surprising participant in the automatic pathway for verbal response selection was the increase over control of activity in the practice condition of a rather extensive area of left medial extrastriate cortex. Previous functional imaging work (Petersen et al 1990), which looked at the response of cortex to the passive presentation of words and word-like stimuli, noted a rather dramatic increase in activity in this area when subjects were visually presented with words and pseudowords but not when they were visually presented with consonant letter strings or false fonts (i.e. letter-like symbols arranged to resemble words). Our interpretation of these results was that a constellation of spatially contiguous areas of peristriate cortex responded uniquely to the presentation of stimuli that behaved according to the rules of the English language (i.e. they were orthographically regular). As such they represented to us the concept of an acquired visual word-form area. There are several reasons why such changes might take place in extrastriate cortex as a result of practice in Raichle et al (1993). It could be that new rules or associations are established in the extrastriate region that allow the performance of the task without further processing taking place in the frontal cortex. It could also be that as the task becomes practiced, resources are shifted from a frontal strategy to a posterior strategy (i.e. attention is directed to this posterior area for the performance of the task). Corbetta et al (1991) discuss such alternative strategies more extensively.

Practical Implications

In our initial study of lexical processing (Petersen et al 1988, 1989) we introduced the concept of hierarchical subtractions to modern functional imaging as a means of isolating the functional anatomy of specific mental operations. The study looked at three levels of change: passive presentation of nouns (compared to no presentation), repetition aloud of nouns (compared to passive presentation), and generation aloud of a verb appropriate to the presented nouns (compared to repetition). The logic of the subtraction analysis in that study was that the passive presentation minus no presentation (i.e. fixation point only) would isolate areas involved in passive sensory processing, the repetition minus passive presentation subtraction would isolate areas involved in articulatory output and motor programming, and the verb generation minus repetition would isolate areas involved in high-level processes such as semantic analysis.

In its simplest form, the type of hierarchical subtraction method used for the design and analysis of modern functional brain imaging studies (e.g. Petersen et al 1988, 1989; Wise et al 1991; Zatorre et al 1992; Raichle et al 1993) involves accepting the assumption that processing done by previously added areas does not change with the addition or deletion of new areas (i.e. each area is functionally isolated). This approach also assumes that the subject does not change strategies with the addition of another task, nor do the task combinations interact with each other (Donders 1969, Sternberg 1969).

The limitations of the additive method were first discussed in terms of reaction time studies of human performance (Donders 1969, Sternberg 1969). For studies of this type, the validity of the underlying assumptions cannot be tested directly and as a result, controversy has occasionally arisen about their interpretation. For functional imaging studies, however, empirical testing is theoretically possible. The locations of areas added at different stages in a task hierarchy can be identified, and the magnitude of their activity at each level in the scan sequence can be monitored. If a brain area is not functionally isolated, then the magnitude of its activity will be modulated by the addition of new tasks. In fact, our study (Raichle et al 1993) had its genesis, in part, because of the discovery that generation aloud of a verb appropriate to a presented noun (compared to repetition of the same noun) modulated areas activated by the repetition of the noun. Furthermore, our results (Raichle et al 1993) now clearly indicate that the actual areas supporting a given task and their relationship with other areas can change dramatically as the result of practice (Figure 2). Such observations underscore the usefulness of combining the hierarchical subtraction method of psychology with modern imaging techniques to further our understanding of the functional anatomy of the normal human brain. They should also impart a note of caution in placing neurobiological interpretations on behavioral data in the absence of direct information about how a process is actually implemented in the brain.

Interpretation of repeated or time intensive within-subject PET measurements must be made with extreme care, because of the potential for rapid changes in the use of brain circuitry resulting from the practice of an unfamiliar task (Figure 2). In our study, 15 min of practice on the verb generation task was sufficient to alter significantly the brain circuitry underlying the task. In fact, changes in the functional anatomy may have occurred even earlier (Raichle et al 1993). Therefore, careful monitoring for changes of behavior as well as in functional anatomical measurements through time are essential.

Of interest as an example of effects of practice is Frith et al's (1991) study, in which three verbal tasks were performed. In the first task the subjects simply repeated the words they heard. In the second task they were asked to generate a word with a meaning opposite to the one that they heard. In the third task the subjects were asked to generate words beginning with the letter *F* each time they heard the word *next.* When the second task was compared to the first task, no difference in cortical blood flow was noted. Based on our earlier results, a clear difference would have been anticipated in task-naive subjects. It is interesting to note that in Frith et al's study "all volunteers practiced producing opposite words beforehand," so they were not really naive. With regard to the actual imaging measurement duration and the effect of practice, the selection of an imaging measurement strategy will also be critical. In Raichle et al 1993, measurement of blood flow was used because of its simplicity and because of the short measurement time. The total measurement time for blood flow with PET is 40 sec (Raichle et al 1983, Fox & Mintun 1989), in contrast to measurement of glucose metabolism, an equally good marker of neuronal activity (Raichle 1987), which requires 30 to 45 min to complete (Sokoloff et al 1977, Reivich et al 1985). Clearly our results would have been quite different had such a lengthy measurement strategy been selected.

Finally, the appearance of a prominent increase in blood flow in the left posterior temporal cortex in the naive and novel conditions of Raichle et al (1993) was quite unexpected. In previous work on the verb generation task (Petersen et al 1988, 1989), we did not observe a blood flow response of significance in this area when subjects either spoke aloud or generated a verb to a visually presented noun. The only difference between these experiments was that in the earlier work words were presented once per second and in the most recent experiment the rate was slowed to one word every 1.5 sec. The reason for this change in presentation rate was that preliminary testing of subjects revealed a much higher success rate in providing an appropriate verb for each noun presented at the slower rate in the naive condition. At the faster rate, subjects often got behind and had to skip a response in order to catch up. This observation indicates the importance that seemingly small details will have on the results of functional brain imaging studies.

Theoretical Implications

Our data (Raichle et al 1993) are consistent with the existence of two pathways for verbal response selection. Although probably first suggested by Jackson (1874), the idea of two circuits or pathways for verbal response selection was presented most clearly by Lichtheim (1885). In an attempt to provide a conceptual framework for the various forms of aphasia, Lichtheim (1885) insightfully devised a scheme centered around three brain systems: a word-form area concerned with the perceptual aspects of language; a center for the motor representations of words, or a motor center of speech; and a very distributed system "for the elaboration of concepts." As he envisioned it, information coming from the word-form system could advance to the motor center for speech either directly or via the concept system. The latter route he characterized as more conscious and less fluent (Lichtheim 1885, p. 474) than the former.

Cast in Lichtheim's conceptual framework, two types of aphasia are of particular theoretical interest to us. The first is conduction aphasia in which the patient has severe and disproportionate difficulty on repetition tasks in the context of intact comprehension and relatively normal spontaneous speech. The second is transcortical motor aphasia in which the patient exhibits the converse pattern: speech production on repetition tasks may be excellent; yet spontaneous speech is difficult to initiate, effortful, and contains a high incidence of phonemic, paraphasic errors (Damasio 1992). Lichtheim postulated that conduction aphasia represented a disruption of the connection between the word-form area and the motor speech area whereas transcortical motor aphasia represented a disturbance in information processing from the word-form area to the motor speech center via the concept system. We suggest that these two routes for verbal response find their neural instantiation in the two circuits revealed in Raichle et al (1993) (Figure 3).

Behavioral dissociations in patients with acquired language deficits are consistent both with Lichtheim's scheme and our results. In an innovative series of studies of patients with conduction and transcortical motor aphasia, McCarthy & Warrington (1984) were able to show that on those repetition tasks designed to maximize active semantic processing, conduction aphasics showed improvement while transcortical motor aphasics showed deterioration. On the basis of this double dissociation, McCarthy & Warrington postulated a dual route model for speech production following Lichtheim's earlier work.

We hypothesize that repetition of words, under conditions that minimize semantic processing, represents an automatic activity that uses the resources of the Sylvian-insular and left, extrastriate visual cortices. We have previously observed the former area to be active during simple repetition of seen or heard nouns (Petersen et al 1988, 1989) and in the present study only with practice when responses have become stereotyped and rapid. We postulate that damage in Sylvian-insular cortices underlies the deficit in patients with conduction aphasia (Figure 3). Before practice, when the performance is less automatic, different cortical areas are used. We postulate that these areas are damaged in patients with transcortical motor aphasia (Figure 3). Under normal circumstances fluent speech is a blend of the activities of the two circuits "in which we are aware of the sense of what we are saying, rather than of every word we say" (Lichtheim 1885).

Several different models have been developed that capture this sort of balance (see Miller et al 1960, Norman & Shallice 1980, Reason & Mycielska 1982). They differ in specifics, but all of these models postulate the existence of one system that operates in a relatively open-loop configuration, with a stimulus or goal leading to a cascade of events that operate in a feed-forward manner to produce a response or sequence of action (i.e. automatic system). The other system operates in a closed-loop manner, using feedback and controlled processing to direct the production of responses (i.e. controlled system).

At a second level of analysis, the effects of practice on our verbal response selection task (Figure 2) can be broken down into item effects (i.e. the effect of practicing particular items) and a more general task effect (i.e. the subjects become familiar with the general demands of the task paradigm). Our observations (Raichle et al 1993) in all areas except right Sylvian-insular cortex suggest that the changes in functional anatomy we observe are item-specific and may underlie the development of learned stimulus-response patterns of behavior. This is consistent with previously developed models of skill learning and the development of automaticity (see Schneider & Shiffrin 1977, Anderson 1982, MacKay 1982, Logan 1988). A critical feature of these models is the ability to develop stimulus-response pairings through repeated practice so that once initiated, a response can be carried through to completion automatically, without further control. Practice allows tasks to be performed using processes that are less attention demanding and allow a sequence of responses to be produced automatically following stimulus presentation.

FUTURE DIRECTIONS

Functional imaging of the normal human brain will advance over the next several years as other techniques join PET. An especially important addition will be functional magnetic resonance imaging (fMRI).

The implications for functional brain imaging result from the fact that an increase in blood flow without a concomitant increase in oxygen consumption leads to an increase in the oxygen concentration in the cerebral venous blood draining the area of brain activation. Changes in the oxygenation of hemoglobin affect its magnetic properties (Pauling 1935) so that there is the potential for increased contrast between the brain and blood in the area of activation in a properly designed magnetic resonance image (Ogawa et al 1990). Several groups have demonstrated that functionally-induced signals could be obtained with MRI (Ogawa et al 1992, Kwong et al 1992). This has led to a great deal of interest in the potential of MRI to do functional brain imaging of the type detailed in this review.

There are several advantages of MRI for functional brain imaging. The technique has no known biological risk except for the occasional subject who suffers claustrophobia in the scanner (the entire body must be inserted into a relatively narrow tube). MRI provides both anatomical and functional information, which permits an accurate anatomical identification of the regions of activation in each subject. The spatial resolution is quite good, approaching the 1–2 mm range. Finally, MRI systems are much more widely available than PET systems, which require not only a scanner but also a small cyclotron and chemistry facility.

At the moment the disadvantages of MRI include some uncertainty about the actual equipment needed. Successful images have been obtained on standard hospital instruments (Schneider et al 1993), but it is unclear whether truly successful functional imaging will require instruments of higher field strength (Ogawa et al 1992) and more rapid imaging capability (Ogawa et al 1992, Kwong et al 1992). Because the subject is confined in a long, narrow tube and is in a very high magnetic field, instruments routinely used to deliver stimuli to subjects in PET cameras cannot be used with MRI. This difficulty will eventually be overcome, but for the moment it is a problem. Because of the very high resolution of MRI, any movement of the subject during an activation scan renders the data useless. Verbal responses have been sufficient to produce image-destroying movement, which is clearly a problem for studies of verbal response selection! Finally, uncertainty remains about the exact nature of the fMRI signal and its relationship to the task-induced changes in neuronal activity (Ogawa et al 1992, Lai et al 1993). In addition to the problems unique to fMRI, there are also some uncertainties shared by fMRI and PET.

Functional imaging with PET and fMRI is based on measuring the changes in local blood flow that are tightly coupled to changes in local neuronal activity (see Raichle 1987 for review). PET can measure these changes in blood flow very accurately (Fox et al 1986, Mintun et al 1989). Estimates of these changes also have been made with fMRI (Belliveau et al 1991). Parallel increases in oxygen consumption do not accompany these transient, task-induced physiological increases in blood flow in the normal brain. As a result, the local cerebral venous oxygen content increases with blood flow (Fox & Raichle 1986). These increases can be detected by fMRI (Ogawa et al 1992, Kwong et al 1992) because the properties of hemoglobin in a magnetic field are affected by the amount of oxygen it is carrying (Pauling 1935, Ogawa et al 1990).

Decreases in both neuronal activity and blood flow from a resting, awake baseline state can also be expected to occur occasionally in functional activation studies (see Squire et al 1992, Figure 3 top and bottom, *Baseline minus Fixation*). Decreases in blood flow are known to accompany decreases in neuronal activity (Sokoloff 1981). However, changes in venous oxygen content have not been observed when neuronal activity is decreased and blood flow is reduced in normal brain. As a result fMRI imaging studies using measurements of change in cerebral venous oxygen content as a basis for functional mapping (e.g. Ogawa et al 1992, Kwong et al 1992) will miss such changes. These absolute local reductions in blood flow and metabolism from a resting, awake baseline state must be distinguished from those observed in subtraction images in which the blood flow in the control state is actually increased more from a resting, awake baseline than in the task state of interest (see Squire et al 1992, Figure 3 middle, *Priming minus Baseline*). In such a situation it is anticipated that a change in venous oxygen content will be observed. However, to my knowledge there are no experimental data available to support this hypothesis.

During functional brain activation, local glucose metabolism increases in parallel to blood flow. Oxygen metabolism changes little, if at all (Fox & Raichle 1986, Fox et al 1988). This uncoupling of neuronal activity and oxidative metabolism during functional activation is consistent with the hypothesis that the energy required for these transient increases in neuronal activity is small relative to the overall energy demands of the brain (Creutzfeldt 1975). Full oxidative metabolism of glucose to carbon dioxide and water, which accounts for the majority of the resting, awake metabolism of the mammalian brain, efficiently produces 36 molecules of ATP for each molecule of glucose consumed. Non-oxidative or glycolytic metabolism produces only 2 molecules of ATP per molecule of glucose consumed. Thus, the physiological uncoupling encountered in functional activation studies leads to a marked increase in glucose consumption relative to energy demands. If we assume that blood flow to the brain is coupled to glucose consumption, and considerable evidence suggests this (Sokoloff 1981, Fox et al 1989), then the shift to glycolysis as a means of energy production could cause up to an 18-fold increase in blood flow change per additional molecule of ATP required. The result is a dramatic signal amplification for functional brain imaging studies.

Our understanding of the basic physiology leading to such shifts in metabolism is incomplete. For example, it is unknown whether uncoupling occurs under all circumstances and in all neuronal systems within the brain. If increased energy demand is supplied under some circumstances by oxidative metabolism of glucose rather than non-oxidative metabolism, it is reasonable to anticipate a much attenuated increase in blood flow and glucose utilization. Such an increase in blood flow response and an absence of an oxygen signal under such circumstances could not be interpreted as less neuronal work! We must vigorously pursue a more complete understanding of these important issues if we are to use functional imaging techniques with confidence. Our window to the brain is only as good as our understanding of the principles upon which it operates.

In the immediate future it is very likely that PET and MRI will operate in parallel, PET providing a survey of the entire brain and a general description of the entire circuit underlying a particular task. MRI will allow us to focus on the details of particular areas within circuits of interest, allowing us a look at the detailed functional anatomy in each subject. Together, they should greatly enhance our understanding of the functional anatomy of the normal human brain. Despite suggestions to the contrary (Kwong et al 1992), it is unlikely that either MRI or PET will provide information on the real time processing within functional circuits in the human brain. The problem is that the signal observed by both MRI and PET is based on change in blood flow, which follows changes in neuronal activity in the cortex by hundreds of msec to sec (Frostig et al 1990). As a result I predict that functional imaging will include some form of brain electrical recording either from scalp electrodes (e.g. see Kutas & Hillyard 1984) or the recording of functionally-induced brain magnetic fields (e.g. Yamamoto et al 1988). Sophisticated work of the future will use some combination of MRI and PET to locate the potential electrical generators in the circuitry underlying a particular task. With this knowledge, electrical techniques will then be used to determine the time course of information flow within the circuit.

These technical advances in localizing and monitoring the activity of local areas and circuits during specific mental tasks in the normal human brain and the data generated thus far suggest that our understanding of the neurobiological basis of behavior is likely to advance rapidly in the Decade of the Brain.

Literature Cited

Akshoomoff NA, Courchesne E, Press GA, Iragui V. 1992. Contribution of the cerebellum to neuropsychological functioning: evidence from a case of cerebellar degenerative disorder. *Neuropsychologia* 30: 315–28

Anderson JR. 1982. Acquisition of cognitive skill. *Psychol. Rev.* 89:369–406

Ballantine HT, Levy BS, Dagi TF, Giriunas IB. 1975. Cingulotomy for psychiatric illness: report of 13 years' experience. In *Neurosurgical Treatment in Psychiatry, Pain, and Epilepsy,* ed. WH Sweet, pp. 333–53. Baltimore: Univ. Park Press

Barris RW, Schuman HR. 1953. Bilateral anterior cingulate gyrus lesions. *Neurology* 3:44–52

Belliveau JW, Kennedy DN, McKinstry RC, Buchbinder BR, Weisskoff RM, et al. 1991. Functional mapping of the human visual cortex by magnetic resonance imaging. *Science* 254:716–19

Berntson GG, Torello MW. 1982. The paleocerebellum and the integration of behavioral function. *Physiol. Psychol.* 10:2–12

Bracke-Tolkmitt R, Linden A, Canavan AGM, Rockstroh B, Scholz E, et al. 1989. The cerebellum contributes to mental skills. *Behav. Neurosci.* 103:442–46

Brush ES, Mishkin M, Rosvold HE. 1961. Effects of object preferences and aversions on discrimination learning in monkeys with frontal lesions. *J. Comp. Physiol. Psychol.* 54:319–25

Corbetta M, Miezin FM, Dobmeyer S, Shulman GL, Petersen SE. 1991. Selective and divided attention during visual discriminations of shape, color and speed: functional anatomy by positron emission tomography. *J. Neurosci.* 11:2383–402

Corkin S. 1980. A prospective study of cingulotomy. In *The Psychosurgery Debate: Scientific, Legal and Ethical Perspectives,* ed. ES Valenstein, pp. 164–204. San Francisco: Freeman

Corkin S, Twitchell TE, Sullivan EV. 1979. Safety and efficacy of cingulotomy for pain and psychiatric disorder. In *Modern Concepts in Psychiatric Surgery,* ed. ER Hitchcock, HT Ballantine Jr., BA Meyerson, pp. 253–72. New York: Elsevier/North Holland

Cormack AM. 1963. Reconstruction of densities from their projections, with applications in radiological physics. *Physics Med. Biol.* 18:195–207

Cormack AM. 1973. Reconstruction of densities from their projections, with applications in radiological physics. *Physics Med. Biol.* 18:195–207

Creutzfeldt OD. 1975. Neurophysiological correlates of different functional states of the brain. In *Brain Work. The Coupling of Function, Metabolism and Blood Flow in the Brain,* ed DH Ingvar, Lassen NA, pp. 21–46. Alfred Benzon Symp. VIII. Munksgaard, Copenhagen.

Damasio AR. 1992. Aphasia. *N. Engl. J. Med.* 326:531–39

Decety J, Sjoholm H, Ryding E, Stenberg G, Ingvar DH. 1990. The cerebellum participates in mental activity: tomographic measurements of regional cerebral blood flow. *Brain Res.* 535:313–17

Donders FC. 1969. On the speed of mental processes. Reprinted in *Acta Psychol.* 30:412–31

Duncan J. 1992. *Selection of Input and Goal in the Control of Behavior.* New York: Oxford Univ. Press

Fiez J, Petersen SE, Cheney MK, Raichle ME. 1992. Impaired non-motor learning and error detection associated with cerebellar damage. *Brain* 115:155–78

Fox PT, Mintun MA. 1989. Noninvasive functional brain mapping by change-distribution analysis of averaged PET images of $H_2{}^{15}O$. *J. Nucl. Med.* 30:141–49

Fox PT, Mintun MA, Raichle ME, Miezen FM, Allman JM, Van Essen DC. 1986. Mapping human visual cortex with positron emission tomography. *Nature* 323:806–9

Fox PT, Mintun MA, Reiman EM, Raichle ME. 1988. Enhanced detection of focal brain responses using intersubject averaging and change-distribution analysis of subtracted PET images. *J. Cereb. Blood Flow Metab.* 8:642–53

Fox PT, Perlmutter JS, Raichle ME. 1985. A stereotactic method of anatomical localization for positron emission tomography. *J. Comput. Assist. Tomogr.* 9:141–53

Fox PT, Raichle ME. 1986. Focal physiological uncoupling of cerebral blood flow and oxidative metabolism during somatosensory stimulation in humanb subjects. *Proc. Natl. Acad. Sci. USA* 83:1140–44

Fox PT, Raichle ME, Mintun MA, Dence C. 1989. Nonoxidative glucose comsumption during focal physiologic neural activity. *Science* 241:462–64

Friston KJ, Frith CD, Liddle PF, Frackowiak RSJ. 1991a. Investigating a network model of word generation with positron emission tomography. *Proc. R. Soc. London Ser. B* 244:101–6

Friston KJ, Frith CD, Liddle PF, Frackowiak RSJ. 1991b. Comparing function (PET) images. The assessment of significant change. *J. Cereb. Blood Flow Metab.* 11:690–99

Friston KJ, Frith CD, Passingham RE, Liddle PF, Frackowiak RSJ. 1992. Motor practice and neurophysiological adaptation in the cerebellum: a positron emission tomographic study. *Proc. R. Soc. London Ser. B* 248:223–28

Frith CD, Friston K, Liddle PF, Frackowiak RSJ. 1991. Willed action and the prefrontal cortex in man: a study with PET. *Proc. R. Soc. London Ser. B* 244:241–46

Frostig RD, Lieke EE, Ts'o DY, Grinvald A. 1990. Cortical functional architecture and local coupling between neuronal activity and the microcirculation revealed by in vivo high-resolution optical imaging of intrinsic signals. *Proc. Natl. Acad. Sci. USA* 87:6082–86

Fuster JM. 1989. *The Prefrontal Cortex.* New York: Raven

Goldman-Rakic PS. 1987. Circuitry of primate prefrontal cortex and regulation of behavior by representational knowledge. *Handb. Physiol.* 5:374–417

Grafton ST, Mazziotta JC, Presty S, Friston KJ, Frackowiak RSJ, Phelps ME. 1992. functional anatomy of human procedural learning determined with regional cerebral blood flow and PET. *J. Neurosci.* 12:2542–48

Haier RJ, Siegel BV Jr, MacLachlan A, Soderling E, Lottenberg S, Buchsbaum M. 1992. Regional glucose metabolic changes after learning a complex visuospatial motor task: a positron emission tomographic study. *Brain Res.* 57:134–43

Herscovitch P, Markham J, Raichle ME. 1983. Brain blood flow measured with intravenous $H_2{}^{15}O$. I. Theory and error analysis. *J. Nucl. Med.* 24:782–89

Herscovitch P, Raichle ME, Kilbourn MR, Welch MJ. 1987. Positron emission tomographic measurement of cerebral blood flow and permeability-surface area product using 15-O water and 11-C butanol. *J. Cereb. Blood Flow Metab.* 7:527–42

Hinshaw WS, Bottomley PA, Holland GN. 1977. Radiographic thin-section image of the human wrist by nuclear magnetic resonance. *Nature* 270:722–23

Hounsfield GN. 1973. Computerized transverse axial scanning (tomography): Part I. Description of system. *Br. J. Radiol.* 46:1016–22

Howard D, Patterson K, Wise R, Brown WD, Friston K, et al. 1992. The cortical location of the lexicons. *Brain* 115:1769–82

Ito M. 1993. How does the cerebellum facilitate thought? In *Brain Mechanisms of Perception and Memory: From Neuron to Behavior,* ed. Ono T, Squire LR, Raichle ME, Perrett DI, Fakuda M. New York: Oxford Univ. Press. In press

Jackson JH. 1874. On the nature of the duality of the brain. *Med. Press Circ.* i:19, 41, 63

James W. 1890. *The Principles of Psychology,* 1:1–113 New York: Holt

Janer KW, Pardo JV. 1991. Deficits in selective attention following bilateral anterior cingulotomy. *J. Cogn. Neurosci.* 3:231–41

Jones AKP, Brown WD, Friston KJ, Qi LY, Frackowiak RSJ. 1991. Cortical and subcortical localization of response to pain in man using positron emission tomography. *Proc. R. Soc. London Ser. B* 244:39–44

Kutas M, Hillyard SA. 1984. Brain potentials during reading reflect word expectancy and semantic association. *Nature* 307:161–63

Kwong KK, Belliveau JW, Chesler DA, Goldberg IE, Weisskoff RM, et al. 1992. Dynamic magnetic resonance imaging of human brain activity during primary sensory stimulation. *Proc. Natl. Acad. Sci. USA* 89:5675–79

Lai S, Hopkins AL, Haacke EM, Li D, Wasserman BA, Buckley P, et al. 1993. Identification of vascular structures as a major source of signal contrast in high resolution 2D and 3D functional activation imaging of the motor cortex at 1.5T: preliminary results. *J. Mag. Res. Med.* In press

Lautebur PC. 1973. Image formation by induced local interactions: examples employing nuclear magnetic resonance. *Nature* 242:1901–191

Leiner HC, Leiner AL, Dow RS. 1991. The human cerebro-cerebellar system: its computing, cognitive, and language skills. *Behav. Brain Res.* 44:113–28

Levin HS, Eisenberg HM, Benton AL. 1991. *Frontal Lobe Function and Dysfunction.* New York: Oxford Univ. Press

Lichtheim L. 1885. On aphasia. *Brain* 7:433–84

Lisberger SG. 1988. The neural basis for learning of simple motor skills. *Science* 241:728–35

Logan GD. 1988. Toward an instance theory of automatization. *Psychol. Rev.* 95:492–527

Luria AR, Tsvetkova LS. 1964. The programming of constructive activity in local brain injuries. *Neuropsychologia* 2:95–107

MacKay DG. 1982. The problems of flexibility, fluency, and speed-accuracy trade-off in skilled behavior. *Psychol. Rev.* 89:483–506

Masdeu JC, Schoene WC, Funkenstein H. 1978. Aphasia following infarction of the left supplementary motor area. *Neurology* 28:1220–23

Mazziotta JC, Grafton ST, Woods RC. 1991. The human motor system studied with PET measurements of cerebral blood flow: topography and motor learning. In *Brain Work and Mental Activity, Alfred Benzon Symp. 31,* ed. NA Lassen, DH Ingvar, ME Raichle, L Friberg, pp. 280–90. Copenhagen: Munksgaard

Mazziotta JC, Phelps ME, Wapenski JA. 1985. Human cerebral motor system metabolic responses in health and disease. *J. Cereb. Blood Flow Metab.* 5(Suppl. 1):S213–14

McCarthy R, Warrington EK. 1984. A two-route model of speech production. *Brain* 107:463–85

Meyer DR, Treichler FR, Yutzey DA, Meyer PM. 1964. Precedence effects in discriminationlearning by normal and frontal monkeys. *J. Comp. Physiol. Psychol.* 58:472–74

Miller GA, Galanter E, Pribram KH. 1960. *Plans and the Structure of Behavior.* New York: Holt

Milner B. 1963. Effects of different brain lesions on card sorting. *Arch. Neurol.* 9:100–10

Mintun MA, Fox PT, Raichle ME. 1989. A highly accurate method of localizing regions of neuronal activation in the human brain with positron emission tomography. *J. Cereb. Blood Flow Metab.* 9:96–103

Mitz AR, Godschalk M, Wise SP. 1991. Learning-dependent neuronal activity in the premotor cortex: activity during the acquisition of conditional motor associations. *J. Neurosci.* 11:1855–72

Nielsen JM, Jacobs LL. 1951. Bilateral lesions of the anterior cingulate gyri. *Bull. L. A. Neurol. Soc.* 16:231–34

Norman DA, Shallice T. 1980. Attention to action: willed and automatic control of behavior. Center for Human Information Processing (Tech. Rep. No. 99). Revised and reprinted 1986 in *Consciousness and Self-regulation,* Vol. 4, ed. RJ Davidson, GE Schwartz, D Shapiro. New York: Plenum

Ogawa S, Lee LM, Kay AR, Tank DW. 1990. Brain magnetic resonance imaging with contrast dependent on blood oxygenation. *Proc. Natl. Acad. Sci. USA* 87:9868–72

Ogawa S, Tank DW, Menon R, Ellermann JM, Kim S-G, et al. 1992. Intrinsic signal changes accompanying sensory stimulation: functional brain mapping with magnetic resonance imaging. *Proc. Natl. Acad. Sci. USA* 89:5951–55

Pardo JV, Pardo PJ, Haner KW, Raichle ME. 1990. The anterior cingulate cortex mediates processing selection in the Stroop attentional conflict paradigm. *Proc. Natl. Acad. Sci. USA* 87:256–59

Passingham RE. 1985. Cortical mechanisms and cues for action. *Philos. Trans. R. Soc. London Ser. B* 308:101–11

Pauling L. 1935. Oxygen equilibrium of hemoglobin and its structural interpretation. *Proc. Natl. Acad. Sci. USA* 21:186–91

Petersen SE, Fox PT, Posner MI, Mintun MA, Raichle ME. 1988. Positron emission tomographic studies of the cortical anatomy of single word processing. *Nature* 331:585–89

Petersen SE, Fox PT, Posner MI, Mintun M, Raichle ME. 1989. Positron emission tomographic studies of the processing of single words. *J. Cogn. Neurosci.* 1:153–70

Petersen SE, Fox PT, Snyder AZ, Raichle ME. 1990. Activation of extrastriate and frontal cortical areas by visual words and word-like stimuli. *Science* 249:1041–44

Phelps ME, Hoffman EJ, Mullani NA, Ter-Pogossian MM. 1975. Application of annihilation coincidence detection to transaxial reconstruction tomography. *J. Nucl. Med.* 16:210–24

Posner MI, Petersen SE. 1990. The attention system of the human brain. *Annu. Rev. Neurosci.* 13:25–42

Posner MI, Petersen SE, Fox PT, Raichle ME. 1988. Localization of cognitive operations in the human brain. *Science* 240:1627–31

Raichle ME. 1987. Circulatory and metabolic correlates of brain function in normal humans. *Handb. Physiol.* 5:643–74

Raichle ME, Fiez J, Videen TO, Fox PT, Pardo JV, Petersen SE. 1993. Practice-related changes in human brain functional anatomy during non-motor learning. *Cereb. Cortex* In press

Raichle ME, Martin WRW, Herscovitch P, Mintun M, Markham J. 1983. Brain blood-flow measured with $H_2{}^{15}O$. II. Implementation and validation. *J. Nucl. Med.* 24:790–98

Reason J, Mycielska K. 1982. *Absent Minded? The Psychology of Mental Lapses and Everyday Errors.* Englewood Cliffs, NJ: Prentice-Hall

Reivich M, Alavi A, Wolf A, Fowler J, Russell J, et al. 1985. Glucose metabolic rate kinetic model parameters determination in humans: the lumped constants and rate constants or (^{18}F)fluorodeoxyglucose and (^{11}C)deoxyglucose. *J. Cereb. Blood Flow Metab.* 5:179–92

Robinson CJ, Furton H. 1980. Organization of somatosensory receptive fields in cortical areas 7b, retroinsula, postauditory, and granular insula of *M. fascicularis. J. Comp. Neurol.* 192:69–92

Roy CS, Sherrington CS. 1890. On the regulation of the blood supply of the brain. *J. Physiol. London* 11:85–108

Schmahmann JD. 1991. An emerging concept. The cerebellar contribution to higher function. *Arch. Neurol.* 48:1178–87

Schneider W, Noll DC, Cohen JD. 1993. Functional topographic mapping of the cortical ribbon in human vision with conventional MRI scanners. *Nature* In press

Schneider W, Shiffrin RM. 1977. Controlled and automatic human information processing: I. Detection, search, and attention. *Psychol. Rev.* 84:1–53

Seitz RJ, Roland PE, Bohm C, Greitz T, Stone-Elander S. 1990. Motor learning in man: a positron emission tomographic study. *NeuroReport* 1:57–66

Sherrington C. 1906. *The Integrative Action of the Nervous System.* New Haven, Conn: Yale Univ. Press

Shima K, Aya K, Mushiake H, Inase M, Aizawa H, Tanji J. 1991. Two movement-related foci in the primate cingulate cortex observed in signal-triggered and self-paced forelimb movements. *J. Neurophysiol.* 65:188–202

Sokoloff L. 1981. Relationships among local functional activity, energy metabolism, and blood flow in the central nervous system. *Fed. Proc.* 40:2311–16

Sokoloff L, Reivich M, Kennedy C, DesRosiers MH, Patlak CS, et al. 1977. The [^{14}C]deoxyglucose method for the measurement of local cerebral glucose utilization: theory, procedure, and normal values in the conscious and anesthetized albino rat. *J. Neurochem.* 28:897–917

Squire LR, Ojemann JG, Miezen, FM, Petersen SE, Videen TO, Raichle ME. 1992. Activation of the hippocampus in normal humans: a functional anatomical study of memory. *Proc. Natl. Acad. Sci. USA* 89:1837–41

Sternberg S. 1969. The discovery of processing stages: extensions of Donders' method. *Acta Psychol.* 30:276–315

Talbot JD, Marrett S, Evans AC, Meyer E, Bushnell MC, Duncan GH. 1991. Multiple representations of pain in human cerebral cortex. *Science* 251:1355–58

Ter-Pogossian MM, Phelps ME, Hoffman EJ, Mullani NA. 1975. A positron-emmission transaxial tomograph for nuclear imaging (PETT). *Radiology* 114:89–98

Thach WT. 1987. Cerebellar inputs to motor cortex. In *Motor Areas of the Cerebral Cortex,* pp. 201–20. Ciba Found. Symp. 132. Chichester, England: Wiley

Thompson RF. 1987. The neurobiology of learning and memory. *Science* 233:941–48

Ungerleider LG, Mishkin M. 1982. Two cortical visual systems. In *Analysis of Visual Behavior,* ed. DG Ingle, MA Goodale, RJQ Mansfield, pp. 549–86. Cambridge, Mass: MIT Press

Vogt BA, Finch DM, Olson CR. 1992. Functional heterogeneity in cingulate cortex: the anterior executive and posterior evaluative regions. *Cereb. Cortex* 2:435–43

Wernicke K. 1874. Der aphasische Symptomenkomplex. Transl. in *Boston Stud. Philos. Sci.* 4:34–97

Wise R, Chollet F, Hadar U, Friston K, Hoffner E, Frackowiak R. 1991. Distribution of cortical neural networks involved in word comprehension and word retrieval. *Brain* 114:1803–17

Worsley KJ, Evans AC, Marrett S, Neelin P. 1992. A three-dimensional statistical analysis for CBF activation studies in human brain. *J. Cereb. Blood Flow Metab.* 12:900–18

Yamamoto T, Williamson SJ, Kaufman L, Nicholson C, Llinas R. 1988. Magnetic localization of neuronal activity in the human brain. *Proc. Natl. Acad. Sci. USA* 85:8732–36

Zatorre RJ, Evans AC, Meyer E, Gjedde A. 1992. Lateralization of phonetic and pitch discrimination in speech processing. *Science* 256:846–49

Annu. Rev. Psychol. 1994. 45:357–88

PERSONALITY ASSESSMENT

Daniel J. Ozer and Steven P. Reise

Department of Psychology, University of California, Riverside, California 92521

KEY WORDS: traits, five-factor model, scale construction, validity, personality

---

CONTENTS

INTRODUCTION

Personality assessment, as a scientific endeavor, seeks to determine those characteristics that constitute important individual differences in personality, to develop accurate measures of such attributes, and to explore fully the consequential meanings of these identified and measured characteristics. We present the recent efforts of personality assessment researchers in three broad domains: 1. achieving a more finely tuned picture of the primary objects of assessment, confronting both substantive and conceptual issues in defining important personality characteristics; 2. developing new methods of data collection while refining older procedures; and 3. generating new methods of evaluating assessment results while maintaining a continued critical scrutiny of established procedures for ascertaining the validity of measurement outcomes.

These three areas provide us with an organizational framework for discussing much recent research, but this trichotomy is of course artificial. Particular kinds of personality characteristics may require data of a specific type or particular methods for validity assessment. As we proceed, we note several of the more crucial interdependencies among these three broad domains of personality assessment research.

A final topic we raise concerns the challenge to personality assessment inherent in our society's growing awareness of gender and cultural diversity. From Allport (1937) to the present, personality assessment has focused on individual diversity while group differences were largely understood as mean differences. Reconciling individual and group diversity issues so the study of one serves the other is among the more important unrealized goals of differential psychology.

THE OBJECT OF ASSESSMENT

Personality assessment is most often trait measurement (Wiggins & Pincus 1992). Although motives, intentions, beliefs, styles, and structures may also constitute the preferred conceptual units of some researchers, the trait model (Funder 1991, Tellegen 1991) remains dominant. Contemporary trait psychologists continue to explore the five-factor model of personality, but this focus has barely slowed the continued invention of new concepts or the exploration of other units. Despite increasing consensus that the five-factor model summarizes the substantive domain of traits, there is also increasing interest in developing alternative ways to define personality variables. After exploring these substantive and conceptual matters, we suggest that personality theory has an irreplaceable role in resolving the issues.

Personality Structure

THE FIVE-FACTOR MODEL The five-factor model of personality structure (Digman 1990, Goldberg 1993a) continues to influence the choice of measures and constructs among personality psychologists and is becoming the predominant representation of global personality dimensions. The NEO Personality Inventory (Costa & McCrae 1989, 1992a) remains the instrument most closely associated with this model, though a carefully selected set of adjective rating scales developed by Goldberg (1992) now offers an alternative for the assessment of extraversion, agreeableness, conscientiousness, emotional stability, and intellect. Briggs (1992) provides a historical and comparative evaluation of these and other scales that might be used to assess these five dimensions.

An explanation of the explosive growth of interest in the five-factor model awaits the attention of future sociologists and philosophers of science. From the myopic perspective offered by the present it is hard to do more than list several accomplishments of the model. Foremost of these is the ability of the five-factor representation to assimilate other representations of personality as they are embedded in multiscale inventories. Some recent examples include the 16PF (Gerbing & Tuley 1991), the Edwards Personal Preference Schedule (Piedmont et al 1992), the Eysenck Personality Questionnaire (Goldberg & Rosolack 1993), and the California Psychological Inventory (CPI) (McCrae et al 1993). The five-factor model also assimilates dimensions of affect (Saucier 1992, Watson & Clark 1992), and provides a basis for integrating circular models of interpersonal traits (Hofstee et al 1992, Saucier 1992). Linkages between the five-factor model and interpersonal processes are also becoming apparent in current research, where the five factors have been related to the use of different manipulation tactics (Buss 1992) and attachment styles (Shaver & Brennan 1992).

The five-factor model also reveals much about familiar constructs with long and troubled histories. Psychological adjustment, broadly conceived, is a prime example. Current research indicates that each of the five factors is related to psychological well-being (McCrae & Costa 1991) and to adjustment in adolescence (Graziano & Ward 1992). In clarifying the constituent elements in multidimensional measures of adjustment, the five-factor model provides a basis for reconciling the diverse and sometimes contradictory findings that exist in the literature. Smith & Williams (1992) describe a parallel application of the five-factor model in health psychology, where the model can be used to order and integrate existing findings relating personality characteristics and health outcomes.

Specific psychopathological syndromes have been illustrated within the model. Each of the five factors is related to one or more components of narcissism (Buss & Chiodo 1991); and the model provides an alternative, dimensional framework for understanding personality disorders (Costa & McCrae 1992b, Soldz et al 1993, Widiger & Trull 1992). McCrae (1991) argues for the general usefulness of the model in various domains of clinical assessment.

Estimation of the five factors from the Personality Research Form (PRF) in various samples has provided additional evidence supporting the cross-cultural generality of the five-factor model (Stumpf 1993). A similar result is reported by Paunonen et al (1992) who also successfully retrieved the five-factor structure using both the PRF and nonverbal stimuli as test items.

Despite these accomplishments, the five-factor model has its critics. Some (e.g. Paunonen et al 1992, Tellegen 1993) assert that the five-factor model is not sufficiently comprehensive, though others (e.g. McCrae & John 1992, Wiggins & Pincus 1992) are at least provisionally satisfied with the model's inclusiveness. Wiggins (1992) suggests that there is consensus on at least two limitations of the five-factor model: 1. by focusing on broad superordinate categories, much detail useful for both description and prediction is lost; and 2. the model is atheoretical and descriptive rather than explanatory. McAdams (1992) shares these concerns but offers a much more severe indictment: Because the five-factor model is capable only of contextless noncontingent comparisons between persons it is inherently a "psychology of the stranger" (p. 348).

Whether the five-factor model subsumes all of the generally recognized and useful trait dimensions seems, at least in part, an empirical question. Our interpretation of the many reported correlates of each of the five factors suggests at least one important group of individual difference variables that should be, but apparently is not, easily assimilated by the five-factor model. These are the variables subsumed by the well-known second factor of the Minnesota Multiphasic Personality Inventory (MMPI), referred to by Block (1965) as ego control. Mroczek's (1993) examination of the MMPI-2 and Goldberg's (1992) one hundred adjective markers of the five factors failed to find any clear relations between scales saturated with ego control and any of the five-factor markers. The CPI Socialization scale, which assesses similar content, is also poorly predicted by five-factor scales (McCrae et al 1993). But even if data continue to suggest that issues relating to impulse regulation cannot be assimilated to the five-factor model, there is little doubt that the model could accommodate to the data, whether by adding facets to existing factors, redefining factors, or even adding factors. Determining whether an alteration of the model is needed is an important part of the future agenda for research in personality structure.

The full five-factor model is more than a short list of broad individual differences variables: It is a highly structured taxonomy (Goldberg 1993b). There are misplaced concerns that the five broad dimensions of the model may limit assessors to using superordinate factors instead of more specific traits within the structure. There is no inconsistency in advocating the five-factor model as a general taxonomy and the use of measures of specific traits for particular predictive or explanatory purposes.

Although settling for the current five-factor model may be premature, concerns about the specific details of the model are less telling than are the in principle reservations expressed in critiques such as McAdams' (1992). In our view, the five-factor model provides a useful taxonomy, a hierarchical coordinate system, for mapping important personality variables. The model is not a theory; it organizes phenomena to be explained by theory, and as Wiggins (1992) notes, several different theories seek to do so. Any claim that the five-factor model is more than a hierarchical coordinate system requires substantive theory based on evidence independent of the factor structure (e.g. such as Eysenck's 1967 cortical arousal theory of extraversion).

Goldberg (1993a) likens the five-factor model to the standard north-south and east-west axes of cartography. Just as latitude and longitude permit the precise description of any location on earth, the five-factor model promises the hope of similarly locating personality dispositions. And just as the discovery of how to measure longitude was crucial to navigation; the invention of the five-factor model is a major contribution to personality assessment. Personality psychologists who continue to employ their preferred measure without locating it within the five-factor model can only be likened to geographers who issue reports of new lands but refuse to locate them on a map for others to find. But just as knowing the exact coordinates of the Grand Canyon provides no insight into the geological principles and processes that created this magnificent formation, the five-factor model, per se, offers no insight into the psychological principles and processes that create a personality. In this sense, McAdams' (1992) characterization of the five-factor model as the psychology of a stranger is fair; a model of structure without process can only be a portion of a psychology of personality.

MEASURES OF PERSONALITY VARIABLES Although much recent assessment research has focused on the overall structure of personality and the five-factor model, researchers have also been revising familiar scales and inventories and developing new measures of familiar constructs. For many years, the MMPI was among the most frequently used and cited measure of personality. The revised version, the MMPI-2 (Butcher et al 1989) is the focus of much research concerned with the assessment of psychopathology (e.g. Butcher et al 1991); but so far, the MMPI-2 is attracting far less interest than its predecessor among those focusing on normal-range personality attributes. Those who prefer specific rather than more global assessment of important traits will find an increasing array of instruments to choose from. For example, Buss & Perry (1992) developed a four-factor measure of aggression, including scales for physical aggression, verbal aggression, anger, and hostility; and the Endler Multidimensional Anxiety Scales provide the ability to discriminate between anxiety and depression (Endler et al 1992).

As our knowledge of personality structure grows, there will be an increasing need to develop instruments that offer various bandwidth-fidelity tradeoffs. For some purposes, global, nonspecific measures will be preferred while in other instances, specific high fidelity low bandwidth measures will be desired. As new instruments are developed, we hope their authors become increasingly careful in locating where their measure falls within the taxonomy of individual difference variables. The current proliferation of measures apparent in the research literature does not correspond to the kind of ordered growth we envision. The collective capacity of personality assessors to invent new personality variables implies an inexhaustible potential supply of measures. This truism should not be taken as license to develop all such measures. A bewildering number of self-report scales are produced each year; but a large portion of the scale development and analysis research leaves much to be desired.

Many recently proposed constructs are of an extremely narrow focus. The measures associated with such constructs run the risk of being bloated specific (Cattell 1966) variables (e.g. dimensions created by having subjects respond to items of almost identical content). Health locus of control (Parcel & Meyer 1978, Wallston et al 1978) or academic self-concept (see Marsh 1990) measures can be considered potential bloated specifics garnered from more general personality variables. Bloated specific measures often lack theoretical utility, have an extremely circumscribed range of prediction, and are typically not linked to broader and more established personality variables. Such narrowly focused measures can be useful for purely predictive purposes. Indeed, both of the examples cited above are clearly useful predictive tools, and this utility justifies their continued use. But most bloated specifics have far less to offer; and no bloated specific contributes to our larger understanding of personality structure.

Although scale interpretation is facilitated when item responses are unidimensional (i.e. observed scores are influenced by only one common dimension), a tendency to elevate this desirable characteristic to a *sine qua non* of assessment has caused much confusion. The existence of multiple factors does not preclude scaling individuals along a common dimension. There is a seeming plague of articles proclaiming the multidimensional nature of measures and constructs; each of which seems to invite debate about the number of factors involved. The recent history of the Self-Monitoring Scale (e.g. Briggs & Cheek 1988, Gangestad & Snyder 1985, Hoyle & Lennox 1991) is an appropriate, but not representative example. Issues pertaining to the dimensionality of the Self-Monitoring Scale were discussed with precision, ingenuity, and attention to larger questions of personality structure. Too often, discussions of scale dimensionality are merely arguments about whether the second (or third) eigenvalue is large enough to justify an additional factor.

A further problem in the scale development and analysis literature is that researchers sometimes do not recognize or appreciate that not all personality constructs are amenable to measurement via a self-report questionnaire. Implicit motives, by definition, are beyond the reach of self-report (McClelland et al 1989). Other constructs, like popularity, cannot be directly measured by self-report, but depend crucially upon the reactions and reports of others (Ozer 1989).

Finally, we note that the methods of establishing reliability and validity are not fully generalizable across different types of variables. Sometimes high internal consistency is important to establish reliability, and sometimes it is not. The type of evidence needed to support the validity of a proposed measure of a taxonomic variable is different from the evidence needed to support a proposed measure of a dimensional variable. Further, a measure used solely for prediction should be evaluated differently than a measure explicitly designed to assess a construct. For example, the type of evidence needed to support a "disposition toward bulimia" measure is different from that required to assess a construct like stress reaction. The need to apply different types of psychometrics to different types of concepts and their associated measures is insufficiently recognized.

The Concept of a "Personality Variable"

Much empirical research has been aimed at identifying the structure of personality traits, but less effort has been directed at resolving conceptual issues involved in defining appropriate units for personality psychology. We present several conceptual distinctions that can be made between personality constructs, and we attempt to discern the implications these distinctions might have in terms of assessment and for testing the measurement and structural models of particular constructs.

THE EMERGENT AND LATENT VARIABLE DISTINCTION Several researchers have raised issues with important implications about conceptualizing and modeling psychological variables that have important implications for personality research. Bollen & Lennox (1991), for example, elaborate a distinction between a causal measurement model and an effect measurement model for representing the structure of psychological variables. In a causal model (similar to a latent factor model), the trait causes variation in its indicators. Conversely, in an effect model (similar to a components model), the trait is caused by, or emerges from, its indicators.

Bollen & Lennox (1991) demonstrate that accepted standards for what constitutes a good measure of a construct (e.g. high internal consistency), are only relevant if a causal measurement model is assumed true. Some of the measured constructs of interest to personality psychologists, however, strike us as being more of the effect type. For example, individual differences in judgability (Colvin 1993) may be considered a function of several more basic personality variables. Evaluation of measures associated with emergent variables requires a different analytic framework. Specifically, the construct validity of measures of emergent variables should be assessed with an emphasis on external rather than internal criteria.

While Bollen & Lennox (1991) describe the implications of latent and emergent measurement models, Cohen et al (1990) discuss how this same distinction impacts the fitting of a structural equation model. Cohen et al argue that applying an inappropriate measurement model (e.g. treating an emergent as if it were a latent variable) can produce misleading estimates of structural coefficients. Erroneous interpretations are then bound to follow.

Not all emergent variables arise from the additive combination of components. Lykken et al (1992) describe a class of emergent variables, which they call emergenic traits, that arise from configural, nonadditive, and nonlinear combinations of components. Each component is necessary but not sufficient for the emergence of the trait. Lykken et al consider genetically mediated emergenic characteristics and present evidence that some personality traits (e.g. extraversion) may be emergenic in nature. There are two defining features of an emergenic trait: 1. it will tend not to run in families, and 2. the traditional polygenic additive model will not adequately explain observed heritability indices. Knowing whether a trait is emergenic or not has immediate implications for the measurement model.

There are characteristics (e.g. leadership) that are often conceptualized as resulting from additive combinations of more basic variables, and modeled through a multiple regression framework. Even if the independent variables have nonlinear or nonadditive effects, linear models will still describe well the relationship between independent and dependent variables. But prediction is not explanation. Recognizing that certain traits are emergenic requires a change in research strategy. Specifically, theories about emergenic traits should be evaluated with nonadditive, nonlinear, or threshold models. Lubinski & Humphreys (1990) elaborate several of the details of evaluating nonadditive models. Whenever one goes beyond the standard linear framework in conceptualizing and modeling traits, new levels of complexity, both theoretical and statistical, are added.

MODELING MULTIFACETED TRAIT CONCEPTS Many popular personality concepts are explicitly postulated to be composed of distinct subcomponents (e.g. hardiness, Kobasa 1979). Several conceptual problems arise in using multifaceted constructs to predict or understand behavior. As Carver (1989) makes clear, the basic problem with multifaceted constructs is how to model a multifaceted variable's relation to a dependent variable. One alternative is to aggregate scores across the subcomponents. This permits the examination of the relationship between the general construct and the dependent variable, but subcomponents may predict criteria better than the general construct. A second option is to relate each subcomponent separately to the dependent variable. The problem with this strategy is that it is often unclear to what extent an effect is due to the specific component or to the variance it may share with some broader variable.

Hull et al (1991) provide a cogent discussion of how to treat multifaceted personality constructs within a structural modeling context. The advantage of structural models is their ability to explicitly represent common variance among subcomponents, specific variance within each subcomponent that remains after common variance has been extracted, and unique or error variation. Specific hypotheses regarding the simultaneous contribution of the general construct and each of the subcomponents toward the prediction of a dependent variable can then be evaluated, and interpretation problems inherent to raw score techniques (e.g. multiple regression) are alleviated.

Caution should be used before viewing structural equation modeling as the statistical representation of choice for multifaceted constructs. Multifaceted constructs are often emergent variables. For example, hardiness may arise from internal locus of control, a sense of commitment, and a sense of challenge; therefore, a causal measurement model is not appropriate (Carver 1989). Current structural equation modeling methods do not easily provide for interactive effects in the measurement model.

TRAITS VERSUS TYPES The identification of distinct entities (taxons) is an important foundational issue in many sciences. In psychology there is great resistance to challenging the received view that all personality structures are dimensional. As a result, we are hard pressed for ways to establish whether a particular psychological concept (e.g. extravert) refers to a qualitatively distinct entity, of which some people are members and some are not, or an extreme level of a dimensional trait.

To address this type of question, Rorer & Widiger (1983) encouraged personality psychologists to become enlightened of taxonomic methods. In a more recent consciousness raising effort, Meehl (1992) summarizes his longstanding views concerning the identification of types in normal and abnormal ranges of personality. One of the important "take home" messages from Meehl is that the identification of taxonomic structures requires a different type of psychometrics than most personality psychologists are used to working with (see Gangestad & Snyder 1991).

Perhaps because of Meehl's continued efforts, a small body of research has questioned the dimensional versus typological status of psychological constructs. Strube (1989) has examined the status of the Type-*A* versus Type-*B* personality distinction. His conclusions support the notion that there is good reason to maintain a typological framework for this concept. Trull et al (1990) have explored the dimensional status of the borderline personality construct, but they uncovered no evidence of taxonicity in this domain.

There is a prevailing attitude among personality psychologists that the trait vs type issue is not central to their concerns. Nevertheless, it is worth emphasizing that the dimensional vs typological status of a concept has implications for (*a*) assessing constructs, (*b*) integrating constructs into a more general theoretical framework, and (*c*) searching for etiological mechanisms (Strube 1989). The burden of proof, however, falls squarely on the shoulders of those who encourage taxonomic questioning, and no clear case has yet been made to bring this issue into the mainstream of personality research.

Although the notion of "type" that concerns Meehl (1992) implies qualitatively different structures or functions between members of different classes, this is not the only view of type that is influential in the personality literature. The concept of a prototype offers an alternative basis for a typology, one especially appropriate for summarizing multifaceted personality constructs. The relative merits of prototype scores, which are a kind of aggregate, vs the use of multiple dimensions, parallels those concerns inherent in modeling any multifaceted trait concept. Broughton et al (1993) and York & John (1992) provide recent demonstrations of the appeal of the prototype approach.

MIDDLE-LEVEL UNITS Personality researchers also use other units for assessing individual differences. Motivational concepts of various kinds occupy a middle-level (Buss & Cantor 1989) of analysis between traits and behavior. These units include explicit motive structures such as life-tasks (e.g. Cantor 1990), personal strivings (e.g. Emmons 1991), and personal projects (e.g. Little et al 1992), as well as implicit needs and motives deriving from Murray's personology (McClelland et al 1989).

Assessment of implicit motives by means of thematic content analysis has a long history, now fully accessible in Smith's (1992) landmark compendium of nearly all of the frequently used scoring manuals in this area. Assessment of explicit motives is a more recent enterprise, and researchers in this area have not yet fully examined and compared the various procedures used in different research programs. Comparative analyses of the reliability and validity of different methods of assessing explicit motives should be an important element of future research in this area.

Emmons & McAdams (1991) explore the relation between implicit and explicit motives, and offer the outlines of a conceptual framework in which broader implicit motives unify and coordinate the more specific explicit motives. Little et al (1992) demonstrate several relations between explicit motives and the five-factor model.

Theory and Assessment

Choices among various kinds of conceptual units for describing individual differences cannot be made arbitrarily, nor will data always be sufficient to guide personality assessors to appropriate units and procedures. Psychological theory has an irreplaceable role in personality assessment. Theory should guide the way a construct is conceptualized, how it is measured, and the way scores are interpreted. A taxonomy of different kinds of individual difference variables is greatly needed.

Modern personality research is predominantly trait-based (Wiggins & Pincus 1992). In the absence of theory, measured traits are static variables, good for describing what someone is like and for predicting important behaviors, but poor at providing a rich and deep understanding of personality processes and dynamics (McAdams 1992). We may learn more from Shapiro's *Neurotic Styles* (1965) than from the empirical trait literature, because Shapiro presents a theory that relates and integrates traits, motives, attitudes, mechanisms, processes, and behaviors. A trait psychograph (Allport 1937) is analogous to a weather report: good for telling you whether to wear a raincoat, but poor in providing a sufficient explanation of why it might rain.

We believe that trait research needs to attend more to motivations, mechanisms, and processes. We have in mind an emphasis on two types of research questions. First, given extant knowledge of personality trait structure, the processes and mechanisms that promote these individual differences must be elucidated. Second, different theoretical accounts of important traits need to be tested explicitly against each other. For example, Block's (1965) ego-resilience, Eysenck's (1967) neuroticism, and Tellegen's (1985) negative affect coexist as importantly different accounts of the emotional stability dimension of the five-factor model. We await explicit comparative theory testing.

A growing body of research explicitly emphasizes personality processes and motivational concepts rather than trait variables (e.g. Cantor 1990, Emmons & McAdams 1991). Such research addresses several of our concerns mentioned above, but there are only sporadic attempts (e.g. Little et al 1992) to integrate these newer conceptual units with well-known and established trait structures. For example, McAdams & de St. Aubin (1992) present a rich process-oriented theory of generativity in which agency and communion are used as higher-order motivational units. Wiggins (1991) discusses the relations between these same motivations and interpersonal traits. As trait researchers continue to appeal to higher-order motive structures, the possibilities for linking personality traits to process-oriented theory may be realized.

Psychological theory is also required as part of the construct validation of trait measures. In a typical validity study, a test score is correlated with external variables. Empirically validating forward inferences (i.e. from measure to outcome) in a construct system is a relatively straightforward process. However, backward validity inferences (from test scores to source mechanisms, structures, traits, and processes) is an equally important but neglected research problem that must be addressed if we are serious about answering the question "what is a test measuring?"

METHODS OF DATA COLLECTION

Personality psychologists employ numerous procedures to collect data; and like Cattell (1973) and Block (1977), we find it convenient to broadly categorize four data collection methods: self-reports, observer reports, life events and outcomes, and performance in standardized, situational tests. We have chosen to review a single important trend, new development, or promising start within each of these domains.

Developments in Personality Scale Construction

The standard methods of self-report scale construction (rational, empirical, and factor analytic), despite minor embellishments to each, have remained fundamentally unchanged for decades. Tellegen & Waller (1993) argue that these approaches can provide acceptable measures of an established construct but are not particularly useful in changing or illuminating the original conceptualization of the construct. When personality concepts are relatively unexamined, poorly understood, or simply too open, a method that can inform the definition of the construct as well as lead to the creation of a scale would be desirable.

Tellegen & Waller (1993) describe a scale construction philosophy designed to promote theoretical development. Their exploratory approach to scale construction and construct elaboration puts to practice Cattell's (1966) inductive-hypothetico-deductive spiral. Briefly, one begins with a rough idea of a personality construct and writes an overinclusive pool of possible items. Data are collected, and the analyses are used not just to refine the scale's psychometric properties, but also to generate new theories about the nature of the construct. A new set of possible trait indicators is then written, more data are collected and analyzed, and theory is again evaluated. This iterative process continues until a satisfactory level of convergence and demarcation of the construct has occurred and is manifested in the final set of items.

The ultimate goal of the exploratory approach is to make construct elaboration an integral part of scale construction. In this regard, the exploratory approach parallels Loevinger's (1993) account in that the interplay of personality theory and empirical data is an integral part of the measure and construct development process. The procedure has been applied in the development of the Multidimensional Personality Questionnaire (Tellegen & Waller 1993), which taps eleven personality constructs historically considered important in the personality field. The forced thoughtfulness inherent to the exploratory approach is a step forward for personality measurement; its implementation should alleviate some of the problems associated with bloated specifics and multidimensional scales. If applied independently in two groups, the procedure may prove to be a valuable tool for uncovering cross-cultural differences in personality trait structure.

The exploratory approach to scale construction and construct elaboration may be viewed as an integration and enhancement of rational and factor analytic scale construction techniques. Similarly, Lippa's (1991, Lippa & Connelly 1990) notion of diagnosticity can be considered a modern extension of the empirical, criterion-keying, approach to scale construction.

As originally conceived, the empirical approach to scale construction is based on establishing a criterion group (e.g. leaders), and then finding items that differentiate the target group from the complementary class (e.g. "all others"). For example, the item "is athletic" may be more frequently endorsed by leaders than by nonleaders, in which case it might be included in a leadership scale. If a number of such items can be identified, they can then be joined to form a measure in which a person's score is the number of keyed responses.

Like the empirical strategy, the diagnosticity approach to measurement requires the establishment of criterion groups. For example, in Lippa's (1991) research, gender is the criterion. In contrast to the empirical approach, responses to indicator variables that potentially differentiate the groups are analyzed by discriminant analysis. A person's score under the diagnosticity strategy is the Bayesian probability that he or she belongs to a criterion classification. Such scores are interpreted as reflecting "the degree to which individuals are prototypic of indexing groups given a set of diagnostic indicators of group membership" (Lippa & Connelly 1990, p. 1063). Much depends on the careful and extensive sampling of attributes that may differentiate between groups, a concern characteristic of the diagnosticity approach and one that sets it apart from older empirical strategies of scale construction.

Both the exploratory and diagnosticity approaches would seem most useful when the goal is to assess constructs that initially are poorly or incompletely understood. Application of the exploratory approach through the necessary iterative steps would result in a more elaborate and specific definition of the construct and a measure aligned to it. But some constructs will necessarily resist this kind of definition, and in such instances, the exploratory approach will not be the optimal strategy. Personality characteristics that are socially constructed rather than psychologically defined may change in meaning over time. The diagnosticity strategy appears more appropriate for scaling individual differences on this sort of personality construct. Gender-related individual differences are a clear example of this type of construct. The diagnosticity approach may prove useful for tapping into important concepts that cannot be measured easily through factor analytically derived scales.

Accuracy in Observers' Ratings

Among the various possible methods of personality assessment, perhaps none has a longer history than observer evaluations. As a personality assessment method, the use of observer ratings presumes that, at least in principle, knowledgeable informants can provide valid information about a target's personality. But because there are no standardized observers, the formal validity of observer judgments must be evaluated each time they are used. Understanding the processes that create accurate observer evaluations is thus a key methodological concern of personality psychologists. This interest, combined with the growing awareness among social psychologists that dominant paradigms in the study of social cognition have emphasized bias and error at the expense of accuracy (Fiske & Taylor 1991) continues to sustain the study of accuracy in observer evaluations of personality.

Studies of accuracy in personality judgment have proceeded past mere demonstrations that observers can provide valid assessments of other persons, and now identify factors influencing accuracy. One clear determinant of judge accuracy is the degree of acquaintance between judge and target. It is hardly surprising that greater acquaintance between judge and target increases judge accuracy (see Wiggins & Pincus 1992 for a review), a result now unambiguously documented by Paulhus & Bruce's (1992) longitudinal study. One recurring and puzzling finding in research examining acquaintance effects on accuracy is the degree of validity in the ratings provided by strangers. In predicting behavior in a specific situation, Colvin & Funder (1991) report that strangers who observed a target's behavior in a similar situation were as accurate as close acquaintances who lacked this observational opportunity. The accuracy of strangers may be explained by Paunonen's (1991) simulation results: If just a few judges observe and use valid cues, then the majority of judges can rate in a random fashion with a resulting correlation of moderate magnitude between self and stranger ratings.

Using Paunonen's simulation study as a basis for developing an explanation for the accuracy of strangers requires a process model of accuracy in observer evaluations. Increasingly, researchers are focusing on observers' use of cues and on the validity of cues, and are placing the study of accuracy within a lens model. Funder & Sneed (1993) report that observers agree on the diagnosticity of different behaviors for the five factors and that diagnostic behaviors are indeed used when making trait inferences. Moreover, the diagnostic behaviors observers use to make inferences are largely valid indicators of all but the Openness (or Intellect) factor. Thus, if strangers are provided with even a few valid cues it is reasonable to expect that at least the more diligent and motivated judges will recognize and use these valid cues in forming their judgements. Observers apparently do more than merely tally valid cues; Borkenau & Müller (1992) conclude that global judgments of personality reflect both confirming and disconfirming evidence as well as the amount of irrelevant evidence. Global ratings appear to reflect the ratio of positive to total available evidence.

The distinction between cue use and cue validity in the lens model provides a conceptual tool useful for a variety of purposes. Asendorpf (1992) reports that judgments of shyness in children and adults are based on the same cues, and that the differential validity of these cues is relatively stable across time. Gangestad et al (1992) hypothesize that cue use should be a function of the importance to the judge of making a correct inference. Gangestad et al's analysis of self-stranger correlations indicates that stranger's ratings of socio-sexuality are more accurate than ratings of social potency and social closeness, which are more accurate than ratings of stress reaction. Thus, a lens model suggesting that accuracy depends on both access to and use of valid cues provides a useful framework for permitting researchers to understand the sources of accuracy in observer ratings.

Examining self-other correlations for moderator effects provides an alternative analytic framework for identifying factors leading to accuracy. Chaplin's (1991) authoritative review of the evolution of this paradigm for examining self-other agreement and his detailed analyses of several proposed moderators lead to a pessimistic assessment of their magnitude of effect. Chaplin acknowledges that these small effects might prove important if linked in a compelling fashion to theory. Allport's (1937) idiographic psychology provided the impetus for Zuckerman et al's (1991) investigation of self-rated uniqueness (similarity vs dissimilarity to others on a trait) as a moderator variable. Uniqueness, relevance, and observability (but not consistency) moderated self-other agreement, though the effect sizes were of a magnitude described by Chaplin.

The moderator variable approach to judge accuracy could be made more useful if placed within a lens model framework. For example, observability should increase cue use (i.e. judges are more likely to use more easily obtained information) but not cue validity (unless there is reason to think that easy observation is related to validity). The moderator variable approach, unless supplemented by additional conceptual tools seems to have run its useful course. However intuitively appealing the notion that for any given trait some persons are easier to predict than others, the yield from such approaches has been meager. At present, the heuristic value and empirical promise of the lens model seems superior to moderator variable approaches for understanding accuracy in observer evaluations.

Assessing Daily Life Events

A biologist interested in a particular animal species would, at some point quite early in the investigative process, seek to determine the nature of the environment inhabited by species members; and to determine patterns of foraging, feeding, sleeping, procreating, and rearing of offspring. In short, a molecular account of the daily life of the animal, as well as a more molar kind of life history typical of species members would be sought. Only recently has this descriptive enterprise, as a goal in itself, become a focal interest in personality psychology.

Systematic examination of daily life events is a relatively new development, but there is a long and fragmented history of studying daily life events. Wheeler & Reis (1991) provide an overview of this history, especially the applications of self-report methods to the recording of life events. The events and experiences of everyday life have been studied for a variety of reasons (e.g. studying behavior in the workplace to improve efficiency), but the differentiating feature of the early study of life events was its emphasis on what Wheeler & Reis describe as the "little experiences" of day-to-day life. This emphasis provides a useful contrast to life outcome data traditionally collected in personality assessment, where important and meaningful data is often extracted from an individual's life history. The difference in analysis level between the little experiences and major life outcomes is not an unbridgeable gap. The Holmes & Rahe (1967) Social Readjustment Rating Scale, and the research that used it, provides a landmark example of a compromise, if not an integration, of these different approaches.

At least three different but clearly overlapping aims characterize daily life event research: 1. to link events in everyday life to mood, affect, and well-being; 2. to relate life events to persons' explicit goals, motives, and intentions; and 3. to find associations between daily life events and personality traits. These are clearly different conceptual goals, but they are intertwined deeply.

Research relating physical well-being recorded daily to trait measures of neuroticism display this interconnected agenda quite clearly. Larsen & Kasimatis' (1991) assessment of the frequency and duration of specific illness episodes shows that neuroticism is associated with the frequency but not duration of illness. Bolger & Schilling (1991) use hierarchical linear modeling to show that differential reactivity, and not differential exposure, provides a link betwen daily stressors and neuroticism. Larsen's (1992) finding that neuroticism contributes to symptom recall independent of concurrent symptom reports demonstrates the importance of assessment techniques like daily reports. Retrospective reports of symptomology may be unduly influenced by subjects' personality characteristics. Assessing symptoms and stressors on a daily basis provides a methodology for developing an explanation of the correlation between physical well-being and neuroticism.

Personality traits other than neuroticism have also attracted the interest of researchers. Watson et al (1992) report that the amount of social activity, recorded daily, is related to extraversion and positive affect, but not to other major personality factors. Wong & Csikszentmihalyi (1991) show that the PRF Affiliation Scale is related to the frequency of wishing to be with friends. Research of this type, which relates scores on a trait measure to the occurrence of everyday behavior, elaborates the meaning of the personality variable and supports the measure's construct validity.

Much of a person's daily behavior reflects the explicit motives and intentions of the individual, but this general observation masks the rich and interesting details of everyday experience. Cantor et al (1991) show how daily events are influenced by subjects' life tasks, and how emotional involvement in daily events is a function of the events' relevance to important life tasks. Cantor et al (1992) further disentangle some complexities of understanding appraisals of daily events. Emmons (1991) also reports a clear relation between intentions and everyday events: Personal strivings are related to the occurrence of events (e.g. persons with affiliative strivings experience more interpersonal events), and the occurrence of events is related to affect (e.g. affiliative strivings are associated with positive affect in response to good interpersonal events).

Assessing life experiences is a problematic task, and no single best method has yet emerged. How to sample experiences (e.g. time vs event sampling); how to record experiences (e.g. checklists vs open-ended formats); how to characterize and summarize the recorded results, determining the frequency and duration of recording; and how to recruit and retain subjects in the relatively arduous procedure are all questions without good, or even standard answers. Stone et al (1991) review the many options available in the design of studies of life experiences, and engage all of the issues noted above.

New measurement and design concerns are not the only hurdle facing the personality assessor interested in the study of life experiences. Data analysis procedures that can adjust to and capitalize on the time-dependent, sequenced nature of the data must be adopted. West & Hepworth (1991) review various time-series approaches for analyzing life events, emphasizing how substantive theory guides the specific foci of analyses.

Many of the phenomena of interest to personality psychologists display variability across time. Perhaps the prototypical example of such a phenomenon is mood or affect (Larsen 1987). Larsen (1990) describes the use of spectral analysis for fitting periodic functions to measures of a single variable collected over time. The objective is to identify periodic components that might underlie across-time variability. One particularly appealing aspect of spectral analysis is that it allows for the characterization of variability within an individual, as well as for representing variability as it occurs in a sample. For example, Larsen & Kasimatis (1990) identify a strong weekly (7-day) cycle for mood fluctuation in a sample of undergraduates. However, adherence to this cycle shows clear individual differences that appear to be associated with individual differences in extraversion. To date, applications of spectral analysis have been used solely in the analysis of mood. We look forward to seeing how the method is used to study behavioral variability in areas outside of the affective realm.

Personality and Psychophysiological Assessment

Psychophysiology, which focuses on the relation between physiological processes and cognition, emotion, and behavior is both the source of perhaps the oldest personality theory (the humoral theory of temperament) and the newest frontier in personality assessment methods. Contemporary neuroscience models do not rely on unidirectional causation and so admit the development of theory that is not simplistically reductionistic; nor do they posit simple one-to-one relations between physiological and psychological processes (Cacioppo et al 1991). This lack of simple isomorphism calls for research that employs multiple measures of both physiological and psychological processes and that attempts to assess possible mediating variables linking physiology to behavior.

Bullock & Gilliland's (1993) examination of Eysenck's (1967) arousal theory of extraversion provides an example of such an assessment procedure. Introverts and extraverts were identified by scores on the Eysenck Personality Inventory (Eysenck & Eysenck 1964) and brainstem auditory evoked responses were assessed under varying conditions of caffeine induced arousal and task demand. Subjective reports of arousal were also obtained. Consonant with Eysenck's theory, introverts exhibited faster neural transmission rates across the various levels of induced arousal; and although caffeine intake affected the reported level of subjective arousal, extraversion was unrelated to subjective arousal. The relation between extraversion and cortical arousal cannot be attributed to differences in the subjective experience of the experimental tasks.

Zuckerman (1991) provides an advanced text organizing and documenting research on the biological basis of personality, and offers an integrated theory of how genotypic differences lead to differences in global dimensions of personality. Zuckerman's model is characterized by multiple levels of mediation: biochemical (e.g. neurotransmitters, enzymes, and hormones); psychophysiological (e.g. cortical excitation), emotional (e.g. positive affect, anxiety), and cognitive-behavioral (e.g. reward and punishment expectations). Although Zuckerman notes the tentativeness of the model, and that many refinements and amendments arising from further research may be anticipated, the overarching framework should be of considerable heuristic value in guiding future investigations.

Systematic use of physiological indicators in personality assessment requires that such measures be scrutinized against the familiar measurement criteria of reliability and validity. Geenen (1991) describes a psychometrically ambitious study of physiological measures and their relation to personality variables. Subjects viewed various films (representing a form of situational variability) on two occasions and eight different indicators of physiological activity were monitored. Analysis of physiological responses using generalizability theory showed that there were indeed consistent individual differences in response to the films, and that individual physiological response patterns were stable over occasions. Geenen's descriptive examination of autonomic responsiveness as a function of persons, situations, and occasions suggests that variation in physiological measures may be decomposed into coherent and interpretable components.

In addition to testing and developing biological theories of personality, psychophysiological assessment can usefully complement personality research by providing an important alternative method of measurement, one that is especially valuable when self-reports may be of questionable validity and the information of interest is intrinsically private, so that observer judgments are of even more dubious value. Buss et al (1992) found gender differences in subjects' selection of emotional or sexual infidelity as the more upsetting alternative. One might question the veracity of subjects' reports since they chose in conformance to societal expectations. In a second study, subjects were asked to imagine specific, hypothetical instances of emotional and sexual infidelity while electrodermal activity, pulse rate, and electromyographic activity associated with facial displays of unpleasant emotions were recorded. The results from this second study parallelled the first: females responded as if they were more upset by emotional rather than sexual infidelity, while males showed the reverse pattern. Buss et al's use of physiological indicators rules out a number of competing, alternative explanations, and provides much firmer evidence that there are indeed gender differences in the types of events that elicit jealousy.

A comparable logic guided three experiments described by Nikula et al (1993), who demonstrated that increased electrodermal activity is associated with subjects' current concerns elicited through both self-generated thoughts and externally presented stimuli. These results suggest several theoretical interpretations, including the hypothesis that arousal is produced by current concern–related thought. Regardless of the specific interpretation of the findings, the psychophysiological assessment results clearly contribute to the construct validity of the psychological methods used to assess current concerns.

EVALUATING ASSESSMENT RESULTS

Assessment data rarely, if ever, unequivocally speak for themselves. Properly interpreting the meaning of subjects' responses is perhaps the most difficult yet familiar task for the assessor. Item response theory provides a rigorous quantitative model for understanding item responses and for using responses to scale individuals. Although applications in personality assessment remain relatively rare, researchers need to remain alert to the possibilities offered by this powerful model. The validity of a subject's responses to items is a primary concern in applied assessment contexts, and after years of neglect, researchers are returning to this topic. Scales and inventories are administered in order to permit inferences about respondents. Justifying inferences based on assessment results requires validation research; and how such research may itself be interpreted is often at issue.

Item Response Theory

In the applied aptitude measurement domain, the last decade has witnessed the virtual replacement of classical test theory (CTT) models and procedures with those from item response theory (IRT) (Lord 1980). The basis for this transformation is simple: IRT models can solve important problems that are unworkable under a CTT framework. Do IRT models provide advantages in the personality assessment domain or are they too complex and cumbersome? Researchers have started to address this question and applications of IRT-based techniques in the personality domain are appearing in the literature.

First, IRT methods have been employed to study the psychometric characteristics of personality test items. For example, Childs et al (1992) used IRT-based procedures to search for differential item functioning (i.e. item bias) between genders on the MMPI-2 Depression scale, and Reise & Waller (1990) report on an intensive analysis of the Multidimensional Personality Questionnaire (MPQ) scales. Further applications of IRT models are found in the domains of alexithymia (Hendryx et al 1992) and depression (Schaeffer 1988) measurement.

A second area of IRT application is in the construction of computerized adaptive assessment systems. IRT models are advantageous in this context because unlike with CTT, examinees need not be administered the same set of items in order to be scaled onto a common metric. Testing systems can thus be designed that locate a person's trait level with as few items as necessary. Examples of IRT applications in this area are Kamakura & Balasubramanian's (1989) computerized adaptive interview schedule, and Waller & Reise's (1989) computerized adaptive test to assess Absorption.

Response Validity Measures

A particular scale can be a good measure of a psychological construct, but a poor measure of the construct for a particular individual (Ben-Porath & Waller 1992). Response validity indicators are measures designed to identify persons who are not measured well by a particular scale. Two recent developments in this area are of general interest. First, Tellegen (1988) has embedded a new type of response validity measure into the MPQ. Each validity scale attempts to identify a specific form of response inconsistency. The variable response inconsistency (VRIN) scale, for example, consists of item pairs that are semantically similar. Examinees who respond to an item pair in opposite directions are scored for inconsistency. The true response inconsistency (TRIN) scale consists of item pairs that are semantically similar if keyed in opposite directions. The TRIN scale is used to identify both indiscriminate True and indiscriminate False responding.

TRIN and VRIN response inconsistency measures have also been built into the MMPI-2 (Butcher et al 1989) and research regarding the effectiveness of these indices can be found in Berry et al (1991) and Graham et al (1991). As Tellegen & Waller (1993) point out, response inconsistency scales, like TRIN and VRIN, can be contrasted with traditional desirability measures (e.g. lie scales, the CPI Good Impression scale). These latter measures are known to be confounded with valid personality trait variance, while TRIN and VRIN appear to show no relationship with other MPQ or MMPI scales.

A second class of response consistency indices has roots in Bem & Allen's (1974) study and the ensuing search for moderator variables (see Chaplin 1991, Tellegen 1988). Several researchers have been experimenting with item response "scalability" measures (Lanning 1988, 1991; Reise & Waller 1993) that attempt to assess how well an individual's responses conform to the measurement model used to interpret individual differences in trait level.

There are three potential applications of scalability indices in personality assessment: 1. to identify examinees who are poorly measured by a particular test (i.e. as test score validity indicators); 2. to increase predictive validity by extracting poorly measured individuals (i.e. as moderator variables); and 3. to assess the fit between an examinee's personality and a nomothetic trait construct (i.e. as traitedness indicators). Lanning (1988, 1991) and Chaplin (1991) are concerned predominantly with the utility of scalability measures as moderator variables. Reise & Waller (1993) emphasize the problems involved when using a scalability measure as an indicator of traitedness.

Global consistency measures (e.g. TRIN and VRIN) and item response pattern scalability indices should be viewed as complementary approaches to response validity testing. The major distinguishing feature is that scalability measures are typically computed and interpreted within a particular trait scale.

This property can be advantageous when one is interested in issues of trait specific response inconsistency. Alternatively, indices like TRIN can identify specific forms of protocol invalidating response sets (e.g. acquiescence) that occur across measures of different traits. Scalability indices probably have limited utility for this purpose.

Evaluating Scale Validity

There are at least two kinds of concerns in the analysis of scale validity. First, individual results must be interpreted, a task more complex than it often appears; and second, patterns of results must be integrated to form a full evaluation. This latter task is often attempted through structural equation modeling of multitrait-multimethod matrices.

INTERPRETING VALIDITY COEFFICIENTS Loevinger (1966) emphasized that measures of two constructs can be highly correlated (e.g. height and weight in humans) without meaning that the constructs are redundant or that variation in one may be explained by variation in the other. More caution is needed in interpreting correlations among measures. For example, equating the degree of correlation between psychological measures with the degree of conceptual linkage between psychological concepts appears to be a trend in research that relates personality disorders to normal-range personality traits.

Costa & McCrae (1990), for example, report a correlation of −.49 between a measure of Antisocial Personality Disorder and a measure of agreeableness. Similar findings have led Wiggins & Pincus (1989, Pincus & Wiggins 1990) to conclude that personality disorders involve maladaptive expressions of some or all of the five factors of personality. These sentiments have been echoed by other authors (e.g. Schroeder et al 1992). This conclusion may be correct, but correlations between measures will not resolve this issue.

There are several reasons why a high correlation between measures of distinct constructs does not determine the constructs' degree of conceptual relatedness. In the present case, measures of personality disorders, like the Millon Clinical Multiaxial Inventory-2 (Millon 1987) and measures of normal-range traits, like the NEO Personality Inventory (Costa & McCrae 1992a), contain highly similar item content. Open concepts such as personality characteristics cannot be defined operationally at the behavioral (i.e. item) level (Meehl 1990). Instead, a concept is explicated by stipulating both descriptive features and source or generating mechanisms. For example, flu and strep throat each contain fever and sore throat as manifestations, but the concepts are distinguished because they have different causal origins. Meehl (1990) provides a more elaborate and eloquent account of open concepts and their implications.

However, unlike concepts from the medical domain, the measurement of psychological constructs usually takes place at the behavioral or symptom level as opposed to the generative or source level. It is not surprising that a measure of schizoid disposition correlates −.62 with a measure of extraversion (Costa & McCrae 1990). Descriptively, schizoids look like extreme introverts. But the psychological, biological, and social mechanisms that generate schizoid behavior may not be the same as those underlying introversion. If the mechanisms that create a schizoid personality structure differ from the mechanisms that create extreme introversion, then the personality disorder is not reducible to the personality trait.

Test score validity is the foundation of personality assessment. Research designed to elucidate mechanisms is needed to shed light on relations among psychological variables and to proceed beyond measurement by description. In particular, well articulated theories of psychological concepts that specify etiological factors (mechanisms), descriptive features, and outcomes are needed. Progress of the kind we envision is exemplified by Block & Gjerde's (1986) demonstration that psychopathy is not redundant with, or explained by, individual differences in ego-control, despite the high correlations between measures of either concept.

MULTITRAIT-MULTIMETHOD MATRICES Since first proposed 35 years ago, the multitrait-multimethod matrix (MTMM)(Campbell & Fiske 1959) has become the quintessential data structure for examining the construct validity of psychological measures. Methods of analyzing such matrices have become increasingly complex and diverse. Kenny & Kashy (1992) describe and compare three different approaches: the now traditional confirmatory factor analysis (CFA) approach specifying both trait and method factors, the correlated uniqueness model, which includes only trait factors and accounts for method effects through correlated uniqueness terms; and the fixed method model, which includes trait and method factors but restricts the number of method factors to one fewer than the number of methods included in the design. After reviewing the assumptions, strengths, and weaknesses of each, Kenny & Kashy recommend the use of the correlated uniqueness model for the analysis of multitrait-multimethod matrices.

One method of analyzing MTMM matrices that was excluded from the Kenny & Kashy (1992) review is the Composite Direct Product (CDP) model, in which trait and method contributions to covariances among measures are regarded as inseparable and multiplicatively related. Goffin & Jackson (1992) provide a comparative review of CFA and CDP models in the analysis of MTMM matrices. In their analysis of four multitrait-multirater matrices, the CDP model provided a better fit than did the traditional CFA approach.

Bagozzi (1993a) details the assumptions, strengths, and weaknesses of the original criteria (Campbell & Fiske 1959) for evaluating MTMM matrices, CFA approaches, the correlated uniqueness model, and the CDP model. Rather than suggest the general superiority of one method over another, Bagozzi offers a set of guidelines for the successive use of these several approaches for analyzing MTMM matrices, and also offers a fully worked example (Bagozzi 1993b).

The general interest in MTMM structures derives from their usefulness in evaluating validity in psychological measurement. Kane's (1992) argument-based approach to validity reminds us that validity is an attribute of an interpretive argument concerning the meaning of a score and not an attribute of the measurement device. In Kane's analysis, a good interpretation of a measure's meaning requires a good argument—one that is clear, coherent, requires only plausible assumptions, and is supported by evidence. In choosing which model to fit to a MTMM matrix for evaluating the meaning of one or more measures included in the matrix, consideration of the type of model that in general typically fits best is a dubious concern. Of greater interest is the relative fit of different models to the specific MTMM under analysis, the plausibility of the model's assumptions as they pertain to the specific measures at hand, and the overall coherence of the model in illuminating the meaning of the measures. Psychologists interested in the validity of interpretive inferences rather than quantitative methods of analysis should consider different models to determine the most plausible and informative one for the data at hand.

Although fitting formal models to MTMM matrices can be informative when testing particular interpretations (e.g. to what extent the correlation between two measures is reflective of substantive overlap in meaning rather than a function of shared method), the general usefulness of formal models for evaluating validity is often exaggerated. Kenny & Kashy (1992) suggest that formal models for analyzing MTMM matrices evolved from two criticisms of the original Campbell & Fiske (1959) formulation. First, the evaluation of a MTMM involves ambiguous criteria; and second, validity inferences involve latent variables, while MTMM matrices contain correlations among measured variables. In our view, formal statistical models, in principle, cannot respond to the first problem; and to the extent that the second criticism is legitimate, formal statistical models suffer from practical limitations.

Kane (1992) notes that validity arguments are practical arguments and do not involve simple yes or no decisions. The search for unambiguous criteria to determine the validity of an interpretation may well be misplaced, but to the extent that clear criteria may be identifiable, formal statistical models are not necessarily superior to inspection of an MTMM matrix. It may be possible to decide whether a particular model does or does not fit the data unambiguously, but it does not follow that the interpretation of an unequivocally good-fitting model is unambiguous. The parameters associated with a measure of interest within such a model may leave quite a bit of doubt about the meaning of the measure.

In most applications, measured and not latent variables are used to make decisions about persons with regard to fallible criteria. In such instances, interpretations associated with the observed rather than latent variable scores are properly invoked. Research designed to elucidate construct validity will be concerned with latent variables. But the number of observed variables that can in practice be used to estimate latent variable scores is small: MTMM matrices that include more than four measures of the same latent trait are rare. Should we really believe that an optimally weighted composite of four variables can generally be regarded as interchangeable with the construct? An answer of yes implies the assertion that the correlation between this latent variable and a second latent variable based on four other measures of the construct would have a correlation of 1.00.

GENDER AND CULTURE IN PERSONALITY ASSESSMENT

One need not accept or endorse the full mismeasurement thesis of Tavris (1992) to recognize that personality assessors historically have been less sensitive to group diversity issues than contemporary standards demand; and however much harm this insensitivity inflicted upon the common weal, it also deeply undermined the scientific agenda of personality assessment. How should we measure important personality constructs in the face of biological, social, and ethnic diversity (Moran 1990)? As usual there is no formulaic answer: It depends on what is being assessed in what population. There are at least three different approaches to conducting measurement operations in ostensibly different populations.

When the construct of interest is assumed to be nomothetic, one may begin by translating an existing measure and administering it in a new population. An example of this etic approach can be found in Noh et al (1992), who examined a Korean version of the Center for Epidemiology Studies Depression Scale (CES-D). This strategy saves researchers the resources that would be involved in developing a new measure, but requires the assumption that the scale is measuring the same thing in the same way among populations. It is better to reformulate this issue as whether members of different populations can be scaled onto the same variable using the test. This phrasing allows hypotheses to be evaluated with modern empirical approaches (e.g. Holland & Wainer 1993).

A second strategy, also assuming the construct of interest is nomothetic, is to develop unique measures within each population. Examples of this more culturally sensitive, emic approach are Haynes et al's (1992) marital satisfaction measure for aged populations and Cheung et al's (1992) global personality measure for use with Chinese populations. The benefit here is that qualitative differences in trait manifestation can be incorporated explicitly into the measurement operations. The obvious problem is that different item content across the different versions of a test may limit the possibility of between-population comparisons. Furthermore, this strategy can lead to an endless proliferation of new measures.

A third and more recent approach recognizes that some important personality constructs are not nomothetic at all, but rather are only applicable to certain populations. For example, African Self-Consciousness (Baldwin & Bell 1985) is a variable that is explicitly only relevant to understanding the psychology of a circumscribed set of individuals. A growing number of personality measures target specific groups [e.g. the Hispanic Stress Inventory (Cervantes et al 1991)]. Such measures have a tremendous advantage in that they allow researchers the freedom to potentially understand and predict behavior differentially in different populations.

We must begin investigating the extent to which commonly used personality measures are biased within populations found in the United States. A biased scale contains items that relate differentially to latent variables depending on group membership. Under this definition, identifying item bias requires the use of technologies such as confirmatory factor and item response theory models (Reise et al 1993). Simply comparing group means on a scale is not germane to the question of bias. Mean differences in the absence of evidence of bias, such as reported ethnicity differences in measures of psychopathology (e.g. Hamberger & Hastings 1992, Hutton et al 1992), might lead to the use of subgroup norms in decision contexts.

Several researchers have explored whether personality scales have different patterns of external correlates for different gender and ethnic groups (e.g. Kline & Lachar 1992). Although such research is valuable, caution must be used to avoid confusing differential prediction with test bias. Tests have both structural (external correlates) and measurement (internal correlates) relations. Identifying test score bias involves analyses of a test's measurement, and not structural, relations, to determine whether or not persons from different populations with the same raw scores have the same level on the latent construct. A test can have completely different patterns of external correlations among different populations, but still measure the same construct in the same way for each population (Drasgow 1984, Drasgow & Kanfer 1985). The existence of different external correlates may require different uses of a test, but do not necessarily indicate the existence of test bias.

Discovering how traits may be differentially structured in different groups is of great importance. It is equally important to note that qualitative differences in structure on a dimensional personality construct may not occur at the manifest level (e.g. gender, ethnicity). Qualitative variation in trait structure may exist among latent types of individuals. Psychometric techniques to identify qualitative variation at the latent level are only now being developed (e.g. Rost 1990). In closing, we suspect that in the next ten years, some of the most interesting assessment research will occur in the group comparison domain.

CONCLUSION

Two years ago Wiggins & Pincus (1992) observed a back-to-basics movement in personality psychology, reflecting a sense of continuity and renewed commitment among researchers, and perhaps a maturing of the subdiscipline. We share this view. Influenced in part by Wiggins & Pincus' emphasis on substantive issues and in part by our own predilections, we have emphasized methodology. Most of the issues we addressed have a long and detailed history that we have not mentioned; and in most instances, a reading of the history, juxtaposed with the present literature, will reveal just how far we have come.

Literature Cited

Allport GW. 1937. *Personality: A Psychological Interpretation.* New York: Holt

Asendorpf JB. 1992. A Brunswikean approach to trait continuity: application to shyness. *J. Pers.* 60:53–77

Bagozzi RP. 1993a. Assessing construct validity in personality research: applications to measures of self esteem. *J. Res. Pers.* 27:49–87

Bagozzi RP. 1993b. An examination of the construct validity of measures of negative affect in the PANAS-X scales. *J. Pers. Soc. Psychol.* In press

Baldwin JA, Bell Y. 1985. The African self-consciousness scale: an africentric personality questionnaire. *West. J. Black Stud.* 9:61–68

Bem DJ, Allen A. 1974. On predicting some of the people some of the time: the search for cross-situational consistencies in behavior. *Psychol. Rev.* 81:506–20

Ben-Porath YS, Waller NG. 1992. "Normal" personality inventories in clinical assessment: general requirements and the potential for using the NEO personality inventory. *Psychol. Assess.: J. Consult. Clin. Psychol.* 4:14–19

Berry DT, Wetter MW, Baer RA, Widiger TA, Sumpter JC, et al. 1991. Detection of random responding on the MMPI-2: utility of F, Back F, and VRIN scales. *Psychol. Assess.: J. Consult. Clin. Psychol.* 3:418–23

Block J. 1965. *The Challenge of Response Sets.* New York: Appleton-Century-Crofts

Block J. 1977. Advancing the psychology of personality: paradigmatic shift or improving the quality of research. In *Personality at the Crossroads,* ed. D Magnusson, NS Endler, pp. 37–63. Hillsdale, NJ: Erlbaum

Block J, Gjerde PF. 1986. Distinguishing between antisocial behavior and undercontrol. In *Development of Antisocial and Prosocial Behavior: Research, Theories, and Issues,* ed. D Olweus, J Block, M Radke-Yarrow, pp. 177–206. New York: Academic

Bolger N, Schilling EA. 1991. Personality and the problems of everyday life: the role of neuroticism in exposure and reactivity to daily stressors. *J. Pers.* 59:355–86

Bollen K, Lennox R. 1991. Conventional wisdom on measurement: a structural equation perspective. *Psychol. Bull.* 110:305–14

Borkenau P, Müller B. 1992. Inferring act frequencies and traits from behavior observations. *J. Pers.* 60:553–73

Briggs SR. 1992. Assessing the five-factor model of personality description. *J. Pers.* 60:253–93

Briggs SR, Cheek JM. 1988. On the nature of self-monitoring: problems with assessment, problems with validity. *J. Pers. Soc. Psychol.* 54:663–78

Broughton R, Boyes MC, Mitchell J. 1993. DIStance-from-the-PROtotype (DISPRO) personality assessment for children. *J. Pers. Assess.* 60:32–47

Bullock WA, Gilliland K. 1993. Eysenck's

arousal theory of introversion-extraversion: a converging measures investigation. *J. Pers. Soc. Psychol.* 64:113–23

Buss AH, Perry M. 1992. The agression questionnaire. *J. Pers. Soc. Psychol.* 63:452–59

Buss DM. 1992. Manipulation in close relationships: five personality factors in interactional context. *J. Pers.* 60:477–99

Buss DM, Cantor N, eds. 1989. *Personality Psychology: Recent Trends and Emerging Directions.* New York: Springer-Verlag

Buss DM, Chiodo LM. 1991. Narcissistic acts in everyday life. *J. Pers.* 59:179–215

Buss DM, Larsen RJ, Westen D, Semmelroth J. 1992. Sex differences in jealousy: evolution, physiology, and psychology. *Psychol. Sci.* 3:251–55

Butcher JN, Dahlstrom W, Graham J, Tellegen A, Kaemmer B. 1989. *Manual for Administering and Scoring the MMPI-2.* Minneapolis: Univ. Minn. Press

Butcher JN, Graham JR, Fowler RD. 1991. Special series: the MMPI-2. *J. Pers. Assess.* 57:203–90

Cacioppo JT, Berntson GG, Anderson BL. 1991. Psychophysiological approaches to the evaluation of psychotheraputic process and outcome, 1991: contributions from social psychophysiology. *Psychol. Assess.: J. Consult. Clin. Psychol.* 3:321–36

Campbell DT, Fiske DW. 1959. Convergent and discriminant validation by the multitrait-multimethod matrix. *Psychol. Bull.* 56:81–105

Cantor N. 1990. From thought to behavior: "having" and "doing" in the study of personality and cognition. *Am. Psychol.* 45:735–50

Cantor N, Acker M, Cook-Flannagan C. 1992. Conflict and preoccupation in the intimacy life task. *J. Pers. Soc. Psychol.* 63:644–55

Cantor N, Norem J, Langston C, Zirkel S, Fleeson W, Cook-Flannagan C. 1991. Life tasks and daily life experience. *J. Pers.* 59:425–51

Carver CS. 1989. How should multifaceted personality constructs be tested? Issues illustrated by self-monitoring, attributional style, and hardiness. *J. Pers. Soc. Psychol.* 56:577–85

Cattell RB. 1966. Psychological theory and scientific method. In *Handbook of Multivariate Experimental Psychology,* ed. RB Cattell, pp. 1–18. Chicago: Rand McNally

Cattell RB. 1973. *Personality and Mood by Questionnaire.* Chicago: Aldine-Atherton

Cervantes RC, Padilla AM, Salgado de Snyder N. 1991. The Hispanic Stress Inventory: a culturally relevant approach to psychosocial assessment. *Psychol. Assess.: J. Consult. Clin. Psychol.* 3:438–47

Chaplin WF. 1991. The next generation of moderator research in personality psychology. *J. Pers.* 59:143–78

Cheung PC, Conger AJ, Hau K, Lew WJF, Lau S. 1992. Development of the multi-trait personality inventory (MTPI): comparison among four chinese populations. *J. Pers. Assess.* 59:528–51

Childs RA, Dahlstrom WG, Kemp SM, Panter AT. 1992. Item response theory in personality assessment: The MMPI-2 Depression Scale. *L. L. Thurstone Psychometric Lab. Res. Rep. 91-1.* Univ. NC, Chapel Hill

Cohen P, Cohen J, Teresi J, Marchi M, Velez NC. 1990. Problems in the measurement of latent variables in structural equations causal models. *Appl. Psychol. Meas.* 14:183–96

Colvin CR. 1993. Childhood antecedents of young-adult judgability. *J. Pers.* In press

Colvin CR, Funder DC. 1991. Predicting personality and behavior: a boundary on the acquaintance effect. *J. Pers. Soc. Psychol.* 60:884–94

Costa PT, McCrae RR. 1989. *The NEO-PI/NEO-FFI Manual Supplement.* Odessa, Fla: Psychol. Assess. Res.

Costa PT, McCrae RR. 1990. Personality disorders and the five-factor model of personality. *J. Pers. Disord.* 4:362–71

Costa PT, McCrae RR. 1992a. *NEO PI-R, Professional Manual.* Odessa, Fla: Psychol. Assess. Res.

Costa PT, McCrae RR. 1992b. The five-factor model of personality and its relevance to personality disorders. *J. Pers. Disord.* 6: 343–59

Digman JM. 1990. Personality structure: emergence of the five-factor model. *Annu. Rev. Psychol.* 41:417–40

Drasgow F. 1984. Scrutinizing psychological tests: measurement equivalence and equivalent realtions with external variables are central issues. *Psychol. Bull.* 95:134–35

Drasgow F, Kanfer R. 1985. Equivalence of psychological measurement in heterogeneous populations. *J. Appl. Psychol.* 70: 662–80

Emmons RA. 1991. Personal strivings, daily life events, and psychological and physical well-being. *J. Pers.* 59:453–72

Emmons RA, McAdams DP. 1991. Personal strivings and motive dispositions: exploring the links. *Pers. Soc. Psycholol. Bull.* 17:648–54

Endler NS, Cox BJ, Parker JDA, Bagby RM. 1992. Self-reports of depression and state-trait anxiety: evidence for differential assessment. *J. Pers. Soc. Psychol.* 63:832–38

Eysenck HJ. 1967. *The Biological Basis of Personality.* Springfield, Ill: Thomas

Eysenck HJ, Eysenck SGB. 1964. *The Eysenck Personality Inventory.* San Diego: Educ. Ind. Test. Serv.

Fiske ST, Taylor SE. 1991. *Social Cognition.* New York: McGraw-Hill. 2nd ed.

Funder DC. 1991. Global traits: a neo-Allportian approach to personality. *Psychol. Sci.* 2:31–39

Funder DC, Sneed CD. 1993. Behavioral manifestations of personality: an ecological approach to judgmental accuracy. *J. Pers. Soc. Psychol.* 64:479–90

Gangestad SW, Simpson JA, DiGeronimo K, Biek M. 1992. Differential accuracy in person perception across traits: examination of a functional hypothesis. *J. Pers. Soc. Psychol.* 62:688–98

Gangestad SW, Snyder M. 1985. On the nature of self-monitoring: an examination of latent causal structure. In *Review of Personality and Social Psychology,* ed. P Shaver, 6:65–85. Beverly Hills, Calif: Sage

Gangestad SW, Snyder M. 1991. Taxonomic analysis redux: some statistical considerations for testing a latent class model. *J. Pers. Soc. Psychol.* 61:141–61

Geenen R. 1991. *Psychophysiological Consistency and Personality.* Tilburg, The Netherlands: Tilburg Univ. Press

Gerbing DW, Tuley MR. 1991. The 16PF related to the five-factor model of personality: multiple-indicator measurement versus the a priori scales. *Multivar. Behav. Res.* 26:271–89

Goffin RD, Jackson DN. 1992. Analysis of multitrait-multirater performance appraisal data: composite direct product method versus confirmatory factor analysis. *Multivar. Behav. Res.* 27:363–85

Goldberg LR. 1992. The development of markers for the big-five factor structure. *Psychol. Assess.: J. Consult. Clin. Psychol.* 4:26–42

Goldberg LR. 1993a. The structure of phenotypic personality traits. *Am. Psychol.* 48: 26–34

Goldberg LR. 1993b. The structure of personality traits: vertical and horizontal aspects. In *Studying Lives Through Time: Approaches to Personality and Development,* ed. DC Funder, R Parke, C Tomlinson-Keasey, K Widaman, pp. 169–88. Washington, DC: Am. Psychol. Assoc.

Goldberg LR, Rosolack TK. 1993. The big-five factor structure as an integrative framework: an empirical comparison with Eysenck's P-E-N model. In The *Developing Structure of Temperament and Personality from Infancy to Adulthood,* ed. CF Halverson, GA Kohnstamm, RP Martin. New York: Erlbaum. In press

Graham JR, Watts D, Timbrook RE. 1991. Detecting fake-good and fake-bad profiles with the MMPI-2. *J. Pers. Assess.* 57:264–77

Graziano WG, Ward D. 1992. Probing the big five in adolescence: personality and adjustment during a developmental transition. *J. Pers.* 60:425–40

Grove WM, Cicchetti D, eds. 1991. *Thinking Clearly About Psychology,* Vol. 2: *Personality and Psychopathology.* Minneapolis: Univ. Minn. Press

Hamberger LK, Hastings JE. 1992. Race differences on the MCMI in an outpatient clinical sample. *J. Pers. Assess.* 58:90–95

Haynes SN, Floyd FJ, Lemsky C, Rogers E, Winemiller D, et al. 1992. The marital satisfaction questionnaire for older persons. *Psychol. Assess.: J. Consult. Clin. Psychol.* 4:473–82

Hendryx MS, Haviland MG, Gibbons RD, Clark DC. 1992. An application of item response theory to alexithymia assessment amount abstinent alcoholics. *J. Pers. Assess.* 58:506–15

Hofstee WKB, de Raad B, Goldberg LR. 1992. Integration of the Big Five and circumplex approaches to trait structure. *J. Pers. Soc. Psychol.* 63:146–63

Holland P, Wainer H. 1993. *Differential Item Functioning.* Hillsdale, NJ: Erlbaum

Holmes TH, Rahe RH. 1967. The social readjustment rating scale. *J. Psychosom. Res.* 11:213–18

Hoyle RH, Lennox RD. 1991. Latent structure of self-monitoring. *Multivar. Behav. Res.* 26:511–40

Hull JG, Lehn DA, Tedlie JC. 1991. A general approach to testing multifaceted personality constructs. *J. Pers. Soc. Psychol.* 61: 932–45

Hutton HE, Miner MH, Blades JR, Langfeldt VC. 1992. Ethnic differences on the MMPI overcontrolled-hostility scale. *J. Pers. Assess.* 58:260–68

Kamakura WA, Balasubramanian SK. 1989. Tailored interviewing: an application of item response theory for personality measurement. *J. Pers. Assess.* 53:502–19

Kane M. 1992. An argument-based approach to validity. *Psychol. Bull.* 112:527–35

Kenny DA, Kashy DA. 1992. Analysis of the multitrait-multimethod matrix by confirmatory factor analysis. *Psychol. Bull.* 112: 165–72

Kline RB, Lachar D. 1992. Evaluation of age, sex, and race bias in personality inventory for children (PIC). *Psychol. Assess.: J. Consult. Clin. Psychol.* 4:333–39

Kobasa SC. 1979. Stressful life events, personality, and health: an inquiry into hardiness. *J. Pers. Soc. Psychol.* 37:1–11

Lanning K. 1988. Individual differences in scalability: an alternative conception of consistency for personality theory and measurement. *J. Pers. Soc. Psychol.* 55: 142–48

Lanning K. 1991. *Consistency, Scalability, and Personality Measurement.* New York: Springer-Verlag

Larsen RJ. 1987. The stability of mood variability: a spectral analytic approach to daily mood assessment. *J. Pers. Soc. Psychol.* 52:1195–204

Larsen RJ. 1990. Spectral analysis of psychological data. In *Statistical Methods in Longitudinal Research,* Vol. II: *Time Series and Categorical Longitudinal Data,* ed. A Von Eye, pp. 319–49. Boston: Academic

Larsen RJ. 1992. Neuroticism and selective encoding and recall of symptoms: evidence from a combined concurrent-retrospective study. *J. Pers. Soc. Psychol.* 62:480–88

Larsen RJ, Kasimatis M. 1990. Individual differences in entrainment of mood to the weekly calendar. *J. Pers. Soc. Psychol.* 58:164–71

Larsen RJ, Kasimatis M. 1991. Day-to-day physical symptoms: individual differences in the occurrence, duration, and emotional concomitants of minor daily illnesses. *J. Pers.* 59:387–423

Lippa R. 1991. Some psychometric characteristics of gender diagnosticity measures: reliability, validity, consistency across domains, and relationship to the big 5. *J. Pers. Soc. Psychol.* 61:1000–11

Lippa R, Connelly S. 1990. Gender diagnosticity: a new Bayesian approach to gender-related individual differences. *J. Pers. Soc. Psychol.* 59:1051–65

Little BR, Lecci L, Watkinson B. 1992. Personality and personal projects: linking big five and PAC units of analysis. *J. Pers.* 60:501–25

Loevinger J. 1966. The meaning and measurement of ego development. *Am. Psychol.* 21:195–206

Loevinger J. 1993. Measurement of personality: true or false. *Psychol. Inq.* 4:1–16

Lord FM. 1980. *Applications of Item Response Theory to Practical Testing Problems.* Hillsdale, NJ: Erlbaum

Lubinski D, Humphreys LG. 1990. Assessing spurious "moderator effects": illustrated substantively with the hypothesized ("synergistic") relation between spatial and mathematical ability. *Psychol. Bull.* 107:385–93

Lykken DT, McGue M, Tellegen A, Bouchard TJ. 1992. Emergenesis: genetic traits that may not run in families. *Am. Psychol.* 47:1565–77

Marsh HW. 1990. Confirmatory factor analysis of multitrait-multimethod data: the construct validation of multidimensional self-concept responses. *J. Pers.* 58:661–92

McAdams DP. 1992. The five-factor model in personality: a critical appraisal. *J. Pers.* 60:329–61

McAdams DP, de St. Aubin E. 1992. A theory of generativity and its assessment through self-report, behavioral acts, and narrative themes in autobiography. *J. Pers. Soc. Psychol.* 62:1003–15

McClelland DC, Koestner R, Weinberger J. 1989. How do self-attributed and implicit motives differ? *Psychol. Rev.* 96:690–702

McCrae RR. 1991. The five-factor model and its assessment in clinical settings. *J. Pers. Assess.* 57:399–414

McCrae RR, Costa PT. 1991. Adding *liebe und arbeit*: the full five factor model and well-being. *Pers. Soc. Psychol. Bull.* 17:227–32

McCrae RR, Costa PT, Piedmont RL. 1993. Folk concepts, natural language, and psychological constructs: the California Psychological Inventory and the five-factor model. *J. Pers.* 61:1–26

McCrae RR, John OP. 1992. An introduction to the five-factor model and its applications. *J Pers.* 60:175–215

Meehl PE. 1990. Schizotaxia as an open concept. In *Studying Persons and Lives,* ed. AI Rabin, RA Zucker, RA Emmons, S Frank, pp. 248–303. New York: Springer

Meehl PE. 1992. Factors and taxa, traits and types, differences of degree and differences in kind. *J. Pers.* 60:117–74

Millon T. 1987. *Millon Clinical Multiaxial Inventory.* Minneapolis, Minn: Interpret. Scoring Syst.

Moran MP. 1990. The problem of cultural bias in personality assessment. In *Handbook of Psychological and Educational Assessment of Children,* ed. CR Reynolds, RW Kamphaus, pp. 524–25. New York: Guilford

Mroczek DK. 1993. *Personality and psychopathology in older men: the five factor model and the MMPI-2.* PhD thesis. Boston Univ.

Nikula R, Klinger E, Larson-Gutman MK. 1993. Current concerns and electrodermal activity: responses to words and thoughts. *J. Pers.* 61:63–84

Noh S, Avison WR, Kaspar V. 1992. Depressive symptoms among Korean immigrants: assessment of a translation of the center for epidemiologic studies-depression scale. *Psychol. Assess.: J. Consult. Clin. Psychol.* 4:84–91

Ozer DJ. 1989. Construct validity in personality assessment. See Buss & Cantor 1989, pp. 224–34

Parcel GS, Meyer MP. 1978. Development of an instrument to measure children's health locus of control. *Health Educ. Monogr.* 6:149–59

Paulhus DL, Bruce MN. 1992. The effect of acquaintanceship on the validity of personality impressions: a longitudinal study. *J. Pers. Soc. Psychol.* 63:816–24

Paunonen SV. 1991. On the accuracy of ratings of personality by strangers. *J. Pers. Soc. Psychol.* 61:471–77

Paunonen SV, Jackson DN, Trzebinski J, Forsterling F. 1992. Personality structure across cultures: a multimethod evaluation. *J. Pers. Soc. Psychol.* 62:447–56

Piedmont RL, McCrae RR, Costa PT. 1992. An assessment of the Edwards Personal Preference Schedule from the perspective of the five-factor model. *J. Pers. Assess.* 58:67–78

Pincus AL, Wiggins JS. 1990. Interpersonal problems and conceptions of personality disorders. *J. Pers. Disord.* 4:342–52

Reise SP, Waller NG. 1990. Fitting the two-parameter model to personality data. *Appl. Psychol. Meas.* 14:45–58

Reise SP, Waller NG. 1993. Traitedness and the assessment of response pattern scalability. *J. Pers. Soc. Psychol.* 65:143–51

Reise SP, Widaman, KF, Pugh, RH. 1993. Confirmatory factor analysis and item response theory: two approaches for exploring measurement invariance. *Psychol. Bull.* In press

Rorer LG, Widiger TA. 1983. Personality structure and assessment. *Annu. Rev. Psychol.* 34:431–63

Rost J. 1990. Rasch models in latent classes: an integration of two approaches to item analysis. *Appl. Psychol. Meas.* 14:271–82

Saucier G. 1992. Benchmarks: integrating affective and interpersonal circles with the big-five personality factors. *J. Pers. Soc. Psychol.* 62:1025–35

Schaeffer NC. 1988. An application of item response theory to the measurement of depression. In *Sociological Methodology,* ed. CC Clogg, pp. 271–307. Washington, DC: Am. Sociol. Assoc.

Schroeder ML, Wormworth JA, Livesley WJ. 1992. Dimensions of personality disorder and their relationships to the big-five dimensions of personality. *Psychol. Assess.: J. Consult. Clin. Psychol.* 4:47–53

Shapiro D. 1965. *Neurotic Styles.* New York: Basic Books

Shaver PR, Brennan KA. 1992. Attachment styles and the "big five" personality traits: their connections with each other and with romantic relationship outcomes. *Pers. Soc. Psychol. Bull.* 18:536–45

Smith CP, ed. 1992. *Motivation and Personality: Handbook of Thematic Content Analysis.* Cambridge: Cambridge Univ. Press

Smith TW, Williams PG. 1992. Personality and health: advantages and limitations of the five factor model. *J. Pers.* 60:395–423

Soldz S, Budman S, Demby A, Merry J. 1993.Representation of personality disorders in circumplex and five-factor space: explorations with a clinical sample. *Psychol. Assess.: J. Consult. Clin. Psychol.* 5:41–52

Stone AA, Kessler RC, Haythornthwaite JA. 1991. Measuring daily events and experiences: decisions for the researcher. *J. Pers.* 59:575–607

Strube MJ. 1989. Evidence for the type in Type A behavior: a taxometric analysis. *J. Pers. Soc. Psychol.* 56:972–87

Stumpf H. 1993. The factor structure of the Personality Research Form: a cross-national evaluation. *J. Pers.* 61:27–48

Tavris C. 1992. *The Mismeasure of Woman.* New York: Simon & Schuster

Tellegen A. 1985. Structures of mood and personality and their relevance to assessing anxiety, with an emphasis on self-report. In *Anxiety and Anxiety Disorders,* ed. AH Tuma, JD Maser, pp. 681–706. Hillsdale, NJ: Erlbaum

Tellegen A. 1988. The analysis of consistency in personality assessment. *J. Pers.* 56:621–63

Tellegen A. 1991. Personality traits: issues of definition, evidence, and assessment. See Grove & Cicchetti 1991, pp. 10–35

Tellegen A. 1993. Folk concepts and psychological concepts of personality and personality disorder. *Psychol. Inq.* 4:122–30

Tellegen A, Waller NG. 1993. Exploring personality through test construction: development of the Multidimensional Personality Questionnaire. In *Personality Measures: Development and Evaluation,* ed. SR Briggs, JM Cheek, pp. Greenwich, CT: JAI. In press

Trull TJ, Widiger TA, Guthrie P. 1990. Categorical versus dimensional status of borderline personality disorder. *J. Abnorm. Psychol.* 99:40–48

Waller NG, Reise SP. 1989. Computerized adaptive personality assessment: an illustration with the absorption scale. *J. Pers. Soc. Psychol.* 57:1051–58

Wallston K, Wallston B, DeVellis R. 1978. Development of the multidimensional health locus of control (MHLC) scales. *Health Educ. Monogr.* 6:161–70

Watson D, Clark LA. 1992. On traits and temperament: general and specific factors of emotional experience and their relation to the five-factor model. *J. Pers.* 60:441–76

Watson D, Clark LA, McIntyre CW, Hamaker S. 1992. Affect, personality, and social activity. *J. Pers. Soc. Psychol.* 63:1011–25

West SG, Hepworth JT. 1991. Statistical issues in the study of temporal data. *J. Pers.* 59:609–62

Wheeler L, Reis HT. 1991. Self-recording of everday life events: origins, types, and uses. *J. Pers.* 59:339–54

Widiger TA, Trull TJ. 1992. Personality and psychopathology: an application of the five-factor model. *J. Pers.* 60:363–93

Wiggins JS. 1991. Agency and communion as conceptual coordinates for the understanding and measurement of interpersonal behavior. See Grove & Cicchetti 1991, pp. 89–113

Wiggins JS. 1992. Have model, will travel. *J. Pers.* 60:527–32

Wiggins JS, Pincus AL. 1989. Conceptions of personality disorders and dimensions of personality. *Psychol. Assess.: J. Consult. Clin. Psychol.* 1:305–16

Wiggins JS, Pincus AL. 1992. Personality: structure and assessment. *Annu. Rev. Psychol.* 43:473–504

Wong MM, Csikszentmihalyi M. 1991. Affiliation motivation and daily experience: some issues on gender differences. *J Pers. Soc. Psychol.* 60:154–64

York KL, John OP. 1992. The four faces of Eve: a typological analysis of women's personality at midlife. *J. Pers. Soc. Psychol.* 63:494–508

Zuckerman M. 1991. *Psychobiology of Personality*. Cambridge: Cambridge Univ. Press

Zuckerman M, Miyake K, Koestner R, Baldwin CH, Osborne JW. 1991. Uniqueness as a moderator of self-peer agreement. *Pers. Soc. Psychol. Bull.* 17:385–91

Annu. Rev. Psychol. 1994. 45:389–418

SEXUAL DIFFERENTIATION OF THE HUMAN NERVOUS SYSTEM

S. Marc Breedlove

Department of Psychology and Graduate Group in Neurobiology, University of California, Berkeley, California 94720

KEY WORDS: sex dimorphism, sex orientation, humans, hypothalamus, homosexuality

---

CONTENTS

INTRODUCTION

There has never been any doubt that female and male humans are structurally distinguishable and there has been little doubt that they sometimes behave differently, but there remains an active debate about whether their behaviors are made different by biological influences or by social influences upon development, as if these were separable forces. The implicit, fallacious premise of such discussions is that biological influences alter neural development in one part of the person's brain while social influences alter psychological development in some other part. Because biological influences are naively perceived as immutable forces, this debate is viewed by some as relevant to whether society can do anything about sex differences in behavior. The debate has recently broadened into consideration of the development of sexual orientation within each gender, again with the question of whether biological or psychosocial factors play the determining role, perhaps with the hope that a resolution could help shape public policy. The recent discoveries of sex differences in structure (i.e. sexual dimorphism) in the human brain, and reports of neural orientation dimorphism (i.e. structural differences between the brains of heterosexual and homosexual men), have rekindled this long-standing argument within the greater nature-nurture debate. These recent findings in humans, examined in the context of research on the sexual differentiation of non-humans, provide no evidence favoring either nature or nurture in the development of human behavioral sex differences. Rather, the non-human literature highlights again the shortcomings of such a facile dichotomy, and suggests concrete means by which social and biological factors interact.

Biological Versus Psychological Measures

One source of confusion is the idea that there are biological influences that are distinct from psychological influences, and the related idea that any change seen in a biological measure cannot be engendered by forces that affect the psychological sphere. But if psychology and biology are simply disciplines that offer different means of describing the same phenomena, it is impossible to separate biological and psychological contributions to behavioral differences. Biologists monitor and describe such events as secretion of a hormone, or change in neuronal number or morphology. Any significant change in neuronal number or connectivity will eventually result in changes in behavior that a psychologist, given sufficient knowledge and access, could detect and describe in purely behavioral terms. Conversely, psychologists describe events such as experiences, stimuli, or learning procedures that reliably alter an organism's behavior. By definition, any significant experience will alter behavior and there must be some physical change within the organism, probably within its brain, in order for future behavior to be changed. Thus an assertion that "homosexuality [is] biologically determined" (J. M. Bailey quoted in Burr 1993) makes the mistake of confusing biological measures with biological influences. It is possible to have psychological and/or biological measures of a given influence, but there are no purely psychological or biological influences that determine behavior. Circumstances altering behavior must change both the psychology and the biology of an individual and because social influences certainly alter behavior, it follows that social stimuli must be able to alter biological measures such as brain morphology.

Genetic Versus Environmental Influences

Alternatively, it is at least theoretically possible to separate genetic and nongenetic contributions to differences in behavior. A difference in genes, specifically whether those found on the Y chromosome are present, undeniably accounts for sex differences in humans. Yet there remains the question of the extent to which social reactions to a child's gender polarize her or his early experiences and thereby give rise to or magnify later sex differences in behavior. Such positive feedback from the social sphere mediates some of the Y chromosome's influence on sex-related behavior even in rats, and doubtless some human cultures serve to magnify sex differences more than others. It will be difficult to determine the net impact of such socially mediated effects on sex differences. Behavior geneticists will not have the luxury of comparing groups of monozygotic twins raised apart, one treated exactly and unambiguously as a boy and the other exactly as a girl.

As for the genetic contribution to sexual orientation within a gender, there is less reason to suspect social feedback effects early in life, since babies that grow up to be heterosexual look much like babies that grow up to be homosexual. Estimates of the heritability of sexual orientation based on comparisons of relatives suggest that about half the variance in sexual orientation is due to variance in the genome in both men (Bailey & Pillard 1991) and women (Bailey et al 1993). These estimates are comparable to those for the heritability of intelligence test performance. It was recently reported that homosexual brothers share, because of maternal inheritance, alleles on a region of the X chromosome more often than would be expected by chance—i.e. in 33 out of 40 such pairs, each brother had coinherited genes in this region (Hamer et al 1993). This result strongly indicates that a gene (or genes) in this region affects the probability of homosexuality. But there remain 7 pairs of homosexual brothers that had *not* coinherited genes in this region and other homosexual men were not selected for this study because their pedigrees were inconsistent with such maternal transmission. These two results indicate that factors other than the implicated gene can result in male homosexuality. There may be converse cases in which men inherit the gene without becoming homosexual, but the design of this study precluded detecting such individuals. Thus heritability estimates and linkage analysis agree that (*a*) genes can indeed alter the probability of one's sexual orientation and that (*b*) even complete knowledge of an individual's genome would not allow perfect prediction of his or her later sexual orientation. As a final demonstration, note that not all monozygotic twins are concordant for sexual orientation (Eckert et al 1986, Green 1987, Buhrich et al 1991). There may well be socially mediated aspects of the genetic contributions to sex orientation (Byne & Parsons 1993). For example, if very young children who display nongender conforming behavior of the sort described as the "sissy-boy" syndrome (Green 1987, Whitam & Zent 1984) are treated differently from other children, then social reactions to the child's behavior could reinforce later nonconformity to traditional sex roles (Hines & Green 1991).

In this review I first describe in purely biological terms sexual differentiation of the body, most of which takes place before there are any behaviors to be described in psychological terms. These early events in somatic sexual differentiation are common to all mammals, including humans. I then review the literature concerning sexual differentiation of the nervous system in non-human species, which fully validates the unity of biological and psychological phenomena—researchers using purely behavioral measures predicted the presence of sexual dimorphism in the nervous system of many species and identified the active agent (i.e. steroid hormones) inducing dimorphism (Phoenix et al 1959). Subsequent biological work confirmed the predictions and provided a rather thorough cellular description of sexual differentiation of the nervous system (see Breedlove 1992a, Tobet & Fox 1992 for recent reviews). However, even in non-human species, early environmental influences and experiences have been found to alter adult behavior, and recent studies have successfully detected changes in biological measures, such as neuronal number and connectivity in specific nuclei of the nervous system, that appear to mediate the behavioral alterations. Some of the examples of sexual dimorphism found in non-human species have also been found in the human central nervous system and two of these models provide a springboard for a more detailed discussion of sexual dimorphism in the human brain. Morphological neural correlates of sexual orientation and a discussion of apparent dissociations between somatic sex and behavior follow. Finally, I summarize the meager yet intriguing evidence that the fetal hormonal stimulation that we know directs sexual differentiation of the human body may also direct sexual differentiation of the human brain.

SEXUAL DIFFERENTIATION OF THE BODY

Basic Principles of Mammalian Sexual Differentiation

The earliest stages of mammalian sexual differentiation take place before there is much observable behavior; therefore, it can only be described in biological terms. A crucial early event is whether the individual received a Y chromosome from its father. If so, the early, indifferent gonads will develop as testes; if not, they will develop as ovaries (for review, see Wilson et al 1981, Breedlove 1992a). Once the sex of the gonads is determined, sexual differentiation of the rest of the body is affected, not by genetic influence directly, but by the hormones secreted from the gonads. In mammals it is clear that testicular hormones are crucial for the development of males. The most important testicular hormones responsible for masculinization of the body are the androgenic steroids, principally testosterone. Providing testosterone to female mammals at the right time in development can result in a completely male exterior. The fetal ovaries, on the other hand, secrete very little hormone and appear to play either a small or a nonexistent role in sexual differentiation, since loss or removal of the ovary does not markedly affect the development of a female body. Conversely, if one removes the testes, or pharmacologically blocks androgen action, in males at the right point in development, they will develop a completely feminine exterior.[1] Thus one may intervene in the sexual differentiation of the body by controling the timing and extent of androgen exposure. Various developmental anomalies make it clear that these same rules apply to the human body—in the presence of androgen a male external phenotype will develop; in the absence of androgenic stimulation, a female phenotype will develop. Intermediate levels of androgen stimulation will result in an intersex phenotype. The fact that manipulation of a single factor, the androgenic steroids, has such wide-ranging consequences for development is fortuitous for researchers interested in sexual differentiation.

Mechanisms of Steroid Hormone Action

Steroid hormones, including androgens such as testosterone, can affect only cells that possess a specialized protein, called a receptor, which recognizes and binds to a specific class of steroids. Thus only cells that possess an androgen receptor will respond to androgen. In such cells, the testosterone binds to the

---

1 Some of the internal female structures, including the fallopian tubes, uterus, and inner vagina, are unaffected by androgens. Development of these structures is normally repressed by another testicular hormone, Mullerian Regression Hormone. In the absence of this hormone, either because the developing gonad is an ovary or the developing testes have been removed, these internal feminine structures will develop.

androgen receptor and the resulting steroid-receptor complex binds to the cell's DNA and thereby alters the production of various proteins by that cell.[2] Such steroid-induced alterations in gene expression can drastically alter the target cell, causing it to divide, alter extensively its morphology and/or function, or even die. If a cell lacks the appropriate receptor, it cannot itself respond to the steroid hormone.[3] There are many kinds of steroid receptors, each responsive to a different subset of steroid hormones (Beato 1989), and each affecting the expression of a different set of genes. Different steroids can therefore have different effects on a given cell population. During fetal development, both males and females possess the appropriate receptors to respond to androgen, but normally only the males are exposed to enough androgen to be masculinized. Therefore XX individuals exposed to fetal androgen can be masculinized. Occasionally XY individuals bear a defective gene for the androgen receptor that results in androgen insensitivity (AI). In such instances testes develop under the influence of the Y chromosome and testosterone is secreted, but the non-gonadal tissues fail to respond to androgen and therefore develop a feminine exterior (Olsen 1992).

Among the many types of cells that possess steroid receptors are neurons. The appropriate steroid hormone can induce the neuron to make new synapses upon its target cells, to discard old synapses from other neurons, to die while other neurons live, or to remain alive while other neurons die (see Breedlove 1992b for review). Thus the same steroidal signals that direct the body to develop in a masculine configuration can direct the nervous system to develop along a masculine pathway and result in sex differences in neural structure. Many such sexual dimorphisms have been found in the nervous system of various vertebrate species.

SEXUAL DIFFERENTIATION OF THE CENTRAL NERVOUS SYSTEM IN NON-HUMAN SPECIES

Behavior as an Index of Brain Morphology: The Organizational Hypothesis

Sexual dimorphism in the brains of rodents was first inferred from sex differences in behavior. W. C. Young and colleagues found that exposing

---

[2] Steroid hormones may have an alternative class of effects on neurons that do not require receptors that interact with DNA directly. Although intriguing, there is no evidence that this form of steroid action is relevant to sexual differentiation, and therefore will not be discussed here (see Schumacher 1990, Paul & Purdy 1992 for review).

[3] Of course, it is possible for a receptor-deficient cell that does not itself respond to a steroid hormone to be indirectly affected as a result of the steroid altering a neighboring, receptor-containing cell (Rand & Breedlove 1991).

female guinea pigs to androgen in utero permanently altered their adult behavior—such females were very unlikely to display the lordosis reflex required for a mounting male to achieve intromission (Phoenix et al 1959). They proposed that early androgens not only masculinized the developing body, but also organized the developing brain in a masculine fashion, making the animals less likely to display feminine behaviors (i.e. to be defeminized) and more likely to display male behaviors (i.e. to be masculinized). The finding that early androgen treatment could alter the adult behaviors of animals was replicated for many other behaviors and in several other species (Beatty 1992). The sensitive periods during which androgen manipulation was effective varied across species and behaviors, but generally coincided with an immature and therefore presumably very malleable nervous system. The organizational hypothesis implied that there would be sex differences in the structure of the nervous system and that whether an animal would possess a masculine or feminine configuration would depend on whether it was exposed to androgens early in development.

Two Examples of Neural Sexual Dimorphism in Rodents

Following the publication of the organizational hypothesis, several examples of subtle sexual dimorphism were indeed found in the rat hypothalamus (Pfaff 1966), including Raisman & Field's (1971) demonstration that females had a greater number of a particular class of synapse in their pre-optic area (POA) than did males. These subtle dimorphisms were soon overshadowed by the pioneering report that the brains of songbirds contained sexually dimorphic regions so prominent they could be detected with the naked eye (Nottebohm & Arnold 1976). These same neural regions had been implicated in the production of song, a primarily male behavior, and were 5–6 times larger in volume in males than in females. This was a startling demonstration that neural sexual dimorphism could be both dramatic and functionally comprehensible. Other sexual dimorphisms have been found in the nervous systems of many species and to date all result from the action of gonadal steroids. Furthermore, except for a few unresolved questions of whether early ovarian secretions are active (Hendricks 1992, Mack et al 1993, Toran-Allerand 1981, Dohler et al 1984), testicular secretions masculinize the brain of males, and the absence of testicular secretions allows the brain to develop in a feminine fashion. While the findings concerning birdsong development are remarkable, and many examples of neural sexual dimorphism have been found (de Vries et al 1984, Tobet & Fox 1992), we focus on two sexually dimorphic regions of the rat nervous system that seem to have counterparts in the human nervous system: the sexually dimorphic nucleus of the preoptic area and the spinal nucleus of the bulbocavernosus.

THE SEXUALLY DIMORPHIC NUCLEUS OF THE PREOPTIC AREA (SDN-POA) Another prominent sexual dimorphism, again visible without a microscope, was described within the rat preoptic area soon after Nottebohm & Arnold's report (Gorski et al 1978). This aggregation of neurons constitutes a nucleus and was therefore named the sexually dimorphic nucleus of the pre-optic area (SDN-POA). The SDN-POA is 5–6 times larger in volume in males than in females and exhibits the predictions of the organizational hypothesis—exposure to androgen around the time of birth results in a large nucleus in adulthood, while perinatal interference with androgen action results in a small, feminine SDN-POA (Gorski et al 1978, Jacobson 1980, Gorski 1988). Masculinization of the rat SDN-POA was accomplished by estrogenic metabolites of testosterone. Similar sexually dimorphic nuclei were found in the POA of gerbils (Commins & Yahr 1984), guinea pigs (Hines et al 1985), and ferrets (Tobet et al 1986). In each case, neither hormone treatment nor castration of animals in adulthood erased the dimorphism. Only perinatal treatment of rats with testosterone resulted in a more masculine (i.e. larger) nucleus in adulthood. The function of the SDN-POA is not well understood, since lesions of the SDN portion of the POA in adult male rats result in little or no discernible changes in behavior (DeJonge et al 1989, Arendash & Gorski 1983). However, because lesions of the greater POA, including the SDN-POA, reliably reduces male copulatory behavior, the SDN portion may nonetheless contribute to such behavior in a manner that is undetected following lesions.

THE SPINAL NUCLEUS OF THE BULBOCAVERNOSUS (SNB) A second example relevant to humans is the spinal nucleus of the bulbocavernosus (SNB), a collection of motoneurons in the lower lumbar spinal cord that control striated bulbocavernosus muscles at the base of the penis in rats. These muscles and their motoneurons aid the application and removal of copulatory plugs that seal over the cervix and thereby aid sperm transport and fertilization (Monaghan & Breedlove 1992). Although the bulbocavernosus muscles and their SNB motoneurons are present in rats of both sexes at birth, the muscles shrink drastically and the motoneurons die in newborn females (Cihak et al 1970, Nordeen et al 1985), resulting in sexual dimorphism in both the periphery and spinal cord in adulthood. If testosterone is administered to the animal before the demise of the muscles and their motoneurons, both can be spared permanently (Breedlove & Arnold 1983). Androgens per se act directly on the bulbocavernosus muscles, which in turn effect the rescue of their motoneurons in the SNB (Fishman et al 1990, Fishman & Breedlove 1992, Forger et al 1992,

1993). The human homologues of the SDN-POA and SNB will be described below.

The Masculinizing Role of Estrogens in the Rodent Brain

An unexpected aspect of the mechanism by which perinatal androgen organizes the rodent brain was the finding that estrogenic hormones such as estradiol are as effective as testosterone. Exposure of developing female rats to estrogen results in adults that fail to ovulate, are unlikely to display the feminine lordosis reflex, are more likely to display male-typical mounting behaviors (Whalen & Nadler 1963, Mullins & Levine 1968, Hendricks 1969), and possess a large, male-like SDN-POA (Dohler et al 1982). It was known that testosterone could be converted to estradiol by a single chemical reaction known as aromatization, while the reverse reaction virtually never occurred. Therefore it was proposed that androgens such as testosterone defeminized and masculinized the developing rodent brain after being aromatized to estrogens, which then interacted with estrogen receptors (Naftolin & MacLusky 1984). The requisite enzyme, aromatase, was found in the hypothalamus of several species and a variety of experiments demonstrated conclusively that estrogens were the active agents organizing the brains of rodents.

Developing female rats are normally protected from maternal estrogens by a plasma protein that sequesters estrogens but not androgens. In developing males, testosterone ignores the binding protein, enters the brain, and is intracellularly aromatized to estrogen, which then alters neuronal fate (see Gorski 1988 for review). Many of the sex differences in rodent behavior (including male copulatory behavior) and sexual dimorphisms in rodent CNS (including the SDN-POA) are instigated by aromatization (i.e. the testes of developing males secrete testosterone, which is aromatized in the brain into one of several estrogens, which then interact with estrogen receptors to alter brain development and later structure and function). A rare exception in the rodent literature is the SNB, which appears to be masculinized by androgens themselves, acting on androgen receptors. Thus, XY rats with defective androgen receptors and consequent androgen insensitivity fail to develop a masculine SNB (Breedlove & Arnold 1981) but, owing to their intact estrogen receptors, nevertheless develop a masculine SDN-POA (Jacobson 1980). In animals other than rodents, the extent to which masculinization or defeminization is mediated by estrogens rather than androgens is unclear. Among non-human primates there is little evidence that estrogen mediates masculinization of rough-and-tumble play or reproductive behaviors. Rather, it is manipulation of androgen receptors that alters the expression of these behaviors (Goy 1968). Nevertheless, in considering the human literature, one must bear in mind from the rodent literature that estrogens can direct masculinization of the nervous system.

The Interaction of Environmental and Hormonal Influences in Non-human Species

FETAL CROSS-TALK One of the earliest indications that gonadal secretions might be responsible for masculinization of the periphery came from studies of cattle. Breeders have known for centuries that freemartins, cows that had a male twin in utero, are often sterile. Lillie (1916) noted that close overlapping of the placentas of the twins was associated with more reproductive tract anomalies and a greater chance of sterility in the female. He concluded that some factor from the male crossed the placentas to masculinize the female fetus and today it seems likely that the factor is androgen. Among the rodents, the presence of large litters and the many available measures of masculinity and femininity offer ample opportunity to study the spillover of testicular secretions from male to female fetuses. There is some disagreement whether simply the number of contiguous males [i.e. whether the female is nestled in the uterus adjacent to no male, 1 male, or 2 males (Clemens et al 1978)] or the number of males "upstream" from the female with respect to uterine blood flow (Meisel & Ward 1981) offers more predictive value (vom Saal 1989), but there is agreement that such exposure can masculinize females as measured by augmented male copulatory behaviors and aggression in adulthood. Elevated levels of androgen have been measured in the amniotic fluid and plasma of such females, and correlates well with expected levels of exposure to their brothers (vom Saal 1989). It is not known whether such in utero contamination of females also affects the development and therefore adult morphology of the SDN-POA or SNB (but see vom Saal 1989 regarding males).

MATERNAL STRESS The morphology of both the SDN-POA and the SNB have been correlated with another prenatal effect—stress experienced by the dam. When pregnant rats are restrained under bright lights each day, their male offspring produce less androgen during the fetal period, and have more feminine (i.e. smaller) SDN-POA's (Anderson et al 1985) and fewer SNB cells (Grisham et al 1991) in adulthood, than males whose mothers were not so restrained. The male offspring of stressed dams also display altered copulatory behavior that is almost certainly the result of reduced fetal androgen production and may be related to the altered adult morphology of the hypothalamus and spinal cord. There is good evidence that these effects are mediated by the following cascade of events: maternal stress releases endogenous opioids that inhibit gonadotropin secretion, which results in decreased androgen production by the fetal testes and reduced activities of aromatase in the brain (Ward 1992). Consequently, the developing brain receives reduced androgenic and estrogenic stimulation. Treating the dam with the opioid blocker naltrexone during stress blocks much of the influence of the stress on later sexual receptivity (Ward et al 1986).

THE ROLE OF EARLY ENRICHMENT Some examples of sexual dimorphism in the fine structure of neurons in the rat cortex are expressed when the animals are raised in enriched environments (i.e. in social housing in large cages with fresh infusions of play objects), but not when raised in more standard laboratory conditions (Juraska 1990). In such cases the level of stimulation provided even by the enriched environment is probably far less than developing rats received prior to domestication. The opportunity for developing males to engage in juvenile play has also proved crucial for later male copulatory behavior in both rats (Ward 1992) and monkeys (Goy & Goldfoot 1974, Goldfoot et al 1984), where rearing males in social isolation, despite normal fetal androgen levels, effectively prevents later copulatory behavior. Social isolation is especially devastating in prenatally stressed male rats that display little copulatory behavior even when later housed for a long period with a female rat. Such social "therapy" significantly ameliorates the deficits in rats that have been exposed to either social isolation or prenatal stress only (Ward 1992). It is intriguing to speculate that differences in the ways that young males and females interact socially may provide differences in experiences shaping brain morphology and behavior in rats, monkeys, and men. There are certainly sex differences in the play behavior of each species, with males displaying a more active, rough-and-tumble type of play (Goy & Wallen 1979, Meaney & Stewart 1981, Berenbaum & Hines 1992). Interestingly, the sex differences in play are magnified when comparing groups of all males with groups of all females, and are somewhat ameliorated when analyzing the play behavior of males and females in mixed-sex groups (Meaney & Stewart 1981, Thor & Holloway 1986).

MATERNAL SOCIAL INFLUENCE Moore and colleagues have found it likely that social stimuli serve as positive feedback to mediate androgenic masculinization of the nervous system in rats. Moore noted that rat dams licked the anogenital region of their male pups more often than their female pups. Such licking stimulates evacuation reflexes of the bladder and colon. Apparently males are normally groomed more often because of their plasma testosterone levels, since castration reduces the attention they get from the dam and testosterone treatment restores it (Moore 1982). Rendering the dam anosmic (unable to smell) resulted in less anogenital grooming directed toward any pups. Males reared by anosmic dams therefore receive much less genital stimulation as pups than do males reared by intact dams and as adults require more time to achieve initial and subsequent ejaculations (Moore 1984). The altered sexual behavior may occur because males reared by anosmic dams have fewer SNB motoneurons in adulthood than do males reared by intact dams (Moore et al 1992). Moore has not yet determined whether altering neonatal anogenital stimulation also affects the adult structure of the SDN-POA. But at least one of the means by which testicular steroids masculinize the nervous system of developing rats is by attracting special attention from the dam, who provides additional anogenital stimulation to the pup, thereby preserving a few more SNB motoneurons from death, which may very well alter later reproductive behavior. Surely the more complex social reaction to gender among humans also sculpts the developing nervous system and therefore adult behavior in our species as well.

SEXUAL DIMORPHISM IN THE HUMAN CENTRAL NERVOUS SYSTEM

As discussed earlier, a sexual dimorphism present in the brains of adults could be the result of (*a*) sex differences in early social experience shaping brain development, or (*b*) the unfolding of neural processes that are normally unaffected by early experience. Thus an important question for each sexual dimorphism is whether it is literally congenital (i.e. already present at birth, the point at which the individual begins social interactions). On the one hand, if the sex difference first arises after birth, it could represent the delayed unfolding of events begun by prenatal hormone exposure, but one must also consider that the different social stimulation provided to males and females may drive sexual differentiation of the trait. On the other hand, any difference that arises before birth could not be the result of differential social stimulation to the sexes. Rather, prenatal sex differences, almost certainly the same differences in steroidal stimulation that drive sexual differentiation of the body, must be responsible for dimorphisms present at birth, although subsequent differential social stimulation might sustain, accentuate, or attenuate the sexual dimorphism into adulthood. Except for the rather small difference in absolute brain weight, we do not know conclusively whether any of the sexual dimorphisms in the human brain are present at birth.

Brain Weight in Absolute Terms and Relative to Body Size

Men have larger bodies and brains than do women. Whether the 120–160 gram difference in brain weight is because of a difference in the number or size of individual neurons or glia has never been demonstrated. This neural sexual dimorphism has been dismissed by some because there is a modest correlation between body size (variously measured as body mass, height, or estimated surface area) and brain weight, either within or between the sexes (e.g. Dekaban & Sadowsky 1978, Ankney 1992; but see also Peters 1991). Nineteenth century neurologists, most of whom were male, made much of the sex difference in absolute brain size (Swaab & Hofman 1984) but when corrected for body size, the sex difference is reduced (Peters 1991, Ankney 1992), eliminated (Gould 1981), or even reversed (Montessori 1913, cited in Swaab & Hofman 1984). Some of these differences of opinion result from different standards of body size (i.e. whether weight, height, or body surface area is the appropriate index for scaling brain weight). The consensus seems to be that no single measure of body size normalizes brain weight sufficiently to eliminate completely the male advantage (Gould 1981, Peters 1991, Ankney 1992). However, Gould (1981) asserts that some as yet unascertained body metric probably would result in equal relative brain size between the sexes (p. 106), an assertion that cannot easily be disputed.

The sex difference in absolute brain weight is present in humans at birth, although much less pronounced than in adulthood (Pakkenberg & Voigt 1964, Dekaban & Sadowsky 1978). Comparisons across the lifespan do not resolve the question of whether brain mass simply reflects body size, because there was no sex difference in either body weight or length among a cohort of newborns that demonstrated a statistically significant albeit modest (5%, representing one fourth of a standard deviation) difference in brain weight (Dekaban & Sadowsky 1978). However, even if a sex difference in body size is not detected at birth, there could well be a latent sex difference, undetected by external measures, that causes a sex difference in subsequent body development. Thus it is not clear whether a sex difference in body morphology precedes, either ontogenetically or causally, a sex difference in brain size. Indeed, the question of how the correlation of body and brain size across the sexes comes about has never been addressed. Does development of a sex difference in the brain guide development of sex differences in the body, does body development guide that of the brain (Purves 1988), or does some third factor such as growth hormone independently guide both?

The difference in both body and brain size becomes more pronounced over the first decade of life. The magnitude of the sex difference in adult body size has been proposed by several authors as a benchmark for other sex differences in humans. The sex difference in body size is readily apparent in everyday life despite the overlap of ranges and represents at least two standard deviations (i.e. the difference between the mean height of women and men is at least twice the mean of the standard deviations for males and that for females). Besides adult brain weight, which could simply represent another body metric, no other sex difference in neuroanatomical or psychological measures (McGlone 1980; Feingold 1988, 1992) approaches this magnitude. It is important to remember that all sex differences among humans, including the slight male superiority in tests of spatial reasoning and the female superiority in verbal fluency (see Levy & Heller 1992 for review) are accompanied by substantial overlap in the distributions of women and men.

The Spinal Cord

The sexual dimorphism described earlier in the rat periphery and spinal cord is also present in humans. Both men and women have a bulbocavernosus muscle. In men, it wraps around the base of the penis, much as it does in male rats, to aid the ejaculation of semen. In women, the muscle encircles and serves to constrict the opening of the vagina, a function female rats forgo since in their case the muscle degenerates shortly after birth. The muscle is larger in men than in women and accordingly, men possess approximately 25% more motoneurons in the spinal nucleus that innervates this and other perineal muscles, known as Onuf's nucleus X or simply Onuf's nucleus (Forger & Breedlove 1986). Because Onuf's nucleus in humans and the SNB in rats control the same perineal musculature, they are homologous sexual dimorphisms. It seems likely that, as is the case for the SNB of rats, fetal androgen guides sexual differentiation of the periphery and the fate of spinal motoneurons follows suit. The evidence in favor of this sequelae is that humans, like rats, undergo a period during which about half the generated motoneurons die (Forger & Breedlove 1987), and this period, completed by the 26th week of human gestation, overlaps the period during which male fetuses secrete testosterone and the external genitalia become differentiated.

Lateralization of Brain Function

There are several psychological tests that are thought to reflect hemispheric specialization for particular cognitive functions. Especially among right-handed individuals, verbal information is usually processed more rapidly and accurately when presented to the left cerebral hemisphere while spatial information is better processed when presented to the right hemisphere. The discrepancy in performance when information is presented to one side or the other is slightly greater in men than in women (McGlone 1980 for review). The effects of strokes also indicate that women have less lateralized brains than do men, since knowing whether the lesion is on the right or left provides more predictive power about the nature and extent of neuropsychological deficit in men patients than in women (see Levy & Heller 1992 for review). Whether this difference in interhemispheric organization is related to sex differences in spatial reasoning (favoring males) and verbal fluency (favoring females) is unknown despite considerable speculation (Voyer 1990, Levy & Heller 1992, Reinisch & Sanders 1992). The reports of sex differences in cerebral lateralization have been disputed (McGlone 1980), but are interesting because the assertion that the cerebral hemispheres of men are more asymmetrical than those of women is at least a century old (Crichton-Brown 1880). More recently, Wada et al (1975) described an asymmetry in the surface area of the so-called planum of the temporal lobe, which is usually slightly larger in the left hemisphere than in the right in both sexes. However, the brains of women were more likely to display symmetry or even a reversed laterality on this measure. Chi et al (1977) assert that some related morphological asymmetries in the temporal lobe develop during the final trimester, but do not distinguish between the sexes, therefore we do not know whether this subtle dimorphism is congenital. However, some other cortical regions have been reported to be more asymmetrical in males than in females before birth (de Lacoste et al 1991).

CAN EARLY ESTROGENS MASCULINIZE BRAIN LATERALIZATION? Studies of women exposed in utero to the estrogenic compound diethylstilbestrol (DES), which was used to prevent miscarriages, indicate that aromatized metabolites of androgen could masculinize human cognitive function. Women who had been exposed to DES in utero showed more lateralized performance on dichotic listening tasks than their non-DES exposed sisters (Hines 1982). This is especially interesting because, unlike the remaining cases of inadvertent hormone exposure, there is little reason to expect any confusion on the part of family or acquaintances of these individuals because their external genitalia are those of normal females. Thus the DES effect, while small, may be a direct result of hormonal stimulation to the developing brain rather than an effect mediated by an altered periphery and therefore an altered social environment. Another indication that aromatized metabolites of testosterone might masculinize the human brain is that although most DES-exposed women are heterosexual, they are more likely to exhibit a homosexual or bisexual orientation than are non-exposed women (Ehrhardt et al 1985).

The Corpus Callosum

Communication between the two sides of the brain is limited to a few structures, several of which have been reported to display sexual dimorphism. Neurologists of the previous century reported that a structure joining the left and right thalamus, the so called massa intermedia, was more commonly present in women than in men, and later reports confirm that 86% of women and 72% of men have this structure (Morel 1948). The fact that many people of each sex lack a massa intermedia (i.e. the left and right halves of the thalamus remain separate in the region of the third ventricle) suggests that the structure and consequently sex differences in the structure are of little consequence to behavior. Whether the sex difference is present at birth has not been reported. There is also a single report that the minor fiber tract connecting the two cerebral hemispheres, the anterior commissure, is larger in midsagittal area relative to brain weight in women than in men (Allen & Gorski 1992).

The major structure connecting the left and right brains is the corpus callosum (CC) and that structure, consisting of neuronal axons crossing the midline, is indisputably crucial for the proper coordination of left and right cerebral function (e.g. Sperry 1977). Thus the report that the CC presented a different midline profile in women than in men (de Lacoste-Utamsing & Holloway 1982) generated considerable interest. While there was no sex difference in the overall midsagittal area of the CC, there was a sex difference in the maximal width and area of the posterior portion of the CC, known as the splenium. The literature concerning the CC and possible sex differences in the CC in humans is filled with contradictory findings (e.g. Weber & Weir 1986, Elster et al 1990, Denenberg et al 1991), which immediately indicates that any sexual dimorphism must be rather subtle.

There are several possible explanations for the contradictory findings. First, there are differences in the protocols used to define CC subregions. Second, there are apparent differences in CC morphology related to handedness (Witelson 1985), which is uncontrolled in some studies. Third, there are indications that CC morphology can change with age and that the changes with age may be more prominent in one sex than the other (Witelson 1989, Allen et al 1991). Fourth, some studies use magnetic resonance imaging (MRI), which provide less distinct borders for measurement, while other studies use postmortem materials, which could be subject to artifacts due to fixation, handling, etc. There is also the difficulty of consistently achieving a perfect midsagittal section for either MRI images or tissue slices. Finally, many of the studies, both those confirming and refuting a sex difference, rely on a small number of subjects.

Regarding the first explanation, it is possible to devise several different, but each quite reasonable, morphometric protocols to define, for example, what constitutes the splenium. Several failures to replicate the original report of a sex difference are also failures to replicate the original measures and thus are difficult to interpret. In one of the few studies that explicitly gathers measurements by different protocols, a sex difference is seen when measured by the method of de Lacoste-Utamsing & Holloway, but is not detected in the same material when measured by another, equally plausible, protocol (Allen et al 1991).

If there is a sexual dimorphism in the human CC, it is a subtle sex difference not in size but in the midsagittal shape such that a greater proportion of the CC is found in the posterior end, resulting in a more bulbous splenium in females (de Lacoste-Utamsing & Holloway 1982, Yoshii et al 1986, Clarke et al 1989, Allen et al 1991). All studies agree that these differences cannot allow one to correctly classify every brain as either male or female, and this shortcoming has been offered as proof that sexual dimorphism in the CC is unworthy of study (e.g. note the title for Byne et al 1988; see also Byne & Parsons 1993). But body height would also fail to meet so stringent a criterion, yet there is no doubt that this sex difference is statistically, scientifically, and socially significant.

When does a sex difference in the CC appear? Despite an early report that the sex difference in splenial width (favoring females) was present in fetal brains (de Lacoste et al 1986), there have been no replications and several failures to detect a sex difference in children (Bell & Variend 1985, Clarke et al 1989, Allen et al 1991), albeit with small sample sizes. Thus there is little reason to believe the dimorphism in the CC is congenital. Nor does anyone know the functional significance of these differences in the CC. It has been suggested that a larger CC subregion might reflect more axons communicating between the left and right portions of the brain and that the shared information results in less functional specialization of either side, such as is seen in women performing lateralization tasks or suffering stroke. However, a sex difference in the midsagittal area of the CC does not necessarily mean there is a sex difference in the number of axons (Juraska & Kopcik 1988, Kopcik et al 1992, Aboitiz et al 1992a,b) and one could as easily argue that specialization of processing within each hemisphere might make sharing of information between them more important and therefore require more axons in men than in women.

The Hypothalamus

One region of the hypothalamus that has been studied is the bed nucleus of the stria terminalis (BNST). Allen & Gorski (1990) report that the volume of the "darkly staining posteromedial component" of the BNST is 2–3 times larger in males than in females. Although their postmortem sample is limited, the sex difference does not appear to be present in individuals younger than 10 years of age. While similar sex differences in the BNST have been seen in other species, the function and ontogeny of this nucleus in any species is poorly understood. Most attention concerning sexual dimorphism in the human hypothalamus has focused on the preoptic area.

THE SDN-POA Swaab & Fliers (1985) first reported a sex difference in the hypothalamus of adult humans, and the difference they described (larger in males than in females), histological appearance, and general location was sufficiently reminiscent of the SDN-POA in rats that they named this nucleus the SDN-POA of humans. Counts of the number of cells found in the nucleus agreed well with volumetric measures. The volume of the nucleus and the number of cells counted within the nucleus declined with age in both sexes. Because the average age of the women in the original report was more than a decade older than that of the men (Swaab & Fliers 1985), it was difficult to gauge the true extent of the sex dimorphism. The same researchers later traced the ontogeny of this nucleus using a larger set of brains and reported a sex difference in cell number that first appeared after 10 years of age (Swaab & Hofman 1988, Hofman & Swaab 1989), and peaked in young adulthood and middle age. Because the sexual dimorphism is first detected well after the watershed event of birth, it could well be the result of social influences upon gender development. Again, it is also possible that a sex difference is present in the SDN-POA before birth, but only becomes apparent as reflected in cell number at the later age. A rapid decline in SDN-POA cell numbers was seen at about age 50 in men, while a much more gradual decline was seen in women after age 70. Thus there are stages in life in which the nucleus is monomorphic (childhood), other stages in which it is modestly dimorphic (60–80 years), and yet other stages (young adulthood and extreme old age) when the nucleus displays the maximum dimorphism, being about twice as large in men as in women.

THE INTERSTITIAL NUCLEI OF THE ANTERIOR HYPOTHALAMUS When Allen, Gorski, and colleagues examined the POA in human brains, they found a more complicated picture than in the rat POA. In addition to the nucleus described by Swaab & Fliers, Allen et al (1989), described three other nuclei in the region of the medial POA and paraventricular nucleus. Rather than try to sort out exactly which human nucleus corresponded to which rat nucleus, they simply numbered the nuclei as the interstitial nuclei of the anterior hypothalamus (INAH) 1 through 4 (INAH-1, -2, -3, -4). INAH-1 corresponds to the previously named SDN-POA of Swaab & Fliers, and while Allen et al confirmed the reduced volume of the nucleus with aging, they did not detect a sex difference in its volume. Because of the sensitivity of the SDN-POA/INAH-1 to age (see discussion above), Allen et al explicitly assembled cohorts of male and female brains that were well matched for age at autopsy, but it is always possible that their sample size was insufficient or age distribution inappropriate to reveal a sexual dimorphism present in INAH-1. INAH-4 was also found to be sexually monomorphic, but both INAH-2 and -3 were reported to be larger in men than in women (Allen et al 1989). There are as yet no studies of the ontogeny of INAH-2, -3, or -4, but we will shortly consider a study that replicated the sex difference in adult INAH-3.

SEXUAL ORIENTATION DIMORPHISM IN THE HUMAN BRAIN

Among human subjects there are other sex-related characteristics such as gender identity, the gender with which individuals identify themselves (Money & Ehrhardt 1972). It is also possible to consider the sexual orientation of an individual (i.e. whether the individual seeks romantic and sexual relationships with individuals of the same or the opposite sex). Because homosexual men and heterosexual women share an attraction to men, several investigators have asked whether the brain structure of homosexual men more closely resembles that of women than that of heterosexual men. One of the obvious regions to examine is the CC, because it can be examined via MRI in living subjects. But there have been no such reports as yet, which may be related to the difficulties and inconsistencies cited earlier. However, there is a report that the anterior commissure (AC), a small tract of axons that, like the larger CC, communicates between the two cerebral hemispheres, is larger in homosexual men than in (presumed) heterosexual men (Allen & Gorski 1992). This may relate to cognitive lateralization, since there have been several reports that homosexual men perform in a female-like manner on tests of cognitive function and are more likely to be non-right handed than the general population (McCormick & Witelson 1991). If instead of absolute size one examines the midsagittal area of the AC relative to brain weight, the difference between homosexual and heterosexual men remains and a sex difference in the AC, favoring women, is revealed among the heterosexual subjects. Furthermore, homosexual men and heterosexual women do not significantly differ in terms of relative AC size. Whether the individuals died of AIDS does not appear to explain the differences. There is no way to discover whether the measured differences in the adult structure of the AC are the results or causes of sexual orientation development.

The Hypothalamus

Most interest in orientation dimorphism has centered on the hypothalamus. The reports of sexual dimorphism in the human hypothalamus gained considerable attention when LeVay examined postmortem materials and reported that INAH-3 was indeed larger in men than in women but was also larger in presumed heterosexual men than in homosexual men (LeVay 1991). LeVay did not detect a sex difference in INAH-1 (SDN-POA of Swaab & Fliers 1985) or INAH-2, putting him somewhat at variance with both the Gorski and Swaab labs. However, small sample sizes and variation in ages examined could easily account for the discordant results. The differences in INAH-3 in LeVay's samples could not be ascribed to AIDS or body size. As in the case of the AC described above, because only adult brains were examined, we do not know whether the difference in INAH-3 is a cause or a result of the development of sexual orientation (LeVay 1993), but most of the public press seems unaware of the latter possibility (Tuller 1991).

The first report of orientation dimorphism in the human brain was in another region of the anterior hypothalamus, the suprachiasmatic nucleus (SCN) (Swaab & Hofman 1990, Swaab et al 1992). Postmortem materials of AIDS victims indicated that the SCN of homosexual men was some 150% larger in volume and contained twice as many cells as the SCN of heterosexual men who also had AIDS. This earlier report did not garner as much attention as that of LeVay because there are no reported sex differences in human SCN structure, nor any reason to expect the SCN to play a role in sexual behavior. Thus it is more difficult to understand the relationship of SCN structure to sexual orientation.

At present, measures of AC, INAH-3, and SCN require postmortem processing of tissue, therefore it will not be possible to test whether measuring these structures early in life (e.g. in utero) could allow one to predict later sexual orientation. However, a morphological index of early fetal testosterone levels may be available. Because the survival of motoneurons in Onuf's nucleus appears to be partly dependent on androgen [men have more of these motoneurons than do women (Forger & Breedlove 1986)], and because the period during which motoneurons die is complete by the 26th week of gestation (Forger & Breedlove 1987), one would predict that the number of surviving motoneurons would roughly correlate with androgen exposure in the first half of gestation. Unless there are other, presently unknown factors that cause motoneurons to die after birth, one could measure early androgen levels by counting Onuf's motoneurons at the end of life.[4] One obvious question is whether lesbians have more Onuf's motoneurons than do heterosexual women. Although some individuals might expect that homosexual men would show evidence of reduced fetal androgen exposure (e.g. Dorner 1985), reports that homosexual men begin puberty at a younger age (Kinsey et al 1948, Manosevitz 1970), and engage in considerably more sexual activity with more partners (Bell & Weinberg 1978) than do heterosexual men, offer considerable support for the opposite prediction.

Limitations of Animal Models for Sexual Orientation

The major limitation of applying the animal literature to human sexual orientation is the absence of readily available behavioral measures that might reveal something like sexual orientation rather than sexual behavior in animals (Beach 1977). The standard measure of feminine receptivity in rodents is the lordosis posture. However, when treated with estrogen and progesterone, adult female rats will display this posture in response to mounting by rats of either sex, or even in response to a human hand providing general stimulation to the flanks and perineum (Pfaff 1981). The reflexive nature of this response to tactile stimuli rather than to partner characteristics seems unrelated to human preferences for partners of a particular gender, regardless of the particular sex act offered. Rodent models of male sexual behavior often measure either the propensity of a male to mount another rat, or the success with which the male achieves intromission or ejaculation. The former measure, as with the lordosis posture, seems relatively unaffected by the sex of the provided partner—male rats will attempt to mount almost any animal or even inanimate objects (Beach 1977). The latter measures may relate simply to the success of achieving

---

4 For example, if there were a slow attrition of motoneurons with aging, the critical measure would be the number of Onuf's motoneurons relative to the age at death. In fact, there is evidence that the number of motoneurons, unlike other neuronal populations, does not decline with aging in rats (Birren & Wall 1956) or cats (Moyer & Kaliszewski 1958), and this question has not been studied in aging humans.

intromission and adequate stimulation to achieve ejaculation rather than any awareness of the partner's characteristics. Some researchers have attempted to measure an individual rat's willingness to work to have access to a potential sexual partner or the rat's choice of companions. Although this clearly measures the animal's motivation to have access to the other rat, it is difficult to decide which characteristics of the stimulus animal provide the attraction. The effects of maternal stress on fetal male testosterone production in rats may also occur in humans and might be responsible for instigating at least some cases of male homosexuality (Dorner 1985). A significant problem with this analogy is that male rats developing in such circumstances display reduced sexual behavior, while homosexual men display no such deficit.

ANOMALIES IN SEXUAL DIFFERENTIATION OF THE HUMAN BODY

One way to determine whether sex differences in behavior are related to prenatal events is to ask whether there are correlations between hormonal stimulation in utero and later behavior. One study found, as expected, that normal human newborn males had higher concentrations of androgens in the umbilical cord blood than did females (Jacklin et al 1988). When these children were studied at six years of age, they did not display a sex difference in spatial ability, but there was a significant correlation in girls between spatial ability at six and plasma androgen levels at birth. However, the direction of the correlation was the opposite that one might expect—the higher the plasma androgen levels, the lower the spatial ability score. It will be interesting to see whether a sex difference in these tests ever develops in this population (Kerns & Berenbaum 1991) and whether the correlation between neonatal hormone levels and spatial ability changes in sign or extent. The sex difference in plasma androgens develops quite early [between the tenth and twentieth weeks of gestation (Reyes et al 1974)] and future studies would benefit from measuring earlier concentrations and later behavior, but methods for safely measuring hormone levels in utero are not yet available.

There are several instances in which developing humans are exposed to an unusual fetal hormonal milieu. In such cases one may ask whether any of those behaviors that display a sex difference in normal subjects is altered in a fashion predicted by the alteration in fetal hormones. Because subjects displaying anomalies are relatively rare and most brain structures can be studied only in postmortem materials, there have not been any investigations of the brain structure of such individuals.

Androgen Insensitivity

As mentioned earlier, mutations in the gene encoding for the androgen receptor can reduce or eliminate the ability of the receptor to bind to androgen; therefore, depending on the degree to which receptor function is disabled, such mutations can cause a more-or-less complete androgen insensitivity (AI) in humans. In humans with complete AI the developing fetus ignores the masculinizing effect of androgen and displays a female exterior (Wilson et al 1981). Humans with complete AI are accepted as girls at birth and raised as girls, but are identified when menses fail to begin. Such individuals are also feminine in their gender identity and sexual orientation, and they are attracted to and marry men (Money et al 1984). Obviously these feminine characteristics could equally be the result of absence of androgenic stimulation of the nervous system or of psychosocial forces at work in development.

Because AI rats and mice have functional estrogen receptors and an unimpaired gene for the aromatase enzyme, any sexually dimorphic features masculinized via the aromatized metabolites would be expected to be male-like, as is the SDN-POA in AI rats (Jacobson 1980). If, as one would expect, AI humans also have functional aromatase and estrogen receptors, the absence of masculinization of sexual orientation argues against any crucial role for aromatized metabolites in sexual differentiation of the human nervous system. There have been a few studies of cognitive function in AI humans, and each found the AI subjects to be similar to normal females (Masica et al 1969). A more recent study likewise reported that AI subjects exhibited higher scores in the verbal comprehension factor than the perceptual organization factor (which includes visuospatial tests) of the Wechsler intelligence scale, as did their normal sisters and in contrast to their normal male kindred who had higher scores in the visuospatial tasks (Imperato-McGinley et al 1991). Further support for the notion that androgens per se aid the development of spatial reasoning comes from human males that, owing to a failure of gonadotropin production, do not undergo the normal exposure to androgen during puberty. Such individuals develop as males prenatally with maternal gonadotropins driving the testes, so they are presumably raised as normal boys and are identified by their failure to undergo puberty. A group of such adults, who did not receive androgen therapy until after 18 years of age, displayed a deficit in spatial ability compared to either normal males or males who had lost gonadotropin function after undergoing normal puberty (Hier & Crowley 1982). Androgen therapy in adulthood did not change spatial performance in either group of gonadotropin-deficient men, indicating that pubertal rather than fetal or adult androgen affects spatial reasoning. The AI studies suggest that either stimulation of androgen receptors per se and/or early socialization normally masculinize these measures, but estrogen receptor stimulation via aromatization does not (but see also earlier discussion of DES studies by Hines 1982).

Congenital Adrenal Hyperplasia

Congenital adrenal hyperplasia (CAH) is another condition in which genetic sex and fetal hormonal stimulation are in conflict. CAH results from a defect in one of several adrenal enzymes that prevents sufficient production of glucocorticoids and, as a secondary result, an enlarged adrenal gland that produces plasma androgen levels intermediate between normal male and female fetuses. When present in an XX individual, the additional androgen partially masculinizes the external genitalia, producing a phallus intermediate between a penis and a clitoris, and partially fused labia that resemble a scrotum. When such individuals are identified at birth, they are treated with glucocorticoids to reduce adrenal enlargement and halt excess androgen production and their external genitalia are surgically altered to more closely resemble those of females. As children, such individuals are more likely to be tomboys, prefer toys normally favored by boys (Berenbaum & Hines 1992), and show interests in careers than are non-CAH girls (Ehrhardt et al 1985). As adults, most CAH females are heterosexual in orientation, but may be more likely to be lesbians than are control females, including non-CAH affected sisters (Money et al 1984, Ehrhardt et al 1968, Ehrhardt et al 1985). There are reports that CAH females perform better than normal females on spatial tasks (Resnick & Berenbaum 1982, Resnick et al 1986, Nass & Baker 1991), but these reports have been disputed (Baker & Ehrhardt 1974). Unfortunately, it is difficult to determine whether the slight behavioral masculinization of the CAH population is the result of prenatal androgen effects on the developing brain or parental confusion about the child's gender, which could produce slightly atypical social influence.

Reductase Deficiency

Some individuals from the Dominican Republic, who, because of a defect in the reductase enzyme that converts testosterone to a more active androgen metabolite, are born with ambiguous, partially masculinized external genitalia—an intermediate sized phallus and labia-like folds of skin that contain testes. These individuals are raised much the way normal girls are, but undergo a transformation at puberty when testicular testosterone secretion rises. The phallus grows further to form a penis and the partially fused labia develop into a scrotum complete with testes (hence the nickname, *guevedoces,* "eggs (testes) at twelve"). There are reports that these individuals are raised as girls, but when they sprout a penis at puberty they display the appearance, behavior, and sexual orientation of most men (Imperato-McGinley et al 1974). One explanation of such results is that fetal testosterone masculinized the brain so that, social rearing notwithstanding, the individuals were destined to think and therefore behave like men. Unfortunately, both the descriptions and the interpretations of these individuals' lives are overly simplistic. Photographs of the genitalia of these individuals as infants portray a clearly intermediate phenotype (i.e. a phallus that resembles either an enlarged clitoris or a small penis). The society obviously recognizes and accepts that some people go through such a change; therefore, it is difficult to rule out the possibility that these individuals are treated differently from normal girls. Furthermore, there may be considerable social pressure for them to behave as men at puberty no matter what their inclinations might be. Thus despite the remarkable characteristics of these individuals, this experiment-of-nature comes with very inadequate control groups to allow any conclusions about the influence of prenatal steroids on sexual orientation in particular or behavior in general.

CONCLUSION

There is certainly sexual dimorphism in the human nervous system. The still unanswered question is the extent to which the sex differences in neural structure are, like sex differences in body morphology, the result of sex differences in prenatal hormone exposure. Besides the slight sex difference in brain weight, none of the sex differences in neural structure have been reliably detected at birth. The SDN-POA/INAH-1 of humans, for example, does not appear dimorphic until several years after birth and therefore could be a consequence of either prenatal steroid action or postnatal social experience. Although few researchers have examined such a possibility, the animal literature has already made it clear that perinatal environmental factors and social stimuli during the development of rats can modulate the degree of adult neural sexual dimorphism measured in biological terms. Since humans are also considered a very social and developmentally malleable species, it is likely that such influences could leave their mark upon our neural structure and consequently our behavior.

Testicular androgens secreted by the fetus direct development of a penis and, after birth, virtually everyone that interacts with that individual will note that he has a penis and will in many instances behave differently than if the individual were a female. These experiences will to some extent shape brain development and result in different behaviors from childhood to adulthood. I find it impossible to classify this chain of events as either purely social or purely biological. Even the most ardent proponent of inborn sex differences in behavior would admit that ignoring the penis and raising the individual as a girl would have some effect on development. But there is no denying that this differential social stimulation is instigated by the effects of fetal androgens, which were in turn the result of the Y chromosome's effects on the developing gonad. This chain of events highlights the futility of trying to separate biological and social influences on sexual differentiation in humans.

Do fetal hormones also directly alter the brain in ways independent of their effects on the body? The best available data are those concerning the masculinizing influence of prenatal DES (Hines 1982, Ehrhardt et al 1985) because this estrogenic hormone does not discernibly masculinize the body and therefore should not elicit male-like attention from others. Yet these effects on cognitive function and sexual orientation are small and contrast with the case of AI humans where, despite presumably normal male-like estrogenic stimulation of the brain, cognitive function and sexual orientation are congruent with sex of rearing (i.e. feminine). Finally, in terms of social policy, the question of whether fetal hormones have any effect on brain morphology, cognitive function, or sexual orientation seems irrelevant. Of course any individual differences in human behavior, either between the sexes or within each sex, could eventually be described in biological terminology and it is difficult to understand why individuals' rights or responsibilities should depend on the degree to which our biological description of their characteristics is comprehensive. It seems obvious that education and experience can affect either verbal or spatial reasoning performance in either sex. Furthermore, as sex roles in our society have become somewhat less polarized, sex differences in performance have waned (Feingold 1988, 1992), and the two phenomena might well be related. The public debate about the ontogeny of sexual orientation seems especially misguided because there is profound agreement between scientists who favor psychosocial theories (e.g. Bieber et al 1962, Byne & Parsons 1993) and those who favor biological theories (e.g. Ellis & Ames 1987, Dorner 1985) that sexual orientation is determined very early in life and is not a matter of individual choice.

Literature Cited

Aboitiz F, Scheibel AB, Fisher RS, Zaidel E. 1992a. Fiber composition of the human corpus callosum. *Brain Res.* 598:143–53

Aboitiz F, Scheibel AB, Zaidel E. 1992b. Morphometry of the sylvian fissure and the corpus callosum, with emphasis on sex differences. *Brain* 115:1521–41

Allen LS, Gorski RA. 1990. Sex difference in the bed nucleus of the stria terminalis of the human brain. *J. Comp. Neurol.* 302:697–706

Allen LS, Gorski RA. 1992. Sexual orientation and the size of the anterior commissure in the human brain. *Proc. Natl. Acad. Sci. USA* 89:7199–7202

Allen LS, Hines M, Shryne JE, Gorski RA. 1989. Two sexually dimorphic cell groups in the human brain. *J. Neurosci.* 9:497–506

Allen LS, Richey MF, Chai YM, Gorski RA. 1991. Sex differences in the corpus callosum of the living human being. *J. Neurosci.* 11:933–42

Anderson DK, Rhees RW, Fleming DE. 1985. Effects of prenatal stress on differentiation of the sexually dimorphic nucleus of the preoptic area SDN-POA of the rat brain. *Brain Res.* 332:113–18

Ankney CD. 1992. Sex differences in relative brain size: the mismeasure of women, too? *Intelligence* 16:329–36

Arendash GW, Gorski RA. 1983. Effects of discrete lesions of the sexually dimorphic nucleus of the preoptic area or other medial preoptic regions on the sexual behavior of male rats. *Brain Res. Bull.* 10:147–50

Bailey JM, Pillard RC. 1991. A genetic study of male sexual orientation. *Arch. Gen. Psychiatry* 48:1089–96

Bailey JM, Pillard RC, Neale MC, Agyei Y. 1993. Heritable factors influence sexual orientation in women. *Arch. Gen. Psychiatry* 50:217–23

Baker SW, Ehrardt AA. 1974. Prenatal androgen, intelligence and cognitive sex differences. In *Sex Differences in Behavior,* ed. RC Friedman, RN Richart, RL Vandewiele, pp. 33–51. New York: Wiley. 423 pp.

Beach FA. 1977. Cross-species comparisons and the human heritage. In *Human Sexuality in Four Perspectives,* ed. FA Beach, pp. 296–316. Baltimore: Johns Hopkins Univ. Press. 330 pp.

Beato M. 1989. Gene regulation by steroid hormones. *Cell* 56:335–44

Beatty WW. 1992. Gonadal hormones and sex differences in nonreproductive behaviors. See Gerall et al 1992, pp. 85–128

Bell AD, Variend S. 1985. Failure to demonstrate sexual dimorphism of the corpus callosum in childhood. *J. Anat.* 143:143–47

Bell AP, Weinberg MS. 1978. *Homosexualities.* New York: Simon & Schuster

Berenbaum SA, Hines M. 1992. Early androgens are related to childhood sex-typed toy preferences. *Psychol. Sci.* 3:203–6

Bieber I, Dain H, Dince PR, Drellich MG, Grand HG, et al. 1962. *Homosexuality: A Psychoanalytic Study.* New York: Basic Books. 472 pp.

Birren JE, Wall PD. 1956. Age changes in conduction velocity, refractory period, number of fibers, connective tissue space and blood vessels in sciatic nerve of rats. *J. Comp. Neurol.* 104:1–16

Breedlove SM. 1992a. Sexual differentiation of the brain and behavior. In *Behavioral Endocrinology,* ed. JB Becker, SM Breedlove, D Crews, pp. 39–68. Cambridge: MIT Press. 574 pp.

Breedlove SM. 1992b. Sexual dimorphism in the vertebrate nervous system. *J. Neurosci.* 12:4133–42

Breedlove SM, Arnold AP. 1981. Sexually dimorphic motor nucleus in the rat lumbar spinal cord: response to adult hormone manipulation, absence in androgen-insensitive rats. *Brain Res.* 225:297–305

Breedlove SM, Arnold AP. 1983. Hormonal control of a developing neuromuscular system. II. Sensitive periods for the androgen-induced masculinization of the rat spinal nucleus of the bulbocavernosus. *J. Neurosci.* 3:424–32

Buhrich N, Bailey JM, Martin NG. 1991. Sexual orientation, sexual identity, and sex-dimorphic behaviors in male twins. *Behav. Genet.* 21:75–96

Burr C. 1993. Homosexuality and biology. *Atlantic Mon.* 271:47–65

Byne W, Bleier R, Houston L. 1988. Variations in human corpus callosum do not predict gender: a study using magnetic resonance imaging. *Behav. Neurosci.* 102:222–27

Byne W, Parsons B. 1993. Human sexual orientation: the biologic theories reappraised. *Arch. Gen. Psychiatry* 50:228–39

Chi JG, Dooling EC, Gilles FH. 1977. Left-right asymmetries of the temporal speech areas of the human fetus. *Arch. Neurol.* 34:346–48

Cihak R, Gutmann E, Hanzlikova V. 1970. Involution and hormone-induced persistence of the muscle sphincter levator ani in female rats. *J. Anat.* 106:93–110

Clarke S, Kraftsik R, van der Loos H, Innocenti GM. 1989. Forms and measures of adult and developing human corpus callosum: Is there sexual dimorphism? *J. Comp. Neurol.* 280:213–30

Clemens LG, Gladue BA, Coniglio LP. 1978. Prenatal endogenous androgenic influences on masculine sexual behavior and genital morphology in male and female rats. *Horm. Behav.* 10:40–53

Commins D, Yahr P. 1984. Acetylcholinesterase activity in the sexually dimorphic area of the gerbil brain: sex differences and influence of adult gonadal steroids. *J. Comp. Neurol.* 224:123–31

Crichton-Browne J. 1880. On the weight of the brain and its component parts in the insane. *Brain* 2:42–67

DeJonge FH, Louwerse AL, Ooms MP, Evers P, Endert E, Van de Poll NE. 1989. Lesions of the SDN-POA inhibit sexual behavior of male Wistar rats. *Brain Res. Bull.* 23:483–92

Dekaban AS, Sadowsky D. 1978. Changes in brain weights during the span of human life: relation of brain weights to body heights and body weights. *Ann. Neurol.* 44:345–56

de Lacoste MC, Holloway RL, Woodward DJ. 1986. Sex differences in the fetal human corpus callosum. *Hum. Neurobiol.* 5:1–5

de Lacoste MC, Horvath DS, Woodward DJ. 1991. Possible sex differences in the developing human fetal brain. *J. Clin. Exp. Neuropsychol.* 13:831–46

de Lacoste-Utamsing MC, Holloway RL. 1982. Sexual dimorphism in the human corpus callosum. *Science* 216:1431–32

Denenberg VH, Cowell PE, Fitch RH, Kertesz A, Kenner GH. 1991. Corpus callosum: multiple parameter measurements in rodents and humans. *Physiol. Behav.* 49:433–37

de Vries GJ, De Bruin JPC, Uylings HBM, Corner MA. 1984. *Sex Differences in the Brain.* Amsterdam: Elsevier. 516 pp.

Dohler KD, Hancke JL, Srivastava SS, Hofmann C, Shryne JE, Gorski RA. 1984. Participation of estrogens in female sexual differentiation of the brain: neuroanatomical, neuroendocrine and behavioral evidence. *Prog. Brain Res.* 61:99–117

Dohler KD, Hines M, Coquelin A, Davis F, Shryne JE, Gorski RA. 1982. Pre- and post natal influence of diethylstilbestrol on differentiation of the sexually dimorphic nucleus in the preoptic area of the female rat brain. *Neurosci. Lett.* 4:361–65

Dorner G. 1985. Sex-specific gonadotrophin secretion, sexual orientation and gender role behaviour. *Exp. Clin. Endocrinol.* 86:1–6

Eckert ED, Bouchard TJ, Bohlen J, Heston LL. 1986. Homosexuality in monozygotic twins reared apart. *Br. J. Psychiatry* 148:421–25

Ehrhardt AA, Evers K, Money J. 1968. Influence of androgen and some aspects of sexually dimorphic behavior in women with the late-treated adrenogenital syndrome. *Johns Hopkins Med. J.* 123:115–22

Ehrhardt AA, Meyer-Bahlburg HFL, Rosen LR, Feldman JF, Veridiano NP, et al. 1985. Sexual orientation after prenatal exposure to exogenous estrogen. *Arch. Sex. Behav.* 14:57–77

Ellis L, Ames MA. 1987. Neurohormonal functioning and sexual orientation: a theory of homosexuality-heterosexuality. *Psychol. Bull.* 101:233–58

Elster AD, DiPersio DA, Moody DM. 1990. Sexual dimorphism of the human corpus callosum studied by magnetic resonance imaging: fact, fallacy and statistical confidence. *Brain Dev.* 12:321–25

Feingold A. 1988. Cognitive gender differences are disappearing. *Am. Psychol.* 432:95–103

Feingold A. 1992. Sex differences in variability in intellectual abilities: a new look at an old controversy. *Rev. Educ. Res.* 62:61–84

Fishman RB, Breedlove SM. 1992. Local perineal implants of anti-androgen block masculinization of the spinal nucleus of the bulbocavernosus. *Dev. Brain Res.* 70:283–86

Fishman RB, Chism L, Firestone GL, Breedlove SM. 1990. Evidence for androgen receptors in sexually dimorphic perineal muscles of neonatal male rats. Absence of androgen accumulation by the perineal motoneurons. *J. Neurobiol.* 21: 694–705

Forger NG, Breedlove SM. 1986. Sexual dimorphism in human and canine spinal cord: role of early androgen. *Proc. Natl. Acad. Sci. USA* 83:7527–31

Forger NG, Breedlove SM. 1987. Motoneuronal death during human fetal development. *J. Comp. Neurol.* 264:118–22

Forger NG, Hodges LL, Roberts SL, Breedlove SM. 1992. Regulation of motoneuron death in the spinal nucleus of the bulbocavernosus. *J. Neurobiol.* 23:1192–1203

Forger NG, Roberts SL, Wong V, Breedlove SM. 1993. Ciliary neurotrophic factor maintains motoneurons and their target muscles in developing rats. *J. Neurosci.* 13:In press

Gerall AA, Moltz H, Ward IL, eds. 1992. *Handbook of Behavioral Neurobiology: Sexual Differentiation.* New York: Plenum. 363 pp.

Goldfoot DA, Wallen K, Neff DA, McBriar MC, Goy RW. 1984. Social influences on the display of sexually dimorphic behavior in rhesus monkeys. *Arch. Sex. Behav.* 13:395–412

Gorski RA. 1988. Hormone-induced sex differences in hypothalamic structure. *Bull. TMIN* 16:67–90

Gorski RA, Gordon JH, Shryne JE, Southam AM. 1978. Evidence for a morphological sex difference within the medial preoptic area of the rat brain. *Brain Res.* 148:333–46

Gould SJ. 1981. *The Mismeasure of Man.* New York: Norton. 352 pp.

Goy RW. 1968. Organizing effects of androgen on the behaviour of rhesus monkeys. In *Endocrinology and Human Behavior,* ed. RP Michael, pp. 12–31. London: Oxford Univ. Press

Goy RW, Goldfoot DA. 1974. Experiential and hormonal factors influencing development of sexual behavior in the male rhesus monkey. In *Neurosciences Third Study Program,* ed. FO Schmitt, FG Worden, pp. 571–81. Cambridge: MIT Press. 1107 pp.

Goy RW, Wallen K. 1979. Experiential variables influencing play, foot-clasp mounting and adult sexual competence in male rhesus monkeys. *Psychoneuroendocrinology* 4:1–12

Green R. 1987. *The Sissy Boy Syndrome and the Development of Homosexuality.* New Haven: Yale Univ. Press. 416 pp.

Grisham W, Kerchner M, Ward IL. 1991. Prenatal stress alters sexually dimorphic nuclei in the spinal cord of male rats. *Brain Res.* 551:126–31

Hamer DH, Hu S, Magnuson VL, Hu N, Pattatucci AM. 1993. A linkage between DNA markers on the X chromosome and male sexual orientation. *Science* 261:321–27

Hendricks SE. 1969. Influence of neonatally administered hormones and early gonadectomy on rats' sexual behavior. *J. Comp. Physiol. Psychol.* 69:408–13

Hendricks SE. 1992. Role of estrogens and progestins in the development of female sexual behavior potential. See Gerall et al 1992, pp. 129–56

Hier DB, Crowley WF. 1982. Spatial ability in

androgen-deficient men. *N. Engl. J. Med.* 306:1202–5

Hines M. 1982. Prenatal gonadal hormones and sex differences in human behavior. *Psychol. Bull.* 92:56–80

Hines M, Davis F, Coquelin A, Goy RW, Gorski RA. 1985. Sexually dimorphic regions in the medial preoptic area and the bed nucleus of the stria terminalis of the guinea pig brain: a description and an investigation of their relationship to gonadal steroids in adulthood. *J. Neurosci.* 5:40–47

Hines M, Green R. 1991. Human hormonal and neural correlates of sex-typed behaviors. *Rev. Psychiatry* 10:536–55

Hofman MA, Swaab DF. 1989. The sexually dimorphic nucleus of the preoptic area in the human brain: a comparative morphometric study. *J. Anat.* 164:55–72

Imperato-McGinley J, Guerrero L, Gautier T, Peterson RE. 1974. Steroid 5 alpha-reductase deficiency in man: an inherited form of male pseudohermaphroditism. *Science* 186:1213–15

Imperato-McGinley J, Pichardo M, Gautier T, Voyer D, Bryden MP. 1991. Cognitive abilities in androgen-insensitive subjects: comparison with control males and females from the same kindred. *Clin. Endocrinol.* 34:341–47

Jacklin CN, Wilcox KT, Maccoby EE. 1988. Neonatal sex-steroid hormones and cognitive abilities at six years. *Dev. Psychobiol.* 21:567–74

Jacobson CD. 1980. *The characterization, ontogeny and influence of androgen on the sexually dimorphic nucleus of the preoptic area.* PhD thesis. Univ. Calif., Los Angeles. 191 pp.

Juraska J. 1990. The structure of the rat cerebral cortex: effects of gender and the environment. In *The Cerebral Cortex of the Rat,* ed. B Kolb, RC Tees, pp. 483–506. Cambridge, MA: MIT Press. 645 pp.

Juraska JM, Kopcik JR. 1988. Sex and environmental influences on the size and ultrastructure of the rat corpus callosum. *Brain Res.* 450:1–8

Kerns KA, Berenbaum SA. 1991. Sex differences in spatial ability in children. *Behav. Genet.* 21:383–96

Kinsey AC, Pomeroy WB, Martin CF. 1948. *Sexual Behavior in the Human Male.* Philadelphia: Saunders

Kopcik JR, Seymoure P, Schneider SK, Kim-Hong J, Juraska JM. 1992. Do callosal projection neurons reflect sex differences in axon number? *Brain Res. Bull.* 29:493–97

LeVay S. 1991. A difference in hypothalamic structure between heterosexual and homosexual men. *Science* 253:1034–37

LeVay S. 1993. *The Sexual Brain.* Cambridge: MIT Press. 168 pp.

Levy J, Heller W. 1992. Gender differences in human neuropsychological function. See Gerall et al 1992, pp. 245–73

Lillie FR. 1916. The theory of the freemartin. *Science* 43:611–13

Mack CM, Fitch RH, Cowell PE, Schrott LM, Denenberg VH. 1993. Ovarian estrogen acts to feminize the female rat's corpus callosum. *Dev. Brain Res.* 71:115–19

Manosevitz M. 1970. Early sexual behavior in adult homosexual and heterosexual males. *J. Abnorm. Psych.* 76:396–402

Masica DN, Money J, Ehrhardt AA, Lewis VG. 1969. IQ, fetal sex hormones and cognitive patterns: studies in the testicular feminizing syndrome of androgen insensitivity. *Johns Hopkins Med. J.* 124:34–43

McCormick CM, Witelson SF. 1991. A cognitive profile of homosexual men compared to heterosexual men and women. *Psychoneuroendocrinology* 16:459–73

McGlone J. 1980. Sex differences in human brain asymmetry: a critical survey. *Behav. Brain Sci.* 3:215–63

Meaney MJ, Stewart J. 1981. Neonatal androgens influence the social play of prepubescent male and female rats. *Horm. Behav.* 15:197–213

Meisel RL, Ward IL. 1981. Fetal female rats are masculinized by male littermates located caudally in the uterus. *Science* 213:239–42

Monaghan EP, Breedlove SM. 1992. The role of the bulbocavernosus in penile reflex behavior in rats. *Brain Res.* 587:178–80

Money J, Ehrhardt AA. 1972. *Man & Woman, Boy & Girl.* Baltimore: Johns Hopkins Univ. Press. 310 pp.

Money J, Schwartz M, Lewis VG. 1984. Adult herotosexual status and fetal hormonal masculinization and demasculinization: 46XX congenital virilizing adrenal hyperplasia and 46XY androgen insensitivity syndrome compared. *Psychoneuroendocrinology* 9:405–14

Moore CL. 1982. Maternal behavior of rats is affected by hormonal condition of pups. *J. Comp. Physiol. Psychol.* 69:403–7

Moore CL. 1984. Maternal contribution to the development of masculine sexual behavior in laboratory rats. *Dev. Psychobiol.* 17:347–56

Moore CL, Dou H, Juraska JM. 1992. Maternal stimulation affects the number of motoneurons in a sexually dimorphic nucleus of the lumbar spinal cord. *Brain Res.* 572:52–56

Morel F. 1948. La massa intermedia ou commissure grise. *Acta Anat. Basel.* 4:203–7

Moyer EK, Kaliszewski BF. 1958. The number of nerve fibers in motor spinal nerve roots of young, mature and aged cats. *Anat. Rec.* 131:681–99

Mullins RF, Levine S. 1968. Hormonal determinants during infancy of adult sexual behavior in the male rat. *Physiol. Behav.* 3:339–43

Naftolin F, MacLusky N. 1984. Aromatization hypothesis revisited. In *Differentiation: Basic and Clinical Aspects,* ed. M Serio. New York: Raven

Nass R, Baker S. 1991. Androgen effects on cognition: congenital adrenal hyperplasia. *Psychoneuroendocrinology* 16:189–201

Nordeen EJ, Nordeen KW, Sengelaub DR, Arnold AP. 1985. Androgens prevent normally occurring cell death in a sexually dimorphic spinal nucleus. *Science* 229:671–73

Nottebohm F, Arnold AP. 1976. Sexual dimorphism in vocal control areas of the songbird brain. *Science* 194:211–13

Olsen KL. 1992. Genetic influences on sexual behavior differentiation. See Gerall et al 1992, pp. 1–40

Pakkenberg H, Voigt J. 1964. Brain weight of the Danes. *Acta Anat.* 56:297–307

Paul SM, Purdy RH. 1992. Neuroactive steroids. *FASEB J.* 6:2311–22

Peters M. 1991. Sex differences in human brain size and the general meaning of differences in brain size. *Can. J. Psychol.* 45: 507–22

Pfaff DW. 1966. Morphological changes in the brains of adult male rats after neonatal castration. *J. Endocrinol.* 36:415–16

Pfaff DW. 1981. *Estrogens and Brain Function.* New York: Springer-Verlag. 281 pp.

Phoenix CH, Goy RW, Gerall AA, Young WC. 1959. Organizing action of prenatally administered testosterone propionate on the tissues mediating mating behavior in the female guinea pig. *Endocrinology* 65:369–82

Purves D. 1988. *Body and Brain: A Trophic Theory of Neural Connections.* Cambridge: Harvard Univ. Press. 231 pp.

Raisman G, Field PM. 1971. Sexual dimorphism in the preoptic area of the rat. *Science* 173:20–22

Rand MN, Breedlove SM. 1991. Androgen locally regulates rat bulbocavernosus and levator ani size. *J. Neurobiol.* 23:17–30

Reinisch JM, Sanders SA. 1992. Prenatal hormonal contributions to sex differences in human cognitive and personality development. See Gerall et al 1992, pp. 221–43

Resnick S, Berenbaum SA. 1982. Cognitive functioning in individuals with congenital adrenal hyperplasia. *Behav. Genet.* 12: 594–95

Resnick SM, Berenbaum SA, Gottesman II, Bouchard TJ. 1986. Early hormonal influences on cognitive functioning in congenital adrenal hyperplasia. *Dev. Psychol.* 22: 191–98

Reyes FI, Boroditsky RS, Winter JSD, Faiman C. 1974. Studies on human sexual development. II: Fetal and maternal serum gonadotropin and sex steroid concentrations. *J. Clin. Endocrinol. Metab.* 38:612–17

Schumacher M. 1990. Rapid membrane effects of steroid hormones: an emerging concept in neuroendocrinology. *Trends Neurosci.* 13:359–62

Sperry RW. 1977. Forebrain commissurotomy and conscious awareness. *J. Med. Philos.* 2:101–26

Swaab DF, Fliers E. 1985. A sexually dimorphic nucleus in the human brain. *Science* 228:1112–15

Swaab DF, Gooren LJG, Hofman MA. 1992. The human hypothalamus in relation to gender and sexual orientation. *Prog. Brain Res.* 93:205–19

Swaab DF, Hofman MA. 1984. Sexual differentiation of the human brain. A historical perspective. *Prog. Brain Res.* 61:361–74

Swaab DF, Hofman MA. 1988. Sexual differentiation of the human hypothalamus: ontogeny of the sexually dimorphic nucleus of the preoptic area. *Dev. Brain Res.* 44: 314–18

Swaab DF, Hofman MA. 1990. An enlarged suprachiasmatic nucleus in homosexual men. *Brain Res.* 537:141–48

Thor DH, Holloway WR. 1986. Social play in juvenile rats: a decade of methodological and experimental research. *Neurosci. Biobehav. Rev.* 8:455–64

Tobet SA, Fox TO. 1992. Sex differences in neuronal morphology influenced hormonally throughout life. See Gerall et al 1992, pp. 41–84

Tobet SA, Zahniser DJ, Baum MJ. 1986. Differentiation in male ferrets of a sexually dimorphic nucleus of the preoptic/anterior hypothalamic area requires prenatal estrogen. *Neuroendocrinology* 44:299–308

Toran-Allerand CD. 1981. Gonadal steroids and brain development. In vitro veritas? *Trends Neurosci.* 7:118–21

Tuller D. 1991. Gays divided over brain study. *San Francisco Chronicle* Sept. 7, p. 1

vom Saal FS. 1989. Sexual differentiation in litter-bearing mammals: influence of sex of adjacent fetuses in utero. *J. Anim. Sci.* 67: 1824–40

Voyer DB. 1990. Gender, level of spatial ability, and lateralization of mental rotation. *Brain Cogn.* 13:18–29

Wada JA, Clarke RA, Hamm A. 1975. Cerebral hemisphere asymmetry in humans. Cortical speech zones in 100 adult and 100 infant brains. *Arch. Neurol.* 32:239

Ward IL. 1992. Sexual behavior: the products of perinatal hormonal and prepubertal social factors. See Gerall et al 1992, pp. 157–79

Ward OB, Monaghan EP, Ward IL. 1986. Naltrexone blocks the effects of prenatal stress on sexual behavior differentiation in male rats. *Pharmacol. Biochem. Behav.* 25:573–76

Weber G, Weis S. 1986. Morphometric analysis of the human corpus callosum fails to reveal sex-related differences. *J. Hirnforsch.* 27:237–40

Whalen RE, Nadler RD. 1963. Suppression of the development of female mating behavior by estradiol administration in infancy. *Science* 141:273–74

Whitam FL, Zent M. 1984. A cross-cultural assessment of early cross-gender behavior and familial factors in male homosexuality. *Arch. Sex. Behav.* 13:427–39

Wilson JD, George FW, Griffin JE. 1981. The hormonal control of sexual development. *Science* 211:1278–84

Witelson SF. 1985. The brain connection: the corpus callosum is larger in left-handers. *Science* 229:665–68

Witelson SF. 1989. Hand and sex differences in the isthmus and genu of the human corpus callosum. *Brain* 112:799–835

Yoshii F, Barker W, Apicella A, Chang J, Sheldon J, Duara A. 1986. Measurements of the corpus callosum on magnetic resonance scans: effects of age sex, handedness and disease. *Neurology* 36(Suppl. 1):133

Annu. Rev. Psychol. 1994. 45:419–49

CHEMICAL SENSES

Linda M. Bartoshuk

Department of Surgery, Section of Otolaryngology, Yale University School of Medicine, New Haven, Connecticut 06520-8041

Gary K. Beauchamp

Monell Chemical Senses Center, 3500 Market Street, Philadelphia, Pennsylvania 19104-3308

KEY WORDS: taste, smell, development, genetics, clinical disorders

---

CONTENTS

INTRODUCTION

Thirty years ago, Lord Adrian gave the opening address at the first International Symposium on Olfaction and Taste (Adrian 1963). In that address he noted that the chemical senses concern "fundamental problems where physiology and psychology meet." Adrian, a pioneer in electrophysiological recordings, was one of the first scientists to gain direct access to the neural mechanisms mediating taste and smell. Recently, major new work has come from two sources. The tools of molecular biology applied to the olfactory and gustatory membranes have begun to provide a detailed picture of interactions between stimulus and receptor and new emphasis on clinical disorders of taste and smell have both helped patients and provided experiments of nature. This review provides an overview of recent results from these two areas and examines the current status of selected problems related to the chemical senses.

INITIAL EVENTS IN OLFACTION AND TASTE

Early Events in Olfaction

Although it has been believed for generations that humans (and other animals) can distinguish and identify a large number of odors, the molecular basis for this presumed ability has until recently been a mystery. It was possible that odor recognition, like color vision, was mediated by a small number of receptors that, depending on the proportion stimulated by a given odorant, resulted in a unique odor sensation analogous to a unique color. More likely was the hypothesis that the system was analogous to the immune system where many receptors are each uniquely responsive to particular chemical structures.

With Buck & Axel's (1991) recent report, it appears that the latter hypothesis is most likely correct. These investigators have identified a family of genes that apparently code for a large number of receptor proteins (hundreds or perhaps thousands) that are located on the membranes of the cilia of olfactory neurons. These receptor proteins are chemically and structurally similar to those that bind neurotransmitters and hormones. They can be divided into subfamilies that may code for perceptually similar odors although this remains to be proved. If this turns out to be true, a rational basis for classifying odors will be available and it will be interesting to see whether it conforms to perceptual similarity and/or to any of the available ad hoc classifying schemes (Cain 1978, Lawless et al 1991).

Following interaction with the receptor, the next step in translating or transducing the chemical energy of an odor into an electrical signal in the brain involves changes in ion fluxes within the receptor cell. Recent studies (see Lancet 1992) have demonstrated that odorants stimulate a cascade of biochemical events within the cell, a cascade that serves both (*a*) to amplify the signal (i.e. activation of a small number of receptor cells can cause a much larger recruitment of chemical changes within the cell) and (*b*) to permit ion flow that ultimately triggers an action potential that carries information to the olfactory bulbs and thence to other portions of the brain.

It is now believed that two different internal signaling systems are involved in olfaction, one using adenosine 3′5′-monophosphate (cAMP) as the internal or second messenger and the other using inositol-1,4,5-trisphosphate (IP_3) and diacylglycerol (DAG) as the second messengers (Miyamoto et al 1991, Nakamura & Gold 1987). Interestingly, an odor seems to involve one or another but not both of these internal systems and the IP_3/DAG system appears in some studies to be stimulated by putrid or otherwise unpleasant odors (to humans) (Breer & Boekhoff 1991). Because these systems could theoretically be altered independently, some clinical complaints about generalized response to bad odors could be a result of modification of one or the other of these cellular messenger systems.

Finally, other events associated with receptor cells could be important in the early events in olfaction. Special odorant binding proteins that have been identified may transport odorants to, or remove them from, receptors (e.g. Pevsner et al 1989). Also, powerful degradative enzymes have been found in the olfactory epithelium. These enzymes may act to detoxify volatile compounds, thus protecting the organism, while at the same time altering the chemical signal.

Early Events in Taste

Consistent with the physiological and psychological evidence that there are basic classes of taste (e.g. salty, sour, sweet, bitter, and perhaps a few others), there appear to be separate and unique receptor/transductive systems for each taste quality. Although much progress has been made in identifying the critical elements in each system, there are still large gaps in our understanding (see Kinnamon 1988).

SALT TASTE In contrast with the olfactory system, where proteinaceous molecular receptors detect odorants, there appears to be no specific receptor for salt (NaCl), which, with the exception of LiCl, provides the only pure salty taste. Instead, specific ion channels in taste cells that allow only Na and Li to pass into the cell itself appear to be responsible for changing the internal electrical state within the cell resulting in secretion of neurotransmitter.

Nonchloride sodium salts do not taste as primarily salty as do NaCl or LiCl because of differing effects of the anion and ionic movements through tight junctions between cells (Ye et al 1991). However, the mechanism of saltiness stimulation by non-sodium salts (e.g. KCl) remains elusive. There may be two separate elements in the detection of saltiness: one specific, responsive only to

Na and Li, and blocked by the specific sodium channel blocker amiloride; and one less specific. As noted below, these two systems may mature at different ages in human infants.

The specificity of this mechanism for detecting Na may account for the difficulty in identifying non-sodium containing salt substitutes. Although there are many chemically different compounds that elicit the sensation of sweetness (see below), and a variety of intensely sweet substitutes for sugars, no pure salt substitute has been identified. Yet, with the increased understanding of the mechanism of salt taste stimulation, it may become possible to develop salt enhancers by learning how to either create additional sodium channels in the taste cells or keep the channels open longer.

SOUR TASTE Like salt taste transduction, sour taste stimuli (acids) probably alter ion channels on the apical end of the taste cell (Kinnamon 1988). Most likely, the hydrogen ion has the major responsibility for altering channel activity, which, in turn, results in ion fluxes within the taste cell that cause release of neurotransmitter. For strong acids (e.g. HCl, H_2SO_4), sourness can be explained completely by the concentration (pH) of the cation; the anion plays no apparent role (P. A. S. Breslin & G. K. Beauchamp, unpublished information). For weak acids (e.g. citric), the anion does influence the taste but the mechanisms for this influence are poorly understood.

SWEET TASTE Because so many apparently chemically disparate substances taste sweet, it has been debated whether there is a single sweet receptor or whether sweetness is actually mediated by multiple types of receptors (see Birch 1987, DuBois et al 1993). This issue has yet to be resolved and probably will not be until the actual receptor(s) is (are) identified. Many investigators expect this event to occur fairly soon since substantial progress has been made with presumably similar receptors for amino acids in aquatic organisms (Caprio et al 1993).

It is now generally assumed that the sweet receptor is a classical proteinaceous molecule analogous to the olfactory receptors. Following the interaction between the ligand (the sweet molecule) and the receptor, there is now evidence that, as in olfaction, there is a cascade of internal cellular events involving cAMP that serves to amplify the signal and eventually to change the ionic status of the taste cell such that neurotransmitter is released across the synapse with the associated taste nerve cell causing it to fire (Naim 1993). Regardless of whether there is one or a family of sweet receptors, this transduction process may be a final common element in the recognition of sweet stimuli.

Although many molecules elicit the sensation of sweetness, there may be differences in their sensory qualities. For example, many of the intense sweeteners (e.g. aspartame, proteins such as thaumatin and monellin) have off-tastes and lingering tastes. Whether this is because they stimulate other receptors and bind more strongly to the sweet receptor is not known. Saccharin is well known to have, to some individuals, both a sweet and bitter component; the ability to detect the latter aspect appears to be related to the genetic ability to taste PTC/PROP (Bartoshuk 1979).

One recent study (Breslin et al 1992) shows that sophisticated psychophysical approaches to taste sensation can provide important data that biophysical studies may illuminate. Borrowing techniques from studies of color matching, it has been found that if one chooses the concentration appropriately, well-trained tasters cannot discriminate glucose from sucrose or glucose from fructose. This indicates that at some point, probably at the receptor, the structures mediating the sensation of these three sweet sugars are identical. Interestingly, at moderate concentrations, another simple sugar, maltose, can be discriminated from glucose regardless of the glucose concentration, indicating that maltose must stimulate a receptor other than, or in addition to, that stimulated by glucose. It will be interesting to see, when the receptor for glucose is identified, if it is identical to that for sucrose and fructose, while maltose binds to other receptors.

BITTER TASTE Bitter sensations are evoked by even more different kinds of molecules than are sweet sensations. There is substantial psychophysical evidence (see McBurney et al 1972), supported by animal model studies (see Lush 1991), that more than one receptor mediates bitterness, although, as for sweetness, no receptor has been definitively identified. Again, following interaction with the presumed proteinaceous receptor (although some bitter compounds could go directly into the cell bypassing traditional receptors), a cascade of intracellular changes involving IP_3 leads ultimately to the release of neurotransmitters.

ODORS AND REPRODUCTION

Chemical signals, often called pheromones, play a central role in regulating sexual and social behavior and endocrine function in many species (see Doty & Muller-Schwarze 1992). These chemicals often are found in urine and/or glandular secretions; however, remarkably few have been chemically identified.

At least two anatomically separate sensory systems are responsible for processing the chemical information. First, there is the main olfactory system with which humans detect and discriminate among odorous chemicals. Second, in many species of vertebrates, an accessory olfactory system is involved in detecting many of the chemical signals mediating changes in sexual behavior and physiology.

The Accessory Olfactory System

This chemosensory system is made up of the paired vomeronasal organs (VNO), and the vomeronasal nerves that synapse in an accessory olfactory bulb, anatomically distinct from the main olfactory bulb. From there, information is transmitted to areas of the brain involved in control of reproductive behavior and physiology (Wysocki 1979, Wysocki & Meredith 1987). Based on this anatomical arrangement, it was predicted many years ago (see Wysocki 1979) that the accessory olfactory system (AOS) would be involved in many of the most dramatic effects of pheromones on animals. For example, chemical signals can influence estrus cycles, regulate the age at reproductive maturation, prevent implantation of fertilized embryos, and signal receptivity of females for mating in a variety of species such as mice, rats, cattle, and pigs (Wysocki & Meredith 1987). Proof that the AOS is involved in many of these reproductive effects comes from studies of animals in which the AOS is damaged or removed. Generally, although the animals' other behavior is normal, their behavioral or physiological responses to pheromones are eliminated. Disruption of the main olfactory system, in contrast, often has little or no effect on these responses. Thus, it appears that for many species, the AOS is the sole or major pathway for pheromonal effects.

Human Chemical Communication

There has been considerable speculation about whether human body odors serve in a communication system analogous or homologous to that of the other mammals. In other words, is there such a thing as a human pheromone? As a possible example of this, it has been found that women who live together tend to become synchronous in their menstrual cycles (McClintock 1971). Preliminary evidence supports the view that this effect is the result of chemical signals transmitted between the women (Preti et al 1986, Russell et al 1980).

The assumption that adult humans lack a functional VNO (Johnson et al 1985, Wysocki 1979) has confounded the idea that chemical signals can play a role in human physiology and behavior analogous to the role played in other animals. However, in several recent studies, it has been demonstrated that humans do possess a VNO, which appears to have nerve-like cells (see Takami et al 1993 and references therein). Several questions remain: Is this organ functional? What are its connections to the central nervous system (CNS)? And what role does it play in processing chemosensory information? Based on its anatomical connections in other mammals, it seems likely that the sensation of chemicals detected by VNO receptors may not be conscious.

DEVELOPMENT OF SENSITIVITY AND AFFECT

Progress has been made in understanding the early development of the senses of smell and taste in humans and other animals. This research was recently reviewed in detail elsewhere (Beauchamp et al 1991b). We now provide an overview of work on human development.

Early Development of Human Olfaction

OLFACTION IN UTERO Like the sense of taste, there is morphological evidence for the existence of functional olfactory as well as vomeronasal and trigeminal structures by at least the twelfth week of gestation (see Beauchamp et al 1991b for a review). Some evidence suggests that at least one of these three chemosensory systems is active in premature infants 28 weeks postconception or older. However, in the absence of careful choice of odorants, it is difficult to determine whether the responses elicited (initiation of sucking or arousal in sleeping infants) are owing to the volatile chemical's odor or to its irritating (trigeminal) qualities.

Animal studies have demonstrated that in utero exposure to odorants can markedly affect postnatal reactions to odor (e.g. Hepper 1987). It is known that flavors of foods mothers consume can be transmitted to the amniotic fluid (Hauser et al 1985). Thus, the infant could first begin to learn about the mothers' diet, her olfactory identity, and so on while still in utero.

NEWBORN INFANTS A number of early studies demonstrated that very young infants are responsive to volatile chemicals and can discriminate among them. Response measures used have included withdrawal, heart rate, and respiratory changes (see Beauchamp et al 1991b for a review). Again, many of these studies have failed to separate olfactory from trigeminal responses.

More recent studies have focused on potentially biologically relevant odors collected mainly from mothers. For example, newborn infants respond with a suppression of general motoric activity when presented with the odor of their mother's breast or neck relative to activity levels in the presence of comparable odors from another lactating female or a no-odor control (e.g. MacFarlane 1975, Schaal 1986). This work suggests exceptional olfactory acuity in the newborn since such discriminations are difficult for adults, if not altogether impossible.

What underlies the newborn's ability to discriminate her mother's odor from the odor of another lactating female? Both early experience and a genetically determined preference for the breast odor of a lactating female may contribute to this ability. The role of experience is suggested by several findings. First, bottle-fed infants do not make similar discriminations (Cernoch & Porter 1985). Since they may lack the intimate contact with the mother that occurs with breast-feeding, this is consistent with a role for experience. Second, these same investigators reported that breast-feeding infants do not discriminate the axillary odors of their own father from those of another father. Third, at seven days breast-fed newborns will turn toward a perfume that has been worn on the mother's breast during feedings in preference to perfumes worn by other mothers (Schleidt & Genzel 1990). Finally, Balogh & Porter (1986) demonstrated that, after 20–24 hours of exposure to an artificial odor (wild cherry or ginger) in the ambient air, female newborns (but not males) less than 2.5 days turned their heads in the direction of that odorant (presented on a gauze pad) as opposed to an equally pleasant (to adults) but unfamiliar odorant.

An innate component mediating neonate ability to discriminate maternal odors has also been suggested (Makin & Porter 1989). Bottle-fed female neonates (2 weeks old) with no prior breast-feeding experience orient toward the breast odor of an unfamiliar lactating female when paired with (*a*) the breast odor of a nonlactating female or a no-odor control; or (*b*) the axillary odor of the same lactating female. These experiments suggest that some unique component of the breast odor such as milk or sebum, and not intensity differences, mediates this effect since infants did not orient selectively toward the more intense of two other stimuli: the odor of a lactating female's axillary odor versus a no-odor control. It is also possible, however, that human milk and formula share volatile components and that babies in this study are orienting toward familiar odor components that have been consistently associated with feeding. Moreover, as alluded to above, the infant may have learned in utero to identify and prefer compounds in this odor. Thus, the evidence for innate preference for odors remains tenuous.

In contrast to the sense of taste, it has been suggested that the most salient characteristic of an odor—its pleasantness or unpleasantness—is learned and that there are no innately pleasant or unpleasant odors (Engen 1982). As indicated above, learning appears to occur very early, perhaps in utero and certainly within the first few days of birth. One context in which odor learning may be very common is during breast-feeding. Not only is the infant exposed to body odors of the mother, but it is also exposed to a rich variety of odors that are transmitted from the food a mother eats to her breast milk and thence to the infant. Thus, like the milk of other mammals, human milk can acquire a variety of odors from the mother's diet. That the breast-feeding infant detects these sensory changes in mother's milk is suggested by the finding that the infant's sucking behavior is altered while the milk is flavored. For example, the infants feed longer and suck more overall when the mother's milk is flavored with garlic (Mennella & Beauchamp 1991a). The mouth movements made during suckling may facilitate the retronasal perception of the garlic volatiles in milk.

Alcohol consumption by the nursing mother also alters the flavor of her milk and the behavior of the infant during breast-feeding (Mennella & Beauchamp 1991b). Unlike the response to garlic-flavored milk, infants did not feed longer when the milk was flavored with alcohol. However, they consumed significantly less alcohol-flavored milk even though they sucked more during the initial minute of the feeds. Whether the infants were responding to the altered milk flavor or whether the alcohol was having pharmacological effects on the nursing mothers is the subject of present investigations.

The finding that the odor of human milk can be altered via transmitted odors might imply that the sensory world of the breast-fed infant is very rich, varied, and quite different from that of the bottle-fed infant. Bottle-fed infants, who experience a constant set of flavors from standard formulas, may be missing significant sensory experiences, which, until recent time in human history, were common to all infants.

One presumes that the evolution of the flavor learning process developed through breast-feeding. Although much research will be required to fully understand the effects of exposure to flavors in mother's milk on the infant's behavior, it is clear that human milk is not a food of invariant flavors. Rather, it provides the potential for a rich source of varying chemosensory experiences to the infant. Based on a variety of animal model studies, the infant's prior exposure to flavors in mother's milk may actually increase the desirability of those flavors through familiarization. Unfamiliar foods, which are often not preferred by children, become preferred as a function of repeated presentation and increased familiarity (Birch 1979). Studies on other animals (e.g. Capretta et al 1975) also suggest that the experience with a variety of flavors during breast-feeding, in contrast to the invariant flavor experienced during formula feeding, predisposes the infants toward an increased willingness to accept novel flavors. And indeed, a recent study reported that breast-fed infants consumed more of a novel vegetable than did formula-fed infants (Sullivan 1992).

Early Development of Human Taste

TASTE IN UTERO Although there is morphological evidence for a functional taste system in utero (Bossey 1980), unambiguous evidence that it is functional in humans is lacking. However, premature infants have been shown to be responsive to sucrose and glucose, discriminating these sugars from water and responding preferentially (e.g. sucking more) to these relative to water (Maone et al 1990, Tatzer et al 1985).

SWEET TASTE There have been several studies of taste in newborn infants. Newborn infants are highly responsive to sweet sugars as determined by a wide range of behavioral measures such as sucking responses, facial expressions, volume of solution consumed, and heart rate (Beauchamp et al 1991b). Thus, the ability to detect sweet sugars seems evident very early in human development and its hedonic tone—that is, its pleasantness—is also well developed at birth. The liking for sweet substances is probably innate in humans and in most herbivores and omnivores, possibly as a consequence of selection favoring animals that consume diets rich in calories (ripe fruits, vegetables) and perhaps associated vitamins and minerals.

Although a liking for sweet substances appears innate, an interacting role for experience in development remains a possibility. However, there is no evidence in humans that variation in early exposure to sweet substances permanently alters preference for sweet tasting substances (see Beauchamp et al 1991b).

BITTER TASTE Newborn infants respond to highly concentrated quinine solutions with facial expressions indicative of distaste or rejection (Rosenstein & Oster 1988, Steiner 1973). However, for at least one bitter compound, urea, there appears to be an early maturational change in response; sensitivity may develop during the first few months of age (Kajiura et al 1992). Because there may be several separate but perhaps overlapping bitter transduction mechanisms, it is possible that they develop at different rates. This needs to be investigated. Nonetheless, it appears that bitter substances are rejected by infants and young children and again there is no evidence that prior experience plays a role in mediating the hedonic response to this taste quality. It has been speculated that innate rejection of bitter substances may reflect the fact that many bitter compounds are toxic. Individuals do come to tolerate and perhaps even like bitter foods and beverages but this is probably the result of learning.

SOUR TASTE The few studies with acids that have been conducted with newborn infants suggest that sour-tasting substances are unpleasant (Desor et al 1973, Rosenstein & Oster 1988, Steiner 1973). In the absence of longitudinal or even cross-sectional studies across an early age range, it is unknown whether there are developmental changes in sensitivity or preference for sour-tasting compounds.

SALTY TASTE The newborn's response to salt is more puzzling. Studies using measures of facial expression and intake relative to water or low concentration sucrose diluents indicate indifference to salt (Desor et al 1973, Rosenstein & Oster 1988). However, when sucking responses have been evaluated, investigators report that salt elicits less sucking than does water, suggesting that salt is unpleasant (Crook 1978). No study demonstrates a preference or liking for salt in the newborn. In light of these ambiguous data and the evidence for a postnatal maturation of salt sensitivity in other species (review: Hill & Mistretta 1990), it seems likely that newborns are relatively insensitive to the saltiness of NaCl. At birth, sodium-specific taste cells may be undeveloped and responsiveness to NaCl at this age may be owing to its stimulation of nonspecific receptors (e.g. those also sensitive to KCl), which could account for its being rejected when sucking measures are taken.

During the first few months of life, responsiveness to NaCl changes dramatically. After 4 months of age, infants prefer salt solutions to water (Beauchamp et al 1986, Cowart & Beauchamp 1986). It has been argued (Beauchamp et al 1991a) that experience with salty tastes probably does not play a major role in the shift from apparent indifference to salt at birth to acceptance in later infancy; rather, this change in response may reflect postnatal maturation of central and/or peripheral mechanisms underlying salt taste perception, allowing for the expression of a largely unlearned preference for saltiness. However, there is some evidence that, at least by 6 months of age, frequency of dietary exposure to high-sodium foods (though not total dietary sodium) may affect the degree of preference for salted versus unsalted cereal.

A number of animal model studies suggest that early depletion of Na, either in utero or during the first few days of life (see Beauchamp et al 1991b for a review) leads to substantial changes in salt sensitivity and preference. It is important to determine whether such phenomena exist in humans; clinical and anecdotal evidence suggests that early profound salt depletion may result in enhanced salt appetite in childhood and adulthood (Beauchamp et al 1991a). Whether some of the individual differences in salt preference and intake seen in children and adults could reflect differential exposure in utero or in infancy remains to be determined.

OTHER TASTES Taste responses to amino acids have been examined in very few studies. In particular, the taste of glutamate (called *umami* taste by Japanese investigators) has been reported to elicit positive facial expressions and to increase solution intake in newborn and young infants but only when the glutamate is present in the context of a low-glutamate soup (Steiner 1987). Monosodium glutamate alone in water does not appear to be hedonically positive either to infants (Beauchamp & Pearson 1991) or to adults (Yamaguchi & Takashai 1984). Thus, if this substance has its sensory effects through unique taste receptors, it is unusual in requiring associated chemosensory stimulation in order for it to be judged as pleasant.

SUMMARY Sensitivity to and preference for various taste modalities develop at different stages during ontogeny. This is further evidence for the independence and specificity of these qualities. Moreover, most of the evidence supports the generalization that the hedonic quality or the pleasantness of a tastant is largely innate. Experience may serve to modulate the inherent pleasantness or unpleasantness of tastes but this sensory system is largely hard-wired, which is not surprising since it is among the last decision points for accepting nutrients likely to be valuable and rejecting substances likely to be damaging.

Infant Olfaction and Taste: Comparison

Although both taste and olfaction are chemosensory systems that play important roles in infant behavior, they are different in several important ways.

Taste appears to be organized into a relatively small number of primary or basic qualities that have been postulated to have been selected because of the central importance of the stimuli that elicit them (sugars, salts, amino acids, toxic compounds) in the acceptance, rejection and utilization of food (Ikeda 1909, McBurney & Gent 1979).

In contrast, olfaction may have multiple functions (e.g. detection and recognition of food, environmental substances, other individuals) and certainly does not have any agreed-upon set of qualities. Indeed, as discussed above, there may be hundreds (or more) of specific receptors, each responsive to different chemical compounds and each capable of mediating the experience of a unique odor.

Associated with this perceptual complexity is the apparently greater importance of individual experience in determining the hedonic valence or pleasantness of odors. There is no unequivocal evidence that any odor is innately pleasant or unpleasant as there is for taste—for example, sweet and bitter. Yet, an absence of evidence does not constitute a strong argument. Recently, it has been demonstrated that when age-appropriate methods are employed, adult-like odor preferences and aversions are evident in children as young as 3 years old (Schmidt & Beauchamp 1988), significantly earlier than previously reported (Engen 1982). Additional work on very young infants is indicated. However, based on the evidence reviewed here and elsewhere in detail (Beauchamp et al 1991b), it appears that experience is more likely to modify the hedonic quality of odors than it is of tastes (see Bartoshuk 1990).

GENETICS OF OLFACTION AND TASTE

Olfaction

GENERAL SENSITIVITY Although anosmia (total inability to smell) is often the result of various pathological factors (see below), genetic differences may also result in anosmia in some individuals. The best known instance of this is Kallman's syndrome, a genetically-determined set of abnormalities that includes failure of normal reproductive organ development, and anosmia owing to the developmental failure of CNS olfactory structures. The molecular genetics of this disease have recently been clarified (Franco et al 1991).

There are individual differences in the ability to smell a wide range of compounds although some recent studies suggest that much of what were thought to be differences between people may instead reflect within subject variation. That is, the sensitivity of a given individual to an odor may vary substantially, often for unknown reasons, so that unless many tests are conducted, stable estimates of sensitivity are often not obtained.

Twin studies are powerful tools in initial investigations of the role of genes in modulating general sensitivity to odors. One study found no support for the view that genes play a role in determining individual differences in sensitivity to odor (Hubert et al 1981); the degree of similarity of identical and fraternal twin pairs was not different. However, as noted above, large individual variance may have obscured a genetic effect. More recently, using twin study methodology, a genetic influence on the ability to identify odors has been reported (Segal et al 1992). In the absence of evidence that this is specific to olfaction (rather than a genetic influence on ability to identify sensations in general) the relevance of this observation to the genetics of olfaction is unclear.

SPECIFIC ANOSMIA Specific anosmia (or often better called specific hyposmia) is defined as the inability of an individual, who has otherwise normal olfactory ability, to smell a specific molecule or related class of molecules. Several specific anosmias have been tentatively identified (see Amoore 1977). It has been suggested that specific anosmias are the consequence of a failure to develop specific receptor proteins because of a genetic change. This remains hypothetical, however, and it is possible that the locus of the defect is beyond the receptor level (but see below). Furthermore, it has been suggested that the number and kinds of specific anosmias may be used to predict the number of different receptor types in olfaction (Amoore 1977); recent progress in molecular genetics of olfaction (see above) will eventually allow a test of this prediction.

Probably the most thoroughly studied example of specific anosmias involves the molecule androstenone. The odor of androstenone is described variously as urinous, sweaty, musky, like sandalwood, or having no smell. Studies have shown that many otherwise normal adults cannot detect this odor at vapor saturation, while others are exquisitely sensitive to it. It is estimated that about 50% of individuals are anosmic to it (Labows & Wysocki 1984). Not only is there vast variation in threshold levels, but different individuals appear to experience the odor as having different qualities.

A twin study was conducted to evaluate the possibility that individual differences in perception of androstenone might be the result of genetic differences between individuals (Wysocki & Beauchamp 1984). The results were straightforward: identical twin pairs were more similar in androstenone sensitivity than were fraternal twin pairs. Specifically, 100% of the identical twin pairs were concordant, that is both either sensitive or insensitive to the smell of androstenone. Only 61% of the fraternal twins were concordant. Although this initial study seemed to suggest a rather simple and elegant model system, other genetic studies indicate a complex mode of inheritance (Pollack et al 1982, Wysocki & Beauchamp 1991).

The issue is even more complex, however. A number of studies (see Beauchamp et al 1991b) indicate that there is a developmental shift in sensitivity to androstenone. Apparently, almost all young children can smell it; at near adolescence the ability to smell this odor seems to disappear in about 50% of individuals. The mechanisms underlying the loss of sensitivity are obscure.

Even more remarkable than the developmental shift in sensitivity is the observation that simple exposure to the odor can induce sensitivity in about 50% of insensitive adults (Wysocki et al 1989). What is altered in individuals who develop a sensitivity to the odor? One hypothesis, presuming a peripheral locus of effect, is that among some individuals who are insensitive to androstenone, receptors do exist and extended exposure induces clonal expansion or selection of such receptors in a manner analogous with immune response to antigen. The consequent change in the receptor number or type would thus raise the odorant stimulation to the level of conscious perception. While this is an attractive idea, the human data cannot exclude more central changes following exposure, for example, in the olfactory bulb or elsewhere in the CNS. Recent animal model studies support the hypothesis of a peripheral effect (Wang et al 1993). These studies have shown that when mice from an inbred (genetically identical) strain that is relatively insensitive to androstenone are exposed to that odor, sensitivity is increased, as measured by summated neural recordings from the olfactory epithelium. This indicates that the effects of exposure in this animal model are on the peripheral structures, most likely the receptors. Moreover, enhanced sensitivity was also observed with another odor suggesting that odor exposure in general may increase sensitivity in individual organisms that are initially relatively insensitive to the odor.

GENETICS OF INDIVIDUAL ODOR Not only is an organism's ability to smell influenced by genes, but its body odor also reflects its genetic constitution. There are well-known disease states that result in abnormal metabolism of various compounds and hence production of stereotypical, diagnostic odorous compounds in urine and elsewhere. An interesting example of this is the condition termed trimethylaminurea, where a presumed genetic flaw results in the functional failure of the enzyme responsible for converting trimethylamine to trimethylamine oxide, which is odorless. As a consequence, individuals afflicted with this problem produce a distinctive unpleasant body odor that has a fishy quality (Al-Waiz et al 1987, Leopold et al 1990).

More generally, a recent series of studies with mice (see Beauchamp et al 1985, Boyse et al 1987 for reviews) and rats (Singh et al 1987), and preliminary work with humans (Ferstl et al 1992), suggest that individuality of normal body odor is influenced by the same set of genes, the Major Histocompatibility Complex (MHC), that is intimately involved in regulating immune function and is responsible for self, non-self recognition within the body. This set of genes, numbering 50 or more, is found in virtually every vertebrate tested. Among other things, these genes code for cell-surface proteins that are critical in allowing the immune system to survey cells for invading microorganisms such as viruses (e.g. Klein 1986). Differences in individual genes in this complex cause differences in urine odors in mice and rats and perhaps humans. Since this set of genes is the most variable of any known—many of the genes have 20 or more alleles or variants maintained in the population—each individual mouse or man, with the exception of identical twins, is uniquely coded by its MHC repertoire, although closely related individuals are more similar than distantly related ones. Hence, these genes also apparently produce an olfactory fingerprint that may be responsible, at least in part, for such feats as the ability of dogs to track humans.

Among the more remarkable recent findings in this area has been the discovery that mice tend to select mates with a different MHC repertoire than themselves, their parents, or probably other closely related individuals. This may assist in the maintenance of genetic diversity in these loci (Potts et al 1991, Yamazaki et al 1988, Yamazaki et al 1976). Such genetic diversity presumably is valuable in withstanding bacterial and viral diseases (Klein 1986). Also, it has been shown recently that the unique olfactory identity of the fetus begins to be expressed approximately halfway through gestation and that the pregnant female mouse smells like a combination of her fetus and herself. The function of this, if any, and whether this is also the case for humans, is unknown.

Taste

TOTAL AGEUSIA Familial dysautonomia is a genetically-determined disorder that is characterized by the absence of overflow tears, reduced reflexes, reduced sensitivity to temperature and pain, and the absence of fungiform and circumvallate papillae and taste buds (Axelrod et al 1974, Henkin 1965, Henkin 1967). For individuals with this disorder, taste is completely absent. Henkin reported that injections of methacholine restored the ability to taste NaCl but that the ability vanished as the drug wore off (Henkin 1965, Henkin 1967). One might question the subjects' ability to identify their sensations as salty when they had never perceived them before; nonetheless, some sensations were apparently produced. This observation deserves additional study.

SPECIFIC AGEUSIA IN ANIMALS Both animal model studies and human studies clearly demonstrate that the ability to taste specific substances has a genetic component. Following extensive work on the genetics of human perception of bitter taste (see below), a series of animal model studies have elegantly explored genetic factors influencing bitter taste perception. These studies using inbred strains of mice (*Mus muscullus*) have implicated several genes in the determination of sensitivity to specific bitter substances. Lush (Azen et al 1986; Lush 1981, 1982, 1984, 1986) postulates at least four separate genes, labeled *Soa, Qui, Rva* and *Cyx,* that control ability to detect specific bitter substances. Studies of sucrose octaacetate (SOA) sensitivity by inbred strains of mice (e.g. Harder et al 1984, Whitney et al 1990) have clearly demonstrated that sensitivity to SOA is under genetic control. Furthermore, Shingai & Beidler (1985) have shown that the strain differences in behaviorally-determined sensitivity are mirrored in parallel electrophysiological differences, supporting the idea that the genes are involved in coding for receptor-associated proteins or other events early in SOA taste transduction.

These studies support the conclusion discussed earlier that bitter perception is not a unitary phenomenon. This is not surprising if one believes that perception and rejection of toxic compounds is the function of a bitter taste system. To date, there is no agreed-upon chemical basis for bitterness and this may be because no common molecular configuration exists for this taste. Instead, as plants and perhaps insects (Brower 1969, Yang & Kare 1968) have evolved substances that are potentially harmful to invertebrates and vertebrates alike, these organisms have evolved means to detect the substances. Specific taste mechanisms have, as a result, developed as a family of different protein-based receptors, all of which are connected to genetic rejection mechanisms and elicit more or less common sensory experience that humans label as bitter and unpleasant (but see Glendinning 1993).

SPECIFIC AGEUSIA IN HUMANS: PTC/PROP BLINDNESS Studies of the inability of certain individuals to taste phenylthiocarbamide (PTC), and its chemical relative 6-*n*-propylthiouracil (PROP), date back to a serendipitous accident in Fox's laboratory (1931). Some PTC he had synthesized blew into the air and a nearby colleague complained of a bitter taste that Fox could not perceive. Since then a variety of family studies have led to the conclusion that tasting is produced by the dominant allele, *T*. Individuals with two recessive alleles, *tt,* are nontasters and individuals with one dominant allele, *Tt,* as well as those with two dominant alleles, *TT*, are tasters (e.g. Blakeslee 1932, Snyder 1931). In the United States, about 25% are nontasters and 75% are tasters. The observation that both nontasters and tasters are able to taste other bitters, lends support to the conclusion from animal studies that bitterness is mediated by more than one receptor mechanism.

Initially a single missing receptor site that could bind the N-C=S chemical group found on both PTC and PROP and some other bitter compounds was believed to explain PTC/PROP nontasting; however, some bitter substances that do not contain the N-C=S group, and even some sweet substances, taste weaker to nontasters (e.g. Bartoshuk et al 1988, Gent & Bartoshuk 1983, Leach & Noble 1986, Mela 1989). Thus the missing receptor site theory cannot explain all of the taste variation.

Two lines of evidence have recently converged to shed some additional light on this genetic variation. Psychophysical evidence suggests that the tasters can be further divided into two groups so there are nontasters, medium tasters, and supertasters (Anliker et al 1991, Bartoshuk et al 1992). Supertasters comprise about 25% of the population. This suggests the possibility that medium tasters are those with one dominant allele and supertasters are those with both dominant alleles. Supertasters perceive stronger taste intensities from several bitter and sweet compounds (Bartoshuk et al 1992). Using videomicroscopy to count the number of taste buds in individuals of varying PROP sensitivities, nontasters had the fewest taste buds per cm^2 on the tongue tip (ave = 96); medium tasters, an intermediate number (ave = 184); and supertasters had the most (ave = 425) (Miller & Reedy 1988, Miller & Reedy 1990, Reedy et al 1993). Despite the impressive differences across these three groups, number of taste buds alone cannot explain the observation that supertasters taste only certain substances as more intense.

Besides perceiving some more intense taste sensations, supertasters also perceive more intense oral burn from capsaicin, the active ingredient in chili peppers (Karrer & Bartoshuk 1991). This may result from the anatomy of the nerves mediating taste and pain. Taste on the anterior tongue is mediated by the chorda tympani, a branch of the facial (*VII*th) nerve. Pain on this same area is mediated by the trigeminal (*V*th) nerve. On the other hand, both taste and pain are mediated by the glossopharyngeal (*IX*th) nerve on the posterior tongue. Trigeminal fibers are found in association with taste buds on the anterior tongue. Since supertasters have more taste buds, they may also have more trigeminal fibers leading to more intense pain sensations. Spatially localized testing with capsaicin showed that supertasters perceived greater pain only on locations innervated by *VII* and *IX*, supporting the view that extra trigeminal fibers may produce the extra pain sensation in supertasters.

CLINICAL ISSUES

Over the last decade, the number of studies on clinical disorders of smell and taste has increased dramatically. Studies have focused on the characterization of chemosensory disturbances as well as possible interventions. The need for clinical evaluation has sharpened psychophysical methodology and the increased participation of basic scientists in studies on clinical problems has led to new insights in the basic work as well (see Getchell et al 1991).

Taste-Olfaction Confusions

There are several sensory modalities with receptors in the oral and nasal cavities. We differentiate most of these easily (e.g. thermal, touch, and pain sensations) but there is confusion between taste and olfaction. Although we generally speak of tasting foods and beverages, much of the sensory input involved is actually olfactory. This confusion arises because there are two routes by which odorants can reach the olfactory cleft and ultimately the odor receptors. The conventional route, orthonasal, is the route taken by the odorant when it is sniffed through the nares. The touch sensations produced by sniffing localize the olfactory sensations to the nose. The less appreciated route, retronasal, is the route taken by the odorant when it is pumped from the mouth up into the nasal cavity by the tongue, cheek, and throat movements resulting from chewing and swallowing. If the odorant in the mouth is pungent, that is, if it stimulates irritation sensations from the touch system, then the odorant reveals its actual path from the oral into the nasal cavity. However, more typically, the food and beverage odors pumped into the nasal cavity do not stimulate touch sensations. The touch sensations produced by contact with the foods and beverages in the mouth apparently serve to localize the composite sensations of taste and retronasal olfaction (i.e. flavor) to the mouth. P. Rozin (personal communication) has coined the term *mouthsense* to characterize the complex of sensations arising when we commonly speak of tasting foods and beverages.

The localization of taste/olfactory sensations via touch can be demonstrated directly. Taste sensations can be localized to areas with no taste receptors by painting (and thereby touching) a path from an area with taste to the area devoid of taste (Todrank & Bartoshuk 1991). Even more dramatic, retronasal olfactory sensations can be localized to the mouth by providing a tactile cue in the mouth. In this latter demonstration (P. Rozin, personal communication), a small tube leading to a reservoir of chocolate syrup was placed in the mouth of a subject who then chewed on gum that had neither odor nor taste. When the experimenter introduced the chocolate odorant into the mouth, the chewing propeled it into the nasal cavity and ultimately to the olfactory receptors. The subject perceived the gum to have suddenly become chocolate. The importance of touch to mouthsense suggests that patients might experience abnormalities in their perceptions of foods and beverages with disturbances in oral touch (Weiffenbach 1993).

Understanding the role of touch in the localization of sensations from other sensory domains owes much to work on the localization of thermal sensations (Green 1977). This effect can be shown by placing two quarters in a freezer and holding one to keep it at body temperature. When the two quarters are cold, the three quarters can be placed on a table in the order cold, body-temperature, cold, spaced so the three middle fingers can easily contact the quarters simultaneously. When the three fingers touch the quarters, all three quarters will feel cold. One sensory domain overriding another is an example of the general category of sensory capture (e.g. McGurk & MacDonald 1976, Rock & Victor 1964, Shimojo 1987, Tastevin 1937).

CONFUSION BETWEEN TASTE AND OLFACTION IN THE CLINIC The confusions between taste and smell produced by the localization of retronasal olfaction to the mouth leads many patients to report that they cannot taste when in fact they suffer only olfactory loss (e.g. see Deems et al 1991, Goodspeed et al 1986, Smith 1991). Total olfactory loss is much more common than total taste loss, and most patients who self-refer because of a loss turn out to suffer from olfactory loss. Patients do not often self-refer with genuine taste loss, because to perceive such a loss, the damage to the system must be extensive (see below).

Confusions between taste and smell also complicate the diagnosis of phantom sensations. One of the best methods for distinguishing between a taste and a smell phantom is to ask the patient to describe the quality of the sensation. True taste phantoms are described as salty, sweet, bitter, or sour. Phantoms described by object names (e.g. gasoline, smoke) or that cannot be described at all are likely to originate from the olfactory system.

Psychophysical Methodology

Some important advances in psychophysical methodology have come about in response to the challenge of finding a way to assess taste and smell losses. Although experiencing elevated thresholds may cause patients some distress, finding their taste and smell worlds diminished in intensity is likely to cause much more distress. This forces psychophysicists to confront an elusive problem: How can we quantify diminished perceived intensities? Comparisons across individuals are ultimately limited because we cannot share one another's experience. One solution is to label the scale with adjectives, like *strong* and *weak,* that we hope reflect the same experience across subjects. Another solution is to use the human's ability to make relative comparisons. Magnitude matching is a new psychophysical method that uses that ability (Marks & Stevens 1980, Stevens & Marks 1980). Subjects are asked to judge on a common scale the intensities of stimuli from two different sensory continua. Subjects are not able to make perfect comparisons (see Marks 1991 for some context effects on such judgments); nonetheless, such judgments can be made. If we can assume that all subjects experience the same intensities from one of the continua, then we can make direct comparisons across subjects on the other continuum. Clearly, we can never be certain of this assumption; however, there are situations where the assumption might hold relatively well. For example, magnitude matching differentiates nontasters from tasters of PROP by assuming that both groups perceive the same intensities from a series of tones varying in intensity (Gent & Bartoshuk 1983) or from a series of gray papers varying in darkness (Marks et al 1992).

Other attributes of sensory responses have also been the focus of study. For example, a subject's consistency across replications of the same stimulus [intraclass correlation coefficient (ICC)] has proved to be a useful measure of sensory performance (Cowart 1991, Gracely et al 1980, Weiffenbach et al 1986). Interestingly, when ICCs were calculated from magnitude estimate data, they did not correlate well with the exponents of the power functions describing the data. For example, even though steep functions seem to indicate better discriminability than flat functions, the ICCs did not universally support this (Cowart 1991).

Psychophysical tests have been modified to provide the information needed by the physician in the diagnosis of chemosensory dysfunction. For example, testing on particular loci allows tests of the function of each of the cranial nerves innervating the taste system (Bartoshuk et al 1987, Tomita et al 1986).

TONGUE MAP Spatial testing has helped to explode the myth that the four basic tastes are spatially distributed such that sweet tastes are perceived on the front of the tongue, bitter on the back, and salty and sour on the sides. The origin of the tongue map was a mistranslation by Boring (1942) of an article published in 1901 in *Philosophische Studien* by a German psychophysicist working in the laboratory of Wilhelm Wundt (Hänig 1901). Spatial testing reveals that all four qualities can be perceived on all tongue loci (Collings 1974, Bartoshuk 1993).

Olfactory Dysfunction

Olfactory loss can result from any condition that blocks the olfactory cleft or damages the olfactory neural structures. Anosmia refers to the total inability to smell all (total anosmia) or some (partial anosmia) odorants. Hyposmia is the decreased ability to smell all (total hyposmia) or some (partial hyposmia). In addition to loss, patients can suffer from dysosmia, olfactory sensations that are inappropriate or that are present in the absence of stimulation (Snow et al 1991). The most common causes of olfactory loss are upper respiratory infection, head trauma, and nasal or sinus disease (Deems et al 1991, Goodspeed et al 1986, Smith 1991).

Nasal or sinus disease is probably most often not a disorder of the olfactory system at all. Rather it is caused by an obstruction that prevents odorants from passing through the olfactory cleft and stimulating the olfactory receptors. Surgical intervention (e.g. Leonard et al 1988) or the use of steroid spray to reduce swelling (e.g. Mott 1991) have successfully restored olfaction in some of these patients.

Head trauma can damage olfaction in three ways: by damaging the nose, thereby blocking access of odorants to the receptors; by damaging the olfactory centers in the brain; or most commonly, by damaging the olfactory neurons at the point where they pass through the cribiform plate of the ethmoid bone on their way to the olfactory bulbs (Costanzo & Zasler 1991). Normally, the neurons penetrate this bone through small openings. Head trauma can tear the neurons away from the bone either by movement of the brain relative to the skull or by fracture of the bone. Olfactory neurons can regenerate but scar tissue at the cribiform plate seems to prevent them from regenerating into the olfactory bulb. Since the regenerating olfactory neurons can survive only if they reach the bulb and form synaptic connections, their inability to cross the cribiform plate leads to degeneration. This can be visualized (Strahan et al 1991) thanks to the development a small instrument (Lovell et al 1982) that can pass through the olfactory cleft to obtain a biopsy of olfactory epithelium in living human subjects.

The common cold can produce a temporary loss of olfaction that is actually a conduction loss if congestion disrupts the pathway through the olfactory cleft. However, viral illnesses can also produce a much more serious, permanent loss of olfaction that may be due to damage produced by viral invasion of olfactory neurons (Leopold et al 1991). Since the virus need not invade all of the olfactory neurons, virus-induced losses can produce hyposmia as well as anosmia. Biopsies of the olfactory epithelium show pathological changes that correlate with the degree of olfactory loss (Jafek et al 1990). In addition to losses, phantom olfactory sensations occur in some cases of upper respiratory infection (Leopold et al 1991).

Taste Dysfunction

Surprisingly enough, considerable damage can be done to the taste system without producing substantial taste loss. Ageusia refers to the inability to taste all (total ageusia) or some (partial ageusia) tastants. Hypogeusia is the decreased ability to taste all (total hypogeusia) or some (partial hypogeusia). In addition to loss, patients can suffer from dysgeusia, taste sensations that are present in the absence of stimulation (Snow et al 1991). Upper respiratory infection and head trauma cause taste loss as well as olfactory loss (Solomon et al 1991).

The sites of damage to the taste system from head trauma are not clear but could involve damage to peripheral nerves (e.g. the chorda tympani nerve could be damaged by fractures of the temporal bone) or to structures in the CNS. Taste loss may be much more common with head trauma than is currently believed. When only part of the system is damaged, subjects' everyday taste experience may be unaffected. Careful spatial testing of patients with head trauma is necessary to assess the extent of the damage.

The mechanism of the taste loss caused by upper respiratory infection is believed to be viral invasion just as with olfaction. The chorda tympani nerve is especially vulnerable to damage from viruses because it passes through the middle ear on its way to the brain. Not surprisingly, infections of the middle ear (otitis media) are associated with taste loss (DiLisio 1990, Urbantschitsch 1876). Bell's palsy, one of the best known causes of taste loss, can also result from viral damage.

The virus that causes chicken pox can, in later years as Ramsey-Hunt's syndrome, damage cranial nerves, including those that mediate taste. This was demonstrated in a particularly dramatic fashion when Pfaffmann, one of the pioneers of research in the chemical senses, developed a taste disorder that he described himself at meetings of the Association for Chemoreception Sciences (Pfaffmann & Bartoshuk 1989, Pfaffmann & Bartoshuk 1990). The disorder is unilateral but can affect several cranial nerves. In Pfaffmann's case, all taste on his left side was abolished by the disorder but he experienced no loss of everyday taste sensations and was unaware of the extent of the damage until spatially tested. Since the taste nerves can regenerate, there was reason to expect at least some taste function to return. Monitoring that return over three years produced a serendipitous discovery about inhibition in the taste system. Ramsey-Hunt's syndrome is unilateral, yet as taste sensations on Pfaffmann's left side began to return, taste sensations on the undamaged right side began to diminish. In light of the anesthesia experiments discussed below, the diminution on the right was interpreted as evidence for inhibition from the left. We thus conclude that taste nerves normally inhibit one another across the midline (the inhibition must be in the brain since the nerves do not contact one another in the periphery). When a nerve is damaged, its ability to inhibit is abolished and the responses previously inhibited increase. During regeneration, the inhibition is restored.

Clinical Anesthesia: A Window into Taste Disorders

Taste is mediated primarily by two cranial nerves: the facial (*VII*th) nerve (the chorda tympani and greater superficial petrosal branches) and the glossopharyngeal (*IX*th) nerve. The vagus (*X*th) nerve also plays a role in taste but has been less studied than the other two. The *VII*th and *IX*th nerves do not appear to cross the midline (that is, they project ipsilaterally) to the cortex (Norgren 1990). From the cortex some descending projections are ipsilateral while others cross the midline (that is, they cross contralaterally) providing one possible mechanism for interaction between the right and left sides (DiLorenzo 1990, London et al 1990, London & Donta 1991). In 1965, a classic observation first suggested inhibitory interactions between *VII* and *IX* (Halpern & Nelson 1965). In that experiment, anesthesia of the chorda tympani branch of the *VII*th nerve produced increased neural responses from the area in the medulla receiving input from the *IX*th nerve. Halpern & Nelson suggested that *VII* might normally inhibit *IX*. Anesthesia of *VII* thus released that inhibition leading to increased responses from *IX*. Recent experiments in human subjects have supported this conclusion. Since the chorda tympani nerve travels with the lingual nerve, which mediates pain in the lower jaw, a dental block, like that used when filling a lower tooth, will abolish taste on the anterior tongue on the side of the injection. Anesthesia of the chorda tympani nerve on one side caused some taste intensities to increase just as the work of Halpern & Nelson predicted (Catalanotto et al 1993, Östrum et al 1985). Spatial testing showed that the location of the increase was the back of the tongue, which is innervated by the *IX*th nerve, also just as Halpern & Nelson predicted. However, the human experiments produced two new observations. The greatest enhancement in the human subjects occurred for the contralateral side (Lehman 1991, Yanagisawa et al 1992). This supports the conclusion that the interaction is central since the two sides of the taste system do not interact in the periphery. Further, about half of the subjects reported spontaneous taste phantoms perceived to come from the contralateral rear of the tongue (the same area where taste stimuli were enhanced) (Yanagisawa et al 1992). Subjects did not all perceive the same quality, but the most commonly reported quality was salty. When a topical anesthetic was painted onto the phantom, it was abolished.

The clinical taste problem most disturbing to patients is dysgeusia. Many cases of dysgeusia actually reflect the presence of unwanted substances in the mouth. For example, traces of medications can enter the saliva from blood and produce a bitter taste; reflux or post nasal drip can produce taste sensations; or blood plasma can enter the mouth through inflamed gums and produce salty or metallic sensations. However, some cases of dysgeusia are phantoms generated in the nervous system. The anesthesia studies suggest that a release-of-inhibition phantom may be induced in some locations by damage at other locations. Another kind of phantom is produced when damage to a taste nerve results in direct stimulation of that nerve (Bull 1965). Topical anesthesia of the mouth enhances this kind of nerve-stimulation phantom presumably because the anesthesia blocks nerves that inhibit the phantom (Bartoshuk et al 1991).

Phantoms can also be elicited by stimulation in the CNS. A tumor in the temporal lobe was associated with a bitter taste phantom (El-Deiry & McCabe 1990) and, although rare, taste phantoms can precede epileptic seizures (Hausser-Hauw & Bancaud 1987).

Aging and the Chemical Senses

Studies on the effects of age on the chemical senses must be read with some caution since some rest on a classic error in the interpretation of magnitude estimation data. Some investigators have given a selected stimulus to both old and young subjects and asked them to assign a particular value to that stimulus and to rate other stimuli relative to it. Although this is a standard technique in magnitude estimation when the goal is to measure the shapes of psychophysical functions, the technique is invalid for a comparison across groups when differences in perceived intensity are of interest.

Age affects some but not all of the individual senses represented in the oral and nasal cavities. One study found that the perception of pressure applied by filaments on the tongue (the modern equivalent of Von Frey hairs) declines with age, but found no evidence for similar declines in the perception of heat, cold, and viscosity (Weiffenbach et al 1990). A variety of studies on taste suggest that perception of sucrose and perhaps NaCl remain remarkably stable across age, but perceptions of citric acid and quinine show some declines (e.g. Bartoshuk et al 1986, Cowart 1983, Hyde & Feller 1981, Murphy & Gilmore 1989, Weiffenbach et al 1986). Studies on olfaction have been done predominantly on orthonasal olfaction and include studies of the ability to identify odorants as well as assessments of the perceived intensities of odorants. The elderly show clear declines in the ability to identify odorants (Doty et al 1984, Wysocki & Gilbert 1989). In addition, perceived intensities of many odorants may dim with age; however, there is some disagreement over the magnitude of the effect (Cowart 1989, Stevens & Cain 1985). The disagreement is related to an observation of behavior in the elderly that is not understood. Most investigators include blanks in any series of stimuli to be evaluated. In the case of olfaction, the blanks consist of the diluent used to dilute the odorants. Young subjects generally report that these blanks have no smell. However, elderly subjects tend to rate odor blanks as if they have smells. Some investigators treat the ratings of the blanks as a kind of cognitive artifact and subtract them from the ratings given other stimuli (Stevens & Cain 1985). This will, of course, increase the apparent size of the loss of olfaction with age.

Age clearly takes a toll on retronasal olfaction (Murphy 1985, Schiffman 1977, Stevens & Cain 1986). Age-related olfactory damage to receptors or to neural structures would obviously affect both orthonasal and retronasal olfaction. However, additional problems resulting in reduced transmission of odorants from the mouth to the nasal cavity take an added toll on retronasal olfaction. Of special interest, some individuals have impairments limited to retronasal olfaction only (Duffy et al 1991, Duffy et al 1993).

We speak of chemosensory losses with age, but age per se may not be totally responsible for the losses. A study in which subjects were healthy showed less olfactory loss than typically found in the literature (Ship & Weiffenbach 1993). This is consistent with the possibility that the olfactory losses seen with age are actually the result of a variety of etiologies and that age simply provides a greater amount of time in which to encounter these etiologies.

SUMMARY

In the last decade, studies using approaches from molecular biology have substantially advanced our understanding of the early events in olfaction and taste. The many odorants that we can recognize may well interact with many distinct receptor proteins. Of the four taste qualities that we recognize, studies on salty and sour suggest that these tastes involve ion channels in the membrane of receptor cells while sweets and bitters bind to receptor proteins.

Some volatiles (pheromones) play special roles in reproductive behavior via the vomeronasal organ (VNO) and the accessory olfactory system. Initial belief that humans lack a VNO has been questioned recently, thus raising the fascinating possibility of human pheromones.

The roles that taste and smell play in the world of the newborn are very different. Acceptance of sweet and rejection of bitter appear to be hard-wired while the affect associated with odors depends much more on experience.

Genetic variation may produce total losses (Kallman's syndrome produces anosmia and familial dysautonomia produces ageusia) or losses specific to certain stimuli. The best known of the specific anosmias is that for androstenone, which has no smell to some, a urinous smell to others, and a smell like sandalwood to still others. Analogous to the specific anosmias, some individuals are unable to taste PROP while others, supertasters, perceive PROP to be exceedingly bitter.

Clinical studies reveal pathologies responsible for total or partial losses. The olfactory system, dependent on one cranial nerve, is more vulnerable than taste, and total anosmia is a relatively common clinical problem. Three cranial nerves carry taste and two of those nerves inhibit one another such that damage to one disinhibits the other and preserves over-all taste function. Total ageusia is very rare.

Throughout these studies we see that taste and olfaction have different properties and often different functions (e.g. odor and reproduction). Yet taste and smell can also be integrated to determine what does or does not enter the body. In Adrian's words, "we are dealing with the sense organs which signal the quality of the air we breathe and that of the food and drink we propose to swallow."

Literature Cited

Adrian ED. 1963. Opening address. In *Olfaction and Taste,* ed. Y Zotterman, 1:1–4. New York: Macmillan

Al-Waiz M, Ayesh R, Mitchell SC, Idle JR, Smith RL. 1987. A genetic polymorphism of the N-oxidation of trimethylamine in humans. *Clin. Pharmacol. Ther.* 42:588–94

Amoore JE. 1977. Specific anosmia and the concept of primary odors. *Chem. Senses* 2:267–81

Anliker JA, Bartoshuk LM, Ferris AM, Hooks LD. 1991. Children's food preferences and genetic sensitivity to the bitter taste of PROP. *Am. J. Clin. Nutr.* 54:316–20

Axelrod FB, Nachtigal R, Dancis J. 1974. Familial dysautonomia: diagnosis, pathogenesis and management. In *Advances in Pediatrics,* ed. I Schulman, pp. 75–96. Chicago: Year Book Med.

Azen EA, Lush IE, Taylor BA. 1986. Close linkage of mouse genes for salivary proline-rich proteins and taste. *Trends Genet.* 2:199–200

Balogh RD, Porter RH. 1986. Olfactory preferences resulting from mere exposure in human neonates. *Infant Behav. Dev.* 9:395–401

Bartoshuk LM. 1979. Bitter taste of saccharin: related to the genetic ability to taste the bitter substance 6-n-propylthiouracil (PROP). *Science* 205:934–35

Bartoshuk LM. 1990. Distinctions between taste and smell relevant to the role of experience. In *Taste, Experience and Feeding,* ed. ED Capaldi, TL Powley, pp. 62–72. Washington, DC: Am. Psychol. Assoc.

Bartoshuk LM. 1993. The biological basis of food perception and acceptance. *Food Qual. Prefer.* 4: In press

Bartoshuk LM, Desnoyers S, Hudson C, Marks L, O'Brien M, et al. 1987. Tasting on localized areas. In *Olfaction and Taste,* ed. S Roper, J Atema, 9:166–68. New York: Ann. NY Acad. Sci.

Bartoshuk LM, Fast K, Karrer TA, Marino S, Price RA, Reed DA. 1992. PROP supertasters and the perception of sweetness and bitterness. *Chem. Senses* 17:594 (Abstr.)

Bartoshuk LM, Kveton J, Lehman C. 1991. Peripheral source of taste phantom (i.e., dysgeusia) demonstrated by topical anesthesia. *Chem. Senses* 16:499–500 (Abstr.)

Bartoshuk LM, Rifkin B, Marks LE, Bars P. 1986. Taste and aging. *J. Gerontol.* 41:51–57

Bartoshuk LM, Rifkin B, Marks LE, Hooper JE. 1988. Bitterness of KCl and benzoate: related to PTC/PROP. *Chem. Senses* 13:517–28

Beauchamp GK, Bertino M, Engelman K. 1991a. Human salt appetite. In *Chemical Senses,* Vol. 4, *Appetite and Nutrition,* ed. MI Friedman, MG Tordoff, MR Kare, pp. 85–108. New York: Dekker

Beauchamp GK, Cowart BJ, Moran M. 1986. Developmental changes in salt acceptability in human infants. *Dev. Psychobiol.* 19:17–25

Beauchamp GK, Cowart BJ, Schmidt HJ. 1991b. Development of chemosensory sensitivity and preference. See Getchell et al 1991, pp. 405–16

Beauchamp GK, Pearson P. 1991. Human development and umami taste. *Physiol. Behav.* 49:1009–12

Beauchamp GK, Yamazaki K, Boyse EA. 1985. The chemosensory recognition of genetic individuality. *Sci. Am.* 253:86–92

Birch GG. 1987. Chemical aspects of sweetness. In *Sweetness,* ed. J Dobbing, pp. 3–13. New York: Springer-Verlag

Birch L. 1979. Dimensions of preschool children's food preferences. *J. Nutr. Educ.* 11:77–80

Blakeslee AF. 1932. Genetics of sensory thresholds: taste for phenyl thio carbamide. *Proc. Natl. Acad. Sci. USA* 18:120–30

Boring EG. 1942. *Sensation and Perception in the History of Experimental Psychology.* New York: Appleton

Bossey J. 1980. Development of olfactory and related structures in staged human embryos. *Anat. Embryol.* 161:255–36

Boyse EA, Beauchamp GK, Yamazaki K. 1987. The genetics of body scent. *Trends Genet.* 3:97–102

Breer H, Boekhoff I. 1991. Odorants of the same odor class activate different second messanger pathways. *Chem. Senses* 16:19–29

Breslin PAS, Pugh EN Jr, Beauchamp GK. 1992. Failure to discriminate chemicals that elicit a similar taste quality: glucose versus fructose. *Chem. Senses* 17:599 (Abstr.)

Brower LP. 1969. Ecological chemistry. *Sci. Am.* 220:20–29

Buck L, Axel R. 1991. A novel multi-gene family may encode odorant receptors: a molecular basis for odor recognition. *Cell* 65:175–87

Bull TR. 1965. Taste and the chorda tympani. *J. Laryngol.* 79:479–93

Cain WS. 1978. History of research on smell. In *Tasting and Smelling,* ed. EC Carterette, MP Friedman, pp. 197–229. New York: Academic

Capretta PJ, Petersik JT, Steward DJ. 1975. Acceptance of novel flavours is increased after early exposure of diverse taste. *Nature* 254:689–91

Caprio J, Brand JG, Teeter JH, Valentinic T, Kalinoski DL, et al. 1993. The taste system of the channel catfish: from biophysics to behavior. *Trends Neurosci.* 15: 191–97

Catalanotto FA, Bartoshuk LM, Östrum KM, Gent JF, Fast K. 1993. Effects of anesthesia of the facial nerve on taste. *Chem. Senses.* In press

Cernoch JM, Porter RH. 1985. Recognition of maternal axillary odors by infants. *Child Dev.* 56:1593–98

Collings VB. 1974. Human taste response as a function of locus of stimulation on the tongue and soft palate. *Percept. Psychophys.* 16:169–74

Costanzo RM, Zasler ND. 1991. Head trauma. See Getchell et al 1991, pp. 711–30

Cowart BJ. 1983. *Direct scaling of the intensity of basic tastes: a life span study.* Presented at Annu. Meet. Assoc. Chemorecept. Sci., Sarasota, Fla.

Cowart BJ. 1989. Relationships between taste and smell across the adult life span. In *Nutrition and the Chemical Senses in Aging: Recent Advances and Current Research Needs,* ed. C Murphy, WS Cain, DM Hegsted, pp. 39–55. New York: Ann. NY Acad. Sci.

Cowart BJ. 1991. Derivation of an index of discrimination from magnitude estimation ratings. In *Ratio Scaling of Psychological Magnitude: In Honor of the Memory of S. S. Stevens,* ed. SJ Bolanowski, GA Gescheider, pp. 115–27. Hillsdale, NJ: Erlbaum

Cowart BJ, Beauchamp GK. 1986. The importance of sensory context in young children's acceptance of salty tastes. *Child Dev.* 57:1034–39

Crook CK. 1978. Taste perception in the newborn infant. *Infant Behav. Dev.* 1:52–69

Deems DA, Doty RL, Settle RG, Moore-Gillon V, Shaman P, et al. 1991. Smell and taste disorders: a study of 750 patients from the University of Pennsylvania Smell and Taste Center. *Arch. Otol. Head Neck Surg.* 117:519–28

Desor JA, Maller O, Turner RE. 1973. Taste in acceptance of sugars by human infants. *J. Comp. Physiol. Psychol.* 84:496–501

DiLisio GJ. 1990. *Taste alteration in subjects with acute otitis media or middle ear fluid/taste preservation in otolaryngologic patients.* MD thesis. Yale Univ. School Med.

DiLorenzo P. 1990. Corticofugal influence on taste responses in the parabrachial pons of the rat. *Brain Res.* 530:73–84

Doty RL, Muller-Schwarze D. 1992. *Chemical Signals in Vertebrates,* Vol. 6. New York: Plenum

Doty RL, Shaman P, Applebaum SL, Giberson R, Sikorski L, Rosenberg L. 1984. Smell identification ability: changes with age. *Science* 226:1441–43

DuBois GE, Walters DE, Kellogg MS. 1993. Mechanism of human sweet taste and implications for rational sweetener design. In *Flavor Measurement,* ed. CT Ho, CH Manley, pp. 239–66. New York: Dekker

Duffy VB, Cain WS, Stevens JC, Ferris AM. 1991. A test of flavor sensitivity. *Chem. Senses* 16:516–17 (Abstr.)

Duffy VB, Ferris AM, Cain WS. 1993. Lower olfactory functioning associates with nutritional risk in elderly women. *Chem. Senses* In press

El-Deiry A, McCabe BF. 1990. Temporal lobe tumor manifested by localized dysgeusia. *Ann. Otol. Rhinol. Laryngol.* 99:586–87

Engen T. 1982. *The Perception of Odors.* New York: Academic

Ferstl R, Egger F, Westphal E, Zavazava N, Muller-Ruchholtz W. 1992. MHC-related odors in humans. In *Chemical Signals in Vertebrates,* ed. RL Doty, D Muller-Schwarze, pp. 205–17. New York: Plenum

Fox AL. 1931. Six in ten "tasteblind" to bitter chemical. *Sci. News Lett.* 9:249

Franco B, Guioli S, Pragliola A, Incerti B, Bardoni B, et al. 1991. A gene deleted in Kalmann's syndrome shares homology with neural cell adhesion and axonal pathfinding molecules. *Nature* 353:529–36

Gent JF, Bartoshuk LM. 1983. Sweetness of sucrose, neohesperidin dihyodrochalcone, and saccharin is related to genetic ability to taste the bitter substance 6-*n*-propylthiouracil. *Chem. Senses* 7:265–72

Getchell TV, Doty RL, Snow JB, Bartoshuk LM, eds. 1991. *Smell and Taste in Health and Disease.* New York: Raven

Glendinning JI. 1993. Pitohui: how toxic and to whom? *Science* 259:582–83

Goodspeed RB, Catalanotto FA, Gent JF, Cain WS, Bartoshuk LM, et al. 1986. Clinical characteristics of patients with taste and smell disorders. In *Clinical Measurement of Taste and Smell,* ed. HL Meiselman, RS Rivlin, pp. 451–66. New York: Macmillan

Gracely RH, Deeter WR, Wolskee PJ, Dubner R. 1980. Does naloxone alter experimental pain perception? *Soc. Neurosci. Abstr.* 6:246

Green BG. 1977. Localization of thermal sensation: an illusion and synthetic heat. *Percept. Psychophys.* 22:331–37

Halpern BP, Nelson LM. 1965. Bulbar gustatory responses to anterior and to posterior tongue stimulation in the rat. *Am. J. Physiol.* 209:105–10

Hänig DP. 1901. Zur Psychophysik des Geschmackssinnes. *Phil. Stud.* 17:576–623

Harder DB, Whitney G, Frye P, Smith JC, Rashotte ME. 1984. Strain differences among mice in taste psychophysics of sucrose octaacetate. *Chem. Senses* 9:311–23

Hauser GJ, Chitayat D, Berns L, Braver D, Muhlbauer B. 1985. Peculiar odors in newborns and maternal prenatal ingestion of spicy foods. *Eur. J. Pediatr.* 144:403

Hausser-Hauw C, Bancaud J. 1987. Gustatory hallucinations in epileptic seizures. *Brain* 110:339–59

Henkin RI. 1965. On the mechanism of the taste defect in familial dysautonomia. In *Olfaction and Taste,* ed. T Hayashi, 2:321–35. New York: Pergamon

Henkin RI. 1967. Sensory mechanisms in familial dysautonomia. In *Symposium on Oral Sensation and Perception,* ed. JF Bosma, pp. 341–49. Springfield, Ill: Thomas

Hepper PG. 1987. The amniotic fluid: an important priming role in kin recognition. *Anim. Behav.* 35:1342–46

Hill DL, Mistretta CM. 1990. Developmental neurobiology of salt taste sensation. *Trends Neurosci.* 13:188–95

Hubert HG, Fabsitz RR, Brown KS, Feinleib M. 1981. Olfactory sensitivity in twins. In *Twin Research III. Proc. 3rd Int. Congr. Twin Studies. Prog. Clin. Biol. Res.,* ed. L Gedda, P Parise, WE Nance, pp. 97–103. New York: Liss

Hyde RJ, Feller RP. 1981. Age and sex effects on taste of sucrose, NaCl, citric acid and caffeine. *Neurobiol. Aging* 2:315–18

Ikeda K. 1909. On a new seasoning. *J. Tokyo Chem. Soc.* 30:820–26

Jafek BW, Hartman D, Eller PM, Johnson EW, Strahan RC, Moran DT. 1990. Postviral olfactory dysfunction. *Am. J. Rhinol.* 4:91–100

Johnson A, Josephson R, Hawke M. 1985. Clinical and histological evidence for the presence of the vomernasal (Jacobson's) organ in adult humans. *J. Otolaryngol.* 14:71–79

Kajiura H, Cowart BJ, Beauchamp GK. 1992. Early developmental changes in bitter taste responses of human infants. *Dev. Psychobiol.* 25:375–86

Karrer T, Bartoshuk L. 1991. Capsaicin desensitization and recovery on the human tongue. *Physiol. Behav.* 49:757–64

Kinnamon SC. 1988. Taste transduction: a diversity of mechanisms. *Trends Neurosci.* 11:491–96

Klein J. 1986. *Natural History of the Major Histocompability Complex.* New York: Wiley

Labows JN, Wysocki CJ. 1984. Individual differences in odor perception. *Perfum. Flavorist* 9:21–26

Lancet D. 1992. Olfactory reception: from transduction to human genetics. In *Sensory Transduction,* ed. DP Corey, SD Roper, pp. 73–91. New York: Rockefeller Univ. Press

Lawless HT, Glatter S, Hohn C. 1991. Context-dependent changes in the perception of odor quality. *Chem. Senses* 16:349–60

Leach EJ, Noble AC. 1986. Comparison of bitterness of caffeine and quinine by a time-intensity procedure. *Chem. Senses* 11:339–45

Lehman C. 1991. *The effect of anesthesia of the chorda tympani nerve on taste perception in humans.* PhD thesis. Yale Univ.

Leonard G, Cain WS, Clavet G. 1988. Surgical correction of olfactory disorders. *Chem. Senses* 13:708 (Abstr.)

Leopold DA, Hornung DE, Youngentob SL. 1991. Olfactory loss after upper respiratory infection. See Getchell et al 1991, pp. 731–34

Leopold DA, Preti G, Mozell MM, Youngentob SL, Wright HN. 1990. Fish-odor syndrome presenting as dysosmia. *Arch. Otol. Head Neck Surg.* 116:354–55

London J, Halsell CB, Barry MB, Donta TS. 1990. An examination of the projection from the gustatory cortex to the NTS in the hamster. *Chem. Senses* 15:609 (Abstr.)

London JA, Donta TS. 1991. Cortical projections to the rostral pole of the hamster NTS exhibit bilateral differences in strength and area of origin. *Chem. Senses* 16:514–15 (Abstr.)

Lovell MA, Jefek BW, Moran DT, Rowley JC. 1982. Biopsy of human olfactory mucosa. *Arch. Otolaryngol.* 108:247–49

Lush IE. 1991. The genetics of bitterness, sweetness and saltiness in strains of mice. In *Chemical Senses.* Vol. 3: *Genetics of Perception and Communication*, ed. CJ Wysocki, MR Kare, pp. 227–42. New York: Dekker

Lush IE. 1981. The genetics of tasting in mice. I. Sucrose octaacetate. *Genet. Res.* 38:93–95

Lush IE. 1982. The genetics of tasting in mice. II. Strychnine. *Chem. Senses* 7:93–98

Lush IE. 1984. The genetics of tasting in mice. III. Quinine. *Gen. Res.* 44:151–60

Lush IE. 1986. The genetics of tasing in mice. II. The acetates of raffinose, galactose, and β-galactose. *Genet. Res.* 47:117–23

MacFarlane AJ. 1975. Olfaction in the development of social preferences in the human neonate. *Ciba Found. Symp.* 33:103–7

Makin JW, Porter RH. 1989. Attractivenss of

lactating females' breast odors to neonates. *Child Dev.* 60:803–10

Maone TR, Mattes RD, Bernbaum JC, Beauchamp GK. 1990. A new method for delivering a taste without fluids to preterm and term infants. *Dev. Psychobiol.* 23:179–91

Marks LE. 1991. Reliability of magnitude matching. *Percept. Psychophys.* 49:31–37

Marks LE, Borg G, Westerlund J. 1992. Differences in taste perception assessed by magnitude matching and by category-ratio scaling. *Chem. Senses* 17:507–18

Marks LE, Stevens JC. 1980. Measuring sensation in the aged. In *Aging in the 1980s: Psychological Issues,* ed. LW Poon, pp. 592–98. Washington, DC: Am. Psychol. Assoc.

McBurney DH, Gent JF. 1979. On the nature of taste qualities. *Psychol. Bull.* 86:151–67

McBurney DH, Smith DH, Shick TR. 1972. Gustatory cross adaptation: sourness and bitterness. *Percept. Psychophys.* 11:228–32

McClintock MK. 1971. Menstrual synchrony and suppression. *Nature* 229:244–45

McGurk H, MacDonald J. 1976. Hearing lips and seeing voices. *Nature* 264:746–48

Mela DJ. 1989. Bitter taste intensity: the effect of tastant and thiourea taster status. *Chem. Senses* 14:131–35

Mennella JA, Beauchamp GK. 1991a. Maternal diet alters the sensory qualities of human milk and the nursling's behavior. *Pediatrics* 88:737–44

Mennella JA, Beauchamp GK. 1991b. The transfer of alcohol to human milk: effects of flavor and the infant's behavior. *N. Engl. J. Med.* 325:981–85

Miller IJ Jr, Reedy FE Jr. 1988. Human taste pore quantification with videomicroscopy. *Chem. Senses* 13:719 (Abstr.)

Miller IJ, Reedy FE Jr. 1990. Variations in human taste bud density and taste intensity perception. *Physiol. Behav.* 47:1213–19

Miyamoto T, Restrepo D, Teeter JH. 1991. Amino acid- and second messenger-induced responses in isolated catfish olfactory neurons. *Biophys. J.* 59:255a

Mott AE. 1991. Topical corticosterois therapy for nasal polyposis. See Getchell et al 1991, pp. 553–72

Murphy C. 1985. Cognitive and chemosensory influences on age-related changes in the ability to identify blended foods. *J. Gerontol.* 40:47–52

Murphy C, Gilmore MM. 1989. Quality-specific effects of aging on the human taste system. *Percept. Psychophys.* 45:121–28

Naim M. 1993. Cellular transduction of sugar-induced sweet taste. In *Food Flavors, Ingredients and Composition,* ed. G Charalambous, pp. 647–56. New York: Elsevier

Nakamura T, Gold GH. 1987. A cyclic nucleotide-gated conductance in olfactory cilia. *Nature* 325:442–44

Norgren R. 1990. Gustatory system. In *The Human Nervous System,* ed. G Paxinos, pp. 845–61. New York: Academic

Östrum KM, Catalanotto FA, Gent JF, Bartoshuk LM. 1985. Effects of oral sensory field loss of taste scaling ability. *Chem. Senses* 10:459 (Abstr.)

Pevsner J, Sklar PB, Hwang PM, Snyder SH. 1989. Odorant-binding protein. In *Receptor Events and Transduction in Taste and Olfaction,* ed. JG Brand, JH Teeter, RH Cagan, MR Kare, pp. 207–42. New York: Dekker

Pfaffmann C, Bartoshuk LM. 1989. Psychophysical mapping of a human case of left unilateral ageusi. *Chem. Senses* 14:738 (Abstr.)

Pfaffmann C, Bartoshuk LM. 1990. Taste loss due to herpes zoster oticus: an update after 19 months. *Chem. Senses* 15:657–58

Pollack MS, Wysocki CJ, Beauchamp GK, Braun DJ, Colloway C, Dupont B. 1982. Absence of HIA association or linkage for variations in sensitivity to the odor of androstenone. *Immunogenetics* 15:579–89

Potts WK, Manning CJ, Wakeland EK. 1991. Mating patterns in semi-natural populations of mice influenced by MHC genotype. *Nature* 352:610–21

Preti G, Cutler WB, Garcia CR, Huggins GR, Lawley HJ. 1986. Human axillary secretions influence women's menstrual cycles: the role of donor extract from females. *Horm. Behav.* 20:474–82

Reedy FE, Bartoshuk LM, Miller IJ, Duffy VB, Yanagisawa K. 1993. *Relationships among papillae, taste pores, and 6-*n*-propylthiouracil (PROP) suprathreshold taste sensitivity.* Presented at Annu. Meet. Assoc. Chemorecept. Sci., 15th, Sarasota, Fla.

Rock I, Victor J. 1964. Vision and touch: an experimentally created conflict between the two senses. *Science* 143:594–96

Rosenstein D, Oster H. 1988. Differential facial responses to four basic tastes in newborns. *Child Dev.* 59:1555–68

Russell MJ, Switz GM, Thompson K. 1980. Olfactory influences on the human menstrual cycle. *Pharmacol. Biochem. Behav.* 13:737–38

Schaal B. 1986. Presumed olfactory exchanges between mother and neonate in humans. In *Ethology and Psychology,* ed. JL Camus, J Conler, pp. 101–10. Toulouse: Private IEC

Schiffman SS. 1977. Food recognition by the elderly. *J. Gerontol.* 32:586–92

Schleidt M, Genzel C. 1990. The significance of mother's perfume for infants in the first weeks of their life. *Ethol. Sociobiol.* 11:145–54

Schmidt HJ, Beauchamp GK. 1988. Adult-like odor preferences and aversions in three-year-old children. *Child Dev.* 59: 1136–43

Segal NL, Brown KW, Topolski TD. 1992. A twin study of odor identification and olfactory sensitivity. *Acta Genet. Med. Gemellol.* 41:113–21

Shimojo S. 1987. Attention-dependent visual capture in double vision. *Perception* 16: 445–47

Shingai T, Beidler LM. 1985. Inter-strain differences in bitter taste responses in mice. *Chem. Senses* 10:51–55

Ship J, Weiffenbach J. 1993. Age, gender, medical treatment and medication effects on smell identification. *J. Gerontol.* 48: M26–M32

Singh PB, Brown RE, Roser B. 1987. MHC antigens in urine as olfactory recogition cues. *Nature* 327:161–64

Smith DV. 1991. Taste and smell dysfunction. In *Otolaryngology, Head and Neck,* ed. MM Paparella, DA Shumrick, JL Gluckman, WL Meyerhoff, pp. 1911–34. Philadelphia: Saunders

Snow JB, Doty RL, Bartoshuk LM, Getchell TV. 1991. Categorization of chemosensory disorders. See Getchell et al 1991, pp. 445–47

Snyder LH. 1931. Inherited taste deficiency. *Science* 74:151–52

Solomon GM, Catalanotto F, Scott A, Bartoshuk LM. 1991. Patterns of taste loss in clinic patients with histories of head trauma, nasal symptoms, or upper respiratory infection. *Yale J. Biol. Med.* 64:280 (Abstr.)

Steiner JE. 1973. The gustofacial response: observation on normal and anencephalic newborn infants. In *Development in the Fetus and Infant,* ed. JF Bosma, pp. 254–78. Washington, DC: US Govt. Print. Off.

Steiner JE. 1987. What the neonate can tell us about umami. In *Umami: A Basic Taste,* ed. Y Kawamura, MR Kare, pp. 97–123. New York: Dekker

Stevens JC, Cain WS. 1986. Smelling via the mouth: effect of aging. *Percept. Psychophys.* 40:142–46

Stevens JC, Cain WS. 1985. Age-related deficiency in the perceived strength of six odorants. *Chem. Senses* 10:517–29

Stevens JC, Marks LE. 1980. Cross-modality matching functions generated by magnitude estimation. *Percept. Psychophys.* 27:379–89

Strahan RC, Jafek BW, Moran DT. 1991. Biopsy of the olfactory neuroepithelium. See Getchell et al 1991, pp. 703–9

Sullivan SA. 1992. *Infant experience and acceptance of solid foods.* PhD thesis. Univ. Ill., Urbana-Champaign

Takami S, Getchell ML, Chen Y, Monti-Bloch L, Berliner DL, et al. 1993. Vomernasal epithelial cells of the adult human express neuron-specific molecules. *Neuroreport* 4:375–78

Tastevin J. 1937. En partant de l'expérience d'Aristote. *Encéphale* 1:57–84, 140–158

Tatzer E, Schubert MT, Timischi W, Simbruner G. 1985. Discrimination of taste and preference for sweet in premature babies. *Early Hum. Dev.* 12:23–30

Todrank J, Bartoshuk LM. 1991. A taste illusion: taste sensation localized by touch. *Physiol. Behav.* 50:1027–31

Tomita H, Ikeda M, Okuda Y. 1986. Basis and practice of clinical taste examinations. *Auris Nasus Larynx (Tokyo)* 13 (Suppl. I): S1-S15

Urbantschitsch V. 1876. *Beobachtungen über Anomalien des Geschmacks der Tastempfindungen und der Speichelsecretion in Folge von Erkrankungen der Paukenhöhle.* Stuttgart: Verlag von Ferdinand Enke

Wang HW, Wysocki CJ, Gold GH. 1993. Induction of olfactory receptor sensitivity in mice. *Science* 260:998–1000

Weiffenbach JM. 1993. Touch and taste in the mouth: presence and character of sapid solutions. *Appetite.* In press

Weiffenbach JM, Cowart BJ, Baum BJ. 1986. Taste intensity perception in aging. *J. Gerontol.* 41:460–68

Weiffenbach JM, Tylenda CA, Baum BJ. 1990. Oral sensory changes in aging. *J. Gerontol.* 45:M121–25

Whitney G, Harder DB, Gannon KS, Maggio JC. 1990. Congenic lines differing in ability to taste sucrose octaacetate. In *Chemical Senses: Genetics of Perception and Communication,* ed. CJ Wysocki, MR Kare, 3:242–62. New York: Dekker

Wysocki CJ. 1979. Neurobehavioral evidence for the involvement of the vomeronasal system in mammalian reproduction. *Neurosci. Biobehav. Rev.* 3:301–41

Wysocki CJ, Beauchamp GK. 1984. The ability to smell androstenone is genetically determined. *Proc. Natl. Acad. Sci. USA* 81:4899–5002

Wysocki CJ, Beauchamp GK. 1991. Individual differences in human olfaction. In *Chemical Senses: Genetics of Perception and Communication,* ed. CJ Wysocki, MR Kare, 3:353–73. New York: Dekker

Wysocki CJ, Dorries KM, Beauchamp GK. 1989. Ability to smell androstenone can be acquired by ostensibly anosmic people. *Proc. Natl. Acad. Sci. USA* 86:7976–78

Wysocki CJ, Gilbert AN. 1989. National Geographic smell survey: Effects of age are heterogeneous. In *Nutrition and the Chemical Senses in Aging: Recent Advances and Current Research Needs,* ed. C Murphy, WS Cain, DM Hegsted, pp. 12–28. New York: Ann. NY Acad. Sci.

Wysocki CJ, Meredith M. 1987. *The Vomeronasal System.* New York: Wiley
Yamaguchi S, Takashai C. 1984. Hedonic functions of monosodium glutamate and four basic taste substances used at various concentration levels in single and complex systems. *Agric. Biol. Chem.* 48:1077–81
Yamazaki K, Beauchamp GK, Kupnlewski D, Bard J, Thomas L, Boyse EA. 1988. Familial imprinting determines H-2 selective mating preferences. *Science* 240:1331–32
Yamazaki K, Boyse EA, Mike V, Thaler HT, Mathieson BJ, et al. 1976. Control of mating preferences in mice by genes in the major histocompatibility complex. *J. Exp. Med.* 144:1332–35
Yanagisawa K, Bartoshuk LM, Karrer TA, Kveton JF, Catalanotto FA, et al. 1992. Anesthesia of the chorda tympani nerve: insights into a source of dysgeusia. *Chem. Senses* 17:724 (Abstr.)
Yang RSH, Kare MR. 1968. Taste response of a bird to constituents of arthopod defense secretions. *Ann. Entomol. Soc. Am.* 61:781–82
Ye Q, Heck GL, DeSimone JA. 1991. The anion paradox in sodium taste reception: resolution by voltage-clamp studies. *Science* 254:724–26

Annu. Rev. Psychol. 1994. 45:451–85

COLOR APPEARANCE: ON SEEING RED—OR YELLOW, OR GREEN, OR BLUE

Israel Abramov

Applied Vision Institute and Psychology Department, Brooklyn College of CUNY, Brooklyn, New York 11210 and Laboratory of Biophysics, The Rockefeller University, New York, New York 10021

James Gordon

Psychology Department, Hunter College of CUNY, New York, New York 10021 and Laboratory of Biophysics, The Rockefeller University, New York, New York 10021

KEY WORDS: color vision, hue, spectrally opponent mechanisms, unique hues, sensory scaling

---

CONTENTS

INTRODUCTION

We see an object by the light it reflects. But the intensity and spectral content of the reflected light can vary greatly, as when a shadow falls across part of the object, or the illumination changes from sunrise to sunset. Similarly, the backgrounds against which objects are seen are rarely uniform. Color is often invoked as the means by which we organize a scene in the face of intensity variations that are not related to boundaries of objects. For example, shared hue helps segregate related elements, such as the patterns seen in the pseudoisochromatic plates of standard color vision tests (Mollon 1989, Mullen & Kingdom 1991). Color may also have a signaling property: it can mark emotional state, sexual readiness, ripeness of a fruit, and so on (Jacobs 1993). This review focuses on the following question: When do things appear to have the same color and what is that color, versus simply when do they appear different? Specifically, we concentrate on descriptions of color appearance (e.g. is something red or yellow) and the associated physiological mechanisms.

BASIC PHYSIOLOGICAL PROCESSES

Photopigments

Vision begins with absorption of light by a photopigment in a receptor. All vertebrate photopigments consist of a chromophore (retinal, in terrestrial species) combined with an opsin (a protein), the particular opsin determining the range of wavelengths that can be absorbed. Any one receptor is univariant: each photon that is absorbed generates the same electrical signal regardless of its wavelength, which only affects the probability that the photon will be absorbed. A receptor signals only the rate at which its pigment absorbs photons. All photopigments have spectral absorbance functions with the same shape when plotted in the appropriate coordinates (MacNichol 1986) and all absorb across large and overlapping spectral ranges. It is highly misleading, therefore, to label any receptor with a color term (e.g. red cone). In this review, we refer to the different pigments by the spectral regions that they absorb best.

The genes for the different opsins have been sequenced in several primates, including humans (Nathans et al 1992). This allows comparison of pigments according to the similarities of their genetic codes, which can be used as a measure of evolutionary closeness. Based on similarities of the gene sequences, it has been estimated that S-cones (short-wavelength-sensitive) diverged from rods about 800 million years ago (MYA). About 200–300 MYA a cone gene formed on the X-chromosome coding either for an M-cone (middle-wavelength-sensitive) or an L-cone (long-wavelength-sensitive), and shortly after the split of New and Old World primates, about 9–35 MYA, this X-gene diverged again to allow for the very closely related M- and L-cones to be present in the same retina (Yokoyama & Yokoyama 1989, Nathans et al 1992).

Any form of color vision requires at least two types of receptors that differ in their spectral sensitivities. However, the responses of different receptor types can still be combined by the nervous system so that the result is univariant (Sirovich & Abramov 1977). For color vision, the responses of the different receptors must be compared by higher order neurons in a way that preserves the differences in the receptors' responses to spectral variations (Zrenner et al 1990). In all known cases this is achieved by spectrally opponent neurons (excited by some wavelengths and inhibited by others) that combine the responses of the receptors with different signs. Spectrally nonopponent neurons may combine receptor responses all with the same sign, or in some weighted fashion so that the net response has the same sign across the spectrum. The former are sometimes called *color-coded,* and the latter *broad-band.* We use *spectrally opponent* to denote an overt change in sign of the response of some higher order neuron.

Contrary to earlier prejudices, the rule for mammals is that they have some form of color vision, usually based on S-cones together with one of M- or L-cones (Jacobs 1993). The choice of M or L may be conditioned by the species' photic environment: pairing S- and M-cones may maximize chromatic differences in leafy environments, while S- and L-cones maximize the differences for the yellows and browns of forest debris (Lythgoe & Partridge 1989). A species with only two cone types is dichromatic. For such a species there will be a spectral neutral point (a wavelength that appears achromatic); furthermore, hue will not appear to vary continuously across the spectrum. Among mammals, only some primates have three cone types, with the attendant lack of a spectral neutral point. In New World primates the M- and L-cones are coded by different alleles at the same gene locus so that only heterozygous females will have three cone types (Jacobs 1993). Of the Old World primates, macaque monkeys are thought to have color vision like that of humans: both have S-, M-, and L-cones with maxima roughly at 430, 530, and 560 nm (Bowmaker et al 1991). However, macaques may not have exactly the same cone types as humans (Jacobs 1991). Also, some humans, mostly males, have only two cone types, but there is no evidence for such polymorphism in macaques (Jacobs & Harwerth 1989).

Human Cones

Human color vision is trichromatic, meaning that in psychophysical studies three independent dimensions are needed to describe completely the appearance of any light. For example, any light can be specified by the particular mixture of three primary lights needed to match it. This is usually ascribed to the relative amounts of light absorbed by three independent cone photopigments. Since only M- and L-cones absorb wavelengths longer than approximately 530 nm, only two primaries are needed to match any wavelength in this spectral range: a spectral light that appears green (G) can be mixed with one that appears red (R) so as to exactly match an intermediate wavelength that appears yellow (Y)—the Rayleigh match. Exciting new findings show that, contrary to previous wisdom, all individuals with normal trichromatic color vision do not necessarily have the same M- and L-cones: the X-chromosome may have several gene loci coding for photopigments in the spectral range of 530–560 nm (Nathans et al 1986, Nathans et al 1992).

According to one model of the various X-linked genes, small variations in the DNA sequences of these genes shift the maxima of the expressed pigments in roughly 6 nm steps between the extremes of 530 and 562 nm (Neitz et al 1991). A priori, individuals with normal color vision and with either the 530 nm or the next longer M-cone and the 562 nm or next shorter L-cone should still be able to make Rayleigh matches within the accepted range for normals and with the same precision. But the precise R/G ratio will depend entirely on the spectra of that person's M- and L-cones (provided there are no wavelength-specific losses in transmission through the ocular media). Because the pigment spectra seem to shift in discrete steps, the matching R/G ratios are also predicted to vary in discrete steps across the population. Such multimodal frequency distributions of R/G ratios have been found and are highly correlated with predictions from analyses of the individuals' DNA sequences (Winderickx et al 1992, Neitz et al 1993). However, many individuals (only males have been tested in order to simplify dealing with X-linked genes) have intermediate R/G ratios that are best predicted by assuming that they express more than two pigments in this spectral range, which, together with their S-cones, would give them at least four cone pigments. Nonetheless, these individuals' ability to use only two primaries to make a normal Rayleigh match shows they are functionally trichromats—trichromacy is not necessarily imposed at the cone pigment level and may be a property of the nervous system (Neitz et al 1993). However, the Rayleigh matches of these individuals are not stable under all conditions and can be disturbed by adding a chromatic adapting light uniformly across the entire field—adding a uniform field would not change the Rayleigh match of an individual with only two cone pigments in the M-to-L range (Neitz et al 1992). Similarly, heterozygous female carriers of red-green color deficiency can make normal Rayleigh matches, and therefore are trichromats, but, as with the above males, their matches can be disturbed by adding uniform chromatic fields. Thus, they too have at least four cone pigments (Nagy et al 1981), which, given the existence of multiple

X-linked pigment genes (Nathans et al 1992), may be a property of normal human color vision in many individuals.

Even with a possible multiplicity of cone pigments, there is no good evidence that trichromacy is violated. Color vision is still describable by three independent spectral weighting functions, at least one of which could be a mixture of two cone pigments, either within a cone, or summed by the nervous system. For normal trichromats, any combinations must be of pigments with similar spectra. Otherwise, they would not make a Rayleigh match within normal limits. For much of the following discussion, we simplify matters by assuming only the canonical three cone types.

Spectrally Opponent and Nonopponent Cells

A higher order neuron usually reports differences in the inputs to it by trading excitation and inhibition (summing the inputs with different signs). When the inputs are from different cone types, the neuron's responses may be overtly spectrally opponent. Spectrally nonopponent cells combine the inputs with the same sign, although some may also include non-overt spectrally antagonistic inputs. Furthermore, for both spectrally opponent and nonopponent types, the inputs from different parts of the receptive field may be antagonistic, making the response spatially opponent. This emphasizes the bottleneck created by the need to compress retinal information into the limited number of optic nerve fibers: responses of retinal ganglion cells are ambiguous—each cell encodes many aspects of a stimulus. There are, however, two clear streams that emerge from the retina: ganglion cells whose axons terminate in the parvocellular (P) layers of the lateral geniculate nucleus (LGN) of the thalamus differ in many of their response properties from those that terminate in the magnocellular (M) layers.[1] For this review, the most important difference between the two cell types is that the great majority of P-cells are spectrally opponent while M-cells are nonopponent (Kaplan et al 1990). This may be overstated, however, since a substantial number of P-cells are not overtly spectrally opponent (De Valois et al 1977) and some M-cells may be spectrally opponent (Lee et al 1989). Much has been written about the sensory and perceptual processes subserved by the parallel P- and M-pathways (Livingstone & Hubel 1988, Shapley 1990, Merigan & Maunsell 1993); we will return to this subject when we consider cortical processing.

Although trichromacy requires that color vision be describable along three independent axes, there is no one set of axes that must be used: there are many possible mappings of color space (Thompson et al 1992). At the earliest level

---

1 The *M* in M-cells refers to neurons whose axons end in a particular part of the thalamus, while the *M* in M-cones refers to the preferred spectral region of a cone type.

the axes might be the relative absorptions by the three cone types, whereas another set of axes might be more appropriate for higher order neurons that combine responses of different cones. A widely used approach for identifying the appropriate axes at levels of spectrally opponent and nonopponent response channels stems from the ability to adapt them separately (second-site adaptation) without necessarily adapting the cone inputs (Krauskopf et al 1982). In this approach, stimuli are temporally modulated in color space (chromaticity and luminance are varied about some starting value); psychophysical thresholds for detecting such changes will be raised only for those channels that respond to the modulation. For example, stimuli could be modulated along a tritanopic confusion line, which is the locus of points on a chromaticity diagram that all appear the same to a person who lacks S-cones. For such an observer, these stimuli can only modulate L- and M-cones and must keep the ratios of their responses constant (otherwise appearance would change). For an observer with all three cone types, these stimuli would modulate the responses only of S-cones. Similarly, other directions can be used to activate channels with different cone combinations.

In the above psychophysical study, stimuli were modulated symmetrically in various directions in color space about a "white" point. Only along three narrowly defined directions were threshold elevations confined to the same direction as the adaptation. Two of these are "cardinal axes" for stimuli that vary only in chrominance; modulation orthogonal to this plane affects only the system that detects luminance changes. The three axes correspond to a luminance channel that sums cone inputs (+L+M), and two spectrally opponent channels: +S–(+L+M), and +L–M (and their inverses), which are often, but misleadingly, referred to as the YB and RG channels (see below). The psychophysically determined chromatic cardinal axes agree quite well with the axes that divide the spectrally opponent P-cells of the LGN into two classes (Derrington et al 1984). Although there are actually four types of spectrally opponent cells, they can be paired to form two spectral classes; those with mirror image inputs from the cones (e.g. cells with either +L–M or +M–L inputs) can be treated as a single class (De Valois et al 1966, Derrington et al 1984).

P-cells, by virtue of their spatially antagonistic receptive fields, show bandpass tuning for patterns varying in luminance; but they are lowpass tuned for patterns that vary only in chrominance—the optimal stimulus for passing chromatic information through these cells is one that uniformly covers the entire receptive field (De Valois et al 1977). The same is true of many of the simple cortical cells in area V1 (Thorell et al 1984). All these cells also respond to uniform fields of white light. What, then, is the role of these cells in determining color appearance? Our psychophysiological linking hypothesis (Teller 1990) is that for any unique category of sensation (e.g. R or Y) there is a neural mechanism with response properties that match those of the related psychophysical functions. Only when that mechanism[2] responds do we experience that sensation. By this criterion, the P-cells are not hue mechanisms, despite their sometimes being called color-coded or labeled with hue terms such as +R–G (De Valois et al 1966, Derrington et al 1984, Livingstone & Hubel 1988).

Consider a few aspects of so-called +R–G cells (more appropriately labeled +L–M): 1. They respond to an achromatic white stimulus and therefore cannot uniquely signal redness. 2. The wavelength at which their spectral response functions cross from excitation to inhibition should correspond to a unique sensation of Y (neither R nor G), but typically are at much shorter wavelengths that would appear GY or chartreuse (Derrington et al 1984). 3. None of these cells have response functions with a second excitatory zone in the short wavelengths, and yet short wavelengths elicit a sensation that includes some R (violet). 4. Modulation along an L-M cardinal axis adapts only cells with inputs from L- and M-cones and has no effect on other cells. But, psychophysically, modulation in every direction of color space markedly shifts the appearance of all chromatic stimuli—i.e. cardinal-axis-adaptation shifts appearance of stimuli on and off the cardinal axis (Webster & Mollon 1991). This means that there is yet another site of adaptation (one that determines appearance), or that adaptation at the level of the LGN changes inputs to higher levels and so changes outputs (appearance) of those levels.

While spectrally opponent P-cells are not by themselves hue mechanisms, they transmit some information about stimulus wavelength and must provide inputs to the sensory/perceptual mechanisms at later stages of the visual system. This, of course, requires disambiguation in order to strip from their responses those components that do not directly determine hue. However, they need not be the only inputs to hue mechanisms. The stimulus that is located in color space at the intersect of the cardinal chromatic axes does not elicit a response from either of the spectrally opponent cell classes because all the spectrally antagonistic inputs cancel each other, but it does elicit responses from spectrally nonopponent cells (Derrington et al 1984). This chromatic-null stimulus, when plotted on a chromaticity diagram, is far from the region of achromatic stimuli and would appear as a somewhat desaturated G or BG. Consistent with this is the following psychophysical observation: the stimulus which neutrally adapts the opponent chromatic channels that contribute to increment-threshold measures of spectral sensitivity is an equal-quantum white, which appears quite B (Fuld et al 1988). But if none of the P-cells respond to a stimulus at the intersect of the cardinal axes and it still appears

[2] Throughout this review we use "mechanism" only in this restricted sense.

colored, then the hue must be signaled by M-cells, the only other class of cells that responds to this stimulus. M-cells cannot always signal this BG hue, or it would be part of the sensation evoked by all stimuli. If this reasoning is correct, we must also postulate an asymmetric interaction: when P-cells are active, they block this chromatic component of M-cells' responses. Such asymmetric gating is not entirely far-fetched: chromatic gratings reduce the visibility of luminance gratings, but not vice-versa (Switkes et al 1988). Except for these possibly atypical conditions, the spectrally nonopponent M-cells are thought to signal intensive aspects of colored stimuli. Their responses match very closely the psychophysical measures of spectral sensitivity that are the basis for specifying stimulus luminance (Lee et al 1990). But M-cells are not the exclusive governors of perceived intensity. The spectral sensitivity function that is obtained either by adjusting nonflickering stimuli to appear equally bright or by measuring their increment thresholds is not the same as the function from M-cells—it includes marked inputs from spectrally opponent P-cells (Sperling 1992).

At the level of the LGN, spectrally opponent cells carry simultaneously the information needed to derive hue responses, together with information used for many other sensory/perceptual functions. Spectrally nonopponent cells are also essential for many aspects of color. Higher levels of the visual system must disambiguate the responses of all these cells and then recombine them to form the mechanisms whose responses then determine color appearance.

COLOR APPEARANCE

Describing Color Appearance

We have argued that the cardinal axes used to describe the responses of LGN cells do not describe the mapping of colored stimuli onto a perceptual color space. Nor can a standard chromaticity diagram be used: a particular stimulus always plots to the same position on it regardless of how its appearance might be distorted by viewing conditions or the adaptation state of an observer. The canonical dimensions of perceived color space are hue, saturation, and brightness (although there are questions about their independence; Burns & Shepp 1988), and many systems have been devised to describe appearance along these, or closely related, dimensions (Derefeldt 1991). Most systems are realized as a set of colored chips varying in discrete steps along the perceptual axes, but there is little agreement on how to segment the hue dimension. We divide hues according to the system first formulated by Hering and elaborated by Hurvich and Jameson (Hurvich 1981): there are four elemental or unique hue sensations that are paired in opponent fashion to form the orthogonal hue dimensions, RG and YB.

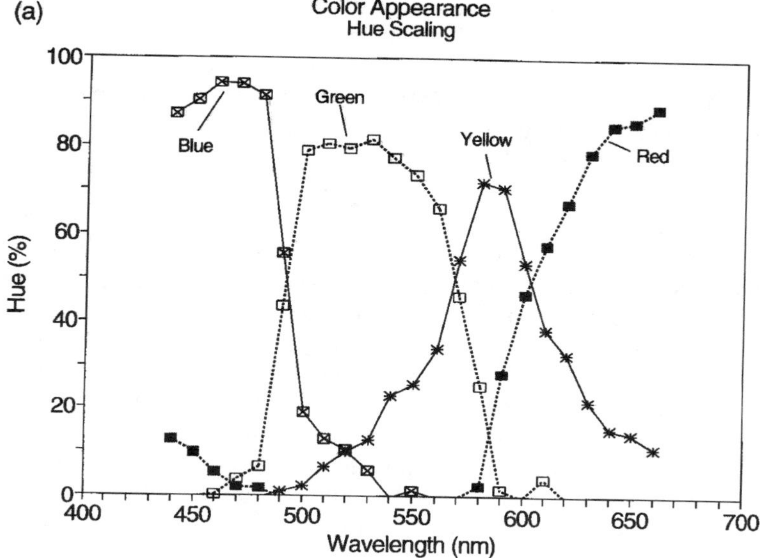

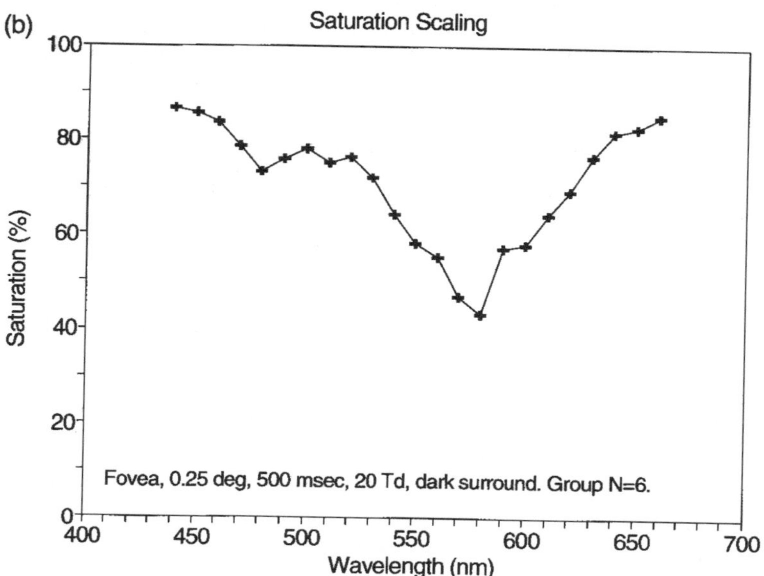

Figure 1 Hue and saturation scaling of monochromatic lights; foveal, 0.25 deg, 500 msec, 20 Td; group means. (*a*) Hue scaling. (*b*) Saturation scaling.

Subjects can directly scale the magnitudes of their sensations of R, G, Y, and B evoked by any stimulus (Jameson & Hurvich 1959). We have systematically explored different procedures for scaling hue and saturation (Gordon & Abramov 1988, Gordon et al 1994), and now use the following: after each stimulus, subjects state the percentages of their hue sensations using any combination of the four unique terms for a total of 100%. They also describe apparent saturation as the percentage of their entire sensation (chromatic and achromatic) that was chromatic. An example is shown in Figures 1a and 1b for monochromatic lights spaced across the spectrum. Note that the four hue terms do not denote separate perceptual categories in the sense that the sensation from a stimulus must belong only to one or another—sensation shades continuously from one to another of the adjacent categories. Also, there is very little overlap of R with G or Y with B—what little there is the result of intersubject and intertrial variability. Thus, R and G form a mutually exclusive pairing of sensations, as do Y and B. To combine hue and saturation, the hue values can be rescaled by their associated saturation values so that the sum of the hue values for each stimulus equals the saturation (Figure 2a). These hue values can be smoothed to remove the small overlaps between opposed pairs and then replotted on a two dimensional uniform appearance diagram (UAD) with orthogonal and bipolar axes Y–B and G–R (Figure 2b). The location of each stimulus defines its hue, and distance from the origin (city-block metric) represents saturation. We refer to this perceptual mapping of the stimuli as uniform because the distances between stimuli are directly proportional to discriminability steps. For example, UADs can be used to derive accurately wavelength discrimination (Abramov et al 1990), as well as the degrees of dissimilarity among widely differing stimuli (Chan et al 1991). A similar scaling procedure was used to derive the samples that constitute the Natural Color System (Hard & Sivik 1981).

Model of Hue Mechanisms

We begin with a simple linear model of how the responses of the different cones may be combined ultimately to yield the hue mechanisms with responses corresponding directly to sensations, such as those shown in Figure 1. (We will discuss later how and where the responses of LGN cells might be combined to produce such mechanisms.) Perceptual considerations place two major constraints on all such models: First, the relative weights of the cones must be such that the null points of the mechanisms, which correspond to the wavelengths that elicit unique hue sensations, are in acceptable regions of the spectrum. Second, these mechanisms must not respond to an achromatic (white) stimulus, or this would violate our linking hypothesis that when a hue mechanism responds, we experience that specific hue. The band of wavelengths associated with each unique hue can be estimated from UADs (Figure

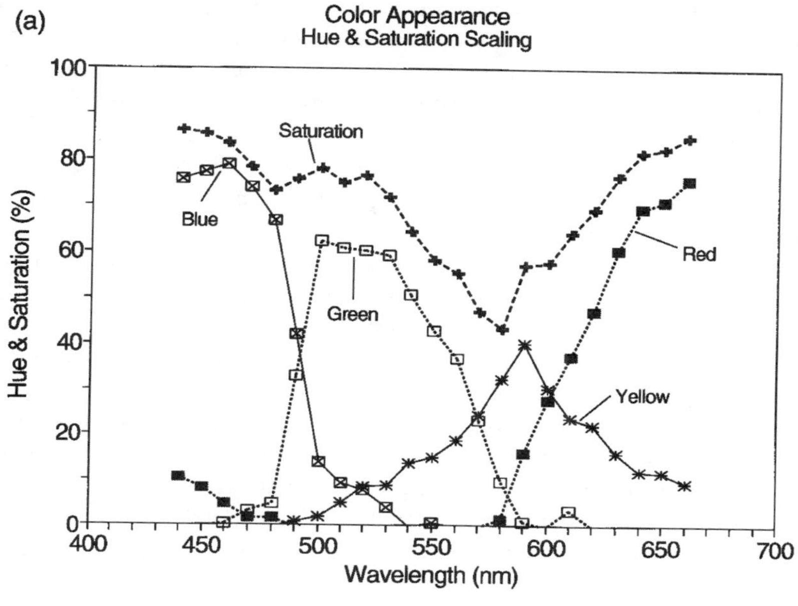

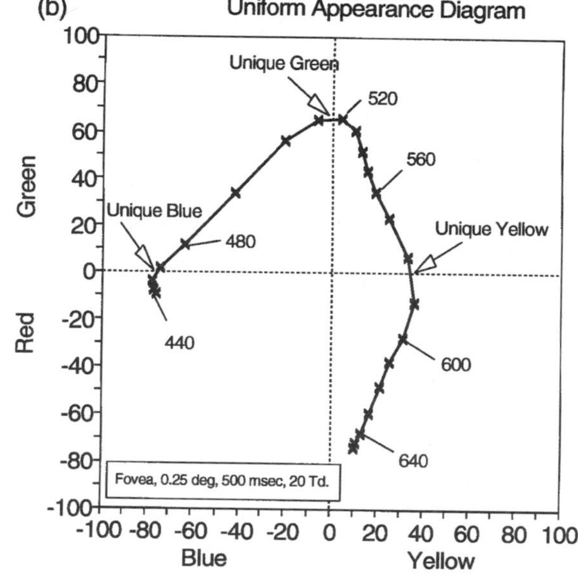

Figure 2 Hue and saturation scaling of monochromatic lights; same data as in Figure 1. (*a*) Combined hue and saturation scaling. (*b*) Smoothed data replotted on Uniform Appearance Diagram.

2b). These wavelengths have also been obtained by adjustment in many studies (Ayama et al 1987); within-subject variability in these settings is markedly less than between-subject variability (Schefrin & Werner 1990). (Between-subject variability may be the result of variations in relative cone weights or of variations in photopigments described earlier.) The best estimates of achromatic stimuli cluster about near equal-energy white lights with equivalent color temperatures of roughly 5500°K (Hurvich & Jameson 1951, Walraven & Werner 1991, Sternheim & Drum 1993).

The responses of the +R–G mechanism, which has inputs +L–M+S, are shown in Figure 3a; the cone functions are from human psychophysical studies (Smith & Pokorny 1975). Consider first the locus of unique-Y, at which point the response of the +R–G mechanism must be zero and only the other hue mechanism (+Y–B) is active. At these wavelengths only L- and M-cones absorb and their responses must be weighted to be equal in order for their inputs to the mechanism to cancel each other. But if only these cones are involved, the mechanism will not produce the R that is part of the sensation at short wavelengths. S-cones must provide this signal and their weighting is now constrained: the combination of all three cones must equal zero at the wavelength of unique-B. The cone weights have been adjusted to keep the null points within the spectral ranges of the unique hues determined by the +R–G mechanism (i.e. unique-Y and -B) and to produce no response to an equal-energy white light (i.e. the integral of the opponent function is zero). Figure 3b shows a similar model for the +Y–B mechanism, which has inputs +L–M–S. The null point of this mechanism corresponds to unique-G, but because all three cones absorb at these wavelengths, the relative weights of their inputs to this mechanism are not tightly constrained, except for the signs of the inputs. It is difficult to find an acceptable set of weights for any other combination of input signs. For the particular version shown, unique-G is appropriately located and there is no response to an equal-energy white. Note that the cone weights we show are for the inputs to these specific mechanisms and cannot both be estimates of the relative numbers of cones in the retina. We return to this later.

Although the major constraints on the above hue mechanisms were imposed by the unique hues, the responses of these mechanisms must also specify the intermediate hues, as well as the apparent saturations of all hues. The precise sensation from any wavelength must be derived at some later stage at which the outputs of the hue mechanisms are compared to each other. For example, the changing ratios of R/Y in hue scaling functions at long wavelengths (Figure 1a) can be derived from the ratios of the responses of +R and +Y hue mechanisms. However, the apparent saturation of those sensations (Figure 1b) requires that the outputs of the hue mechanisms be combined in

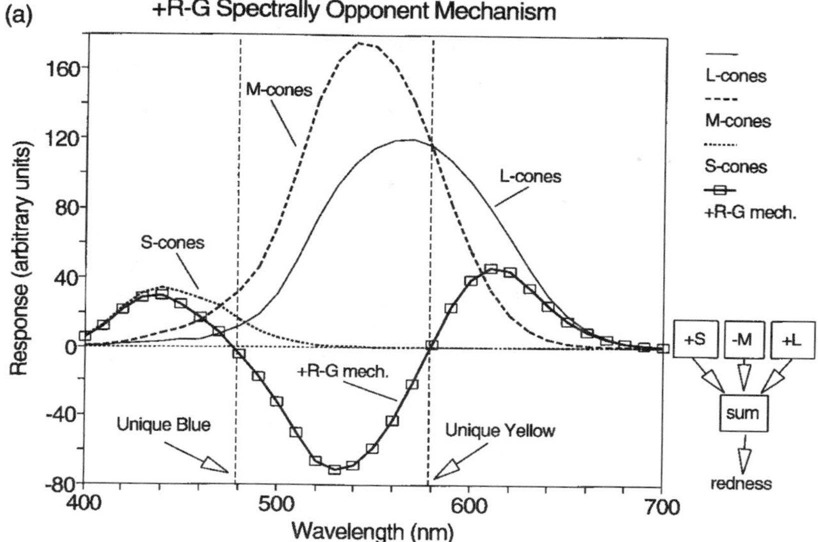

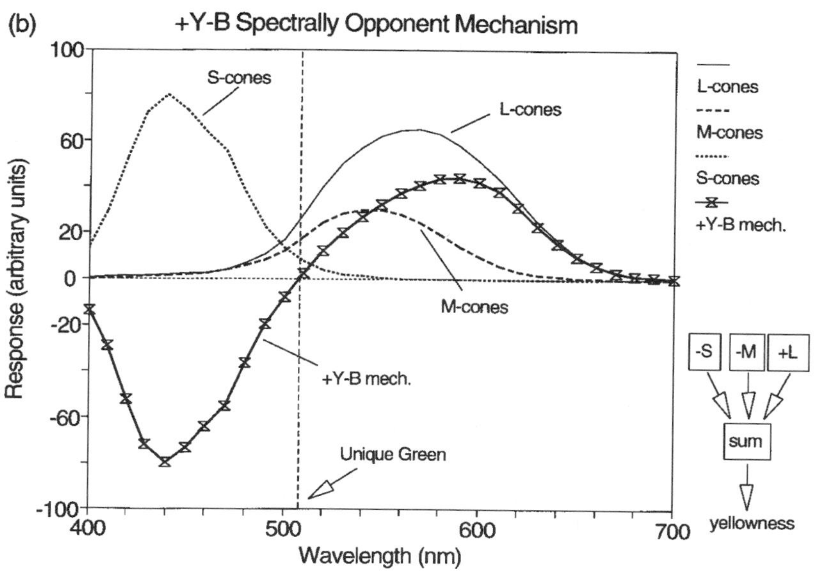

Figure 3 Spectrally opponent hue mechanisms. (*a*) +R–G hue mechanism. (*b*) +Y–B hue mechanism.

yet another way to give some overall measure of chromatic content, which can then be compared to the response of achromatic mechanisms.

We now consider additional constraints that must be placed on these models. First, the different cones cannot be specific color receptors: S-cones contribute to both B and R, M-cones contribute to both B and G, and L-cones contribute to both R and Y (Drum 1989, Shevell 1992). The only factors that determine the spectral loci of the unique hues are the relative magnitudes of the cone inputs to the opponent hue mechanisms.

In the model, we have shown only two hue mechanisms, with the implication that when the +R–G mechanism is excited, for example, we experience R and when it is inhibited, we experience G. However, since there are four types of spectrally opponent LGN cells and cortical neurons have low spontaneous response rates, it is likely that for each of the hue mechanisms in Figure 3 there is also an inverse mechanism (e.g. +G–R). Low cortical spontaneous rates (or half-wave cortical response-rectification) effectively eliminate overt inhibitory responses (Movshon et al 1978, Spitzer & Hochstein 1988). Thus, a more complete model is that R is seen when the +R–G mechanism is excited and G is seen when +G–R is excited, inhibition serving only to limit the spectral ranges of the excitatory responses. Having four separate hue mechanisms permits each to have different properties along other stimulus dimensions, such as size (Abramov et al 1991; see below). But, a mechanism such as +R–G must still have precisely the same cone inputs as its inverse, +G–R; otherwise, for that subject, the sensations of R and G either would not be mutually exclusive, or there would be a wide range of wavelengths that appears unique-Y.

Responses of the various elements of the models are affected by changes in stimulus intensity. In Figures 3a and 3b, as with many similar models, we assume that all responses are linear, which immediately poses a difficulty. The responses shown are to spectral lights equated for energy. In most psychophysical studies stimuli are equated for luminance and not energy, which makes the stimuli at the spectral extremes vastly more energetic. In Figure 4 we show how our postulated mechanisms would respond to such stimuli. The loci of the unique hues are, of course, not affected by intensity changes and neither are the ratios of the mechanisms' responses at any wavelength. But the responses of all hue mechanisms to short wavelengths are increased so massively that the nervous system may lack the precision to compute accurately the ratios of the relatively small responses to the rest of the spectrum. Some form of response compression may be needed.

Varying stimulus intensity produces changes in the appearance of non-unique, intermediate hues (Bezold-Brucke hue shift), which means that the intensity-response functions of the R, G, Y, and B mechanisms cannot be the same (Hurvich 1981); moreover, at least some must be nonlinear (Valberg &

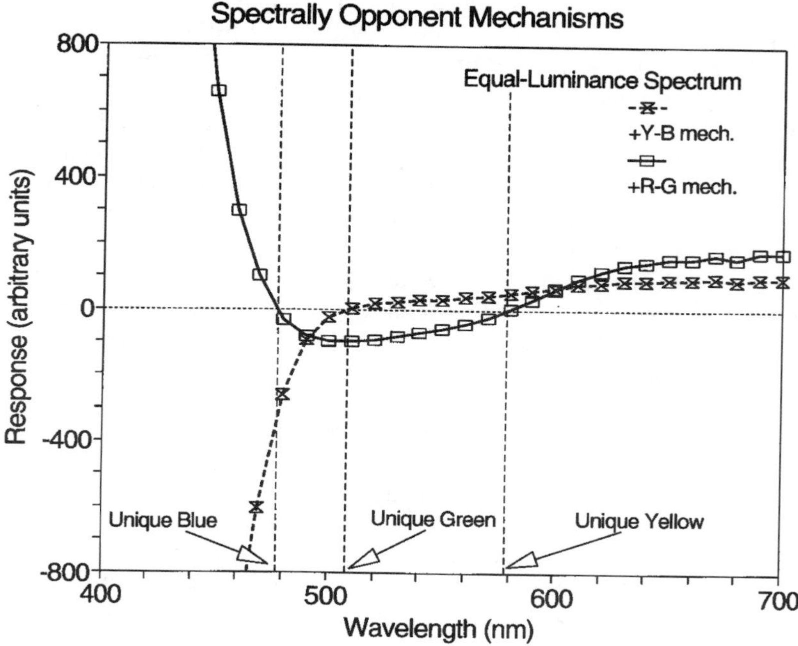

Figure 4 Responses of hue mechanisms to equal-luminance spectrum.

Seim 1991). Either the mechanisms have different thresholds or some response functions are compressive. For example, R could have a compressive function so that as intensity increases, R tends toward a ceiling while Y continues to grow; at higher intensities, longer wavelengths appear more Y. This change in the intermediate hues does not preclude linear cone inputs to the hue mechanisms. It is possible that the cones themselves are linear over very large intensity ranges (Schnapf et al 1990, Hood & Birch 1993); an initial linear stage is followed by a cone-specific compressive stage, which is one of the sites of adaptation (Finkelstein et al 1990). But if the inputs to the hue mechanisms from the cones are linear, the spectral loci of the unique hues must be invariant over intensity, as must the stimulus that appears achromatic; the cancellations of cone inputs that determine these sensations occur before any nonlinearity imposed on the outputs of the opponent hue mechanisms. It is difficult to see how nonlinear cone inputs could still produce invariant unique hues: for example, at the wavelength of unique-Y, the L-cones absorb more than do the M-cones and their responses, therefore, would be further along any nonlinear curve than those of the M-cones. Increasing intensity would have less incremental effect on L- than M-cones, which must shift the locus of the unique hue. While it has been widely accepted that the unique hues are invariant, this is now being questioned (Ayama et al 1987). In particular, the unique loci seem relatively invariant for long stimulus durations, but shift considerably for very short durations (Nagy 1979). A possible explanation is that the longer stimulus durations used in most psychophysical studies are sufficient to produce adaptation (Graham & Hood 1992), thereby resetting the cone responses and keeping the unique hues relatively invariant over intensity. This could also explain the impressive intensity-invariance of achromatic white (Walraven & Werner 1991).

Finally, when the spectrum of the illuminant changes, the spectrum reflected by an object changes, but its color appearance remains relatively stable—we seem to be able to discount the illuminant. Although models of hue mechanisms must ultimately incorporate this ability, we can only hint at the vast material in this area (Pokorny et al 1991). Much of the work has been devoted to the computations necessary to achieve constancy (Brainard & Wandell 1992). In practice, color constancy is much less than perfect, even in the complex scenes needed to obtain enough information about the illuminant in order to discount it. This may not be a failure of visual processing (Jameson & Hurvich 1989). It may be important to identify correctly an object's color under different conditions, but it is also important to know whether the object is being viewed under dawn's early light or the noonday sun. Furthermore, the changes in reflectance of real-world objects may not produce very large visual effects (Dannemiller 1993) and, in any case, the perceived changes depend strongly on the observer's perceptual set (Arend et al 1991).

Color Appearance and Color Words

The perceptual axes of hue space (e.g. Figure 2b) are defined by the words attached to them: red, yellow, green, and blue. Although we assume a continuous linkage from the earliest retinal events to the linguistic response of an observer, it is possible that the specific terms that are used may change or rotate the axes of the hue mechanisms when different linguistic or cultural groups are tested. A related issue is whether the axes we have used are indeed unique.

Starting some 20 years ago, a major challenge was raised to the prevailing tradition of cultural relativism of all linguistic terms (Sapir-Whorf hypothesis): at least the common color words have universal meanings (Berlin & Kay 1969, Kay & McDaniel 1978). Applying linguistic criteria to many languages, 11 basic color terms were identified. The English equivalents are white, black, red, yellow, green, blue, brown, purple, pink, orange, grey. Furthermore, these terms seem to have evolved in a particular sequence since a fixed set of rules seems to specify which terms would be present in any language with less than the full set. Languages with only two basic terms have white and black, while those with three have white, black, and red; but beyond this there are some variations in the sequence of inclusion of terms. In these studies linguistic informants were presented with an ordered array of some 300 Munsell color chips and asked to delineate the boundaries within which any term applied and also to identify the best exemplars of each term.

Regardless of the number of terms, color space is always fully divided among the basic terms. As languages evolve, new subdivisions occur in a lawful sequence (although the original evolutionary sequence of terms has needed some modification): red always appears before other hue terms, a term that initially covers both red and yellow always divides before blue-green; the six fundamental terms (white, black, red, yellow, green, blue) emerge before the others; and so on (Kay & McDaniel 1978, Kay et al 1991). Indeed, across more than 100 languages, less than 30 specific sequences have been found out of the more than 2000 possible sequences of 1 to 11 terms. Part of the argument that basic color terms reflect universal properties of the human nervous system rests on the existence of a common evolutionary sequence. The other component of the universalist thesis is the similarity of the denotations of the basic color terms across languages. The range of colors to which a term applies must vary with the number of basic terms a language has, but within that range there is a privileged location, the focus. Across languages that have equivalent terms, these foci fall on the same tight regions of color space. The existence of common foci shows that color categories are not exclusive—sensation shades continuously from one focus to the next. This may break down at detection threshold, at which point stimuli are distinguishable only when they lie across a category boundary (Mullen & Kulikowski 1990). Fuzzy-set theory has been used to accommodate this division of color space among a few categories that shade continuously into their neighbors (Kay & McDaniel 1978).

There are two major on-going extensions of the original surveys—the World Color and Meso-American Surveys—that already have field data from several thousand informants covering well-over 100 languages (Kay et al 1991, MacLaury 1992). Although there are some differences among the various surveys in the methods of eliciting responses from informants, the effects are small, as are the effects of using Munsell chips. These chips do not cover all of color space and, unlike the OSA Uniform Color Scale chips, are not equally spaced perceptually. In either case, more saturated samples are preferred as examples of basic colors (Boynton et al 1989). Also, all these surveys implicitly assume that color terms can always be dissociated from all other perceptual or cognitive attributes—that color exists as an abstract, independent category. In fact, responses of individuals, or even of local communities, may be influenced by these non-color factors (MacLaury 1991). For us, the most important findings are that, with only small variations, the conclusions about the universality of the foci of color terms continue to hold. The universality is strikingly seen in languages with terms covering more than one English focus. Individual native speakers may not agree with each other in what they choose as the focus, but each of these multiple foci still corresponds to one of the foci common to other languages. Finally, we note that it is not possible to separate laundry correctly unless a culture has all 11 basic terms (Shirriff 1991).

Universal color terms have been explicitly linked to spectrally opponent physiological mechanisms (Ratliff 1976). Specifically, the spectrally opponent and nonopponent cells in the LGN (De Valois et al 1966) have been used to justify the grouping of white, black, red, yellow, green, and blue as fundamental terms (Kay & McDaniel 1978, Kay et al 1991, MacLaury 1992). However, as we have pointed out, these cells are not hue mechanisms and their detailed response properties should not be used to justify particular linguistic models of the development of color terms. But if linguistic terms are universal, they should correspond to certain pre-determined physiological mechanisms. Our point is that while we can infer such mechanisms and their properties, they have not as yet been directly observed.

Unique Perceptual Axes

We turn now to the question of whether there is a necessary pair of perceptual axes that must be used to represent hue space. Stemming from Hering's original work, the accepted bipolar hue axes are RG and YB (in our convention, Figure 2b, the signs are arbitrary: +G–R and +Y–B). But are these the necessary axes? In this tradition, hue cancellation studies demonstrate that hue is organized in opponent fashion: any stimulus that elicits some sensation of G can be added to one eliciting R in order to cancel the R; the intensity of the added canceler is the measure of the sensation that was canceled (Hurvich 1981). The spectral functions of the RG and YB mechanisms obtained from hue cancellation are approximately the same as those from hue scaling; the discrepancies are mostly for YB and are probably owing to nonlinearities in that mechanism (Werner & Wooten 1979). However, there is no obvious a priori justification for these precise axes; the axes might be chartreuse-violet and teal-cherry, which are approximately the hues to which the LGN cardinal axes point. Introspectively, however, we find it virtually impossible to think of canceling or scaling all hues in these terms and ultimately this is the principal justification for using RG and YB as the axes.

Several other lines of evidence converge on the fundamental nature of R, Y, G, B. No one line is conclusive, but together they are convincing. Multidimensional scaling can be used to order the ratings of the similarities of stimuli that elicit a range of color sensations; they are distributed on a two-dimensional plane on which R and G, and Y and B are complementary and orthogonal—but so are other sets of terms (Gordon & Abramov 1988, Shepard & Cooper 1992). More evidence comes from the linguistic studies above: in almost all cases, separate terms for R, Y, G, and B emerge before the other basic hue terms (Kay et al 1991). There is also a series of studies testing which terms are necessary and sufficient to describe hue appearance of a series of stimuli. Subjects begin with red, yellow, green, and blue, together with other basic terms; after using all terms to scale their sensations, individual terms are omitted in order to test whether the remaining ones are still sufficient to describe the sensation completely. Red, yellow, green, and blue are necessary and sufficient—orange, violet, purple, brown are not necessary (Sternheim & Boynton 1966, Fuld et al 1981, Quinn et al 1988). However, consistency and reaction times for applying color terms show that all the 11 basic color terms given above form a separate class and are probably all associated with universal physiological processes—in particular, orange is as salient as the four fundamental terms (Boynton & Olson 1990).

CORTICAL MECHANISMS

We have already pointed out that the responses of neurons through the LGN are ambiguous: they respond equally well along many different sensory dimensions. Since we are capable of separating dimensions such as chromatic from achromatic, these responses must somehow be separated (disambiguated) at higher levels of the visual system. We assume that hue mechanisms like those in our model in Figures 3a and 3b exist somewhere; we now examine them from a physiological perspective. Anticipating some of our conclusions, we note that as yet no cells with the appropriate properties have been recorded. Also, we may not find in the visual system any one cell whose responses alone determine, for example, R—that sensation may be the convergence of several different visual cells onto a common response.

P- and M-pathways

The streams of responses that begin with the P- and M-cells of the LGN may form parallel functional divisions that continue through the visual system: the P-pathway is said to deal mainly with form and color, while the M-pathway subserves motion, stereoscopic depth, etc (Hubel & Livingstone 1987, Livingstone & Hubel 1988). Because these findings have been reviewed recently (Merigan & Maunsell 1993), we summarize only those aspects relevant to color appearance. Anatomically, the pathways are clearly segregated up to their terminations in cortical area V1, but thereafter the distinctions become blurred. Nonetheless, there is general agreement on two subsequent pathways. One pathway includes parietal cortex and area MT, whose neurons are especially responsive to motion (Movshon et al 1985). This pathway probably subserves direction of perceived motion, visual tracking, etc. The other, temporal, pathway includes infero-temporal cortex and area V4, many of whose neurons are "color-coded" (Zeki 1983). This pathway probably deals with color and object recognition. Tests of this organization typically involve one or more of the following procedures: 1. holding constant the responses either of LGN P- or M-cells, 2. ablating P- or M-cells or their cortical projections, or 3. examining effects of neurological damage in clinical populations.

The most common test of these parallel pathways is to hold constant the responses in one of them. This is often done by using isoluminant chromatic stimuli (i.e. stimuli varying in chrominance and equated for photopic spectral sensitivity): since M-cells respond equally to such stimuli (Lee et al 1990), any response function that cannot be sustained by P-cells alone will be degraded. The main attraction of this technique is that it should work equally well for physiological recording from cortical cells and for psychophysical studies. This seemingly straightforward method has generated an entire industry showing that most functions are changed in some way at isoluminance and that pure chromatic stimuli can sustain most functions (Cavanagh 1991). For example, according to the simple two-pathway hypothesis, stereopsis depends on M-cells and should vanish at isoluminance; however, isoluminant, chromatic, random-dot stereograms can yield depth (or coherent motion) percepts without any form percept—no cyclopean object is seen, just pure impression of depth or motion (Kovacs & Julesz 1992). Similarly, most so-called color-coded cells in V1 are not obviously orientation-tuned (they do not have elongated receptive fields) and so color channels should not be orientation-specific (Livingstone & Hubel 1988). However, changes in orientation or spatial frequency of stimuli can be detected almost as readily with isoluminant as with luminance-varying stimuli—purely chromatic channels are also frequency- and orientation-tuned (Webster et al 1990).

There are, however, problems with the interpretations of many of the studies that use isolumnant stimuli. The fact that a function is degraded or changed at isoluminance does not necessarily demonstrate that M-cells are essential for that function. The various models of cortical processing of P-cells' responses show that not only can they be combined to isolate chromatic responses, but also to respond to spatial variations in intensity (Mullen & Kingdom 1991, De Valois & De Valois 1993). For example, when responses of spectrally opponent LGN cells with excitatory L-cone centers are summed with those from cells with excitatory M-cone centers, the resulting channel would be spatially opponent (bandpass spatial tuning) and would have a spectral sensitivity function very similar to that of the spectrally nonopponent M-cells. Thus, isoluminant stimuli could also degrade some of the diverse functions to which P-cells contribute (Logothetis et al 1990, Gur & Akri 1992). Furthermore, isoluminant stimuli cannot modulate the responses of M-cells, but can elicit a constant response from those M-cells capable of sustained activity. Additionally, although there is a generally accepted definition of luminance contrast, chromatic contrast can be specified in a variety of ways (Webster et al 1990, Mullen & Kingdom 1991), which makes it difficult to assess the effects of isoluminance. One approach to comparing stimuli that vary either in luminance or chrominance is to reduce both to similar units, such as cone contrasts (i.e. the amount of light absorbed by each cone type from a stimulus relative to the amount it absorbs from the background). Surprisingly, when this is done for the fovea at detection threshold, sensitivity to chromatic stimuli is almost an order of magnitude greater than for luminance stimuli (Chaparro et al 1993).

The only fool-proof way to examine the contributions of P-cells by themselves is to physically eliminate M-cells. In recent work with macaques, lesions have been made in either the P- or M-layers of one LGN; using eye-tracking systems, stimuli in behavioral tests can be confined to the region of the field projecting either to the lesioned or to the intact LGN for comparison (Schiller et al 1990, Merigan et al 1991, Merigan & Maunsell 1993). When M-layers are lesioned, there are no losses of visual acuity or chromatic contrast sensitivity; losses are confined mostly to luminance-varying stimuli that change rapidly and are relatively large. Lesions in P-layers, on the other hand, reduce sensitivity to relatively small and slowly changing stimuli that vary in luminance; most importantly, much of color vision is lost. But these lesion studies must be considered with caution: it is always possible that a few cells are spared and can continue to support a particular function. Thus, with M-lesions, the sensitivity to luminance contrast of small, slowly varying stimuli is unaffected and is much higher than might be expected from individual P-cells. This could either be due to a few spared M-cells, or to summation across a large ensemble of P-cells (Merigan et al 1991).

The lesion studies confirm that P-cells carry information about both chromatic and intensity variations, while M-cells contribute little to chromatic systems. Thus, in most color vision studies that use isoluminant stimuli, not only are M-cells' responses held constant, but also the intensive aspects of P-cells' responses are minimized.

Primary Visual Cortex

We now turn to the earliest cortical areas that might deal with the chromatic components of the P-cells' responses. Unfortunately it is difficult to characterize fully the responses of cortical neurons. Since most cells are orientation- and spatial-frequency–tuned, response properties must be explored with a variety of grating or bar stimuli, as well as chromatic stimuli. We do not have complete spectral responses for cortical neurons—only broad classifications based on stimuli that cover only a limited part of color space. We present only a brief summary and note that there is considerable variation across studies.

Some reports state that the majority of V1 cells are not spectrally opponent, except for some of the cells in the cytochrome-oxidase blobs, and that these cells do not have oriented (elongated) receptive fields. Even at the next processing stage (V2) few of the cells are obviously spectrally opponent (Hubel & Livingstone 1987). Others assert that the majority of V1 cells (oriented as well as non-oriented) respond both to isoluminant chromatic patterns as well as to luminance patterns; the spatial tuning of the same cells changes with stimulus type, tending more to lowpass for chromatic patterns and bandpass for luminance patterns (Thorell et al 1984). As to color specificity, there are reports that all spectrally opponent cells in a particular blob share the same spectral properties—either RG or YB (Dow & Vautin 1987, Ts'o & Gilbert 1988). Others find that spectrally opponent cortical neurons (in blobs and elsewhere) do not cluster around specific directions in color space, as do LGN cells, or as might be expected of hue mechanisms—there is a continuous distribution of spectral null-points (Thorell et al 1984, Lennie et al 1990). In short, the responses of cells in V1 and even V2 do not show the disambiguation needed to separate hue from other aspects of responses coming from P-cell inputs. Most cells still respond to achromatic patterns and lack the spectral specificity of hue mechanisms. However, some of the necessary recombinations may have been initiated: some cells have tripartite spectral response functions, as would be needed for a RG mechanism (Thorell et al 1984, Dow & Vautin 1987).

Achromatopsia

Although many of the physiological systems examined above are obviously part of the pathways that lead to color sensations, none have all the properties to make them perceptual color mechanisms. Also, the perceptual hue mechanisms may not be easily identifiable with single neurons—they may be more readily associated with patterns of responses across ensembles of cells. Moreover, looking for a color location or center assumes that visual sensations can be subdivided into separate processes and that color sensations can be dissociated from other sensory and perceptual dimensions; most current perceptual and cognitive theories treat color as such a separable entity (Davidoff 1991). Reports of achromatopsias may help establish the separability of color and locate the hue centers. Achromatopsia is a major loss of color vision associated with damage to some area of the central nervous system and not to obvious retinal factors. Nor is it a loss of color knowledge. The affected individuals retain linguistic color terms, color memories, and associations—they can correctly state that leaves are usually green, or the sky is blue. But they cannot correctly identify the color of the particular object currently being viewed.

There are, of course, wide variations in severity and purity of the deficits, which are often associated with specific perceptual losses such as the inability to see faces (prosopagnosia) and visual field losses (Mollon 1989, Zeki 1990, Davidoff 1991, Plant 1991). However, there is a consensus that pure achromatopsia can exist.

Interestingly, severe achromatopsia may not be the same as complete loss of color vision, which is usually defined as the ability to discriminate spectrally different stimuli regardless of intensity. Some individuals with achromatopsia can still discriminate among spectrally different stimuli (e.g. identifying the digits in Ishihara plates) without being able to identify the hues (Victor et al 1989). It is even possible to retain hue discrimination without luminance discrimination in an otherwise cortically blind area (Stoerig & Cowey 1989). Such discrimination without identification might be related to responses of some complex cells in area V1 that respond to all equiluminant chromatic patterns, regardless of hue pairings and direction of chromatic change—these cells detect any chromatic pattern (Thorell et al 1984). This raises an interesting issue. We have shown that our hue and saturation descriptions of color appearance (Figure 1) can be used to derive traditional wavelength discrimination functions (Abramov et al 1990, Chan et al 1991), and have implicitly assumed that discrimination is based on identifiable differences in appearance. But color discrimination does not necessarily imply color identification—the spectral information for these processes may be dealt with in parallel.

From reports of achromatopsias, candidate areas for the hue or color centers are the lingual and fusiform gyri that border primary visual cortex and are probably the homologs of area V4 in macaques (Zeki 1990, Plant 1991). In normal subjects, PET scans have been used to identify cortical areas that respond strongly to complex chromatic patterns. As expected, V1 responds to both luminance and chromatic patterns, but V4 responds only to the chromatic patterns (Lueck et al 1989). It is useful, therefore, to examine the responses of neurons in V4 of the macaque. Many of the macaque's V4 neurons respond only to relatively narrow spectral ranges, probably representing only the excitatory responses of the spectrally opponent channels at lower levels like the LGN (Zeki 1983, Schein & Desimone 1990). It has been claimed that these V4 neurons are truly color-coded: when stimulated with complex colored patterns, they seem to respond to the color-appearance and not the mix of wavelengths coming from a particular patch, which could change as the illuminant changes. They exhibit some form of color constancy since they respond mostly to the reflectance of the object and discount the illuminant (Zeki 1983), as confirmed in some behavioral tests (Wild et al 1985). But V4 cells by themselves cannot be the hue mechanisms we are looking for. Most of them respond well to achromatic stimuli and so their color responses are still ambiguous (Schein & Desimone 1990). Also, the representation of the visual field on V4 is largely confined to the central 30° (Zeki 1990), and yet color vision can still be very good at far greater eccentricities (Van Esch et al 1984, Abramov et al 1991). Furthermore, lesions of V4 disrupt many forms of learned visual discriminations (not just color), but these can all be relearned. V4 may be most important for learning visual tasks in general and not just for color (Schiller & Lee 1991).

Physiological Model of Hue Mechanisms

As already discussed, the spectrally opponent LGN cells cannot be the hue mechanisms because they respond not only to chromatic variations but also to achromatic stimuli and to spatial patterns. Many strategies have been proposed for separating and disambiguating the responses of the different LGN cells (Mullen & Kingdom 1991, Valberg & Seim 1991). A major problem is that most LGN cells have inputs only from M- and L-cones, whereas both RG and YB hue mechanisms must be associated with all three cone types (Figures 3a and 3b). This is nicely dealt with in the recent model of De Valois & De Valois (1993), which we now consider in some detail. As an example, we show schematically in Figure 5 how their +R–G hue mechanism might be assembled, starting with three basic types of spectrally opponent LGN cells. The center component of each receptive field is driven by only one cone type. For generality, all surrounds are shown with the same inputs from all three cone types, with relative weights reflecting their numbers in the retina. Weighted outputs of these cells are then combined in two stages to yield a +R–G hue mechanism. The net weighting of the cone responses at the final stage produces a spectrally opponent response function that is almost exactly the same as that from our perceptual model (Figure 3a). S-cones provide most of the excitatory responses that signal R at short wavelengths, the response null-points fall nicely within the spectral ranges for unique-Y and unique-B, and the excitatory and inhibitory inputs cancel in response to a near equal-energy white. In other words, responses to achromatic stimuli have been removed and the cardinal axes that characterize responses of LGN cells have been rotated to coincide with the perceptual axes.

To ensure spectral opponency, all cone connections to centers and surrounds of the LGN cells in the model cannot be randomly selected from among L-, M-, and S-cones. In the fovea, spectral opponency is assured: the center of each receptive field receives its input from a single cone (L, M, or S), while the surround has a spectrally different input. The surround could receive a random selection of cone types (Lennie et al 1991), or could be connected specifically with a single cone type that is different from the one in the center (Reid & Shapley 1992). To maintain color vision outside the fovea, where receptive fields are larger, the centers of the receptive fields must still be

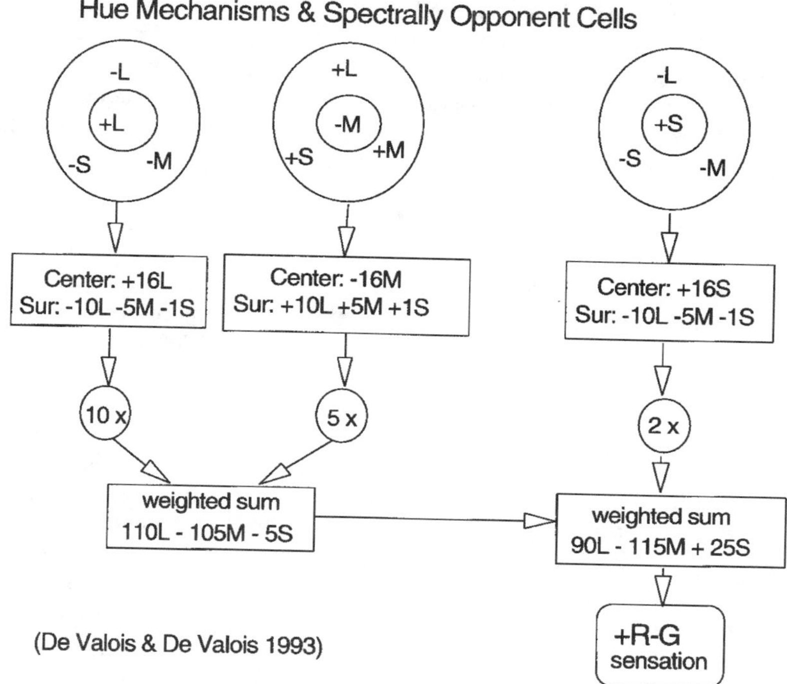

Figure 5 Physiological model of +R–G hue mechanism.

connected to a single type of cone. In addition, LGN cells with L- or M-cone centers probably do not receive any S-cone inputs (Abramov 1968, Derrington et al 1984), but the model of De Valois & De Valois (1993) is not greatly affected by small changes in the inputs to the surrounds, as its proponents point out.

We have used the +R–G mechanism as an example of how this particular physiological model extracts the hue component from the responses of LGN cells (Figure 5). The other hue mechanisms are obtained by changing the signs of the cone inputs to produce other LGN cells, whose outputs are then combined. Inverting the signs of the cone inputs to all the LGN receptive fields in Figure 5 produces a +G–R mechanism. To produce a +Y–B mechanism, only the sign of the receptive field with the S-cone center (Figure 5) need be inverted, making its center –S. However, it may be too simple to assume that only three types of LGN cells (and their inverses) are sufficient for all hue mechanisms. The weightings applied to the outputs of the LGN cells at the model's later stages cannot be the same for all hue mechanisms. The given weights (Figure 5) ensure that RG mechanisms do not respond to white, but YB mechanisms need different net cone weights to meet this criterion for a hue mechanism (see Figures 3a and 3b). This is a minor problem. More seriously, the model's hue mechanisms should never respond to any stimuli that appear white; however, this will hold only when the stimuli cover the receptive fields uniformly. Adding the cone weights for the centers and surrounds (Figure 5) separately through all combination stages shows that the resulting perceptual mechanisms will be spatially opponent and will respond vigorously to spatial patterns, as might be the case for a black/white grating whose period was appropriately matched to the receptive field.

As it stands, this model is incomplete and does not disambiguate the responses of spectrally opponent channels under all conditions, which further emphasizes the difficulty of creating such models. A more complete model must consider the spatial structure of neurons' receptive fields together with changes in color appearance when stimulus size varies, etc. The problem may lie in part with the assumption that all spectrally opponent LGN cells must contribute in some way to hue mechanisms. Some of these cells may in fact contribute more to form perception than to color. It has been suggested that hue is derived only from those spectrally opponent LGN cells that do not have spatially antagonistic receptive fields (Rodieck 1991). Combining outputs only of spectrally, but not spatially, opponent cells would effectively remove any difficulties regarding spatial structure of proposed hue mechanisms. However, since relatively few spatially nonopponent cells have been recorded, it is not clear that they form a subgroup. They may be examples of the end of a continuum of variation in the relative sizes of centers and surrounds of receptive fields.

RECEPTIVE AND PERCEPTIVE FIELDS

The hue mechanisms we described earlier (Figures 3a and 3b) are derived from psychophysical considerations; however, they must be formed from combinations and interactions among neural channels, as suggested by some of the physiological models (Figure 5). Physiological units that correspond to the hue mechanisms have yet to be observed. One of our goals is to identify the necessary properties of hue mechanisms and place constraints on them in ways that can readily be related to physiology. We now return to the postulated hue mechanisms to propose additional constraints that must be met by physiological candidates.

Cone Distributions

Since the retina is not a uniform sheet of photodetectors, we examine what happens to color appearance as stimuli are shifted away from the fovea. Recent anatomical work has shown that packing density of cones is indeed highest in the fovea, falls rapidly with eccentricity out to some 10° and then more gradually to the retinal margin. The decline is symmetrical for the vertical meridian, but there is a clear naso-temporal asymmetry along the horizontal meridian—density is greater on the nasal retina for eccentricities exceeding approximately 20° (Curcio et al 1990). Moreover, there are large differences among individuals; especially in the fovea there can be at least threefold differences in packing densities. A similar picture exists for macaque monkeys (Packer et al 1989). The important factor for color vision is how the different cone types are distributed in the cone mosaic. Many functions depend on the precise ratios, which may be imposed by the anatomical ratios or by weighting the responses of the different cones. For example, ratios of M- and L-cone inputs to +R–G or +Y–B hue mechanisms cannot be the same if the unique hues are to be seen at the correct spectral loci. However, the primary constraint must be imposed by the numbers of the different cones available in the retinal mosaic.

We consider first the distribution of S-cones. When individuals with normal color vision view small, foveal targets, they behave like tritanopes, suggesting a relative paucity of S-cones in the fovea (Williams et al 1981). The opsin of S-cones is sufficiently different from the opsins of other photopigments that it is possible to stain them with specific antibodies. As expected from psychophysics, the packing density of human S-cones is greatest in a ring immediately around the central fovea, which has an S-cone-free zone subtending 1/3° (Curcio et al 1991). This zone is surprisingly large: all hues are seen and are fully saturated for centrally fixated targets as small as 1/4° (Abramov et al 1991, see also Figure 1). Color appearance suggests a considerably smaller zone of reduced S-cone density, which agrees with data from macaques (Wikler & Rakic 1990), as well as other human data based on morphological identification of S-cones (Ahnelt et al 1987). Also, orientation discrimination of gratings that affect only S-cones is better than might be expected from the sparseness of these cones (Webster et al 1990).

As yet there are no anatomical ways to differentiate M- and L-cones—their morphologies and their opsins are too similar. An alternative is to identify each cone unequivocally from microspectrophotometric (MSP) measures of its spectral absorbance. From samples across several species of monkeys, M- and L-cones are roughly equally prevalent, but this may be due to sampling biases (Bowmaker et al 1991). Exhaustive sampling of all cones in small patches of retina is free of such sampling problems, but seems to have been done only for talapoin monkeys. In this species, S-cones are roughly 2% of the total; the remainder are equally divided between M- and L-cones (Mollon & Bowmaker 1992). However, talapoin monkeys may not be entirely representative of either humans or the commonly studied macaques.

Psychophysical measures have been used to estimate the ratio of L/M-cones in humans. The photopic spectral sensitivity curve is best fit by an L/M ratio of almost 2, with no S-cones (Smith & Pokorny 1975), which is unlike the ratios determined by MSP in monkeys. But strictly speaking, psychophysical measures give only the ratios of the inputs of the different cones to the particular channel driving the responses being tested. For example, the ratio required in any model of unique-Y is not the same as for unique-G (see Figure 3). Therefore, attempts have been made to find a general method. When one cone type is isolated with chromatic adaptation and stimuli are very small and brief, the number of cones contributing to detection can be estimated from slopes of the psychometric functions. In the fovea and parafovea, the L/M ratio is approximately 2 with a range of 1.5 to 2.4 across subjects (Cicerone & Nerger 1989, Nerger & Cicerone 1992). Using closely related methods, others have also found more L- than M-cones, but with a much greater inter-observer range—of 1.6 to 7.3 (Wesner et al 1991). Physiological measures (electroretinograms) with rapid heterochromatic flicker have also yielded an average L/M ratio of roughly 2, and with a range of 0.7 to 9 (Jacobs & Neitz 1993). These methods assume that all cones, or all cones of an isolated type, contribute equally to the response measures, but individual cones could contribute with different weights or some might not contribute to the process that drives responses in these experiments. Also, the large range of ratios across individuals raises problems for color appearance. For example, the spectral loci of the unique hues, especially unique-Y, should be shifted drastically in individuals with extreme L/M ratios; however, the unique loci seem tightly constrained across individuals (Schefrin & Werner 1990). This raises the unattractive possibility that whatever assembles the hue mechanisms must somehow "know" the ratio in an individual and compensate for it.

Perceptive Fields

The structures of the receptive fields of the neurons in the visual pathway determine the spatial properties of their responses. When the outputs of various neurons are combined at higher levels to form perceptual mechanisms, their receptive fields combine to form the perceptive fields of the mechanisms; these perceptive fields determine the spatial response properties of the perceptual process being tested. Thus, if the combination rules preserve an antagonistic center-surround arrangement, increasing stimulus size will first increase response of that mechanism, but further size increases will decrease responses—the mechanism will have bandpass spatial tuning.

The overall contrast sensitivity function (CSF) of the luminance system is bandpass, whereas that of chromatic mechanisms is lowpass; however, the individual channels that comprise the CSF of the chromatic mechanisms may themselves be bandpass tuned (Switkes et al 1988, Webster et al 1990, Mullen & Kingdom 1991). Most recent studies of spatial properties use grating stimuli, which, in studies of chromatic systems, are typically isoluminant R/G patterns. As chromatic contrast of such gratings is reduced to find threshold, color appearance changes continuously from a R/G pattern toward a uniform field of intermediate hue. From our perspective this means that these gratings stimulate several of the hue mechanisms we have postulated. The results may be useful for comparing achromatic and chromatic systems in general, but are less useful in the perceptual scheme we propose if the hue mechanisms differ in their spatial properties. It may be difficult to stimulate one hue mechanism by itself, but it is possible to isolate a mechanisms' responses: hue scaling, we have argued, separates the responses of the four hue mechanisms.

We have examined how hue and saturation scaling responses vary as stimulus size is increased (Abramov et al 1991). For example, consider only the R component of the hue sensation at all those wavelengths that elicit some amount of R. We use the amount of R relative to all other responses (i.e. apparent saturation of the R component of the sensation) to test how the R sensation grows with stimulus size. These responses, for any of the hue mechanisms, grow monotonically to an asymptotic value and the curves for all the wavelengths that elicit a given hue, say R, differ only by a scale factor. Thus, the size of stimulus that elicits a near-asymptotic response (critical size) is the same for all wavelengths, even though the value of the asymptotic maximum varies with wavelength. Hence, a given hue mechanism has a uniform spatial structure across wavelengths. The perceptive fields of hue mechanisms do not seem to have spatially antagonistic surrounds: there is no reduction in responses with increases in stimulus size beyond the size eliciting the maximal response at any wavelength. The four hue mechanisms are all spatially lowpass tuned. However, their size-scales are not all the same: the critical sizes of the perceptive fields of the R and B mechanisms are similar and much smaller than those of G and Y. The spatial uniformity of perceptive fields for hue must be qualified when more complex stimuli are used, such as those producing color contrast. In such cases there are, of course, considerable spatial interactions, and these may be nonlinear (Zaidi et al 1992).

It is difficult to study size effects in the fovea because of its high resolution. We examined the perceptive fields of the hue mechanisms across the retina to horizontal eccentricities of 40° (Abramov et al 1991). Everywhere the results were qualitatively as in the fovea, except that the critical sizes increased systematically with eccentricity (beyond 15°). The field sizes were larger on the temporal retina, which accords with the lower packing density of cones in that hemiretina (Curcio et al 1990). Also, at any retinal locus, the fields for R were always relatively small while those for G were the largest, which agrees with findings that relatively small stimuli in the periphery yield lower thresholds for L-cone than for M-cone contrast (Stromeyer et al 1992). At eccentricities at least up to 40° nasal and 30° temporal, a stimulus whose size was equal to the local critical value of the mechanism with the largest perceptive field (a size that exceeds the critical sizes for all the other mechanisms) elicited color sensations very similar to those from foveal stimuli. Similarly, wavelength discrimination in the peripheral retina approximates that in the fovea when field sizes are increased appropriately for each eccentricity (Van Esch et al 1984, Nagy & Doyal 1993). Thus, the spectral properties of the hue mechanisms are approximately the same across most of the retina. When stimuli are made smaller, color sensations not only decrease, but also change qualitatively. The best preserved hues tend to be R and B because of their locally smaller perceptive fields; also, unique-G shifts to longer wavelengths and B spreads across the spectrum towards the usual location of unique-Y (Gordon & Abramov 1977, Abramov et al 1991). We use the term *tritan-B* to describe this tendency to split the spectrum between R and B and for B to extend its spectral range when stimuli are locally small. The term is derived from the two hues, R and B, seen by a tritanope (Alpern et al 1983), which, incidentally reinforces the notion that S-cones cannot be B-cones. Our results from the periphery also show that "small-field tritanopia" is a general property of color vision and is not restricted to the fovea. This study of perceptive fields was done with a dark surround, but adding a white surround, thereby raising adaptation state, had little effect except that all perceptive fields were slightly smaller (Abramov et al 1992).

The above studies of the hue mechanisms across the retina add the following constraints to any hue models: 1. The increase in critical sizes of perceptive fields with eccentricity is too rapid to be accounted for by retinal anatomy. The number of cones covered by equivalent fields (of local critical size) are different, with peripheral fields requiring many more cones. Similarly, the sizes of perceptive fields increase more rapidly with eccentricity than do receptive field sizes in the retina, LGN, and cortical area V1 (Shapley & Perry 1986, Tootell et al 1988). However, perceptive field sizes may resemble those of some V4 neurons (Desimone & Schein 1987). 2. Any physiological scheme for recombining LGN spectrally opponent cells cannot preserve their spatial antagonisms—the perceptive fields of hue mechanisms are not spatially opponent. 3. The fact that R and G perceptive fields are not the same size demonstrates that +R–G and +G–R mechanisms are not simply inverses of each other (nor are B and Y mechanisms). There are separate R, Y, G, and B hue mechanisms. 4. Since the spectral properties of the hue mechanisms remain the same across much of the retina, the cone ratios must be constant and neurons' local receptive fields cannot be assembled by random sampling of cones. They must preserve at all eccentricities the same relative weights of spectrally-opponent inputs that constitute the foveal hue mechanisms. 5. The existence of tritan-B adds to the evidence cited earlier that M-cones must also be associated with the sensation of B. 6. Anatomically, S-cones are sparse everywhere and yet their contributions to hue mechanisms must be substantial, which suggests that at some stage their responses are greatly amplified. Also, the physiological models for combining P-cells to obtain unambiguous hue mechanisms require that each mechanism receive an input from a cell associated with S-cones; but these cells at the level of the LGN are relatively uncommon.

ACKNOWLEDGMENTS

Preparation of this review as partly supported by NIH Grant EY01428 and PSC/CUNY Faculty Research Award Program Grants 662224 and 664238.

Literature Cited

Abramov I. 1968. Further analysis of the response of LGN cells. *J. Opt. Soc. Am.* 58:574–79

Abramov I, Gordon J, Chan H. 1990. Using hue scaling to specify color appearance and to derive color differences. Perceiving, Measuring, and Using Color. *Proc. Soc. Photo Opt. Instrum. Eng.* 1250:40–51

Abramov I, Gordon J, Chan H. 1991. Color appearance in the peripheral retina: effects of stimulus size. *J. Opt. Soc. Am.* A8:404–14

Abramov I, Gordon J, Chan H. 1992. Color appearance across the retina: effects of a white surround. *J. Opt. Soc. Am.* A9:195–202

Ahnelt PK, Kolb H, Pflug R. 1987. Identification of a subtype of cone photoreceptor, likely to be blue sensitive, in the human retina. *J. Comp. Neurol.* 255:18–34

Alpern M, Kitahara K, Krantz DH. 1983. Perception of colour in unilateral tritanopia. *J. Physiol.* 335:683–97

Arend LE Jr., Reeves A, Schirillo J, Goldstein R. 1991. Simultaneous color constancy: papers with diverse Munsell values. *J. Opt. Soc. Am.* A8:661–72

Ayama M, Nakatsue T, Kaiser PK. 1987. Constant hue loci of unique and binary balanced hues at 10, 100, and 1000 Td. *J. Opt. Soc. Am.* A4:1136–44

Berlin B, Kay P. 1969. *Basic Color Terms: Their Universality and Evolution.* Berkeley: Univ. Calif. Press

Bowmaker JK, Astell S, Hunt DM, Mollon JD. 1991. Photosensitive and photostable pigments in the retinae of old world monkeys. *J. Exp. Biol.* 156:1–19

Boynton RM, MacLaury RE, Uchikawa K. 1989. Centroids of color categories compared by two methods. *Color Res. Appl.* 14:6–15

Boynton RM, Olson CX. 1990. Salience of basic chromatic color terms confirmed by three measures. *Vision Res.* 30:1311–17

Brainard DH, Wandell BA. 1992. Asymmetric color matching: how color appearance depends on the illuminant. *J. Opt. Soc. Am.* A9:1433–48

Burns B, Shepp BE. 1988. Dimensional interactions and the structure of psychological space: the representation of hue, saturation, and brightness. *Percept. Psychophys.* 43:494–507

Cavanagh P. 1991. Vision at equiluminance. In *Limits of Vision,* Vol. 5: *Vision and Visual Dysfunction.* ed. JJ Kulikowski, V Walsh, IJ Murray, pp. 234–50. Boca Raton, FL: CRC

Chan H, Abramov I, Gordon J. 1991. Large and small color differences: predicting them from hue scaling. Human vision, visual processing, and digital display II. *Proc. Soc. Photo Opt. Instrum. Eng.* 1453:381–89

Chaparro A, Stromeyer CF III, Huang EP, Kronauer RE, Eskew RT Jr. 1993. Colour is what the eye sees best. *Nature* 361:348–50

Cicerone CM, Nerger JL. 1989. The relative numbers of long-wavelength-sensitive to middle-wavelength-sensitive cones in the human fovea centralis. *Vision Res.* 29:115–28

Curcio CA, Allen KA, Sloan KR, Lerea CL, Hurley JB, et al. 1991. Distribution and morphology of human cone photoreceptors stained with anti-blue opsin. *J. Comp. Neurol.* 312:610–24

Curcio CA, Sloan KR, Kalina RE, Hendrickson AE. 1990. Human photoreceptor topography. *J. Comp. Neurol.* 292:497–523

Dannemiller JL. 1993. Rank orderings of photoreceptor photon catches from natural objects are nearly illuminant-invariant. *Vision Res.* 33:131–40

Davidoff J. 1991. *Cognition Through Color.* Cambridge, MA: Bradford/MIT Press

Derefeldt G. 1991. Colour appearance systems. In *The Perception of Colour.* Vol. 6: *Vision and Visual Dysfunction.* ed. P Gouras, pp. 218–61. Boca Raton, FL: CRC

Derrington AM, Krauskopf J, Lennie P. 1984. Chromatic mechanisms in lateral geniculate nucleus of macaque. *J. Physiol.* 357: 241–65

Desimone R, Schein SJ. 1987. Visual properties of neurons in area V4 of the macaque: sensitivity to stimulus form. *J. Neurophysiol.* 57:835–68

De Valois RL, Abramov I, Jacobs GH. 1966. Analysis of response patterns of LGN cells. *J. Opt. Soc. Am.* 56:966–77

De Valois RL, De Valois KK. 1993. A multistage color model. *Vision Res.* 33:1053–65

De Valois RL, Snodderly DM, Yund EW, Hepler NK. 1977. Responses of macaque lateral geniculate cells to luminance and color figures. *Sens. Process.* 1:244–59

Dow VM, Vautin RG. 1987. Horizontal segregation of color information in the middle layers of foveal striate cortex. *J. Neurophysiol.* 57:712–39

Drum B. 1989. Hue signals from short- and middle-wavelength-sensitive cones. *J. Opt. Soc. Am.* A6:153–57

Finkelstein MA, Harrison M, Hood DC. 1990. Sites of sensitivity control within a long-wavelength cone pathway. *Vision Res.* 30: 1145–58

Fuld K, Sparrow JE, Daning R, Slade CW. 1988. Background stimulus for invariant spectral sensitivity. *Color Res. Appl.* 13: 219–25

Fuld K, Wooten BR, Whalen JJ. 1981. Elemental hues of short-wave and spectral lights. *Percept. Psychophys.* 29:317–22

Gordon J, Abramov I. 1977. Color vision in the peripheral retina. II. Hue and saturation. *J. Opt. Soc. Am.* 67:202–7

Gordon J, Abramov I. 1988. Scaling procedures for specifying color appearance. *Color Res. Appl.* 13:146–52

Gordon J, Abramov I, Chan H. 1994. Describing color appearance: hue and saturation scaling. *Percept. Psychophys.* In press

Graham N, Hood DC. 1992. Modeling the dynamics of light adaptation: the merging of two traditions. *Vision Res.* 32:1373–93

Gur M, Akri V. 1992. Isoluminant stimuli may not expose the full contribution of color to visual functioning: spatial contrast sensitivity measurements indicate interaction between color and luminance processing. *Vision Res.* 32:1253–62

Hard A, Sivik L. 1981. NCS—Natural Color System: a Swedish standard for color notation. *Color Res. Appl.* 6:129–38

Hood DC, Birch DG. 1993. Human cone receptor activity: the leading edge of the a-wave and models of receptor activity. *Visual Neurosci.* In press

Hubel DH, Livingstone MS. 1987. Segregation of form, color, and stereopsis in primate area 18. *J. Neurosci.* 7:3378–3415

Hurvich LM. 1981. *Color Vision.* Sunderland, MA: Sinauer

Hurvich LM, Jameson D. 1951. A psychophysical study of white. I. Neutral adaptation. *J. Opt. Soc. Am.* 41:521–27

Jacobs GH. 1991. Variations in colour vision in non-human primates. In *Inherited and Acquired Colour Vision Deficiencies.* Vol. 7: *Vision and Visual Dysfunction,* ed. DH Foster, pp. 199–214. Boca Raton, FL: CRC

Jacobs GH. 1993. The distribution and nature of colour vision among the mammals. *Biol. Rev.* 68:413–71

Jacobs GH, Harwerth RS. 1989. Color vision variations in Old and New World primates. *Am. J. Primatol.* 18:35–44

Jacobs GH, Neitz J. 1993. Electrophysiological estimates of individual variation in the L/M cone ratio. In *Colour Vision Deficiencies XI,* ed. B Drum, pp. 107–12. Dordrecht, Netherlands: Kluwer

Jameson D, Hurvich LM. 1959. Perceived color and its dependence on focal surrounding, and preceding stimulus variables. *J. Opt. Soc. Am.* 49:890–98

Jameson D, Hurvich LM. 1989. Essay concerning color constancy. *Annu. Rev. Psychol.* 40:1–22

Kaplan E, Lee BB, Shapley RM. 1990. New views of primate retinal function. In *Progress in Retinal Research,* ed. NN Osborne, GJ Chader, 9:273–336. New York: Pergamon

Kay P, Berlin B, Merrifield W. 1991. Biocultural implications of systems of color naming. *J. Linguist. Anthropol.* 1:12–25

Kay P, McDaniel CK. 1978. The linguistic significance of the meanings of basic color terms. *Language* 54:610–45

Kovacs I, Julesz B. 1992. Depth, motion, and static-flow perception at metaisoluminant color contrast. *Proc. Natl. Acad. Sci. USA* 89:10390–94

Krauskopf J, Williams DR, Heeley DW. 1982. Cardinal directions of color space. *Vision Res.* 22:1123–31

Lee BB, Martin PR, Valberg A. 1989. Nonlinear summation of M- and L-cone inputs to phasic retinal ganglion cells of the macaque. *J. Neurosci.* 9:1433–42

Lee BB, Pokorny J, Smith VC, Martin PR, Valberg A. 1990. Luminance and chromatic modulation sensitivity of macaque ganglion cells and human observers. *J. Opt. Soc. Am.* A7:2223–36

Lennie P, Haake PW, Williams DR. 1991. The design of chromatically opponent receptive fields. In *Computational Models of Visual Processing,* ed. MS Landy, JA Movshon, pp. 71–82. Cambridge, MA: MIT Press

Lennie P, Krauskopf J, Sclar G. 1990. Chromatic mechanisms in striate cortex of macaque. *J. Neurosci.* 10:649–69

Livingstone M, Hubel D. 1988. Segregation of

form, color, movement, and depth: anatomy, physiology, and perception. *Science* 240:740–49

Logothetis NK, Schiller PH, Charles ER, Hurlbert AC. 1990. Perceptual deficits and the activity of the color-opponent and broad-band pathways at isoluminance. *Science* 247:214–17

Lueck CJ, Zeki S, Friston KJ, Deiber M-P, Cope P, et al. 1989. The colour centre in the cerebral cortex of man. *Nature* 340: 386–89

Lythgoe JN, Partridge JC. 1989. Visual pigments and the acquisition of visual information. *J. Exp. Biol.* 146:1–20

MacLaury RE. 1991. Social and cognitive motivations of change: measuring variability in color semantics. *Language* 67:34–62

MacLaury RE. 1992. From brightness to hue. *Curr. Anthropol.* 33:137–86

MacNichol EF Jr. 1986. A unifying presentation of photopigment spectra. *Vision Res.* 26:1543–56

Merigan WH, Katz LM, Maunsell JHR. 1991. The effects of parvocellular lateral geniculate lesions on the acuity of macaque monkeys. *J. Neurosci.* 11:994–1001

Merigan WH, Maunsell JHR. 1993. How parallel are the primate visual pathways? *Annu. Rev. Neurosci.* 16:369–402

Mollon JD. 1989. "Tho' she kneel'd in that place where they grew..." The uses and origins of primate colour vision. *J. Exp. Biol.* 146:21–38

Mollon JD, Bowmaker JK. 1992. The spatial arrangement of cones in the primate retina. *Nature* 360:677–79

Movshon JA, Adelson EH, Gizzi MS, Newsome WT. 1985. The analysis of moving visual patterns. In *Pattern Recognition Mechanisms,* ed. C Chagas, R Gattass, C Gross, pp. 117–51. Rome: Vatican. Reprinted 1986 in *Exp. Brain Res.* 11:117–51 (Suppl.)

Movshon JA, Thompson ID, Tolhurst DJ. 1978. Spatial summation in the receptive fields of simple cells in the cat's striate cortex. *J. Physiol.* 283:53–77

Mullen KT, Kingdom FAA. 1991. The perception of colour. In *The Perception of Colour.* Vol. 6: *Vision and Visual Dysfunction,* ed. P Gouras, pp. 198–217. Boca Raton, FL: CRC

Mullen KT, Kulikowski JJ. 1990. Wavelength discrimination at detection threshold. *J. Opt. Soc. Am.* A7:733–42

Nagy AL. 1979. Unique hues are not invariant with brief stimulus durations. *Vision Res.* 19:1427–32

Nagy AL, Doyal JA. 1993. Red-green color discrimination as a function of stimulus field size in peripheral vision. *J. Opt. Soc. Am.* A10:1147–56

Nagy AL, MacLeod DIA, Heyneman NE, Eisner A. 1981. Four cone pigments in women heterozygous for color deficiency. *J. Opt. Soc. Am.* 71:719–22

Nathans J, Merbs SL, Sung C-H, Weitz CJ, Wang Y. 1992. Molecular genetics of human visual pigments. *Annu. Rev. Genet.* 26:403–24

Nathans J, Thomas D, Hogness DS. 1986. Molecular genetics of human color vision: the genes encoding blue, green and red pigments. *Science* 232:193–202

Neitz J, Neitz M, Jacobs GH. 1992. Molecular genetic basis of polymorphism in normal color vision. Advances in color vision. *Opt. Soc. Am. Tech. Digest* 4:14–16

Neitz J, Neitz M, Jacobs GH. 1993. More than three different cone pigments among people with normal color vision. *Vision Res.* 33:117–22

Neitz M, Neitz J, Jacobs GH. 1991. Spectral tuning of pigments underlying red-green color vision. *Science* 252:971–74

Nerger JL, Cicerone CM. 1992. The ratio of L cones to M cones in the human parafoveal retina. *Vision Res.* 32:879–88

Packer O, Hendrickson AE, Curcio CA. 1989. Photoreceptor topography of the adult pigtail macaque (*Macaca nemestrina*) retina. *J. Comp. Neurol.* 298:472–93

Plant GT. 1991. Disorders of colour vision in diseases of the nervous system. In *Inherited and Acquired Colour Vision Deficiencies.* Vol. 7, *Vision and Visual Dysfunction,* ed. DH Foster, pp. 173–98. Boca Raton, FL: CRC

Pokorny J, Shevell SK, Smith VC. 1991. Colour appearance and colour constancy. In *The Perception of Colour.* Vol. 6, *Vision and Visual Dysfunction,* ed. P Gouras, pp. 43–61. Boca Raton, FL: CRC

Quinn PC, Rosano JL, Wooten BR. 1988. Evidence that brown is not an elemental color. *Percept. Psychophys.* 43:156–64

Ratliff F. 1976. On the psychophysiological bases of universal color terms. *Proc. Am. Philos. Soc.* 120:311–30

Reid RC, Shapley RM. 1992. Spatial structure of cone inputs to receptive fields in primate lateral geniculate nucleus. *Nature* 356: 716–18

Rodieck RW. 1991. Which cells code for color? In *From Pigments to Perception,* ed A Valberg, BB Lee, pp. 83–93. New York: Plenum

Schefrin BE, Werner JS. 1990. Loci of spectral unique hues throughout the life span. *J. Opt. Soc. Am.* A7:305–11

Schein SJ, Desimone R. 1990. Spectral properties of V4 neurons in the macaque. *J. Neurosci.* 10:3369–89

Schiller PH, Lee K. 1991. The role of the primate extrastriate area V4 in vision. *Science* 251:1251–53

Schiller PH, Logothetis NK, Charles ER. 1990.

Role of the color-opponent and broad-band channels in vision. *Vis. Neurosci.* 5:321–46

Schnapf JL, Nunn BJ, Meister M, Baylor DA. 1990. Visual transduction in cones of the monkey *Macaca fascicularis. J. Physiol.* 427:681–713

Shapley R. 1990. Visual sensitivity and parallel retinocortical channels. *Annu. Rev. Psychol.* 41:635–58

Shapley R, Perry VH. 1986. Cat and monkey retinal ganglion cells and their visual functional roles. *Trends Neurosci.* 9:229–35

Shepard RN, Cooper LA. 1992. Representation of colors in the blind, color-blind, and normally sighted. *Psychol. Sci.* 3:97–104

Shevell SK. 1992. Redness from short-wavelength-sensitive cones does not induce greenness. *Vision Res.* 32:1551–56

Shirriff K. 1991. Laundry and the origin of basic color terms. *J. Irreprod. Results* 36:10

Sirovich L, Abramov I. 1977. Photopigments and pseudopigments. *Vision Res.* 17:5–16

Smith VC, Pokorny J. 1975. Spectral sensitivity of the foveal cone photopigments between 400 and 500 nm. *Vision Res.* 15: 161–71

Sperling HG. 1992. Spatial discrimination of heterochromatic stimuli: a review and a new experimental approach. In *Colour Vision Deficiencies XI,* ed. B Drum, pp. 35–50. Dordrecht, Netherlands: Kluwer

Spitzer H, Hochstein S. 1988. Complex-cell receptive field models. *Prog. Neurobiol.* 31: 285–309

Sternheim CE, Boynton RM. 1966. Uniqueness of perceived hues investigated with a continuous judgmental technique. *J. Exp. Psychol.* 72:770–76

Sternheim CE, Drum B. 1993. Achromatic and chromatic sensation as a function of color temperature and retinal illuminance. *J. Opt. Soc. Am.* A10:838–43

Stoerig P, Cowey A. 1989. Residual target detection as a function of stimulus size. *Brain* 112:1123–39

Stromeyer CF III, Lee J, Eskew RT. 1992. Peripheral chromatic sensitivity for flashes: a post-receptoral red-green asymmetry. *Vision Res.* 32:1865–73

Switkes E, Bradley A, De Valois KK. 1988. Contrast dependence and mechanisms of masking interactions among chromatic and luminance gratings. *J. Opt. Soc. Am.* 5A: 1149–1162

Teller DY. 1990. The domain of visual science. In *Visual Perception: The Neurophysiological Foundations,* ed. L Spillmann, JS Werner, pp. 11–21. San Diego, CA: Academic

Thompson E, Palacios A, Varela FJ. 1992. Ways of coloring: comparative color vision as a case study for cognitive science. *Behav. Brain Sci.* 15:1–74

Thorell LG, De Valois RL, Albrecht DG. 1984. Spatial mapping of monkey V1 cells with pure color and luminance stimuli. *Vision Res.* 24:751–69

Tootell RBH, Switkes E, Silverman MS, Hamilton SL. 1988. Functional anatomy of macaque striate cortex. II. Retinotopic organization. *J. Neurosci.* 8:1531–68

Ts'o DY, Gilbert CD. 1988. The organization of chromatic and spatial interactions in the primate striate cortex. *J. Neurosci.* 8:1712–27

Valberg A, Seim T. 1991. On the physiological basis of higher colour metrics. In *From Pigments to Perception,* ed. A Valberg, BB Lee, pp. 425–36. New York: Plenum

Van Esch JA, Koldenhoff EE, Van Doorn AJ, Koenderink JJ. 1984. Spectral sensitivity and wavelength discrimination of the human peripheral visual field. *J. Opt. Soc. Am.* A1:443–50

Victor JD, Maiese K, Shapley R, Sidtis J, Gazzaniga MS. 1989. Acquired central dyschromatopsia: analysis of a case with preservation of color discrimination. *Clin. Vision Sci.* 4:183–96

Walraven J, Werner JS. 1991. The invariance of unique white; a possible implication for normalizing cone action spectra. *Vision Res.* 31:2185–93

Webster MA, De Valois KK, Switkes E. 1990. Orientation and spatial-frequency discrimination for luminance and chromatic gratings. *J. Opt. Soc. Am.* A7:1034–49

Webster MA, Mollon JD. 1991. Changes in colour appearance following post-receptoral adaptation. *Nature* 349:235–38

Werner JS, Wooten BR. 1979. Opponent chromatic mechanisms: relation to photopigments and hue naming. *J. Opt. Soc. Am.* 69:422–34

Wesner MF, Pokorny J, Shevell SK, Smith VC. 1991. Foveal cone detection statistics in color-normals and dichromats. *Vision Res.* 31:1021–37

Wikler KC, Rakic P. 1990. Distribution of photoreceptor subtypes in the retina of diurnal and nocturnal primates. *J. Neurosci.* 10: 3390–3401

Wild HM, Butler SR, Carden D, Kulikowski JJ. 1985. Primate cortical area V4 important for colour constancy but not wavelength discrimination. *Nature* 313:133–35

Williams DR, MacLeod DIA, Hayhoe MM. 1981. Foveal tritanopia. *Vision Res.* 21: 1341–56

Winderickx J, Lindsey DT, Sanocki E, Teller DY, Motulsky AG, Deeb SS. 1992. Polymorphism in red photopigment underlies variation in colour matching. *Nature* 356: 431–33

Yokoyama S, Yokoyama R. 1989. Molecular

evolution of human visual pigment genes. *Mol. Biol. Evol.* 6:186–97

Zaidi Q, Yoshimi B, Flanigan N, Canova A. 1992. Lateral interactions within color mechanisms in simultaneous induced contrast. *Vision Res.* 32:1695–1707

Zeki S. 1983. Colour coding in the cerebral cortex: the reaction of cells in monkey visual cortex to wavelengths and colours. *Neuroscience* 9:741–65

Zeki S. 1990. A century of cerebral achromatopsia. *Brain* 113:1721–77

Zrenner E, Abramov I, Akita M, Cowey A, Livingstone M, Valberg A. 1990. Color perception: retina to cortex. In *Visual Perception: The Neurophysiological Foundations,* ed. L Spillmann, JS Werner, pp. 163–204. San Diego, CA: Academic

Annu. Rev. Psychol. 1994. 45:487–516

LANGUAGE SPECIFICITY AND ELASTICITY: BRAIN AND CLINICAL SYNDROME STUDIES

Michael Maratsos and Laura Matheny

Institute of Child Development, University of Minnesota, Minneapolis, Minnesota 55455-0345

KEY WORDS: brain and language, language development, modularity, language syndromes, innateness and language

CONTENTS

INTRODUCTION

Language is currently the highest human mental function for which faculty-specific biological programming seems plausible (Fodor 1983). Although this hypothesis was not favored initially, opinion has typically shifted to a more

0066-4308/94/0201-0487$05.00

nativist orientation (e.g. Bates et al 1991a, Flavell et al 1993, Maratsos 1989, Pinker & Bloom 1990, Slobin 1985).

As evidence begins to favor specific human faculties that make language possible, it becomes important to establish what linguistic nativism might mean. For many years the prototype of what innateness means has been set by nativists such as Chomsky (1965, 1986), who stresses the putative independence of language as a functioning mental faculty, claims both mirrored and elaborated by Fodor (1983). For example, Fowler (1990) writes "one cannot conduct language development research without at least acknowledging the hypothesis that language is acquired, processed, and represented independently of other cognitive domains" (p. 303). Snow, an anti-nativist, believes "the nativists think language is acquired very fast, very easily, and that it's very much a child's responsibility, while we think it requires a relationship with an adult, and a whole set of cognitive abilities" (quoted in Rymer 1992). Fowler and Snow both agree that nativism is likely to entail a belief in a nonsocial, noncognitive language acquisitional process; this belief, we think, is widely shared, even though at least some nativist analysts believe that use of extra-linguistic cognitive processes is an essential part of innate biological specification of language (e.g. Bickerton 1981, Maratsos 1989, Pinker 1984, Slobin 1985).

Probably another common view is that the notion of an innate endowment for language implies a specific biological home for language, the left hemisphere. Dennis & Whitaker (1976) seem to believe the biological specificity of language requires belief in the unique language-analytic properties of left hemispheric language. On the basis of what is known, however, it seems likely to us that biologically-specific language capacity only shows preference for certain brain tissues. Ultimately its code is more central than is the use of highly particular tissues.

This review examines these questions of faculty and tissue specificity by looking at current work on brain localization and clinical syndromes. We begin with a preliminary discussion of the related problems of modularity, and its realization in linguistic models. We concentrate especially on two concepts—encapsulatedness and the role of autonomous syntax in language descriptions—in which we feel misleading impressions have been widely influential. Following these discussions, we proceed to empirical reviews of work in aphasia, hemispheric localization, language and modality, and clinical syndromes such as Williams' and Down syndromes.

Encapsulatedness and Syntactic Autonomy

The key concept in modularity theory is encapsulation (Fodor 1983), a claim that certain mental systems are largely formed of hard-wired independent sets of operations. Encapsulated implies something completely cut off from other systems; encapsulate means "to enclose as in a capsule." (*American Heritage Dictionary* 1975, p.429). But obviously language as a whole could not function this way. Language is used to translate a speaker's concepts, feelings, intentions (or at least what the speaker wishes to present of them) into a public medium in order to amuse, persuade, impress, mislead, or inform others. Indeed, one of the major questions in the study of chimpanzee signing has been whether the chimpanzees really intend to communicate information to another being (Seidenberg & Petitto 1979).

In fact, encapsulation always means partial encapsulation, systems of operations to which other systems have only limited access, and which have only limited access to other systems. A modern corporation is a good example of a modular organization. It has limited access to systems in the outside world, and other systems have limited access to it, especially to parts of its internal workings. But its overall goals (and goals of other parts of society) require some access in both directions.

For many, however, the dominant part of the claim that language is encapsulated lies with what is thought to be its qualitatively unique heart, a modular component of rules often called autonomous syntax (Chomsky 1965, McNeill 1970). We think, however, that the generative semanticists (e.g. Fillmore 1968, Lakoff 1971, Postal 1972) who revolted against Chomskyan autonomous syntax were correct in perceiving it to be an odd hypothesis resting upon considerable descriptive artifice. Some introductory terminology will be useful for discussing this problem, as well as for the empirical review that follows.

PHONOLOGY This refers to the inventory of sounds of which language is composed, and their patterns of arrangement into linguistic sequences.

MORPHEMES AND MORPHOLOGY For our purposes, a morpheme is the smallest sound sequence that has or adds meaning. *Dogs* is comprised of two morphemes, *dog* and noun plural *-s*. Morphology is the analysis of how morphemes are put together to make words.

SYNTAX Syntax is the set of patterns governing how words can be put together into sentences.

LEXICAL SEMANTICS Lexical semantics means word meaning.

GRAMMATICAL SEMANTICS This refers to the meanings that arise from the combinations of morphemes into words and sentences. For example, "John likes Mary," specifies that John is the experiencer, and Mary the source, of the pleasant feelings denoted by *like*, information that *likes, Mary,* and *John* do not convey by themselves as an unordered set of words.

PRAGMATICS This refers to social factors that enter into language use. For example, one would not walk up to a stranger and say the perfectly well-formed sentence "I like dogs," unless in an appropriate context.

GRAMMAR Grammar refers to the total set of rules that relate meanings to morpheme and sound sequences (Chomsky 1965, Fillmore 1968, Lakoff 1971).

All of these draw off of nonlinguistic primitives and concepts. In phonology, humans categorically perceive voiced-unvoiced boundaries that differentiate */b/* from */p/* or */d/* from */t/*. Most languages use this boundary, and infants innately perceive it as do adults (Eimas et al 1971). But minks and monkeys also perceive this boundary (Newport 1982); thus, human languages use an innate mammalian auditory boundary.

Furthermore, sounds are grouped by whether or not differences among them are semantically different. For example, as adults, Japanese speakers do not hear */l/* vs */r/* as different phonemes because the sounds do not differentiate different words in Japanese as they do in English (e.g. *ball* vs *bar*). Pitch contours are controlled by many semantic or pragmatic factors such as questions vs statements.

Morphology widely uses conceptual and social meanings. A child who does not differentiate one vs more than one object in using noun plural *-s* is not given credit for having the morpheme, whether or not she uses it (Brown 1973); past tense refers to past events; first, second, and third person, commonly used to control morphology, refers to whether the subject participates in the conversation as speaker, listener, or talked about. Across languages, morphology encodes matters like who did or felt what, whether or not an object was moving into a specific location or was already there, object shape qualities, and many other conceptual meanings.

Meaning also controls syntax in many ways. A speaker who produced well-ordered sentences like "the dog chased the cat" without regard to which was doing the chasing would not be credited with commanding English syntax (Brown 1973). More subtly, semantic variables often permeate matters such as whether an active sentence has a corresponding passive. Passives like "fifty dollars were cost by this hat" are ruled out by subtle semantic-structural restrictions of English (Jackendoff 1972). Less subtle restrictions include disallowance of nonactional passives like "Mary was liked by Jane" in Northern Russian (Timberlake 1977), or disallowance of passives unless they refer to a bad result in historical Chinese (Erbaugh 1982).

Language acquisition and use thus obviously require a whole set of cognitive abilities. What, then, does independence of language, or autonomous syntax, actually mean? Autonomous syntax is used two ways. The first use refers to the fact, almost certainly true, that some categories of grammar, which we call formal syntactic categories, cannot be defined only by the semantic properties of their members. For example, many verbs refer to actions, but so do many nouns (e.g. *explosion, trip*) and many verbs refer to non-actions [e.g. *feel* (good), *belong, like, consist, have*)]. At least part of the definition of such categories, and the phrases that revolve around them, must lie in nonsemantic structural properties (Maratsos & Chalkley 1980).

To most psychologists, however, it is likely that autonomous syntax refers to the idea that a whole central module of language, the syntactic, that specifies word and morpheme orders, is made up of rules that use only formal syntactic elements, making no reference to semantics or pragmatics at all. But as we have seen, much of the control of word and morpheme order in language is semantic and pragmatic in nature. Part of any human language consists of how semantics is mapped onto syntactic orders. To capture this mapping, some rules must mix both syntactic and semantic representations.

How, then, can be there be an autonomous syntax component with no semantic elements in it? There are two chief devices for doing this. First, a separate component of the grammar is devised to which are exported all rules that have to mix semantics and syntax. For example, consider the sentence "John likes tables." The autonomous syntactic bloc of rules randomly generates a configuration of words and categories for this sentence, roughly identifying *John* as the first noun phrase, followed by a verb phrase made up of the verb *likes* and the noun phrase *table*. For aspects in which semantics controls word order, this meaningless configuration is sent to an interpretive component. This component uses lexical information that for *like* in particular, the first noun phrase denotes an experiencer of pleasant feelings towards the referent of the postverbal noun phrase, a description that obviously mixes syntactic elements (categories and order) and semantic elements.

Formally, the autonomous syntactic bloc of rules is often designated the generative part of the grammar. But this designation has no psychological meaning; no one generates sentences by randomly generating syntactic word configurations and interpreting them until one happens to generate the desired meaning (Chomsky 1965, Katz & Postal 1964). In terms of psychological processes, a speaker probably begins with a meaning to express, and some idea of the major words to use. The meaningful relations among the words, in combination with the syntactic and semantic specifications of the lexicon and semantic-syntactic mapping rules, are then used to control word order. Simply put, formally interpretive rules are really more the generative rules psychologically. Thus autonomous syntax is preserved partly by formally segregating out necessary rules that mix semantic and formal syntactic elements into another component.

A second major device is to rename syntax-controlling semantic properties as purely formal ones while they are operating in autonomous syntax. For example, in Chinese, to control the passive, a purely formal, nonsemantic feature that might be called +BAD could be created; only verbs marked +BAD could undergo the passive. Naturally the semantic interpretive component could then interpret +BAD as meaning bad. As an example closer to home, English subject-verb agreement for person and number are generally treated as syntactic rules; these involve what look like semantic-pragmatic concepts like singular, plural, speaker, spoken-to, etc. But in the generative autonomous syntax, formal features like +SINGULAR or +THIRD PERSON can be created to control agreement; again, of course, the semantic interpretive component will say these mean singular, or person or thing not a speaker or listener. All this essentially corresponds exactly to practices in Chomsky (1965).

Generative semanticists like Fillmore (1968), Lakoff (1971), and Postal (1972) were fully aware that in reality one can only be certain that some rules in a grammar mix formal syntax and semantics. They were also fully aware of the formal artifices required to maintain a purely syntactic bloc of rules, and proposed that in reality, grammatical description employs rules that mix formal syntactic, semantic, pragmatic, and phonological descriptions throughout. Newmayer (1980), in his excellent history of American transformational grammar, holds that in the end, Chomskyan formal approaches won largely on methodological grounds. Generative semanticists wanted to mix semantic and real-world knowledge into the grammar throughout, which Newmayer estimates was not as easy for linguists to work with as the pure syntax approach of Chomsky. As a result, Chomskyan approaches have predominated on largely methodological grounds, and the result has been presented ever since as a known fact about the way grammar centrally works. Ironically, in current Chomskyan approaches, the purely formal autonomous syntactic component has a trivial role (Rizzi 1985); it overgenerates syntactic word sequences, generating both good and bad sequences. The interpretive components, which mix formal syntax and other, more semantic and pragmatic entities, assume the bulk of the work of controlling word order, weeding out most of the generated syntactic sequences as leading to anomalous interpretation. This implies agreement with the generative semanticists that autonomous syntax in reality comprises little of grammar as a whole.

In our view, autonomous syntax always was a problematic hypothesis at best, and remains so, though in a somewhat peculiar universe nothing can be ruled out a priori. From a psychologist's point of view, it should be considered a strong hypothesis that requires empirical support, not something to be assumed as a basic fact about language.

In reality, all fully worked out models of grammar involve mixtures of formal syntactic, semantic, pragmatic, and phonological elements. This implies that grammar can only be learned by recourse to nonlinguistic elements in some form, but this does not mean that there is nothing biologically specific or modular to language acquisition. At a general level, flooding an organism with information does not necessarily make its analytic job easier. In fact, a system that has no means of choosing selectively among information, or among ways of interpreting it, is probably unable to make conclusions about the information (Chomsky 1965, Pinker 1984, Maratsos 1992). Some of the interpretive systems that make these analytic choices may not be specific to language (Markman 1992), but some may well be specifically adapted to language. In fact, there are already some highly structured acquisitional linguistic innatist theories that deal directly with the semanticized nature of syntax and morphology. For example, Pinker (1984) proposes that a morphological learning module only allows a specific set of about thirty to forty conceptual meanings as candidates for controlling morphological structure. This is a proper modular structure, because it allows limited access by nonlinguistic elements (meanings) to a specific acquisitional device. Such a proposal, of course, itself requires empirical support.

In our view, rhetorical claims about autonomous syntax have always obscured the fact that language is fundamentally a system for translating and coordinating nonlinguistic elements, though such a system may have evolved qualitatively unique elements or organizational elements for doing so. The study of the makeup and acquisition of language must rely partly on analyses of the nature of language itself, but convincing evidence on these matters must also come from other kinds of empirical data as well. We now turn to a review of some of the relevant evidence.

APHASIA AND BRAIN LOCALIZATION IN SPEAKING ADULTS

Results from a variety of sources—effects of lesion within hemispheres, study of split-brain patients (whose corpus callosum connecting the hemispheres has been cut), studies of separately anesthetized hemispheres, brain scanning techniques—indicate that for most human adults, the left hemisphere is dominant for language functions (Kolb & Whislaw 1990). Within this hemisphere, the classic language area is in a large part of the brain more or less in the middle of the hemisphere on a front-to-back axis; within this area are two major language areas, Broca's (toward the front) and Wernicke's (toward the rear), the functions of which are still being debated.

Looking at the important work concerning brain hemispherization as a whole may seem the most logical place to start our review, but we begin by looking at attempts to fix localization-function correlations within the left hemisphere in hearing adults. This provides a useful framework, both substantive and methodological, for the consideration of the work in different language modalities (sign) and acquisition, before moving on to work concerning elasticity and acquisition more directly.

Words and Concepts in the Left Hemisphere

Some current work reflects on how language can function both separately from and together with general cognition and perception, at least at the level of lexical concepts. At the word meaning level, it seems that language systems have to be coordinated with nonlinguistic brain areas that represent object and perceptual meanings. More generally, Damasio & Damasio's (1989, 1993) work with lesioned patients indicates three major nonlinguistic areas for object classes, colors, and semantic word categories: 1. an area representing colors or object concepts of different kinds nonlinguistically; 2. areas controlling the articulation of language sounds; 3. areas that specifically connect the first two areas. For example, lesion to a particular area in the lower-posterior part of the brain, partly in the lower occipital lobe, can cause loss of the ability to see color differences. Damage to Wernicke's area damages the ability to articulate words in general, with no loss of the ability to see color. Damage to areas in between may leave intact the ability to perceive color differences and think about colors, and also the ability to articulate words in general. But the subject may lose the ability to remember color names in particular. Similarly, subjects may lose conceptual knowledge of particular individuals and events, or of certain general classes of objects (e.g. animals or tools), without any language-particular loss, through lesions in the lower temporal and parietal lobes [which also seem to encode much of the information about detailed object shape patterns (Stiles & Thal 1992)]. If tissue between the conceptual and language articulation areas is lesioned, subjects may retain conceptual knowledge, but lose much of the general ability to name particular individuals, or to name animals or musical instruments. Such evidence supports the common-sense notion that language systems draw off of nonlinguistic conceptual analysis.

Apparently one cannot learn a language without using other cognitive abilities. However, there may be language-particular programming for the growth of connections between such conceptual-perceptual areas and areas for constructing words and sentences, and there also may be specific normal paths for conducting conceptual-perceptual information to other functioning systems. This would comprise biological specificity of the coordination system, though not in a way that makes language completely independent. If such paths conveyed somewhat different information from the conceptual-perceptual areas to different functions, such a system would be a form of modularity (though not completely encapsulated).

Localization results from the study of lesions and brain scanning techniques both point to more anterior regions for the storage of non-noun concepts encoded by words such as verbs, adjectives, prepositions, and other kinds of words. In fact, such concepts seem close to, or part of, the usually found sentence construction areas (Damasio & Damasio 1992). Such words are usually inherently grammatical in a way many nouns are not, in that they semantically have relational roles that grammar realizes. For example, *like* indicates a liker and likee, and sentences with *like* have particular referents for these roles. Semantics and grammar here are practically inextricable; hence, the absence of physical separation would not be surprising.

Broca's and Wernicke's Aphasia and Functional Profiles

The most interesting claim made about Broca's vs Wernicke's aphasics is that their dysfunctions show some dissociation of formal syntactic vs semantic function. Wernicke's aphasics, who have posterior lesions, speak fluently. But they may scramble up sounds within words, or substitute one word for another, or use pronouns without clear reference. Extreme cases can look like "syntax without meaning," because their syntactically fluent speech may fail to convey much meaning to a listener.

Broca's aphasics, conversely, often have halting, slurred speech. Though their words and utterances are meaningful and connected to context, they may suffer a range of problems from some deletion of morphological markers and small functors (like prepositions or auxiliary verbs), to barely being able to sequence more than one or two words at a time. But they apparently can understand reversible sentences like "the cat chased the dog," which indicates that their deficiency is a production problem. (Schwartz et al 1985).

Matters became more interesting, however, when Zurif & Caramazza (1976) found that various comprehension problems accompany the production problems Broca's aphasics have with small morphemes (morphological markers and functors). Agrammatic speakers (those whose speech shows little grammatical structure) often fail to understand reversible passives. For example, "the cat is chased by the dog," differs from the active only by the small morphemes *is, -ed,* and *by.* Some agrammatics also have trouble with simple active sentences (Schwartz et al 1985). It began to look as though Broca's aphasics lack formal syntactic (particularly functor-related) modules and Wernicke's aphasics lack semantic modules.

Although this view was dominant throughout the 1970s (Schwartz et al 1985), it is no longer widely believed (Bates et al 1991b, Swinney et al 1989; D Swinney, personal communication). The reasons are surprising and instructive. Linebarger et al (1983) found agrammatics who could neither produce nor comprehend sentences well, but who nevertheless showed considerable skill in judging the grammaticality of sentences, distinguishing "is he enjoy it?" from "did he enjoy it?" or "we ate the bread that Mary made" from "we ate the bread that Mary made the cake." Such judgments require considerable knowledge of how small functors work in grammar among other things.

Heeschen (1985) reports that subjects who commonly omitted small functors could nevertheless perform perfectly at a Cloze test in which they had to say which morpheme came next after part of the sentence had been given. He also reports results in which agrammatics who could not comprehend reversible passives could comprehend both actives and passives if the sentences were given as follows: "Look, here's Mary. Mary was kissed by John," thus setting up the grammatical subject of the passive as the topic of discourse. Bates et al (1991) find that across languages, speakers tend to preserve morphological markers if they are more informative or functionally important in a given language. For example, German articles convey more information than English articles and are more likely to be preserved.

Furthermore, Wernicke's aphasics are less asemantic than previously thought. They usually substitute semantically related words for other words (Heeschen 1985) and show the same sentence processing semantic context lexical priming effects as normal speakers (Swinney et al 1989). Their syntax also shows problems if analyzed carefully (Kolk et al 1985), and their underlying syntactic knowledge may be no better than that of agrammatic Broca's aphasics. There are also interesting population variables. Wernicke's aphasics are almost never found among brain-lesioned children or young adults who incur brain lesion in the posterior areas.

Thus what seemed like a promising demonstration of syntactic vs semantic syndrome schism has turned into essentially a mystery. Current attempts to explain dysfluent-fluent aphasia examine differences in basic processing variables like excitation vs inhibition functions (Bates et al 1991b), or temporal integration differences (D Swinney, personal communication). These results serve as important methodological cautions against hasty interpretation of either laboratory experimental results or even apparently clear behavioral syndromes as indications of an underlying lack of knowledge. Such results also make one wonder where in the left hemisphere is knowledge of grammar or even whether this is the appropriate way to think of the question.

LOCALIZATION AND ELASTICITY IN DEVELOPMENT

Aphasia and Hemispheric Localization in Sign Language Users

Work with deaf humans who learn sign language has clear significance for studies of localization, development, and elasticity. Though our main concern is with lateralization results, some remarks on the general nature and significance of sign languages are initially relevant.

NATURE AND SIGNIFICANCE OF SIGN LANGUAGES Sign languages, once thought to be simplified derivatives of spoken languages like English, are now recognized as fully developed natural languages. Like spoken languages, they operate by associating internal concepts with a public medium, in this case hand gestures.

Like spoken languages, sign languages divide events and relations into different parts and make reference to them in sentences; they are propositional. American Sign Language, like sign languages in general, apparently, does not use word order very much (S Goldin-Meadow, personal communication). But sign languages typically include simultaneous modulations of the hand gesture, such as specific kinds of simultaneous motion, to encode subject-verb agreement, noun-verb derivational inflection, and other meanings or grammatical properties typically encoded by morphological markers in spoken languages.

Sign language also has its own characteristic structural properties. Spoken languages typically use pronouns like *she* and *it* to refer back to earlier, more fully established referents, as in "John came in, and he was upset," where *he* refers to the person established initially by *John*. In American Sign Language (ASL), one signs a referent to a particular location; then future signings at that location refer to the referent without overt mention. For example, one might sign the equivalent of "Bob is coming" near the right shoulder. A future proposition "is tall" signed there would mean "Bob is tall." For a subset of verbs, subject-object relations can be signaled by making the sign directionally from one referent location to another; signing *love* directionally from a *Bob* location to a *Mary* location would mean "Bob loves Mary." (Klima & Bellugi 1979, Bellugi 1988).

Although it is a non-spoken language with a somewhat iconic nature, the acquisition of sign looks a lot like spoken languages. Deaf children apparently begin to "babble" sign (make signing motions without word meaning) in the first year, and start to produce meaningful words at the end of the year, as hearing children usually do (Petitto 1988). Signing children tend to make word sequences and morphologically marked words at times comparable to the range for speaking children (Bellugi 1988), and they tend to make comparable grammatical errors like overregularization.

This comparability is surprising in some ways given the evidence we have that there has been specific adaptation for spoken language in humans. The mature human larynx is arranged in the windpipe lower than it is for animals, including other primates, and human infants; in the latter, the location changes with physical maturation. This lower position creates a far better resonance chamber for the production of language sounds. It also makes humans the only organism at all likely to choke to death on food. Obviously the selective advantage of speaking better caused this change, and was enough to overcome the selective disadvantage of being more likely to die. (Lieberman 1989). The fantastic complexity of human oral-facial neuromuscular functioning also makes it likely there has been specific selection for the auditory-articulatory mode. Yet it turns out that sign can realize propositional, grammatical language in another mode. Unless the biological representation of language also includes gestural devices as part of its specification, the very existence of elaborated sign languages points to a significant amount of flexibility in the processes that produce language.

Thus the nature of sign language and its acquisition points to a partly fixed nature for human language (because of its characteristics shared with spoken languages), and a partly flexible one (because of the ability of such properties to transfer to a new medium) (see e.g. Bates et al 1991a, Maratsos 1991, Petitto 1993, Pinker & Bloom 1990, Rispoli 1991, Slobin 1985 for broader discussion of such a mixed nature of language).

LATERALIZATION IN SIGNERS Perhaps the same combination of fixedness and flexibility is to be seen in the lateralization patterns for sign language. Despite its highly spatialized nature, which might indicate a home in the spatially dominant right hemisphere, evidence indicates that sign language is mostly housed in the left hemisphere, as are spoken languages (Poizner et al 1987). This finding resolves one of the possibilities for explaining lateralization of spoken language because certain types of auditory pattern analysis are dominant in the left hemisphere (Poizner et al 1987), and this could attract spoken language associative processes to that hemisphere for most speakers.

Aphasia studies provide the evidence for the left localization of sign language. Poizner et al (1987) studied three left- and three right-lesioned aphasics. Right hemisphere lesions led to the usual kinds of perceptual-spatial difficulties, but fluent and grammatical signing was undisturbed. Left hemisphere lesions led to Broca- and Wernicke-like aphasic symptoms, including word substitutions and contextually problematic fluent speech in one speaker, overuse of unclear pronominal references in another, and very severe Broca aphasic symptoms in a third speaker. Thus it appears that something like a language faculty finds whatever spatial-perceptual resources it needs in the left hemisphere, despite the dominance of the right hemisphere for most spatial functions (but see Kosslyn 1992).

Such evidence does not completely resolve why language functions usually appear dominantly in the left hemisphere. Other possibilities include dominant processing of symbolic processes in general in the left hemisphere (Goldstein 1948), and dominant processing of detailed gestural movements in the left hemisphere [e.g. Kimura (1976) found left-hemisphere sign aphasia typically associated with motor apraxias].

These issues are not easy to settle. Poizner et al (1987) noted that their left-hemisphere aphasics retained the ability to interpret signers' pantomime art forms, which counters the symbol-interpretation hypothesis [see also

Corina et al (1992) for further evidence]. Two of their three left-hemisphere aphasics were not manually apraxic according to Kimura's (1976) criteria, though one of them was very near the boundary. Work will undoubtedly continue on these difficult interpretive problems, but for now we believe that Poizner et al's results do point to some independence of language function and simple modality functions in lateralization. This seems valid, though we must remember that our evidence concerns language implementation systems rather than language knowledge systems per se, the location and nature of which we still do not understand.

Poizner et al, however, do point to one interesting non–left hemispheric language function in signers that differs from those typical in auditory language. As mentioned above, sign has a lot of heavily spatialized grammar for pronominal reference and certain subject-object constructions. Poizner et al gave their subjects comprehension tests for various morphological and spatial grammatical aspects of sign. For comprehension of spatial grammar, as opposed to production, right hemisphere lesions caused problems, while left hemisphere lesions did not. In fact, their left-lesioned Broca-like aphasic, who could barely produce simple uninflected individual signs, and could not comprehend inflectional processes, could comprehend spatial grammar quite well. Poizner et al note that the parietal region of the right hemisphere is particularly dominant for perception of spatial relations at a distance, which is what one needs for comprehending (as opposed to producing) spatial grammar, and they hypothesize that the language faculty does go to the right hemisphere to find what it needs, so to speak.

The results have two major interpretations. One is that most grammatical knowledge and processing is still based in the left hemisphere, but the particular perceptual input is recruited to aid this processing from the right hemisphere. The other interpretation is that a significant amount of comprehension of grammar is actually in the right hemisphere. This possibility is particularly attractive for one of the left-lesioned aphasics, a Broca's aphasic with widespread left hemisphere lesion who had severely impaired grammatical productive processes and inflectional comprehension processes as well, but still retained good comprehension of spatial grammar. Because of the severity of her condition, it seems plausible that real grammatical competence was retained in the right hemisphere after lesion; by extension this could be attributed to the other signers as well. But among auditory language users, severe left hemispheric agrammatism in production and comprehension is compatible with significant retained grammatical knowledge, so we cannot make this stronger conclusion; Poizner et al's agrammatic patient may have retained significant left hemispheric grammatical knowledge even if most of it could not be expressed. On the other hand, there is evidence that the right hemisphere can support significant language functioning.

The work we have reviewed so far has concentrated on adult speakers, though we use this to make inferences about how development has proceeded. We turn now to localization and aphasia results from infants and children, where issues of brain elasticity become central.

Early Elasticity of Language in the Brain

INFANT HEMISPHERECTOMIES Research on speakers and signers supports the conclusion that generally, the left hemisphere is the natural home of language processes. But the signers' recruitment of right hemisphere processes in an especially opportune fashion raises the possibility that there is some important flexibility to this process. Indeed, in left-handers, language is lateralized in the right hemisphere, or represented bilaterally for one third of speakers (Kolb & Whislaw 1990), a finding showing some flexibility of localization in normal development. We now look at further evidence in development for brain organization flexibility, beginning with the dramatic example of children who lose their left hemispheres completely.

Sometimes children develop extreme seizures in one hemisphere, and the only known treatment is to remove the hemisphere. In the case of left hemisphere seizures, if this treatment is performed in early infancy, children with an intact right hemisphere typically develop normal language, showing no qualitatively different pattern of development and becoming fluent speakers. Although this condition is associated with lower intellectual functioning (Huttenlocher 1993), at least one known case has finished college and entered a professional career (Smith 1984). Even though there is evidence for specialized language-related functioning in the left hemisphere at birth, (Molfese 1977), language function as a whole can apparently be developed successfully in the right hemisphere. Given that such extreme left hemispheric seizures probably cause some trauma to the right hemisphere, these results appear remarkable. Liver failure does not usually lead to one of the kidneys taking over liver functions, for example.

Some investigators, however, question whether the right brain really implements language as effectively as the left brain. Dennis and colleagues (Dennis 1980, Dennis & Whitaker 1976) show subtle deficits in experimental comprehension of linguistic structures like reversible passives, and especially negative reversible passives (e.g. "the cat isn't chased by the dog"), and other syntactic test deficits among left hemispherectomized patients; right hemispherectomized patients tend not to show these deficits. But there are good reasons to not take these objections seriously. First, methodologically, we have seen earlier how susceptible laboratory comprehension processes are to general functioning difficulties. Bishop (1983) shows that many young people of dull or even normal intelligence may fare poorly on similar laboratory comprehension tests. There is some retardation associated with loss of a hemisphere in most subjects because the brain is operating with fewer overall resources.

Second, and more to the point, such patients function normally in everyday language use. As we have noted, Chomsky argues with undeniable logic that for any set of input data, there is a theoretically unlimited number of conclusions an organism could draw. To draw any conclusion at all, the organism must have some kind of internal structure. Even for the command of basic formal categories like noun, verb, and adjective, and their associated grammatical behaviors, or basic yes/no questions and interrogatives (*who, what, why, where,* and *when*), there are many reasonable interpretations the child could make from the input data. Most of these interpretations would result in a child who both in acquisition and final state would look qualitatively different from a normal speaker; the child would not just be a little slow, or show subtle deficits in experimental comprehension tests (Chomsky 1981, Maratsos & Chalkley 1980, Pinker 1984). This is certainly true for systems like case-gender systems, which such speakers also master fluently (P Huttenlocher, personal communication). A child who was just getting by with a variety of other strategies and tricks in language, would be like someone who actually had no musical ability trying to get by with other strategies as a member of a string quartet. No one around them would fail to notice serious problems.

We conclude that even though language is usually instantiated largely in the left hemisphere, this is not the result of tissue specificity that commands the basic shape of language abilities. Indeed, it seems that language, when shifting into the right hemisphere, occupies tissue that would have been otherwise occupied by perceptual-spatial analyses (P Huttenlocher, personal communication). Thus what is central in language processes is not determined by particular tissues; rather there must be central programs that have tissue preferences, but that can convert tissues otherwise likely to be used for other purposes.

HYDROCEPHALY AND LANGUAGE Perhaps even more striking are results from infants born hydrocephalic, a condition in which fluid fills the internal vascular cavity. In particular, Lorber (1980) reports that normal to superior development often occurs even with the most severe cases (CAT scans showing ventricular expansion occupying 95% of the cranium); one of these patients "gained a first-class honours degree (Sheffield University) degree in mathematics and is socially completely normal. And yet the boy has virtually no brain" (quoted in Lewin 1980, p. 1232).

EARLY FOCAL LESIONS Children may also suffer from focal lesions (confined to part of the hemisphere) early on. As might be expected, recovery is generally good (Stiles & Thal 1992). Problems from early lesion are fairly global, and language-localization associations do not match adult models very well, in fact (Thal et al 1991). Within the left hemisphere, in one-year olds, both anterior and large posterior lesions are likely to cause expressive language problems, unlike adults for whom anterior lesions affect expression more. This could arise from basic maturational differences during the period of acquisition, or reflect differences in the support processes that must be recruited. For example, children might have less efficient posterior-related nonlinguistic conceptual representations at this time, so damage here might cause them more difficulties in word use than it would adults. Though the left hemisphere is already dominant for language expression, around a year old, lesions to the right hemisphere affect comprehension as much as left hemisphere lesions do. This result is supported by an ERP (event-related-potential) analysis of results in a purely auditory word recognition task (Mills et al 1993), so it is doubtful that task-specific processing variables are at work. ERP results indicate differential hemispheric reaction to familiar words by 18–20 months, suggesting that maturational processes, or the interaction of the hemispheres with language experience, have changed the comprehension balance by then.

Interestingly, early perceptual-spatial lesions in various parts of the brain match adult models of lesion effects better than do early language-area lesions (Stiles & Thal 1992). This may mean that perceptual functions, evolutionarily older, are also more hard-wired for their preferred types of tissue and place of operation than are language functions.

Recovery and Localization of Functions in Older Children

Even by one year of age, left hemisphere lesions produce more expressive language problems, as seen above. In the years after this, left hemispheric lesions are far more likely than right lesions to produce aphasic symptoms in children, possibly even more so than in adults (Hecaen et al 1984). Interestingly, posterior lesion rarely causes aphasia in children, and Wernicke-like symptoms (fluent aphasia, word substituion, within-word scrambled phonology) are very rare. Symptoms are more likely to concentrate on dysarthia and mutism (Hecaen et al 1984), and the relative likelihood of anterior lesion causing such symptoms, compared to temporal lobe lesion, is higher in children. It would certainly be interesting to have interpretations for these developmental differences.

Though possibly more likely to occur in children, aphasias are also likely to be transient (Guttman 1942). The resilience of language to various lesions is considerable, and Broca (1865) noted instances in children of language being retained when Broca's area itself was lost.

Hemispherectomies may be performed on children after infancy. Typically, however, the operation occurs after fairly long periods of seizure or disability, and it is unlikely that the remaining hemisphere has been unaffected; long-range impairment indeed appears more serious with children who had more severe preoperative seizure histories (RE Stark, K Bleile, J Brandt, J Freeman, & EPG Vining, unpublished manuscript). Perhaps most surprising is that some children show normal everyday language functioning in long-term recovery (J Windsor, personal communication), even if they show effects of long-term intellectual impairment (though such impairment typically has occurred before the operation).

Recovery in Adults: Hemispheric Involvements

Although lesion is more likely to result in long-term aphasic symptoms in adults, both short-term and longer-term recovery are common (Smith 1984). Some of this may arise from recovery of language tissue temporarily traumatized during the cause of the lesion (e.g. stroke in one area). But some of it may result from actual reorganization of brain resources. The remaining language functioning areas of the left hemisphere may recruit resources of some kind from the right hemisphere, and the prospects for recovery may depend greatly on whether the left hemisphere can recruit such resources from the right (Smith 1984). For example, Russell & Espir (1961) found more recovery in young adult aphasics with brain missile left lesion, even extensive lesion, than in cases with less extensive bilateral lesions, or left hemisphere lesions involving the corpus callossum. This indicates the importance of right hemispheric resources being available from which to recruit. In older patients, even when only left hemisphere lesion is detectible, absence of right hemisphere problems as indicated by left-side sensory-motor functioning is a central predictor of recovery from left hemisphere lesion (Smith 1984). We do not know what is being recruited from the right hemisphere in such cases; it could be more peculiarly linguistic, or could be nonlinguistic support processes. In any case, the degree of potential recovery even in adulthood is fairly substantial, though less assured than in childhood.

Overall Comments on Elasticity: Language and Perception

There is no question that for most speakers, language naturally localizes its functions in the left hemisphere. Yet even among speakers without any pathological conditions, one third of left-handers have right hemispheric or bilateral language, indicating that something about organizational processes is more robust than tissue fixation. In fact, normal language function probably involves more variation than is commonly believed in other respects. Men, for example, appear to be susceptible to aphasia from lesions in many brain areas, while for women, lesions are most likely for anterior regions (Kimura 1992). More generally, localization of many functions besides language probably shows significant individual variation (Gazzaniga 1989) as do basic matters of morphology and brain configuration. As an example of the latter, Stensass et al (1974) found that primary visual sensory cortex areas vary as much as 400% in a sample of 25 normal brains!

We have also seen great elasticity for language under various conditions, including transfer of language functions to the right hemisphere, or selective recruitment of other within-hemisphere or cross-hemisphere tissue in less stressful conditions such as focal lesion or deafness. In fact, simple localization programs associating certain tissue with certain functions in a fixed manner are probably inaccurate. Stein (1988) notes evidence that even for well-established locus-function relations, fast lesion may be associated with severe function loss, but slow lesion may typically result in no loss of function at all. While controversial, evidence indicates that in conditions of slow lesion, surrounding or other tissue can be converted to the function that is being lost. Dax, in the nineteenth century, had noted the same thing (Smith 1984), and Broca pointed to such cases for language. Often the limiting factor for such elasticity may be the availability of unoccupied other tissue (Goldman 1974), which naturally diminishes with age, though possibly never vanishing. For many biological functions, the notion of fixed tissue seems inappropriate. Rather, what seems central is some kind of underlying program for using tissue; functions like language, in effect, are not hardware but software.

Such elasticity may be even more marked for language than other functions. We have already noted that when language moves to the left hemisphere, language functions may survive better than perceptual-spatial ones (Huttenlocher 1994; but see RE Stark, K Bleile, J Brandt, J Freeman, & EPG Vining, unpublished manuscript). Stiles & Thal (1992) find that the specific effects of early lesion to spatial-perceptual areas are more lasting than those to language tissues, which essentially show recovery of all functions. Indeed, Smith (1984) notes that even in adults, left hemispherectomics may show some recovery for language in the few years they survive the operation (usually undertaken only for tumors so severe they typically spread and kill the patient within a few years of the operation); the perceptual-spatial impairments from right hemispherectomy, in contrast, last for decades after the operation. If there is anything to this generalization of greater flexibility for language, this may reflect further both the evolutionary comparative newness of language, resulting in its being even less of a hard-wired function than other functions, or it may reflect its nature as a higher-order function that coordinates many evolutionarily earlier functions.

Could such results mean that what we call language is really just the summary result of many independent systems that are resilient, responding to environmental regularities? Although this is arguable, it seems unlikely. First, environmental regularities must be interpreted selectively to give organized function; so environmental regularities per se cannot account for continued resilience of the qualitative shape of functioning. The nonlinguistic linguistic functions that are coordinated to comprise language may have their own selectively biased systems, resulting in part of the qualitative shape of language function; but what is impressive is how an overall language function is preserved across many changes of the physical structural underpinning, including both those of normal variation (e.g. left-handed vs right-handed localization patterns) and more serious modality and pathological changes. This indicates the robustness of an overall coordinated function beyond a simple summation of independent abilities, one that shows its nature both in the partial fixedness of normal development, and the qualitative preservation under conditions of change.

LANGUAGE AND CLINICAL SYNDROMES

Finally, we review some recent prominent attempts to find further evidence of language-particular functional subsystems dissociating under conditions of clinical syndrome: that is, does development show language-specific functions being particularly spared, or impaired, compared to other perceptual and intellectual functions? We look at two major problems: another search for a specific cognition-independent syntactic or grammatical component, and an hypothesis about a specific coordinative component of language devoted to translating certain conceptual meanings into morphological form.

Williams' and Down Syndromes

In recent years, arguments have been made from one old syndrome, Down syndrome, and a more newly investigated one, Williams' syndrome, for separation of particular syntactic abilities. Work on Williams' syndrome in particular has inspired much belief in independence of language and cognition. For example, Damasio & Damasio (1992) write:

> ...the maturation of language processes may not always depend on the maturation of conceptual processes, since some children with defective conceptual systems have nonetheless acquired grammar. The neural machinery for some syntactic operations does seem capable of developing autonomously (p. 89).

Flavell et al (1993) label the subheading under which they discuss recent results from Williams' syndrome studies as "language independent of cognition."

The facts are quite dramatic. Williams' syndrome is a severe retardation syndrome, like Down syndrome, in which overall IQs of around 50 are common. The organic and behavioral syndromes, however, are quite different. Organically, Down syndrome children are known to have three chromosomes for chromosome pair 22. The presumed genetic basis of Williams' syndrome is not known, though those with it are known to have abnormal calcium metabolism. Brain sizes are smaller than average for both, but the frontal and cerebellar (motor control) areas are relatively larger in Williams' syndrome. In appearance, Down syndrome children are born with cleft palates (usually surgically repaired) and slanted eyes; Williams' syndrome children have a somewhat elfin look. Children of both kinds are socially quite friendly, and Williams' syndrome parents have to watch them carefully, because the children cannot successfully be told not to talk to strangers.

Of most interest are their differing intellectual profiles. In perceptual recognition and motor tasks, they show different patterns of deficits. Williams' syndrome children, given a letter made of small copies of itself to draw (e.g. an *m* made of small *m*s), draw only the smaller letters and miss the larger form. Their drawings of bicycles are disconnected parts, often looking like unrecognizable squiggles. They do poorly at the Benton line orientation task, but have good facial memory and recognition. In contrast, Down syndrome children draw primitive but recognizable whole shapes; they draw the larger letter and miss the small ones in the letter-copying task; their facial recognition and memory performance is impaired. These results confirm the separability of various perceptual and perceptual-motor tasks from each other (Bellugi et al 1991). These perceptual dissociations in turn are dissociated from language functioning, the central interest here. Williams' syndrome children, though acquiring vocabulary slowly, eventually achieve relatively normal vocabularies, while Down syndrome children do not (Miller 1992). In grammar and other skills, Williams' syndrome children become far more fluent. Thus their language skills contrast greatly with their eventual perceptual and perceptual-motor skills.

There is a fairly large tradition by now, however, of perceptual and perceptual-motor tasks showing a great deal of faculty specificity. In brain lesions, language-related and perceptual-spatial functions are often differentially affected, depending on the sites of hemispheric lesion (Kolb & Whislaw 1990). Functionally, autistic children occasionally turn up with artistic skills like those of adults, even as other skills, including language skills, are enormously retarded (Gardner 1983). Such results thus contribute to understanding of dissociations between language vs perceptual-spatial and perceptual-motor functions, and of dissociations among specific perceptual-spatial-motor abilities (for discussion of the latter, see Kosslyn & Koenig 1992).

What has perhaps attracted more attention is the claim that Williams' and Down syndromes show at least partial independence of language as a whole from higher cognitive processes, in particular the coherent resilience of grammar or syntax within language, as in the quotations from Damasio & Damasio (1992) and Flavell et al (1993) cited above. What are the chief grounds for this possible demonstration? The major evidence is a dissociation between aspects of the children's linguistic abilities and their performance on Piagetian concrete operational tasks that are typically passed by normal children seven to nine years old. By adolescence, Down syndrome children may be found who pass the Piagetian tests, but whose language remains retarded in grammatical, pragmatic, and vocabulary level. In contrast, Williams' syndrome children have become fluent speakers, but characteristically fail to pass the Piagetian tasks. So general cognitive and language achievement apparently need not covary, giving them some independence. This characterization must be generally true, but in order to evaluate its significance, we must look more specifically at the performance of the children.

WILLIAMS' SYNDROME CHILDREN Their language begins slowly, but grammatal development begins with about the same vocabulary that normal children have when they begin making sentences. This development then proceeds relatively quickly. They develop relatively extensive vocabularies, and even use uncommon words. Indeed, one of their peculiarities is that they may give uncommon words immediately in word listing or association tasks (e.g. saying "bird, trochonodon,...") when asked to name animals (Bellugi et al 1991, Rossem 1993). They fail to achieve some subtleties of prepositional semantic use (ES Klima, unpublished information), but basically develop vocabulary that encodes normal word meanings.

Grammatically, Williams' syndrome children become largely fluent speakers by adolescence, though they sometimes still make overregularization errors like *falled.* They comprehend and use constructions like the passive and conditional, often spontaneously used by normal English-acquiring children by age seven or eight. Pragmatically, they can be good narrators, and fluently and skillfully tell a story about a picture book (Rossem 1993; see below for analysis of the Frog story narration). They can talk intelligibly about the nature and function of bicycle parts even if they cannot draw a bicycle, and can talk fluently and reasonably about what it is like to be brain scanned, and what brain scanners do (Bellugi et al 1991). In fact, they can even learn to read at a normal time (Neville et al 1993). They thus become rather mature speakers, even though their "defective conceptual systems" (Damasio & Damasio 1992) are not capable of sustaining middle childhood performance on Piagetian tasks.

What do these findings show? First, do they show "language without cognition," or "language independent of cognition?" This seems unlikely. Williams' syndrome children do not use syntactically correct but semantically meaningless sentences like "colorless green ideas sleep furiously" [to use the semi-famous example of asemantic syntactic regularity from Chomsky (1957)]. Their vocabulary encodes the same concepts as that of normal speakers; their sentences are sensible, comprehensible sentences about normal events, locations, feelings, and object properties.

Nor do they show cognition restricted to those basic aspects needed for vocabulary and grammar. They can learn to read, and surely reading is not a skill wired into basic biological programs. As mentioned above, they show considerable narrative skill. An example from Rossem (1993) is worth analyzing briefly. In the Frog story, a frog escapes from a bottle a boy had put him in. The boy sees the frog is gone, and in the flurry, the boy's dog breaks the bottle. The boy and his dog go looking for the frog, have many adventures, and find the frog with his family. In telling the story, one subject says that the boy wanted to find the frog to tell him that his bottle had been broken. The subject obviously had good event memory for the initial part of the story. But more impressively, the subject selected this event for the boy to tell because the boy would know general pragmatic principles that you should tell someone else something of interest to that person. Furthermore, the subject inferred the frog might be interested in the fate of his bottle, so this is what the boy would tell. Obviously such a subject has considerable cognitive and social knowledge beyond that required for basic sentence construction.

What is striking, however, is the failure of Williams' syndrome children on Piagetian cognitive developmental tests that normal children so regularly pass. These well-known tasks test knowledge of mathematical constancy under perceptual change (conservation of number, conservation of liquid quantity), knowledge of class-subclass relations, transitive reasoning, and other cognitive skills. So one might infer that Williams' syndrome children achieve excellent language knowledge while not having basic abilities to analyze causal relations, mathematical constancy, classification relations, and so on, which might show considerable independence of language from basic cognition.

But the last 25 years of cognitive developmental studies have shown that normal preschool children who fail the Piagetian concrete operational tests nevertheless have considerable knowledge of causal, mathematical, classificatory, and transitive reasoning relations (Flavell 1985, Gelman & Baillargeon 1983). It is now widely suspected that children fail the tests because of particular memory or attentional demands the tests make (Gelman & Baillargeon 1983, Trabasso 1975), not because the children lack the basic cognitive skills. So failure on the tests does not show absence of central causal, classificatory, and other reasoning skills at all. It only shows specific deficits in little-understood cognitive, attentional, and possibly motivational developments that continue in normal children. In fact, on the whole, Williams' syndrome children could be described as children who have become fluent speakers while not being able to pass Piagetian Concrete Operation Tasks; but this, in fact, is an excellent characterization of most normal children, who at the age of five are largely in the same condition.

Bellugi et al (1991) however, argue that there is special resilience of syntactic-grammatical development. They note that Williams' syndrome children develop expressive and comprehension proficiency with certain grammatical constructions, the passive and conditional, that typically normal children only develop around the time they show concrete operational behavior. This might show specific sparing of qualitatively new middle childhood language abilities in the absence of cognitive abilities that normally develop around the same time.

The passive and conditional, however, do not represent grammatical developments qualitatively different from what preschool children can do. Preschool children can use both constructions. Sesotho children hear passives frequently in the earlier years [unlike English-speaking children (Maratsos et al 1985)], and they use passives at ages three and four throughout a wide semantic-structural range (Demuth 1990). English-speaking children of three and four do not typically use conditionals spontaneously, but they comprehend and use them if their parents or experimenters use conditionals in questions to the children (Kuczaj & Daly 1979). The passive and conditional constructions thus do not represent anything qualitatively more advanced.

Are there other central language functions that are qualitatively spared, compared to general middle childhood cognition? Williams' syndrome children do continue to develop vocabulary past typical preschool levels. But this may simply arise from the interaction of preschool cognitive abilities with more experience. Certainly preschool children can come to use uncommon words if such words are used around them. Thus, while there is some dissociation in concrete operational task abilities and language abilities, this dissociation does not show the specific sparing of a coherent language faculty. If anything, it is possible that language relies on or coordinates a number of preschool abilities, and what is fractionated off is that realm of cognitive development (whatever it is) responsible for the ability to do concrete operational tasks. We must conclude that for the present, the language development of Williams' syndrome children shows serious continuing evidence of dissociation of language-related cognition vs perceptual competences; but independence of a spared coherent language faculty from a pool of possible pre-concrete operational cognitive competencies has not been shown.

DOWN SYNDROME CHILDREN Down syndrome children can achieve concrete operational task performance without achieving linguistic fluency. Perhaps this does conclude the case for double dissociation; perhaps they do lack basic language skills, showing the coherence of such language components by their relative absence of such skills.

To summarize an account that is still being worked on (Chapman et al 1992, Chapman et al 1993, Fowler 1990, Miller 1992), Down syndrome children vary widely in final productive language level in adolescence. They vary in average sentence length measured in morphemes (MLU) from 2.0 through about 6.0, levels characteristic of children two-and-a-half to five or six years old. The slower children typically have serious articulation deficits (Miller 1992) that could easily slow down language acquisition in a several ways, including making attention to language itself more aversive, and reducing others' interactive feedback.

There is little argument that language development in Down syndrome children is qualitatively different from that of normal children. Both progress through roughly the same major paths, making essentially the same kinds of errors. In adolescense, they produce approximately the same proportion of complex sentences (conjunctions, embedded sentences) as children with similar mean sentence lengths (Chapman et al 1992, 1993). The main qualitative-looking difference in grammar is that they tend to leave out more small morphological affixes and functors at a given sentence length. This difference reminds one of Broca's asphasics dealing with output implementations, which Down syndrome children also have problems with.

Fowler (1990), however, argues that the specific slowness of rate, and not the manner of grammatical development in particular, shows syntax as a function separate from general mental development for Down syndrome children. Indeed, in many of them, expressive grammar seems worse than general mental test results (Miller 1992). But this is not true of vocabulary and syntactic comprehension, which keep pace with nonverbal mental test results (Chapman et al 1992, 1993). The deficits appear to be specific to the production of language. Such implementational deficits could point to something specific in language implementation systems, or they might be characteristic of more general temporal integration problems in producing complex structures (Miller 1992). In any case, a straightforward isolated problem in syntactic development in particular has not been demonstrated at this point.

A Last Syndrome: Morphological Paradigm Formation Deficit?

We turn now to a language-specific deficit that is not claimed to be one of autonomous syntax or language without cognition, but rather is claimed to be one in the specific coordination of concepts with language systems. Gopnik (1990) reports on a family in which 16 of 30 related members show, by various tests, specific problems with morphological suffixes like plural noun *-s* or past tense *-ed.* The family members do use semantically appropriate individual instances of words with these endings, and certainly show general understanding of the general relevant concepts, such as numerosity or past events. But they often leave the endings off, and more important, Gopnik & Crago (1991) argue at length that various test results, including comprehension tests with novel words and other tests, show that at best, family members memorize individual instances but fail to make generalized morphological paradigms, a language-specific learning ability proposed in Pinker (1984). Thus what is proposed is a specific deficit in a language coordination system for translating meaning into morphology, rather than language independent of cognition.

The results have attracted both support (Pinker 1991) and counterexplanation and controversy. Leonard et al (1993) note that morphology is generally one of the language abilities most vulnerable to lower-level deficits (as we have noted throughout), and proposes two particular different hypotheses. One, called Sparse Morphology, suggests that children who are having general language processing difficulties, may devote less attention to a less frequently and consistently realized structural feature of a language, and in English, morphology has just this status compared to most other languages. A second hypothesis is that English morphological markers are generally unstressed and nonsyllabic, making production and perception more vulnerable for someone with limited resources. Leonard et al 1993 have found children with specific language deficits (that is, who perform normally on non-language mental tests) in languages like Italian and Hebrew, languages that have more consistent use of morphology, and that mark many of the same meanings with full, often stressed syllables. Such children retain such morphological markers in these languages, while omitting ones with less full phonological realization. Leonard suggests that Gopnik & Crago's subjects may thus be responding to the sparse and less marked morphology of English.

Other criticisms more specific to Gopnik & Crago's original results have appeared. M Seidenberg (personal communication) notes that tests that supported the claims were given many trials; tests of nonmorphological aspects of language were given fewer, giving more opportunity for differences to emerge between afflicted and normal family members on the morphological tests. The family inheritance pattern furthermore does not fit inheritance of a single genetic difficulty. Perhaps most important, Vargha-Khadem & Passingham (1990), who also have worked on studies of other language difficulties in the family, write that the "family has a severe congenital speech disorder" by no means confined to morphological expression, but extending to semantic problems in naming tasks, and a number of phonological disorders.

Thus, we obviously do not have a full profile for morphological paradigm formation deficits, and the overall configuration may suggest something different than what is outlined in Gopnik & Crago (1991); further study of the family itself seems like an obvious future course, as does further investigation of cross-linguistic language impairment syndromes.

CLOSING REMARKS

We have concentrated on two closely related matters: the search for specificity of language in the brain and clinical syndromes, and problems of localization and elasticity. Regarding the latter, we think the evidence shows an interesting mixture of flexibility and fixedness in language as a biological system. On the whole, current localization results seem to show a lot of resilience for a central language coordinative function, especially given the combination of partial biological fixedness, and yet opportunistic flexibility of language functions. We consider the interesting facts about both the existence and localization patterns of sign language as part of such a general conclusion.

We have argued on grounds of linguistic analysis itself that a wholly independent language function, or wholly independent subpart corresponding to autonomous syntax is at best a strong and problematic hypothesis. We have found no evidence corresponding to the specificity of such a subpart in aphasia or clinical syndrome studies; the possibility of finding such evidence cannot be ruled out, but we find it doubtful that any part of language has such a character. In general, given the likely nature of evolution, in which present developments opportunistically use past ones (Bates et al 1991a, Bickerton 1981, Glassman & Wimsatt 1984, Mayr 1980) it is unlikely that language is completely independent as an entity. We know of nothing that supports such complete independence for a whole coherent subpart, though nothing should be ruled out a priori. It seems to us most promising to look for specificity of subparts of language in specific systems that exist to coordinate nonlinguistic elements with each other. These coordinations may have specific programming to avoid the conceivable overload of data that might otherwise occur. Current work with lexical concept-word mediation paths (Damasio & Damasio 1992) seems to us consistent with such an approach, and also offers reasonable possibilities about what modular systems might look like (as opposed to ones implying complete encapsulation).

Considerable biological specificity is likely to be found in the core domains of grammar, though probably in a form we would not necessarily recognize at present. Despite our apparent opposition to the view that language as a whole, or in major subparts, is independent of cognition, we do not think there are no specific mechanisms, or specific elements, that form a program for language aquisition and use. More broadly, we think evidence from normal development shows that people are quite good at some functions, such as language use, many perceptual functions, or various weighted category formation tasks (e.g. Medin & Schaffer 1978), and not very good at others, such as logical reasoning, baseline probability reasoning, accurate self-assessment (Dawes 1988, Nisbett & Ross 1980), or ability to see or reason about certain combinations of physical forces (Siegler 1985, Russell 1950). For example, children are likely to analyze without instruction the nature of the seven or eight (at least) semantic, pragmatic, and structural factors that enter simultaneously into the choice of an appropriate case-and-gender marked definite common noun article in German (Maratsos & Chalkley 1980). As adults, experts before Galileo could not analyze or see the simultaneous operation of forward and downward forces operating on an arrow shot from a box (Russell 1950). There is not much real improvement in most adults who have been taught Galilean physics (Siegler 1985). Language seems likely both to comprise an instance of, and to have drawn off of, the privileged domains in human thought processes, and we expect future work will bear out the particular nature of its privileges, whatever they look like.

ACKNOWLEDGMENTS

Many persons contributed valuable help to us in writing this review, in either supplying information or considering arguments with us, and we would like particularly to thank Elizabeth Bates, Robin Chapman, Gedeon Deak, Susan Goldin-Meadow, Peter Huttenlocher, Jon Miller, Rachel Stark, Mark Seidenberg, Maria Sera, Joan Stiles, David Swinney, and Jennifer Windsor.

Literature Cited

American Heritage Dictionary. 1975. Boston: Houghton Mifflin

Bates E, Thal D, Marchman V. 1991a. Symbols and syntax: a Darwininan approach to language development. In *Biological and Behavioral Determinants of Language Development,* ed. NA Krasnegor, D Rumbaugh, R Schiefelbusch, M Studdert-Kennedy, pp. 29–66. Hillsdale, NJ: Erlbaum

Bates E, Wulfeck B, MacWhinney B. 1991b. Cross-linguistic research in aphasia: an overview. *Brain Lang.* 41:123–48

Bellugi U. 1988. The acquisition of a spatial language. In *The Development of Language and Language Researchers*, ed. F Kessel, pp. 153–86. Hillsdale, NJ: Erlbaum

Bellugi U, Bihrle A, Corina D. 1991. Linguistic and spatial development: dissociations between cognitive domains. In *Biological and Behavioral Determinants of Language Development,* ed. NA Krasnegor, D Rumbaugh, R Schiefelbusch, M Studdert-Kennedy, pp. 363–98. Hillsdale, NJ: Erlbaum

Bickerton D. 1981. *The Roots of Language.* Ann Arbor, MI: Karoma

Bishop DVM. 1983. Linguistic impairment after left hemidecortication for infantile hemiplegia? A reappraisal. *Q. J. Exp. Psychol.* 35A:199–207

Broca P. 1865. Sur la siege de la faculte du language articule. In *La Naissance de la Neuropsychologie du Language (1825–1865),* ed. H Hecaen, J Dubois. Reprinted from *Bull. Soc. Anat. Paris* 6:336–57

Brown R. 1973. *A First Language: The Early Stages*. Cambridge: Harvard Univ. Press

Chapman RS, Ross DR, Seung H-K. 1993. *Longitudinal differences in language production of children and adolescents with Down syndrome.* Poster at Univ. Wisc. Symp. Res. Child Lang. Disord., Madison, Wisc.

Chapman RS, Schwartz SE, Kay-Raining Bird E. 1992. *Cross-sectional differences in language production of children and adolescents with Down syndrome.* Poster at Univ. Wisc. Symp. Res. Child Lang. Disord., Madison, Wisc.

Chomsky AN. 1957. *Syntactic Structures.* The Hague: Mouton

Chomsky AN. 1965. *Aspects of the Theory of Syntax.* Cambridge, MA: MIT Press

Chomsky AN. 1981. *Lectures on Government and Binding*. Dordrecht: Foris

Chomsky AN. 1986. *Knowledge of Language.* New York: Praeger

Corina DP, Vaid J, Bellugi U. 1992. The linguistic basis of left hemisphere specialization. *Science* 255:1258–60

Damasio AR, Damasio H. 1992. Brain and Language. *Sci. Am.* 117:89–95

Damasio H, Damasio AR 1989. *Lesion Analysis in Neuropsychology*. London: Oxford Univ. Press

Dawes R. 1988. *Rational Choice in an Uncertain World*. New York: Harcourt, Brace, Jovanovich

Demuth K. 1990. Subject, topic and Sesotho passive. *J. Child Lang*. 17:67–84

Dennis M. 1980. Capacity and strategy for syntactic comprehension after left or right hemidecortication. *Brain Lang*. 10:287–317

Dennis M, Whitaker H. 1976. Language acquisition following hemidecortication: linguistic superiority of the left over the right hemisphere. *Brain Lang*. 3:404–33

Eimas P, Siqueland ER, Jusczyk P, Vigorito J. 1971. Speech perception in infants. *Science* 171:303–6

Erbaugh M. 1982. *The acquisition of Mandarin Chinese*. PhD thesis. Ann Arbor, MI: Univ. Microfilms Int.

Fillmore CJ. 1968. The case for case. In *Universals in Linguistic Theory*, ed. E Bach, RT Harms pp. 1–90. New York: Holt, Rinehart, Winston

Flavell JH. 1985. *Cognitive Development*. Englewood Cliffs, NJ: Prentice-Hall

Flavell JH, Miller PH, Miller SA. 1993. *Cognitive Development*. Englewood Cliffs, NJ: Prentice-Hall

Fodor J. 1983. *Modularity of Mind*. Cambridge, MA: MIT Press. 2nd ed.

Fowler AE. 1990. Language abilities in children with Down syndrome. In *Children with Down Syndrome: A Developmental Perspective*, ed. D Cicchetti, M Beeghly, pp. 302–28. New York: Cambridge Univ. Press

Gardner H. 1983. *Frames of Mind: The Theory of Multiple Intelligences*. New York: Basic Books

Gazzaniga MS. 1989. Organization of the human brain. *Science* 245: 947–52

Gelman R, Baillargeon R. 1983. A review of Piagetian concepts. In *Handbook of Child Development*. Vol. 3: *Cognitive Development*, ed. JH Flavell, E Markman, pp. 167–230. New York: Wiley

Glassman RB, Wimsatt WC. 1984. Evolutionary advantages and limitations of early plasticity. In *Brain Damage*. Vol. 1: *Research Orientations and Clinical Observations*, ed. CR Almli, S Finger, pp. 35–58. New York: Academic

Goldman PS. 1974. Plasticity of function in the CNS. In *Plasticity and Recovery of Function in the Central Nervous System*, ed. DG Stein, JJ Rosen, N Butters, pp. 149–74. London: Academic

Goldstein K. 1948. *Language and Language Disturbance*. New York: Grune & Stratton

Gopnik M. 1990. Feature-blind grammar and dysphasia. *Nature* 344:715

Gopnik M, Crago M. 1991. Familial aggregation of a developmental language disorder. *Cognition* 39:1–50

Guttman E. 1942. Aphasia in children. *Brain* 65:205–19

Hecaen H, Perenin MT, Jeannerod M. 1984 The effects of cortical lesions in children: Language and visual functions. In *Early Brain Damage*. Vol. l: *Research Orientations and Clinical Observations*, ed. CR Almi, S Finger, pp. 277–98. New York: Academic

Heeschen C. 1985. Agrammatism versus paragrammatism: a fictitious opposition. See Kean 1985, pp. 207–48

Huttenlocher P. 1994. Synaptogeneis, synapse elimination, and neural plasticity in human cerebral cortext. In *Infants and Children at Risk*, ed. C Nelson. Hillsdale, NJ: Erlbaum

Jackendoff RS. 1972. *Semantic Interpretation in Generative Grammar*. Cambridge, MA: MIT Press

Katz JJ, Postal PM. 1964. *An Integrated Theory of Linguistic Descriptions*. Cambridge, MA: MIT Press

Kean M, ed. 1985. *Agrammatism*. New York: Academic

Kimura D. 1976. The neural basis of language qua gesture. In *Studies in Neurolinguistics*, ed. H Whitaker, D Whitaker, pp. 97–121. New York: Academic

Kimura D. 1992. Sex differences in the brain. *Sci. Am*. 135:119–25

Klima ES, Bellugi U. 1979. *The Signs of Language*. Cambridge: Harvard Univ. Press

Kolb B, Whislaw I. 1990. *Fundamentals of Human Neuropsychology*. New York: Freeman

Kolk HHJ, Van Grunsven MJF, Keyser A. 1985. On parallelism between production and comprhension in agrammatism. See Kean 1985, pp. 165–206

Kosslyn S & Koenig K. 1992. *Wet Brain*. Cambridge: Harvard Univ. Press

Kuczaj SA II, Daly J. 1979. The development of hypothetical reference in the speech of young children. *J. Child Lang*. 6:573–79

Lakoff G. 1971. On generative semantics. In *Semantics: An Interdisiplinary Reader in Philosophy, Linguistics, and Psychology*, ed. DD Steinberg, LA Jakobovitz, pp. 232–96. Cambridge: Cambridge Univ. Press

Leonard L, Bortolini U, Caselli M, McGregor K, Sabbadini L. 1993. Two accounts of morphological deficits in children with Specific Language Impairment. *Lang. Acquis*. In press

Lewin R. 1980. Is your brain really necessary? *Science* 210:1232–34

Lieberman P. 1989. Some biological constraints on universal grammar and learnability. In *The Teachability of Language*, ed. M Rice, R Schiefelbusch, pp. 167–203. Baltimore: Brookes

Linebarger MC, Schwartz MF, Saffran EM. 1983. Sensitivity to grammatical structure in so-called agrammatic aphasics. *Cognition* 13:361–92

Lorber J. 1980. Is your brain really necessary? *World Med.* May 3:21–24

Maratsos M. 1989. Innateness and plasticity in language development. In *The Teachability of Language,* ed. M Rice, R Schiefelbusch, pp. 109–25. Baltimore: Brookes

Maratsos M. 1991. *Non-innate grammatical category formation.* Paper presented at Meet. Int. Child Lang. Assoc., Budapest, Hungary

Maratsos M. 1992. How the acquisition of nouns may be different from that of verbs. In *Biological and Behavioral Determinants of Language Development,* ed. N Krasnegor, D Rumbaugh, R Schiefelbusch, M Studdert-Kennedy, pp. 67–88. Hillsdale, NJ: Erlbaum

Maratsos M, Chalkley MA. 1980. The internal language of children's syntax: the nature and ontogenesis of syntactic categories. In *Children's Language,* ed. K Nelson, 2:127–213. New York: Gardner

Maratsos M, Fox CD, Becker J, Chalkley MA 1985. Semantic restrictions on children's passives. *Cognition* 19:167–91

Markman E. 1992. Constraints on word learning: speculations about their nature, origins, and domain specificity. In *Modularity and Constraints in Language and Cognition. The Minnesota Symposia on Child Pychology,* ed. M Gunnar, M Maratsos, 23:59–102. Hillsdale, NJ: Erlbaum

Mayr E. 1980. *The Growth of Biological Thought: Diversity, Evolution, and Inheritance.* Cambridge, MA: Belknap

McNeill D. 1970. *The Acquisition of Language: The Study of Developmental Psycholinguistics.* New York: Harper & Row

Medin DL, Schaffer MM. 1978. Context theory of classification learning. *Psychol. Rev.* 85:207–38

Miller J. 1992. Development of speech and language in children with Down syndrome. In *Down syndrome: Advances in Medical Care,* ed. I Lott, E McCoy, pp. 23–41. New York: Wiley

Mills DL, Coffey SA, Neville HJ. 1993. Variability in cerebral organization during primary language acquisition. In *Human Behavior and the Developing Brain,* ed. G Dawson, K Fischer. New York: Guildford. In press

Molfese DL 1977. Infant cerebral assymetry. In *Language Development and Neurological Theory,* ed. SJ Segalowitz, FA Gruber, pp. 21–35. New York: Academic

Neville H, Mills DL, Bellugi U. 1993. Effects of altered auditory sensitivity and age of language acquisition on the development of language-relevant neural systems: preliminary studies of Williams Syndrome. In *Cognitive Deficits in Developmental Disorders: Implications for Brain Function,* ed. S Broman. Hillsdale, NJ: Erlbaum. In press

Newmayer J. 1980. *A History of Transformational Grammar in America.* New York: Academic

Newport E. 1982. Task specificity in language learning? Evidence from speech perception and American Sign Language. In *Language Acquisition: The State of the Art,* ed. E Wanner, L Gleitman, pp. 450–86. Cambridge: Cambridge Univ. Press

Nisbett R, Ross L. 1980. *Human Inference: Strategies and Shortcomings.* Englewood Cliffs, NJ: Prentice-Hall

Petitto L. 1988. "Language" in the prelinguistic child. In *The Development of Language and Language Researchers,* ed. F Kessel, pp. 187–222. Hillsdale, NJ: Erlbaum

Petitto L. 1993. On the ontogenetic requirements for early language acquisition. In *Developmental Neurocognition: Speech and Face Processing in the First Year of Life,* ed. J de Boysson-Bardies, R Schoenen, P Jusczyk, P MacNeilage, J Morton, pp. 108–29. New York: Kluwer Academic

Pinker S. 1984. *Language Learnability and Language Development.* Cambridge: Harvard Univ. Press

Pinker S. 1991. Rules of language. *Science* 253:530–35

Pinker S, Bloom P. 1990. Natural language and natural selection. *Behav. Brain Sci.* 13:723–824

Poizner H, Klima ES, Bellugi U. 1987. *What the Hands Reveal about the Brain.* Cambridge, MA: MIT Press

Postal P. 1972. The best theory. In *Goals of Linguistic Theory,* ed. S Peters, pp. 102–76. Englewood Cliffs, NJ: Prentice-Hall

Rispoli M. 1991. Mosaic theory of grammatical acquisition. *J. Child Lang.* 18:517–51

Rizzi L. 1985. Two notes on the linguistic interpretation of Broca's aphasia. See Kean 1985, pp. 153–64

Rossem R. 1993. *The fractionation of language and cognition in Williams Syndrome.* Colloq. presented at Univ. Minn., May 1993

Russell B. 1950. *Unpopular Essays.* New York: Simon & Schuster

Russell WR, Espir MLE. 1961. *Traumatic Aphasia.* London: Oxford Univ. Press

Schwartz MF, Linebarger MC, Saffran EM. 1985. The status of the syntactic deficit theory of agrammatism. See Kean 1985, pp. 83–124

Seidenberg M, Petitto L. 1979. On the evidence for linguistic ability in signing apes. *Brain Lang.* 8:72–88

Siegler R. 1985. *Children's Thinking.* Englewood Cliffs NJ: Prentice Hall

Slobin DI. 1985. Crosslinguistic evidence for the language- making capacity. In *The Crosslinguistic Study of Language Acquisition,* ed. DI Slobin, 2:1157–1256. Hillsdale, NJ: Erlbaum

Smith A. 1984. Early and long-term recovery from brain damage in children and adults: evolution of concepts of localization, plasticity, and recovery. In *Early Brain Damage.* Vol. 1: *Research Orientations and Clinical Observations,* ed CR Almi, S Finger. New York: Academic

Stein DG. 1988. In pursuit of new strategies for understanding recovery from brain damage: problems and perspectives. In *Clinical Neuropsychology and Brain Function: Research Measurement and Practice,* ed. T Boll, B Bryant. Washington, DC: Am. Psychol. Assoc.

Stensass S, Eddington D, Dobelle W. 1974. The topography and variability of the primary visual cortext in man. *J. Neurosurg.* 40:747–55

Stiles J, Thal D. 1992. Linguistic and spatial cognitive development following early focal brain injury: patterns of deficit and recovery. In *Brain Development and Cognition: A Reader,* ed. M Johnson, pp. 77–98. Oxford: Blackwell

Swinney D, Zurif E, Nicol J. 1989. The effects of focal brain damage on sentence processing: an examination of the neurological organization of a mental module. *J. Cogn. Neurosci.* 1:274–90

Thal DJ, Marchman V, Stiles J, Aram D, Trauner D, et al. 1991. Early lexical development of children with focal brain injury. *Brain Lang.* 40:491–527

Timberlake A. 1977. Reanalysis and actualization in syntactic change. In *Mechanisms of Syntactic Change,* ed. CH Li, pp. 163–82. Austin: Univ. Texas Press

Trabasso T. 1975. Representation, memory, and reasoning: How do we make transitive inferences. In *Minnesota Symposia on Child Psychology,* ed. A Pick, 9:135–72. Minneapolis: Univ. Minn. Press

Vargha-Khadem F, Passingham R. 1990. Speech and language defects. *Nature* 346:226

Zurif EB, Caramazza A. 1976. Psycholinguistic structures in aphasia: studies in syntax and semantics. In *Studies in Neurolinguistics,* ed. H Whitaker, HA Whitaker, 1:147–74. New York: Academic

Annu. Rev. Psychol. 1994. 45:517–44

REPRESENTATIONS AND MODELS IN PSYCHOLOGY

P. Suppes

Ventura Hall, Stanford University, Stanford, California 94305-4115

M. Pavel

Department of Psychology, New York University, New York, New York 10003

J.-Cl. Falmagne

School of Social Sciences, University of California, Irvine, California 92717

KEY WORDS: representation, concept, knowledge, language, measurement

---

CONTENTS

0066-4308/94/0201-0517$05.00

INTRODUCTION

A representation of something is an image, model, or reproduction of that thing. References to representations are familiar and frequent in ordinary and scientific discourse. Following are some typical examples:

> This furniture is representative of the period.
> Visual representation enhances learning.
> This is a representation of the triumphal arch erected by Augustus.
> An intuitive representation of atomic forces is not possible.

A representation often improves our understanding of the object represented. We certainly understand the proportions of a building better—especially the layout of the interior—after examining its architectural drawings. The use of models in science provides many examples of representations. Such models are used primarily to enrich understanding, although they also have other functions that are nearly as important. For instance, numerical representations of measurement procedures are used to make computations more efficient. In the formal sense to be discussed here, representation has also been associated closely with reduction of the unknown to the known.

A claimed reduction of great importance in the history of ideas is Descartes' reduction of geometry to algebra. In the opening lines of his *La Géométrie* (1637; 1954, p. 2), he explained that:

> Any problem in geometry can easily be reduced to such terms that a knowledge of the lengths of certain straight lines is sufficient for its construction. Just as arithmetic consists of only four or five operations, namely, addition, subtraction, multiplication, division and the extraction of roots, which may be considered a kind of division, so in geometry, to find required lines it is merely necessary to add or subtract other lines; or else, taking one line which I shall call unity in order to relate it as closely as possible to numbers, and which can in general be chosen arbitrarily, and having given two other lines, to find a fourth line which shall be to one of the given lines as the other is to unity (which is the same as multiplication); or, again, to find a fourth line which is to one of the given lines as unity is to the other (which is equivalent to division)...

Descartes' detailed mathematical treatment constituted one of the most important conceptual breakthroughs of early modern mathematics. On the other hand, controversies arise when claims about reduction are ideological rather than scientific in character. Descartes' attempted reduction of matter to nothing but extension in his *Principles of Philosophy* (1644) was in its way just as speculative as many current theses about reduction of psychology to neurophysiology.

In this review, representation is typically defined in the restricted sense as a description of an empirical structure in a convenient scientific language. This sense of representation is closely related to the concept of a model. Even though the two concepts are different, we do not attempt to draw a sharp distinction.

We use four partially overlapping categories to organize the various justifications for the use of representations in science:

REDUCTION Most representations in a scientific context result in some reduction of the original structure. It is important to distinguish two essentially different forms of reduction. The first one arises when the original structure takes the form of data regarded as noisy. A random representation may then be used to describe the data in terms of parameters capturing the main tendencies. Among the many examples in psychology, consider a psychophysical situation in which a subject has to discriminate between two stimuli x and y, and decide which of the two appears to exceed the other from the viewpoint of some sensory attribute such as brightness or loudness. Suppose that the pair (x,y) has been presented N times in the course of the experiment, and let $n(x,y)$ be the number of times that x has been judged to exceed y. (Thus $n(x,y + \mathrm{n(y,x)} = \mathrm{N}$.) Typically these empirical frequencies will be represented by binomial random variables, with parameters N and $P(x,y)$, the latter symbolizing the probability of judging that x exceeds y. The reduction consists of the representation of a distribution of empirical frequencies by two parameters to be estimated from the data. Furthermore, in many cases, these probabilities are constrained to satisfy some model or law. The second sense of reduction is that of characterizing one set of theoretical concepts in terms of another. Descartes' reduction of geometry to algebra is a clear example. In psychology the attempted reduction of mental concepts to behavioral concepts has had considerable historical importance, even if the success of the attempted reduction is not now widely accepted.

BETTER UNDERSTANDING The representation may sometimes be summarized by a small number of illuminating principles formalized by axioms or by important empirical laws. Pursuing the psychophysical discrimination example, we may consider a special case in which the discrimination probabilities are strictly positive and satisfy the multiplication condition $[P(x,y)/P(y,x)] \times [P(y,z)/P(z,y)] \times [P(z,x)/P(x,z)] = 1$ (Suppes & Zinnes 1963, Falmagne 1985). When this equation is satisfied for all pair comparisons, then we may represent each stimulus x by a response strength $v(x)$ such that $P(x,y)= [v(x)]/[v(x) + v(y)]$. The representation may also focus the attention on important aspects, or invariants, of the data. The representation of a class of detection probabilities by a receiver operating characteristic curve is an example of such an invariant (Green & Swets 1966).

COMPUTATION AND MANIPULATION Another important motivation for a representation alluded to earlier leads to search for an embedding into a rich structure, endowed with a powerful calculus. A prime example is measurement theory, which involves representing an empirical structure by an appropriately selected numerical structure. When such a representation has been achieved, one may then apply the operations available in the embedding numerical structure in order to derive predictions about the empirical structure.

Germane to the issue of computation are situations in which the embedding structure has been chosen because it is capable of a specific type of manipulation, not necessarily of a numerical character. For instance, two different codings of the same empirical structure may correspond to different techniques for the analysis of essentially the same data. We provide an example of such a situation later, in our discussion of the equivalent representation of a language by a grammar and an automaton.

CLASSIFICATION Representations are particularly useful when individuals or objects must be placed in significant categories. Examples may be found in all the sciences, but such representations are especially characteristic of the social sciences. Well known cases are concept learning, multidimensional scaling (Carroll & Arabie 1980, Kruskal & Wish 1978), and psychometrics (Lord & Novick 1974). The typical outcome of such a representation is a description of a collection of objects (individuals, stimuli, etc) in terms of a small number of significant dimensions or attributes.

We examine four major areas of psychology in which there has been an extended focus on matters of representation: knowledge representation, concept representation and learning, language representation and learning, and representational theory of measurement.

KNOWLEDGE REPRESENTATION

Suppose that we wish to represent what an individual knows about some topic at a given time. For example, we may want to determine the knowledge of a student in elementary algebra. In practice, this type of assessment is important to ascertain the student's strengths and weakesses, to decide which material is most suitable at a particular time, and more generally, to monitor the student's future course of learning. The ability to represent an individual's knowledge is essential for our understanding of most cognitive functions because most of these functions depend critically on the available knowledge and its form. We focus our discussion on assessment in order to illustrate the variety of approaches with a simple example.

It would be impractical, if not impossible, to ask the subject all the questions pertinent to the topic of algebra. An efficient assessment procedure must take advantage of the inherent redundancy of the questions. For example, based on incorrect responses to some questions, one may be able to infer incorrect responses to other questions, thereby eliminating the need to ask them.

The problem is how to represent the student's knowledge in a suitable structure in which the kind of redundancies outlined above are also represented. Adequate knowledge representation is useful in many areas besides education: e.g. diagnoses of mental or physical dysfunctions, infectious diseases, faults in broken automobile engines, or errors in scientific theories. In these cases, the diagnosis is performed by considering available data, and making new measurements and tests. The effectiveness of the diagnosis depends, in part, on the capability of the knowledge representation to capture existing structures.

The desire for a simple and effective knowledge representation can sometimes lead to oversimplification. For example, a concept of question difficulty can be used to construct a unidimensional representation of knowledge. The difficulty of each problem and the ability of each student is represented by a single number (Guttman 1944). This difficulty scale can then be used to jointly order the questions and the students: a student is assumed to have mastered all questions represented by numbers smaller or equal to his or her ability. This unidimensional representation, which is basic to many psychometric models, has a number of virtues. The scale is relatively easy to construct from the test results of a large number of individuals. Uncertainty can be incorporated by assuming that both the difficulty and ability are random variables with specified distributions.

Unfortunately, this unidimensional structure is not a faithful representation of the knowledge in most areas of interest. For example, not all pairs of questions can be ordered with respect to their difficulty. Moreover, providing a correct answer may require more than one type of ability. For example, to answer a word problem, a student must have the necessary language skills, the ability to transform a problem into an algebraic representation, and sufficient knowledge of algebra to solve it.

More complex knowledge representations (KR) are needed in order to capture the intricacies of relations between various concepts. Two different types of such representations, deterministic and probabilistic, have been developed by scientists from diverse fields, e.g. psychologists studying human memory or the ability to reason and solve problems, and researchers in artificial intelligence who have been trying to develop knowledge representations that would enable autonomous agents to reason and solve problems.

Deterministic Approaches

FIRST-ORDER LOGIC A potentially powerful approach to KR in psychology, cognitive science, and artificial intelligence (Nilsson 1981) is based on first-order logic (FOL). In FOL facts are represented by predicates. Predicates denote functions that map their arguments into two values: *true* or *false*. The statement *Integer*(x) is a typical example of an unary predicate that is true if x is an integer, and *Plus*(x,y,z) is a predicate that is true whenever $z = x + y$. *First-order* refers to the fact that there is only quantification over arguments of predicates, not over predicates themselves.

Reasoning that corresponds to generating predictions is performed in an FOL system by proving theorems. In fact, one of the advantages of using FOL to represent a cognitive system is its powerful tools for reasoning about a variety of concrete or abstract objects and ideas. For example, a student's knowledge of algebra could be represented by first specifying a set of questions Q and defining a predicate $A\ (x)$ to represent the fact that a student can answer question x. Similarly, the negation $-A(x)$ would represent an incorrect response to question x. The knowledge structure could be then represented in FOL formulas.

For example, $A(y) \rightarrow A(x_1) \wedge A(x_2) \wedge A(x_3)$ would represent the fact that if a student can answer correctly question y then he is expected to answer correctly questions x_1, x_2, x_3. Thus the concepts addressed by x_1, x_2, and x_3 are prerequisites for y. On the other hand, if $[A(x_1) \wedge -A(x_2)] \vee [-A(x_1) \wedge A(x_2)] \rightarrow A(y)$ then an answer to y is expected only if the student knows one or the other question, but not both. This statement represents the case when two different skills interfere with each other.

Although the FOL knowledge representation can, in principle, perform all the required functions of a KR, it has several disadvantages. Perhaps the most critical shortcoming of FOL, and of any other system of this or greater generality, is that reasoning (i.e. theorem proving) is computationally intractable, i.e. it requires an impractically large number of computations. In general, the number of computations grows exponentially as a function of the number of predicates. This complexity arises from the fact that the system must typically examine all combinations of variables and values.

The computational complexity of FOL is a result of its power to express a very broad range of facts (Levesque & Brachman 1985). Because FOL lacks inherent constraints, it is generally impractical to determine the knowledge structure and the knowledge of the individual only from empirical observations or tests. To have a computationally tractable system, restricting assumptions grounded in theory or prior empirical findings must be added. Recognizing the tradeoff between the expressiveness of a KR and its computational tractability, Levesque & Brachman (1985) described several types of restrictions that can make FOL more useful. For example, a restricted KR that they called database form contains only positive instances and does not use negation, disjunction, or existential quantifiers. By limiting the types of predicates, and reducing the expressiveness of the complete FOL to a database form, acceptable performance is achievable.

Although such restrictions might be useful in some artifical intelligence applications, this approach is not regarded as leading to reasonable models in psychology. For example, human subjects seem to have difficulties in conditional reasoning ($A \rightarrow B$) (Rips 1983). Even after a semester course in logic, college students did not perform well in application of Modus tollens (Cheng et al 1986).[1] Cognitive scientists, therefore, have considered different approaches to represent knowledge and reasoning. Johnson-Laird (1983) proposed and simulated a model in which people confronted with a reasoning problem construct a small, concrete "world" that seems consistent with the given premises. According to this model, people reason by inspecting what is true about this world. This model reproduces several major errors found in experiments concerned with human reasoning. See Johnson-Laird & Byrne (1991) for more on this use of mental models. The examples of reasoning used in these studies are quite elementary. The cognitive study of more advanced mathematical reasoning has scarcely begun.

Aside from issues of complexity, FOL is a monotonic reasoning system. The applicability of FOL reasoning processes depends on the correctness and the consistency of the hypotheses used in all possible contexts. Since this is rarely the case, hypotheses that are no longer correct have to be removed from the FOL representation. The FOL system of logical inference has no convenient ways of removing axioms or hypotheses that need to be weakened or changed in some other way. This problem led researchers in artificial intelligence to develop so-called nonmonotonic reasoning (McCarthy 1980). For a recent excellent survey, see Reiter (1987). The use of probabilistic representation of human reasoning is an alternate approach to nonmonotonic reasoning (see below).

PROPOSITIONAL, SEMANTIC, AND ASSOCIATIVE NETWORKS One appealing way to reduce computational complexity and the expressiveness of a full FOL is to constrain the kinds of predicates and formulas in the knowledge representation to a graph structure. In particular, consider a representation in which the

1 The form of Modus tollens is from *If P then Q* and *It is not the case Q* infer *It is not the case P*.

predicates are limited to unary predicates (called types), and binary predicates (called attributes), with occurrences of quantifiers also limited. Then, the resulting structure can be represented in a graph as a propositional or semantic network (e.g. Collins & Quillian 1969). The nodes are constants or types, and the edges are either labeled with attributes or types. The advantage of the graph-based representation is that it permits certain kinds of inferences to be performed by efficient, graph-based algorithms. In addition to the efficiency of searching, the graph-theoretical representation can be used to quantify a relation between any two nodes in terms of their distance in the graph.

Associative networks are based on similar principles except that the edges connecting concepts are not necessarily labeled by attributes or types. Rather, the edges are given numerical values or strengths. Associative networks are used primarily to model human processes underlying the retrieval of information. An individual's long-term knowledge of a concept is given by the strength associated with the node representing that concept. Recall of a proposition is mediated by the activation that is propagated via the edges in the network. A correct response to a question is predicted if the strength combined with the activation of the corresponding proposition exceeds a threshold. Some relevant experimental studies are Dosher & Rosedale (1989) and Dosher (1991). For a closely related approach to associative memory, Kanerva (1988) has developed a detailed mathematical theory of sparse distributed memory.

PRODUCTION RULES One approach that appeared feasible for capturing human knowledge and problem-solving behavior is the concept of a production system, first given currency by Newell & Simon (1972), and used later by many researchers. A production rule is an example of knowledge represented in terms of procedures and actions.

Although the primary purpose of a production-rule system is to solve problems or to model human problem-solving behavior, its ability to represent knowledge is one of its most critical components. In a production-rule system, knowledge is represented in terms of condition—action production rules. Production rules are essentially if–then statements in which the *if* part consists of one or more conditions and the *then* part is a set of actions. At any point during execution of the problem-solving process, the system identifies all rules whose *if* part is satisfied—all preconditions are *true*. The system selects one of these rules and executes the corresponding actions. The selection of the rule to use at any given time is performed by a conflict–resolution strategy.

Thus, knowledge in the production system is represented by the set of production rules combined with the conflict–resolution strategy. Production systems can be used to model the rules of inference in FOL. They have also been used to model learning (see below).

An implementation of KR in terms of production rules has several shortcomings. Perhaps the most critical problem is that if a production system has more than a few hundred rules, its behavior is difficult to predict, because it will depend critically on the particular conflict–resolution strategy used. Another shortcoming of both the production system and of FOL is their deterministic nature. There are several rule-based decision-making systems that deal with uncertainty, but explicitly rule-based representation is not particularly convenient for the representation of randomness, and therefore, for the detailed statistical analysis of experimental data.

Probabilistic Approaches

Knowledge in most domains is uncertain, i.e. we hold hypotheses that are more or less likely. Even in those domains with certain knowledge, e.g. elementary algebra, responses may still have a stochastic component, and the chances that an individual knows a given concept may depend on the particular population. Therefore, a realistic knowledge representation must have uncertainty as a part of the basic structure.

One principled way to represent the stochastic nature of the world is in terms of probability theory. In particular, consider a structure, such as FOL, in which the truth values of all predicates have a probabilistic interpretation; each is associated with a random variable. An outcome in this system is a particular truth assignment to all the random variables. Therefore, a complete description of this system would require a specification of the joint probability of all combinations of the truth values.

In practice, the construction and evaluation of such joint probabilities raise intractable computational difficulties akin to those encountered by early researchers in choice and decision-making, who recognized the need for approximations and simplifications to decision-theoretic formulations (Simon 1955), and in expert systems for medical diagnosis (Gorry & Barnett 1968). In the case of diagnosis, the input features were symptoms and test results. The outputs were the possible diseases. To simplify the calculation, Gorry & Barnett assumed that the diseases were mutually exclusive and that the features were conditionally independent.

Because the simplifying assumptions were regarded as too constraining, these early attempts to use probabilistic representations were abandoned (Henrion et al 1991). Instead, artificial intelligence researchers began developing rule-based systems for reasoning. To incorporate uncertainty, researchers allowed for propositions to assume intermediate values between *true* and *false*. The same graded-truth assumption was made about the applicability of each rule in rule-based expert systems. Examples of these approaches include MYCIN (Buchanan & Shortliffe 1984) and PROSPECTOR (Duda et al 1979). These systems used a heuristic, such as a certainty factor in MYCIN, to approximate a complete probabilistic representation. For a variety of reasons, including irreversibility of uncertain inference (Shachter & Heckerman 1987) and inappropriate treatment of prior probabilities, these heuristics were found to be inappropriate (Heckerman & Horvitz 1987). Such drawbacks have led researchers to explore probabilistic representations with somewhat richer structures than their earlier counterparts.

BAYESIAN NETWORKS One convenient way to represent probabilistic knowledge and reasoning is based on Bayesian networks. These networks are structures that represent subjective probabilities (e.g. prior probabilities), together with the rules for updating them as new evidence becomes available. Although subjective, the assignments of probabilities usually depend heavily on all available evidence and data. Structurally, a Bayesian network (BN) is a graph with nodes that represent random variables and directed edges that represent stochastic dependence (Pearl 1988). An edge between two nodes indicates conditional dependency. In particular, the probability distribution of the variable corresponding to a terminating node can be completely specified in terms of conditional probability, given the values of all its ancestors. Thus, BN is a representation that by itself does not impose any constraints, but provides a convenient language for the formulation of such constraints.

For example, a constraint specifying that two nodes are conditionally independent is represented by the absence of an edge between the two nodes. The basic idea of conditional independence can be illustrated using the elementary algebra example. Here *a, b,* and *c* are three questions represented by three nodes. Suppose that there are two edges (c,a) and (c,b) indicating that the probability distribution of the answers to questions *a* and *b* depends on the ability to answer question *c*. If we know the response to question *c,* then the answers to *a* and *b* are conditionally independent of each other, i.e. $P(a,b|c) = P(a|c)\ P(b|c.)$ The assumed independence between variables is a crucial property that can be used to reduce the computational complexity of the representation.

The graph-theoretic probabilistic KR has a number of advantages. Perhaps the most significant is the applicability of many powerful tools developed for graph-theoretic data structures that permit the development of computationally tractable algorithms that can be used to approximate the probability of various outcomes. In addition, researchers in the area of decision-making have developed several methods to construct Bayesian networks from observations. For example, Cooper & Herskovits (1991) constructed BN from data with the objective of minimizing the overall entropy of the representation.

There have been many advances in simplification of the computation associated with Bayesian networks, but the evaluation process is often still too complex. Therefore, researchers are investigating ways to further constrain the representation.

Knowledge spaces, surmise systems, and entail relations

Doignon, Falmagne, and their colleagues (Doignon & Falmagne 1985; see Falmagne et al 1990, for an overview) have developed the various parts of a comprehensive theory for the efficient assessment of the state of a system. The paradigm motivating this work comes from computer-assisted instruction: the system is a student, whose knowledge state consists of all notions mastered at a given time. A computer program sequentially selects questions to ask, and verifies whether the student's responses are correct or false, gradually narrowing down the possible knowledge states. In general, the state of a system can be described by a collection of features, indicating the functioning parts. The theory underlying the assessment algorithms is quite extensive.

KNOWLEDGE SPACES The basic concept is a pair (Q,K), in which Q is a finite set of questions or items in a particular area of information, and K is a distinguished family of subsets of Q. The set Q is the domain of the knowledge structure, and the elements of K are referred to as (knowledge) states. Both the empty set and Q are assumed to be states. The pair (Q, K) is called a knowledge structure or, equivalently, K is a knowledge structure (on Q). An example of a knowledge structure with domain Q of four questions q_1, q_2, q_3 and q_4 is:

$$K = \{\varnothing \{q_1\}, \{q_2\}, \{q_1, q_2\}, \{q_1, q_3\}, \{q_2, q_3\}, \{q_1, q_2, q_3\}, \{q_1, q_2, q_4\}, \{q_1, q_2, q_3, q_4\}\} \quad \text{Equation 1}$$

It is assumed implicitly that a student begins learning the material with either question q_1 or question q_2; the second item mastered is either q_2 or q_3, etc.

An important axiom is that the collection of states is closed under union: if K and K' are states, then $K \cup K'$ is also a state. A knowledge structure satisfying this axiom is called a knowledge space. (Note that the knowledge structure K defined by Equation 1 satisfies the axiom.) The goal of the assessment procedure is to uncover a subject's knowledge state by asking appropriate questions.

In practice, it is possible that a student tested on the questions in the domain Q may respond in a manner not exactly consistent with the nine knowledge states given in Equation 1. Such patterns of responses are regarded as resulting from careless error or lucky guesses. In fact, a probabilistic theory is also given, which is capable of explaining such response patterns (Falmagne 1989, 1993).

Two other concepts, surmise systems and entail relations, provide exactly the same information as a knowledge space, but they have a very different structure, i.e. representation.

SURMISE SYSTEMS What can we infer from the fact that a subject has mastered some item q? Specifically, what are the possible sets of items preceding q in the learning history of a subject? The formal concept relevant here is that of a surmise system, which we now define. Let Q be a finite set of questions, and let σ be a mapping associating to each question q of Q, a nonempty family $\sigma(q)$ of subsets of Q. Each C in $\sigma(q)$ is called a clause for q. The pair (Q,σ) is called a surmise system if the following three conditions are satisfied for any two questions q, q' in Q:

S1. Every clause for q contains q;
S2. If q' belongs to a clause C for q, then there is a clause for q' included in C;
S3. If C and C' are two distinct clauses for q, we cannot have $C' \subset C$.

The function σ is then said to be a surmise function on Q. Thus, if C is a clause for q, then $C - \{q\}$ may be regarded as a possible, but not necessarily unique, set of prerequisites for q. Under this interpretation, the axioms S1, S2, and S3 seem reasonable. Conceptually, a surmise function is different from a knowledge space. Nevertheless, any knowledge space can be represented uniquely as a surmise function, and vice-versa.

ENTAIL RELATIONS Empirical knowledge spaces may be obtained either by extensive testing of students or by questioning experts (teachers). In practice, the expert is asked to respond to queries such as: "Suppose that a student has failed to solve questions $q_1,\ldots,q_n$. Would this student also fail to solve question q_{n+1}?" There is a unique knowledge space consistent with all of these questions. Various inference rules use the considerable redundancy between queries so, in fact, only a minute fraction of all the possible queries is actually asked (Kambouri et al 1991). From a formal standpoint, the responses to the full set of questions specifies an entail relation P between subsets of Q, with the interpretation that the relation P holds between A and B if failing all the questions in the set B entails failing all the questions in the set A.

More generally, each of the three concepts introduced here—knowledge space, surmise function, and entail relation—provide an information preserving representation of the other two (see Doignon & Falmagne 1985, Koppen & Doignon 1990, Koppen 1993). An algorithm for constructing a knowledge space on a given set of questions by querying a human expert, e.g. an experienced teacher, is also developed in Koppen 1993.

CONCEPT REPRESENTATION AND LEARNING

With the major exception of perception, experimental psychology was dominated prior to 1965 by behaviorism and learning theories derived from behavioristic concepts. In the mid-1960s there was a strong shift to cognitive psychology, in particular to symbol processing, as the most important way to think about the cognitive abilities of organisms, especially humans. In 1985, a new form of behaviorism, based on connectionism and the development of neural networks, began to challenge the preeminence of cognitive ideas and especially symbol processing as the main way to think about either the mental representation of concepts or concept learning. The major conflict in psychological theories of concept representation is between those theories treating humans as symbol systems and those treating them as neural networks. We examine this conflict as well as the somewhat older intensive debate on whether the internal processing of perceptual concepts is propositional in character or often involves perceptual images. This is a debate that in certain ways is as old as psychology itself as a science, but has had a recent flurry of attention.

Humans as symbol systems

The central dogma of this view is that the process of cognition is mainly a process of manipulating symbolic expressions, modeled in general on the way such symbolic operations are performed by digital computers. The heyday of this view was around 1980 (see Fodor 1976, 1987; Newell 1980, 1982; Pylyshyn 1980, 1984, 1985). Although variations may be found, the three central tenets of humans as symbol systems can be summarized as follows: 1. Brains, as well as digital computers, are physical symbol systems. The symbols must be realized physically; there cannot be a purely mental disembodied concept of symbol. 2. There is a formal or combinatorial syntax and semantics for mental representations. The formality of these representations is what distinguishes symbol systems in their structure from, for example, the usually incomplete descriptions of atomic or neural structures as such. The syntax and semantics of mental representations are implied to be much closer in principle to the formal systems of mathematical logic than to the structural descriptions of physiology or chemistry. 3. The formal syntax of mental representations is manipulated, as in the case of formal mathematical systems, by explicit syntactic rules.

Two excellent defenses of this cognitivist viewpoint are in articles collected by Pinker & Mehler (1988), especially the first article by Fodor & Pylyshyn, and also in the extensive analysis of the cognitivist viewpoint in Newell's last work (1990). The major weakness of the cognitivist position is that the claim for the formality or combinatorial character of the syntax and semantics of mental representations has not been established satisfactorily. Yet there are many pieces of evidence from human cognition that provide positive evidence that something like inference, in terms of a formal syntax, is often used in mental computations.

In the framework of the central thesis stated above, cognitivists have also developed learning theory, especially in the form of production systems (see above), which are a class of computer simulation models formulated in terms of condition-action rules, like conditional jump instructions for a computer. A representative collection of articles on this approach to learning is found in Klahr et al (1987).

Connectionism

Connectionists and cognitivists are both representational in spirit, but they have radically different views about how concepts and computations about concepts are represented in the mind. Connectionists would deny that the three cognitivist theses listed above are necessary components of human thinking. They emphasize that much is subsymbolic in ordinary cognition and that there is an important role for associations, which in an earlier period provided the dominant mechanism of learning. The most important criticism made by connectionists is that a great deal of evidence exists at different functional levels that the kinds of representation and computation characteristic of the human brain are radically different from those postulated by the symbol-processing approach of cognitivists. Connectionists also are critical of the cognitivists' ability to give a detailed account of learning. Cognitive theories are most vulnerable in this respect, especially from an evolutionary perspective anchored in animal learning. Within the last decade the literature on connectionism and neural networks has rapidly expanded across disciplines from physics to operations research. The realization within psychology that connectionism was to become a major force in current psychological theorizing followed the publication of Rummelhart et al's (1986) two-volume work. A further defense of the neural viewpoint toward mental computation was effectively set forth in Nadel et al's (1989) collection of articles.

Studies of perception make the most impressive case for neural networks as fundamental to human cognitive processing: e.g. Grossberg's work on the analysis of classical and instrumental learning in terms of neural networks (1974) and on a theory of visual coding, memory, and development (1978), and Grossberg & Kuperstein's (1986) extended study of the neural dynamics of ballistic eye movements. It is obvious that extensive computations must be made by the perceptual system for it to be of any use, and such work is elaborate and complicated in character. The symbol-processing orientation has not led to any scientific developments as significant as the contributions the neural network approach have had to vision. Hummel & Biederman's (1992) extensive development of neural networks for shape recognition exemplifies an important strand of current intensive research in psychology, but their work is not isolated. In neural studies of the visual system, Marr's (1982) impact should also be noted. According to the paradigm Marr introduced, an organism or machine performing an information-processing task, especially one as complex as vision, should be understood on three levels: computational theory; representation and algorithms; and neural implementation, biological or artificial. As Marr emphasizes, there is no single representation characteristic of the visual system, but rather a set of representations and one naturally maps into another. The depth of problems faced in carrying out the Marr program can be seen especially at the level of understanding the actual computational activity of biological neurons.

Tuckwell's (1989) examination of stochastic modeling of neuron behavior illustrates that even in schematic form, the detailed understanding of such behavior is still out of reach. The complexity of Tuckwell's theoretical monograph, which is itself a simplified version of the actual biological behavior of neurons, shows that it is going to be a long time before we have a full understanding of the computational nature of actual neurons.

There is also a rapidly growing literature relating the asymptotic statistical performance of artificial neural networks to standard statistical methods (e.g. Hampshire & Pearlmutter 1991, Whittle 1991).

Mental Imagery

The nature of our mental representations of physical objects or physical phenomena, such as the motion of objects, has been the subject of discussion for many centuries. Within experimental psychology, a new paradigm of experimentation can bring new and original insights to an old subject. This is certainly true of Shepard's introduction in 1971 of experiments concerned with the "mental rotation" of a physical object (Shepard & Metzler 1971, Cooper & Shepard 1973). Shepard and his students found that in determining whether two objects presented in different orientations were judged the same or different in intrinsic shape, subjects imagined one object rotated to the orientation of the other at a limited rate of angular rotation. They also found evidence that during this process of mental rotation, individuals passed through mental representations of the intermediate orientations of the object. [See Shepard & Cooper (1982) for an extensive review of studies of this type.] Georgopoulos et al (1989) reported neurophysiological support for these findings in electrical activity recorded from the brains of monkeys planning rotational movements.

More recently, Shepard and his students have studied in detail mental conceptions of how a physical object might rigidly move between any two positions in space. A central question investigated, as in the case of mental rotations, is to what extent do such mental motions imagined for objects have the characteristics of an analogue simulation? More generally, in what sense are such mental processes governed by internalizations of the laws of physics? [See Carleton & Shepard (1990a, b) for a detailed study and excellent reviews of the literature.]

Three very readable general books on mental imagery are by Kosslyn (1983), Rollins (1989), and Tye (1991). The first stresses computer analogies and the other two give a critical yet sympathetic assessment of the recent psychological research on imagery from a philosophical perspective. Finke (1989) provides another good critical survey of the proposed principles of mental imagery. Of particular interest is Pylyshyn's (1985) defense of the symbol-processing view as an interpretation of the mental representation of rotation and motion, despite the apparent analogue character of many experiments. In its starkest terms, the Pylyshyn view is that all mental images are ultimately linguistic in character. Obviously, anyone with connectionist leanings would strongly deny such a claim. Scientific resolution of these strongly conflicting theories clearly requires formulation of more detailed and formally explicit pictorial and linguistic theories of mental imagery.

LANGUAGE REPRESENTATION AND LEARNING

Syntactic Representation

Recent work on languages continues to use ideas of representation that Chomsky (1959) introduced many years ago. We begin with his general concept of an arbitrary phrase-structure grammar. By adding restrictions we get grammars whose powers of expression are more limited. Let V be a finite, nonempty set. Then V^* is the set of all finite sequences of elements of V. Let 0 be the empty sequence. Then $V^+ = V^* - 0$. V is the vocabulary. V^+ is the set of strings or sentences. A structure $G = (V, N, P, S)$ is a phrase-structure grammar if and only if 1. V, N, and P are nonempty finite sets; 2. $N \subset V$; 3. $P \subset V^+ \times V^*$; and 4. $S \in N$. In standard terminology: The set N is the set of nonterminal symbols, or variables. $V_T = V - N$ is the set of terminal symbols or words. P is the set of productions. If $(\alpha, \beta) \in P$ we ordinarily write: $\alpha \rightarrow \beta$, to indicate that from α we may produce β. Finally, S (for sentence) is the start symbol with which derivations begin. $L(G)$ is the language, generated by finite sequences of the rules of the grammar, i.e. $L(G)$ is the set of all sentences in the terminal vocabulary V_T generated by G. The weakness of the axioms matches the great generality of the definition. Most interest centers around various restricted classes defined below.

Formal languages are meant to represent the syntactic structure of natural languages. It can be claimed that natural languages fit within the hierarchy defined here, although we do not examine the rather complicated question of whether this is really true. There is substantial evidence that important fragments of natural languages can be analyzed with the grammatical concepts introduced below.

TYPES OF GRAMMARS Type 0 grammars are characterized by the definition of phrase structure grammars. To obtain type 1, or context-sensitive grammars, we add the restriction that for every production $\alpha \rightarrow \beta$, $\mid \Omega 9\alpha \mid \leq \mid \beta \mid$, whereΩ9 $\mid \Omega 9\ \alpha \mid$ is the length of α or the number of symbols in α. To obtain type 2, or context-free grammars, we add the stronger restriction: if $\alpha \rightarrow \beta$, is in P then 1. α is a variable, i.e. α is in N; 2. $\beta \neq 0$. A typical context-free production rule is: $S \rightarrow NP + VP$, where S intuitively stands for sentence, NP for noun phrase, VP for verb phrase, and the plus sign is used to show concatenation.

To obtain type 3, or regular grammars, we add the still stronger restriction: any production must be of the form 1. $A \rightarrow aB$ or 2. $A \rightarrow a$, with A, B in N, a in V_T. (Instead of 1., we can have 1′ $A \rightarrow Ba$, but the change from right-linear to left-linear is trivial, even though all rules of form 1. must be changed.)

FINITE AUTOMATA Subtly different definitions of finite automata are found in the literature. For example, according to Rabin & Scott (1959), a structure (A,V,M,s_0,F) is a finite (deterministic) automaton if and only if 1. A is a finite, nonempty set (the set of states); 2. V is a finite, nonempty set (the alphabet or vocabulary); 3. M is a function from the Cartesian product $A \times V$ to A (M defines the transition table); 4. s_0 is in A (s_0 is the initial state); and 5. F is a subset of A (F is the set of final states). The generality of this definition is apparent. Among the few restrictions are that the sets A and V be finite, but these finite restrictions are critical.

Perhaps the simplest nontrivial example of a finite automaton is the following: In a two-letter alphabet, with the symbols 1 and 0, and two internal states, s_0 and s_1. The transition function of the automaton can be defined informally as follows: given state s_0 and input 0, the transition is to s_0; given s_0 and 1, it is to s_1; given s_1 and 0, it is to s_1; and given s_1 and 1, it is to s_0.

Finally, we select the internal state s_1 as the only member of the set F of final states. By calling this the simplest nontrivial automaton we mean that the transition table depends both on the internal state and the input letter. From a more general conceptual standpoint, it is clear that the device is itself trivial.

Following is the pair of theorems characterizing the mutual representation relation between regular grammars and finite automata:

> Theorem 1. If G is a regular grammar, there is a finite automaton that will accept $L(G)$.
>
> Theorem 2. Given a finite automaton A, there exists a regular grammar G such that $L(G) = L(A)$.

Theorems 1 and 2 together provide a procedural account for regular grammars, but a perusal of the proofs of the two theorems shows that the representing structures are too close to the original ones to substantively represent how a regular grammar works. However, Theorem 1 does show that a regular grammar can be processed by a strictly finite machine, and this is not necessarily obvious from the form of such grammars.

PUSHDOWN AUTOMATA AND CONTEXT-FREE LANGUAGES A new and important idea is that of the pushdown store, which is a restricted form of memory. The automaton can store structured information of finite but unbounded extent in this store, but it can make state transitions only in terms of the top symbol on the store—the store operates like a stack of cafeteria trays on the principle of "first-in and last-out." A special store vocabulary is provided the machine. The transition function depends now, not just on the input symbol and the current state, but also on the top symbol on the store. Again, we have a pair of mutual representation theorems:

> Theorem 3. If a language is context-free then there is a pushdown automaton that accepts the language.
> Theorem 4. If A is a pushdown automaton then $L(A)$ is a context-free language.

Similar theorems can be proved for type 0 and type 1 grammars. In particular, a grammar is of type 0 if and only if the language it generates is accepted by some Turing machine.[2]

For more recent developments of syntactic representations of natural language, see especially the large volume edited by Bresnan (1982) on the mental representation of grammatical relations. However, in spite of the great linguistic interest in this work, the use of purely psychological concepts is limited. The volume does present in very accessible form, lexical functional grammars as developed by Bresnan and her colleagues. A useful survey of three of the main forms of contemporary syntactic theories, namely, government-binding theory, generalized phrase-structure grammars, and lexical-functional grammars, is to be found in Sells (1985). None of these three has yet led to significant representation theorems like the four cited above, but they are all greatly concerned with the empirical inadequacies of the earlier work.

Semantic Representations

Set-theoretical and model-theoretic semantics developed in mathematical logic since the early 1930s, especially since the appearance of Tarski (1936), has

---

[2] Intuitively, a Turing machine is a finite automaton with the addition of a tape of unbounded length that may be used in computations; any particular computation uses only a finite amount of tape.

dominated much of the discussion of the semantics of natural language. This is very much a case of the incursion of logic into linguistics and psychology (see Montague 1974). Research prior to the early 1970s is well summarized in the volume edited by Davidson & Harman (1972) but such formal semantics does not provide any kind of psychological theory of how language is comprehended or produced in meaningful speech or writing. There has naturally arisen a desire for a more procedural semantics to provide a more detailed and realistic theory of meaning (e.g. Suppes 1991).

The formal semantics of logicians is almost entirely structural in character and emphasizes the desirability of rules of structural composition, i.e. the composing of the meaning of a sentence from its parts. Empirical studies and theories emphasizing lexical semantics, that is the semantics of words, have also been of great importance to linguistics and psychology [e.g. Miller & Johnson-Laird's (1976) study of perceptual words]. Other generalizations of semantic ideas, having significant impact on psychological research, are Barwise & Perry's (1983) generalization of model-theoretic semantics to situation semantics, and the work by a number of individuals on discourse analysis and discourse semantics (Brown & Yule 1983, Seuren 1985). Another important influence from outside psychology has been philosopher Paul Grice's work on conversational implicatures or presuppositions (Grice 1957, 1968, 1975). Levelt (1989) and the recent volume of papers by Clark (1992) exemplify the extensive psychological research on the actual nature of speaking and conversation. This research, important for understanding of meaningful speech by either speakers or listeners, goes far beyond the formal semantics of logicians, and also points the way for much of the future psychological research on meaning. Suppes (1991) makes an extended case for variable-free semantic representations being much closer to natural language than the standard logical ones.

Language Learning

The literature on language acquisition in children in now voluminous. Empirical studies of aspects of language learning by children in the case of many different languages now number in the thousands. A lively and controversial summary of many of the issues is found in the edited volume of papers on the debate between Piaget and Chomsky (Piattelli-Palmarini 1980). Many informative and detailed empirical studies are found in two collections of articles, Wanner & Gleitman (1982) and MacWhinney (1987).

Although studies of language learning have a long history, we can date the mathematical theory to an important paper by Gold (1967). He established the following important theorem: Regular or context-free classes of grammars are not "text-learnable" (i.e. the grammar cannot be taught just by presenting instances of text to the learner). On the other hand, by making the stronger assumption that one could ask an informant whether something were grammatical in the language being spoken, Gold proved the positive theorem: Regular or context-free classes of grammars are "informant-learnable." Of course, Gold's framework is completely non-psychological but it has provided a framework for much formal theorizing on language learning.

Gold's work forms a general background for the formal psychological theory of language learning presented by Wexler and his associates [e.g. Hamburger & Wexler (1975) on the mathematical theory of learning transformational grammars]. Wexler & Culicover's (1980) book shows that if we assume that the learner has already given a context-free language as the carrier of meaning, then a reasonable theory of the learning of a transformational grammar can be formulated in technical detail. This work represents an important milestone, but it is far from providing a realistic theory of language learning that can be tested against experimental data. In particular, quantitative evidence about the rate of learning is missing.

Pinker moves closer to the data by building his ideas (1984) on the theory of lexical functional grammars (Kaplan & Bresnan 1982), which are generalizations of the phrase-structure grammars characterized above, and more recently by using Chomsky's government-binding theory (Pinker 1989). Pinker's work is full of insightful remarks about the problems of theorizing in this area. He considers a variety of psycholinguistic experimental and naturalistic data, but he does not formulate a detailed formal theory. Consequently, he cannot establish whether his theoretical ideas are sensible from the standpoint of computations about rates of learning, formal structure of semantics, formal grammatical generalizations, etc. Wexler also has moved closer to linguistic data in his recent work (e.g. Avrutin & Wexler 1993, Hyams & Wexler 1993).

In contrast, Osherson et al (1986) perhaps best exemplify the development of "formal learning theory," which is concerned not with children but more generally with any systems that learn. The authors have some important results about the learnability of computable functions and they have some general formal theorems about restrictions on the kind of languages that can be learned, but their work is closer in spirit to the earlier formal work on learnable functions by Ehrenfeucht & Mycielski (1973a,b; 1977) than to studies of language learning.

Suppes (1969) originated another line of formal work that proves the theorem that given any finite automaton, there is a stimulus-response model that under appropriate learning conditions asymptotically becomes isomorphic to the finite automaton. This theorem is further clarified and extended to universal computation in Suppes (1989), but this work also suffers from the difficulty of relating the formal theory to detailed data. The recent work by Suppes et al (1992) on machine learning of natural language strongly suggests that much more detailed theoretical ideas are needed. Earlier stimulus-response concepts of association play a role in this research, but equally important are internal formal procedures for grammatical and semantical generalization.

As detailed theoretical developments and the vast variety of empirical studies of children's language acquisition continue unabated, we can anticipate a more detailed and fruitful comparison of theories and empirical studies, both experimental and naturalistic, in the decades ahead.

REPRESENTATIONAL THEORY OF MEASUREMENT

The theory of measurement has a long and significant history in psychology. Early examples are Thurstone's (1927) law of comparative judgment and Stevens' (1946, 1951) explicit analysis of various types of measurement. Because the concept of numerical representation has been used extensively in the development of psychological theories of measurement, we begin with a brief exposition of the central mathematical concepts of isomorphism and homomorphism used in characterizing numerical representations of measurement procedures. The representational framework we outline is the basis for most of the current research on fundamental measurement.

Isomorphism of Models

One of the most general and useful concepts that may be applied to a theory is that two models or structures of the theory may be isomorphic, i.e. exhibiting the same structure from the standpoint of the basic concepts of the theory. The formal definition of isomorphism for a particular theory makes this notion of same structure precise. The definition of isomorphism of models of a theory is not dependent on the detailed nature of the theory, but in fact is independent enough to be termed "axiom free," depending only on the set-theoretical character of models of a theory. Thus two theories with models having the same set-theoretical character, but with quite different substantive axioms, would use the same definition of isomorphism.

These ideas may be made more definite by considering the ordinal theory of measurement. Models of this theory are customarily called weak orderings and we use this terminology in defining the appropriate predicate.

The set-theoretical structure of this theory's models have a nonempty set A and a binary relation R defined on this set. Let us call such a pair $\mathfrak{A} = (A,R)$ a simple relation structure. A simple relation structure $\mathfrak{A} = (A,R)$ is a weak ordering if and only if for every a, b, and c in A: 1. if $a\ R\ b$ and $b\ R\ c$, then $a\ R\ c$; 2. $a\ R\ b$ or $b\ R\ a$.

The definition of isomorphism of simple relation structures makes it apparent that the definition of isomorphism depends only on the set-theoretical structure of the simple relation structures and not on any of the substantive axioms imposed. A simple relation structure $\mathfrak{A} = (A,R)$ is isomorphic to a simple relation structure $\mathfrak{A}' = (A', R')$ if and only if there is a function f such that: 1. the domain of f is A and the range of f is A'; 2. f is a one-to-one function; 3. if x and y are in A, then $x\ R\ y$ if and only if $f(x)\ R'\ f(y)$.

To illustrate this definition of isomorphism let us consider the question, "Are any two finite weak orderings with the same number of elements isomorphic?" Intuitively it seems clear that the answer should be negative, because all the objects could stand in the relation R to each other in one of the weak orderings and not in the other. It will be interesting to find the counterexample with the smallest domain we can construct to show that such an isomorphism does not exist in general. It is clear that two one-element sets will not do, because within isomorphism there is only one weak ordering with a single element, namely, the ordering that makes that single element stand in the given relation R to itself. However, a counterexample can be found by adding one more element. In one of the weak orderings we can let R be the universal relation, i.e. $R = A \times A$, the Cartesian product of A with itself, and in the other, let R' be a "minimal" relation satisfying the axioms for a weak ordering. More formally, let $A = \{1,2\}$, $R = \{(1,1),(2,2),(1,2),(2,1)\}$, $A' = A$, and $R' = \{(1, 1), (2, 2), (1, 2)\}$. Then it is easily checked that $\mathfrak{A} = (A, R)$ and $\mathfrak{A}' = (A', R')$ are both weak orderings with domains of cardinality two, but $\mathfrak{A}$ cannot be isomorphic to $\mathfrak{A}'$.

Representation Theorems

In attempting to characterize the nature of the models of a theory, the notion of isomorphism enters in a central way. Perhaps the best and strongest characterization of the models of a theory is expressed in terms of a representation theorem (i.e. a certain class of models of a theory represents to within isomorphism every model of the theory). More precisely, let $\mathfrak{M}$ be the set of all models of a theory, and let $\mathfrak{B}$ be some distinguished subset of $\mathfrak{M}$. A representation theorem for $\mathfrak{M}$ with respect to $\mathfrak{B}$ would consist of the assertion that given any model M in $\mathfrak{M}$ there exists a model in $\mathfrak{B}$ isomorphic to M. In other words, from the standpoint of the theory, every possible variation of model is exemplified within the restricted set $\mathfrak{B}$. A trivial representation theorem can always be proved by taking $\mathfrak{B} = \mathfrak{M}$. A representation theorem is only as interesting as the intuitive significance of the class $\mathfrak{B}$ of models. An example of a simple and beautiful representation theorem is Cayley's theorem that every group is isomorphic to a group of transformations. One source of the concept of a group, as it arose in the nineteenth century, comes from consideration of the one-to-one functions that map a set onto itself. Such functions are usually called transformations. It is interesting and surprising that the elementary axioms for groups are sufficient to characterize transformations in this abstract sense that any model of the axioms, i.e. any group, can be shown to be isomorphic to a group of transformations.

Certain cases of representation theorems are of special interest. When the set $\mathfrak{B}$ can be taken as a unit set, i.e. a set with exactly one element, then the theory is said to be categorical. Put another way, a theory is categorical when any two models are isomorphic. Thus, a categorical theory has within isomorphism only one model. Examples of categorical theories are the elementary theory of numbers when a standard notion of set is used, and the elementary theory of real numbers with the same standard notion of set. It has been asserted that one of the main differences between nineteenth- and twentieth-century mathematics is that nineteenth-century mathematics was concerned with categorical mathematical theories while the latter deals with noncategorical theories. It is doubtful that this distinction can be made historically, but there is certainly a rather sharp conceptual difference between working with categorical and noncategorical theories. There is a clear sense in which noncategorical theories are more abstract, because there is not just one intuitive model.

Homomorphism of models

In many cases a representation theorem in terms of isomorphism of models is less interesting than a representation theorem in terms of the weaker notion of homomorphism. A good example of this latter sort within psychology is provided by theories of measurement, and the generalization from isomorphism to homomorphism can be illustrated in this context. When we consider general practices of measurement it is evident that in terms of the structural notion of isomorphism we would think of the isomorphism as being established between an empirical model of the theory of measurement and a numerical model. An empirical model is one in which the basic set is a set of empirical objects, stimuli, or other phenomena; a numerical model is one in which the basic set is a set of numbers. However, a slightly more detailed examination of the question indicates that difficulties about isomorphism arise quickly. In measurement, distinct empirical phenomena are frequently assigned the same number, and thus the one-to-one relationship required for isomorphism of models is destroyed. Fortunately, this weakening of the one-to-one requirement for isomorphism is the only respect in which we must change the general notion in order to obtain an adequate account for theories of measurement of the relation between empirical and numerical models. The general concept of homomorphism is designed to accommodate this situation. To obtain the formal definition of homomorphism for two simple relation structures as previously defined, we need only drop the requirement that the function establishing the isomorphism be one-to-one. When the function is many-to-one instead of one-to-one, we have a homomorphism that is not an isomorphism.

These remarks may be made more concrete by considering the theory of weak orderings as a theory of measurement. It is easy to give a simple example of two weak orderings such that the first is homomorphic to the second, but not isomorphic to it. Let $A = \{1,2\}$, $R = \{(1, 1), (2, 2), (1, 2), (2, 1)\}$, $A' = \{1\}$, and $R' = \{(1, 1)\}$, and $f(1) = 1, f(2) = 1$. From these definitions it is obvious that the weak ordering $\mathfrak{A} = (A, R)$ is homomorphic under the function f to the weak ordering $\mathfrak{A}' = (A', R')$.

On the other hand, it is clear, on the basis of cardinality considerations, that $\mathfrak{A}$ is not isomorphic to $\mathfrak{A}'$, because the set A has two elements and the set A' has one element. It is also evident that $\mathfrak{A}'$ is not homomorphic to $\mathfrak{A}$. This also follows from cardinality considerations, because there is no function whose domain is the set A' and whose range is the set A. As this example illustrates, the relation of homomorphism between models of a theory is not an equivalence relation; it is reflexive and transitive, but not symmetric.

By a numerical-weak ordering we mean a weak ordering $\mathfrak{A} = (A,\leq)$ where A is a set of numbers. The selection of the numerical relation $\leq$ to represent the relation R in a weak ordering is arbitrary, in the sense that the numerical relation $\geq$ could just as well have been chosen. However, choice of one of the two relations $\leq$ or $\geq$ is the only intuitively sound possibility. The following theorem provides a homomorphic representation theorem for finite weak orderings, and thus makes the theory of finite weak orderings a theory of measurement:

> Theorem 5. Every finite weak ordering is homomorphic to a numerical weak ordering.

Theorem 5 was restricted to finite weak orderings for good reason; it is false if this restriction is removed. The classic counterexample is the lexicographical ordering of the plane. Extension to infinite weak orderings is, however, straightforward, but since it is rather technical, it is here omitted.

Types of Measurement

For the sake of simplicity we have only discussed ordinal measurement in detail, but other types of measurement are obviously of fundamental importance in science. The classic example is extensive measurement, which requires some kind of empirical operation of addition (as in the measurement of weight using a standard equal-arm balance, for example), or in the case of the subjective concept of probability, using the union of disjoint events, i.e. the subjective probability of two disjoint events should correspond to their numerical sum in the intended numerical representation. Equally or even more important in psychology have been intensive measurements, which lead to new representations if one considers not only the ordinal comparison of the intensity of stimuli but also the ordinal comparison of differences in the intensity of stimuli. Sufficiently strong assumptions about these comparisons of differences leads us to the expected numerical representation. A different kind of intensive measurement can be made in terms of conjoint comparisons of pairs of stimuli ordinally, or in the case of utilities, comparisons of standard gambles with each member of the pair having a probability of 1/2 of being realized. A third familiar kind of measurement is the psychophysical method of bisection where it is assumed that one stimulus is judged to lie at the midpoint of the interval between two other stimuli. This kind of measurement is standard in psychophysical experiments, but no assumptions about physical measurement are needed to test the psychological axioms yielding a standard numerical representation of bisection.

These various types of measurement also give rise to a fundamental formal problem of the uniqueness of the representation. For example, in the case of extensive measurement we expect uniqueness up to the fixing of a unit. In the case of intensive measurement, we expect uniqueness up to fixing both a unit and an arbitrary origin. The formal analysis of a theory is not satisfactory until the appropriate uniqueness and existence of numerical representations have been proven.

The most extensive standard treatment of representational theory of measurement is the three-volume treatise *Foundations of Measurement* (Krantz et al 1971, Suppes et al 1989, Luce et al 1990) with a large number of references to the current literature. Other good resources are Roberts' (1979) excellent survey of the field, and Narens' (1985) book, which contains some important abstract results.

Many fundamental problems about the foundations of measurement remain open. Luce & Narens (1993) provide an excellent current survey of problems concentrating on the nature of the representational view of measurement and on the use of continuum representations in measurement.

CONCLUDING COMMENTS

What we hope to have shown in this review is that the concept of representation has an important explicit role in many different parts of psychology. Moreover, many of the most fundamental problems can be formulated as problems of representation, e.g. how are linguistic utterances or visual images represented in the mind. This recognized prominence of representation is relatively recent in psychology, but there are many reasons for thinking that this aproach to psychological issues is not just a passing fad.

The explicit use of representations is to be found in every developed domain of science. The current focus on representations of psychological phenomena is consonant in a broad conceptual fashion with many other scientific disciplines. This is because the effort to give a structural representation of phenomena in a given domain has become central to our modern search for scientific understanding.

Literature Cited

Avrutin S, Wexler K. 1993. Developments of principle B in Russian: coindexation at LF and coreference. *Lang. Acquis.* 2:In press

Barwise J, Perry J. 1983. *Situation and Attitudes.* Cambridge, Mass: MIT Press

Brown G, Yule G. 1983. *Discourse Analysis.* Cambridge: Cambridge Univ. Press

Bresnan J, ed. 1982. *The Mental Representation of Grammatical Relations.* Cambridge, Mass: MIT Press

Buchanan B, Shortliffe E, eds. 1984. *Rule-based Expert Systems: The Mycin Experiments of the Stanford Heuristics Programming Project.* Reading, Mass: Addison-Wesley

Carleton EH, Shepard RN. 1990a. Psychologically simple motion as geodesic paths: I. asymmetric objects. *J. Math. Psychol.* 34:127–88

Carleton EH, Shepard RN. 1990b. Psychologically simple motion as geodesic paths: II. symmetric objects. *J. Math. Psychol.* 34:189–228

Carroll JD, Arabie P. 1980. Multidimensional scaling. *Annu. Rev. Psychol.* 31:607–49

Cheng PW, Holyoak KJ, Nisbett RE, Oliver LM. 1986. Pragmatic versus syntactic approaches to training deductive reasoning. *Cogn. Psychol.* 18:293–328

Chomsky N. 1959. On certain formal properties of grammars. *Inf. Control* 2:137–67

Clark HH. 1992. *Arenas of Language Use.* Stanford, Calif./Chicago: CSLI/Univ. Chicago Press

Collins AM, Quillian MR. 1969. Retrieval time from semantic memory. *J. Verb. Learn. Verb. Behav.* 8:240–47

Cooper GF, Herskovits E. 1991. *A Bayesian method for the induction of probabilistic networks from data.* Tech. Rep. KSL-91–02. Knowledge Systems Lab., Med. Comp. Sci., Stanford University

Cooper LA, Shepard RN. 1973. Chronometric studies of the rotation of mental images. In *Visual Information Processing*, ed. WG Chase, pp. 75–176. New York: Academic

Davidson D, Harman G, eds. 1972. *Semantics of Natural Language.* Dordrecht, The Netherlands: Reidel

Doignon JP, Falmagne JC. 1985. Spaces for assessment of knowledge. *Int. J Man-Mach. Stud.* 23:175–96

Dosher BA. 1991. Bias and discrimination in cuing of memory: a weighted decisions model. In *Relating Theory and Data in Memory*, ed. W Hockley, S Lewandowsky, pp. 14-1--30

Dosher BA, Rosedale G. 1989. Integrated retrieval cues as a mechanism for priming. *J. Exp. Psych: Gen.* 118:191–218

Duda R, Gasching J, Hart P. 1979. Model design in the PROSPECTOR consultant system for mineral exploration. In *Expert Systems in the Microelectronics Age*, ed. D Michie, pp. 153–67. Edinburgh: Edinburgh Univ. Press

Ehrenfeucht A, Mycielski J. 1973a. Interpolation of functions over a measure space and conjectures about memory. *J. Approx. Theory* 9:218–36

Ehrenfeucht A, Mycielski J. 1973b. Organisation of memory. *Proc. Natl. Acad. Sci. USA* 70:1478–80

Ehrenfeucht A, Mycielski J. 1977. Learnable functions. In *Foundational Problems in the Special Sciences,* Proc. 5th Int. Congr. Logic Method. Philos. Sci., London, Ontario, Canada, Vol 2, ed. RE Butts, J Hintikka, pp. 251–56. Dordrecht, The Netherlands: Reidel

Falmagne JC. 1985. *Elements of Psychophysical Theory.* New York: Oxford Univ. Press

Falmagne JC. 1989. A latent trait theory via stochastic learning theory for a knowledge space. *Psychometrika* 53:283–303

Falmagne JC. 1993. Stochastic learning paths in a knowledge structure. *J. Math. Psychol.* In press

Falmagne JC, Villano M, Doignon JP, Johannesen JP. 1990. Introduction to knowledge spaces: how to build, test, and search them. *Psychol. Rev.* 97:201–24

Finke RA. 1989. *Principles of Mental Imagery.* Cambridge, Mass: MIT Press

Fodor J. 1976. *The Language of Thought.* Sussex: Harvester

Fodor J. 1987. *Psychosemantics.* Cambridge, Mass: MIT Press

Georgopoulos AP, Lurito JT, Petrides M, Schwartz AB, Massey JT. 1989. Mental rotation of the neuronal population vector. *Science* 243:236–36

Gold EM. 1967. Language identification in the limit. *Inf. Control* 10:447–74

Gorry G, Barnett G. 1968. Experience with a model of sequential diagnosis. *Comp. Biomed. Res.* 1:490–507

Green DM, Swets JA. 1966. *Signal Detection Theory and Psychophysics.* New York: Wiley

Grice HP. 1957. Meaning. *Philos. Rev.* 66:377–88

Grice HP. 1968. Utterer's meaning, sentence meaning and word meaning. *Found. Lang.* 4:225–42

Grice HP. 1975. Logic and conversation. In *Syntax and Semantics.* Vol 3: *Speech Acts*, ed. R Cole, JL Morgan, pp. 41–58. New York: Academic

Grossberg S. 1974. Classical and instrumental learning by neural networks. In *Progress in Theoretical Biology*, ed. R Rosen, F Snell, pp. 51–141. New York: Academic

Grossberg S. 1978. A theory of visual coding, memory and development. In *Formal Theories of Visual Perception*, ed. ELJ Leeuwenberg, HFJM Buffart, pp. 7–26. New York: Wiley

Grossberg S, Kuperstein M. 1986. *Neural Dynamics of Adaptive Sensory-motor Control.* Amsterdam: North-Holland

Guttman AL. 1944. A basis for scaling of qualitative data. *Am. Sociol. Rev.* 9:139–50

Hamburger H, Wexler S. 1975. A mathematical theory of learning transformational grammar. *J. Math. Psychol.* 12:137–77

Hampshire JB, Pearlmutter B. 1991. Equivalence proofs for multi-layer perception classifiers and the Bayesian discriminant function. In *Connectionist Models*, ed. DS Touretsky, JL Elman, TJ Sejnowski, GE Hinton, pp. 159–72. San Mateo, CA: Kaufmann

Heckerman D, Horvitz E. 1987. On expressiveness of rule-based systems for reasoning under uncertainty. In *Proc. 6th Natl. Conf. Artif. Intell.*, pp. 121–26

Henrion M, Breese JS, Horvitz EJ. 1991. Decision analysis and expert systems. *Artif. Intell.* 12:64–91

Hummel JE, Biederman O. 1992. Dynamic binding in a neural network for shape recognition. *Psychol. Rev.* 3:480–517

Hyams N, Wexler S. 1993. On the grammatical basis of null subjects in child language. *Linguist. Inq.* 24:In press

Johnson-Laird PN. 1983. *Mental Models.* Cambridge: Harvard Univ. Press

Johnson-Laird PN, Byrne RMJ. 1991. *Deduction.* London: Erlbaum

Kambouri M, Koppen M, Villano M, Falmagne J-Cl. 1991. *Knowledge Assessment: Tapping Human Expertise.* Irvine Res. Unit Math. Behav. Sci., Univ. Calif., Irvine

Kanerva P. 1988. *Sparse Distributed Memory.* Cambridge, Mass: MIT Press

Kaplan R, Bresnan J. 1982. Lexical-functional grammar: A formal system for grammatical representation. In *The Mental Representation of Grammatical Relations*, ed. J Bresnan, pp. 173–281. Cambridge, Mass: MIT Press

Klahr D, Langley P, Neches R. 1987. *Production System Models of Learning and Development.* Cambridge, Mass: MIT Press

Koppen M. 1993. Extracting human expertise for constructing knowledge spaces: an algorithm. *J. Math. Psychol.* 1:1–20

Koppen M, Doignon JP. 1990. How to build a knowledge space by querying an expert. *J. Math. Psychol.* 34:311–31

Kosslyn SM. 1983. *Ghosts in the Mind's Machine.* New York: Norton

Krantz D, Luce RD, Suppes P, Tversky A. 1971. *Foundations of Measurement*, Vol. I. New York: Academic

Kruskal JB, Wish M. 1978. *Multidimensional Scaling.* Newbury Park, Calif: Sage

Levelt WJM. 1989. *Speaking.* Cambridge, Mass: MIT Press

Levesque HJ, Brachman RJ. 1985. A fundamental tradeoff in knowledge representation and reasoning. In *Readings in Knowledge Representation*, ed. RJ Brachman, HJ Levesque. pp. 41–70. San Mateo, CA: Kaufmann

Lord FM, Novick MR. 1974. *Statistical Theories of Mental Tests Scores.* Reading, Mass: Addison-Wesley

Luce RD, Krantz DH, Suppes P, Tversky A. 1990. *Foundations of Measurement*, Vol. III. San Diego: Academic

Luce RD, Narens L. 1993. Fifteen problems concerning the representational theory of measurement. In *Patrick Suppes: Scientific Philosopher*, ed. P Humphreys. Dordrecht, The Netherlands: Kluwer Academic

MacWhinney B, ed. 1987. *Mechanisms of Language Acquisition.* Hillsdale, NJ: Erlbaum

Marr D. 1982. *Vision.* San Francisco: Freeman

McCarthy J. 1980. Circumspection—a form of non-monotonic reasoning. *Artif. Intell.* 13:41–72

Miller GA, Johnson-Laird PN. 1976. *Language and Perception.* Cambridge: Harvard Univ. Press/Belknap

Montague R. 1974. *Formal Philosophy*, ed. RH Thomason. New Haven, Conn: Yale Univ. Press

Nadel L, Cooper L, Culicover P, Harnish M, eds. 1989. *Neural Connections, Mental Computation.* Cambridge, Mass: MIT Press

Narens L. 1985. *Abstract Measurement Theory.* Cambridge, Mass: MIT Press

Newell A. 1980. Physical symbol system. *Cogn. Sci.* 4:135–83

Newell A. 1982. The knowledge level. *Artif. Intell.* 18:87–127

Newell A. 1990. *Unified Theories of Cognition.* Cambridge: Harvard Univ. Press

Newell A, Simon H. 1972. *Human Problem Solving.* Englewood Cliffs, NJ: Prentice Hall

Nilsson NJ. 1981. *Principles of Artificial Intelligence.* Tahoe City, Calif: Tioga

Osherson DN, Stob M, Weinstein S. 1986. *Sys-*

tems That Learn. Cambridge, Mass: MIT Press

Pearl J. 1988. *Probabilistic Reasoning in Intelligent Systems: Networks of Plausible Inference.* San Mateo, CA: Kaufmann

Piattelli-Palmarini M, ed. 1980. *Language and Learning.* Cambridge: Harvard Univ. Press

Pinker S. 1984. *Language Learnability and Language Development.* Cambridge: Harvard Univ. Press

Pinker S. 1989. *Learnability and Cognition.* Cambridge, Mass: MIT Press

Pinker S, Mehler J, eds. 1988. *Connections and Symbols.* Cambridge, Mass: MIT Press

Pylyshyn ZW. 1980. Cognition and computation: issues in the foundations of cognitive science. *Behav. Brain Sci.* 3(1):154–69

Pylyshyn ZW. 1984. Why computation requires symbols. *Proc. 6th Annu. Conf. Cogn. Sci. Soc.*, Boulder, Colo. Hillsdale, NJ: Erlbaum

Pylyshyn ZW. 1985. *Computation and Cognition: Toward a Foundation for Cognitive Science.* Cambridge, Mass: MIT Press/Bradford. 2nd ed.

Rabin MO, Scott D. 1959. Finite automata and their decision problems. *IBM J. Res. Dev. 3:114–25. Reprinted 1964 in Sequential Machines*, ed. EF Moore, pp. 63–91. Reading, Mass: Addison-Wesley

Reiter R. 1987. Nonmonotonic reasoning. *Annu. Rev. Comp. Sci.* 2:147–86

Rips LJ. 1983. Cognitive processes in propositional reasoning. *Psychol. Rev.* 90:38–71

Roberts FS. 1979. *Measurement Theory with Applications to Decision Making, Utility and the Social Sciences.* Reading, Mass: Addison-Wesley

Rollins M. 1989. *Mental Imagery: On the Limits of Cognitive Science.* New Haven, Conn: Yale Univ. Press

Rumelhart DE, McClelland JL, PDP Research Group. 1986. *Parallel Distributed Processing: Explorations in the Microstructure of Cognition*, Vols. 1, 2. Cambridge, Mass: MIT Press

Sells P. 1985. *Lectures in Contemporary Syntactic Theories.* Stanford, Calif: Center Stud. Lang. Inf.

Seuren PAM. 1985. *Discourse Semantics.* Oxford: Blackwell

Shachter R, Heckerman D. 1987. Thinking backwards for knowledge acquistion. *Artif. Intell.* 8:55–63

Shepard RN, Cooper LA. 1982. *Mental Images and their Transformations.* Cambridge, Mass: MIT Press

Shepard RN, Metzler J. 1971. Mental rotation of three-dimensional objects. *Science* 171:701–3

Simon H. 1955. A behavioral model of rational choice. *Q. J. Econ.* 69:99–118

Stevens SS. 1946. On the theory of scales of measurement. *Science* 103:677–80

Stevens SS. 1951. Mathematics, measurement and psychophysics. In *Handbook of Experimental Psychology*, ed. SS Stevens, pp. 1–49. New York: Wiley

Suppes P. 1969. Stimulus-response theory of finite automata. *J. Math. Psychol.* 6:327–55

Suppes P. 1989. Current directions in mathematical learning theory. In *Mathematical Psychology in Progress*, ed. EE Roskam, pp. 3–28. Berlin: Springer Verlag

Suppes P. 1991. *Language for Humans and Robots.* Cambridge, Mass: Blackwell

Suppes P, Boettner M, Liang L. 1992. Comprehension grammars generated from the machine learning of natural language. In *Proc. 8th Amsterdam Colloq., Inst. for Logic, Language and Computation, Univ. Amsterdam*, ed. P Dekker, M Stokhof, pp. 93–112

Suppes P, Krantz DH, Luce RD, Tversky A. 1989. *Foundations of Measurement*, Vol. II. San Diego: Academic

Suppes P, Zinnes JL. 1963. Basic measurement theory. In *Handbook of Mathematical Psychology*, Vol. 1, ed. RD Luce, RR Bush, E Galanter, pp. 1–76. New York: Wiley

Tarski A. 1936. Der Wahrheitsbegriff in den formalisierten Sprachen. *Stud. Philos.* 1:261–405 [In German]

Thurstone LL. 1927. A law of comparative judgment. *Psychol. Rev.* 34:273–86

Tuckwell HC. 1989. *Stochastic Processes in the Neurosciences.* Philadelphia: SIAM

Tye M. 1991. *The Imagery Debate.* Cambridge, Mass: MIT Press

Wanner E, Gleitman LR, eds. 1982. *Language Acquistion: The State of the Art.* New York: Cambridge Univ. Press

Wexler S, Culicover PW . 1980. *Formal Principles of Language Acquisition.* Cambridge, Mass: MIT Press

Whittle P. 1991. Neural nets and implicit inference. *Ann. Appl. Prob.* 1:173–88

Annu. Rev. Psychol. 1994. 45:545–80

SOCIAL EXPERIMENTS: SOME DEVELOPMENTS OVER THE PAST FIFTEEN YEARS

Thomas D. Cook

Departments of Sociology and Psychology, Northwestern University, Evanston, Illinois 60208

William R. Shadish

Department of Psychology, Memphis State University, Memphis, Tennessee 38152

KEY WORDS: causation, randomization, quasi-experiments, causal generalization, selection modeling

---

CONTENTS

0066-4308/94/0201-0545$05.00

INTRODUCTION

The *Annual Review of Psychology* has never published a chapter on causal inference or experimentation. This is surprising, given psychology's traditional concern with establishing causal relationships, preferably through experiments. Our own expertise is in social experiments, as practiced not only in psychology but also in education, economics, health, sociology, political science, law and social welfare. Philosophers and statisticians are also involved with such experiments, but more to analyze them than to do them. This review concentrates on important developments from this multidisciplinary spectrum during the 1980s and early 1990s.

Experiments can be characterized both structurally and functionally (Cook 1991a). The more prototypical structural attributes of experiments include a sudden intervention; knowledge of when the intervention occurred; one or more post-intervention outcome measures; and some form of a causal counterfactual—that is, a baseline against which to compare treated subjects. Functionally, experiments test propositions about whether the intervention or interventions under test are causally responsible for a particular outcome change in the restricted sense that the change would not have occurred without the intervention.

Social experiments take place outside of laboratories and therefore tend to have less physical isolation of materials, less procedural standardization, and longer-lasting treatments when compared to experiments in laboratory settings. Social experiments are usually designed to test an intervention or treatment that is usually better characterized as a global package of many components than as a presumptively unidimensional theory-derived causal construct. This is because the usual aim of field researchers is to learn how to modify behavior that has proven to be recalcitrant in the past (e.g. poor school performance, drug abuse, unemployment, or unhealthful lifestyles) as opposed to testing a theoretical proposition about unidimensional causes and effects. There are two types of social experiments, each of which has the sudden intervention, knowledge of intervention onset, posttest, and causal counterfactual component that characterize all experiments. Randomized experiments have units that are assigned to treatments or conditions using procedures that mimic a lottery, whereas quasi-experiments involve treatments that are assigned nonrandomly, mostly because the units under study—usually individuals, work groups, schools or neighborhoods—self-select themselves into treatments or are so assigned by administrators based on analysis of who merits or needs the opportunity being tested.

We cover four experimentation topics that are currently of interest: 1. modifications to the dominant theory of social experimentation; 2. shifts in thinking about the desirability and feasibility of conducting randomized field experiments; 3. modifications to thinking about quasi-experiments; and 4. recent concerns about justifying generalized causal inferences.

CHANGES IN THE DOMINANT THEORY OF SOCIAL EXPERIMENTATION

Theories of Causation

Experimentation is predicated on the manipulability or activity theory of causation (Collingwood 1940, Mackie 1974, Gasking 1955, Whitbeck 1977), which tries to identify agents that are under human control and can be manipulated to bring about desired changes. This utilitarian conception of causation corresponds closely with common-sense and evolutionary biological understandings of causation, and it assumes that cause-effect connections of this kind are dependable enough to be useful. Experiments have this same purpose. They probe whether a force that is suddenly introduced into an ongoing system influences particular outcomes in a way that would not have occurred without the intervention. The aim of experiments is to describe these causal consequences, not to explain how or why they occurred.

Experiments can be made more explanatory, though. This is achieved primarily by selecting independent and dependent variables that explicitly explore a particular theoretical issue or by collecting measures of mediating processes that occurred after a cause was manipulated and without which the effect would presumably not have come about. But few social experiments of the last decades were designed to have primarily an explanatory yield, and nothing about the logic of experimentation requires a substantive theory or well-articulated links between the intervention and outcome, though social experiments are superior if either of these conditions is met (Lipsey 1993).

Understanding experiments as tests of the causal consequences of manipulated events highlights their similarity with the manipulability theory of causation. But it also makes them seem less relevant to the essentialist theories of causation (Cook & Campbell 1979) to which most scholars subscribe. These theories seek either a full explanation of why a descriptive causal connection comes about or the total prediction of an effect. Thus, they prioritize on causal explanation rather than causal description, on isolating why a causal connection comes about rather than inferring that a cause and effect are related. Such explanatory theories are likely to be reductionistic or involve specifying multiple variables that co-condition when a cause and effect are related. Each of these is a far cry from the "if X, then Y" of the manipulability theory of causation. Mackie (1974)—perhaps the foremost theorist of causation—sees the manipulability theory as too simplistic because it assumes a real world characterized by many main effects that experiments try to identify. For

Mackie and the essentialists, the real world is more complex than this. However, Mackie doubts whether essentialist theories are epistemologically adequate, however ontologically appropriate they may be. He postulates that all causal knowledge is inevitably "gappy," dependent on many factors so complexly ordered that full determination of the causal system influencing an outcome is impossible in theory and practice. Thus, he contends that essentialists seek a complete deterministic knowledge they are fated never to attain.

Conceiving of all causal relationships as embedded within a complex context that co-determines when an effect is manifest implies the need for a methodology sensitive to that complexity and embeddedness. Yet individual experiments are designed to test the effects of one or a few manipulable independent variables over a restricted range of treatment variants, outcome realizations, populations of persons, types of settings, and historical time periods. To be sure, in their individual studies, researchers can measure attributes of treatments, outcomes, respondents, and settings and then use these measures to probe whether a particular outcome depends on the treatment's statistical interaction with such attributes. This strategy has been widely advocated, especially in education (Cronbach & Snow 1976). But the variability available for analysis in individual studies is inherently limited, and tests of higher-order interactions can easily lead to data analyses with low statistical power (Aiken & West 1991). As a result, interest has shifted away from exploring interactions within individual experiments and toward reviewing the results of many related experiments that are heterogeneous in the times, populations, settings, and treatment and outcome variants examined. Such reviews promise to identify more of the causal contingencies implied by Mackie's fallibilist, probabilistic theory of causation; and they speak to the more general concern with causal generalization that emerged in the 1980s and 1990s (e.g. Cronbach 1982, Cook 1993, Dunn 1982).

With its emphasis on identifying main effects of manipulated treatments, the activity theory of causation is too simple to reflect current philosophical thinking about the highly conditional ways in which causes and effects are structurally related. The experimentalist's pragmatic assumption has to be either (*a*) that some main effects emerge often enough to be dependable, even if they are embedded within a larger explanatory system that is not fully known; or (*b*) that the results of individual experiments will eventually contribute to a literature review identifying some of the causal contingencies within this system.

Theories of Categorization

The descriptive causal questions that experimenters seek to answer usually specify particular cause and effect constructs or categories to which generalization is sought from the manipulations or measures actually used in a study.

Philosophical work on categorization is currently dormant, while in psychology there is considerable productive chaos. Classic theories of categorization postulate that instances belong in a class if they have all the fixed attributes of that class. This approach has been widely discredited (Rosch 1978, Lakoff 1987, Medin 1989), and there is now recognition that all categories have fuzzy rather than clearly demarcated boundaries (Zimmerman et al 1984), that some elements are more central or prototypical than others (Smith & Medin 1981), and that knowledge of common theoretical origins is sometimes more useful for classifying instances than the degree of initially observed similarity (Medin 1989). In biology, plants or animals used to be assigned to the same class if they shared certain attributes that facilitate procreation. But classification now depends more on similarity in DNA structure, so that plants or animals with seemingly incompatible reproductive features but with similar DNA, are placed in the same category. This historical change suggests that seeking attributes that definitively determine category membership is a chimera. The attributes used for classification evolve with advances elsewhere in a scholarly field, as the move from a Linnean to a more microbiological classification system illustrates in biology.

Categorization is not just a logical process; it is also a complex psychological process (or set of processes) that we do not yet fully understand. Ideally, social experiments require researchers to explicate a cause or an effect construct, to identify its more prototypical attributes, and then to construct an intervention or outcome that seems to be an exemplar of that construct. Explicit here is a pattern-matching methodology (Campbell 1966) based on proximal similarity (Campbell 1986). That is, the operation looks like what it is meant to represent. But the meanings attached to similar events are often context-dependent. Thus, if a study's independent variable is a family income guarantee of $20,000 per year, this would probably mean something quite different if the guarantee were for three years versus twenty. In the first case individuals would have to think much more about leaving a disliked job because they do not have the same financial cushion as someone promised the guarantee for 20 years. Also, classifying two things together because they share many similar attributes does not imply they are theoretically similar. Dolphins and sharks have much in common. They live exclusively in water, swim, have fins, are streamlined, etc. But dolphins breathe air out of water and give direct birth to their young—both features considered prototypical of mammals. Hence, dolphins are currently classified as mammals rather than fish. But why should breathing out of water and giving birth to one's young be considered prototypical attributes of mammals? Why should it not be the fit between form and function that unites dolphins and fish? Another example of this complexity comes from social psychology. Receiving very little money to do something one doesn't want to do seems different on the surface from being asked to choose between two objects of similar value. Yet each is supposed to elicit the same theoretical process of cognitive dissonance. Should the attributes determining category membership depend on physical observables linked to particular classes by a theory of proximal exemplification or prototypicality? Or should the attributes instead reflect more latent and hence distal theoretical processes, such as those presumed to distinguish mammals from fish or those that make financial underpayment and selecting among objects of similar value instances of the same class called cognitive dissonance?

Experimenters have to generalize about causes, effects, times, settings, and people. If the best theories from philosophy and psychology are not definitely helpful, researchers can turn instead to statistics where formal sampling theory provides a defensible rationale for generalization. However, in experimental practice it is almost impossible to sample treatment variants, outcome measures, or historical times in the random fashion that sampling theory requires; and it is extremely difficult to sample persons and settings in this way. So, in individual experiments, generalization depends on the purposive rather than random selection of instances and samples to represent particular categories of treatment, outcome, people, or settings. Unfortunately, in current sampling theory, purposive selection cannot justify generalization to a category—only random selection can.

Relabeling Internal Validity

Among social scientists, Campbell (1957) was the first to systematically work through the special issues that arise when probing causal hypotheses in complex field settings. As he recounts it (Campbell 1986), his analysis originated from concerns with the low quality of causal inferences promoted by the field research of the time and with the questionable generalizability of the cause-testing laboratory research of the time. So he invented a language for promoting more confident causal inferences in contexts that better resembled those to which generalization is typically sought. He coined the term *internal validity* to refer to inferences about whether the relationship between two operationalized variables was causal in the particular contexts where the relationship had been tested to date; and he invented *external validity* to express the extent to which a causal relationship can be generalized across different types of settings, persons, times, and ways of operationalizing a cause and an effect. These two terms have now entered into the lexicon of most social scientists.

But many scholars did not understand internal validity in the way Campbell intended. It was widely taken to refer, not just to the quality of evidence about whether an obtained relationship between two variables was causal, but also to whether the relationship was from a particular theoretically specified causal agent to a particular theoretically specified effect (Kruglanski & Kroy 1975,

Gadenne 1976). Thus, labeling the cause and effect were smuggled in as components of internal validity. Cronbach (1982) went even further, adding that internal validity concerns whether a causal relationship occurs in particular identifiable classes of settings and with particular identifiable populations of people—each an element of Campbell's external validity. To discuss validity matters exactly, Cronbach invented a notational system. He used *utos,* to refer to the instances or samples of units *u,* treatments *t,* observations *o,* and settings *s* achieved in a research project probing a causal hypothesis. He used *UTOS,*[1] to refer to the categories, populations, or universes that these instances or samples represent and about which research conclusions are eventually drawn. Translating Campbell's internal validity into these terms we see that it refers only to the link between *t* and *o* at the operational level. What *t* stands for (i.e. how the cause or *T* should be labeled) is irrelevant, just as it is irrelevant what *o* stands for (i.e. how the effect or *O* should be labeled). For Campbell, these are matters of external validity, as are concerns about the types of units and settings in which the *t-o* relationship can be found (Campbell 1957, Campbell & Stanley 1963).

After critics eventually understood how restricted Campbell's description of internal validity was, they decried it as positivistic (Gadenne 1976), irrelevant to substantive theory (Kruglanski & Kroy 1975), and insensitive to the contingency-laden character of all causal conclusions (Cronbach 1982). Cronbach persisted in describing his internal validity in terms of generalization from all parts of *utos* to all parts of *UTOS,* thus subsuming under his version of internal validity all the elements Campbell had included as elements of his external validity! To reduce this ambiguity, Campbell (1986) sought to invent more accurate labels for internal validity. He invented *local molar causal validity* to replace internal validity, hoping to highlight with *local* that internal validity is confined to the particular contexts sampled in a given study. By *molar* he hoped to emphasize that his internal validity treated interventions and outcomes as complex operational packages composed of multiple microelements or components. (The contrast here is with more reductionist approaches to causation that place most weight on identifying the microelements responsible for any relationship between a more molar treatment and a more molar outcome.) Finally, with the *causal* part of his new label, Campbell sought to highlight the centrality of assertions about whether the *o* in Cronbach's *utos* formulation would change without variation in *t,* thereby downplaying the aspiration to learn about other facets of this link, especially its generalizability. Campbell's new name for internal validity has not been widely adopted, despite its greater precision. Internal validity is still widely

---

1 We ignore here Cronbach's discussion of the difficulty of drawing inferences about populations or settings.

used and misused, though clarification is now at hand for those willing to seek it.

Relabeling External Validity

Campbell's concept of external validity also came to be modified. His early work described external validity in terms of identifying the contexts in which a given causal relationship holds, including ways that the cause or effect were operationalized. Cook & Campbell (1979) distinguished between generalizing to theoretical cause and effect constructs and generalizing to populations of persons and settings, using construct validity to refer to the former and external validity to refer to the latter. More importantly, Cronbach (1982) differentiated between two types of generalization that were obscured in the work of Campbell and his colleagues. The first involves generalizing from *utos* to *UTOS*—using attributes of the sampling particulars to infer the constructs and populations they represent. This is what Cronbach calls internal validity. The second involves generalizing from *UTOS* to **UTOS* (star-*UTOS*), with **UTOS* representing populations and constructs that have manifestly different attributes from those observed in the sampling details of a study. At issue with **UTOS* is extrapolation beyond the sampled particulars to draw conclusions about novel constructs and populations. Cronbach calls this external validity.

To clarify his own different understanding of external validity, Campbell relabeled it as *proximal similarity* (Campbell 1986). He chose this label to emphasize a theory of generalization based on using observable attributes to infer whether a particular sample of units, treatments, observations, or settings belonged in a particular class or category as that class or category is usually understood within a local research community or in ordinary English-language usage. Similarity between the specific instances sampled and the more general classes they are supposed to represent is the order of the day, and Campbell is adamant in classifying instances on the basis of observable characteristics linked to a theory specifying which characteristics are prototypical. *Proximal* is part of his new label for external validity to emphasize that other characteristics are more distal for him, particularly those where the similarity is not immediately evident but is instead derived from substantive theory—e.g. classifying dolphins as mammals rather than fish. Like local molar causal validity, proximal similarity has failed to catch on among social scientists. Campbell's old external validity lives on, seemingly as vigorous as ever. However, the need he felt in 1986 to create new labels to clarify the constructs first introduced in 1957 suggests growing dissatisfaction about the clarity or content of his validity types. However worthy the underlying ideas, the terms themselves cannot now be considered as unproblematic and as sacrosanct as they once were.

Debates about Priority among Validity Types

One debate about priorities among validity types concerns the warrant for Campbell's preference for internal over external validity. Campbell & Stanley (1963) argued that it is only useful to explore how generalized a causal connection is if very little uncertainty remains about that connection. How would theory or practice be advanced, they reasoned, if we identified limits to the generalization of a relationship that might later turn out not to be causal? Cronbach (1982) asserted that this priority reflects the conservative standards scientists have traditionally adopted for inferring causation, and he questioned whether these standards are as relevant for other groups as they are for individuals with a stake in the results of a social experiment. His own experience has convinced him that many members of the policy-shaping community are more prepared than scholars to tolerate uncertainty about whether a relationship is causal, and they are willing to put greater emphasis than scholars do on identifying the range of application of relationships that are manifestly still provisional. Cronbach believes that Campbell's preference for internal over external validity is parochial. Chelimsky (1987) has offered an empirical refutation of Cronbach's characterization of knowledge preferences at the federal level. But research on preferences at the state or local levels is not yet available, and Cronbach's characterization may be more appropriate there. Time will tell.

Dunn (1982) has criticized the validity typology of Campbell and his colleagues because neither internal nor external validity refers to the importance of the research questions being addressed in an experiment. He claims that substantive importance can be explained just as systematically as the more technical topics Campbell has addressed, and he has proposed some specific threats that limit the importance of research questions. Dunn is correct in assuming that there is no limit to the number of possible validity types, as Cook & Campbell partially illustrated when they divided Campbell's earlier internal validity into statistical conclusion validity (are the cause and effect related?) and internal validity (is the relationship causal?), and when they divided his external validity into construct validity (generalizing from the research operations to cause and effect constructs) and external validity (generalizing to populations of persons and settings). Cook & Campbell also proposed new threats to validity under each of these headings, and their validity typology is widely used (e.g. Wortman 1993). Thus, Campbell and his colleagues agree with Dunn, only criticizing him on some particulars about threats to the importance of research questions (see especially Campbell 1982).

Though his higher-order validity types came under attack, Campbell's specific list of threats to internal and external validity did not. Internal validity threats like selection, history, and maturation continue to be gainfully and regularly used to justify causal inferences, under whichever validity label they might be fit. This is probably because researchers, in their daily work, have to rule out specific threats to particular inferences. Debates about validity types are more abstract and remote. Campbell's identification of specific validity threats constitutes one of his most enduring contributions to social science methodology.

Raising the Salience of Treatment Implementation Issues

Cook & Campbell (1979) distinguished between construct and external validity because (*a*) the means for promoting construct validity are rarely, if ever, based on the random sampling procedures so often advocated for generalizing to populations of persons and settings; and (*b*) experience has indicated how problematic treatment implementation can be in nonlaboratory contexts where researchers are more often guests than hosts, where researchers are not always the providers of services, where program theory is often poorly explicated, and where unexpected difficulties often arise to compromise how well an intervention is mounted (Boruch & Gomez 1977; Sechrest et al 1979; Bickman 1987, 1990; Chen & Rossi 1983; Gottfredson 1978). Hence, Cook & Campbell (1979) outlined a new list of threats describing some of the ways the complex intervention packages implemented in practice differ from the often more theoretical intervention procedures outlined in a research protocol (Lipsey 1993). Their concern was to identify which parts of the research protocol were actually implemented; which were not implemented; which were implemented but without the frequency or intensity detailed in the guiding theory; and which unplanned irrelevancies impinged on the research and might have influenced research outcomes.

Experiments test treatment contrasts rather than single treatments (Holland 1986). Cook & Campbell (1979) drew attention to four novel threats that affect the treatment contrast without necessarily influencing the major treatment purportedly under test. All these threats touch on diffusion of one treatment to other treatments. *Resentful demoralization* occurs when members of control groups or groups receiving less desirable treatments learn that other groups are receiving more. If they become resentful because of this focused comparison their performance might decrease and lead to a treatment-control difference. But this is because the controls are getting worse rather than the experimentals getting better. They also postulated that *compensatory rivalry* can arise if the focused inequity that so many experimental contrasts require leads members of the groups receiving less to respond by trying harder to show that they do not deserve their implicitly lower status. Such a motivation obscures true effects occurring in treatment groups because performance in the control groups should improve. *Compensatory equalization* occurs when administrators are not willing to tolerate focused inequities and they use whatever discretionary resources they control to equalize what each group receives. This also threatens to obscure true effects of a treatment. Finally, *treatment diffusion* occurs when treatment providers or recipients learn what other treatment groups are doing and, impressed by the new practices, copy them. Once again, this obscures planned treatment contrasts. These four threats have all been observed in social experiments, and each threatens to bias treatment effect estimates when compared to situations where the experimental units cannot communicate about the different treatments. Statisticians now subsume them under the general rubric of SUTVA—the stable-unit-treatment-value assumption (Holland & Rubin 1988)—in order to highlight how much the interpretation of experimental results depends on the unique components of one treatment group not diffusing to other groups and hence contributing to the misidentification of the causal agent operative within a treatment contrast. Is it the planned treatment that influences the outcome, or is it serving in a control group?

This is only one of many arguments in favor of documenting the quality of treatment implementation in all treatment conditions, including no-treatment controls. "Black box" experiments without such documentation are potentially counterproductive (Lipsey 1993). If they result in no-difference findings, it is not clear whether the intervention theory was wrong, the particular treatment implementation was weak, or the statistical power to detect a given effect was inadequate. In the absence of documentation of treatment integrity, even positive results do not make it clear what role the intended processes played in bringing about outcome changes. Realizing this, experimenters have devoted more resources over the last decade to describing implementation quality and relating this to variability in outcomes.

The Epistemology of Ruling Out Threats

All lists of validity threats are the product of historical analyses aimed at identifying potential sources of bias. They are designed to help researchers construct the argument that none of these threats could have accounted for a particular finding they wish to claim as causal. The epistemological premise here is heavily influenced by Popper's falsificationism (1959). But Kuhn's (1962) critique of Popper on the grounds that theories are incommensurable and observations are theory-laden makes it difficult to believe that ruling out such threats is easy. So, too, does Mark's (1986) observation that ruling out validity threats often depends on accepting the null hypothesis—a logically tenuous exercise. Campbell has always emphasized that only plausible threats need ruling out and that plausibility is a slippery concept, adding to the impression that falsification is logically underjustified.

However, in the real world of research there have to be some mechanisms for certifying which threats are plausible in local contexts and for establishing which procedures will probably rule out a particular threat. The scientific community is not likely to prefer methods for ruling out threats that depend only on professional consensus. Logically justifiable procedures are the preference. This is why causal inferences from quasi-experiments are less convincing than from randomized experiments. They depend on a larger set of accompanying arguments, including many that are weaker because they postulate that particular threats are implausible in the context under analysis or have been ruled out on the basis of statistical adjustments of the data that themselves are assumption-laden. Is it not better to control threats via random assignment, with its clear rationale in logic? Realization of the epistemological difficulties inherent in ruling out alternative interpretations has strengthened calls both to sample persons, settings, treatments, and outcomes at random and also to assign units to treatments at random (Kish 1987). There is no debate about the desirability of this in principle; however, there are legitimate debates about the feasibility of random assignment and random selection when testing causal hypotheses, and especially about the degree of confidence merited by different methods that do not use some form of randomization for inferring cause and estimating its generalizability.

RANDOMIZED EXPERIMENTS IN FIELD SETTINGS

The strength of the randomized experiment seems to be that the expected mean difference between randomly created groups is zero. This is merely a special case of the more general principle that unbiased causal inference results whenever all the differences between groups receiving treatments are fully known (Rubin 1977, Trochim 1984). Statisticians like to remind us that unbiased causal inference results if individuals are assigned to conditions by the first letter of their surname, by whether they are left or right handed, or by the order in which they applied to be in a particular social program. The key is that the assignment process is fully known and perfectly implemented; random assignment is only one instance of this more general principle.

Though random assignment involves considerable ethical, political, and legal problems (detailed in Coyle et al 1991), assertions that such assignment can rarely be used outside the laboratory have been disproved by the long lists of experiments Boruch et al (1978) have compiled. Cronbach (1982) has reclassified some of the studies on these lists as quasi-experiments or failed randomized experiments; nonetheless, the lists leave the impression that random assignment is already common in social science and could be even more widely used if researchers were better informed about how to circumvent objections to it. Researchers wanting to use other means of assignment now find it more difficult to justify their plans than even a decade ago. There are still cases where a randomly created control group is impossible (e.g. when studying the effects of a natural disaster), but the last decade has witnessed a powerful shift in scientific opinion toward randomized field experiments and away from quasi-experiments or non-experiments. Indeed, Campbell & Boruch (1975) regret the influence Campbell's earlier work had in justifying quasi-experiments where randomized experiments might have been possible. In labor economics, many critics now advocate randomized experiments over quasi-experiments (Ashenfelter & Card 1985, Betsey et al 1985, LaLonde 1986). In community-based health promotion research, randomized experiments have now replaced the quasi-experiments that were formerly used to reduce the high cost of mounting interventions with the larger sample size of whole towns or cities that random assignment requires. Indeed, in biostatistics much emotional strength is attached to random assignment and alternatives are regularly denigrated (e.g. Freedman 1987).

Much of the recent discussion about randomized experiments deals with implementing them better and more often. Little of this discussion has appeared in scholarly outlets. So the following exposition of the factors making randomized experiments easier to implement depends heavily on informal knowledge among practicing social experimenters as well as on such published sources as Boruch & Wothke (1985).

Mounting a Randomized Experiment

The best situation for random assignment is when the demand for the treatment under evaluation exceeds the supply. The treatment then has to be rationed and can be allocated at random. If demand does not exceed supply naturally, experimenters can often induce the extra demand by publicizing the treatment. In a pilot study of multiracial residential housing in a university, CM Steele (unpublished research proposal) found in the pilot year that too few whites volunteered for the program to make random assignment possible. So, the next year he publicized the residential units through the campus housing office. Such publicity creates a tradeoff. It makes random assignment easier; but because of it, those who eventually enter the control or placebo conditions have learned of the multiracial housing alternative for which they applied but were not selected. This knowledge might lead to treatment diffusion, compensatory rivalry, compensatory equalization, or resentful demoralization. Although such threats can operate in any type of study, the question for field experimenters is whether they operate more strongly because of the publicity required to stimulate extra demand (Manski & Garfinkel 1992) or because random assignment provides a less acceptable rationale for experimental inequities when compared to allocation by need, by merit, or on a "first come, first served" basis (Cook & Campbell 1979).

When using random assignment in field settings, a key concern is when respondents are assigned to treatments. Riecken & Boruch (1974) identified three options: before respondents learn of the measurement burdens and treatment alternatives; after they learn of the measurement demands, but before they learn of the content of the treatments being contrasted; and after they know of the measurement demands and treatments and agree to be in whatever treatment condition the coin toss (or equivalent thereof) determines for them. Opinion has long favored the last alternative because it reduces the likelihood that refusals to serve in the experiment will be related to the treatments, thus creating the nonequivalence that random assignment is designed to avoid. However, the cost to such delayed randomization is that some persons may drop out of the study when they realize they are not guaranteed the treatment they most desire. Thus, the potential gain in internal validity (in Campbell's original sense) entails a potential loss in external validity.

Some scholars now question the wisdom of placing such a high premium on internal validity that treatment assignment is delayed. For policy contexts, Heckman & Hotz (1988) question the usefulness of strong causal conclusions if they only generalize to those who are indifferent about the treatments they receive, because personal belief in a treatment might be an important contributor to its effectiveness. This critique highlights the advantages that follow from linking a randomized study of persons willing to undergo any treatment with a quasi-experimental study of persons who self-select themselves into treatments, controlling for self-selection in the quasi-experiment as well as the statistical state of the art allows (Boruch 1975). Otherwise, advocates of delayed random assignment have to argue that it is better to have limited information about the generalization of a confident causal connection than it is to have considerable information about the generalizability of a less certain connection.

Using random assignment in complex field settings is all the more difficult because researchers often do not do the physical assignment process themselves. They may design the process and write the protocols determining assignment, whether as manuals or computer programs implementing a complex stratification design. But the final step of this assignment process is often carried out by a social worker, nurse, physician, or school district official. It is up to these profesionals to explain to potential volunteers the rationale for random assignment, to detail the alternatives available, and then to make the actual treatment assignment. Sometimes, implementers at the point of service delivery misunderstand what they are supposed to do—which is mostly a matter of improved training. At other times, however, professional judgment predominates over the planned selection criteria and assignment occurs by presumptions about a client's need or merit instead of by lottery.

Professionals are trained to judge who needs what, when. It is not always easy for them to let a manual or computer protocol decide. Indeed, we have heard anecdotes about workers in early childhood development centers who came in surreptitiously at night to modify a computer so that it made the assignments they believed were professionally correct rather than the random assignments that were supposed to be made! To prevent professional judgment from overriding scientific assignment requires giving better explanations of the necessity for random assignment, having local research staff carry out the assignment rather than service professionals, instituting earlier and more rigorous monitoring of the selection process, and providing professionals with the chance to discuss special cases they think should be excluded from the assignment process.

Random assignment can be complicated, especially when social programs are being tested. In such cases, the organization providing benefits could lose income if all the places in the program are not filled. This means a waiting list must be kept; however, it is unrealistic to expect that all those on the waiting list will suspend self-help activities in the hope they will eventually enter the program. Some will join other programs with similar objectives or will have their needs met more informally. Thus, even a randomly formed waiting list changes over time, often in different ways from the changes occurring in a treatment group as it experiences attrition. Though no bias occurs if persons from the waiting list are randomly assigned to treatment and control status when program vacancies occur, it can be difficult to describe the population that results when people from the ever-changing waiting list are added to the original treatment group. Bias only occurs with more complex stratification designs where program needs call for making the next treatment available to a certain category of respondent (e.g. black males under 25). If there are fewer of these in the pool than there are treatment conditions in the research design, then program needs dictate that this person enters the program even if no similar person can be assigned to the control status. If researchers belatedly recruit someone with these characteristics into a comparison group, this vitiates random assignment and introduces a possible selection bias. But if they exclude these persons from the data analysis because there are no comparable controls, this reduces external validity.

Outside the laboratory, random assignment often involves aggregates larger than individuals (e.g. schools, neighborhoods, cities, or cohorts of trainees). This used to present problems of data analysis since analysis at the individual level fails to account for the effects of grouping, while analysis at the higher level entails smaller sample sizes and reduced statistical power. The advent of hierarchical linear modeling (Bryk & Raudenbush 1992) should help reduce this problem, particularly when more user-friendly computer programs are available. But such modeling cannot deal with the nonequivalence that results when, despite random assignment, the number of aggregated units is low. After all, it can be costly to assign whole cities to treatments and obtain stable estimates for each city at each measurement wave. To counter this, researchers now almost routinely match larger units on pretest means or powerful correlates of the outcome before assigning them to the various treatments. Since the highest single research cost is likely to be mounting the intervention, researchers sometimes select more control than intervention sites (Kish 1987). This reduces the statistical power problem associated with small sample sizes, but it does not guarantee initial group equivalence if the treatment is still assigned to a small sample of randomly selected and aggregated units. So the preferred solution is to move to a study with more schools or cities. The National Heart, Lung and Blood Institute now seems to have adopted this point of view, preferring multimillion dollar, multisite studies of smoking cessation and women's health over smaller studies. Yet these studies will inevitably be homogeneous in some components that reduce generalization, and critics will inevitably suggest some study factors that need to be varied in subsequent research. Moreover, the expense of such multisite experiments entails opportunity costs—meritorious studies that deserve to be funded cannot be.

Maintaining a Randomized Experiment

Unlike laboratory experimenters, field experimenters are usually guests in somebody else's organization. The persons they study are usually free to come and go and pay attention or not as they please, lowering the degree of treatment standardization. Some individuals will leave the study long before they were expected to, having had little exposure to the treatment. This increases the within-group variability in treatment exposure and also decreases the exposure mean for the group overall. All these processes reduce statistical power. Standard practice now calls for describing the variability in treatment exposure, determining its causes, and then relating the variability to changes in the dependent variable (Cook et al 1993). Describing the quality of treatment implementation has now become central; even explaining this variability seems to be growing in importance.

Treatment-correlated respondent attrition is particularly problematic because it leads to selection bias—a problem exacerbated in social experiments because the treatments being contrasted often differ in intrinsic desirability and attrition is generally higher the less desirable the intervention. Field experimenters have now accumulated a set of practices that reduce the severity of treatment-correlated attrition, though none is perfect. Taken together, they are often effective. They include making generous payments to controls for providing outcome data; monitoring attrition rates early to describe them, to elicit their possible causes, and to take remedial action; following up drop-outs in whatever archival databases relevant information is located; and designing the experiment to contrast different treatments that might achieve the desired outcome as opposed to contrasting a single treatment group with a no-treatment control group. The presumption is that rival contenders as effective interventions are likely to be more similar in intrinsic desirability than are a treatment and a no-treatment control group.

Social experimenters cannot take for granted that a perfect random assignment plan will be perfectly implemented. Social experiments have to be closely monitored, even if this means adding to the already complex set of elements that might explain why a treatment impacts on an outcome. Note the two purposes of monitoring: to check on the quality of implementation of the research design, including random assignment; and to check on the quality of implementation of the intervention program itself. Variability in program implementation quality is serious, but probably not as serious as the confounding that arises when components of one treatment are shared by another. Occurring in complex field contexts, social experiments rarely permit experimental isolation and so treatments can diffuse in response to many quite different types of forces. For example, cultural mores change with the result that in one disease prevention study, members of the control group began to exercise more, eat better, and avoid drugs in response to national trends (RV Luepker et al, submitted for publication). Alternatively, no-treatment controls can and do seek alternative sources of help; educational professionals get together and share experiences so that principals from a control school may learn what is happening in an intervention school; and participants in a job training program might tell program personnel about details of the job training their friends are experiencing in other programs. Whatever the impetus, treatment diffusion is not rare, so experimenters have to look for opportunities to study groups that cannot communicate with each other. But even this does not avoid the problem that social experiments are probably most likely to be funded when a social issue is already on national policy agendas so that other solutions are simultaneously being generated in the public or private sectors. Monitoring what happens in both treatment and control groups is a *sine qua non* of modern social experiments.

QUASI-EXPERIMENTATION

In quasi-experimentation, the slogan is that it is better to rule out validity threats by design than by statistical adjustment. The basic design features for doing this—pretests, pretest time series, nonequivalent control groups, matching, etc—were outlined by Campbell & Stanley (1963) and added to by Cook & Campbell (1979). Thinking about quasi-experiments has since evolved along three lines: 1. toward better understanding of designs that make point-specific predictions; 2. toward predictions about the multiple implications of a given causal hypothesis; and 3. toward improved analysis of data from quasi-experiments. These more recent developments are general, whereas the alternative interpretations that must be ruled out in any cause-probing study are particular to the given study (Cook & Campbell 1986). In quasi-experimental work, the local setting must be carefully examined to determine which validity threats are plausible and to identify any such threats that might be operating. With this caution in mind, we now discuss the three more recent developments mentioned above.

Designs Emphasizing Point-Specific Causal Hypotheses

In interrupted time series, the same outcome variable is examined over many time points. If the cause-effect link is quick acting or has a known causal delay, then an effective treatment should lead to change in the level, slope, or variance of the time series at the point where treatment occurred. The test, then, is whether the obtained data show the change in the series at the prespecified point. Statistical conclusion validity is a potential problem because errors in a time series are likely to be autocorrelated, biasing ordinary least-squares estimates of the standard error and hence statistical tests. But internal validity is the major problem, especially because of history (e.g. some other outcome-causing event occurring at the same time as the treatment) and instrumentation (e.g. a change in record keeping occurring with the treatment). Fortunately, the point specificity of prediction limits the viability of most history and instrumentation threats to those occurring only when the treatment began. Such threats are often easily checked, are rarer than threats occurring elsewhere during the series, and can sometimes be ruled out on a priori grounds.

Plausible threats are best ruled out by using additional time series. Especially important are (*a*) control group series not expected to show the hypothesized discontinuity in level, slope, or variability of an outcome; and (*b*) additional treatment series to which the same treatment is applied at different times so we expect the obtained data to recreate the known differences in when the treatment was made available. During his career, Campbell has provided many good examples of the use of control time series and multiple time series with different treatment onset times (e.g. Campbell 1976, 1984, and other papers reproduced in Overman 1988). The design features also help when a time series is abbreviated, lacking the roughly 50 pretest and 50 posttest data points that characterize formal time series analysis. Extensions using from 5 to 20 pretest and posttest assessments are common in single-subject designs (Barlow & Hersen 1984, Kratochwill & Levin 1992).

Despite their strengths for causal hypothesis-testing, interrupted time series designs are infrequently used. Most use data already in archives because it is often costly to gather original data over long time periods. But relevant dependent variables are not always available in archives. Moreover, the relevant statistical analyses are not familiar to many social scientists, with ARIMA modeling (Box & Jenkins 1970) and spectral analysis (Granger & Newbold 1977) being particularly foreign to psychology's ANOVA tradition. But where the necessary archives exist, researchers have quickly learned these methods; and analytic strategies continue to develop (Harrop & Velicer 1985, 1990). In time series research, causal inference depends on effects occurring shortly after treatment implementation or with a known causal lag. When a possible effect is delayed, causal inference is less clear—as when job training affects income years later. Causal inference is also less clear when an intervention slowly diffuses through a population (e.g. when an AIDS prevention program is first provided to a small proportion of local needle-sharing drug users and then slowly extends to others as they are found and program resources grow). With unpredicted causal lags, time series have an ambiguous relationship to the point of treatment implementation—a problem that is compounded whenever treatment implementation is poor or highly variable. Nonetheless, interrupted time series rightly enjoy a special status among quasi-experimental designs wherever they are feasible.

Like interrupted time series studies, regression discontinuity studies also rely on the hypothesis that observations will depart from an established pattern at a specified point on a continuum. In this case the continuum is not time, but rather the regression line characterizing the relationship between outcome and an assignment variable. The regression discontinuity design depends on units on one side of an eligibility cutoff point being assigned one treatment, while units on the other side are not so assigned (e.g. income defines eligibility for Medicaid and grades determine who makes the Dean's List). More complex assignment strategies are possible using multiple cutoffs or multiple assignment variables (Trochim 1984). But in all cases, the assignment variables must be observed (not latent), and adherence to the cutoff must be strict.

The regression discontinuity design is so named because a regression line is plotted to relate the assignment and outcome variables. If the treatment is effective, a discontinuity in the regression line should occur at the cutoff point. Individuals whose income is just above and just below the eligibility point for Medicaid should differ in health status if the program is effective. The point specificity of such a prediction makes regression discontinuity resemble time series, but it is also like a randomized experiment in that the assignment of subjects to conditions is completely known. As a result, Mosteller (1990, p. 225) defines regression discontinuity as a true experiment and Goldberger (1972a,b) and Rubin (1977) have provided formal statistical proofs that regression discontinuity provides an unbiased estimate of treatment effects, just like the randomized experiment.

The widespread endorsement of the regression discontinuity design and its frequent reinvention in different disciplines suggests its usefulness whenever merit or need determine treatment assignment. But regression discontinuity studies are unfortunately even rarer than interrupted time series studies. This is partly because assignment is not always done according to strict public criteria. Professional judgment and cronyism play some role, as does the use of multiple criteria, some of which are judgmental. The low use may also be because the analysis requires accurate modeling of the functional form of the assignment-outcome relationship. Researchers typically plot linear relationships between the two variables, but if the underlying relationship is curvilinear, such modeling will yield inaccurate estimates of the discontinuity at the cutoff. Since the randomized experiment is not subject to this problem, Trochim & Cappelleri (1992) argue for combining regression discontinuity with randomized assignment, using the latter to verify the functional form at the points most open to doubt. If such a combination is not feasible, then ad hoc analyses may be needed to model functional form (Trochim 1984) or statistical tests can be used that do not make strong assumptions about such form (Robbins & Zhang 1988, 1989). However, these last tests are still in their infancy and should be treated with caution. Finally, regression discontinuity is less used because it requires 2.5 times as many subjects to achieve as much power as randomized experiments that use the pretest as a covariate, although in the absence of the pretest covariate, the power of the two designs is similar (Goldberger 1972a). In practice, power is further eroded in regression-discontinuity designs as (*a*) as the cutoff point departs from the assignment variable mean; (*b*) cases are assigned in violation of the cutoff, as with the fuzzy cutoff design discussed by Trochim (1984); or (*c*) the units assigned to a treatment fail to receive it. While these problems are also found with randomized experiments, they are likely to have more serious practical consequences for regression-discontinuity designs because researchers using such designs usually have less control over the treatment assignment implementation processes. Experimenters are therefore correct to prefer random assignment over regression-discontinuity.

The promise of the regression-discontinuity design is that it can be used whenever policy dictates that special need or merit should be a prerequisite for access to the particular services whose effectiveness is to be evaluated. In this circumstance, the treatment and control group means will almost certainly differ at the pretest, seeming to create a fatal selection confound. But this is not the case with regression-discontinuity designs because the effect estimate is not the difference between raw posttest means. It is the size of the projected discontinuity at the cutoff, which is unaffected by the correlation between the assignment and outcome variables. The design is also flexible in that many variables other than quantified need or merit can be used for treatment assignment, including the order with which individuals apply to be in a social program or the year they were born (Cain 1975). Despite the design's flexibility and impeccable logic, many practicing researchers are still skeptical. It seems implausible to them that a cutoff-based assignment process that necessarily creates a selection difference can rule out selection! Yet this is the case. Realizing that the major impediment to greater use of this design are issues of its implementability and persuasiveness in ruling out selection, Trochim & Cappelleri (1992) recently have described several variations of the design that are particularly useful for practitioners and that create the groundwork for increased use of this design in the medical context from which their examples come.

Designs Emphasizing Multivariate-Complex Causal Predictions

Successful prediction of a complex pattern of multivariate results often leaves few plausible alternative explanations. The design elements to be combined for such prediction include (*a*) nonequivalent dependent variables, only a subset of which is theoretically responsive to a treatment, though all the dependent variables are responsive to the other plausible alternative explanations of an outcome change; (*b*) designs where a treatment is introduced, removed, and reintroduced to the same group; (*c*) nonequivalent group designs that have two or more pretest measurement waves providing a pre-intervention estimate of differences in rates of change between nonequivalent groups; (*d*) nonequivalent group designs with multiple comparison groups, some of which initially outperform the treatment group and some of which underperform it (Holland 1986); (*e*) cohort designs that use naturally occurring cycles in families or educational institutions to construct control groups of siblings or next year's freshmen that are initially less different than controls constructed in almost any other way; (*f*) other designs that match units on demonstrably stable attributes to reduce initial group nonequivalence without causing statistical regression (Holland 1986); and (*g*) designs that partition respondents or settings—even after the fact—to create subgroups that differ in treatment exposure levels and so in expected effect size.

These design features are often discussed separately. But the better strategy is to combine many of them in a single research project so as to increase the number and specificity of the testable implications of a causal hypothesis. Cook & Campbell (1979) give two examples. One example is an interrupted time series (*a*) to which a no-treatment control series was added; (*b*) where the intervention was later given to controls; and (*c*) where the original treatment series was partitioned into two nonequivalent series, only one of which the treatment should theoretically have influenced. A second example is a regression-discontinuity study of Medicaid's effects on physician visits. Medicaid eligibility depends on household income and family size. The regression-discontinuity design related income (the assignment variable) to the number of physician visits after Medicaid was passed, and it supplemented this with data on income and physician visits from the prior year. A discontinuity in the number of physician visits occurred at the cutoff point in the year after Medicaid was introduced but not in the year before.

Meehl (1978) has lamented the social sciences' dependence on null hypothesis testing, arguing that with large enough samples any null hypothesis can be rejected under some conditions. He counsels testing exact numerical predictions. Among social scientists, his advice has largely fallen on deaf ears, presumably because, outside of some areas within economics, so few theories are specific enough to make point predictions. The quasi-experimental emphasis on point-specific and multivariate-complex causal predictions approaches the spirit of Meehl's counsel, but substitutes specificity of time point predictions and pattern matching for numeric point predictions. Both point-specific and multivariate-complex predictions preserve the link to falsification because the pattern of obtained relationships facilitates causal inference only to the extent no other theory makes the same prediction about the pattern of the outcome data. Point-specific and multivariate-complex predictions lower the chance that plausible alternatives will make exactly the same prediction as the causal hypothesis under test; but they cannot guarantee this.

Statistical Analysis of Data from the Basic Nonequivalent Control Group Design

Despite the growing advocacy of designs making point-specific or multivariate complex predictions (Cook 1991a), the most frequently employed quasi-experiment still involves only two (nonequivalent) groups and two measurement waves, one a pretest and the other a posttest measured on the same instrument. This design is superficially like the simplest randomized experiment and is easy to implement, perhaps explaining its great popularity. However, causal inferences are not easy to justify from this design.

Interpretation depends on identifying and ruling out all the validity threats that are plausible in the specific local context where a treatment has been implemented. But many researchers fail to consider context-specific threats, relying instead on Campbell & Stanley's (1963) checklist of validity threats when this design is used, though such threats are general and may fail to reflect unique local threats. Unfortunately, causal inferences from the design have proven far more vulnerable to model misspecification than was originally hoped. In principle, a well-specified model requires complete knowledge and perfect measurement either (*a*) of the selection process by which respondents end up in different treatment groups; or (*b*) of all causes of the outcome that are correlated with participation in treatment. The hope was that such knowledge might become available or that approximations would allow us to get quite close to the correct answer. But few social researchers who study the matter closely now believe they can identify the completely specified model, and the 1980s and early 1990s were characterized by growing disillusionment about developing even adequate approximations. Nearly any observed effect might be either nullified or even reversed in the population, depending, for example, on the variables omitted from the model (whose importance one could never know for certain) or on the pattern of unreliability of measurement across the variables in the analysis. As a result, it proved difficult to anticipate with certainty the direction of bias resulting from the simpler types of nonequivalent control group studies. But there has been much work on data analysis for this design (see Moffitt 1991, Campbell 1993).

SUGGESTIONS ABOUT DATA ANALYSIS FROM THE QUASI-EXPERIMENTAL TRADITION Most of the scholars writing about the analysis of quasi-experimental data from within the Campbell tradition are reluctant apologists for their work, preferring randomized experiments but realizing that they are not always possible. Moreover, even if such experiments are implemented initially, treatment-correlated attrition often occurs, leaving the data to be analyzed as though from a quasi-experiment. Initially, the obvious solution seemed to be to measure pretest differences between the groups under contrast and then to use simple analysis of covariance to adjust away these differences (Reichardt 1979). But two problems arise here. First, unreliability in the covariates leads to biased estimates of treatment effect (Lord 1960) so that a preference emerged for using latent variable models in which multiple observed measures of each construct are analyzed, thereby reducing measurement error and permitting an analysis only of the shared variance (Magidson 1977, Magidson & Sorbom 1982; but for a dissenting voice, see Cohen et al 1990). However, this does not deal with the second and more serious problem—that of validly specifying either the selection process or the outcome model. For this, the recommendation has been that investigators must rely on their best common sense and the available research literature in the hope of including in the analysis all likely predictors of group membership (the selection model) or outcome (the outcome model), or both (although either by itself is sufficient). Since the latent variable tradition offers no guarantee that all group differences have been statistically adjusted for, members of the theory group around Campbell turned instead to strengthening causal inference by design rather than statistical analysis (e.g. Cook 1991a) or by conducting multiple data analyses under different plausible assumptions about the direction and nature of selection bias instead of relying on a single analysis (Reichardt & Gollub 1986, Rindskopf 1986, Shadish et al 1986). The one perfect analysis remained an impossible dream, given only two nonequivalent treatment groups and two measurement waves.

SUGGESTIONS FROM LABOR ECONOMISTS At the same time, some labor economists developed an alternative tradition that sought to create statistical models that do not require full model specification and that would apply to all nonexperimental research where respondents are divided into levels on some independent variable. The best developed of this class of analyses is the instrumental variable approach associated with Heckman (Heckman 1980, Heckman et al 1987, Heckman & Hotz 1989). The probability of group membership is first modeled in a selection equation, with the predictors being a subset of variables that are presumably related to selection into the different treatment conditions. When this equation correctly predicts group membership, it is assumed that a correct selection model has been identified. The results of this model are then used as an instrumental variable in the main analysis to estimate treatment effects by adjusting for the effects of selection. Conceptually and analytically, this approach closely resembles the regression discontinuity design because it is based on full knowledge and perfect measurement of the selection model. However, in approaches like Heckman's, the selection model is not fully known. It is estimated on the basis of fallible observed measures that serve to locate more general constructs. This limitation may explain why empirical probes of Heckman's theory have not produced confirmatory results. The most compelling critiques come from studies where treatment-effect estimates derived from Heckman's selection modeling procedures are directly compared to those from randomized experiments—presumed to be the gold standard against which the success of statistical adjustment procedures should be assessed. In a reanalysis of annual earnings data from a randomized experiment on job training, both LaLonde (1986, LaLonde & Maynard 1987) and Fraker & Maynard (1987) have shown that (*a*) econometric adjustments from Heckman's work provide many different estimates of the training program's effects; and (*b*) none of these estimates closely coincides with the estimate from randomized controls. These reanalyses have led some labor economists (e.g. Ashenfelter & Card 1985, Betsey et al 1985) to suggest that unbiased estimates can only be justified from randomized experiments, thereby undermining Heckman's decade-long work on adjustments for selection bias. Other labor economists do not go quite so far and prefer what they call natural experiments—what Campbell calls quasi-experiments—over the non-experimental data labor economists previously used so readily (e.g. Card 1990, Katz & Krueger 1992, Meyer & Katz 1990; and see especially Meyer 1990 for an example that reinvents regression-discontinuity).

In Heckman & Hotz's (1989, Heckman et al 1987) rejoinder to their critics, they used the same job training data as LaLonde to argue that a particular selection model—based on two separate pretreatment measures of annual income—met certain specification tests and generated an average causal effect no different from the estimate provided by the randomized experiment. Unfortunately, their demonstration is not very convincing (Cook 1991a, Coyle et al

1991). First, there is a problem of model generality since the two-wave selection process that fit for youths who were just entering the labor market did not fit for mothers enrolled in the Aid to Families with Dependent Children Program (AFDC) who were returning to the job market. Heckman invoked a simpler cross-sectional model to describe the selection process for AFDC mothers, but this model could not be subjected to restriction tests and was assumed to be correct by fiat. Second, close inspection of the data Heckman presented reveals that the econometric analyses yielded such large standard errors that finding no difference between the two methods reflects a lack of statistical power in the econometric approach. Finally, the procedure that Heckman & Hotz found to be better for their one population had been widely advocated for at least a decade as a superior quasi-experimental design because the two pretest waves allow estimation of the preintervention selection-maturation differences between groups (Cook & Campbell 1979). Moffitt's (1991) rediscovery of the double-pretest design should be seen in the same historical light that exemplifies the quasi-experimental slogan: better to control through design than measurement and statistical adjustment. To conclude, empirical results indicate that selection models usually produce different effect estimates than do randomized experiments, and if researchers using such models were close to the mark in a particular project, they would not know this unless there were also a randomized experiment on the same topic or some better quasi-experiment. But then the need for less interpretable selection modeling would not exist!

SUGGESTIONS FROM MATHEMATICAL STATISTICIANS Historically, statisticians have preferred not to deal with the problems arising from quasi-experiments (which they call observational studies). They almost monolithically advocate randomized designs unless prior information is so reliable and comprehensive that Bayes' theorem is obviously relevant. This situation changed a little in the 1980s, and a flurry of publications appeared guided by the realization that quasi-experiments were rampant and might be improved upon even if never perfected (Holland 1986; Rosenbaum 1984; Rosenbaum & Rubin 1983, 1984).

The statisticians provided four major suggestions for improving the analysis of quasi-experimental data. The first emphasized the need for selecting study units matched on stable attributes, not as a substitute for random assignment, but as one of a series of palliatives that reduce bias (Rubin 1986, Rosenbaum 1984). The second was a call to compute a propensity score, an empirical estimate of the selection process based, to the extent possible, on actual observation of which units enter the various treatment groups being contrasted (Rosenbaum & Rubin 1983, 1984). The intent is to generate the most accurate and complete description of the selection process possible rather than to find a proxy for the entire selection process. The third improvement the statisticians counseled was the use of multiple comparison groups to increase statistical power; to rule out construct validity threats through the use of placebo controls, for example; and to vary the direction of pretest group differences and hence the assumptions made about growth rate differences between groups. The statisticians want to avoid having a single comparison group that outperforms or underperforms a treatment group before the treatment and might be changing over time at a different rate from the treatment group. The final suggestion was that multiple data analyses should be conducted under different explicit and plausible assumptions about factors that might influence posttest performance in one group more than another. Clearly, the statisticians see quasi-experimental analysis as involving a more complicated, thoughtful, theory-dependent process of argument construction than is the case when analyzing data from randomized experiments.

It is interesting to note some convergences across all the different traditions of dealing with group nonequivalence. One is the advocacy of directly observing the selection process so as to have a more fully specified and more accurate model. Confidence in instrumental variables or single pretest measures as adequate proxies is waning. A second convergence is the advocacy of multiple control groups, especially to make heterogeneous the direction of pretest bias. A third is the advisability of using several pretreatment measurement waves to observe how the different groups might be changing spontaneously over time. A fourth is the value of using matching to minimize initial group noncomparability provided that the matching will not lead to statistical regression. The final point of convergence is that multiple data analyses should take place under very different (and explicit) assumptions about the direction of bias. The aim is to test the robustness of results across different plausible assumption sets. We see here the call for an honest critical multiplism (Cook 1985, Shadish 1989); a lack of confidence in the basic two-group, two-wave quasi-experimental design that is so often used in social experiments; and the need for more specific causal hypotheses, supplementing the basic design with more measurement waves and more control groups.

During the years we are examining, the use of empirical research on experiments has been increasing. From the beginning, Campbell (1957) argued that his lists of validity threats could be shortened or lengthened as experience accumulated about the viability of particular validity threats or the necessity to postulate new ones. Today we see even more focused research on design issues, as with the labor economists who contrast the results from randomized experiments and quasi-experiments. The use of empirical research to improve design is also evident in meta-analysis, particularly as it explores how methodological decisions influence effect size estimates. For example, do published studies yield different estimates from unpublished studies (Shadish et al 1989)? Does the presence of pretest measurement change effect size estimates

(Willson & Putnam 1982)? Do randomized experiments yield different estimates than quasi-experiments in general or than certain types of quasi-experiments in particular (Heinsman 1993)? We expect explicit meta-analytic studies of design questions to become even more prevalent in the future.

GENERALIZING CAUSAL RELATIONSHIPS

Cronbach's (1982) *UTOS* formulation suggests that experimenters often hope that the causal inferences they claim (*a*) will generalize to specific populations of units and settings and to target cause and effect constructs; and (*b*) can be extrapolated to times, persons, settings, causes, and effects that are manifestly different from those sampled in the existing research. Campbell's (1957) work on external validity describes a similar but less articulated aspiration. But such generalization is not easy. For compelling logistical reasons, nearly all experiments are conducted with local samples of convenience in places of convenience and involve only one or two operationalizations of a treatment, though there may be more operationalizations of an outcome. How are Cronbach's two types of generalization to be promoted if most social experiments are so contextually specific?

Random Sampling

The classic answer to this question requires randomly sampling units from the population of persons, settings, times, treatments, or outcomes to which generalization is desired. The resulting samples provide unbiased estimates of the population parameters within known sampling limits, thereby solving Cronbach's first causal generalization problem. Unfortunately, this solution is rarely applicable. In single experiments it is sometimes possible to draw a formal probability sample of units and even settings. However, it is almost impossible to draw probability samples of treatments or outcomes because no enumeration of the population can be achieved given that the treatment and outcome classes can seldom be fully defined. Occasionally, an enumeration of settings or units is possible, as with studies intending to generalize to elementary school children in a particular city, or to all community mental health centers in the nation. But for dispersed populations, there are enormous practical difficulties with drawing the appropriate sample in such a way that the treatment can be implemented with high quality. Even if these difficulties could be surmounted, the experiment would usually still be restricted to those individuals who agreed to be randomly assigned—surely only a subpopulation of all those to whom generalization is sought. Moreover, attrition is likely after an experiment has begun, making the achieved population even less similar to the target population. For all these reasons, formal probability sampling methods seem unlikely to provide a general solution to Cronbach's first framing of the causal generalization problem, though they are desirable whenever feasible.

Proximal Similarity

Campbell's solution to Cronbach's first generalization problem is implicit in his tentative relabeling of external validity as proximal similarity, by which he means that "as scientists we generalize with most confidence to applications most similar to the setting of the original research" (Campbell 1986, p. 75). He believes that the more similar an experiment's observables are to the setting to which generalization is desired, the less likely it is that background variables in the setting of desired application will modify the cause-effect relationship obtained in the original experiment. Cronbach appears to agree with this. But applying this rationale requires knowledge of which attributes must be similar, and this presumably depends on good theory, validated clinical experience, or prior relevant experimental results. Alas, good substantive theory is not always available, intuitive judgments can be fickle, and prior findings are often lacking. What can be done in such cases?

St. Pierre & Cook (1984) suggest two related purposive sampling options that are useful in planning generalizable cause-probing experiments. In modal instance sampling, the researcher uses background information or pilot work to select experimental particulars that proximally resemble the kinds of unit, setting, treatment, and outcome variants that are most commonly found in the settings to which generalization is sought. The strategy here is to capture the most representative instances (Brunswick 1955). In sampling to maximize heterogeneity, the aim is to sample as widely as possible along dimensions that theory, practice, or other forms of speculation suggest might codetermine the efficacy of a treatment. If a treatment is robustly effective at widely differing points on such dimensions, then generalization over them is facilitated. If the treatment is not general in its effects, then the researcher can conduct subgroup analyses to identify some of the specific boundary conditions under which the treatment is effective. Since power is potentially a problem when examining statistical interactions, St. Pierre & Cook (1984) also suggest probing whether a cause-effect relationship can be demonstrated across whatever heterogeneity is deliberately allowed into the sampling plan. Purposive sampling either to increase heterogeneity or to capture modal instances does not justify generalization as well as random sampling does, but it should increase insights into how broadly a causal relationship can be generalized.

Probes for Robust Replication over Multiple Experiments

A collection of experiments on the same or related topics can allow even better probes of the causal contingencies influencing treatment effectiveness. This is because each experiment is likely to involve a different population of persons and settings, a different time, and unique ways of conceptualizing and measuring the cause and effect. A search can then take place to identify which causal relationships are robust across the obtained variation in all these dimensions and also to identify those contexts that limit generalization because no cause-effect relationship can be found in them. Meta-analysis is the best-known exemplar of this approach to causal generalization (Cook 1991b, Cook et al 1992).

Consider meta-analytic work on the effects of psychotherapy. This suggests that effect sizes do not differ across such seemingly crucial dimensions as therapist training and experience, treatment orientation, and duration of treatment (Smith et al 1980, Berman & Norton 1985). However, effect sizes do differ by outcome characteristics, with larger effects emerging for outcomes that receive the most attention in treatment (Shadish et al 1993), suggesting one restriction to the generality of psychotherapy effects. Empirical efforts to probe the robustness of a cause-effect relationship require the pool of available studies to vary on factors likely to moderate the relationship. But sometimes there is little or no variability. For example, in psychotherapy literature there are very few experimental studies of psychoanalytic orientations, so we still do not know if the general finding about therapist orientation making little difference to client outcomes also applies to psychoanalysis as a particular form of treatment.

Still, with the greater range and heterogeneity of sampling that literature reviews promote it is often possible to probe whether a causal relationship is reproduced in contexts that are proximally similar to particular, defined contexts of intended application. This speaks to Cronbach's first framing of causal generalization. Important for his second framing is that when a causal relationship demonstrably holds over a wide array of different contexts (e.g. Devine 1992), it seems reasonable to presume that it will continue to hold in future contexts that are different from past ones. The warrant for such extrapolation is logically flawed; nonetheless, it is pragmatically superior to the warrant for extrapolation when a relationship has only been tested within a narrow range of persons, settings, times, causal manipulations, and effect measures.

Causal Explanation

We cannot expect all relevant causal contingencies to be represented in the body of studies available for synthesis. Hence, we need other methods for extrapolating a causal connection to unstudied populations and classes. Cronbach believes that causal explanation is the key to such generalization, and that causal explanation requires identifying the processes that follow because a treatment has varied and without which the effect would not have been produced. Identifying such micro-mediating processes usually involves decomposing the molar cause and effect constructs into the subsets of components thought to be most critically involved in the molar causal link and then examining all micro-mediating processes that might link the causally efficacious treatment components to the causally impacted outcome components.

The presumption is that once such knowledge has been gained, the crucial causal processes can be transferred to novel contexts of application. Cook & Campbell (1979) use the example of a light switch to illustrate this. Knowledge that flicking the switch results in light is the type of descriptive knowledge about manipulanda that experiments promote; more explanatory knowledge requires knowing about switch mechanisms, wiring and circuitry, the nature of electricity, and how all these elements can be combined to produce light. Knowing so much increases the chances of creating light in circumstances where there are no light switches, providing one can reproduce the causal explanatory processes that make light in whatever ways local resources allow. One need not be restricted to what can be bought in a hardware store or to what was available when one first learned about electricity. Another example concerns the murder of Kitty Genovese, who was stabbed repeatedly for over half an hour, with nearly forty neighbors watching and not offering to help. Latane & Darley (1970) hypothesized that this apathy resulted from a process they called the diffusion of responsibility—everyone thought someone else would surely help. Latane & Darley experimentally demonstrated that this process was common to a host of other situations as diverse as when a woman falls and sprains her ankle, smoke comes into a room from a fire, someone has an epileptic seizure, or a cash register is robbed (Brown 1986). Once micro-mediating processes are identified, they are often broadly transferable, certainly more so than if the research had shown that helping is reduced only following a stabbing and then only in New Jersey and only with apartment dwellers.

Identifying causal explanatory processes is not easy. Randomized experiments were designed to provide information about descriptive causal connections and not about processes accounting for these connections. Hence, the methods for exploring causal mediation must be added to experimental frameworks. Within quantitative research traditions, potential mediators can be assessed and used in some form of causal modeling. Alternatively, respondents might be assigned to treatments that vary in the availability of a hypothesized explanatory mechanism. However, experience with complex randomized experiments has not been salutary in field research. The Negative Income Tax experiments are among the most complex ever designed with respect to the number of factors examined, the number levels on each factor, and the unbalanced distribution of respondents across factors and levels (Kershaw & Fair 1976). Preserving all these distinctions in field settings has proven quite difficult, though some fairly complex planned variation studies have been carried out successfully (Connell et al 1985). Cronbach (1982) has proposed that the qualitative methods of the ethnographer, historian, or journalist should also be used to generate and defend hypotheses about micro-mediating processes. Although we personally have a lot of sympathy for this qualitative approach, it is likely to fall on deaf ears in the social science community at large.

CONCLUSIONS

Field experiments are now much more commonplace than they were twenty years ago. The pendulum has swung to favor randomized experiments over quasi-experiments—and strongly so in all areas except perhaps intervention research in education. Considerable informal information is now available about the many factors that facilitate the implementation of random assignment and about factors that promote better randomized studies. As a result, fields like labor economics and community health promotion that fifteen years ago were characterized by the use of statistical adjustments to facilitate causal inference now use more (and larger) experiments and fewer quasi-experiments.

Though quasi-experiments have lost some of their warrant, some progress has been made toward improving them. More attention has been directed to two designs that promote point-specific causal inferences—the regression-discontinuity and interrupted time series designs (Marcantonio & Cook 1994). Also more often advocated are somewhat elaborate quasi-experimental designs that predict a complex pattern of results emanating from the causal agent under analysis. At issue here are more pretest measurement waves, more control groups, better matched controls (including cohorts), and removing and reinstating the treatment at known time points (Cook et al 1990).

Much work has also gone into the statistical analysis of data from quasi-experiments in order to model selection biases. There are several different traditions that, unfortunately, rarely communicate with each other (see Campbell 1993). This is sad because they are growing ever closer together. None of these traditions is sanguine about finding the elusive demonstrably valid counterfactual baseline unless the selection model is completely known, as with randomized experiments or the regression-discontinuity design. All traditions agree, though, that causal inference is better warranted the more closely the comparison groups are matched, the more information there is to describe the selection process, the more comparison groups there are (particularly if they bracket the treatment group mean at the pretest), and the more robust are the results generated from multiple statistical analyses made under different plausible assumptions about the nature of selection bias.

But selection is not the only inferential problem researchers need to worry about. Campbell's (1957) internal validity threats of testing, instrumentation, and history are often relevant, as are Cook & Campbell's (1979) threats of treatment diffusion, resentful demoralization, compensatory rivalry, and compensatory equalization. Statistical research on selection modeling has been dominant in the past, and rightly so. But it should not crowd out research into these other relevant threats to valid causal inference.

Work on the generalization of causal relationships has historically been less prevalent than work on establishing causal relationships. There is ongoing work on the generalization of causal inferences in two modes. One is meta-analytic and emphasizes the empirical robustness of a particular causal connection across a wide range of persons, settings, times, and cause and effect constructs. The second is more causal-explanatory, and it emphasizes identifying the micro-mediating processes that causally connect a treatment to an outcome, usually through a process of theoretical specification, measurement, and data analysis rather than through the sampling strategy that characterizes meta-analysis. Causal generalization is now more of an issue in social experiments than it was fifteen years ago (Cook 1991a, 1993; Friedlander & Guerin 1992).

Literature Cited

Aiken LS, West SG. 1991. *Multiple Regression: Testing and Interpreting Interactions.* Newbury Park, CA: Sage

Ashenfelter O, Card D. 1985. Using the longitudinal structure of earnings to estimate the effect of training programs. *Rev. Econ. Stat.* 67:648-60

Barlow DH, Hersen M, eds. 1984. *Single Case Experimental Designs: Strategies for Studying Behavior Change.* New York: Pergamon. 2nd ed.

Berman JS, Norton NC. 1985. Does professional training make a therapist more effective? *Psychol. Bull.* 98:401–7

Betsey CL, Hollister RE, Papageorgiou MR, eds. 1985. *Youth Employed and Training Programs: The YEDPA Years.* Washington, DC: Natl. Acad. Press

Bickman L. 1987. Functions of program theory. In *Using Program Theory in Evaluation: New Directions for Program Evaluation,* ed. L Bickman, 33:5–18. San Francisco: Jossey-Bass

Bickman L, ed. 1990. *Advances in Program Theory: New Directions for Program Evaluation,* Vol. 47. San Francisco: Jossey-Bass

Boruch RF. 1975. On common contentions about randomized experiments. In *Experimental Tests of Public Policy,* ed. RF Boruch, HW Riecken, pp. 107–42. Boulder, CO: Westview

Boruch RF, Gomez H. 1977. Sensitivity, bias and theory in impact evaluations. *Prof. Psychol. Res. Pract.* 8:411–34

Boruch RF, McSweeney AJ, Soderstrom EJ. 1978. Randomized field experiments for program planning development and evaluation. *Eval. Q.* 2:655–95

Boruch RF, Wothke W, eds. 1985. *Randomization and Field Experimentation: New Directions for Program Evaluation,* Vol. 28. San Francisco: Jossey-Bass

Box GEP, Jenkins GM. 1970. *Time-series Analysis: Forecasting and Control.* San Francisco: Holden-Day

Brown R. 1986. *Social Psychology: The Second Edition.* New York: Free Press

Brunswik E. 1955. *Perception and the Representative Design of Psychological Experiments.* Berkeley: Univ. Calif. Press. 2nd ed.

Bryk AS, Raudenbush SW. 1992. *Hierarchical Linear Models: Applications and Data Analysis Methods.* Newbury Park, CA: Sage

Cain GG. 1975. Regression and selection models to improve nonexperimental comparisons. In *Evaluation and Experiment: Some Critical Issues in Assessing Social Programs,* ed. CA Bennett, AA Lumsdaine, pp. 297–317. New York: Academic

Campbell DT. 1957. Factors relevant to the validity of experiments in social settings. *Psychol. Bull.* 54:297–312

Campbell DT. 1966. Pattern matching as an

essential in distal knowing. In *The Psychology of Egon Brunswik,* ed. KR Hammond, pp. 81–106. New York: Holt, Rinehart, Winston

Campbell DT. 1976. Focal local indicators for social program evaluation. *Soc. Indic. Res.* 3:237–56

Campbell DT. 1982. Experiments as arguments. *Knowl.: Creation Diffus. Util.* 3:237–56

Campbell DT. 1984. Hospital and landsting as continuously monitoring social programs: advocacy and warning. In *Evaluation of Mental Health Service Programs,* ed. B Cronhom, L von Korring, pp. 13–39. Stockholm: Forskningsraadet Medicinska

Campbell DT. 1986. Relabeling internal and external validity for applied social scientists. See Trochim 1986, pp. 67–77

Campbell DT. 1993. Quasi-experimental research designs in compensatory education. In *Evaluating Intervention Strategies for Children and Youth at Risk,* ed. EM Scott. Washington, DC: US Govt. Print. Office. In press

Campbell DT, Boruch RF. 1975. Making the case for randomized assignment to treatments by considering the alternatives: six ways in which quasi-experimental evaluations tend to underestimate effects. In *Evaluation and Experience: Some Critical Issues in Assessing Social Programs,* ed. CA Bennett, AA Lumsdaine, pp. 195–296. New York: Academic

Campbell DT, Stanley JC. 1963. *Experimental and Quasi-Experimental Designs for Research.* Chicago: Rand-McNally

Card D. 1990. The impact of the Mariel boatlift on the Miami labor market. *Ind. Labor Relat.* 43:245–57

Chelimsky E. 1987. The politics of program evaluation. *Soc. Sci. Mod. Soc.* 25(1):24–32

Chen HT, Rossi PH. 1983. Evaluating with sense: the theory-driven approach. *Eval. Rev.* 7:283–302

Cohen P, Cohen J, Teresi J, Marchi M, Velez NC. 1990. Problems in the measurement of latent variables in structural equations causal models. *Appl. Psychol. Meas.* 14(2):183–96

Collingwood RG. 1940. *An Essay on Metaphysics.* Oxford: Clarendon

Connell DB, Turner RT, Mason EF. 1985. Summary of findings of the school health education evaluation: health promotion effectiveness, implementation, and costs. *J. School Health* 85:316–17

Cook TD. 1985. Post-positivist critical multiplism. In *Social Science and Social Policy,* ed. RL Shotland, MM Mark, pp. 21–62. Beverly Hills, CA: Sage

Cook TD. 1991a. Clarifying the warrant for generalized causal inferences in quasi-experimentation. In *Evaluation and Education at Quarter Century,* ed. MW McLaughlin, D Phillips, pp. 115–44. Chicago: NSSE

Cook TD. 1991b. Meta-analysis: its potential for causal description and causal explanation within program evaluation. In *Social Prevention and the Social Sciences: Theoretical Controversies. Research Problems and Evaluation Strategies,* ed. G Albrecht, H-U Otto, S Karstedt-Henke, K Bollert, pp. 245–85. Berlin-New York: de Gruyter

Cook TD. 1993. A quasi-sampling theory of the generalization of causal relationships. In *Understanding Causes and Generalizing About Them: New Directions for Program Evaluation,* ed. L Sechrest, AG Scott, 57:39–82. San Francisco: Jossey-Bass

Cook TD, Anson A, Walchli S. 1993. From causal description to causal explanation: improving three already good evaluations of adolescent health programs. In *Promoting the Health of Adolescents: New Directions for the Twenty-First Century,* ed. SG Millstein, AC Petersen, EO Nightingale, pp. 339–74. New York: Oxford Univ. Press

Cook TD, Campbell DT. 1979. *Quasi-Experimentation: Design and Analysis Issues for Field Settings.* Chicago: Rand-McNally

Cook TD, Campbell DT. 1986. The causal assumptions of quasi-experimental practice. *Synthese* 68:141–80

Cook TD, Campbell DT, Perrachio L. 1990. Quasiexperimentation. In *Handbook of Industrial and Organizational Psychology,* ed. MD Dunnette, LM Hough, pp. 491–576. Palo Alto, CA: Consult. Psychol. Press. 2nd ed.

Cook TD, Cooper H, Cordray D, Hartmann H, Hedges L, Light R, Louis T, Mosteller F, eds. 1992. *Meta-Analysis for Explanation: A Casebook.* New York: Russell Sage Found.

Coyle SL, Boruch RF, Turner CF, eds. 1991. *Evaluating AIDS Prevention Programs: Expanded Edition.* Washington, DC: Natl. Acad. Press

Cronbach LJ. 1982. *Designing Evaluations of Educational and Social Programs.* San Francisco: Jossey-Bass

Cronbach LJ, Snow RE. 1976. *Aptitudes and Instructional Methods.* New York: Irvington

Devine E. 1992. Effects of psychoeducational care with adult surgical patients: a theory-probing meta-analysis of intervention studies. See Cook et al 1992, pp. 35–84.

Dunn WN. 1982. Reforms as arguments. *Knowl. Creation Diffus. Util.* 3(3):293–326

Fraker T, Maynard R. 1987. Evaluating the adequacy of comparison group designs for evaluation of employment-related programs. *J. Hum. Res.* 22:194–227

Freedman DA. 1987. A rejoinder on models, metaphors, and fables. *J. Educ. Stat.* 12:206–23

Friedlander D, Gueron JM. 1992. Are high-cost services more effective than low-cost services? In *Evaluating Welfare and Training Programs,* ed. CF Manski, I Garfinkel, pp. 143–98. Cambridge: Harvard Univ. Press

Gadenne V. 1976. *Die Gultigkeit psychologischer Untersuchungen.* Stuttgart, Germany: Kohlhammer

Gasking D. 1955. Causation and recipes. *Mind* 64:479–87

Goldberger AS. 1972a. Selection bias in evaluating treatment effects: some formal illustrations. In *Discussion Papers No. 123–172.* Madison: Inst. Res. Poverty, Univ. Wisc.

Goldberger AS. 1972b. Selection bias in evaluating treatment effects: the case of interaction. In *Discussion Papers No. 123–172* Madison: Inst. Res. Poverty, Univ. Wisc.

Gottfredson SD. 1978. Evaluating psychological research reports: dimensions, reliability and correlates of quality judgments. *Am. Psychol.* 33:920–34

Granger CW, Newbold P. *Forecasting Economic Time Series.* New York: Academic

Harrop JW, Velicer WF. 1985. A comparison of alternative approaches to the analysis of interrupted time series. *Multivariate Behav. Res.* 20:27–44

Harrop JW, Velicer WF. 1990. Computer programs for interrupted time series analysis: 1. A qualitative evaluation. *Multivariate Behav. Res.* 25:219–31

Heckman JJ. 1980. Sample selection bias as a specification error. In *Evaluation Studies Review Annual,* ed. EW Stromsdorfer, G Farkas, 5:13–31. Newbury Park, CA: Sage

Heckman JJ, Hotz VJ. 1988. Are classical experiments necessary for evaluating the impact of manpower training programs? A critical assessment. *Ind. Relat. Res. Assoc. 40th Annu. Proc.,* pp. 291–302

Heckman JJ, Hotz VJ. 1989. Choosing among alternative nonexperimental methods for estimating the impact of social programs: the case of manpower training. *J. Am. Stat. Assoc.* 84:862–74

Heckman JJ, Hotz VJ, Dabos M. 1987. Do we need experimental data to evaluate the impact of manpower training on earnings? *Eval. Rev.* 11:395–427

Heinsman D. 1993. *Effect sizes in meta-analysis: does random assignment make a difference?* PhD thesis. Memphis State Univ., Tenn.

Holland PW. 1986. Statistics and causal inference (with discussion). *J. Am. Stat. Assoc.* 81:945–70

Holland PW, Rubin DB. 1988. Causal inference in retrospective studies. *Eval. Rev.* 12:203–31

Katz LF, Krueger AB. 1992. The effect of minimum wage on the fast-food industry. *Ind. Labor Relat.* 46:6–21

Kershaw D, Fair J. 1976. *The New Jersey Income-Maintenance Experiment.* Vol. 1: *Operations, Surveys and Administration.* New York: Academic

Kish L. 1987. *Statistical Design for Research.* New York: Wiley

Kratochwill TR, Levin JR, eds. 1992. *Single-Case Research Design and Analysis.* Hillsdale, NJ: Erlbaum

Kruglanski AW, Kroy M. 1975. Outcome validity in experimental research: a re-conceptualization. *J. Represent. Res. Soc. Psychol.* 7:168–78

Kuhn TS. 1962. *The Structure of Scientific Revolutions.* Chicago: Univ. Chicago Press

Lakoff G. 1987. *Women, Fire, and Dangerous Things: What Categories Reveal About the Mind.* Chicago: Univ. Chicago Press

LaLonde RJ. 1986. Evaluating the econometric evaluations of training programs with experimental data. *Am. Econ. Rev.* 76:604–20

LaLonde RJ, Maynard R. 1987. How precise are evaluations of employment and training experiments: evidence from a field experiment. *Eval. Rev.* 11:428–51

Latane B, Darley JM. 1970. *The Unresponsive Bystander: Why Doesn't He Help?* New York: Appleton-Century-Crofts

Lipsey M. 1993. Theory as method: small theories of treatments. In *Understanding Causes and Generalizing About Them: New Directions for Program Evaluation,* ed. LB Sechrest, AG Scott, 57:5–38. San Francisco: Jossey-Bass

Lord FM. 1960. Large-scale covariance analysis when the control variable is fallible. *J. Am. Stat. Assoc.* 55:307–21

Mackie JL. 1974. *The Cement of the Universe.* Oxford: Oxford Univ. Press

Magidson J. 1977. Toward a causal model approach for adjusting for pre-existing differences in the non-equivalent control group situation. *Eval. Q.* 1(3):399–420

Magidson J, Sorbom D. 1982. Adjusting for confounding factors in quasi-experiments. *Educ. Eval. Policy Anal.* 4:321–29

Manski CF, Garfinkel I, eds. 1992. *Evaluating Welfare and Training Programs.* Cambridge: Harvard Univ. Press

Marcantonio RJ, Cook TD. 1994. Convincing quasi-experiments: the interrupted time series and regression-discontinuity designs. In *Handbook of Practical Program Evaluation,* ed. JS Wholey, HP Hatry, KE Newcomer. San Francisco: Jossey-Bass. In press

Mark MM. 1986. Validity typologies and the logic and practice of quasi-experimentation. See Trochim 1986, pp. 47–66

Medin DL. 1989. Concepts and conceptual structure. *Am. Psychol.* 44:1469–81

Meehl PE. 1978. Theoretical risks and tabular asterisks: Sir Karl, Sir Ronald, and the slow progress of soft psychology. *J. Consult. Clin. Psychol.* 46:806–34

Meyer BD. 1990. Unemployment insurance and unemployment spells. *Econometrica* 58:757–82

Meyer BD, Katz LF. 1990. The impact of the potential duration of unemployment benefits on the duration of unemployment. *J. Public Econ.* 41:45–72

Moffitt R. 1991. The use of selection modeling to evaluate AIDS interventions with observational data. *Eval. Rev.* 15(3):291–314

Mosteller F. 1990. Improving research methodology: an overview. In *Research Methodology: Strengthening Causal Interpretations of Nonexperimental Data,* ed. L Sechrest, E Perrin, J Bunker, pp. 221–30. Rockville, MD: AHCPR, PHS

Overman ES. 1988. *Methodology and Epistemology for the Social Sciences: Selected Papers of Donald T. Campbell.* Chicago: Univ. Chicago Press

Popper KR. 1959. *The Logic of Scientific Discovery.* New York: Basic Books

Reichardt CS. 1979. The statistical analysis of data from nonequivalent group designs. See Cook & Campbell 1979, pp. 147–205

Reichardt CS, Gollob HF. 1986. Satisfying the constraints of causal modelling. See Trochim 1986, pp. 91–107

Riecken HW, Boruch RF, eds. 1974. *Social Experimentation.* New York: Academic

Rindskopf D. 1986. New developments in selection modeling for quasi-experimentation. See Trochim 1986

Robbins H, Zhang C-H. 1988. Estimating a treatment effect under biased sampling. *Proc. Natl. Acad. Sci. USA* 85:3670–72

Robbins H, Zhang C-H. 1989. Estimating the superiority of a drug to a placebo when all and only those patients at risk are treated with the drug. *Proc. Natl. Acad. Sci. USA* 86:3003–5

Rosch E. 1978. Principles of categorization. In *Cognition and Categorization,* ed. E Rosch, BB Lloyd. Hillsdale, NJ: Erlbaum

Rosenbaum PR. 1984. From association to causation in observational studies: the role of tests of strongly ignorable treatment assignment. *J. Am. Stat. Assoc.* 79:41–48

Rosenbaum PR, Rubin DB. 1983. The central role of the propensity score in observational studies for causal effects. *Biometrika* 70:41–55

Rosenbaum PR, Rubin DB. 1984. Reducing bias in observation studies for causal effects. *J. Educ. Psychol.* 66:688–701

Rubin DB. 1977. Assignment to treatment group on the basis of a covariate. *J. Educ. Stat.* 2:1–26

Rubin DB. 1986. Which ifs have causal answers? *J. Am. Stat. Assoc.* 81:961–62

Sechrest L, West SG, Phillips MA, Redner R, Yeaton W. 1979. Some neglected problems in evaluation research: strength and integrity of treatments. In *Evaluation Studies Review Annual,* ed. L Sechrest, SG West, MA Phillips, R Redner, W Yeaton, 4:15–35. Beverly Hills, CA: Sage

Shadish WR. 1989. Critical multiplism: a research strategy and its attendent tactics. In *Health Services Research Methodology: A Focus on AIDS. DHHS Pub. No. PHS89-3439,* ed. L Sechrest, H Freeman, A Mully. Rockville, MD: NCHS, USDHHS

Smith EE, Medin DL. 1981. *Categories and Concepts*, Cambridge: Harvard Univ. Press

Shadish WR, Cook TD, Houts AC. 1986. Quasi-experimentation in a critical multiplist mode. See Trochim 1986, pp. 29–46

Shadish WR, Doherty M, Montgomery LM. 1989. How many studies are in the file drawer? An estimate from the family/marital psychotherapy literature. *Clin. Psychol. Rev.* 9:589–603

Shadish WR, Montgomery LM, Wilson P, Wilson MR, Bright I, Okwumabua TM. 1993. The effects of family and marital psychotherapies: a meta-analysis. *J. Consult. Clin. Psychol.* In press

Smith EE, Medin DL. 1981. *Categories and Concepts*. Cambrigde: Harvard Univ. Press

Smith ML, Glass GV, Miller TI. 1980. *The Benefits of Psychotherapy.* Baltimore: Johns Hopkins Univ. Press

St. Pierre RG, Cook TD. 1984. Sampling strategy in the design of program evaluations. In *Evaluation Studies Review Annual,* ed. RF Conner, DG Altman, C Jackson, 9:459–84. Beverly Hills, CA: Sage

Trochim WMK. 1984. Research design for program evaluation: the regression-discontinuity approach. Newbury Park, CA: Sage

Trochim WMK, ed. 1986. *Advances in Quasi-experimental Design Analysis: New Directions for Program Evaluation,* Vol. 31. San Francisco: Jossey-Bass

Trochim WMK, Cappelleri JC. 1992. Cutoff assignment strategies for enhancing randomized clinical trials. *Control. Clin. Trials* 13:190–212

Whitbeck C. 1977. Causation in medicine: the disease entity model. *Philos. Sci.* 44:619–37

Willson VL, Putnam RR. 1982. A meta-analysis of pretest sensitization effects in experimental design. *Am. Educ. Res. J.* 19:249–58

Wortman PM. 1993. Judging research quality. In *Handbook of Research Synthesis,* ed. HM Cooper, LV Hedges. New York: Russell Sage Foundation. In press

Zimmermann HJ, Zadeh LA, Gaines BR, eds. 1984. *Fuzzy Sets and Decision Analysis.* New York: Elsevier

AUTHOR INDEX

C

D

E

F

G

H

I

J

M

N

Q

R

S

X

Y

Z

SUBJECT INDEX

A

B

C

D

E

F

G

J

K

L

M

N

Q

R

CUMULATIVE INDEXES

CONTRIBUTING AUTHORS, VOLUMES 35–45

I

J

K

L

M

N

O

P

Q

R

S

CHAPTER TITLES, VOLUMES 35–45

ANNUAL REVIEWS

a nonprofit scientific publisher
4139 El Camino Way
P.O. Box 10139
Palo Alto, CA 94303-0139 • USA

ORDER FORM

ORDER TOLL FREE
1.800.523.8635
from USA and Canada

Fax: 1.415.855.9815

Annual Reviews publications may be ordered directly from our office; through booksellers and subscription agents, worldwide; and through participating professional societies. **Prices are subject to change without notice. We do not ship on approval.**

- **Individuals:** Prepayment required on new accounts. in US dollars, checks drawn on a US bank.
- **Institutional Buyers:** Include purchase order. Calif. Corp. #161041 • ARI Fed. I.D. #94-1156476
- **Students / Recent Graduates: $10.00 discount from retail price, per volume.** ***Requirements:*** **1.** be a degree candidate at, or a graduate within the past three years from, an accredited institution; **2.** present proof of status (photocopy of your student I.D. or proof of date of graduation); **3.** Order direct from Annual Reviews; **4.** prepay. This discount **does not** apply to standing orders, *Index on Diskette,* Special Publications, ARPR, or institutional buyers.
- **Professional Society Members:** Many Societies offer *Annual Reviews* to members at reduced rates. Check with your society or contact our office for a list of participating societies.
- **California orders** add applicable sales tax. • **Canadian orders** add 7% GST. Registration #R 121 449-029.
- **Postage paid** by Annual Reviews (4th class bookrate/surface mail). UPS ground service is available at $2.00 extra per book within the contiguous 48 states only. UPS air service or US airmail is available to any location at actual cost. UPS requires a street address. P.O. Box, APO, FPO, not acceptable.
- **Standing Orders:** Set up a standing order and the new volume in series is sent automatically each year upon publication. Each year you can save 10% by prepayment of prerelease invoices sent 90 days prior to the publication date. Cancellation may be made at any time.
- **Prepublication Orders:** Advance orders may be placed for any volume and will be charged to your account upon receipt. Volumes not yet published will be shipped during month of publication indicated.

NOTE: For copies of individual articles from any *Annual Review,* or copies of any article cited in an *Annual Review,* call **Annual Reviews Preprints and Reprints (ARPR)** toll free 1-800-347-8007 (fax toll free 1-800-347-8008) from the USA or Canada. From elsewhere call 1-415-259-5017.

ANNUAL REVIEWS SERIES *Volumes not listed are no longer in print*			**Prices, postpaid, per volume. USA/other countries**	Regular Order Please send Volume(s):	Standing Order Begin with Volume:
❑ *Annual Review of*		ANTHROPOLOGY			
Vols.	1-20	(1972-91)	$41 / $46		
Vols.	21-22	(1992-93)	$44 / $49		
Vol.	23	(avail. Oct. 1994)	$47 / $52	Vol(s). ______	Vol. ______
❑ *Annual Review of*		ASTRONOMY AND ASTROPHYSICS			
Vols.	1, 5-14, 16-29	(1963, 67-76, 78-91)	$53 / $58		
Vols.	30-31	(1992-93)	$57 / $62		
Vol.	32	(avail. Sept. 1994)	$60 / $65	Vol(s). ______	Vol. ______
❑ *Annual Review of*		BIOCHEMISTRY			
Vols.	31-34, 36-60	(1962-65,67-91)	$41 / $47		
Vols.	61-62	(1992-93)	$46 / $52		
Vol.	63	(avail. July 1994)	$49 / $55	Vol(s). ______	Vol. ______
❑ *Annual Review of*		BIOPHYSICS AND BIOMOLECULAR STRUCTURE			
Vols.	1-20	(1972-91)	$55 / $60		
Vols.	21-22	(1992-93)	$59 / $64		
Vol.	23	(avail. June 1994)	$62 / $67	Vol(s). ______	Vol. ______

ANNUAL REVIEWS SERIES *Volumes not listed are no longer in print*	**Prices, postpaid, per volume. USA/other countries**	Regular Order Please send Volume(s):	Standing Order Begin with Volume:

❑ *Annual Review of* CELL BIOLOGY
Vols. 1-7 (1985-91)................................$41 / $46
Vols. 8-9 (1992-93)................................$46 / $51
Vol. 10 (avail. Nov. 1994).... ....$49 / $54 Vol(s). ______ Vol. ______

❑ *Annual Review of* COMPUTER SCIENCE (Series suspended)
Vols. 1-2 (1986-87)................................$41 / $46
Vols. 3-4 (1988-89/90)............................$47 / $52 Vol(s). ______
Special package price for
Vols. 1-4 (if ordered together)....... ....$100 / $115 ❑ Send all four volumes.

❑ *Annual Review of* EARTH AND PLANETARY SCIENCES
Vols. 1-6, 8-19 (1973-78, 80-91)............. ....$55 / $60
Vols. 20-21 (1992-93)................................$59 / $64
Vol. 22 (avail. May 1994).... ....$62 / $67 Vol(s). ______ Vol. ______

❑ *Annual Review of* ECOLOGY AND SYSTEMATICS
Vols. 2-12, 14-17, 19-22..(1971-81, 83-86, 88-91)...$40 / $45
Vols. 23-24 (1992-93)................................$44 / $49
Vol. 25 (avail. Nov. 1994).... ....$47 / $52 Vol(s). ______ Vol. ______

❑ *Annual Review of* ENERGY AND THE ENVIRONMENT
Vols. 1-16 (1976-91)................................$64 / $69
Vols. 17-18 (1992-93)................................$68 / $73
Vol. 19 (avail. Oct. 1994).... ....$71 / $76 Vol(s). ______ Vol. ______

❑ *Annual Review of* ENTOMOLOGY
Vols. 10-16, 18, 20-36 (1965-71, 73, 75-91).......... .$40 / $45
Vols. 37-38 (1992-93) ....$44 / $49
Vol. 39 (avail. January 1994).... ....$47 / $52 Vol(s). ______ Vol. ______

❑ *Annual Review of* FLUID MECHANICS
Vols. 2-4, 7 (1970-72, 75)
9-11, 16-23 (1977-79, 84-91)... ....$40 / $45
Vols. 24-25 (1992-93) ....$44 / $49
Vol. 26 (avail. January 1994).... ....$47 / $52 Vol(s). ______ Vol. ______

❑ *Annual Review of* GENETICS
Vols. 1-12, 14-25 (1967-78, 80-91)... ....$40 / $45
Vols. 26-27 (1992-93)................................$44 / $49
Vol. 28 (avail. Dec. 1994).... ....$47 / $52 Vol(s). ______ Vol. ______

❑ *Annual Review of* IMMUNOLOGY
Vols. 1-9 (1983-91) ....$41 / $46
Vols. 10-11 (1992-93)................................$45 / $50
Vol. 12 (avail. April 1994).... ....$48 / $53 Vol(s). ______ Vol. ______

❑ *Annual Review of* MATERIALS SCIENCE
Vols. 1, 3-19 (1971, 73-89) ....$68 / $73
Vols. 20-23 (1990-93) ....$72 / $77
Vol. 24 (avail. August 1994).... ....$75 / $80 Vol(s). ______ Vol. ______

❑ *Annual Review of* MEDICINE: Selected Topics in the Clinical Sciences
Vols. 9, 11-15, 17-42 (1958, 60-64, 66-42) ....$40 / $45
Vols. 43-44 (1992-93) ....$44 / $49
Vol. 45 (avail. April 1994).... ....$47 / $52 Vol(s). ______ Vol. ______